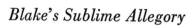

Blake's Sublime Allegory

Blake's Sublime Allegory

ESSAYS ON

The Four Zoas
Milton
Jerusalem

EDITED BY

Stuart Curran

AND

Joseph Anthony Wittreich, Jr.

THE UNIVERSITY
OF WISCONSIN
PRESS

Published 1973
The University of Wisconsin Press
Box 1379, Madison, Wisconsin 53701

The University of Wisconsin Press, Ltd.
70 Great Russell Street, London

First printing
Printed in the United States of America
For LC CIP information see the colophon

ISBN 0–299–06180–9

Many, indeed, of those [forms of allegory] which I have produced on this last occasion, might more properly be referred to that sublimer kind of allegory, *which in its principal view looks forward to a meaning much more important than that which is obvious and literal; and under the ostensible subject, as under a rind or shell, conceals one interior and more sacred.*

—ROBERT LOWTH

Of the epic plan, the loftiest species of human conception, the aim is to astonish whilst it instructs; it is the sublime allegory of a maxim.

—HENRY FUSELI

Thus I hope that all our three years' trouble Ends in Good Luck at last & shall be forgot by my affections & only remember'd by my Understanding; to be a Memento in time to come, & to speak to future generations by a Sublime Allegory, which is now perfectly completed into a Grand Poem. I shall praise it, since I dare not pretend to be any other than the Secretary; the Authors are in Eternity.

—WILLIAM BLAKE

Contents

List of Illustrations

The illustrations, when referred to
in the text, are cited by number within braces: {1}.

Preface

It would be small comfort to William Blake to realize that the neglect his poetry suffered during his own time was only a facet in a general cultural reaction lasting from the onset of the French Revolution until the late 1820s, when he died. Unlike the eighteenth century or the Victorian period, which offered honors that are still largely recognized, the Romantic period gave its accolades to a class of writers Shelley characterized as "the illustrious obscure," bards of the weight of Campbell, Rogers, and Southey. Of the great poets only Byron forged a reputation equal to his talents. While the others fought their way as best they could, Blake quietly relinquished his hopes for a contemporary reputation as a poet. His retirement to the calm of Felpham and the protective patronage of William Hayley bears the reluctant admission of that failure. A prophet without honor in his own country, at Felpham Blake returned to those sprawled overflowings of his genius, the fragments of *The Four Zoas*, to redeem his myth and vision in major prophetic poems. He created *Milton* and *Jerusalem*, he asserted, "to be a Memento in time to come, & to speak to future generations by a Sublime Allegory."

Blake's abiding faith in his divine vision is nowhere more inimitably expressed. He entrusted his sublime allegory to a handful of copies, ten of which survive to this day. Apart from the sheets to *The Four Zoas*, fortunately preserved in the British Museum, four copies of *Milton*, each different, and five of *Jerusalem* descend from Blake's time. A further copy of *Jerusalem* has disappeared sometime in the past fifty years and may yet be recovered. The survival of these works we owe to the dedicated loyalty of artists like Cumberland, Linnell, and Varley, who gathered around Blake in his last years, to the pre-Raphaelites in midcentury, and to two eccentric minds, one a genius, who at last published the major prophecies in a form designed to gain them readers, Edwin J. Ellis and William Butler Yeats. Since that edition in 1893, one may separate the critical emphases on Blake's most abstruse poems into two distinct phases. The first period, lasting from the Ellis-Yeats edition until the middle of the twentieth century and presided over by two devoted scholars, Geoffrey Keynes in England and S. Foster Damon in the United States, concentrated on elucidating the significance of Blake's mythic machinery. If efforts to denote analogies in Blake's life were at times excessive, and if many identifications have since been enlarged in scope or proven inadequate, their value is unquestionable. They established in the minute particulars of Blake's art the basis for its understanding. The modern phase of Blake scholarship dates from 1946–47, with the publication of Mark Shorer's *William Blake: The Politics of Vision* and Northrop Frye's *Fearful Symmetry*. The new generation of Blake scholars has been more rigorous in its methodology and less interested in biographical referents than in comprehending the prophecies within the total design of Blake's life work. The modern scholar speaks to an ever-growing audience: no longer a cult as it was fifty years ago, it is a responsive readership, sufficiently disciplined and persevering to endure the education Blake demands of those who enter his realms.

Although the last twenty-five years have witnessed an extraordinary alteration in Blake's reputation, much of it surely the result of a concerted effort by critics and scholars to unravel his system, we easily lose sight of Blake's broad appeal to these "future generations" who have rediscovered him. That appeal derives from the nearly endless depths to which Blake's sublime allegory, his self-created, complex, and subtle myth, resounds in the modern mind. W. H. Auden once noted that the essential truths of Freudian psychology are prefigured in *The Marriage of Heaven and Hell*. One might amplify this insight by observing that the major prophecies are themselves profound excursions into depth analysis, with the mythic structure revealing progressively internal layers of consciousness. With such a basis for interpretation, Blake's relevance to Jungian psychology is also evident. Among many areas of mutual concern, the most obvious are Jung's fascination with the mandala, or squared circle, and his assertion of synchronicity in which spiritual agencies underlie the causal relationships of the phenomenal world. Modern mythic criticism, derived from the researches of Frazer and Jung, owes much of its actual existence to Blake, who taught Northrop Frye to anatomize literature; and there are clear links with the conceptions of modern anthropologists and linguists, like Claude Levi-Strauss and Noam Chomsky. Blake's focus on the split between the self and its emanation, between one's actuality and potentiality, has become firmly rooted in modern sociological and political notions of alienation. It also suggests his closeness to Marx. For all Blake's fundamental disagreement with a Marxist reliance on materialistic forces, his emphasis on progress as resulting from interacting contraries, as well as on the self-defeating dialectic that forces a materialistic culture to disintegrate, are firmly within a Marxist perspective. With the logical positivists Blake would have nothing to do, but with the entire tradition of idealist philosophy, deriving in England from Bishop Berkeley, in Germany from Kant and Hegel, and still very much alive in existentialism and phenomenology, Blake is in sympathetic accord. With radical Christian theology Blake would also find much in common, as is attested to by the discriminating study of his religious values by Thomas J. J. Altizer. A recital such as this does not pretend to completeness, nor does it presuppose that poets must be judged by their relevance to this last third of the twentieth century, which is acutely aware of being betrayed by a simple-minded trust in that industrial revolution whose beginnings Blake attacked so steadfastly. But it does predicate Blake's kinship with the great poets of Western culture—with those like Dante, Spenser, Milton, and Goethe—who defined their vision as encyclopedic and their role as that of cultural syncretizers. All scholarship aspires to a similar end, that of preserving the continuity of human civilization: if modern humanistic and social disciplines often remain unintegrated, they are built on synoptic structures long established. Thus, to see Blake's affinity with Freudians or Marxists, with modern psychology, political theory, anthropology, linguistics, theology, and philosophy, is to claim only that his vision is far-reaching and true to human life. That is sufficient claim for any man.

But to assert such a claim is also in some measure to explain the combined effort represented by this volume. The modern period of Blake scholarship has fixed its attention on those poems that have appeared most congenial to close reading. And if there are now some two dozen valid interpretations of "The Tyger," one may exclaim with Dryden—perhaps less enthusiastically —"here is God's plenty" and assimilate the poem in the richness of its variety. The Songs of Innocence and of Experience are not simple poems, as even a contemporary like Hazlitt realized; but by Blake's own standards they are limited by their brevity and by their mode. The minor prophetic poems—America, Europe, or the Urizen, Ahania, Los sequence—suggest a restless mind seeking a form capable of adequately expressing its ideas. They are thus self-evidently limited. Blake's poetic career represents the building of a canon; it drives continuously toward supreme and summary works, toward the sublime allegory of The Four Zoas, Milton, and Jerusalem. Increasingly it has become evident that bridges must be built across this seeming chaos, both for the headstrong, fearless, Romantic student who comes to Blake with an inquisitive mind and will not be put off by being told that some works are beyond the limitations of mortal intellects, and for the less headstrong but probably more Romantic scholar who wishes to move from the civilized east of the Songs to the great vistas of the mountainous and unsettled west. Miltonists view *L'Allegro* and *Il Penseroso* from the heights of *Paradise Lost* and *Paradise Regained*. Blakeans have too long gazed up at *Milton* and *Jerusalem* from the vantage point of the *Songs of Innocence and of Experience*. The purpose of this collection of original essays is to assist in altering our perspective by offering a multitude of interpretations from which both students and scholars can construct a critical basis at once stable and varied.

The interests of the contributors are generous in their diversity; often they extend beyond the specific confines of the major prophecies. Still, the essays themselves are dominated by concerns, somewhat neglected in past Blake criticism, which find fullest expression in Blake's largest visionary and poetic structures. Particular attention focuses on Blake's form of epic-prophecy, on its traditions, its structure, aesthetics, and metaphysics. A related concern is the emphatic, if complex, relationship Blake sought to establish with his audience, a question as old as art itself, but generally thought of minor import to the selfconscious, independent literature of the Romantic period. The meaning of basic terms and values in Blake's mature vision is reassessed, particularly his concentration on the fundamental role of sexuality in human life. And a concerted attempt has been made to extend the recent, significant advances in our comprehension of the interaction of Blake's verbal and visual designs. Such varied interests and perspectives, of course, preclude a definitive statement on the major prophecies. But the prophecies are themselves, in the fullest sense of the word, their own and only definitive statement. The variety of conceptions in these essays seems peculiarly appropriate to the encompassing vision of the poems they treat. For few works in Western literature demand such creativity from their readers. To explore the essential language and form of such a response is the purpose of this volume. If the essays open many doors, we hope it can justly be said that they close none.

The editors have accumulated many debts in the process of planning and preparing this volume. David V. Erdman responded quickly and helpfully to several queries, and Walter B. Rideout provided encouragement at a time when encouragement—more than anything else—was needed. To Diane Boland, Pat Carrington, and Daphne Rowe, who maintained remarkable accuracy in their typing of large parts of the manuscript, we express our thanks.

The editors also wish to acknowledge the following persons and institutions for their kind permission to reproduce the illustrations in the volume: the Trustees of the British Museum for the drawings and engravings to *Vala* and the engraving, *Moore and Co. Advertisement*; the Victoria and Albert Museum for the pencil drawing called *Theotormon Woven*; the Huntington Library, San Marino, California, for the set of designs to

Comus; Lessing J. Rosenwald and the Library of Congress for the reproductions from copy D of *Milton*; and Mr. and Mrs. Paul Mellon for those
from copy E of *Jerusalem*.

S. C.

J. A. W.

Madison, Wisconsin
19 January 1972

ABBREVIATIONS

A	*America, a Prophecy*
DC	*A Descriptive Catalogue*
E	*Europe, a Prophecy*
EG	*The Everlasting Gospel*
FZ	*The Four Zoas*
J	*Jerusalem*
Job	*Illustrations for the Book of Job*
L	*The Book of Los*
M	*Milton*
Marg.	*Marginalia*
MHH	*The Marriage of Heaven and Hell*
NT	*Illustrations for Young's Night Thoughts*
PA	*Public Address*
SE	*Songs of Experience*
SI	*Songs of Innocence*
Thel	*The Book of Thel*
U	*The [First] Book of Urizen*
V	*Vala*
VDA	*Visions of the Daughters of Albion*
VLJ	*A Vision of the Last Judgment*

All quotations of Blake's poetry and prose, unless otherwise indicated, are from *The Poetry and Prose of William Blake*, ed. David V. Erdman, rev. ed. (Garden City, N.Y.: Doubleday, 1970); and in order to avoid any confusion, all page references to this edition, when they appear within the text of any essay, are given in italics. Citations are usually to plate and line number; thus, *M* 5: 15–19 means *Milton*, Plate 5, lines 15–19. On occasion, it was impossible to give a line number, or a line number that was meaningful; in these cases, the *italicized* number given after the plate or "Night" designation refers to the page in the Erdman edition on which the quotation appears. Thus, *M* 1: *95* means *Milton*, Plate 1, page 95, in the Erdman edition, and *FZ* VIIB: *395* means *The Four Zoas*, Night VIIB, page 395, in the Erdman edition. For convenience, and because of the complexities of citation for this fragmentary manuscript, references to *The Four Zoas* generally allude to the pages of the Erdman text rather than to the pages of the manuscript.

Blake's Sublime Allegory

The Aim of Blake's Prophecies and the Uses of Blake Criticism

JEROME J. McGANN

It is equally fatal to the spirit to have a system and not to have a system. Thus one must come to the decision to contain both.

Friedrich Schlegel, *Athenaeumsfragmente 53*

Though we have had many discussions of Blake's theory of the imagination, few relate that theory to what used to be called, in more innocent ages, the rhetorical purposes of his works. That is to say, whereas many areas of "meaning" in Blake's poetry have been exhaustively explored, few critics have tried to explain precisely how his poems aim to work. This question seems a crucial one, perhaps especially for the epics, which are poems designed to set in motion that elaborate set of relations known as Blake's "system," or his personal mythology.

The problem, which is both simple and fundamental, can be stated in this way. Do we not violate Blake's poetry by encouraging, in ourselves or in others, an analytic or systematic approach to it? Or is it true, as some readers have hinted, that Blake's own attacks upon Urizenic attitudes are themselves belied by his poetry, and thrown back by his complex "system"? Is it all, in fact, no more than another Satanic mill with complicated wheels?

I shall try to face these questions in this essay, and to propose an answer for those who find Blake's own work based upon hidden systematizing principles. At the same time I shall be entering a caveat not only for Blake criticism as such, but also for criticism in general, especially for those critics who agree with Blake's philosophic positions. My study of Blake has led to the conclusion that, to the degree that one regards Blake's art as an object of analysis and interpretation, to the degree that any criticism fosters

3

such a view, to that degree has Blake been misused, even, I would venture to say, misread. Such uses disregard Blake's explicit aims, and certainly do not treat his work in the same spirit that the author writ.

Much of what follows here is intended to be rigorously analytic. I can only say, at this point, what I hope will be borne out by the essay: that I have tried throughout to enlist analysis in the service of vision and, in Blake's words, to pierce Apollyon with his own bow.

I

Students of Blake often speak of his *prophetic* art, and they are right to do so. A prophet does not speak for himself, as orthodox conceptions of prophecy make very clear. The prophet is God's spokesman. This fact about prophetic speech has important aesthetic consequences for Blake. Blake believed that God was a man, incarnated in Jesus but imprisoned as well in every individual psyche. We are all divine children, as "The Lamb" so delicately recalls: "I a child, & thou a lamb, / We are called by his name" (*SI, p. 9*). Yet such a poem offers not an explanation of, but an occasion for experiencing, the oneness of man and God and their creations. Like so many of Blake's lyrics, "The Lamb" is properly called prophetic rather than personal because its "I" and "thou" do not locate the sort of personal encounter typical of the lyrics of Cowper, Burns, Coleridge, or Keats. "I" and "thou" are points of relation describing the circling unities of child, lamb, Christ, and Everyman. The art of the poem is to seem *not* to interpret the relations of its own signs, to offer those signs without a point of view from which to understand their significance. The poem seems hermetically sealed, and for this very reason makes a special demand upon those of us who desire it to establish communication. The poem, in fact, requires its meaning from the reader, the only personality which can experience in vision that for which the poem is the occasion.

In "Frost at Midnight" or "Bright Star" the poet is so completely in his poem that we as readers must observe everything at one remove. Our experience is mediated by the poetically enacted lives of Coleridge and Keats. But in the Blake poem no such mediation occurs. The reader is forced to a direct experience of a verbal process which can have no precise significance, not even an intermediary one, until he himself has given the language his own personal meaning.[1]

1. The distinction I am drawing is between the aesthetic strategies of two types of lyric, the one "personal," the other not. Though the "Coleridge" in "Frost at Midnight" is only a virtual presence, Blake's poem does not dramatize its materials psychologically at all, whereas Coleridge's poem does. Like "The Lamb," nearly all of

"The Lamb" is typical of Blake, and its special character explains why so many critics have resorted to the analytic constructs of "voices" and "personae" to explain Blake's poems. Such terms suggest the depersonalizing inertia in the works. But one must see, in addition, that the prophetic and visionary aspect of the poem is similarly depersonalized. The poem fulfills its prophecy and vision only in man the reader. We do not properly call Blake's art visionary if we merely mean by this that it records Blake's personal visions. His art is visionary not because it records but because it induces vision. For this reason Blake set out as epigraph to *Milton* the passage from Numbers: "Would to God that all the Lords people were Prophets" (1:95).

The whole of Blake's commentary on his painting *A Vision of the Last Judgment* repeats the idea that art is a vehicle for vision rather than an object of perception. In describing his work Blake says simply: "I have represented it [*The Last Judgment*] as I saw it[.] to different People it appears differently . . . as every thing else does.' He then goes on to explain carefully "The Nature of Visionary Fancy or Imagination." The power "is very little Known," Blake says,

& the Eternal nature & permanence of its ever Existent Images is considerd as less permanent than the things of Vegetative & Generative Nature yet the Oak dies as well as the Lettuce but Its Eternal Image & Individuality never dies. but renews by its seed. just . . . ⟨so⟩ the Imaginative Image returns . . . ⟨by⟩ the seed of Contemplative Thought the Writings of the Prophets illustrate these conceptions of the Visionary Fancy by their various sublime & Divine Images as seen in the Worlds of Vision.

(pp. 544–545)

What Blake means here is explained later when he elaborates on the nature of "Contemplative Thought." First he describes some of the scenes in his painting, which is itself a visionary response to certain biblical scenes and images. He then explains what is required of the viewer of his painting:

If the Spectator could Enter into these Images in his Imagination approaching them on the Fiery Chariot of his Contemplative Thought if he could Enter into Noahs Rainbow or into his bosom or could make a Friend & Companion of one of these Images of wonder which always intreats him to leave mortal things as he must know then would he arise from his Grave then would he meet the Lord in the Air & then he would be happy General Knowledge is Remote Knowledge it is in Particulars that Wisdom consists & Happiness too.

(p. 550)

Blake's lyrics are psychically neutralized. They cannot be approached in terms of models of psychological realities, whereas such models precisely *define* the major type of so-called Romantic lyric.

Such pronouncements explain why Blake thought that art alone could restore man to his golden age. Blake's ideal art released every man to the
achievement of his own fullest powers. Thus he could extol *"the Art of Invention not of Imitation"* (*PA, p. 569*), not so much to aggrandize his own
practice as to remind us that the end of all art, in every man, is not analysis
but vision.

All three of Blake's surviving epics are explicit attempts to recover the
Divine Vision for, in, and through the world. He does not compose his
poetry for himself but for "the Divine Humanity," the brotherhood of all
men. Thus he will say: "I will not cease from Mental Fight . . . Till we have
built Jerusalem" (*M* 1: 95). That is, "I" (Blake) struggle that "we" (Man)
may together, in vision, recover our emanation Jerusalem, who is the image
of every man's infinite desire. Blake is not simply being modest here. The
lyric states the literal fact of his belief, that the original state of blessedness
is recovered only when every man lives in vision, that is, when every man
beholds the universe in his own active imagination. An "external world" is
a delusion just as any "generalized" conception of reality is a shadow. To
find the world one must find oneself.

For all are Men in Eternity. Rivers Mountains Cities Villages,
All are Human & when you enter into their Bosoms you walk
In Heavens & Earths; as in your own Bosom you bear your Heaven
And Earth, & all you behold, tho it appears Without it is Within
In your Imagination, of which this World of Mortality is but a Shadow.
(J 71: 15–19)

Milton and *Vala* carry the same message. Since imagination "is the Human Existence itself" (*M* 32: 32), to be without imagination is to be inhuman, dead. But Blake does not rationalize, he images this condition.
Satan cannot exercise vision and is himself invisible:

his bosom grew
Opake against the Divine Vision: the paved terraces of
His bosom inwards shone with fires, but the stones becoming opake!
Hid him from sight, in an extreme blackness . . .
(M 9: 30–33)

This is the Satan who, as Prince of this World, darkens the minds of all
men:

Every thing in Eternity shines by its own Internal light: but thou
Darkenest every Internal light with the arrows of thy quiver . . .
That every thing is fixd Opake without Internal light.
(M 10: 16–20)

Though its style is rooted in poetic conventions of the eighteenth century, *Vala* dramatizes the same condition.

With trembling horror pale aghast the Children of Man
Stood on the infinite Earth & saw these visions in the air
In waters & in Earth beneath they cried to one another
What are we terrors to one another. Come O brethren wherefore
Was this wide Earth spread all abroad. not for wild beasts to roam
But many stood silent & busied in their families
And many said We see no Visions in the darksom air
Measure the course of that sulphur orb that lights the darksom day
Set stations on this breeding Earth & let us buy and sell
Others arose & schools Erected forming Instruments
To measure out the course of heaven.

(FZ II: 312)

Against such blindness was *Milton*, like *Vala* and *Jerusalem*, composed, to help man recover his own highest vision of himself:

Seest thou the little winged fly, smaller than a grain of sand?
It has a heart like thee; a brain open to heaven & hell,
Withinside wondrous & expansive; its gates are not clos'd,
I hope thine are not: hence it clothes itself in rich array;
Hence thou art cloth'd with human beauty O thou mortal man.
Seek not thy heavenly father then beyond the skies:
There Chaos dwells & ancient Night & Og & Anak old.

(M 20: 27–33)

Through all three epics the theme is relentlessly pursued: "Turn inwardly thine Eyes & there behold the Lamb of God" (*FZ VIIA: 330*).

The insistence upon every man's possession of his own Divine Vision is basic to everything Blake wrote. In their fulfilled, or, as Blake would have it, Edenic condition, all men are united in Jesus, that is, all men are creative visionaries who interchange their vital energies and continually regenerate themselves through each other.

... Man subsists by Brotherhood & Universal Love
We fall on one anothers necks more closely we embrace
Not for ourselves but for the Eternal Family we live
Man liveth not by Self alone but in his brothers face
Each shall behold the Eternal Father, & love & joy abound.

(FZ IX: 386–387)

Though this homely description of Blake's visionary paradise contrasts markedly with the splendid concluding passages of *Jerusalem*, it nevertheless expresses the same event.

Blake's task in his poetry, then, will not be to impose himself single-mindedly upon the company of those who agree to hear him. His poetry offers no solutions but can be, if rightly apprehended, the vehicle for our discovery of the solutions we each require:

> I rest not from my great task!
> To open the Eternal Worlds, to open the immortal Eyes
> Of Man inwards ... into Eternity ...
>
> (*J* 5: 17–19)

"To recover Art has been the business of my life," he declared (*PA, p. 569*), which meant the encouragement of vision in the "[*Imaginative Eye*] of Every one according to the situation he holds" (*VLJ, p. 544*). To do this requires an enormous act of self-effacement:

> Visions of ... eternal principles or characters of human life appear to poets, in all ages; the Grecian gods were the ancient Cherubim of Phoenicia. ... These gods are visions of the eternal attributes, or divine names, which, when ... erected into gods, become destructive to humanity. They ought to be the servants, and not the masters of man, or of society.
>
> (*DC, p. 527*)

Blake is not talking about theology here but about art, and about human life which is the creation of art. As he said in *The Marriage of Heaven and Hell*, all great visions court the danger of enslaving vulgar minds into worship and imitation. Indeed, the history of fallen man is the record of successive acts of creative vision which repeatedly became debased in cultural transmission. Blake believed he was divinely marked to usher in the final stages of fallen man's history, and that hence he was called upon to introduce an art that could be received only in vision. He aimed for an imaginative vehicle which would preclude his imposing himself on his audience.

His purpose was not to lead men to copy him but, through his example, to "copy Imagination" (*PA, p. 563*). No one, not even an inspired artist, can arrogate to himself the responsibilities which properly belong to every several individual. To assume such a prerogative is to pretend to righteousness and to become thereby the slave of one's selfish will. Good intentions here mean nothing. "There can be no Good-Will. Will is always Evil It is pernicious to others or selfish" (*Marg., p. 591*). Blake wrote *Milton* expressly to show the artistic weaknesses of the great Puritan whose name was given to the poem. Blake's *Milton* is a man who allowed his pure act of vision to be corrupted by personal commitments to certain ideas, that is, to what Blake calls moral law. History is full of different sets of ideas about the nature of man and his world, Blake said, but all such notions are the creations of man's perishing memory. They devour each other successively, which is for Blake the proof of their insubstantial character. Thus Milton, like so many before him, "shut the doors of mind and of thought, by placing Learning above Inspiration" (*DC, p. 537*). Milton himself admits that "I in my Selfhood" (*M* 14: 30) have been the cause of much human misery. The prophets Rintrah and Palamabron rightly say that his ideas and moral precepts introduced sequences of cultural horror (*M* 22: 38–45). In Blake's poem, Milton voluntarily sends his continuing spectrous life to annihilation.

Blake was determined not to fall into Milton's error, which amounted to the formation of a Urizenic system from what Milton's "enlarged & numerous senses" (*MHH* 11: 37) had perceived in true vision. Blake's program was to free man forever from the domination of intellectual programs. His aim was this, by "Striving with Systems to deliver Individuals from those Systems" (*J* 11: 5). Blake believed that all systems waged reductive attacks upon the multiplied particulars of life: "One Law for the Lion & Ox is Oppression" (*MHH* 24: 43). One may well wonder, therefore, why Blake should have created his own elaborate system and how he expected it to serve the arts of creation rather than destruction. What protects the reader from the powerful system announced by Blake's prophet at the beginning of *Jerusalem*?

I must Create a System, or be enslav'd by another Mans
I will not Reason & Compare: my business is to Create.
(10: 20–21)

II

Coming to terms with this apparent paradox in Blake's work demands that we grasp what Blake means by creation. Whether seen in a historical or an aesthetic frame of reference, creation can only be for Blake both an act of divine mercy and a delusion of the Satanic will. He states his views very explicitly in *A Vision of the Last Judgment*. Creation is generative and changing, whereas eternity is permanent and infinite. Therefore Blake insists that "Error is Created Truth is Eternal Error or Creation will be Burned Up & then & not till then Truth or Eternity will appear" (*p. 555*). Creation and eternity are two different conditions altogether, the one having a beginning and an end while the other remains a simple existent. "Eternity Exists and All things in Eternity Independent of Creation which was an act of Mercy" (*pp. 552–553*). In terms of Blake's biblical view of history, creation began with the fall of man from his eternal home in imagination. Before that catastrophe there was no "Error or Creation":

Earth was not: nor globes of attraction . . .
Death was not, but eternal life sprung.
                    (*U* 3: 36–39)

But if eternity and creation are two different conditions of being, the divine mercy, or imagination, can transform creation and error into the means of recovering true vision.

The Sexes sprung from Shame & Pride,
Blow'd in the morn; in evening died;
But Mercy chang'd Death into Sleep;
The Sexes rose to work & weep.
                    ("To Tirzah," *SE, p. 30*)

Ultimately aesthetic and historical creation are imaginatively transformed into a "Vision of the Science of the Elohim" (*M* 29: 65). The Elohistic science is precisely the system which Los seeks to manipulate, the means of piercing Apollyon with his own bow. It is a system driving itself and all things forward to Eternal Death, where changing forms will finally be "Burned up."

What is true in terms of natural and historical images is likewise true of art. The twenty-seven churches, or the successive intellectual and religious systems which man's fallen imagination has created, all solidify into destructive systems under the image of the Covering Cherub. Milton's Shadow is another avatar of this ultimate demon, for Blake argued that all men, even, like Milton, the most artistic and powerful, were subject to its transformations. Milton's own work fostered idolatry rather than life to the degree that it accepted certain pre-established systems of thought, or urged a wisdom that could be commonly accepted rather than one that had to be instantly gained.

What was needed was an art that could not be turned into an abstraction, an art that no one would fall down and worship. It must be an art that would urge no programs and offer no systems. He found it in an art which was ultimately committed not to creation but, paradoxically, to destruction, an art that would not be seen but would be seen through. Through it men would be made, like the Milton of Blake's poem, to "go to Eternal Death" (*M* 14: 14).

The chief metaphor for an art of this sort, as all of Blake's major epics show, is a Christian one: redemption through death and the annihilation of the righteous selfhood. The life of Jesus, along with all the economies of the Christian mystery, properly stands at the pivot of what Blake sought to accomplish. Blake's purposes, of course, have nothing to do with religion as we commonly know it, nor with philosophy or ethics. All these things comprised "the Wastes of Moral Law" (*J* 24: 24), those very sets of

abstractions which had closed man's infinite senses in the forests of the
night of Bishop Watson and under the sign of the Covering Cherub. The
life of Jesus is a poetic tale, not a form of worship; it does not introduce
into the world a new system but is the definitive method for deliverance
from all system. Blake represented this in the Jesus who lived to break all
the commandments. He himself strove to produce an art that would bring
no messages, consolatory or otherwise. His poetry issued a call to life not
through visionary ideas, which are a contradiction in terms, but through
visionary forms, poetic tales. In this sense his poetry must be said to have
no meaning.

The great Australian poet A. D. Hope has written, alike of poetry and
criticism: "Criticism in these years has undoubtedly become sharper and
more probing. . . . But it has also suffered from a certain over-confidence.
. . . The poem is always under the critic's microscope, and he seems never
to reflect that while he is testing the poem the poem may in fact be testing
him. Sometimes, if he were aware of it, a very sardonic eye is gazing back
at him through his lens."[2] Blake felt that all art, even the most debased,
could only be called art if it thus put men to the test. In this sense Blake
defines all poetry as prophecy, that is, the issuance of a call to judgment,
the declaration of a state of affairs in which men have to choose either the
light or the darkness. Echoing Isaiah 8: 15, Los declares:

But still I labour in hope, tho' still my tears flow down.
That he who will not defend Truth, may be compelld to defend
A Lie: that he may be snared and caught and snared and taken . . .
                                        (*J* 9: 28–30)

"He who has ears to hear, let him hear." Blake's prophetic art is in the first
place a revelation. It exposes the inner condition of the listener. But beyond
this, his art demands a choice. One must either take up the responsibility
for one's newly revealed life or let it go. These are the prophet's functions.
He does not teach, he declares that the time of choice has come.

The particular "testing" quality of Blake's art suggests why his work is
more closely allied to the *symboliste* method of later writers than to the
allegorical techniques of his intellectual forebears. Blake insisted his work
was not allegory because he correctly saw that all allegory "is Formd by
the daughters of Memory" (*VLJ, p. 544*), that it involves systems of signs
and things signified. Allegory counts upon "remembered" things—conventional meanings and publicly accepted ideas and forms of thought
which the poet can build upon.[3] But *symbolisme* came into being precisely

2. Alec Derwent Hope, *The Cave and the Spring* (Chicago: Univ. of Chicago Press,
1970), p. 76.
3. Thus Blake naturally associated allegory with his hated systems of thought (or

because the systems of publicly acceptable ideas and forms of thought had broken up. Art after the French Revolution especially registers Western man's cataclysmic sense of his loss of his traditional forms of order. In this process of cultural disintegration, often described in the rubric "dissociation of sensibility," men found themselves faced with the terror of an isolation they had not known before.

Many cultural prophets have lamented this descent into what could be called "mere anarchy." But Blake, along with a number of other writers, transformed it into an image of blessedness. For Blake it was an image of "Divine Mercy." A terrible beauty was seen to be born of such disintegration—the aesthetic man—and art broke away from that form of symbolism we now call allegory. Blake's notoriously private symbolism (and in contrast to allegory, all symbolism is private) is merely the sign of a new state of artistic affairs. His mythology is privately apocalyptic in the sense that any meaning which one derives from it will reveal more about the commentator than about the artifact or its maker. It is an art of creative obscurity because its obscurity repels generalized conceptions. The poetry carries meaning only along the grammars of individual assent.

Thematic criticism of "The Tyger," for example, has been both massive and contentious; and there is no reason to think that the quarrels about the meaning of the poem will soon be resolved. But once a reader no longer requires a definitive experience of the poem in cognitive terms, it ceases to pose a problem (though it must always remain a conundrum). As with so many of Blake's lyrics, part of the poem's strategy is to resist attempts to imprint meaning upon it. "The Tyger" tempts us to a cognitive apprehension but in the end exhausts our efforts. It teases us out of thought and either drives us on to vision or away from it, back to old habits of perception. "The Fly" operates similarly. "The Clod & the Pebble" is yet another, unpretentious example of a poem designed to confound intellectual apprehension. This modest, yet treacherous, lyric perfectly balances its opposing sets of assertive symbols. Tempting us to approach it as if it were an allegory about ethics, in the end it baffles the inherited content of its images. Like "The Tyger," the poem has no meaning. The attitudes represented through the clod and the pebble face each other to a standoff.

In this respect, I should perhaps mention that Blake's method has analogues in the work of other Romantic and Romantically influenced post-Romantic writers. Shelley's *Alastor*, Keats's "La Belle Dame sans Merci" or "Ode on a Grecian Urn," Coleridge's *Kubla Khan*, are all works which produce extreme critical controversy. But, as in Blake, these poems are

---

what he calls "Moral Law"). "Allegories are things that Relate to Moral Virtues Moral Virtues do not Exist they are "Allegories & dissimulations" (*VLJ, p. 614*).

precisely designed to foster ambivalent perspectives. To decide that Keats's fairy child is a Circe or a visionary ideal, or neither, is to have passed a judgment upon one's self. Poems like these are silent forms teasing us into and out of our own thoughts. A Byronic hero is a similar figure—one cast into antithetical sets of terms whose significance can only be determined by a reader's self-implicating decision. One could also cite, as examples of this technique, many of Tennyson's poems, especially the earlier ones like "Mariana" and "The Lady of Shalott."

Thus, the extreme diversity of opinion among critics of Blake about the meaning of particular poems and passages of poems is perhaps the most eloquent testimony we have to the success of his work. Interpretations of the meanings of Blake's poems are necessarily legion, since his poetry was written to break in upon the centers of individual life and call their meanings into the open. Like Jesus, Blake came to send not peace but a sword. His work is a sign of contention.

I I I

When Blake says, in a letter to Dr. Trusler, that the most useful art "rouzes the faculties [of others] to act" (*p. 676*),[4] he not only tells us about the peculiar orientation of his poetry; he suggests as well what it involves. Vision and imagination are not merely a method of thought or even a way of life. <u>Vision *is* life, the only life.</u> When he says, as a relatively young man writing *There Is No Natural Religion*, that the poetic genius is "the faculty which experiences" (*p. 2*), he formulates a lifelong conviction: "Inspiration & Vision was then & now is & I hope will always Remain my Element my Eternal Dwelling place" (*PA, p. 650*). The two remarks have in common the belief that one does not *know* through imagination, one lives in it. Ideas are gained but life is lived. Correspondingly, the imaginative life carries us not to achievements but experiences. When Blake praises Shakespeare and the Bible, it is not for the ideas they give us but for the poetic tales they present. Their art is exemplary rather than prescriptive. It offers forms upon which imagination can feed and grow.[5]

4. The entire passage surrounding this quotation emphasizes how deeply Blake was committed to the tradition of allegorical prophecy. His poetic obscurity is a deliberate device, he says, and he appeals to the practice of the ancients. For a fine concise discussion of these traditions see Michael Murrin's *The Veil of Allegory* (Chicago: Univ. of Chicago Press, 1969), especially chapters 1 and 2.

5. The basis of Blake's criticism of Swedenborg in relation to Dante and Shakespeare is that the latter offer poetic tales to release imagination in their audiences, whereas too much of Swedenborg is mere intellectualizing: "a recapitulation of all superficial opinions, and an analysis of the more sublime, but no further" (*MHH* 22: 42). Blake

Blake holds up an exemplary art, an art of poetic tales, because such forms are neutral. They can mean anything. To be presented with them—to read "The Mental Traveller," for example—is to be exposed and tested. Imaginative life is not comfortable; it is strenuous, trying. Urizen initiates the fall of man precisely because he shrinks from the furious wars of eternity.

I have sought for a joy without pain,
For a solid without fluctuation
Why will you die O Eternals?
Why live in unquenchable burnings?
                    (U 4: 10–13)

Ultimately *Jerusalem* has only one aim: to lead us toward vision in the infinite world. Though the elaboration of this simple purpose is astonishing, one can grasp the essential method by looking closely at one of the poem's symbols, the world of Generation. Accumulating the different images which make up this symbolic complex, we discover an essentially contrarious situation. We have, on the one hand, the destructive mills of generation, the Satanic wheels which produce the inhuman city of Babylon. Related to these are the nets of female religion, themselves allied to the vast polypus of death images recurring everywhere. Blake deliberately presents these images as parodic versions of an alternative, heroic set associated with the prophet Los. The mills correspond to the furnaces of Los which build the city of art, Golgonooza, just as Rahab's nets correspond to Enitharmon's golden looms in Cathedron. These latter creations are called "the sublime Universe of Los & Enitharmon" (J 59: 21).

The world of Generation, then, in its lethal aspect, is a sea of time and space, a delusive state of cycles and flux, perpetuating bondage and dismemberment. Blake's famous Arlington Court tempera painting depicts such a world. As the joyfully declared "[*Image*] of regeneration" (J 7: 65), however, the world of flux is a patent symbol of divine grace. For creation is also an act of mercy.

For Blake, the man of imagination lives in neither of these worlds but in eternity. The sublime world of Los and Enitharmon is merely the world of deadly generation turned inside out. Thereby the world is *revealed*, exposed, so that men may be led on to death and vision. Los's world, in Blake's terms, is a current which runs opposed to the current of vegetative existence. Blake has some marvelous ways of imaging this interacting set of opposing movements.

always praises art that is exemplary rather than art which urges opinion, for the same reasons. See for example his "Annotations to Watson," especially *p. 607*; or, even more emphatically, *A Descriptive Catalogue, p. 534.*

Terrific ragd the Eternal Wheels of intellect terrific ragd
The living creatures of the wheels, in the Wars of Eternal life
But perverse rolld the wheels of Urizen & Luvah back revers'd . . .
(*FZ* I: *309*)

In *Milton* the same image is brilliantly refined in terms of a set of mechanical cogs, the "evil" one turning in one direction but the "redemptive" one, attached to it, fatally reversing the effective inertia through death toward life.

This Wine-press is call'd War on Earth, it is the Printing-Press
Of Los; and here he lays his words in order above the mortal brain
As cogs are formd in a wheel to turn the cogs of the adverse wheel.
(*M* 27: 8–10)

The whole of the last movement of the first chapter of *Milton* (23: 31— 29: 65) is an elaborate illustration of this doubled perspective upon "the World of Los the labour of six thousand years" (29: 64). For example, the remark that the wine-press of Los "is call'd War on Earth" spins off a double set of images, one of a horrifying cast, the other suggestive of the Great Harvest and Vintage, the Communion of Saints. Los, the generative form of the eternal prophet Urthona, forces us to hold the two perspectives in a single field. Doing so, we participate in the redemption of creation (ourselves), and even perceive wherein the created "Nature is a Vision of the Science of the Elohim" (29: 65).

At the end of the first chapter of *Jerusalem* (23: 29—24: 60), Albion repeats the experience of Los's Spectre at the beginning of the chapter (7: 9–50—10: 37–59). Both the Spectre of Los and Albion, perceiving the murderous aspects of Nature and History, curse their lot and counsel despair. The situation seems hopeless to both of them. As Albion laments: "But Albion is cast forth to the Potter his Children to the Builders / To build Babylon because they have forsaken Jerusalem" (24: 29–30). Like Los's Spectre, he will wish "that Death & Annihilation were the same" (23: 40).

But such a view is what Blake calls "single vision," and he composes his epics to raise men, initially, into the double vision that is the generative symbol of the fourfold vision in eternity. To perceive not only that nature is a prison house but that it is a garden of delights ("the sublime Universe of Los & Enitharmon") is to perceive through "contraries." Threefold vision, which Blake associates with the land of Beulah, is a further advance still. In this condition men perceive the identity of the contraries.

There is a place where Contrarieties are equally True
This place is called Beulah, It is a pleasant lovely Shadow
Where no dispute can come. Because of those who Sleep.
(*M* 30: 1–3)

The verse enacts its own principle by demanding that we rouse our faculties to see beyond the differences to the equalities (both for good and evil) between the terrible sleep of death and the benevolent sleep of Beulah. But to be in Beulah is to possess only its consolatory perspective. Beulah is a place of "mild & pleasant Rest" (30: 14) for Blake's pilgrims of eternity.

Fourfold vision is not rest but activity. Its first demand is that all things be forsaken, since only by thus fostering a condition of total perceptual indigence can one begin the preparation for infinite vision. Possessing nothing, one discovers that all things are possible. But if to describe fourfold vision in this way is almost to parody it, Blake's poems resort to enactment and dramatization. However this is done, it always occurs in the "Moment in each Day that Satan cannot find" (M 35: 42). (Note how Blake's statement assures us that such visionary, timeless moments are continually borne to us through fallen time, even by Satan's "Watch Fiends" themselves.) Between the pulsations of an artery, suspended from time in time, such a moment contains an experience of dying to an old form of thought and gaining a new world of perception.

Blake's poems aim to establish the conditions which will rouse the faculties of his readers to this very death and release. He sets out contrarious perspectives on the universe, and by violent acts of juxtaposition forces us "To build the Universe stupendous: Mental forms Creating" (M 30: 20). The demand is that we set the poem's terms into successively different types of relations with each other. Blake's art is a sort of Glass-Bead Game. To "make sense" of his works we establish in and for them different forms of order based upon shifting sets of dissociations and associations, contrasts and analogies. To cease the act of creating these sets of relations, or of ironically unbuilding them again, is to lapse into single vision. For example, to perceive the similarity between the Spectre of Los and Albion in the first chapter of *Jerusalem* is to have gained a perception that is already a dangerous temptation to single vision and Newton's sleep. That sense of an analogy itself establishes the terms for a further demand: the perception of distinctions and contrasts. And these additional experiences call for still further constructions and destructions. As far as Blake is concerned, the process is clearly infinite. His favorite image for it is, characteristically, an optical one.

Albion! Our wars are wars of life, & wounds of love,
With intellectual spears, & long winged arrows of thought:
Mutual in one anothers love and wrath all renewing
We live as One Man; for contracting our infinite senses
We behold multitude; or expanding: we behold as one,
As One Man all the Universal Family . . .

(*J* 34: 14–19)

Blake's epics aim to promote such acts of imaginative perception on both a large and a small scale. Every line ought to be an opportunity for outwitting Satan's watch fiends, while the poem as a whole is designed as a spiritual exercise for the encouragement of universal prophecy. To illustrate the method in slightly greater detail, let us take the famous speech of Enion at the end of the second night of *Vala*.

I am made to sow the thistle for wheat; the nettle for a nourishing dainty
I have planted a false oath in the earth, it has brought forth a poison tree
I have chosen the serpent for a councellor & the dog
For a schoolmaster to my children
I have blotted out from light & living the dove & nightingale
And I have caused the earth worm to beg from door to door
I have taught the thief a secret path into the house of the just
I have taught pale artifice to spread his nets upon the morning
My heavens are brass my earth is iron my moon a clod of clay
My sun a pestilence burning at noon & a vapour of death in night

What is the price of Experience do men buy it for a song
Or wisdom for a dance in the street? No it is bought with the price
Of all that a man hath his house his wife his children
Wisdom is sold in the desolate market where none come to buy
And in the witherd field where the farmer plows for bread in vain

It is an easy thing to triumph in the summers sun
And in the vintage & to sing on the waggon loaded with corn
It is an easy thing to talk of patience to the afflicted
To speak the laws of prudence to the houseless wanderer

To listen to the hungry ravens cry in wintry season
When the red blood is filld with wine & with the marrow of lambs
It is an easy thing to laugh at wrathful elements
To hear the dog howl at the wintry door, the ox in the slaughter house moan
To see a god on every wind & a blessing on every blast
To hear sounds of love in the thunder storm that destroys our enemies house
To rejoice in the blight that covers his field, & the sickness that cuts off his
  children
While our olive & vine sing & laugh round our door & our children bring fruits
  & flowers

Then the groan & the dolor are quite forgotten & the slave grinding at the mill
And the captive in chains & the poor in the prison, & the soldier in the field
When the shatterd bone hath laid him groaning among the happier dead

It is an easy thing to rejoice in the tents of prosperity
Thus could I sing & thus rejoice, but it is not so with me!

(*pp. 318–319*)

The first ten lines are self-accusation of the same sort that Albion makes in the passages from *Jerusalem* cited above. The final seventeen lines are Enion's justification for her "lamentation" and feelings of despair: her life having been blighted, she will not rejoice. What she says is, in fact, a trenchant criticism of the ordinary sort of mortal "joy," which is really no more than a reflex movement toward an external condition of prosperity (just as her own despair is a reflex movement toward an external condition of poverty and evil). This implicit criticism of the ignorantly joyful is analogous to the just accusations hurled against the world by Los's Spectre in *Jerusalem*.

As with Los's Spectre, however, Enion's "just cause" for sorrow is of an unredemptive sort from her perspective. It remains a function of a reflexive existence. The famous central lines of the passage underline this for us and are intended by Blake to rouse up our faculties to a new perspective on Enion's speech. For Enion, the "price of Experience" is far too dear to pay, since it involves the loss "Of all that a man hath." The perception that her life has been a source of destruction and misery is an "Experience" she has gained at what she regards as too terrible a cost. It has left her utterly "desolate." But the lines, with their implicit allusion to the New Testament admonishment to sell all that one hath in order to follow Jesus, drive the reader toward an expansion of his understanding of Enion's speech. Through her words we come to perceive what she cannot see but what Blake is constantly iterating: that the poetic genius is the faculty which experiences, and that all imaginative growth entails, in Blake's characteristically Pauline way of expressing it, a self-annihilation, a voluntary death to the old man and a waking to the new. This "Experience," which Enion laments, becomes for her a failed invitation to apocalypse. To rejoice in the corrosive fires of self-discovery would be to have experienced what Blake understands by the life of imagination.

For us, the perception of larger significances in Enion's speech is an imaginative exercise establishing the ground for a habitual humanity. But we must recall that such imaginative acts have little to do with cognition as such. Meaning is not the issue in such matters, nor could it be, since experienced worlds are perpetually crossed with networks of warring ideas and systems of ideas. All ideas have their contraries, and the sets of contraries are indefinitely expandable within worlds mapped along four dimensions. For Blake, the essence of human life is not thought but experience, the imaginative apprehension of the unseen worlds which we believe will always exist for the joy of man's discovery. These may as well be worlds of thought, but for Blake the experience of discovering them rather than the intellectual possession of them is paradise, Eden, fourfold vision.

I V

Like the angel of the Annunciation and the prophets of the Good News, Los exists to prepare the way for the coming of the Lord, and one of his most difficult functions is to give way before the Redeemer. This final gesture is the justification of the prophet's life. Los's career in *Jerusalem* follows such a pattern of life, which is clearly derived from the example of Saint John the Baptist.[6] In *Jerusalem*, Plate 75, we read:

And Rahab Babylon the Great hath destroyed Jerusalem . . .

And all her Twenty-seven Heavens now hid & now reveal'd,
Appear in strong delusive light of Time & Space drawn out
In Shadowy pomp by the Eternal Prophet created evermore

For Los in Six Thousand Years walks up & down continually
That not one Moment of Time be lost & every revolution
Of Space he makes permanent in Bowlahoola & Cathedron . . .
But Jesus, breaking thro' the Central Zones of Death & Hell
Opens Eternity in Time & Space; triumphant in Mercy.

(ll. 1–22)

The passage helps to explain other things besides the relation of Los and Jesus. The universe of Los in space and time is created in order to expel all such natural boundaries from man's life forever. Near the opening of the poem Los, seeing the melancholy duty placed upon him to create a world of spatial and temporal forms, yet hopes against his fears.

Yet why despair? I saw the finger of God go forth
Upon my Furnaces from within the Wheels of Albion's Sons,
Fixing their Systems, permanent: by mathematic power
Giving a body to Falsehood that it may be cast off for ever
With Demonstrative Science piercing Apollyon with his own bow!

(*J* 12: 10–14)

In the end, Los will himself undergo the death through which his own dire but merciful inventions drive all things. When this event is told, the natural world of space and time ends forever. Los himself goes to Eternal Death along with all his invented worlds, in order to advance the redemption of Albion. When the risen Albion says to Jesus, the Divine Vision: "I see thee

---

6. In *Milton*, on the other hand, the relation of Blake and Milton is patterned on that of Elijah and Elisha (see the opening chapters of 2 Kings). The "Chariot of fire," which presides over *Milton* (1:95), is a direct echo of Elijah's chariot described in 2 Kings 2:11.

in the likeness & similitude of Los my Friend" (*J* 96: 22), we understand
that art itself has finally been redeemed to the Divine Vision. This entails
the annihilation of "art" for "Vision" and hence means that in *Jerusalem*
Los must pay "the price of Experience" if he would truly live; that is, he
must give up all he has. His death is the heroic gift which he passes on to his
friend Albion, the example according to which Albion must live his life. As
Albion received it from his friend Los, Los received it from Jesus.

We live imagination as Jesus did, though we live in it through the exercise
of all our giant faculties, in particular the faculty of aesthetic prophecy.
Imagination does not create time and space, Los does. Imagination conceives
the transformation of these terrifying and deadly manufactures into the
mercies of eternity, a transformation in which the fearful Los yet courage-
ously hopes. In this process Los is Jesus' instrument, just as Los's Spectre is
the instrument of Urthona's vehicular personality. When Blake speaks of
Los "Creating Space, Creating Time according to the wonders Divine / Of
Human Imagination" (*J* 98: 31–32), the very grammar draws the distinction I have been pointing to. For, to Blake, imagination is not creation; it is,
rather, life, existence, and—in the metaphor most characteristic of Blake's
own faculties—vision. All creation is a *felix culpa* according to imagination
(in any other view it is mere Hell) and will be, as Blake said, annihilated
in the Last Judgment that ushers in Human Existence. For this was all creation permitted: death. Golgonooza, Los's city, is not Jerusalem but the means
toward it, and the function of his city of art is to reveal the whorish aspects
of all creation. Golgonooza too must go to Eternal Death, for it stands not
only as the promise of Jerusalem, but also as the last great temptation to
retreat from vision. Golgonooza is the house whose windows of the morning
open out to the worlds of eternity, where Jesus dwells. We were never meant
to live in it, or with it, but through it.

Like Shelley, Blake understood the magnificent, if agonizing, truth that
when composition begins inspiration is already on the wane, for the function of imagination is the life of activity rather than the pleasures of possession. We cannot live in art: Tennyson's commonplace friend never dreamed
what a profound truth was ironically hinted in that officious remonstrance.
The task Blake set himself was the revelation of a form of art which would
not imprison later generations of men the way so much of art, even Milton's,
had done. Blake aimed to foster a fellowship of creative spirits, not a world
of corpses paralyzed within a dream of life. To regard Blake's vision of life
as an object of study or perception is to transform it into a shadow of death.
Thus he designed his work to be a means of vision in us, to "rouze" our faculties to act the way his had been roused. For the only communion that men
share in Jesus is the exercise of imagination. The vehicular forms of the
imaginative life, that is, the worlds of Los, are as varied as human existence

itself; and men must be encouraged to their continual production. To do so, artists must approach the world not with creations that will trap men but with visions that will encourage imaginative activity. The model for such an art, in Blake's mind, was his notion of a Christian death, that is, the gaining of life not by possessing it but by fostering it. Men live only when they help life to spring everywhere and eternally. So Blake waged war on the Selfhood continually, knowing that his visions were not ours any more than his own perceptions were ritually repeatable. Thus he developed an intensely private mythology, to protect both himself and us: for we can live in that mythology only to Blake's shame and our destruction. For himself, he had continually to subject his own visions to revisions and imaginative renewals. "William Blake," he could sign himself, "Born 28 Novr 1757 in London & has died several times since."

Opening the Seals:
Blake's Epics
and the Milton Tradition

JOSEPH ANTHONY WITTREICH, JR.

The genius of the prophetic poetry is to be explored by a due attention to the nature and design of prophecy itself.

—Robert Lowth

When Blake, in a letter, admonished Dr. Trusler, "you ought to know that What is Grand is necessarily obscure to Weak men. That which can be made Explicit to the Idiot is not worth my care" (*p. 676*), he committed himself to a poetry of obscurity and invited the criticism that, in his epics, a vast idea is lost in confusion and verbiage. Bernard Blackstone epitomizes over a century of response to Blake when he concludes that "the *aesthetic* impact of the symbolic books on the reader—on the careful and persistent reader . . . is one of confusion and obscurity. We cannot enjoy *Jerusalem* as we enjoy

This essay is a revised and expanded version of the lecture I delivered at the Henry E. Huntington Library and Art Gallery on August 28, 1971. Research for the essay was carried out, in part, during my tenure as a Fellow of the Folger Shakespeare Library. For this award, I am grateful to the Trustees of Amherst College and also to the University of Wisconsin Graduate School that, by a supplementary grant, made my semester at the Folger feasible. Another paper, " 'Sublime Allegory': Blake's Epic Manifesto and the Milton Tradition," *Blake Studies*, 4 (1972), 15–44, provides a context for this one; and still another, "Domes of Mental Pleasure: Blake's Epics and Hayley's Epic Theory," *Studies in Philology*, 69 (1972), 101–129, offers an illuminating footnote to it. Several other studies provide incisive statements on the Romantic epic, and all of them have important implications for Blake: (1) Karl Kroeber, *Romantic Narrative Art* (Madison: Univ. of Wisconsin Press, 1960), esp. pp. 78–112; (2) Brian Wilkie, *Romantic Poets and Epic Tradition* (Madison: Univ. of Wisconsin Press, 1965), esp. pp. 3–29; (3) Thomas A. Vogler, *Preludes to Vision: The Epic Venture in Blake,*

Paradise Lost or *The Prelude*."[1] Behind Blackstone's comment is the belief
that Blake, unlike Milton or Wordsworth, disregarded tradition, locking
his "vision" from generations of readers. What Blackstone does not comprehend (and few besides William Butler Yeats have) is that, while spurning
eighteenth-century poetical traditions, Blake still took his place within the
margins of what he regarded, and we should recognize, as the Milton tradition. In the process, Blake created a poetry of contexts with Milton's poems
serving as a backdrop for his own.

Throughout most of this century, Blake's admirers and detractors alike
have noisily asserted his radical independence of mind, his iconoclastic
spirit, which allegedly isolates him from poetical traditions and from "a
framework of accepted and traditional values."[2] For the Blake cult, the
poet's "isolationism" has been cause for celebration; but for T. S. Eliot,
who argues that without strong ties with tradition a poet is speechless,
Blake's "isolationism" has resulted in the silencing of a major talent. Like
Eliot, Yeats affirms the value of tradition, but Yeats's tradition is differently
constituted than Eliot's: whereas Eliot pushes Milton outside the main tradition of English poetry and says that Blake deliberately took a place beyond
its boundaries, Yeats places Milton at the center of the same tradition and
Blake within its margins. To think otherwise, says Yeats, is to have "glass
screwed into one eye."[3] Until recently, Yeats's perception has gone untested.

In *Blake and Tradition*, Kathleen Raine argues that we may come "to a
deeper understanding of Blake through knowledge of his traditional roots,"[4]
which she locates, not in poetical tradition, but in the heterodox tradition
that embraces Neoplatonism and hermeticism. Despite its considerable
learning and its considered interpretations, Raine's book is disappointing,
and disappointing for precisely the reason formulated by Jean Hagstrum:
"The shadowy and insubstantial pageant of Neoplatonism is an inappropri-

---

Wordsworth, Keats, and Hart Crane (Berkeley and Los Angeles: Univ. of California
Press, 1971), esp. pp. 1–59; (4) Stuart Curran, "The Mental Pinnacle: *Paradise Re-
gained* and the Romantic Four-Book Epic," in *Calm of Mind: Tercentenary Essays on
Paradise Regained and Samson Agonistes in Honor of John S. Diekhoff*, ed. J. A.
Wittreich, Jr. (Cleveland: Press of Case Western Reserve Univ., 1971), pp. 133–162.
The first three studies, all of them intelligent pieces of criticism, share a common
fault: they attribute to the Romantics what should rightly be attributed first to Milton.
Curran's essay sets the record straight and, in doing so, becomes the starting point for
any future study of the Romantic epic.

1. *English Blake* (Cambridge: Cambridge Univ. Press, 1949), p. 69.
2. T. S. Eliot, *The Sacred Wood* (London: Methuen, 1934), p. 157.
3. *The Letters of William Butler Yeats*, ed. Alan Wade (New York: Macmillan,
1955), p. 853.
4. Bollingen Series 35: 11 (Princeton: Princeton Univ. Press, 1968), I, xxxii.

ate and inadequate analogue to Blake's vision."[5] The Neoplatonic influence on Blake is qualitatively different from the impulses that came to him from the Bible and Milton, or from Michelangelo and Raphael: "These four sources are in a class by themselves; Blake is humble before them since they constitute the Bible of humanity. What Kathleen Raine says of Blake's Neoplatonic and hermetic sources can properly be said of these four and perhaps no others. These authors and artists Blake reflects with pride, and is not above receiving their 'dictation.'"[6] Hagstrum's understanding is shared by John Grant, who observes that "Blake must not be relegated to his former state of splendid and irrelevant isolation from the main currents of thought," but cautions that an understanding of Blake and tradition will not take us far if we are restricted to Kathleen Raine's tradition. "When we come to Blake and Milton," however, "there really is something to talk about."[7] Hagstrum and Grant fasten attention to the relationship that this essay will explore. Blake's deepest roots are planted in the epic tradition that by Spenser and Milton was tied to the tradition of prophecy. These are the traditions, unexplored by Raine but continually invoked by Blake, that stand behind his poetry from *Poetical Sketches* to *Jerusalem* and that provide the best guide to understanding it.

Blake understood that "Poetry was a tradition like religion and liable to corruption,"[8] and he saw the corrupted forms of both traditions emerging in his own century. Unsurprisingly, Blake turned from the poets of the eighteenth century, who seemed more adept at theorizing about epics than writing them, to the examples of Spenser and Milton, who, harnessing prophecy to epic, created a new kind of epic poetry. Spenser, because he fostered the experimentation that Milton continued, requires notice; but it is finally Milton who made the great advances, forging a new tradition out of the old one—a tradition that Blake could embrace as his own and, once mastering, could use as the informing context for his epic endeavors—*The Four Zoas*, *Milton*, and *Jerusalem*.

Blake was not interested in the Milton tradition as T. S. Eliot understood it: as a tradition of eighteenth-century imitators who proved that Milton could be only a bad influence on those who would follow in his footsteps. For Blake, the Milton tradition was comparable to the classical epic tradition; it was created by Milton with the hope that his successors would use it

5. "Kathleen Raine's Blake," *Modern Philology*, 68 (1970), 82.

6. Ibid., p. 79.

7. John E. Grant, "Blake's Designs for *L'Allegro* and *Il Penseroso*," *Blake Newsletter*, 4 (1971), 118.

8. William Butler Yeats, "Introduction," *The Oxford Book of Modern Verse 1892–1935* (Oxford: Clarendon Press, 1936), p. ix.

in the same way that he used the poems of Homer, Virgil, and Ovid—imaginatively, not imitatively. Milton's own epics refuted the notion that "the *epic process* was stayed at a particular point," a moment at which "its development . . . [its] movement was arrested." Blake perceived that most epic poets were "followers . . . [and] copyists of a pattern long ago laid down in antiquity";[9] but this perception also provided him with the basis for distinguishing between "most" epic poets and Milton: they followed the classical patterns that Milton subverted, and they were tyrannized by the very traditions from which Milton liberated epic poetry. The Milton tradition, for Blake, was characterized not by its bonds with the past but by its freedom from them—not by its compliance with precedents but by its disregard of them. To write within the Milton tradition was to write without fetters, and thus Blake was able to give an allegiance to Milton that he could not properly give to any other poet. Blake could go to school to Milton just as Milton had gone to school to Spenser. Like Spenser, Milton joined epic to prophecy; but what was more important, from Blake's point of view, was that Milton took a radical stance against *all* traditions—poetical and intellectual. Poets like Spenser, Herbert, and Milton transmuted the forms they inherited, but what distinguished Milton from other poets was the fact that he used his newly created forms to undermine rather than to uphold the reigning orthodoxies. Spenser and Herbert took their values from the audiences they addressed, but Milton (and Blake following him) rejected the prevailing values in order to create new ones.

The Milton tradition, as understood by Blake, reflects a perfect coincidence between form and content: radically altered forms become the vehicles for revolutionary ideals; the humanistic mind becomes an instrument of reformation, celebrating liberty in all its aspects and thereby prompting artistic, political, social, and theological change. Milton, the revolutionary, lived through crises and disillusionment and wrested from the old order a design for a cohesive and creative society. The image of that order is not any individual poem but rather the total vision to which various poems contribute. An architect of new forms, a generator of values nobler than those his culture already possessed, a maker of new myths rather than a recorder of old ones, Milton projected a portrait of the artist that Blake emulated; and, more than any other writer of epics, Milton showed that the evolution of epic poetry involved a progress toward intellectual and imaginative freedom. Before Milton, epic was a hybrid form, subsuming under one cover diverse forms. In *Paradise Lost*, Milton explodes this conception of epic by exploiting all forms within his one grand form and thus opens the way for the quintessential form that he creates with the publication of *Paradise Re-*

9. William Macneile Dixon, *English Epic and Heroic Poetry* (London: J. M. Dent and Sons, and New York: E. P. Dutton, 1912), pp. 13, 16.

gained. In this poem, even more than in *Paradise Lost*, Milton pushes beyond the tradition of mimetic art, disrupting the free movement of narration with the mental exertions characteristic of visionary art. In the process, epic conventions give way to prophetic structures, and the epic poem becomes less a dome of pleasure and more a palace of wisdom.

This essay treats incidentally these various aspects of the Milton tradition, but it is concerned centrally with just one element in that tradition—the fusion of epic and prophecy. Though greatly misunderstood by neoclassical poets (and some modern ones), the Milton tradition was comprehended at the end of the eighteenth century by William Cowper and William Hayley and was relayed to Blake by them. Together Hayley and Cowper sharpened Blake's comprehension of Milton and of the tradition that he shaped, and, in turn, the Milton tradition steadily became a more and more prominent context in Blake's poetry. This is my understanding, but it was also the understanding of Blake's first commentator. Having observed that the Book of Revelation and Milton "may well be supposed to engross much of Mr. Blake's study," Benjamin Malkin concluded that Blake's later poetry is "altogether *epic* in its structure."[10] Blake's "later" poetry achieves the same kind of union between epic and prophecy that Milton achieved in his epics. Many of Blake's early poems are explicitly or implicitly "prophecies" (Blake designates *America* and *Europe* as such); yet many of his early poems (*The Book of Urizen*, for instance) reveal an epic impulse that does not become prominent until he writes *The Four Zoas*. Within this poem, Blake's rather nebulous conception of epic evolves to the point where he can attempt a meaningful coalescence of epic and prophetic elements, a coalescence that is grandly realized in *Milton* and *Jerusalem*.

Recently it has been suggested that while Milton "produced epic expressions . . . on which both the poet and the audience could agree" Blake confronted a new challenge: his task involved "finding, rather than preserving, an acceptable collective ideology."[11] This view of Milton was not held by Cowper and Hayley. As they read Milton, *Paradise Lost* and *Paradise Regained* were new swords forged on old anvils; Milton's epics were designed to destroy specious orthodoxies and to create new ones. Cowper finds in Milton a precedent for most of the "doctrines" (literary and theological)

10. Benjamin Heath Malkin, *A Father's Memoirs of His Child* (London, 1806), pp. xxx, xl (my italics).

11. Vogler, *Preludes to Vision*, pp. 8–9. Christopher Caudwell presents a view that contradicts Vogler's and that corresponds with my own: the effect of revolution on an artist, like Milton, was profound, says Caudwell; "Poet and audience were separated" (*Romance and Realism: A Study of English Bourgeois Literature*, ed. Samuel Hynes [Princeton: Princeton Univ. Press, 1970], p. 43).

represented in his own time as "modern";[12] and like Cowper, Hayley sees
Milton as the shaper of a new Christianity. Locating in *Paradise Regained*
the truly revolutionary moment in the history of epic poetry, Hayley discovers in the poem "a purer religion" accompanied by "the truest heroism,
and the triumph of Christianity."[13] This perception is shared by Blake, but
not by most historians of epic poetry and students of Milton. When the revolutionary character of Milton's art is discussed (and that is too seldom),
Paradise Lost is represented as "the nodal point in the history of the English
epic," as "the really revolutionary moment," as "the first and, at the same
time, the last example of a really modern 'heroic' poem."[14] Hayley and
Blake would concede that *Paradise Lost* is "a glorious and perfectly staged
suicide"[15] which leaves the classical epic in ruins; but they perceived, too,
that in *Paradise Regained* Milton brings out of those ruins a new kind of
epic that gathers into focus and minutely particularizes the radical version
of Christianity given form but not body in *Paradise Lost*. This perception
is behind Blake's comment to Henry Crabb Robinson: "Milton . . . in his
old age . . . returned back to God whom he had had in his childhood."[16] It is
also the perception behind Blake's second set of designs to *Paradise Lost*
and his illustrations to *Paradise Regained*; it is an informing idea in
Milton.[17] Milton, the revolutionary, turns the wheel of corrupted Christianity back into the New Testament; his radical Christian vision, as it was
embodied in *Paradise Regained*, is there articulated by Christ and his Apostles in a sublime allegory that Milton newly interprets. So doing, Milton
becomes the prototype of the epic poet who is simultaneously an interpreter
of Scripture and a prophet of Christianity. From Blake's point of view,
Milton is an interpreter and a prophet in the same sense that Moses, Ezekiel,
Isaiah, and John are interpreters and prophets. Milton's poems, besides
being "criticisms" of their literary predecessors, are "interpretations" of
the prophecies that precede them.

12. *Milton's Life and Poetical Works with Notes by William Cowper*, ed. William
Hayley (Chichester, 1810), II, 469.
    13. William Hayley, *The Life of Milton*, 2nd ed., with Introduction by J. A. Witt-
reich, Jr. (1796; rpt. Gainesville, Fla.: Scholars' Facsimiles and Reprints, 1970), pp.
220, 277.
    14. Peter Felix Hägin, *The Epic Hero and the Decline of Heroic Poetry: A Study
of the Neoclassical English Epic with Special Reference to "Paradise Lost,"* ed. H.
Lüdeke (Basel: Cooper Monographs, 1964), pp. 14, 44, 146.
    15. T. J. B. Spencer, "*Paradise Lost*: The Anti-Epic," in *Approaches to Paradise
Lost*, ed. C. A. Patrides (Toronto: Univ. of Toronto Press, 1968), p. 98.
    16. *The Romantics on Milton: Formal Essays and Critical Asides*, ed. J. A. Witt-
reich, Jr. (Cleveland: Press of Case Western Reserve Univ., 1970), p. 96.
    17. For elaboration of this point, see my essay, "William Blake: Illustrator-Interpreter
of *Paradise Regained*," in *Calm of Mind*, ed. Wittreich, pp. 93–132.

The new role of prophet and interpreter that Milton assumes for the epic poet is analogous to the role assumed by biblical commentators, especially those who would divine the Book of Revelation. Like Milton, the two major eighteenth-century commentators on the last great scriptural prophecy noted the corruption of religion and strove for its restoration to the state in which "it was at first settled by the Apostles from *Christ*, and received and practised by the primitive Churches."[18] To the extent that Isaac Newton failed in his purpose he failed because he rationalized the sublime allegory of Revelation until its vision was lost, rather than perceiving in that allegory the lineaments of one true religion and one true mythology. This point Blake makes ironically when he has Newton sound the trumpet of apocalypse that introduces a new cycle of devastation rather than announcing liberation from it (*E* 13: 4–8). Newton is a type of Saint Paul's "prophet" who trumpets "an uncertain sound" and prepares no one for battle; he utters "words easy to be understood," but meaning nothing they "speak into the air" (1 Cor. 14: 8–9).[19]

A similar point is made, with equally biting irony, about Swedenborg in *The Marriage of Heaven and Hell*. Swedenborg had announced a "new heaven" in 1757, but as Blake looks around himself he discovers that Swedenborg's "heaven" is "the Eternal Hell revive[d]," that Swedenborg is, by his own definition, the devil in that hell (*MHH 3: 34*). In *The Apocalypse Revealed*, Swedenborg distinguishes between the hell called "the Devil," by which he means the hell created by those "who are in the love of self," and the hell called "Satan," by which he means the hell created by those who live by "falsities" and "who are in the pride of their own intelligence."[20] Swedenborg begins *The Apocalypse Revealed* with a proclamation: "There are many who labored in the explanation of the *Apocalypse*; but, as the spiritual sense of the Word had been hitherto unknown they could not see the arcana which lie concealed therein, for the spiritual sense alone discloses these." Then he makes a pronouncement: *I* am the visionary with "a particular enlightenment" and will now reveal the Book of Revelation.[21] From Blake's viewpoint, Swedenborg "conciev'd himself as much wiser" than he really was. Swedenborg "shews the folly of churches, & ex-

18. William Whiston, *Six Dissertations* (London, 1734), p. 268; cf. Isaac Newton, *Observations Upon the Prophecies of Daniel, and the Apocalypse of St. John* (London, 1733), p. 252.

19. I am grateful to Florence Sandler, University of Puget Sound, for showing me the appropriateness of this biblical quotation to Blake's representation of Newton; I am even more grateful to her for stimulating conversations at the Huntington Library, which helped me to sharpen many of the perceptions that have gone into this essay.

20. Translated by John Whitehead (New York: Swedenborg Foundation, 1931), I, 113.

21. Ibid., p. iii.

poses hypocrites, till he imagines that all are religious, & himself the single one on earth that ever broke a net." However, this is the "plain fact," says Blake: "Swedenborg has not written one new truth: Now hear another: he has written all the old falshoods" (*MHH* 21–22: *41–42*). *The Marriage of Heaven and Hell* is structured around the opposition between the true and false prophet represented in the satire by Milton and Swedenborg respectively. Like Newton, Swedenborg tried to reduce the spiritual sense, the sublime allegory, of Revelation to corporeal understanding and thereby perverted true religion into a corrupt orthodoxy. Like Milton, Blake preserves the visionary dimension of prophecy, even if doing so requires transforming all the Lord's people into prophets. Rather than perverting sublime allegory into falsehood, Blake would convert an entire civilization into a nation of visionaries. This Newton refused to do and Swedenborg failed to do, both of them by bruising Saint John's minute articulations, and Newton by denying that God ever designed to make people into prophets.[22]

Even so, if Newton and Swedenborg were seen by Blake, on occasion, as types of the false prophet, they were also seen by him, on other occasions, in the posture of the redeemed man. Both Newton and Swedenborg articulated conceptions of prophecy compatible with Blake's own, which explains why in *Milton* Swedenborg is represented as "strongest of men" (22: 50) and why in *Jerusalem* Newton rides a chariot when, "at the clangor of the Arrows of Intellect," the apocalypse occurs (98: 7). Precisely because Newton was bound to his own religious culture, he understood that the Book of Daniel and the Book of Revelation were related not only to one another but to all other scriptural prophecies, "so that all of them together make but one complete Prophecy" that "consists of two parts, an introductory Prophecy, and an Interpretation thereof."[23] Each prophet is both creator of his visions and interpreter of them; and every subsequent prophet repeats the pattern but, in the process, becomes an interpreter both of his own visions and of the visions of his predecessors. Behind Newton's understanding is the perception that the Apocalypse subsumes all previous prophetic structures. The Apocalypse is simultaneously an interpretation and a prophecy; by way of repeating all previous prophecies it comments on them, but it also introduces a series of seven new visions, each of which interprets the one it supersedes until in the final vision all things burst into clarity. Swedenborg reveals exactly this understanding when he depicts chapter 22 of Revelation as both an individual vision and a revelation of the total meaning of the Apocalypse.

From Newton and Swedenborg incidentally and from Spenser and Milton

22. See Newton, *Observations*, esp. pp. 251–252, where he says that "the folly of Interpreters" has been to speak "as if God designed to make them Prophets," and then argues that "the design of God was much otherwise."

23. Ibid., p. 254.

quite centrally, Blake took his prophetic stance; and from them all he learned that prophecy had a structure, which epic poetry could appropriate and accommodate. Austin Farrer has observed quite perceptively that in composing the Book of Revelation "St. John was making a new form of literature," but he concludes quite mistakenly that John "had no successor."[24] In Blake's epics, conventional structures are subdued, though not fully eliminated, and the living form of Revelation prophecy imparts the "new" epic structure. Blake's epics turn to Saint John, the last great prophet in Scripture, and to John Milton, the last great prophet in the epic mode; and then they turn, for their structural model, to the culminating vision of each prophet: Milton's vision of paradise regained and John's of apocalypse. In those prophecies, "the summe of Religion is shewed," and it is Blake's task to reveal the essence of those visions, which commentators on Revelation understood as "allegories," penetrable by only the initiated, and which eighteenth-century commentators on Milton seemed not to have understood at all.[25]

William Halloran has observed of *The French Revolution* that "when the work is set against its principal source and approached not as a truncated epic but as a visual and dramatic prophecy, its structure becomes clearer and its place in the Blake canon more central than most critics have recognized or allowed." He concludes, "the poem . . . is not an epic, but a prophecy; and its main source is not *Paradise Lost*, but the Book of Revelation." To the extent that Blake's poems, especially *The Marriage of Heaven and Hell* and the epics, are "an imaginative recasting of Revelation" Halloran's essay is helpful; but to the extent that the essay sharply dichotomizes epic and prophecy it is misguided.[26]

The structure of Revelation involves, to be sure, an "interaction between . . . two kinds of motion—vertical and linear." It may be described as a recording of twenty-one events with the last chapter forming "a frame or envelope," though it is probably more to Halloran's point that the Book of Revelation was understood to be composed of seven visions and that Blake, in adopting its structure, projected "A Poem in Seven Books." It may be described as "a series of verbal pictures" without "a strong narrative line," but with persistent repetition that both "links events . . . and provides a sense

24. *A Rebirth of Images: The Making of St. John's Apocalypse* (London: Dacre Press, 1949), p. 305.

25. See Hugh Broughton, *A Revelation of the Holy Apocalypse* ([London], 1610), and my Introduction to *Milton's "Paradise Regained": Two Eighteenth-Century Critiques by Richard Meadowcourt and Charles Dunster* (Gainesville, Fla.: Scholars' Facsimiles and Reprints, 1971).

26. *"The French Revolution*: Revelation's New Form," in *Blake's Visionary Forms Dramatic*, ed. David V. Erdman and John E. Grant (Princeton: Princeton Univ. Press, 1970), pp. 31–32.

of order," though to do so requires Halloran to blur the division that he establishes between epic and prophecy.[27] Nothing in Halloran's "review" of the main features of the structure of the Book of Revelation distinguishes it from the conventional epic structure of *The Faerie Queene* or of *Paradise Lost*; nor, for that matter, does anything in the "review" cut to the heart of Revelation's structure and reveal the actual points of structural correspondence between the Apocalypse and the apocalyptic poems of Spenser, Milton, and Blake. Halloran's thesis is controverted by his evidence, and it implies an estimate of *Paradise Lost* that Blake probably would reject. To say that *The French Revolution* is not "a traditional epic but . . . a visual and dramatic prophecy" is to imply, through the context given the statement, that *Paradist Lost* is "a traditional epic" and that its structure is unlike that of "a visual and dramatic prophecy."[28] The contrary is true. The effect of Milton's "experiment" in *Paradise Lost* is to cross and intervolve epic and prophecy, and to intervolve them so completely that the commonly recognized distinctions between the two previously distinct literary types are obscured. *Paradise Lost* and *Paradise Regained*, therefore, are more than epics that contain prophecies—they are *epic prophecies*. This is the nature of the Miltonic experiment in *Paradise Lost* that Halloran does not perceive, though Blake himself seems to have comprehended it.

It is as an experimental artist that Milton managed to elicit so much of Blake's attention. In every genre that he assays, Milton engaged in "generaic competition" and sought an "ultimate performance." Milton, therefore, assumes a relationship with his predecessors which, when defined, illuminates the one that exists between Blake and Milton. As Angus Fletcher reminds us, the relationship between Milton and his two great models, Spenser and Shakespeare, is "archetypal for the poetry of transcendental forms," and the desire to outdo his predecessors, when understood as "a single complex need, reveals the nature of the transcendental process" that involves joining various literary types, various symbolic modes, and then "hold[ing] them under pressure, in a state of high, even ecstatic tension." Milton, as Blake understood him, learned how to create "transcendental" and "virtuoso" forms[29] because he knew that "poetry is a sword of lightning, ever unsheathed, which consumes the scabbard that would contain it."[30] Milton

27. Ibid., pp. 32–34.
28. Ibid., p. 35.
29. Angus Fletcher, *The Prophetic Moment: An Essay on Spenser* (Chicago: Univ. of Chicago Press, 1971), p. 301, and also his book *The Transcendental Masque: An Essay on Milton's Comus* (Ithaca: Cornell Univ. Press, 1971), esp. pp. 116–146.
30. I quote from Shelley's "A Defence of Poetry," in *Shelley's Prose or the Trumpet of a Prophecy*, ed. David Lee Clark (Albuquerque: Univ. of New Mexico Press, 1954), p. 285.

knew that laws governing poetry, like laws governing human life, "are death / To every energy of man, and forbid the springs of life" (*J* 31: 11–12). This is a point Milton himself makes in *Reason of Church-Government* when he wonders whether, in writing epic poetry, "the rules of *Aristotle* . . . are strictly to be kept," and concludes that, for those who "know art and use judgment," following nature (i.e., individual genius) "is no transgression, but an inriching of art" (I, 813–814).[31] It is a point reiterated in *Of Education*, when Milton refers to Aristotle, Horace, and certain Italian critics as the teachers of "what the laws are" of epic, dramatic, and lyric poetry and of "what decorum is, which is the grand master peece to observe" (II, 404–405). The context of this statement is important; for Milton is not merely encouraging the study of genre but is saying that from such a study will come a knowledge of the inadequacies of the "kinds" as they exist and, with that knowledge, will emerge a *new* decorum for making secular forms serve spiritual needs. Remarks like these, together with Milton's practice, encouraged Blake and his contemporaries to spurn established maxims (the rules devised for epic poets by eighteenth-century theorists); but in eschewing the epic tradition that emerged in his own century Blake reverts to what he regarded as the mainline tradition in England—a tradition initiated by Spenser and perfected by Milton.

In an important sense, *Paradise Lost* is an anti-epic. Milton, from a very early point in his career, recognized that literary forms were structural principles, providing the poet with a set of conventions by which he could structure his insights and define his discoveries; and he recognized, too, that literary forms carried ideologies, what William Empson calls "rough world-views,"[32] every form projecting its own identifiable attitude toward human existence. In *Paradise Lost* Milton exploded the epic conventions, and through them the values they customarily supported, leaving the epic tradition in ruins; but in the same poem he established a "new" structural principle used prominently in *Lycidas, Paradise Regained*, and *Samson Agonistes*—the structure of prophecy as it was understood by the famous commentator David Pareus.[33] Out of the epic ruins of *Paradise Lost*, Milton

31. All quotations of Milton's prose follow the text of *Complete Prose Works of John Milton*, ed. Don M. Wolfe et al. (New Haven: Yale Univ. Press, and London: Oxford Univ. Press, 1949–). References to this edition are given parenthetically within the text, citing volume number and pagination. References to Milton's poetry are also given parenthetically within the text, and they follow the text of *The Works of John Milton*, ed. Frank Allen Patterson (New York: Columbia Univ. Press, 1931–38). I have used the following abbreviations for Milton's works: *Apology* for *Apology for Smectymnuus, Divorce* for *The Doctrine and Discipline of Divorce*, PL for *Paradise Lost*.

32. See *English Pastoral Poetry* (New York: W. W. Norton, 1938), p. 21.

33. *A Commentary Upon the Divine Revelation of the Apostle and Evangelist John,*

created a new form, free of the *impedimenta* of convention and distinguishable by the union achieved between epic and prophecy. Milton learned from Spenser, as Blake was to learn from Milton, the possibilities for accommodating epic and prophecy; Blake also learned from Milton, as Milton learned from Pareus, the basic elements in prophetic structure.

In *Reason of Church-Government* (a work from which Blake quotes and from which he takes the themes and structure of *The Marriage of Heaven and Hell*), Milton describes "the Apocalyps of Saint John" as "the majestick image of a high and stately Tragedy, shutting up and intermingling her solemn Scenes and Acts with a sevenfold *Chorus* of halleluja's and harping symphonies." This is "my opinion," says Milton, which "the grave autority of *Pareus* . . . is sufficient to confirm" (I, 815). In the Preface to *Samson Agonistes*, Milton comments similarly, explaining that Pareus divides the Book of Revelation "as a Tragedy, into Acts distinguist each by a Chorus of Heavenly Harpings and Song between." When Pareus applies the label of tragedy to Revelation, he does not mean the same thing each time, nor does he mean primarily what we would understand by the designation. In the sense that John records "the Tragedie of Antichrist" and represents "Tragicall motions and tumults," his book encompasses the ideology we commonly associate with tragedy. But in the sense that Revelation is a dramatic structure, it also merits the label of tragedy. This latter meaning is the primary sense conveyed by Pareus's designation. His point is simply that Reve-

---

tr. Elias Arnold (Amsterdam, 1644). Since Milton is referring to Pareus before this edition appeared, he probably read Pareus's commentary in *Operum Theologicorum* (Frankfurt, 1628). All quotations of Pareus in this essay are from the 1644 edition, and citations are given parenthetically within the text. This edition has separate pagination for the front matter and the commentary; therefore pages referring to the front matter are in italics and those referring to the commentary itself are in the usual form.

Several recent studies have explored connections between Milton's poetry and the Book of Revelation; see especially my essay, "Milton's 'Destin'd Urn': The Art of *Lycidas*," *PMLA*, 84 (1969), 60–70; Michael Fixler's essay. "The Apocalypse within *Paradise Lost*," in *New Essays on Paradise Lost*, ed. Thomas Kranidas (Berkeley and Los Angeles: Univ. of California Press, 1969), pp. 131–178; and Barbara Lewalski's study, "*Samson Agonistes* and the 'Tragedy' of the Apocalypse," *PMLA*, 85 (1970), 1050–1060. As Claus Westermann observes, even though today "the investigation into the forms and history of the prophetic speeches has passed too much into the background," we must acknowledge that the eighteenth century marks the beginning of a *concerted* effort of research into prophecy that "came to flower in the nineteenth century" (*Basic Forms of Prophetic Speech*, tr. Hugh Clayton White [Philadelphia: Westminster Press, 1967], p. 13). But at the same time we should recognize that the three Milton essays alluded to in this note constitute a reminder that the *pioneering* effort to research prophecy was begun the century before and that Milton was aware of the conclusions emerging from it.

lation is a tragedy because it is dramatically structured (pp. *20, 23, 26*), and this is the idea that Milton punctuates in his two references to the commentator. It is also the point of correspondence between Revelation as a tragic structure and Revelation as an epic structure.

Tragedy and epic alike view the same experience but respond differently to it. Thomas Vogler observes that "*Job* can be read as a tragic drama or as a 'brief epic,' depending on whether we are reacting to the sense of despair in the early part or to the triumph . . . at the end."[34] What Vogler says of the Book of Job is equally true of Genesis and of the different ways Milton responded to the story of Adam's Fall. Initially he projected a tragedy on the subject of Adam's Fall and lingered with the conception long enough to begin a tragedy called *Adam Unparadised* from which he lifted materials for *Paradise Lost*. Milton's diffuse epic obviously marks a change in his conception of the Genesis story, though his original understanding of it is preserved in Book IX when he says that he "must change" his "Notes to Tragic" (ll. 5–6). Significantly, at the very moment that Milton returns to a purely epic mode in Book XI, *Paradise Lost* gives way to the kind of prophetic-dramatic structure described by Pareus. Like Job and *Paradise Lost*, the Book of Revelation has its tragic story, but it also culminates in a moment of triumph that succeeds the cycles of defeat.[35] In this sense—and in the sense that Revelation has the cosmic dimensions of no other scriptural book—it is a suitable model for epic, especially as Milton came to understand the genre. Shorter than the ordinary epic, the brief epic, as exemplified by *Paradise Regained*, had to rely upon typology to create its encyclopedic compass, but the brief epic also magnified the dramatic element in the diffuse epic—and magnified it so greatly that the brief epic poem became an intensely dramatic poem, the interest of which was psychological and the structure of which was created by contending perspectives (the various interpretations of Christ's baptism) and by a series of gradually sharpening antitheses (the confrontations between Christ and Satan) that culminate in the vision on the pinnacle, in the moment when Christ apprehends his divinity and when Satan, smitten with amazement, exposed for what he is, falls.

It is by no means clear that Blake was familiar with Pareus, though he doubtless had read Milton's references to the commentator. The important point is this: Pareus sums up a century of commentary on Revelation by

34. *Preludes to Vision*, p. 6.
35. The same dualism pervades *Jerusalem*. In "The Structure of Blake's *Jerusalem*," *Bucknell Review*, 11 (1963), E. J. Rose makes the same point when he calls attention to the tragic disunity in Chapter II and opposes it to the apocalyptic reintegration in Chapter IV. As one moves through *Jerusalem*, says Rose, "the tragic becomes the apocalyptic" (p. 40).

regarding the prophecy as a poem with a carefully articulated structure, and he provides confirmation—and probably amplification—for an understanding that Milton regarded as his own. Milton's observation in *Reason of Church-Government* makes clear that he regarded Pareus as the confirmer, not the shaper, of his understanding of Revelation. If Blake did not know Pareus firsthand, he could have inferred much of the commentator's thinking from Milton's practice, and he could have known much of it that had been absorbed into eighteenth-century commentaries on Revelation and treatises on prophecy. A spate of such books was published in England between 1780 and 1800, and Hayley's library contained some of them.[36]

There is a twofold premise behind most commentary on Revelation (but not Newton's) : the obscurity of the prophecy is not invincible, and so it should be sought out; the "Propheticall Progression"[37] is from obscurity to clarity, from, in Milton's words, "shadowy types to truth" (*PL* XII: 303). However, there is another premise that Newton does share with his predecessors and successors, namely that the Book of Revelation is a gathering of previous prophecy and an articulation of a new one. To the extent that it is a "gathering" it offers interpretation, and to the extent that it is an "articulation" it requires interpretation.

Repeatedly, in both his prose and his poetry, but nowhere more persistently than in *Jerusalem*, Blake invokes the tradition of prophecy and, doing so, creates the impression that, like Elijah, he "comprehends all the Prophetic Characters" whom he supersedes (*VLJ*, p. 550). Like epic poetry as Milton wrote it, prophecy is a tissue of "Imaginative Images" perpetually reborn through contemplation. Just as Revelation is a rebirth and reinterpretation of images used by John's predecessors, so in Blake's epics images gathered from previous prophecies are reborn in the poems and continually reborn in the minds of those who read those poems creatively. Since the prophet takes his inspiration from the Lord, receiving the prophet as a prophet becomes both a test and an obligation of civilization; and because receiving the prophet is a duty of civilization it is "most wicked in a Christian Nation / For any Man to pretend to Inspiration" ("Cowper," p. 498). One responsibility of the true prophet is to expose the false ones; but his

36. Hayley's library contained a large selection of Milton volumes and a number of eighteenth-century treatises on prophecy; see *A Catalogue of the Very Valuable and Extensive Library of the Late William Hayley, Esq.* (Sold at auction by Mr. Evans), February, 1821. There is a copy of this catalogue in the University of Wisconsin Rare Book Room; and the catalogue is reproduced in the second volume of *Poets and Men of Letters: Sale Catalogues of Libraries of Eminent Persons*, ed. A. N. L. Munby (London: Mansell, 1971).

37. I take the phrase from George Sandys' *Sacrae Heptades, or Seven Problems Concerning Antichrist* ([London], 1625), p. 57.

other, more important, duty is to serve his nation as a seer rather than as a dictator. The true prophet prepares men for the future; he does not predict it. "Raging with the inspirations of a prophetic mind," the true prophet acts "from conscious superiority" but always in accordance with "divine decrees" passed on to him (*DC, p. 535*).

When Blake says, at the beginning of *Jerusalem*, that his poem is a "consolidated & extended Work" (3: *143*) he sets himself firmly within the tradition of prophecy. What becomes immediately apparent upon negotiating the plates of the poem is that *Jerusalem* is not only a consolidation and continuation of Blake's previous poems, especially *The Four Zoas* and *Milton*; it is also a consolidation of the visions contained in Milton's epics and in Revelation prophecy. If *The Four Zoas* takes its structure from *Paradise Lost* and if *Milton* takes its from *Paradise Regained*, *Jerusalem* also derives its form from Milton's four-book epic, from the four gospel accounts as they were interpreted by Milton's brief epic, and from the Book of Revelation. The Miltonic and Apocalyptic contexts are invoked immediately by Blake through the posture he assumes. "I see the Saviour over me / Spreading his beams of love, & dictating the words of this mild song" (*J* 4: 4–5; cf. 74: 40–41) recalls both the proem to *Paradise Regained*, where Milton describes his brief epic as a "prompted Song" that tells of deeds "unrecorded . . . through many an Age" (I: 12, 16), and Saint John's repeated assertions (of which Pareus reminds us) "that he received his *Revelation from Christ*, and wrote the same by the Angels command" (p. 8). Blake comprehends the momentous significance of Revelation's beginning with Christ standing at the door and knocking, and alludes to this key event on Plate 1 of *Jerusalem* {33} where Los, the new "Spirit of Prophecy" with whom Blake identified himself in *Milton*, is shown entering a door with a lantern in his hand. John's point, and Blake's, is that revelation descends from God to Christ, and from Christ to his servants; and in the process the servant, whether John, Los, or Blake, becomes a prophet and his book a prophecy. This "continuity of apocalyptic postures"[38] is underscored by the concluding paragraph of the address "To the Public," which ends with a manifesto similar to the one Milton appended to *Paradise Lost*. Blake's "revolutionary" manifesto invokes the Milton tradition, where the orator and poet are one and, as a consequence, urges the discrimination of styles and the accommodation of them all to the appropriate parts of the poem; and it pushes a step beyond that tradition by spurning "English Blank Verse" with the same contempt that Milton exhibits in abandoning the "modern bondage of Riming." Blake's manifesto begins, literally, where Milton's terminated.

38. I borrow the phrase from Frank Kermode's *The Sense of an Ending: Studies in the Theory of Fiction* (New York: Oxford Univ. Press, 1967), p. 123.

By invoking the concept of the "true Orator" whose prototype is Blake's Muse, the poet recalls the figure of the orator that emerges from Milton's prose works[39] and that finds its fullest definition in Augustine's *De Doctrina Christiana*, where the concept of the true orator is mounted upon John's methods in Revelation. This is a point that Pareus understood; for, following Augustine, he explains that in the Book of Revelation "are contained many darke things, that the Readers mind might be exercised, and in it are a few things, by the clearnesse whereof the rest with labour may be sought out, chiefly, because it so repeateth the same things after a diverse manner." The visions of the prophetic orator, he continues, are "intricate": they are "Images" of "some secret thing" whose "mysteries . . . are so obscure, as they cannot be found out by the understanding of mortall man" (p. 9). In *Jerusalem*, as in Revelation, there are two principal characters: John or Blake, who are actors throughout; and Jesus, who in both cases is the author of the Revelation, the true maker of the poem. Prophecies, Blake knew, come from God only: they are divinely inspired, which is to say that "all created things are altogether insufficient to reveale these heavenly secrets . . . . This honour appertains to the Lambe onely. His weeping was not in vaine," and from it both prophet and audience should understand "that the mysteries contained in Gods word . . . are not to be understood without weeping: that is, desire, study, [and] labour" conjoin to effect an understanding of prophecy (Pareus, p. 99). The Apocalypse, then, is an act of poetic creation; and John, like Blake following him, must go through all the agonies and all the labors of the archetypal poet Los—and so must his audience.

This conception of prophecy, shared by Blake, accounts for the calculated obscurity that hides the poet's visions from corporeal understanding but not from "the Divine Arts of Imagination" (*J* 77: 229). Blake's obscurity is like John's, and like Milton's as it was described by Coleridge:

A reader of Milton must be always on his Duty: He is surrounded with sense; it rises in every line; every word is to the purpose. There are no lazy intervals: all has been considered and demands & merits observation.

If this be called obscurity, let it be remembered tis such a one as is com-

39. For an extended discussion of this point, see my essay, " 'The Crown of Eloquence': The Figure of the Orator in Milton's Prose Works," in *Achievements of the Left Hand: Essays on the Prose Works of John Milton*, ed. Michael Lieb and John T. Shawcross (Amherst: Univ. of Massachusetts Press, 1973), in press. Joseph Anthony Mazzeo's remarks are also illuminating; see *Renaissance and Seventeenth-Century Studies* (New York: Columbia Univ. Press, and London: Routledge and Kegan Paul, 1964), pp. 1–28. One should also compare Blake's notion of mixed styles (see *J* 3: 144) with Milton's conception, which has recently been elucidated by Irene Samuel, "Milton on Style," *Cornell Library Journal*, 9 (1969), [39]–58.

plaisant to the Reader: not that vicious obscurity, which proceeds from a muddled head.[40]

Milton himself cites the Christian oratorical tradition, represented by Christ and Saint Paul, as his authority for requiring mental gymnastics from his reader:

... there is scarse any saying in the Gospel, but must be read with limitations and distinctions, to be rightly understood; for Christ gives no full comments or continu'd discourses, but ... speaks oft in Monosyllables, like a maister, scattering the heavenly grain of his doctrin like pearle heer and there, which requires a skilfull and laborious gatherer ....

(*Divorce*, II, 338)

Like Augustine, Milton regarded the obscurity of Scripture as part of God's design: through it God exercises the mind, leading it from the realities of this world to those of the next. At the same time that God is exercising Milton's mind, and the minds of Milton's protagonists, Milton is forcing difficult mental exertions upon his audience, hoping through those exertions to cleanse the doors of perception and thereby move his audience to vision and his nation to apocalypse.

The exercise of intellect in pursuit of truth is, for Blake too, "that Talent which it is a curse to hide." So that the imagination may achieve "the Harvest of ... its Labours," Blake provides, amidst the obscurity of *Jerusalem* and of his other epics, moments of "clearnesse," what he calls "the end of a golden string" that winds into the "Divine Vision" his poem contains (*J* 77: 229). With Pareus and Milton, Blake understood that God not only revealed visions "but would have them written for the understanding of all"; and with them he distinguished between the "message" of the vision and its "mystery." The message of the vision should be set down for all; this Blake does in the addresses that preface each chapter of *Jerusalem*. But the mysteries of the visions should be hidden in an obscurity that is impenetrable to "vulgar minds" but accessible to "the godly" who "by the obscurity" will be all "the more stirred up to searching out the divine mysteries" (Pareus, p. 9). The mysteries of vision Blake "organizes" into his poem.

Blake's technique of using darkness as the way to light, obscurity as the vehicle for vision, though more pronounced in his poems than in Milton's,

40. *Romantics on Milton*, ed. Wittreich, p. 159. James Thorpe was the first to observe that in these lines Coleridge is making a "transcription of disconnected sentences" from Jonathan Richardson's *Explanatory Notes and Remarks on Milton's Paradise Lost* (1734)—a work that Blake himself may have read; see "A Note on Coleridge's 'Gutch Commonplace Book,'" *Modern Language Notes*, 63 (1948), 130–131.

is still in keeping with Milton's practice—more so than Geoffrey Hartman would have us believe. For Hartman, the point of distinction between Blake and Milton as visionaries rests in Milton's theory of accommodation, which involves "two different, even contradictory ideas." When Milton allows Raphael to liken spiritual to corporeal forms, "Raphael brings truth down to earth" but does so, says Hartman, as a way of lifting "an earthly mind to heaven." Because the first aspect of accommodation is "authoritarian and condescending," the Romantics (especially Blake) are represented as opposing it; and since the second aspect of accommodation is "initiatory," the Romantics (especially Blake) are seen embracing it: the idea of leading men through darkness into light is the Romantic "obverse" to "the principle of accommodation," which depicts God darkening light that human eyes are too weak to behold.[41] Hartman's distinction is as shrewd as it is illuminating, but it is also misleading both as it relates to Milton's art and as it relates to the Romantics' understanding of Milton's art.

The Romantics quote Milton's line, "fit audience find, though few" (PL VII: 31), with astonishing frequency. Blake quotes it in his 1809 Advertisement, and doing so insinuates the kind of distinction that Hartman draws without implying that Milton's is a poetry of "condescension" as opposed to his own poetry of "initiation." Hartman's distinction is analogous to the one Blake makes between the true and the false prophet: the one creates a symbolic language, and the other reduces the language of symbolism to a set of signs. Milton's whole purpose in frustrating narrative movement with authorial intrusions, in impeding narrative structure with "the traverse action" of imagery, is to lift his reader to the level of vision rather than to accommodate his vision to the reader's lesser understanding.[42] Blake's poetry

41. See Geoffrey Hartman, "Adam on the Grass with Balsamum," in ELH: Essays in Honor of D. C. Allen, 36 (1969), 178.

42. I quote from Robert Martin Adams' rejoinder to Hartman's essay, "Contra Hartman: Possible and Impossible Structures of Miltonic Imagery," in Seventeenth-Century Imagery: Essays on Uses of Figurative Language from Donne to Farquhar, ed. Earl Miner (Berkeley and Los Angeles: Univ. of California Press, 1971), p. 130.

Insisting upon "the mortal limitation of all sight and so of all poems," Kathleen Williams' essay, "Vision and Rhetoric: The Poet's Vision in The Faerie Queene," in ELH: Essays in Honor of D. C. Allen, 36 (1969), reminds us that all poetry involves an act of accommodation. "The vision, although it is something given, is also something achieved," says Williams; it comes not through "dreamlike ease" but through "difficult, concentrated, sometimes even painful attention. The vision has to be won," first by the poet, then by his audience, through "devoted exercise" (p. 132); the vision is achieved through an "arduous process of contemplation" (p. 134). Though tied to Spenser's poetry, these observations, and the following one, have relevance for Milton's poetry, and for Blake's: "The poet's voice [Williams is speaking of The Faerie Queene] is controlled by two purposes . . . : that of being faithful to . . . [his] vision . . . and

is not without a narrative line, but more pointedly than Milton's, it sub-ordinates "narrative . . . to hermeneutic structure."[43] Milton and Blake use this technique to transform their audiences from a theater of readers into a house of interpreters.

Insofar as any conclusions can be drawn about either poet's procedures in composition, those conclusions reveal striking similarities in method. It appears that Milton wrote his narrative in strictly chronological order, and then disrupted the chronology in order to achieve his folded structure and his hermeneutic emphasis. It also appears that Blake, in early versions of his illuminated books, preserved his narrative line but, in later versions, subdued and all but concealed it, first, by rearranging plates so that narrative continuity is broken and then by redistributing full-page designs so that these ruptures in the narrative do not go unobserved. (The early copies of *Milton* [A and B] in comparison with the later ones [C and D] are a case in point.) Through this process, both poets preserve the integrity of their visions; yet neither poet locks his vision from those not immediately able to comprehend it. Milton's authorial intrusions in *Paradise Lost* serve the same function as the songs and full-page designs in *Jerusalem*: they exercise the mind into understanding by lifting it to the level of vision and by providing instruction in how to decipher what it will behold.

The Book of Revelation offered to poets like Milton and Blake not only a prophetic stance but a prophetic structure. As Austin Farrer observes, the apocalyptic tradition, of which Virgil is the initiator, "contains nothing like the form of the Christian Apocalypse. It supplies plenty of the material, but it does not supply the form."[44] Thus Milton, and later Blake, must turn for

---

that of achieving the fullest possible communication of the vision to his readers, who must be shown how to receive it, how to do their part. . . . the poet-narrator [makes us] aware of poetry as . . . a divine rhetoric. The thing seen by the poet . . . requires all his care and skill to convey it and ours as readers to receive it. It is vision and rhetoric, the Orphic poet leading his instructed and responsive listeners through the complex metaphor in which he has captured his sight of harmonious order" (p. 144). Importantly, Williams' essay underscores the point that prophecy, besides being a poetical form, is a rhetorical form; cf. Westermann, *Basic Forms of Prophetic Speech*, p. 15. For further amplification of Williams' point and for a brilliant counter-statement to Hartman, see S. K. Heninger, Jr., *Touches of Sweet Harmony: Pythagorean Cosmology and Renaissance Poetics*, a forthcoming publication of the Henry E. Huntington Library (1973).

43. Hartman, "Adam on the Grass," p. 191.

44. *A Rebirth of Images*, p. 305. The element of prophecy is introduced to epic by Virgil and figures prominently in Book VI of the *Aeneid*, where it stretches the dimensions of the poem into the distant "future" which is Virgil's "present"; it is equally important in Tasso's *Gerusalemme Liberata*, where the prophet-priest Pietro is cast as a man of God rather than as just a deliverer of oracles. Yet prophecy as used by

prophetic structures from epic to prophetic tradition. The Book of Revelation, as described by Pareus and many other commentators on the Apocalypse, was composed of a preface (1: 1–9), a prophecy composed of seven visions (1: 10–22: 5), and a conclusion (22: 6–21).[45] The form of this structure, says Pareus, is "plainly . . . *Dramaticall* . . . hence the Revelation may truely be called a *Propheticall Drama*." The confrontations between characters in a usual drama are replaced with a confrontation of perspectives; the usual dramatic interludes are replaced with songs that, instead of lessening "the wearisomness of the spectators" (p. *20*), increase the intellectual demands placed upon them. The process involved here is presented in bold relief in what has been called Blake's "new, loose, antimimetic form" of *The Four Zoas*, the poem in which Blake invokes Milton's "anti-epic" as a precedent for his abandonment of "the associative obligations of major poetry, and by so doing threatens the mimetic mode itself."[46] This is precisely the threat that *Paradise Lost* posed to eighteenth-century theorists, and it is their reason for insisting that epic be mimetic of the poems of Homer and Virgil. In *The Four Zoas*, confrontations of character give way to confrontations of perspective that involve "an intense exchange of action and reaction, statement and counter-statement." What has been called an "epic of situations"[47] might more appropriately be described as an epic of contending, but complementary, perspectives that, instead of isolating itself by innovation from *Milton* and *Jerusalem*, anticipates the innovations that are subdued into the structure of Blake's later epics. The repeated "violent,

---

Virgil and Tasso differs decidedly from prophecy as utilized by Spenser and Milton. The former poets assume a prophetic stance without devising a prophetic structure, and for them prophecy is simply predictive of the future. Spenser and Milton, on the other hand, continue the prophetic stance and use a prophetic structure derived from the Book of Revelation; for them prophecy, instead of simply predicting the future, provides an understanding of the past and the present and prepares man for facing the future. Moreover, prophecy, though it may have reference points in history, is primarily concerned with the inner life of man which it mythologizes. As Westermann observes in *Basic Forms of Prophetic Speech*, "the prophetic message is closely related to the time in which it was proclaimed and for which it was intended" (p. [11]); but Kermode, in *The Sense of an Ending*, provides the necessary qualification when he says of prophecy that "the historical allegory is always having to be revised; time discredits it" (p. 8).

45. See especially p. 19, where Pareus identifies the Seven Visions of Revelation as Christ walking among the candlesticks (1: 10–3), God's majesty sitting upon the throne (4–7), Seven trumpets (8–11), Woman and man-child (12–14), Seven angels (15–16), Judgment of the Great Whore (17–19), Binding and judgment of the Beast and the descent of the heavenly Jerusalem (20–22: 6).

46. Helen T. McNeil, "The Formal Art of *The Four Zoas*," in *Blake's Visionary Forms Dramatic*, ed. Erdman and Grant, pp. 379, 390.

47. Ibid., p. 373.

absolute confrontations"[48] in all Blake's epics are reminiscent of the repeated confrontations within and between perspectives in Revelation.

The visions of Revelation, though they seem continuous, are not so, since
they push the reader back into contemplation and interpretation of what he
has just beheld; but the visions "do all cohere one with another" (Pareus,
p. 20). Each vision looks back to and epitomizes what precedes it, with the
result that certain motifs are tenaciously repeated. In Revelation, Pareus
reminds us, "most of the Visions doe end with the last Judgement" and the
effect of this repetition is to create "the forme of an Harmonie" with each
new vision saying the same thing as those that precede it but in a different
manner (pp. 22–23). The early visions are more obscure than the later ones
so that there is a sense of progression within the repetitions: individual
events, like the Last Judgment, that are persistently repeated are also "shadowed out by more manifest Types":

The last Judgement is more darkly shadowed out towards the end of the *second*
and *third* Visions: but more clearely towards the end of the *fourth*, by the
Type of the *Harvest* and *Vintage*, and of the fift [sic] Vision by the Type of a
great *Earthquake*: but most clearely towards the end of the *sixth*: and most
properly in the *seventh*.

(p. 24)

In Revelation structure, as described by Pareus and more recently by Farrer,
the darker types go before, and the clearer follow after; the darker are revealed by the clearer and may, with some labor, be understood. In both the
epics of Milton and those of Blake, the "form" of Revelation prophecy is
observed: there is the same "many-sidedness" of "the continuous symbolic
theme"; there is "the internal building up of pattern out of the elements of
previous pattern"; there is the same persistent use of echo and refrain and
the same skill in "piling up climax," at least in *Paradise Regained* and
Jerusalem.[49] With greater precision than Milton, Blake defines multiple
perspectives contending with one another as characters in a drama, which he
personifies as "One Man reflecting each in each" (*J* 98: 39). Just as every
part of the Eternal Man reflects every other part of him, so every part of
Blake's poem reflects every other part of it.

Though each vision in Revelation repeats the same event and represents
it in relation to all time, it does so without reiterating the same details or
the same totality. Some visions figure "the whole, others some certain distances." In Revelation, says Pareus, there "are four remarkable distances"
that represent "the whole period" (p. 25). The first period depicts the

48. Ibid.
49. See Farrer, *A Rebirth of Images*, p. 305.

church flourishing, then groaning under tyranny; the second shows the
church reigning and rioting under the Christian emperors until the rising
of the Western Antichrist; the third describes the church trodden upon and
oppressed by Antichrist; and the last figures the church reformed from
popery and extends its vision to the end of all time. The four time-periods
of Revelation correspond roughly with the four time-periods identified in
"The Argument" to *The Marriage of Heaven and Hell*, and more exactly
with the time-periods invoked in the four chapters of *Jerusalem*. When it is
understood that, for Blake, Jesus is Imagination and his throne is in every
man rather than in the tabernacles of the churches, it becomes clear that
Blake is paralleling the church's struggle for survival in Revelation with
the imagination's struggle for articulation in *Jerusalem*. At the same time,
the parallels between the "four distances" of Revelation and those of *Jerusalem* become conspicuous. Just as the church flourishes until it comes under
tyranny, so the creative aspect of man dominates until the spectre is formed
to tyrannize it. Just as the church tries to extricate itself from the Christian
emperors, so the creative man tries to extricate himself from the cycle of
nature and history that suppresses him. Just as the church (or Christ's
emanation) is trodden upon and oppressed by Antichrist as it becomes distinct from Him, so the creative man is inarticulate when his emanation is
separated from him and tyrannized by her shadow in the same way that the
creative man is tyrannized by his spectre. Los's dilemma, and Blake's, is
figured by Albion, who falls into the sleep of death when Jerusalem separates from him and becomes enveloped by Rahab. And just as the church,
when reformed from popery, can extend its vision to the end of time, so
Los and Blake, once they expel their spectres and retrieve their emanations,
can organize their visions and ready mankind for apocalypse. This is Blake's
sublime allegory that derives *definite* form from the Book of Revelation
and *minute particularization* from Blake's own imagination.

Some of the visions of Revelation are "Universal Visions" that embrace
all time; others are "Particular Visions" that gather into focus a distinct
period of time. Regardless of the kind of vision articulated, each one has
two facets: "What is *Dramaticall*," by which Pareus means the songs that,
establishing an antagonism between the prophet and his audience, inspire
the intellectual exercise necessary to raise an audience to the level of vision;
and "what [is] Propheticall," by which he means the vision itself that represents what eternally exists, whether it be "open or hid" (pp. *25–26*). When
it is understood that there are three distinguishable kinds of vision—"cor-
porall," or those we behold with our bodily eyes; "spirituall," or those we
behold as apparitions either while waking or sleeping; and "intellectual," or
those beheld by "the minde being illuminated," enabling it to penetrate
"the mysteries of those things . . . presented" (Pareus, p. 17)—when this is

understood it becomes clear that it is the last form of vision with which John the prophet and Milton and Blake the poets are concerned. The prophet who, like Milton, portrays himself as clothed in "the light of the divine countenance" (*Defensio Secunda*, IV, i, 589–590) or who, like Blake, represents himself in a letter as "drunk with intellectual vision" (*p. 703*) will understandably refer to himself in the course of laying down his prophecy. It is one thing, says Pareus, "to write a historie, another thing to write a prophesie"; for "the truth of an *historie* requireth not the authority of the writer" but "a *prophesie*" does. Without that authority, a prophecy will go unheard and thus will not stir up the audience "as soldiers" who, by the trumpet of a prophecy, are "emboldened" to engage in the mental warfare that produces apocalypse (p. 18).

These elements of prophecy, described by Pareus, provide a background for understanding Blake's epic endeavors, which have proved to be the greatest obstacle to understanding his one grand poem to which all his individual poems contribute. These elements of prophecy also clarify—and often correct—previous analyses of Blake's epic structure, especially as it unfolds in *Jerusalem*. Blake's epics are no more "patchwork" than the Revelation prophecy. What has been called the "suspicious symmetry" of *Jerusalem* is not an effort to substitute an "artificially inveterate structure" for "living form" but part of Blake's design to follow Revelation structure, even in its smallest details.[50] Like Milton, Blake uses symmetrical structure

50. W. H. Stevenson, "Blake's *Jerusalem*," *Essays in Criticism*, 9 (1959), 254, 257. It is interesting and instructive to set Stevenson's observations on Blake's "suspicious symmetry" and "artificially inveterate structure" against a recent description of the structure of Homer's *Iliad*. Stevenson likens the structure of *Jerusalem* to a "balloon" into which Blake puffs "air . . . until it has reached the required size." Blake, says Stevenson, "has not enlarged the [poem's] theme, but adds frills and flounces to it. The necessary length is produced by interpolation" (p. 255). In *The Iliad, The Odyssey, and the Epic Tradition* (London and Melbourne: Macmillan, 1968), Charles Rowan Beye says of the *Iliad*'s structure that it "seems to have developed like churned butter, bits and pieces sticking together until a perceptible amount, clearly butter and no longer cream, clings to the paddle. By simple accretion, new words and phrases come which explained or defined more fully what had gone before." And Beye concludes, "This theory of composition does not necessarily require a strong sense of unity" (p. 111). However crude these metaphors may be, they serve as a *rough* analogy for the kind of prophetic structures that Milton and Blake imitate. Both poets would, of course, resist the idea that their structures deny "a strong sense of unity," for unity was for each poet a paramount concern. When we recall that the *Iliad* was not divided by its poet into books but that Blake's poems, and Milton's, were, it becomes clear that while all three poets used mechanical structures, Milton and Blake used them more conspicuously than Homer, and more deceptively. In the *Iliad* mechanical structure is the primary structure; in Milton's epics, and in Blake's, mechanical structure is supportive to the organic or prophetic structure. This is not only my understanding, it is Blake's (see "On Homers Poetry," and "On Virgil," *p. 267*).

without sacrificing organic form; the one structure merely conceals the other, which will eventually supersede it. To say that "the reader's failure to follow Blake through *Jerusalem* is due less to his own ignorance than to Blake's uncertainty about what he really means to do" is quite to miss the mark.[51] Blake worked with confidence, with certainty; he knew what he wanted to do, and that was to create prophetic structures modeled on those created by Milton in his epics and by John in the Book of Revelation. Such structures used artificial forms to support living forms. In writing their respective epics, Milton and Blake confronted the same questions that Ezra Pound's *Cantos* posed for Yeats: Can a poem which gives "the impression that all is living" have "a mathematical structure"? "Can impressions that are in part visual, in part metrical, be related like the notes of a symphony . . ."? Having raised these questions, Yeats chose "to suspend judgment";[52] but Milton and Blake had to answer those questions before they wrote their epics, and they answered them affirmatively. Instead of having "no idea of the techniques involved, or even of the problems he was facing,"[53] Blake seems to have had a deeper knowledge of both epic and prophetic traditions than his critics have supposed. Not only is the fourth chapter of *Jerusalem* "like Revelation,"[54] but the entire epic derives its patterns and themes from the biblical prophecy of John. It is through persistent repetition of motifs, each time with greater elaboration, it is through the movement from obscurity to clarity and through the gradually sharpening perspectives, that Blake creates the "idea" and imitates the "structure of growth."[55] When Pareus writes that "Revelation is a Propheticall and

---

In view of Blake's juxtaposition of "Mathematical Form" and "Gothic Form," it is instructive to look at Eugène Vinaver's description of romance structure, where seeming faults in construction and lapses in coherence are regarded as "part of the poet's design"; they are accompanied, says Vinaver, by a "process of coalescence": the chaotic surface-structure hides "a structure more complete than any that has been seen before." Individual panels of the large structure are held together by "the device of interweaving." The large structure, then, is like "the fabric of matting or tapestry," its *"acentric composition"* possessing "as much internal cohesion as one would find in any centralized pattern." This description of romance (i.e., Gothic) structure bears a strong resemblance to the prophetic structures of Spenser and Milton, which are accommodated to and amplified in Blake's epics. When this kind of structure is pursued to its logical conclusion (and this is precisely what Blake does), it embraces and justifies "the very things that our conventional poetics condemn outright"—"expansion and diversity . . . [and] growth" (see *The Rise of Romance* [New York: Oxford Univ. Press, 1971], esp. pp. 40, 56, 66, 71–72, 75–76).

51. Ibid., pp. 254–255.
52. "Introduction," *The Oxford Book of Modern Verse*, pp. xxiv–xxv.
53. Stevenson, "Blake's *Jerusalem*," pp. 254–255.
54. Rose, "The Structure of Blake's *Jerusalem*," p. 53.
55. See Karl Kiralis, "The Theme and Structure of William Blake's *Jerusalem*," in

dramaticall representation distinguished into certaine visions, and subdivided into certain *visionall Acts*" (p. 475) he epitomizes the tradition of prophecy joined to epic by Milton and invoked by Blake in the climactic moments of *Jerusalem* where he speaks of "Visionary forms dramatic" redounding from "Tongues in thunderous majesty, in Visions / In new Expanses, creating exemplars of Memory and of Intellect, / Creating Space, Creating Time according to the wonders Divine / Of Human Imagination . . ." (98: 28–32).

The tradition of prophecy, as it was represented by Pareus, not only provided poets with instruction in how to write it but offered audiences instruction in how to read it. Prophecy, though it is not history, has a historical dimension to it. Pareus's first counsel is to compare principal historical events with types in the vision, remembering that the vision transcends its types by gathering them into a mythology. This is the level at which Blake's prophecies are most immediately accessible; it is not, however, the level at which he wanted them to be read. Pareus's second counsel is related to the first: use the experience of the present moment, but weigh it equally with "events past, present, and to come" (p. *11*). Like God in Book III of *Paradise Lost*, the prophetic poet sees all aspects of time—past, present, and future—collapsing into a single moment. What Angus Fletcher describes as "the prophetic moment" occurs "when the prophetic order of history is revealed."[56] This is, for Blake, the "Period" when "the Poets Work is Done":

Events of Time start forth & are concievd in such a Period,
Within a Moment: a Pulsation of the Artery.

(*M* 29: 2–3)

In such moments "the poet collaborates with all the forces of the world spirit" and is brought to the "prophetic threshold."[57]

Pointedly, *Milton* concludes in the same moment from which *Jerusalem* unfolds, the end of the first poem and the beginning of the second having their primary referent in the first chapter of Revelation. *Jerusalem* begins, like Revelation (and this point we have already observed) with Christ standing at the door knocking, with Blake taking in the vision of which his poem is an articulation. *Jerusalem* begins, that is, in the same moment with which *Milton* ends. Beholding Jesus in "Felphams Vale clothed in Clouds of blood" and hearing "Four Trumpets . . . sounded to the Four Winds," Blake is "Terror struck" and, trembling, falls "outstretchd upon the path" (*M* 42: 20–25), just as John of Patmos, turning to see the voice that speaks

---

The Divine Vision: Studies in the Poetry and Art of William Blake, ed. Vivian de Sola Pinto (London: Victor Gollancz, 1957), pp. 158–159 n.

56. *The Prophetic Moment*, p. 45.
57. Ibid.

to him and beholding the vision of Jesus, falls "to his feet as dead" (Rev.
1: 17). *Milton* anatomizes the moment when the vision is taken in by the
poet; but that moment, for Blake, is merely a portal to the moment when
the poet can give his vision form. The struggle recorded in *Jerusalem* is not
a struggle to achieve vision (the vision has been achieved) but rather a
struggle to organize it into what Blake calls "Minute Particulars." This
moment of translation is the moment when vision, given form, becomes act
and when act holds out the possibility of realizing—of concretizing—the
vision.[58]

The best guides to explicating prophecy, according to Pareus, are the
general prologues to prophetic books and the particular prologues to individual visions contained within them. In terms of Blake's *Jerusalem*, this
means the prose statements and lyrics that precede each chapter and the
full-page designs that conclude each of the four chapters.[59] Finally, since
the Book of Revelation is a gathering of individual prophecies—a consolidation especially of those visions presented by Ezekiel, Daniel, and Zechariah
—these early visions provide analogues and clues to understanding the consolidated vision. Just as the sublime allegory of Revelation is impenetrable
without a comprehension of previous prophecy, so Blake's *Jerusalem* is not
fully comprehensible without having previously penetrated all that it consolidates—biblical prophecy, Milton's epic prophecies, and Blake's earlier
prophecies, especially *The Four Zoas* and *Milton*.

Blake's final prophecy not only subsumes and interprets previous prophecy, scriptural and literary, especially the Book of Revelation and *Paradise
Regained*, but it takes its structure from these books, picking up where John
the prophet and Milton the poet leave off. The final vision of each prophet—
in Revelation the Last Judgment and Jerusalem descending, in *Paradise
Regained* the return of Jesus to civilization—provides the point of departure for Blake's last epic. The four chapters of *Jerusalem* find their structural
analogue in *Paradise Regained* and in Revelation where each vision preserves the analogy with drama and is divided into four acts. The last vision
is not "a vaine repetition" of what was revealed in the previous visions "but
a most profitable revealing of things divers from the former mysteries"
(Pareus, p. 501). *Jerusalem* is an anatomy of the culminating moments in
both *Paradise Regained* and the Apocalypse; it is a revelation of the "mysteries" enclosed in Blake's previous prophecies, and it is a new vision that
requires the same kind of interpretation that it provides for previous prophe-

58. See Northrop Frye, "The Road of Excess," in *The Stubborn Structure: Essays
on Criticism and Society* (Ithaca: Cornell Univ. Press, 1970), p. 174.

59. See Henry Lesnick's essay, "Narrative Structure and the Antithetical Vision of
Jerusalem," in *Blake's Visionary Forms Dramatic*, ed. Erdman and Grant, pp. 391–412,
which elaborates this point.

cies. Coleridge's sources stand in the same relation to *Kubla Khan* as the Old Testament does to the Book of Revelation and as all previous prophecy, Blake's own and his predecessors', does to *Jerusalem*. These prophetic contexts give way to one another unexpectedly; and by this process *Jerusalem* achieves coherence. The relationship between John's Gospels and the Apocalypse, moreover, is identical with the relationship between *Paradise Lost* and *Paradise Regained*, between *Milton* and *Jerusalem*: the differences in style spell differences in vision; the latter work looks back to the former but proceeds beyond it by stamping a new vision out of the old one. Milton radically transforms the images, themes, and patterns he inherits from his sources just as Blake transforms many of those that he derives from his sources, including Milton. But these transformations should be regarded less as efforts to spurn tradition and more as attempts to invoke the precedent of "the Christian revolution" which involved the "transformation of images" with Christ himself as architect of much of the "transforming work." [60]

Counsels for reading prophecy, like those offered by Pareus, have been followed by Blake's critics with varying degrees of success. The last of those counsels, which fastens attention to prophetic structure, has just recently been discovered as a tool for shaping an understanding of Blake's epics. With it Harold Bloom forges an important interpretation of *Jerusalem* but also a partial one, inasmuch as he suggests that epic and prophetic structures are somehow incompatible and believes, therefore, that in his "definitive poem" Blake abandons the former for the latter by going "at last for prophetic form to a prophet, to the priestly orator, Ezekiel, whose situation and sorrow most closely resemble his own." [61]

In the context of Bloom's observation, several points merit reiteration. Blake's epics are like Milton's—poems of many structures rather than poems of a structure. *The Four Zoas, Milton,* and *Jerusalem* possess both epic and prophetic structures; the epic structure of *The Four Zoas* derives from *Paradise Lost*; and the epic structures of *Milton* and *Jerusalem* derive from *Paradise Regained*. The prophetic structure of each poem derives from the Book of Revelation, but the immediate precedent for conjoining the structure of prophecy with epic is to be found in *Paradise Lost* and *Paradise Regained*. Ezekiel's prophecy provides one significant analogue for the structure of *Jerusalem* and is also one clue to the poem's meaning; but *Jerusalem*, like the Book of Revelation, is a series of visions, an amalgamation of

---

60. Farrer, *A Rebirth of Images*, p. 15.

61. "Blake's *Jerusalem*: The Bard of Sensibility and the Form of Prophecy," *Eighteenth-Century Studies*, 4 (1970), 6. Bloom's essay is reprinted in his book, *The Ringers in the Tower: Studies in Romantic Tradition* (Chicago: Univ. of Chicago Press, 1971), pp. 65–79.

perspectives, which, gathering into themselves previous prophecies, still maintain their integrity as "visions." Blake's task is greater than that of John the prophet, for the biblical prophet had only to contend with the prophecies of Scripture. Blake as poet, prophet, and orator must contend with scriptural prophecies (most importantly John's) and with the epic prophecies of Milton. The greater task holds out the possibility for the greater *artistic* achievement.

What Bloom says of Ezekiel can properly be said of only John and Milton: ". . . in regard to Blake's *Jerusalem*, [they are] like Homer in regard to the *Aeneid*: the inventor, the precursor, the shaper of the later work's continuities. From Ezekiel [I would say from John the prophet and Milton the poet] . . . Blake learned the true meaning of prophet, visionary orator, honest man who speaks into the heart of a situation to warn: if you go on so, the result is so . . . ."[62] The prophecy of Ezekiel, Bloom tells us, derives its form from the initial vision of glory; however, Blake is still searching for his vision when *Jerusalem* commences. All he sees about him is "an image of salvation [that] has been abandoned to destruction."[63] Blake, in short, has adopted the pattern of Ezekiel but has inverted it. To say that Blake is still searching for "vision" when he writes *Jerusalem* is mistaken, but what Bloom says of Blake's inverting the pattern of Ezekiel's vision is true enough. Indeed, such inversions are typical of the way prophets treat their predecessors, shifting their accents and presenting reverse images of earlier prophetic patterns. One need only recall that on virtually every occasion when Milton derives a pattern from Homer or Virgil it is a pattern presented in reverse; the new pattern becomes a way of defining, through irony, the poet's unique discoveries. Blake follows the same "ironic epic strategy"[64] that Milton employs, but with a difference. Milton would not take "dictation" from Homer, Virgil, and Dante. Neither did Blake. But in the same way that Milton serves as God's secretary and takes dictation from all those biblical prophets who had previously recorded the word of God, Blake takes dictation from Milton—less from the poet who wrote *Paradise Lost* than from the poet who wrote *Paradise Regained*. Like Milton, Blake was not beyond shifting the accents and patterns of biblical prophecy: Blake does it in *Jerusalem*, and Milton does it most noticeably in *Paradise Regained*. Yet both poets have scriptural precedent for what they do. This is precisely what John does in the Apocalypse, and his practice both poets adhere to.

Blake learned from Milton and John the true meaning of "prophet," but

62. Ibid., p. 7.
63. Ibid., p. 8.
64. The phrase is Brian Wilkie's; see "Epic Irony in *Milton*," in *Blake's Visionary Forms Dramatic*, ed. Erdman and Grant, p. 363.

he also learned from them the true meaning of "orator." The kind of ideal relationship that the orator sought with his audience was represented during the Renaissance by Hercules, who is portrayed as "a lustie old man with a long chayne tyed by one end at his tong, by the other end at the peoples eares." The people, standing "farre of," seem "to be drawen to him by force [sic] of that chayne fastned to his tong, as . . . by force of his perswasions."[65] The image is one of many used by rhetoricians to define the orator's "legislative" responsibilities, as well as the relation between "vision and action." However much Milton and Blake may alter oratorical patterns, they still embrace the ideology of the form, and each testifies to that ideology through his insistence upon mastering the various styles, which oratorical tradition had bound to the three classes of men that comprise the social order. However opposed both poets were to what Milton calls the *"expediency of set formes"* or "the compelling of set formes" (*Apology*, I, 936, 938,), each continues the oratorical tradition because it is the expression of political and moral forces and the vehicle for translating the misery, fever, and fret of human existence into the ideal.

If the "histrionic" mode is understood as a "theatre of mind" wherein the poet is both actor and audience, then the prophetic orator-poet must necessarily struggle to transcend it. "The prophet retains a sense of himself as actor, but he ceases to be his own audience. A passage from solipsism to otherness is made, the theatre of mind dissolves, and the actor stands, as a warner of *persons*,"[66] and as their awakener and redeemer. Blake, Bloom rightly says, followed Milton "to the line of prophecy." But Bloom's remarks on "the anxiety of influence" confuse matters—not by seeing Blake following his sources "at a distance," fearing that their "Hebraic theism . . . would make his apocalyptic humanism impossible"; but by suggesting that, for this reason, Blake "held back from identifying himself wholly with Milton," and by insinuating, too, that Milton was, in Blake's mind, allied with the "lesser mode" of eighteenth-century poetry from which Blake, in *Jerusalem*, disengages himself, "cross[ing] over . . . from the theatre of mind to the orator's theatre of action."[67] This last assertion, insofar as it relates to Blake, is valid; but it also misrepresents Milton and Blake's relationship to him.

It has been said that *Paradise Regained* "hardly exists as a tradition demanding allegiance."[68] It should be said that, for Blake, *Paradise Regained* was the one poem in epic tradition to which he could give his allegiance, the

---

65. George Puttenham, *The Arte of English Poesie* (1589; rpt. London, 1811), p. 118.
66. Bloom, "Blake's *Jerusalem*," pp. 9–10.
67. Ibid., pp. 7, 15–16, 20.
68. Wilkie, "Epic Irony in *Milton*," p. 361.

one poem from which he could accept "dictation." The form of Blake's *Milton* and the form of Blake's *Jerusalem* emphasize return. Both poems pick up where *Paradise Regained* leaves off—with the true poet-prophet-orator (Milton-Los-Blake), having annihilated selfhood, which is Satan, returning to civilization to begin the work of its redemption. By withstanding the temptation on the pinnacle, Christ displays his enormous love for God; be returning to his mother's house he displays his enormous love for man. This moment of return is Christ's deed above heroic, and it constitutes *the moment* when contemplation, having unfolded into vision, is translated into form and action. *Jerusalem* may take its form from the Book of Revelation but it takes its meaning, as Bloom defines it, from the final moments in *Paradise Regained*. Blake's designs to that poem—the last complete set of illustrations to Milton that Blake did (and he did them during the time when *Jerusalem* was being etched)—fasten attention to the moment on the pinnacle and to the moment of return. *Milton* and *Jerusalem* not only recall these moments; they anatomize them and define their significance. *Milton* is to *Jerusalem* what *Paradise Regained* is to *Samson Agonistes*: "a calm before the storm . . . the stillness as one enters the eye of the hurricane" that is apocalypse.[69] *Jerusalem* culminates in a vision of apocalypse and *Samson* in a moment that adumbrates it.

Jerusalem not only has a definable relationship to *Paradise Regained*, *Samson Agonistes*, and the Book of Revelation, but has a similar relationship to Blake's own canon. Its vision is a continuation of or, better, a complement to the one articulated in *Milton*. There Blake repeated with Milton the journey of Christ into the wilderness and participated in his predecessor's redemption. Now, like Christ, he must return to the world with his superior illumination and build "Jerusalem, / In Englands green & pleasant Land" (*M* 1: 15–16). With Los, he must now hammer out a vision of eternity. Like the Bible, Blake's canon is "a wholly concordant structure, the end is in harmony with the beginning, the middle with the beginning and end."[70] The end, which is *Jerusalem*, subsumes the whole structure.

Blake learned yet another quality of the "true orator" from Milton and John. The orator, says Milton, fulfills his role by "making a creation like to Gods" (*Apology*, I, 721)—a creation wherein discords and enmities, the agony and strife of contraries, are resolved into a unity. Imitating God, the orator-poet attempts to bring "the due likeness and harmonies of his works together" (*Divorce*, II, 272). Such a harmony could be realized in individual poems, but in no genre more fully than in the epic.[71] It could also be achieved between poems, integrating them all in such a way as to create

69. Fletcher, *The Prophetic Moment*, p. 49.
70. Kermode, *The Sense of an Ending*, p. 6.
71. In a famous passage, Tasso likens God and the epic poet as creators; the passage

one grand poem, one harmonious vision. Following Milton's example, Blake interrelated his works—and so completely that one poem can scarcely be read without contending with the others. The Bible provided an analogy— and a mythic structure—for the encompassing unity that Blake and Milton sought.

Blake doubtless discerned this analogy in Milton's poetry, where it is an informing principle; but Blake could also have found encouragement for pursuing it in a work by Anselm Bayly, published in 1789. Observing that, with Milton, epic combines forces with oratory and prophecy, Bayly describes the Bible, in the way that Saint Jerome described it, as "one grand epic poem"; and he urges epic poets to follow Milton's lead by imitating its large design and also the structure of its various prophecies. Epic poems, Bayly explains, are "Poetic Prophecies," which employ "allegories" that are neither "easy, nor conspicuous." By "expand[ing] our thoughts" and "sublim[ing] our interpretations" of eternal realities, which the poet can best do by going to the Book of Revelation, the epic poem effects a purification of religion and directs men back to pristine Christianity.[72] For Bayly, as for Blake, all religions, all mythologies, are one; and the history of both begins the moment that "the Unity of Godhead . . . divided, and the Plurality of Personality was multiplied." The history of religion and of mythology continues with the story of how, corrupted by fragmentation, they became "varied" and "multiform."[73] This history is recorded in Scripture and, Blake would say, in *Paradise Lost*; the purpose of the new epic poet, akin to the purpose of John in Revelation, is to record this history but also to add chapters to it, which point men back to original Christianity and to the unified vision of life that it supports.

In *The Marriage of Heaven and Hell*, Blake promised a Bible of Hell. While *The Book of Urizen* is often described as Blake's rewriting of Genesis and *The Book of Ahania* as his Exodus, it is usually assumed that with *The Four Zoas* the pursuit of this analogy between his individual poems and scriptural books is terminated. On the contrary, the analogy is appropriate to Blake's epic poems and illuminating to any study of the structure of their mythology. As Blake read the Bible he saw three central myths pulled together to comprise the total Christian mythology—a myth of creation and fall, a myth of wandering, and a myth of return. The first was detailed in Genesis, the last in Revelation, while the story of man's wandering in the wilderness occupied the intervening books of the Bible. This design of

---

is quoted and discussed by E. M. W. Tillyard, *The English Epic and Its Background* (London: Chatto and Windus, 1954), pp. 231–232.

72. *The Alliance of Musick, Poetry, and Oratory* (London [1789]), pp. 132, 135, 265, 267.

73. Ibid., p. 244.

Christian mythology provides a rough outline for the one Blake adopts for his three epic poems, each of which pivots on one of the three myths that is seen under the aspect of a total mythology. That mythology, by preserving points of contact with traditional ones, uses mythic differentiation as the way to mythic condensation. *The Four Zoas* employs the story of creation and fall but, in the shorthand of its final books, recounts the myth of exodus and, with apocalyptic fury, moves into a description of the Last Harvest. *Milton*, poised between Blake's first and last epic venture, refers to the creation in its opening lines and the apocalypse in its closing ones; but it also takes its central action from the pattern of experience that dominates the rest of biblical history, that time from the Book of Numbers to the Epistles of Saint John that immediately precede the Book of Revelation, and derives its structural patterns from those books in the same way that *Jerusalem* derives its from the Book of Revelation.[74]

Blake's last epic, while surveying both the creation-fall and exodus myths, is concerned preeminently with the myth of apocalypse. It does for its age what Milton's epics did for the seventeenth century. Unfulfilled promises of apocalypse in both centuries broke the expectations of the nation: 1666 was one predicted date for apocalypse, 1757 another. Both Milton and Blake shared in their culture's malaise, not because either poet had undaunted faith in naive apocalyptism but because both poets saw their expectations for reformation through revolution dashed. The French Revolution failed Blake in the same way that the Puritan Revolution failed Milton: at their outsets, both revolutions presented the image of a cohesive and creative society and promised to realize it; but as each revolution followed its course, this image was scarred into the demonic image of a society more fragmented and more oppressed than it was before the revolution ensued. The epic efforts of Milton and Blake alike are designed to effect a "readjustment of expectations" in a culture frustrated and fragmented by the failure of a promise. *Paradise Regained* and *Jerusalem* are the culminations of those efforts, both poems bursting out of "eschatological despair"[75] to present radically new versions of Christianity by which their authors are able to make sense of the world. In these final visions, to which *Paradise Lost* and

74. For an elaboration of this point, see Northrop Frye, *A Study of English Romanticism* (New York: Random House, 1968), pp. 3–49, and my essay, "Domes of Mental Pleasure," pp. 101–129.

75. This phrase, as well as the one in the preceding sentence, is borrowed from Kermode's *The Sense of an Ending*, pp. 8, 18. Since completing my essay, I have read the important study by M. H. Abrams, *Natural Supernaturalism: Tradition and Revolution in Romantic Literature* (New York: W. W. Norton, 1971). Abrams recognizes that "the preoccupation with Apocalypse" in Spenser and Milton has "important consequences for their Romantic successors [including Blake] in the prophetic tradition" (p. 38). Pages 19–70 present insights that complement my own, and pages 329–356

Milton are "preludes," the prophetic poet tries to originate an order: both poets clarify the confusion of their cultures by transforming a barren wilderness into Jerusalem and hope that "Empire" with follow them to its portals.

"To create one's own support," to create one's own form, says Martin Price, is "an exercise of liberty" made by William Blake, but accompanied "by a loss of those forms of authority that both limit and support."[76] Price misses the significance of Milton for Blake and for the rest of the Romantics. Blake's epics "are part of the whole Romantic attempt to refurbish epic" and should be seen in the context of Spenser's experimentation and Milton's. "It is obvious that Blake enters the epic arena in order both to enlist Milton's aid as a brother prophet and to confute or convert him," but it is not so obvious that Blake does essentially "the same thing" as Milton "with the whole general tradition of literary epic."[77] The epic poems of Milton, and later of Blake, are an extended allusion to the entire tradition of epic poetry, which both poets regard as a form corrupted by mimetic rule and which both poets attempt to "refurbish" by spurning the boundaries of mimetic art, knocking away its usual underpinnings, the conventions the form accumulated, in order to create epic anew. Like Milton, Blake inverts whatever patterns he inherits from tradition—his art is continually engaged in inversional transformations. Beyond that, Blake, following another Miltonic lead, attempts another consolidation of epic tradition, achieved in *Jerusalem* not just by echoing his predecessors, nor by resorting to conspicuous imitation, but by allowing his poem to intersect with the endings of three separate Renaissance epics. *Jerusalem* is, as we have seen, an ampli-

---

offer an extended treatment of what I have suggested here in abbreviated form.

Morton Bloomfield's *Piers Plowman as a Fourteenth-Century Apocalypse* (New Brunswick: Rutgers Univ. Press, 1962) also provides an interesting perspective on my essay and on Blake's apocalyptic epics. Bloomfield's reluctance to define *Piers Plowman* as an "apocalypse" stems from his belief that "we cannot clearly accept this form of literature as an established genre" (p. 10). This is true enough if we are thinking of the fourteenth century, but not true at all if we are thinking of Milton: one achievement of Renaissance commentators on Revelation was to establish "apocalypse" as a literary genre. Most interesting for Blake are Bloomfield's comments on "The Problem of Imaginatif" (pp. 170–174). The *problem* lies in the fact that imagination, regarded as a lesser faculty and thus accorded little attention in medieval psychology and philosophy, is elevated to a prominent position in *Piers Plowman*. Bloomfield explains this unusual treatment of imagination by turning to the tradition of medieval prophecy—a tradition that emphasizes and enhances the power of imagination. This point helps to clarify the roles assumed by Los and imagination in Blake's epics, poems which represent the culmination—indeed the apotheosis—of the tradition outlined and explained by Bloomfield.

76. "Introduction," *Eighteenth-Century Studies*, 4 (1970), 5.

77. Wilkie, "Epic Irony in *Milton*," p. 359.

fication and continuation of *Paradise Regained*; but it is also a completion of Spenser's unfinished epic and an extension of Tasso's culminating vision in *Gerusalemme Liberata*. Blake, then, soars beyond the models he invokes but not without establishing continuity between his vision and the visions of his predecessors nearest him in time and purpose. In both respects, Milton's poems are the ones closest to those that Blake himself wished to write.

When experimentation with epic resumed at the end of the eighteenth century, theorists and poets alike turned instinctively to Milton, and understandably so: Milton charged atrophied forms with life and used those forms to discharge the lightning that rolled the dark clouds of ignorance into the distance. In his poetry and prose alike, Milton sowed the seeds that, having since taken root, were "now growing up to a glorious harvest." As artist and as intellect, Milton was the chief agent responsible for "those revolutions" in which men were "now exulting"; he prepared men for the recovery of lost liberty, and he precipitated "the overthrow of priestcraft and tyranny."[78] Milton inculcated a culture with the values it was ready to adopt, and he created a radical aesthetic to support them. In Milton's works, there was no disjunction between form and content. Milton lived through a period which saw the shattering of forms and of the beliefs with which they were invested, but he also saw beyond the usual categories of art and of morality and out of his vision created new forms and new values to replace those that had been shattered. Milton achieved a perfect unity between form and content and thus demanded of those who would follow in his tradition the unity of religion and art, "the unity of politics and art . . . , the unity of revolutionary . . . content and the highest possible perfection of artistic form."[79] The twentieth century has just begun to recover the understanding of Milton that dominated the late eighteenth and early nineteenth centuries. We have become accustomed to thinking of Milton's epics "as *being* the norm" of their age, while, as E. M. W. Tillyard suggested some time ago, those epics "*created* the norm, doing thereby an original . . . a daring thing."[80]

A brilliant architect and a brilliant creator of myth, Milton—more so than any other poet—taught Blake what it meant to be a revolutionary artist. Through his study of Milton's art, Blake came to distinguish between mathematical and organic form. The conventions accumulated by poetry provided the former and myth provided the latter. In the case of epic,

78. Richard Price, "A Discourse on the Love of Our Country," in *British Radicals and Reformers 1789–1832*, ed. Wilfried Keutsch, English Texts (Tübingen: Max Niemeyer Verlag, 1971), p. 11.

79. Mao Tse-Tung, *On Literature and Art* (Peking: Foreign Language Press, 1967), p. 30.

80. *The English Epic and Its Background*, p. 434.

when conventions were purged from the venerable mode, design came to provide its external form, while myth continued to supply its internal form.[81] This is part of the lesson that Blake sought to record, verbally and pictorially, and to transmit to posterity. The other part of the lesson emerges from his belief, shared with Milton, that poetry is doctrinal to a nation and that the poet is a legislator. This belief had its corollary: if literature did not exist apart from social activity, neither did social activity exist in isolation from literature; rather social activity, revolution, was an influence on literary forms. Milton's poetry showed Blake that the shape of a poem was de-

---

81. I have suggested in another essay (see "William Blake: Illustrator-Interpreter of *Paradise Regained*," in *Calm of Mind*, ed. Wittreich, p. 122), and earlier in this essay, that with *Paradise Regained* conventions are purged from the venerable tradition of epic poetry. In an important sense this is true, but the "truth" also requires qualification. In *Paradise Regained*, most of the epic conventions disappear, and the few that persist are there in abbreviated form. Two conventions, however, are seized upon, joined together, and then transmuted: I am thinking of (1) the descent into the underworld, through which the hero comes to terms with the dark side of human existence and (2) the descent of the heavenly messenger, who brings divine illumination to the hero. The brief epic (as *Paradise Regained* exemplifies it) is an internalized drama that these epic conventions, transformed, clarify and support. The descent into the underworld is modulated into Christ's descent into himself; the descent of the heavenly messenger is modulated into Christ's willing descent from the pinnacle (a type of the Incarnation) to begin the work of man's redemption. The first descent involves the acquisition of knowledge by the hero; the second, the extension of that knowledge to mankind. The same conventions, similarly combined and transformed, persist in Blake's epics, most notably in *Milton*, where the hero descends into himself to annihilate selfhood and, accomplishing that, descends into the world to become its "Awakener."

If the initiatory experience is but one aspect of the diffuse epic, it is absolutely central to the brief epic. The hero and the audience are together "Initiated Into The Mysteries," which is to say that both are brought to the threshold of "vision." The language is William Warburton's, and I borrow it from "A Dissertation on the Sixth Book of Virgil's Æneis," in *The Works of Virgil*, ed. Joseph Warton (London, 1753), III, 10, 34. Warburton continues by equating initiation with beholding "the divine lights" that reveal "the great *secret* of the *unity*" (III, 53, 59) and by paralleling that "initiation' with "death." "TO DIE," says Warburton, is "TO BE INITIATED"; and the initiation occurs in three stages: (1) the hero is filled with uncertainties (Christ in *Paradise Regained*) and/or an awareness of his errors (Milton in *Milton*) and "wander[s] . . . through night and darkness" (Christ and Milton); (2) all that the hero confronts "wears a dreadful aspect: it is all horror, trembling . . . affrightment" (note especially Christ's confronting the spectres of the night and Milton's confronting his own spectre, which is Satan); (3) suddenly the divine light displays itself, revealing "holy visions" (III, 60–61). This is the moment on the pinnacle in Milton's poem, and the moment of which Blake's *Milton* is an anatomy. This description of the initiatory experience is as relevant to *Paradise Regained* as it is to *Milton* and *Jerusalem*; Warburton's observations are so appropriate to Blake's epics that it is difficult not to assert that Blake read and was influenced by them.

termined by cultural forces "just as the sea is determined in its shape by the land, [and] in its surface by the wind." [82] Milton's verse forms were no less revolutionary than the ideologies they projected, though the revolutionary character of both was, in Blake's time as in our own, "not . . . always perceived." [83] Revolutions reduce cultures to chaos: not only are values and ideologies lost but so are the aesthetic systems that once supported them. Thus those very artists who construct a new scheme of values, a new worldview, must also create a new aesthetic. This Milton did, and for this reason the very poets who reverted to him for their ideological framework adopted from him their literary aesthetic as well. Blake was one such poet.

With Blake, the poetry of allusion gives way to a poetry of contexts. Blake knew that poetry cannot "speak for itself anymore than any other symbol system can, but takes its meaning from its contexts, both those to which it specifically refers and those which it attempts to exclude from the reader's attention." [84] Through the contexts exposed to or excised from the reader's attention, Blake guides his audience toward relevant contexts and steers it away from irrelevant and misleading ones. Blake's poetry excludes fewer contexts than is usually assumed, and its contexts are often defined pointedly; seldom are they defined cryptically. And the one context that is a constant in Blake's poetry is Milton; in the background of virtually everything he writes is a work, or a complex of works, by Milton. To consider Blake in relation to the Milton tradition is to end in something of a paradox: to define the revolutionary character of Milton's art is to reveal the traditionalism of Blake's. [85] For many, such an effort will seem to take us a step beyond T. S. Eliot (he denied Blake the stature of a "classic") by now denying him individual genius. The fact of the matter is this: to locate Blake within the Milton tradition is not to deny him genius but to describe the character of his genius more precisely. It is to place Blake within the great tradition of English poetry—the line of vision, not the line of wit—a tradition in which startlingly few poets have had the imagination, the historical sense, or the *genius* to participate; it is also to open the seals that have hidden Blake's prophecies from generations of readers.

82. Caudwell, *Romance and Realism*, p. 130.
83. Ibid., p. 47.
84. Rosalie L. Colie, *Paradoxia Epidemica: The Renaissance Tradition of Paradox* (Princeton: Princeton Univ. Press, 1966), p. 190.
85. To a greater extent than Blake, Milton invokes tradition, but usually to subvert it. The effect of this subversion is to liberate his successors from the fetters of tradition. Therefore, Blake and many other Romantic poets can appropriate the revolutionary elements in Milton's art while ignoring its traditionalism. In the process, Romantic poetry involves itself in a paradox: the revolutionary aspects of Milton's art, so often represented as distinguishing elements in Romantic art, are, by virtue of Milton's use of them, traditional.

Time and Space
in Blake's
Major Prophecies

RONALD L. GRIMES

In an earlier era of Blake studies it was not unusual to hold that Blake was a mystic with no real interest in the affairs of mundane, historical time. As a mystic he was thought to be interested only in the eternal. Today, however, one cannot make such a claim without massive support and reinterpretation. That Blake both knew and poetically utilized the events of his day is accepted by most modern critics, largely as a result of the work of David V. Erdman. Erdman's book has had such an impact that Edward J. Rose, reviewing the second edition of *Blake: Prophet Against Empire*, must remind a critic of Erdman (Martin Price) that Blake carries on a debate not only with his times but with all times: "Blake does not simply read the 'Times' he reads the Eternities."[1] If there was once the danger that interpreters would overlook Blake's interest in time, there now seems to be the possibility that a reader might miss his interest in eternity, hence Rose's reminder.

If one accepts as proven the argument that Blake's prophecies are not timeless in the sense that they ignore or disdain events occurring in space and time, but, in fact, are firmly rooted in Blake's own time, the interpreter still has the responsibility for showing precisely how the prophecies are related to space and time. A thorough treatment of Blake's understanding of time and space would have to include a careful study of his employment of verb tense in relation to time, his use of prepositions in relation to space, and his use of connective devices in relation to the unity of space and time.

1. "Reviews: David V. Erdman, *Blake: Prophet Against Empire*, 2nd ed.," *Blake Newsletter*, 4 (1970), 48.

Furthermore, a study of what Blake does with artistic space in the designs needs to be linked to what is said of space in the poetry. And still further, what is said of time in the prophecies needs to be integrated into the larger questions of the chronology, unity, and "plot" of the prophecies. In order to establish the premises for a more thorough consideration, I have in this essay limited my discussion to what Blake says about space and time in the poetry of *The Four Zoas, Milton,* and *Jerusalem.*

I

The importance of the question of time's role in the prophecies is indicated by the association of time with Blake's prime protagonist, Los. Los is unquestionably Blake's crucial figure when inquiry is made into the relationship between time and imagination. Not only does Los control the times, seasons, and years (*FZ* I: *301*), he is named "Time" by men (*M* 24: 68). However, the association of Los with time should not be taken too literally or just allegorically. For example, even after "times are ended" on page 131 of *The Four Zoas,* Los is subsequently still very much in the middle of the action on page 137, so a purely allegorical interpretation is doomed to failure.

Los is supposed to be in control of time. Over space his Emanation, Enitharmon, is made mistress. *The Four Zoas* does little to develop this theme other than frequently to refer to Los's anvils as "the Anvils of time and space" (VIII: *361*). Ideally, space and time are tools which Los uses, rather than conditions to which he must subject himself. One such use is his forging of days, years, and hours into a chain with which to bind Urizen (*FZ* IV: *328–329*), but these "chains of sorrow" fly out of Los's control and entangle his own Emanation. So, in fact, time and space often do become conditions which overwhelm Los.

Only in *Milton* do the implications of Los's role as "watchman of eternity" become explicit, because Blake is struggling with the meaning of historical influence and with the problem of the relation between visionary poetry and history.

Milton enters Blake's foot, but Blake does not immediately recognize him,

. . . for man cannot know

What passes in his members till periods of Space & Time
Reveal the secrets of Eternity: for more extensive
Than any other earthly things, are Mans earthly lineaments.

And all this Vegetable World appeard on my left Foot,
As a bright sandal formd immortal of precious stones & gold:
I stooped down & bound it on to walk forward thro' Eternity.

(*M* 21: 8–14)

Blake clearly affirms the necessity, perhaps even the inevitability, of man's being rooted in space and time. Revelation may be *from* eternity but it is *in* time. Space and time are the media and location of revelation. The "vegetable world," the world of time and space, is not left behind in a flight to the timeless but becomes the foundation for a walk through eternity. One is reminded of the aphorism from *The Marriage of Heaven and Hell*: "Eternity is in love with the productions of time" (7: 35). Even though Blake "stoops down" and binds the sandal to his "left" foot, the connotations are not purely negative. The sandal is precious as long as it serves man's entry into eternity. And significantly, Los enters Blake's soul when he hears ". . . what time I bound my sandals / On; to walk forward thro' Eternity . . ." (*M* 22: 4–5).

The assimilation of Milton and then Los to Blake himself is recognition that a figure from the past, a poetic character, and a man of the present are not sealed off from one another in visionary perception. One must beware, however, of jumping to the fallacious conclusion that imaginative time is reversible or that sequence is being denied. Blake is not attempting to wreck the fabric of chronology. He knows quite well that Milton lived historically before him and that Los lives in the "virtual" present of literature. Nevertheless, he insists that no historical moment is necessarily irretrievable, though it will wither and die outside an imaginative milieu:

I am that Shadowy Prophet who Six Thousand Years ago
Fell from my station in the Eternal bosom. Six Thousand Years
Are finishd. I return! both Time & Space obey my will.
I in Six Thousand Years walk up and down: for not one Moment
Of Time is lost, nor one Event of Space unpermanent.
But all remain: every fabric of Six Thousand Years
Remains permanent: tho' on the Earth where Satan
Fell, and was cut off all things vanish & are seen no more
They vanish not from me & mine, we guard them first & last[.]
The generations of men run on in the tide of Time
But leave their destind lineaments permanent for ever & ever.
(*M* 22: 15–25)

Two modes of time are contrasted in this passage: time which preserves and time which sweeps all things into oblivion. Blake's distinction must not be confused with the distinction sometimes made between mythical and historical time. Mythical time is often characterized as primordial time made present. It is the time of the beginning as indefinitely recoverable, indefinitely repeatable.[2] Historical time is said to be different, inasmuch as

2. Mircea Eliade, *The Sacred and the Profane* (New York: Harper and Row, 1961), pp. 68–69.

events follow one another in linear succession and are therefore unique and unrepeatable.

Preserving, or imaginative, time, as Blake sees it, is not static; but neither does it flow in uniform units like seconds or minutes. Time obeys his will; it is flexible. It bends under the impact of men like Milton who leave their "lineaments" impressed upon it. But time does not obey Los/Blake's will in any absolute sense; otherwise, Blake would have prevented the Puritan of the past, Milton, from influencing him at all. Blake cannot will who or what his history was, but he can will, if sufficiently imaginative, how that history's course will be affected by the present.

In contrast to imaginative time, the time of the Satanically dominated earth is atomistically divided. An event blazes like a flame and is then snuffed out without a trace of smoke. Such time is a kind of ordered, mechanized chaos. Nothing is connected with anything else, but all things follow a fixed sequence. This Blake calls "the Sea of Time & Space" (*M* 15: 39). Blake conceives of time as linear and irrevocable; but linearity does not imply homogeneity, nor does irrevocability imply that history is forever locked in a room somewhere behind us. Time cannot be lost. Either it will become a Satanic horror in memory, or it will become a visionary inspiration in imagination. History is not finished; it does not die in the doing of the event. Instead history becomes the raw material for re-creation both of and by the next generation. One has no choice; he cannot choose his own past. But he can choose whether to live the past again or to live the past forward. To live it again is Satanic. To live it forward is visionary. In *Milton* the imaginative Los/Blake "lives forward" the history of John Milton in such a way that both Milton and Blake escape the shackling elements of time.

Time does not run down for Blake as it does in some religious mythologies. There is no solstice or equinox celebration to insure the continuance of the yearly cycle. Hence, he resists our New Year's symbols for time, the old man and the newly born babe:

Los is by mortals nam'd Time Enitharmon is nam'd Space
But they depict him bald & aged who is in eternal youth
All powerful and his locks flourish like the brows of morning
He is the Spirit of Prophecy the ever apparent Elias
Time is the mercy of Eternity; without Times swiftness
Which is the swiftest of all things: all were eternal torment:
All the Gods of the Kingdoms of Earth labour in Los's Halls.
Every one is a fallen Son of the Spirit of Prophecy.
                                   (*M* 24: 68–75)[3]

3. In *VLJ, p. 553*, Blake confesses, "The Greeks represent Chronos or Time as a very Aged Man this is Fable but the Real Vision of Time is in Eternal Youth I have

Los is the eschatological forerunner of the Divine Vision, Jesus; and he prepares the way for the inbreaking of eternity by proclaiming that now is the
time, that the times are ripe. The messenger of eternity who proclaims his
message in time mercifully brings the promise of prophecy to the tormented.
Since the possibility of an eschaton of imagination is ever-present, not, as
in some first-century eschatologies, just a possibility at the historical end
of the world, Los is said to be the eternal youth. He is the time of imagination, not the time of atomistically conceived history or the time of restless
sleep.

The "when" of Blakean eschatalogical time is "in between," not "at the
beginning" or "after the end," as the following passage makes clear:

But others of the Sons of Los build Moments & Minutes & Hours
And Days & Months & Years & Ages & Periods; wondrous buildings
And every Moment has a Couch of gold for soft repose,
(A Moment equals a pulsation of the artery)
And between every two Moments stands a Daughter of Beulah
To feed the Sleepers on their Couches with maternal care.
And every Minute has an azure Tent with silken Veils.
And every Hour has a bright golden Gate carved with skill . . .

Every Time less than a pulsation of the artery
Is equal in its period & value to Six Thousand Years.
For in this Period the Poets Work is Done: and all the Great
Events of Time start forth & are concievd in such a Period
Within a Moment: a Pulsation of the Artery.
                                    (*M* 28: 46—29: 3)[4]

The sleep of Ulro into which Albion falls is the sleep which is but a re-
version to the chaos of the primeval womb. Such sleep-time is the shapeless
stuff which has not yet felt the impact of the creative act. But there is another kind of sleep which is not the sleep of night and darkness and which
does not merely antedate the creative act but instead is a prelude to it. This
is the "sleep of Beulah," which is no longer than the pulsation of an artery.
The moment of poetic inspiration is so short that the poet does not have to
become oblivious to the realities of a time-laden world. The time of imagination and renewal, then, is not literally speaking at "the" beginning or at
"the" end. Blake's vision has nothing whatever to do with archaic myths of
cosmogony and theogony, which are based on circular views of time and
which seek renewal by a ritualistic return to the time between chaos and

---

⟨however⟩ somewhat accomodated my Figure of Time to ⟨the⟩ Common opinion as I
myself am also infected with it & my Visions also infected & I see Time Aged alas too
much so."
4. Cf. *J* 56: 9–10.

history, namely, to the time of "the" creation. Blake's interest is not creation but creativity.

The moment of imaginative dawning, the moment of creativity, can be any moment. More accurately, such time is "between" the tick and the tock of a clock's moment. Frank Kermode in his book *The Sense of an Ending* shows how literature tries to bridge the distance between "tick" and "tock," between beginning and end, by using what he calls "fictions of concord."[5] A crucial problem in reading Blake is the opacity of Blake's fiction of concord. Blake forever struggles to devise a fiction with which to link the "before" and "after" of the eschaton of imagination. He labors to keep from being perpetually hung *zwischen den Zeiten*. One cannot sleep too long in Beulah without awakening in Ulro; yet one must go to Beulah. The muses are there. All great events begin there. Later I will say more about the problem of linking beginning and ending. Meanwhile, it must suffice to note that the major prophecies end suddenly and surprisingly, or else they end on the brink of the eschaton. Their endings are either eschatological or realistically indecisive but hopeful.

What prevents the prophecies from being eschatological in the strict sense of the word is that the time of renewal is not the new aeon which succeeds the old, evil aeon. Rather the time of renewal is the instant between aeons. The time of transition *is* the time of imagination; it is not merely the time preceding the time of imagination. Blake's writing style is peculiarly appropriate to such a view (despite the fact that it is hard on plot-sketching readers). Connective devices are muted, if not missing altogether. The "spaces" between events seem to be blank, as if inviting the reader to fill them in by himself. Why one event follows another or even why an event occurs at all is seldom evident. The reader must sleep the inspirational sleep of Beulah between two moments if he wants to know "how" and "why." The causal and developmental linkage that one might expect of epic is simply not there. The "wherefores" do not tell "why," and the "thens" seem only to mean "and." Blake relies heavily on the biblical stylistic habit of parataxis, the linking of elements with co-ordinate rather than subordinate conjunctions, leaving the reader to discover logical connections for himself as he wanders between events. Blake emphasizes the problem of transition in its literary, psychological, and social manifestations precisely by muting or omitting connective devices. Characters do not develop biographically. Events do not proceed from one another developmentally. One might infer that vision is none other than the breaking down of strict chronological and causal sequences. Visionary relationships are the opposite of deterministic relationships, and each event is a

5. New York: Oxford Univ. Press, 1967, pp. 57–59.

"miracle" in the sense that its cause is not immediately evident if one looks only on an empirical level.[6] Events are somehow related, but not causally related. The problem is to find out exactly how they are related.

The Blakean "moment" has as its primary characteristic flexibility. A passage closely related to the one immediately above makes this explicit:

There is a Moment in each Day that Satan cannot find
Nor can his Watch Fiends find it, but the Industrious find
This Moment & it multiply. & when it once is found
It renovates every Moment of the Day if rightly placed[.]
In this Moment Ololon descended to Los & Enitharmon
Unseen beyond the Mundane Shell Southward in Miltons track.
                              (*M* 35: 42–47)

This renewing moment is moveable and multipliable; and if rightly used, it can renew every moment of the day. Imaginative time is not a single instant, nor is it time isolated from the chronological divisions which constitute a day. The time of imagination is not merely one part among other parts. Hence Blake can remark, "The Imagination is not a State: it is the Human Existence itself" (*M* 32: 32). Visionary time is not so much a segment of a uniformly divided line as it is a quality of perception. It is the quality of renovation, renewal, regeneration. Blake's "sacred" time is the imaginatively informed present which has pressed upon it the imaginatively appropriated past and the imaginatively envisioned future. The flexibility of such time is, for Blake, dependent upon the capacity for variation in man's "Organs of Perception."[7] Erin complains, "The Visions of Eternity, by reason of narrowed perceptions, / Are become weak Visions of Time & Space, fix'd into furrows of death" (*J* 49:21–22).

This passage raises a very important question, namely, the meaning of eternity. For Blake, eternity is not sheer chronological sequence without beginning or end, because he does not hesitate to speak of the beginning or ending of eternity. He can do so because he identifies eternity with the world of imagination.[8] The imagination, far from being filled with the fleeting and temporary, opens one to the permanent; it is, according to Blake, infinite and eternal. When Blake speaks of "throwing off the temporal that the Eternal might be Established" (*VLJ, p. 545*), it sounds as if time and eternity are opposites; but we have already seen how Blake distinguishes between preservative and destructive time. So perhaps it is not unfair to

6. This is perhaps the best clue to interpreting Blake's statement in *J* 3: *144*, "We who dwell on Earth can do nothing of ourselves, every thing is conducted by Spirits, no less than Digestion or Sleep."

7. See, e.g., *J* 98: 31–38.

8. See, e.g., *M* 1: *94*; and cf. *VLJ, p. 545*.

identify preservative time and eternity. The essential point, in any case, is that "eternal" does not equal "static." One may die continually in eternity; there are wars in eternity; and one travels in eternity (*M* 11: 18, 30: 19, 15: 22). Change is essential to eternity. What is permanent about eternity is the nature of change. All changes have regenerative possibilities and therefore can be used for man's benefit. Something is eternal for Blake only when it is capable of continually participating in time's flow as a renewing factor. Blake would reject the usual understanding of eternity as changelessness. In fact, the essential point about a transition from time as a sea to time as eternity is creative transformation; eternity can be defined as "time which is flexible and open to change." Eternity is a continual process that forever depends upon flux. Though the "Times are ended," Blake nevertheless speaks of "Eternal times" (*FZ* VI: *344*, IX: *385*). Eternity, therefore, should be understood as a quality of time. The "times which are ended" is the time of sheer loss, the time which, like a sea, sweeps everything under itself.

That our understanding of Blake's use of the term "eternity" needs further qualification is evident when he speaks of eternity's appearing "as One Man." What sense can we make of this association of a temporal category with a category of identity? Eternity can appear as one man, the man of course being Jesus, because eternity is harmoniously unified. In eternity all actions and characters are, as it were, linked together by a common nervous system. Blake, in fact, sometimes speaks of imagination as "the Divine Body" (*J* 5: 59), and probably is drawing from the body-of-Christ image in Paul's first letter to Corinth. So if Blake identifies imagination with eternity and Jesus with imagination, the vision of eternity as one man is not surprising.[9] One of the primary characteristics of eternal time is its being a particularly human time, and the figure of Jesus is the one man whom Blake considers to be all that is essentially human. Eternity, then, combines unity and humanity into a single vision which renews and awakens those lost in the sea of time and space.[10] It is because of Jesus that eternity does not remain "above" or "behind" or "in front of"[11] us but is

9. Blake explicitly humanizes time and space by saying, "But Time & Space are Real Beings a Male & a Female Time is a Man Space is a Woman & her Masculine Portion is Death" (*VLJ, p. 553*).

10. One merciful act of eternity is to bring creation into being. Blake notes, "Many suppose that before [*Adam*] ⟨the Creation⟩ All was Solitude & Chaos This is the most pernicious Idea that can enter the Mind as it takes away all sublimity from the Bible & Limits All Existence to Creation & to Chaos To the Time & Space fixed by the Corporeal Vegetative Eye & leaves the Man who entertains such an Idea the habitation of Unbelieving Demons Eternity Exists and All things in Eternity Independent of Creation which was an act of Mercy" (*VLJ, pp. 552–553*).

11. There may be one exception to my argument that eternity is neither the time

present with us. Blake says, "But Jesus breaking thro' the Central Zones of Death & Hell / Opens Eternity in Time & Space; triumphant in Mercy" (*J* 75: 21–22).

One is struck by the spatial metaphors Blake uses in speaking of time, so perhaps I should note here that eternity is given a spatial connotation in addition to its personal connotation. Eternity is located at the center, and it expands outward.[12] I will say more about spatial expansion later. That eternity is "inside" reminds one of imaginative time's being located "between" pulses of the heartbeat. In both cases Blake is closing up the divine/human distance and straining toward a vision of the unity of God and man. The journey toward the transcendent is none other than the journey into the immanent. The flexibility, the expansion and contraction, of time is the means whereby man and God become as one man and one family (*J* 55: 44–46).

Having sketched the relation between Blake's imaginative time and eternal time, I want to complete the picture by inquiring in what sense time is eschatological for Blake.[13] The end of time must not be identified simply with the future. The confusion of imaginative vision with an attempt to see the future is typically associated with Urizen. Vision is not prediction, since prediction presupposes the very determinism which imaginative vision rejects.

Urizen saw & envied & his imagination was filled
Repining he contemplated the past in his bright sphere
Terrified with his heart & spirit at the visions of futurity
That his dread fancy formd before him in the unformd void.
(*FZ* II: *316*)

---

of pre-history nor post-history. In *M* 13: 10–11, Blake says, "The Sin was begun in Eternity, and will not rest to Eternity / Till two Eternities meet together." This, however, is not Blake's typical attitude.

12. See, e.g., *M* 31: 48.

13. I use the term "eschatological" rather than "apocalyptic," since "apocalyptic" is a particular kind of eschatology, a type which insists on the absence of the divine from the present while Satan is in control and which expects the total destruction of the world as a prelude to redemption. Both words refer to end-time, but "apocalyptic" is a specific view of the nature of that time, whereas "eschatology" is a more general term. A distinction is sometimes made between prophetic eschatology and apocalyptic eschatology. The former employs proclamation, diatribe, and historical narrative, whereas the latter tends to be more visionary and ecstatic. Blake is stylistically closer to apocalyptic eschatology, but he would never accept the dualism necessary for apocalyptic. Hence, it seems appropriate simply to speak of Blakean eschatology and to recognize that his is a third species of eschatology, neither wholly prophetic nor wholly apocalyptic. For further discussion of eschatology and apocalyptic see Martin Rist, "The Revelation of St. John: Introduction," in *Interpreter's Bible*, ed. George Buttrick (New York: Abingdon Press, 1957), XII, 347ff.

Ironically, Urizen looks into the crystal ball of the past in order to discern the future. Eschatological vision is, of course, an impossibility if one holds a view of time as homogeneous. Predictions can only bring terror and further suffering if the paradigms of the past are all one can hope for. Blake is sharply critical of this kind of positivistic historiography:

The reasoning historian, turner and twister of causes and consequences, such as Hume, Gibbon and Voltaire; cannot with all their artifice, turn or twist one fact or disarrange self evident action and reality. Reasons and opinions concerning acts, are not history. Acts themselves alone are history, and these are neither the exclusive property of Hume, Gibbon nor Voltaire, Echard, Rapin, Plutarch, nor Herodotus. Tell me the Acts, O historian, and leave me to reason upon them as I please; away with your reasoning and your rubbish. All that is not action is not worth reading. Tell the What; I do not want you to tell me the Why, and the How; I can find that out myself, as well as you can, and I will not be fooled by you into opinions, that you please to impose, to disbelieve what you think improbable or impossible. His opinions, who does not see spiritual agency, is not worth any man's reading; he who rejects a fact because it is improbable, must reject all History and retain doubts only.

(*DC*, p. 534)

This polemical passage is surprising and deceptive. It at once rejects and presupposes an ability to separate fact from interpretation. The passage appears ill-advised, since historians are being condemned for doing what Blake himself does with Milton and with Jesus: interpreting their "Acts." On the one hand, Blake says that only factual reporting is worth reading. On the other hand, nothing is worth reading that does not recognize the crucial role of "spiritual agency" (i.e., vision and imagination). This apparent contradiction stems from Blake's disgust with historians who propose to present the "real" facts by eliminating references to spiritual causality.

Blake is convinced that the reference to spiritual causality found in some historical documents is an integral, important part of the fact. When Blake demands the "fact" or the "Acts themselves alone," he wants the document in its entirety. What Blake resists is historical scholarship that covertly interprets by selecting what it considers probable as the only legitimate fact. Blake demands that historical documents be dealt with in their integrity or not at all. The historians violate the texts by substituting their own "Whys" and "reasons" for the "Whys" and "reasons" implicit in the texts themselves. Of course, Blake also interprets events differently than the texts themselves do (e.g., the virgin birth and Milton's Puritanism). The difference between Blake's interpreting and the historians' interpreting lies in Blake's assumption that he reinterprets on the basis of a more profound understanding of the goal of the text itself, whereas the historians reinterpret on the basis of a principle taken with them to the texts, namely, that the improbable (the mythical, the imaginative, "spiritual agency") must be separated from the historical and then eliminated. Visionary historiography in contrast to positivistic historiography resembles what Ernst Cassirer calls "symbolic memory": "Symbolic memory is the process by which man not only repeats his past experience but also reconstructs the experience. Imagination becomes a necessary element of true recollection."[14]

Blake knows that imaginative vision is as efficacious in man's achievements as political or economic factors. And interpretations of history may have as much effect on the consequent, lived history as any war or decision of government has. To put the matter in psychological terms, history's direction is determined as surely by the improbabilities of imaginative unconsciousness as by the probabilities of conscious decision. Blake calls on the historians to give him the What and not the Why, because he thinks their Why is superficial and deterministic. But the What that Blake is demanding is, of course, not the What the historians would give him, because theirs does not include an account of "spiritual agency."

Blake is critical of any view of time and history which precludes an eschatology by insisting that the future can only develop analogously to the past. In short, he rejects the view of time which does not recognize genuine possibility for regeneration. In contrast to such a view Blake develops his own peculiar eschatalogical vision, and this vision has important consequences for his view of the historicity of the Bible.

In *The Everlasting Gospel*, for example, Blake rewrites the Gospel eschatalogically in terms of its own "end" or "essence." The Gospel, like Milton, comes to its own only through an imaginative present. The Gospel can be a present Word only through Jesus' presence in vision. The Jesus of vision is a re-living forward of, not a repetition of, the Jesus of history. An illustration will help. Blake rewrites the virgin birth in visionary fashion:

Was Jesus Chaste or did he
Give any Lessons of Chastity
The morning blushd fiery red
Mary was found in Adulterous bed
Earth groand beneath & Heaven above
Trembled at discovery of Love
Jesus was sitting in Moses Chair
They brought the trembling Woman There
Moses commands she be stoned to death
What was the sound of Jesus breath . . .

14. Ernst Cassirer, *An Essay on Man* (1944; rpt. New York: Bantam Books, 1970), p. 57.

Hide not from my Sight thy Sin
That forgiveness thou maist win
Has no Man Condemned thee
No Man Lord! then what is he
Who shall Accuse thee . . .

(*pp. 512–513*)

The woman whom Jesus forgives for her adultery seems to be his own mother.[15] The adultery which he forgives is the hardest of all to forgive: the one which issued in his own birth. Blake thinks that the principle for rewriting this story forward (i.e., writing eschatologically, writing toward its own implicit goal) is that the truth of any account of Jesus depends solely on the extent to which it embodies the vision of forgiveness. Blake rewrites Jesus' past in terms of his present meaning, and meaning is the continuation of history into the present.

To give another example of eschatological "rewriting forward," Plate 61 of *Jerusalem* rewrites the angel's appearance to Joseph after he learns of Mary's pregnancy. The angel declares that Mary is "with Child by the Holy Ghost." Blake's visionary Joseph understands quite well what this means: he is to forgive Mary for her adultery. Mary's "virginity" and Jesus' birth "by the Holy Spirit" are sacred because they issue from a wedlock of forgiveness.

Blake's eschatology, we might say, is first of all a literary and perceptual eschatology and only secondarily a historical eschatology. The end which is anticipated is not the kind to be waited upon with patience in the face of martyrdom. Rather the *telos* of past and present is written and imagined forward in such a manner that the vision of the "end" breaks back in upon the present and past and reshapes them. What one *does* in response to such a literary eschatology is to see, to envision, to perceive anew. Thus it has its social and political consequences, but it is not the same as a first-century eschatology in which the primary *deed* is either rebellion or patient forbearance.

We may summarize by saying that for Blake eschatological time, or end-time, is the time when a man perceives the ends or possibilities implicit in past and present.

The idea of the future plays little role in Blake; and when it does appear, it is largely negative. "Seeing the vision" does not equal "seeing the future." The future when seen once by Los is full of swords and spears. And Urizen must cast off his obsession with the future before he can be regenerated:

Then Go O dark futurity I will cast thee forth from these
Heavens of my brain nor will I look upon futurity more

15. *EG, p. 794.*

I cast futurity away & turn my back upon that void
Which I have made for lo futurity is in this moment.

(FZ IX: 375–376)[16]

The last line is particularly significant because it captures Blake's eschatology. The term "futurity" does not refer to a time which is yet to come, as
it does in each of the three preceding lines. The future, which once dangled
like corn in front of a hungry donkey, becomes that which shapes this very
moment. The eschatological future is none other than a present pregnant
with imaginative possibility. Hence, Blake subtly warns his reader not to
identify vision with speculation about the future.

We cannot leave questions of end-time without looking at Blake's handling of death, for death is one's own personal ending, and death/rebirth is
usually associated with the end of time. Inevitably, one must also inquire
whether cessations of any kind in myth or poetry are final or are simply new
beginnings or returns to *the* beginning.

If one looks at those passages which narrate the death of some character,
he soon learns not to take them literally. The death of a character does not
mean that his time is ended and that he will therefore no longer be in the
fray of battle, despite Albion's assertion, "Rent from Eternal Brotherhood
we die & are no more" (*FZ* III: *321*). Apparently, dying and being are not
mere synonyms for nonexistence and existence. One can hardly regard dying
as the stoppage of personal time, and still speak, as Blake does, of dying
"throughout all Eternity" (*M* 11: 18). When Vala is commanded to slay
Albion so that he will rise no more, she succeeds only in "embalming him
in moral laws" and begs Jesus not to revive the dead. This exclamation rises,
". . . such thing was never known / Before in Albions land, that one should
die a death never to be reviv'd! / For in our battles we the Slain men view
with pity and love: / We soon revive them in the secret of our tabernacles"
(*J* 80: 23–26).[17]

As in some ancient mythologies, death, for Blake, is like sleep. One does
not undergo a single death and cease to exist. One dies periodically, just as
one sleeps periodically. *The Four Zoas*, subtitled ". . . the Death and Judgment of Albion . . . ," is about the Ancient Man who "sleep[s] in the dark
of Death" (*FZ* II: *309*). To sleep is to fall into the sea of space and time
rather than to fall "beyond" or "out of" time, as it is in some views of death.
Keeping in mind that we have already seen how Blake differentiates the
sleep of Albion from the sleep of Beulah, we may regard death as the state
of spatial and temporal formlessness. Death is sheer transition. As such, it

16. Cf. *FZ* VIIA: *347*.

17. Cf. *FZ* I: *307*, where Blake speaks of Eden rather than Albion as the place where
reviving always follows dying.

needs but does not have organization; hence it is symbolized by the sea or
by restless sleep. Earlier I pointed to the problem of connectives in vision
and noted that the transition from moment to moment is a kind of blank spot,
the sleep of Beulah, in which the poet finds the freedom and inspiration to
create. So even the divine imagination must pass through death. But when
imagination passes through death, it begins to organize and envision from
the inside so the chaos cannot become permanent. Blake's fear is that death
may become permanent. Therefore, those who are awake to vision, like Los,
persistently try to invade Albion's sleep of death and plant the seeds of
wakefulness.

Blake's prophecies are sometimes compared to dreams. *The Four Zoas* is
"a DREAM of Nine Nights." One must be careful, however, because the
eschatological goal is to awaken from dream-time. The difference between
dreaming and prophetic perception is not that one is visionary and the other
not. The difference is that dream is vision fallen into chaotic time, whereas
prophecy is vision organized and humanized.

Blake's eschatological treatment of time, then, is not really concerned
with death in the usual sense of the term, nor with the end of the world,
nor with one's dream-life, because each of these, far from being integral to
the achieving of true vision, is the destruction and disorganization of vision.
The temporal focus of visionary imagination is not post-mortem, not post-
history, and not at night. The time of vision is now. The crucial factor which
determines whether one falls into Ulro or builds Jerusalem is how one
handles the gaps between successive "nows." Fall and redemption hinge on
transition. To go to sleep in the in-between is to fall. To refuse to enter the
in-between is to fall. To build a bridge across the in-between is to be
redeemed.

I I

Bridging the in-between is such a pervasive problem for eschatological
vision that the structure, as well as the content, of the major prophecies is
affected. The poetic, structural parallels of primordial, present, and eschatological time are beginning, middle, and ending. How Blake handles the
beginnings, middles, and endings of the major prophecies reveals as much
about his view of time as his direct reflection on the subject does. *The Four
Zoas*, for instance, begins *in medias res*. A daughter of Beulah is commanded
to tell of Los's fall into division and his resurrection to unity, and to begin
the story with Tharmas. We do not see Tharmas fall. He has already fallen,
so we never see an Edenic beginning into which division intrudes. The poem
begins in the middle, and the middle only occasionally recalls what the
beginning was like. The beginning is either remembered or envisioned as

being like the end. It is important to note that Blake does not begin his poem at *the* beginning, nor does the image of an undifferentiated or primordial unity ever occur. The unity which is posited of Eden is the unity of organized plurality, not the simple, undifferentiated identity of Neoplatonism. We do not see either Edenic harmony or the fall. The poem begins with the Zoas having already fallen, and later we are told various versions of the story of the fall.[18]

Night IX is designated by Blake as the Last Judgment. It is his ending and resembles in many ways the Apocalypse of Saint John. Trumpets are blown, the dead are raised, nature pours torrents of blood and fire, the beasts flee. When Albion awakens and realizes his plight, he links together beginning and ending by crying, "When shall the Man of future times become as in days of old" (IX: *374*). This is one of Blake's most overt appropriations of a circular notion of time in which beginning and ending coincide.[19] The circularity seems to be emphasized by his repeated references to time's "revolving." This would seem to militate against my previous observation that Blake does not think of time as primordial and circular but rather as teleological and eschatological. But as we have already seen, futurity for Blake is a metaphoric term referring to the present as it is imaginatively informed. The same must be said of beginning-time. Therefore, the circularity involved is simply the path traced by straying away from the imaginative in-between moment and back again. To say that, "All things Begin & End in Albion's Ancient Druid Rocky Shore" (*J* 27: *169*), is both a spatial and temporal way of insisting that the creative moment is now and the creative place is here. There is no point in searching for some better time and place to do the poet's imaginative work. We will always find ourselves ending where we began until we begin right now, right here.

Night IX of *The Four Zoas* does not end where the poem began. It ends where the poem says universal brotherhood began. Structurally, then, the poem cannot be called circular despite Blake's references to "revolving" times. To be sure, the poem ends speaking of war and there has been war from the outset, but the war has shifted levels from the "war of swords" to "intellectual War." If we want a more appropriate spatial image, only the spiral will suffice.

The action in *Milton* has a twofold beginning: one is the content of the Bard's Song, the other is Milton's descent. I do not propose to solve the structural problems involved with the Bard's Song, but only to refer to the notion of time reflected in this way of beginning the poem. In the Song again we encounter the action already in progress: Albion has been slain, Urizen is in chains, Los is laboring. The fall is in process, and Blake only

18. See, e.g., *FZ* I: *301*, and III: *320*.
19. See also *FZ* II: *314*, IX: *376*, and VIIB: *392*.

presupposes a beginning of harmony, but it is previous to the limits of his poem.

In Plate 14 where Milton's deed begins, the action originates in heaven, but it is not the heaven which precedes creation, Eden, and the fall. Milton is dissatisfied. There will be no fall because Milton has already fallen into the sea of history's space and time and has already risen into heaven. Instead there will be a regenerative descent into history to reclaim and revitalize his own vision. Blake apparently decides that a fall at the beginning—even if it is not a fall from undifferentiated unity—does not sufficiently suggest the dialectic of history and imagination or of middle and end. So in *Milton* the action begins in a heaven already preceded by and influenced by history.

Milton ends on the brink, after a middle composed of a battle between Palamabron and Satan and of a quest by Milton for Ololon. The Palamabron–Satan battle has ended indecisively. Milton and Ololon have reunited in Blake. As Blake recovers from the shock and returns to his "mortal state," eschatological clouds roll, and the harvest is ready for reaping. There is a sense of conclusion, a sense of ending, insofar as Blake, Milton, and Ololon have gone from a beginning of alienation (the state of negation) to an ending of productive tension (the state of contraries). On the other hand, this ending is more properly a culmination, for it opens into the ongoing middle of an eschatological battle still in process. The open "end" of *Milton* parallels the open "end" of the Bard's Song. Thus the poem stops without really ending. Aesthetically, it is finished, but socially and psychologically the reader can hardly stop moving.

The action in *Jerusalem*, as in both the preceding prophecies, starts in the middle of the sea of space and time. Jesus is calling Albion, who has long been asleep in this sea. It is recalled that things were different once when "Albion covered the whole earth" and London "walkd in every Nation mutual in love & harmony" (*J* 24: 43–44). The middle of *Jerusalem* focuses largely on the efforts of Los to rescue Albion, subdue his own Spectre, and reclaim his Emanation. The transition from middle to end is marked by the declaration, "Time was Finished" (94: 18). In *The Four Zoas* end-time is precipitated by Los as he suddenly reaches up and tears down the sun and moon (IX: 372). In *Jerusalem* there is no precipitating factor, only an immediate supporting event: the divine breath breathes over Albion (94: 18). *Jerusalem* is the most nearly eschatological of the three major prophecies because of its refusal to suggest a causal link between middle and end, between history and eschaton. In biblical eschatology there is no earthly cause; no one can bring the end a moment closer or postpone it a single hour. One can only proclaim that the time is here, now. To write eschatologically, then, implies (to recall Blake's polemic against the historians) that the Why and How of regeneration be accounted for only by "spiritual agency." The poetic consequence is a break in developmental continuity. This is a stylistic means of handling eschatological time. Blake only gives us the What: the declaration that the middle, the sea of space and time, is over and that the time of awakening is here. Blake, like Los, is an "ever present Elias" who proclaims but does not explain. The arrival of regeneration is a miracle; that is, an event in which the imaginative man can participate but which he cannot create by sheer exertion of energy and will. One can only be ready for the inspirational end-time by reclaiming his spectre and emanation and by reawakening his senses.

The concluding plates of *Jerusalem* are filled with images of awakening and expansion (see {35}–{38}). But there are "Wars of mutual Benevolence Wars of Love" (97:14), so conflict is still present, though now the conflict makes possible growth rather than causing destruction. The ending is more conclusive than that of *Milton* and not so fully developed as that of *The Four Zoas*.

To summarize these conclusions about the structural consequences of Blake's view of time, one can say that none of the major prophecies ends where it started. There is no Innocence–Experience–Return-to-Innocence sequence. Instead the sequence is Experience–(Remembrance of Innocence)–Brotherhood. It is of immense importance, I think, that Blake does not structurally follow the threefold "chronological" order Innocence–Experience–Return-to-Innocence, even though that order may be logically implied by the remembrance of "times of old" by characters in the experiential sea of space and time. The fact that the ancient days are remembered by characters rather than narrated by Blake casts Innocence into the middle, into history, into time, and supports Blake's spatial image of imaginative time as the in-between of two pulses of the artery. To repeat the chorus of this essay, the diagram Experience–(Remembrance of Innocence)–Brotherhood leaves blank the connective in between, for that is the eschatological space and time of imagination. The Blakean middle, like Blakean connective, is difficult to grasp because it consists only of the interplay of beginning and end. Yet, the middle is all-important because it is the here and now where visionaries must take their stand.

III

Thus far I have used numerous spatial designations to describe time. The virtual impossibility of discussing time apart from space accords with Blake's insistence that regeneration occurs only with the reunion of Los and Enitharmon, watchman of eternity and mistress of space. Time apart from space is a sea that drowns imagination, and space apart from time is a cavelike cell that blocks off the reach of vision.

Space, like time, is metaphorically recast. Consequently, spatiality is primarily a quality of imaginative perception; only secondarily does it refer to pure location. Hence Blake writes,

What is Above is Within, for every-thing in Eternity is translucent:
The Circumference is Within: Without, is formed the Selfish Center
And the Circumference still expands going forward to Eternity.
And the Center has Eternal States!

$$(J 71: 6–9)$$

The heavenly "above" of orthodox religious imagery is identified with the Blakean "within." The door to eternity is not in the sky but inside man himself. Blake chooses the image of an expanding circumference to suggest the imaginative space within the self; and the goal of such spatial motion is eternity, a temporal category. The profane space of obstructed vision is symbolized by the center which is outside man, suggesting that man's only appropriate center is within himself. "Center" and "within" are not synonyms for Blake, because man's "within," his imagination, cannot be moved outside himself, even though its limits are expanding, whereas one can shift his "center" elsewhere and thus be self-alienated, off center. The symbol of the center is not fully positive as it usually is in myth. In myth the center is the sacred space where one builds his sanctuary and around which he organizes his life.[20] In Blake's vision Golgonooza is built by Los and Enitharmon at the center, but it is important to recognize that this central "hole" in the fabric of the cosmos is exactly the fault created by the collapse and fall of the Zoas (*M* 19: 21–25). The fall is not away from the center but is toward the center. So the center is a point of coincidence. It is the zero point toward which the blind rush and from which the visionary proceed. It is the point at which the prototype of the sacred city and the fault in the cosmos converge.

The center can be either within or without. When it is within, it is positive; it is visionary. When it is without, it is fallen. It is from the center that eternity expands outward.[21] Visionary space is dynamic, so only as the center "rolls out into an expanse" and opens within itself is the center a regenerative place. When the center of a man is inside himself, eternity is there also, and space and time are one.

To have one's center in oneself is not the same as being selfish. The selfish center is formed without, Blake reminds us. When one is self-centered, or selfish, he is contracted into a tiny involved mass outside of himself and consequently outside of others. When he has his center within himself, its cir-

20. See Eliade, *The Sacred and the Profane*, pp. 36ff.
21. *M* 31: 47–48; cf. *J* 13: 34–35, and 57: 17–18.

cumference expands into eternity to include others. Blake says that the sanctuary of Eden is located in the outline, in the circumference (*J* 69: 41), probably because it reaches out constantly toward inclusiveness without limit:

There is a limit of Opakeness, and a limit of Contraction;
In every Individual Man, and the limit of Opakeness,
Is named Satan: and the limit of Contraction is named Adam.
But when Man sleeps in Beulah, the Saviour in mercy takes
Contractions Limit, and of the Limit he forms Woman: That
Himself may in process of time be born Man to redeem
But there is no Limit of Expansion! there is no Limit of Translucence.
In the bosom of Man for ever from eternity to eternity.

(*J* 42: 29–36)

To contract is to withdraw from relation and to lose the ability to see the imaginative identity of all things. To contract is to become increasingly bound by space until the imagination can no longer "see" beyond its own location. The light of eternity cannot penetrate the dense, contracted organs of perception. Therefore, limits are set on contraction and opacity. Contraction and opacity are never allowed to become absolute. Furthermore, Jesus has taken on the limit of contraction and is working from within to push man's circumference outward again. This is Blake's version of the doctrine of grace. However, Jesus can do his work only during the sleep of Beulah, the time of imagination's renewal. And this is Blake's version of faith. Regeneration, the conjunction of grace and faith, is the opening of man's center into an expanding circumference.[22]

Motion inward is almost always positive for Blake. One must not, however, mistake this for the mystic's systematic withdrawal from the sensory world, because, in fact, it is the opposite. Man reaches out to man by indirection, never directly. Imagination, or the within, is the means of joining brother to brother. Repeatedly a character will be said to be "in" another character. Jesus declares:

I am in you and you in me, mutual in love divine . . .
I am not a God afar off, I am a brother and friend;
Within your bosoms I reside, and you reside in me.

(*J* 4: 7, 18–19)

Blake does leave open the possibility of an opening from outside to inside by having Beulah be present "On all sides within and without . . ." (*FZ* I: *299*).[23] Even though the outside is usually negatively treated, it is not

22. See *J* 48: 38; cf. *FZ* I: *300*.
23. Cf. *M* 30: 8–10.

entirely beyond hope. In fact, the creation of any space is a merciful act.
Even Ulro is a space created to prevent one's falling into Eternal Death. The
creation of "locations" is a limit-setting activity necessary to prevent the
absolute Blakean horror, indefiniteness. The indefinite and the infinite are
not at all the same thing. The indefinite is the unbounded; whereas the infinite, when Blake uses the term to refer to imagination, denotes the unlimited possibilities of any minute particular. So to speak of the outline of
infinity is no contradiction. One concept demands the other. Unlimited relation, unlimited metaphoric identification of one thing with another, depends on clear spatial outline or circumference.[24]

Vision-crushing space is sometimes called by Blake "Female Space." It is
the space which imprisons and shrinks man's perception.

The nature of a Female Space is this: it shrinks the Organs
Of Life till they become Finite & Itself seems Infinite.
And Satan vibrated in the immensity of the Space!   Limited
To those without but Infinite to those within . . .
(M 10: 6–9)

The destructiveness of Female Space is that it draws infinity to itself and
away from man. To simplify, Female Space is a purely "locational" category, whereas imaginative space (and therefore imaginative infinity) is an
anthropomorphic and perceptual category. Female Space is not subservient
to man's infinitude. Instead it dwarfs that infinitude into a private finitude.
But, Blake reminds us, it is really Female Space that is finite, as those not
in its trap perceive clearly. Female Space surrounds man like an infinite
trap, but regenerative space is surrounded by man. It is within. Blake's
"sacred" space always has an anthropomorphic quality—the more human,
the more sacred; the less human, the more profane.

So far, I have referred to Blake's understanding of center, circumference,
within and without. Even more clearly anthropomorphic is his directional
symbolism: east/west, north/south, right/left, up/down. These are not
merely neutrally descriptive geographical co-ordinates. Every position and
location has its own accent. One cannot be indifferent to location because
location is essential, not accidental. One's being is something different in the
south than in the north. To be in a certain place is to have that place in one's
own self. Spatial references in Blake are organized on the basis of one's
intuition of his own body. East is associated with the nostrils; west is associated with the tongue; north is associated with the ears; south is associated with the eyes (J 12: 59–60). The disorganizing fall of the Zoas
takes the form of directional confusion, and the Zoas forget their proper
places.

24. See, e.g., J 98: 20–23.

Because location is essential, the loss of vision comes through what one might call "situational arrogance." When a character acts as if his location is not defined in relation to a center shared by other locations or when he would destroy directional distinctions by violating boundaries, he loses vision. Blake re-asserts the continuity and complementarity of different "places." Locational distinctions are real but relative. The relativity of each location to every other location implies that no place is inherently sacred. No spot is automatically the place to be for vision to occur. But any place may become sacred, so Blake symbolically superimposes a map of Palestine on a map of Britain and both, then, on a cosmic map.[25] In imagination more than one object can occupy the same space at the same time, and no place is more sacred than the "here."

Blake has considerably less to say about infinity than he does about eternity, but his most fully developed description is as follows:

The nature of infinity is this: That every thing has its
Own Vortex; and when once a traveller thro' Eternity
Has passed that Vortex, he percieves it roll backward behind
His path, into a globe itself infolding; like a sun:
Or like a moon, or like a universe of starry majesty,
While he keeps onwards in his wondrous journey on the earth
Or like a human form, a friend with whom he livd benevolent.
As the eye of man views both the east & west encompassing
Its vortex; and the north & south, with all their starry host;
Also the rising sun & setting moon he views surrounding
His corn-fields and his valleys of five hundred acres square.
Thus is the earth one infinite plane, and not as apparent
To the weak traveller confin'd beneath the moony shade.
Thus is the heaven a vortex passd already, and the earth
A vortex not yet pass'd by the traveller thro' Eternity . . .

      . . . the Sea of Time & Space thunderd aloud
Against the rock, which was inwrapped with the weeds of death
Hovering over the cold bosom, in its vortex Milton bent down
To the bosom of death, what was underneath soon seemd above . . .
      . . . so Miltons shadow fell,
Precipitant loud thundring into the Sea of Time & Space.
          (*M* 15: 21–46)

The image of the vortex symbolizes one's perspective from a particular space-time complex. Each minute particular is situated and therefore is seen and can see only within the limits of a point of view. That a vortex can be passed through suggests that one can transcend any particular space-time situation, but to do so is not to escape being situated altogether. It is to

25. See *J* 16: 1–69.

be faced with another vortex. This is the situation of the traveler through eternity: he must always envision reality from a perspective (i.e., from a space and a time), but no particular perspective is binding. In contrast is Urizen, who cannot escape his own single vortex:

For when he came to where a Vortex ceasd to operate
Nor down nor up remaind then if he turnd & lookd back
From whence he came twas upward all. & if he turnd and viewd
The unpassd void upward was still his mighty wandring
The midst between an Equilibrium grey of air serene
Where he might live in peace & where his life might meet repose

But Urizen said Can I not leave this world of Cumbrous wheels
Circle oer Circle nor on high attain a void
Where self sustaining I may view all things beneath my feet
Or sinking thro these Elemental wonders swift to fall
I thought perhaps to find an End a world beneath of voidness
Whence I might travel round the outside of this Dark confusion
When I bend downward bending my head downward into the deep
Tis upward all which way soever I may course begin
But when A Vortex formd on high by labour & sorrow & care
And weariness begins on all my limbs then sleep revives
My wearied spirits waking then tis downward all which way
So ever I my spirits turn no end I find of all.

(FZ VI: 342)

Urizen is inescapably bound to live only in the eye of his private hurricane. Even on an infinite plane where no vortex operates, the sides of the cone rise up behind and in front. Unlike the traveler through eternity, Milton, Urizen cannot pass through a vortex so that he may attain a perspective on his perspective; that is, so he can see the three-dimensional cone from beyond one end, thus making it appear to be a disc, the sun. Urizen desires to be self-sustaining; he wants to be either totally above or totally below. His mistake lies in thinking that this would make him omnipresent and therefore ruler of all things. Perspective is imaginative when one can enter into the vortex of another and thus take on a new perspective. Urizen does not seek a new perspective; he seeks to be outside of perspective. But to be outside of a perspective-bound world is itself the most confining of perspectives. Every thing is uphill in waking and downhill in sleep. It is very much in keeping with Blake's emphasis on minute particularity to insist that vision does not deny the space/time situation which we call perspective. A man may pass out of one vortex into another, but there is no place beyond vortexes. The poet is one who can enter the vortex of another. He not only can see the other, he can see *as* the other. For this reason, Jesus is not merely the *object* of visionary perception, he is also its *subject*. This is the meaning of Blake's calling Jesus "The Divine Vision," "The Divine Body," and "The Poetic Genius."[26] Jesus is not only beheld *by* imagination, he becomes incarnate *as* imagination. So we might summarize by saying that visionary space is space in which one participates in the other. I am in visionary space when I am "inside" my neighbor seeing as he sees.

Northrop Frye suggests that in every imaginative act space and time are reunited and become one as when oxygen and hydrogen unite to become water.[27] When Los who is time and Enitharmon who is space reunite, eternity and infinity are perceived simultaneously as one. The locus of union is the here and now of imaginative vision or, as Frye notes, "the eternal Now" and "the eternal Here."[28]

I would suggest that Blake's medium is intended to be a point of coincidence between space and time. He strives for total engagement by rendering his prophetic "Illuminated" works in both poetic lines and artistic engravings. The lines of poetry are imagination's descent into time. The designs are examples of imagination's descent into space. Time's medium unites with space's medium to form an Illuminated work. Blake strives to precipitate visionary perception by reuniting space and time, masculine and feminine, individual and society, and finally, poetry and painting. Poetry and painting were respectively diverted into religion and "Physic & Surgery" (*M* 27: 60), so the professions are, in Blake's view, the mechanizing and routinizing of the arts. The Illuminated works, or prophecies, are intended to reunify the professions with the arts by reuniting space with time. So Blake's eschatological vision does not entail either a destruction of the professions or a naive return to art, as that word is usually understood. Rather it envisions life lived as art, a life fully and imaginatively participating in space and time.

26. For characteristic uses of the terms, see *FZ* I: *303*, II: *315*, and *J* 91: *9*.
27. *Fearful Symmetry: A Study of William Blake* (Princeton: Princeton Univ. Press, 1947), p. 46.
28. Ibid., p. 48; cf. *Marg.*, p. *581*.

Los, Pilgrim of Eternity

EDWARD J. ROSE

When Blake deleted the words "gave visions toward heaven" in the first Night of *The Four Zoas* and replaced them with "made windows into Eden," he was searching (as he does elsewhere) for an effective metaphorical expression of the underlying purpose and the fundamental aim of his life's work. He was seeking to create a literary version of the easel picture he was later to call "portable fresco." While his opinions on current events may have changed with the changing times at the end of the eighteenth century, his opinions on art and the aims and function of the artist grew steadily without deviation towards the views expressed in the *Laocoön* aphorisms. It is the purpose of this essay to examine some of the most important ways in which Blake made his ideas about art and perception the subject of his work and to explain how the figure of Los embodies these ideas, for Los is the act of perceiving. In this discussion, Blake's philosophy of time and its relation to imagination will be emphasized because this inter-relationship tells us much about what Blake meant by "Eternity" and why and how he spoke of imagination as he did.

I

"Kairos," says Paul Tillich, "points to unique moments in the temporal process, moments in which something unique can happen or be accomplished."[1] It is in such moments that the fallen and the unfallen worlds meet or intersect. Such moments are those in which the poet's work is done (*M* 28–29: *124–127*). "Kairos, for biblical writers," Tillich writes, "is fulfilled time— the time in which the appearance of Christ was possible because in spite of

1. "Kairos," in *A Handbook of Christian Theology* (Cleveland: World Publishing Co., 1965), pp. 193–197.

actual rejection, all the conditions of his reception are prepared." Blake would say that "because of actual rejection" is more exactly the case. The consolidation of error, of oppression, of compulsion, is at any time preparation for its own overthrow, the "Overwhelming of Bad Art & Science" by "The Imagination" which is "God himself." That is why "Jesus & his Apostles & Disciples were all Artists" (*The Laocoön, p. 271*). To Tillich, "The one real Kairos is the moment of history in which the preparatory period of history comes to an end because that for which it was a preparation has become historical reality. In this sense, Kairos implies that the central event—the appearance of Christ—is not an isolated happening falling, so to speak, from heaven; but that it is an event which is prepared for by history and by the 'timing' of historical providence." This is essentially the ground of all Blake's art, especially if we mean by "historical reality" the perception obtained through "Kairos"-oriented action or experience, and if we *see* that "central event" as "One Central Form" (*Marg., p. 367*). Tillich's next point is even more applicable to Blake than the previous one: "One can express this by saying that 'the great Kairos' presupposes many smaller *kairoi* within the historical development by which it was prepared. From this statement one can derive the other; that in order for 'the great Kairos' to be received many smaller *kairoi* are required in the historical development following it." All the "smaller *kairoi*" like "All Forms," of course, "are Perfect in the Poet's Mind, but these are not Abstracted nor compounded from Nature, but are from Imagination." The *one* window into Eden which is "Within a Moment" when "the Poets Work is Done" is the *many* windows into Eden, "and all the Great / Events of Time start forth & are concievd in such a Period" (*M* 29: 1–3).

The relation between the "smaller *kairoi*" and "the great Kairos" is the subject of *Milton* and *Jerusalem*, but it is observable in Blake's work as early as the *Songs*. A smaller kairos is an epiphany, a revelation of reality, like any one of the illustrated songs. It is also the honoring of God's gifts in another man; it is the recognition of the Holy Spirit when one sees it in others.[2] The "Moment in each Day that Satan cannot find" and the "Grain of Sand in Lambeth that Satan cannot find" (*M* 35: 42; *J* 35: 1–2) are symbols in terms of time and space of the manifestation of "smaller *kairoi*," of, in fact, Los's fabricated "forms sublime" which Blake records in Lambeth. The city or palace of art and eternity, which rises out of vision's minute particulars, is a house of many mansions, the Lamb's house. The artist preserves them in imagination. Blake's furnace-brain is like the Tyger's or like Los's "infinite wombs."[3] In his art there comes into being the new Jerusalem

2. See *MHH* 22–23: 42; *J* 91: 1–17.
3. See *FZ* VIIA: *356*; *L* 5: 35–40.

(*Jerusalem*) and the spiritual fourfold London. His palace of Art stands opposed to that of the Archbishop. The re-creation or resurrection of time and space and history is achieved by applying "Divine Vision" to the world of compulsions, and by embodying in a work of art the iconographical words that describe the events of six thousand years. Satan cannot find the moment or the grain because he is a "Generalizer"; but the "True" artist, whose moment and grain they are, can, because he is the "Particularizer" (*Marg., p. 650*). His is a "decisive act of spiritual freedom";[4] it is individual and existential. Blake writes that "Jerusalem is calld Liberty among the Children of Albion," that "every particular Form . . . Emanates Its own peculiar Light." Jerusalem in every man is particular and unique.

In Great Eternity, every particular Form gives forth or Emanates
Its own peculiar Light, & the Form is the Divine Vision
And the Light is his Garment. This is Jerusalem in every Man.
(*J* 54: 1–3)

This description of the particular form describes an act of spiritual freedom which bestows, and is a product of, absolute liberty. The outward embodiment of the inward is the resurrection of man in God's eye—the "Divine Vision." Art is a window *into* the human form in Eden because it is a window *in* the human form itself.

Blake's last long poem, *Jerusalem*, is about "smaller *kairoi*" and "the great Kairos" (the many windows into Eden). It *is* an artistic point of view which Blake perfected in his illustrations for the *Songs of Innocence and of Experience* and the shorter prophetic books. In *Jerusalem* in one way and in the Job illustrations in another, Blake was able, literally and figuratively, to *frame* his point of view in a way that expressed that point of view. Blake's poems are the concrete embodiments of imaginative or creative existence and as such are one with that existence. This partly suggests the perception of the fallen world, by a fallen creature, with an *unfallen* perspective. The creature is in two places at once, just as time as Kairos is within time as Chronos. The perception thereby obtained is capable of seeing the one central event and all events, of seeing the "One Central Form" and all forms. That perception is called LOS.

Los's descent into Albion in *Jerusalem* is a process of self-exploration. It is a pilgrimage through history, but it is experienced as Kairos rather than as Chronos. It is the search for identity through a vision of the particular man in his infinite variety. The labor of Los is the imagination's view of itself. Blake's vision of the reality of the creative mind is based upon his

4. Northrop Frye, *Anatomy of Criticism* (Princeton: Princeton Univ. Press, 1957), p. 94.

understanding of man's ability to imagine, as Shelley says, "intensely and comprehensively";[5] and the imagery of his poetry and the iconography of his designs dramatize that vision. His symbolic figures are, therefore, not allegorical abstractions or mythological people and gods, but energizing images in action.

I I

Blake's poetry is mythopoeic; that is, it is a structure of metaphors, images, and symbols that expresses a point of view. Instead of only expressing his theories discursively or assertively, Blake develops his ideas *in* the imagery of his poems *as* images. His system of symbols, often and mistakenly called his mythology, *is* the process by which he examines the nature of art and of man. Because his ideas are images, his symbolic figures are not mythological personages. To Blake's mind, a mythological figure is as general or abstract as a mathematical sign or natural law and as equally one-dimensional, hence his comment on Rubens' rickety princes and princesses and worn-out lumber of mythology. Neither in theory nor in practice does Blake adopt the techniques of the fable or of simple allegory. For Blake, as for Wallace Stevens in his "Notes Toward a Supreme Fiction,"

There was a myth before the myth began
Venerable and articulate and complete.

There is no reason for Blake to generalize the concrete or reduce his imagery to one-dimensional allegory, since to do so would be to weaken the visualizing and energizing character of myth itself. It is the mythic perception of reality that he compares to the generalizations of rationalistic moral and scientific law. He understands that the poem is an expression, unified and complete, of the creative act which is in the beginning and in the end a single eternal act, the world bathed in the blood of the imagination. Blake writes about the "ur-myth"—the one that was before myth began. But to write about it is to write with it. For the "ur-myth" is the creative experience which is timeless and beyond us in any strictly personal way.

Blake stresses the wholeness and oneness of the creative process, which is forever organic, while emphasizing the liberating character of particularity; that is what he means by identity. This process by which paradox is resolved, yet retained and sustained, is a seeming paradox itself. Blake names this process LOS, but also speaks of it as mental war or mental fight or mental travel. Each expression of the imagination is unique because it is

5. "A Defence of Poetry," in *The Complete Works of Percy Bysshe Shelley*, ed. R. Ingpen and W. E. Peck (New York: Charles Scribner's Sons, 1926–30), VII, 118.

identical with that which it expresses. In the opening part of *Jerusalem*, Blake defines briefly the creative response as an individual commitment:

I must Create a System, or be enslav'd by another Mans
I will not Reason & Compare: my business is to Create.
(*J* 10: 20–21)

The creative process, as opposed to the reasoning power, is eternal life, the business of man. It is a system only because it is striving with systems, laboring to remake the flesh into word, art's response to or reversal of the incarnation according to natural religion. Eternal existence is thereby the imaginative re-creation of man, what man is from the point of view of the creative act, not what he is from a natural or even a supernatural point of view. The imagination, as Blake understands it, has nothing to do with allegoric dissimulations. Los's pilgrimage is not like any man's, but all of human kind must make that pilgrimage, since it is the progress of time itself to eternity. As such, Los's mental travel is distinctly different from human wandering. To be inspired is to know and to search or explore, not to hypothesize and experiment.

The creative act is not an abstraction, but instead the resurrection of life from death or nonentity which is itself abstraction or "Allegoric Generation." Blake says that the "Sons of Albion," Locke and other British empiricists,

. . . take the Two Contraries which are calld Qualities, with which
Every Substance is clothed, they name them Good & Evil
From them they make an Abstract, which is a Negation
Not only of the Substance from which it is derived
A murderer of its own Body: but also a murderer
Of every Divine Member: it is the Reasoning Power
An Abstract objecting power, that Negatives every thing
This is the Spectre of Man: the Holy Reasoning Power
And in its Holiness is closed the Abomination of Desolation.
(*J* 10: 8–16)

This passage sums up many important arguments in Blake's work, because his philosophical principles (if they can be called that) are fused with the imagery of his poetry so completely that they become one form, one protest.

First, there are the contrary states of innocence and experience. As "contraries" innocence and experience are a kind of ying and yang totality, or two kinds of epiphany presented in the *Songs* in various guises. For Blake contraries are not secondary qualities; they are equally true in imagination. Blake's use of contraries has no more to do with Hegel than it has to do with Locke. In Blake the synthesized union of contraries is hermaphroditic. When they are equally true (as in Beulah) they are married in the sense in which

Buber speaks of *Ich und Du*. They are one in relation, and consequently threefold.

Second, there is the abstract negation which Blake associates with perverted or rationalistic distortions of imaginative truth. In the history of English thought, abstract negation is to be observed in the empirical and experimental theories of Blake's demonic trinity—Bacon, Newton, and Locke—and in the allegorical imitations of nature found in the works and theories of Reynolds. In the history of religion in the Western world, the influence of the abstract negation is to be observed in the rituals of Judaism and Druidism or any experience or religion given over to "Outward Ceremony" or a moral code (holy and mysterious), which Blake says is "Antichrist" or "oppression," such as the "Modern Church" that "Crucifies Christ with the Head Downwards" (*VLJ, p. 554*). Although Blake reinforces his analogical patterns with Semitic and Celtic parallels, he does not confine his patterns to these two alone. The three manifestations—the English, the Judaic, and the Celtic—are parallel images of a broad analogical pattern centered upon the sacrifice or murder of the divine imagination in man.

In this passage from Plate 10 of *Jerusalem*, we also see the "spectre," who as man's negative power is ultimately to be identified with the state of Satan. This is the mentality that reduces man to a lonely wayfarer who seeks general laws in order to create a false identity of contraries. Finally, we find an association of a reasoning Satanic power with the "Abomination of Desolation," the Babylonian Whore, that establishes the state of life-in-death.

Auden has used Blake to call attention to the central importance of this imagery and of the imagination to the celebration of individualism in Romanticism by saying that "The Deist religion of reason had a catholic myth, that of the Goddess of reason, but no cultus, no specifically religious acts; all rational acts were worship of the Goddess." The imagery is Blake's. "Cartesian metaphysics," he continues, "Newtonian physics and eighteenth-century theories of perception divided the body from the mind, and the primary objects of perception from their secondary qualities, so that physical nature became, as Professor Collingwood says, 'matter, infinite in extent, permeated by movement, devoid of ultimate qualitative differences, and moved by uniform and purely quantitative forces', the colorless desert from which Melville recoils. . . ." And like Melville, Blake sees "All deified nature" as a *painted harlot*. She is ironically a virgin harlot, "whose allurements cover nothing but the charnel house within," while her painted surface is a perversion of the artist's palette. "Such a view," says Auden, "must naturally affect the theory of artistic composition, for it involves a similar division between the thing to be expressed and the medium in which it is expressed." The Romantic reaction, which Auden subsequently describes, is Blake's, since Blake also stressed "imagination and vision; i.e., the less conscious side of artistic creation, the uniqueness of the poet's individual experience, and the symbolic rather than the decorative or descriptive value of images."[6]

III

Because the poet-prophet is the most individualistic of individuals and is also the "representative" man (as Emerson says), the poet becomes his own hero and stands as a concrete identity in opposition to the abstract and general indefinite. He is "greatly good," as Shelley says, because he is of imagination. The growth of the poet's mind, his personal imaginative apocalypse, becomes, therefore, archetypal. According to Blake, such mental growth culminates in a Last Judgment, the forsaking of error and the establishment of truth "continually." The poet unifies subject and object because he becomes in Emerson's sense, the "world's eye" and the "world's heart" and is able to contain subject and object in "Worlds of Vision" which overwhelm "Bad Art & Science." Time and space obey him, instead of subjecting him to their laws. Los is so described in *Milton*. He stands in opposition to the power of the world of threefold compulsion, which, in Shelley's words, is described "usurping and uniting in our own persons the incompatible characters of accuser, witness, judge and executioner,"[7] a symbolic pattern describing the enemies of art which Blake also invokes. As a fellow celebrant of imagination and as a spokesman for Promethean freedom, Shelley draws the enemies of the individual visionary after the image of the pharisaical judges of Socrates—Shelley's "Jesus Christ of Greece." Blake does so on Plate 93 of *Jerusalem*.

Blake thinks of Los as shaping the world into human form. Therefore, it is the function of Blake's artist to create imaginative forms that are permanent. He strives with "Systems to deliver Individuals from those Systems" (*J* 11:5), to deliver identity from "indefinite" death, which manifests itself in each and every form of tyranny over the mind of man. Thus while man's perception must be unique, it must also be free. Los compels his Spectre to turn the ore "into the clay ground prepar'd with art" (*J* 11:4) because the artist prepares the clay ground (natural man) in order to form his art (real man). It is in this way that Blake prepares his plates for etching or his panels and canvases for painting. The "Eye of Imagination, The Real Man" creates real form by perceiving the "Imaginative Image" on the copper body on which a ground has been prepared (*Marg.*, p. 654). The plate, panel, or canvas begins as a "terrible" blank surface without lineaments and untouched by the image-making human hand and intellect.

6. W. H. Auden, *The Enchafèd Flood* (New York: Random House, 1950), pp. 58–61.
7. "A Defence of Poetry," *Works*, VII, 138.

Since imaginative images are definite and are to be contrasted with indefinite abstractions, Blake associates the artist's initial act with the visionary's effort to delineate form on indefinite space—to mercifully give time to space, to draw a line. In his long poems, Blake's recurrent epithets for the spectre are "deform'd" and "indefinite." This is indicative of the spectre's relationship to the "Female Will," which is always associated with space and with tyranny. The Babylonian Whore figure—the goddess Nature, Vala, Rahab, the painted leper—is mystery, an ironical and demonic virgin. The correlation between the "scientific" indefinite and "religious" mystery is consistent in Blake's work. He associates the negative destructiveness of the rational faculty with the loss of identity in an industrial society which is a Satanic mill of gears and cogs or a universe subject to destiny or fate or holy mystery. The division of life into avocation and vocation, the rise of wage slavery amidst potential plenty, and starvation amidst gluttony, the simultaneous complexity of disorganization and over-organization which destroys unity and simplicity, the loss of self-realization through work without any knowledge of its purpose, describe in brief conditions in the fallen world. They are the product of the arts of Reason, which is a virgin science. Their effect is to leave their victims "deform'd," created so to speak according to the images of the "Arts of Death":

And all the Arts of Life.   they changd into the Arts of Death in Albion.
The hour-glass contemnd because its simple workmanship.
Was like the workmanship of the plowman, & the water wheel,
That raises water into cisterns: broken & burnd with fire:
Because its workmanship.   was like the workmanship of the shepherd.
And in their stead, intricate wheels invented, wheel without wheel:
To perplex youth in their outgoings, & to bind to labours in Albion
Of day & night the myriads of eternity that they may grind
And polish brass & iron hour after hour laborious task!
Kept ignorant of its use, that they might spend the days of wisdom
In sorrowful drudgery, to obtain a scanty pittance of bread:
In ignorance to view a small portion & think that All,
And call it Demonstration: blind to all the simple rules of life.
                                                              (J 65: 16–28)

The relevance of this passage to the rise of industrial slavery is especially clear in the last six lines. Blake is describing the mills of him who grinds meal and man with intricate wheels and ratios of any sort, whether those mills are owned by millers of flour or millers of textiles.

Blake's social revolution is part of the resurrection to unity, and this unity is the unique one man. Furthermore, it is part of Blake's life-long "Spiritual War" which he described as "Israel deliverd from Egypt," or "Art deliverd from Nature & Imitation" (The Laocoön, p. 272). Wage-slavery is simply another form of human bondage for which the only solution is Milton's "strenuous liberty." One law for the lion and the ox is oppression because simple reconciliation on fallen terms is tyranny. Any single abstract which ignores individual idiosyncrasies is a "generalizing Demonstration" of "the Arts of Death." For Blake, *one* already embraces *two*; any attempt to reconcile a contrary with a negative is error, for the rational falsely divides and falsely unites. By dividing that which is indivisible and uniting that which is not unifiable, the rational fails to achieve either identity or wholeness and certainly obscures individuality. In the imagination each thing is what it is and thus all things; for, from the creative point of view, anything is what it is and no other thing because there are no other things. The imagination is "the Human Existence itself" (*M* 32: 32).

"Exuberance is beauty," says Blake. That seems to me a practically definite solution, not only of the minor question of what beauty is, but of the far more important problem of what the conceptions of catharsis and ecstasis really mean. Such exuberance is, of course, as much intellectual as it is emotional. Blake himself was willing to define poetry as "allegory addressed to the intellectual powers." We live in a world of threefold external compulsion: of compulsion on action, or law; of compulsion on thinking, or fact; of compulsion on feeling, which is characteristic of all pleasure whether it is produced by the *Paradiso* or by an ice-cream soda. But in the world of imagination a fourth power, which contains morality, beauty, and truth but is never subordinated to them rises free of all their compulsions. The work of the imagination presents us with a vision, not of the personal greatness of the poet, but of something impersonal and far greater: the vision of a decisive act of spiritual freedom, the vision of the re-creation of man.[8]

Blake calls this "fourth power" and this vision LOS.

I V

In his essay "Life Without Principle," Thoreau writes, "All great enterprises are self-supporting. The poet, for instance, must sustain his body by his poetry, as a steam planing-mill feeds its boilers with the shavings it makes. You must get your living by loving."[9] Such a comment on love and creativity is a succinct description of the nature of creativity as Blake un-

8. Frye, *Anatomy of Criticism*, p. 94. See my article, "Blake's *Milton*: The Poet as Poem," *Blake Studies*, 1 (1968), 16–38. For a discussion of the number symbolism and the kind of vision or perspective involved in the final paragraph of this section, see my article, "Blake's Fourfold Art," *Philological Quarterly*, 49 (1970), 400–423.

9. *The Writings of Henry David Thoreau* (Boston: Houghton Mifflin, 1906), IV, 461.

derstood it. Los sustains the body of man because he is the spirit of prophecy and of self-regeneration in Albion. He is the aesthetic and moral agent of rebirth.

Los creates something beyond himself that is truly himself, "The Eternal Body of Man." Whereas Thoreau says after his fashion that we get our living by loving, and whereas Shelley characteristically writes, "A man, to be greatly good, must imagine intensely and comprehensively," Blake writes that "Imagination is the Divine Body in Every Man." Los is the "vehicular" energy of this divine body.

In *Jerusalem* man is enwombed in time, but his imagination (Los) turns the "little lovely Allegoric Night" (*J* 88: 31) of this world into a "Divine Analogy." Los takes the space around the winding worm (fallen embryo man) and gives it a "Time & Revolution." He is the kinetic force of mental travel or mental war acting on the static condition of man. He is time in space, lending a circumference to the indefinite.

Divine analogy is the womb-tomb world which looks like an egg or a skull, depending on whether it is viewed from Lambeth or Golgotha, the inside or the outside, the beginning or the end. This womb-tomb existence is our horizon, our sky-surrounded world—Shelley's many-colored dome. It is also the internal space of human psychology. It is the "Mundane Shell" into which man is born (like Reuben, "his head downwards") so that he may be born out of it. Geographically it is external space—Canaan. In still another way it is "thought," which Blake says, changes "the infinite to a serpent," the kind of thinking which shuts up the "image of infinite" in "finite revolutions" (meaning geometric *and* political revolutions), makes "Heaven a mighty circle turning" and "God a tyrant crown'd" (meaning the King of Heaven *and* the King of England). The artist's vision breaks these serpentine mental coils ("The mind-forg'd manacles" the bard of experience hears) by banishing, in Coleridge's words, its "viper thoughts, . . . Reality's dark dream" with the "shaping spirit of Imagination."[10] Blake's poet is a kind of Samson in the circular "serpent temple" of the Philistinian Druid, Albion. Inwardly illumined, he sees through windows into Eden (the picture-eyes of Albion), and the metaphor of temporal existence becomes "Permanent" in his vision, in the art of the nation: "all that has existed in the space of six thousand years" is "seen in the bright Sculptures of Los's Halls" from which "every Age renews its powers" (*J* 13: 59, 16: 61–62). And since every age is a Canterbury Pilgrimage, every age must turn to the human imagination in order to renew itself by exploring its interiors. This experience is forever original because each man is, as Emerson says, "a unique." This kind of self-exploration characterizes *Milton* and

10. "Dejection. An Ode," in *The Complete Works of Samuel Taylor Coleridge*, ed. W. T. G. Shedd (New York: Harper, 1858), VII, 192–193 (ll. 94–95, and 86).

Jerusalem, because it is the poet's search for identity, the Human Form Divine. Los conducts that search in Albion. It is a continual and never-ending quest in the eternity and infinity of man.

In *The Marriage of Heaven and Hell*, Blake defined creative activity ironically by praising excess. "The road of excess leads to the palace of wisdom," he wrote in the "Proverbs of Hell," because "He who desires but acts not, breeds pestilence" (7: 35). A fool persisting in his folly becomes wise because "What is now proved was once, only imagin'd" (8: 36). For Blake, the creative act is one in which the individual encompasses the totality of things by reaching the circumference at every point on the ever-expanding perimeter of self until he is like the peacock, eyed all over (*J* 98: 14) ; and his selfhood or ego is destroyed by expansion, not by contraction. Man becomes all, therefore, not by generalizing himself, but by particularizing himself. He increases his dimensions until he has no dimensions and cannot be measured. Having achieved such dimensions, man's imagination is unaffected by the ratios of reason which have no *raison d'être* for him because they can measure only that which permits itself to be measured, reasoned, and compared. That is why "Exuberance is Beauty" (*MHH* 10: 37), why "The whole Business of Man Is The Arts" (*The Laocoön, p. 271*), and why Los's system is no system but instead a continual pilgrimage to eternity.

From Blake's conception of the creative process, certain important themes emerge. First, the creative process is necessarily a unifying action which integrates every facet of a fully experienced totality imaged forth as a human body becoming divine through self-realization. Second, Blake's eternity of art presupposes an eternity of mind whose perpetual striving identifies word and act in a dialogue of the self. Third, Blake's poet is one who achieves a continual renewal through a revelation or vision of "All that Exists." Fourth, the poet is that kind of prophet who effects the identification of the personal and the impersonal. Finally, the essentially mythopoeic structure of poetry enables the poet to describe in any age the creative experience itself, because he is able to draw upon eternal forms of imagination. Blake implies a series of "linked analogies," such as Melville assumes, "O Nature, and O soul of man! how far beyond all utterance are your linked analogies! not the smallest atom stirs or lives on matter, but has its cunning duplicate in mind." Because reality is "linked analogies," Melville tells his readers not to read *Moby-Dick* as a "hideous and intolerable allegory."[11] It is precisely hideous and intolerable allegories that Blake seeks to replace with an "Allegory address'd to the Intellectual powers," the system which it is his business to create. This system is LOS.

The final design of *Jerusalem*, {38}, like the whole poem, portrays Los

11. *Moby-Dick*, ed. H. Hayford and H. Parker (New York: Norton, [1967]), Chapters 70 and 45, pp. 264 and 177.

as the creative agent or principle in Albion. Man is re-created according to
imagination through the one long night of the soul. Like everything else
which only appears to be real, the cyclical nature of existence proves also
to be delusion, an allegorical generation. When the long night ends, only
the imaginative *forms*, the mental acts of man, remain; and these (his emanations) are now themselves one with man. Awakening to identity, man is
fourfold and the seasons of his sleep are no longer sequential but simultaneously present. Viewed from eternity, the pilgrimage is the creative
moment—an apocalypse. Viewed from time, the pilgrimage is recurrent—
that is, cyclical. Much misunderstanding of Plate 99 of *Jerusalem* {37} can
be traced to the reader's failure to maintain the healthy twofold vision Blake
says he himself "Always" possesses. In Los, time comes to eternity through
the window ornamented with art. Los is the eye of the artist, the eye that
sees more than the heart knows.

V

The fullest description of Los as time appears in *Milton* (24: 68–76):

Los is by mortals nam'd Time Enitharmon is nam'd Space
But they depict him bald & aged who is in eternal youth
All powerful and his locks flourish like the brows of morning
He is the Spirit of Prophecy the ever apparent Elias
Time is the mercy of Eternity; without Times swiftness
Which is the swiftest of all things: all were eternal torment:
All the Gods of the Kingdoms of Earth labour in Los's Halls.
Every one is a fallen Son of the Spirit of Prophecy
He is the Fourth Zoa, that stood around the Throne Divine.

In *A Vision of the Last Judgment* Blake writes about the actual eternal
youthfulness of Time in connection with Time's usual aged appearance:
"The Greeks represent Chronos or Time as a very Aged Man this is Fable
but the Real Vision of Time is in Eternal Youth I have ⟨however⟩ somewhat accomodated my Figure of Time to ⟨the⟩ Common opinion as I myself am also infected with it & my Visions also infected & I see Time
Aged alas too much so" (*VLJ*, p. 553).[12] That "All the Gods of the Kingdoms of Earth" are laborers in Los's halls certainly connects them with the
bright sculptures (*J* 16: 61–62) from which "every Age renews its powers."
Because every one of these laboring gods is a fallen son of Los, who is the
spirit of prophecy, each is a temporal and limited (because fallen) extension

12. In *Milton, Jerusalem,* and *A Vision of the Last Judgment,* the figure of Elijah
(associated with Los in the two poems) underscores the relation of time to prophecy.

of Los's visionary power that does not age in itself, although time seems to grow old in passing by. Mortals see only Chronos and hence depict Time as Blake does in his illustrations for Young's *Night Thoughts*;[13] but when Time is seen as Kairos, Blake draws Los in creative action. For these reasons Los is the point of view of "The Mental Traveller" poem, a point of view that can see all of time sequentially *and* simultaneously. He passes on while the country remains permanent: men come and go, but mental states remain (*J* 73: 45). He "who sees this mortal pilgrimage in the light" that Blake sees it knows that "Duty to his country is the first consideration & safety the last" (*Marg. p. 601*). One has to know, however, what is indeed one's duty.[14] In examining Bishop Watson's reply to Paine, Blake says to "Read patiently" because "The consideration of these things is the whole duty of man & the affairs of life & death trifles sports of time. But considerations business of Eternity" (*Marg., p. 601*).[15] Blake would certainly have understood Thoreau's levels of perception and perspective:

Seen from a *lower* point of view, the Constitution, with all its faults, is very good; the law and the courts are very respectable; even this State and this American government are, in many respects, very admirable, and rare things, to be thankful for, such as a great many have described them; but seen from a point of view a *little higher*, they are what I have described them; seen from a *higher* still, and the *highest*, who shall say what they are, or that they are worth looking at or thinking of at all? [16]

Thoreau's speculative transcendentalism, his ability to see things both from time and from (or under the form of) eternity, is symbolized in Blake's work by the certain vision of Los.[17] Whether we see through Los as Chronos or Los as Kairos influences our understanding of what it is we are perceiving, including time itself, and how we are perceiving:

Thus is the earth one infinite plane, and not as apparent
To the weak traveller confin'd beneath the moony shade.

13. See the water colors, nos. 36, 45, 46, 49, 50, 102, 182, and 192, where Time is portrayed in the recognizable and, perhaps, conventional way. See, also, in the engraved versions, the title page to Night II and pp. 24–26.

14. Emerson is confronted with the same Puritan-Protestant problem vis-à-vis secular affairs. It was, of course, Milton's problem, too.

15. Cf. *PA, p. 569*: "I am really sorry to see my Countrymen trouble themselves about Politics. If Men were Wise the Most arbitrary Princes could not hurt them. If they are not Wise the Freest Government is compelld to be a Tyranny. Princes appear to me to be Fools Houses of Commons & Houses of Lords appear to me to be fools they seem to me to be something Else besides Human Life."

16. "Civil Disobedience," *Writings*, IV, 383.

17. See my article, "'A World with Full and Fair Proportions': The Aesthetics and the Politics of Vision," in *The Western Thoreau Centenary: Selected Papers*, ed. J. Golden Taylor (Logan, Utah: Utah State Univ., 1963), pp. 45–53.

Thus is the heaven a vortex passd already, and the earth
A vortex not yet pass'd by the traveller thro' Eternity.
                                        (*M* 15: 32–35)

Los's ability to see time as a finished totality yet act in time is pronounced unmistakably in *Milton* and reconfirmed near the end of *Jerusalem* (Plates 92 and 94). In *Jerusalem*, in an exchange between Los and Enitharmon, Blake writes of the amalgamation of one nation in Los's furnaces, declaring that the poem is coming to a conclusion by way of a delicate but symbolic double-entendre on the verb "draws." At the same time he invokes a Shakespearean pun on "period." And just prior to Albion's resurrection from the living dead, he writes that "Time was Finished." In *Milton* he has Los proclaim

I am that Shadowy Prophet who Six Thousand Years ago
Fell from my station in the Eternal bosom.   Six Thousand Years
Are finished.   I return!   both Time & Space obey my will.
I in Six Thousand Years walk up and down: for not one Moment
Of Time is lost, nor one Event of Space unpermanent.
But all remain: every fabric of Six Thousand Years
Remains permanent: tho' on the Earth where Satan
Fell, and was cut off all things vanish & are seen no more
They vanish not from me & mine, we guard them first & last[.]
The generations of men run on in the tide of Time
But leave their destind lineaments permanent for ever & ever.
                                        (*M* 22: 15–25)

In writing at the end of *Jerusalem* that "The Poet's Song draws to its period & Enitharmon [Space] is no more," Blake indicates that it is Los who is the ancient bard. Furthermore, whereas in the *Songs* the bard sees past, present, and future, in *Jerusalem* he sees time as a single form in which he can act mercifully and creatively.

   Los's attempt to accumulate "minute particulars" and to preserve them by opposing the generalizing and abstract attempts of the ratiocinative mind to combine them in a hideous, bloated aggregate is based upon another delicate and symbolic double-entendre: mi-*nute* is also *min*-ute. The minute particulars are the moments that Satan and his watch fiends cannot find but frantically search for, since Satan can only pursue the victimization of minute particulars in men in the State of Satan where time is a mathematical illusion. By killing time, as Thoreau remarks, such a mentality attempts to injure eternity. It is clear from *Milton* how fully responsible Los is for the mercy of time (as opposed to the tyranny of time) and how he *draws* time to eternity by creating and making permanent each *min*-ute.

But others of the Sons of Los build Moments & Minutes & Hours
And Days & Months & Years & Ages & Periods; wondrous buildings
And every Moment has a Couch of gold for soft repose,
(A Moment equals a pulsation of the artery)
And between every two Moments stands a Daughter of Beulah
To feed the Sleepers on their Couches with maternal care.
And every Minute has an azure Tent with silken Veils.
And every Hour has a bright golden Gate carved with skill.
And every Day & Night, has Walls of brass & Gates of adamant,
Shining like precious stones & ornamented with appropriate signs:
And every Month, a silver paved Terrace builded high:
And every Year, invulnerable Barriers with high Towers.
And every Age is Moated deep with Bridges of silver & gold:
And every Seven Ages is Incircled with a Flaming Fire.
Now Seven Ages is amounting to Two Hundred Years
Each has its Guard. each Moment Minute Hour Day Month & Year.
All are the work of Fairy hands of the Four Elements
The Guard are Angels of Providence on duty evermore
Every Time less than a pulsation of the artery
Is equal in its period & value to Six Thousand Years.

(M 28: 44–63) [18]

Time is described in terms of duration or Chronos, but the smallest, most mi-*nute* segment of time (that which is "less than a pulsation of the artery") is equal to the whole of time "in its period & value" because it is time as Kairos. And all is created by the spirit of Los, who is Time itself because he is prophecy.

While Los builds the stubborn structure of the language (*J* 36: 59), his Sons (attributes and extensions of his spirit) [19] create segments of time. Los's world of imagination "is no country for old men" and hence he makes permanent or gathers "Into the artifice of eternity" all time (Chronos), but that time (Kairos) always was, else Chronos could not exist.[20]

18. The number symbolism in Blake is consistent even to subtle divisions: Seven ages amount to two hundred years, which means that each age is twenty-eight and four-sevenths years.

19. That is, when they do not to themselves attribute "Universal Characteristics" (see *J* 90: 28–29) but remain unperverted extensions of the spirit or power of Los. As such they are to Los as segments of time are to all of time.

20. Blake is always relevant to "Sailing to Byzantium," and Yeats is often relevant to Blake; however, the most important factor is the line of the Almighty that Los draws on the shining heavens because he is that line: Kairos informing Chronos. "Leave out this l[i]ne and you leave out life itself; all is chaos again, and the *line of the almighty* must be drawn out upon it *before man or beast can exist*" (*DC, p. 540*; my italics). See my article "The Spirit of the Bounding Line: Blake's Los," *Criticism*, 13 (1971), 54–76.

For in this Period the Poets Work is Done: and all the Great
Events of Time start forth & are concievd in such a Period
Within a Moment: a Pulsation of the Artery.

(*M* 29: 1–3)

Los is the watchman of man's mental night or winter,[21] the visionary spirit
abroad in the temporal world of mortal men. He works in time through the
human imagination. His pilgrimage is a kind of intellectual love of God[22]
that has no object or end but itself and is expressed in the creative acts of
creative men in time.[23] As a true prophet crying in the wilderness, Los is
the ultimate "Pilgrim of Eternity . . . veiling all the lightnings of his song"
in an allegory addressed to the intellectual powers of a dehumanized Albion.
Hence, from the point of view of Chronos, Los speaks "In sorrow." From
the point of view of Kairos, however, he speaks in joy. Blake addressed *The
Ghost of Abel* to Shelley's "Pilgrim of Eternity," but his own Los crying in
the same wilderness is at the end of *Jerusalem* no longer *lost*.

At the beginning of this essay I wrote that Los is the act of perceiving,
and I have suggested briefly elsewhere that Los is (among other things)
"Lo" in the plural, LOs.[24] When man *los*, he sees under the form of eternity,
that is, he is in Los and *los* are in man. This internalizing of time as Chronos
and time as Kairos makes man's temporal mental acts into babes in Eternity.
It also permits the poet (especially the Romantic poet) to invent techniques
by which he can go outside (into the external landscape) and draw that
which is outside inside. The human imagination thereby overcomes the
limitations man's mortality places upon him. With imagination he can cir-
cumcise space as well as time.[25] The act of overcoming his limitations is
dramatized or illuminated by the works of art that embody those unique
moments in which man experiences this leap beyond his limitations—his
Urizenic circumference. With Los he opens his center to his circumference.[26]

To *behold* God or the divine in man is to act with Los, since it is impossible to recognize the Holy Spirit in others unless one acts with and in the
Holy Spirit. Not only is Los identified with that spirit and with the ever-
apparent Elias, he is described as of the similitude and likeness of Jesus.

21. See my article, "'Eternal Forms Exist For-ever': The Covenant of the Harvest
in Blake's Prophetic Poems," in *Blake's Visionary Forms Dramatic*, ed. David V.
Erdman and John E. Grant (Princeton: Princeton Univ. Press, 1970), pp. 443–462.

22. Cf. Spinoza, *Ethic*, V, propositions 33, 36, and 42.

23. Cf. Shelley, "A Defence of Poetry," *Works*, VII, 140.

24. See "The Spirit of the Bounding Line: Blake's Los" and "The Meaning of Los,"
Blake Newsletter, 1 (1967), 10–11.

25. See my article, "Circumcision Symbolism in Blake's *Jerusalem*," *Studies in
Romanticism*, 8 (1968), 16–25.

26. See my article, "The Symbolism of the Opened Center and Poetic Theory in
Blake's *Jerusalem*," *Studies in English Literature, 1500–1900*, 5 (1965), 587–606.

And he is also Time. All action in Los, therefore, is eternal energy whether or not it is measured by the clock or the yardstick. Los's pilgrimage in man is the creative activity of men in every age.

Blake's distinction between the wanderer and the pilgrim is related to his distinction between memory or allegory and vision. Memory records and recalls unredeemable time; that is, memory *is* unredeemable time—time past. Allegory is the major form that memory or unredeemable time most often takes. Vision, on the other hand, records redeemed time; that is, vision *is* redeemed time—eternal time. Vision also takes the form of allegory, but it is an allegory addressed, as Blake writes, to the intellectual powers and not to the corporeal powers. That is why many allegories, like *Pilgrim's Progress*, have some vision in them. When Christian ceases to be a cold earth wanderer (especially in the mind of the reader) and becomes a true pilgrim, we see Blake's point. All corporeal pilgrimages are only mental wanderings if the traveler remains mentally within generation. All corporeal pilgrimages become allegories without vision if the poet is limited by the manner in which he addresses his poem to the reader-spectator and the way in which the reader-spectator responds to the poem. From his own experience as a reader-spectator, Blake knew there was a special kind of reading just as there was a special kind of writing. In his own way, he anticipates Emerson, who writes, "There is then creative reading as well as creative writing. When the mind is braced by labor and invention, the page of whatever book we read becomes luminous with manifold allusions. Every sentence is doubly significant, and the sense of our author is as broad as the world. We then see, what is always true, that as the seer's hour of vision is short and rare among heavy days and months, so is its record, perchance, the least part of his volume."[27] Whereas in Blake's work the least part becomes a "minute particular" or a moment, the "luminous" page becomes an "illumination." In Blake's work the "manifold allusion" is commonplace, for the mental traveler's pilgrimage is in Los. He no longer wanders and he is no longer dependent upon memory or unredeemable time, because he, as a pilgrim of eternity, redeems all time. Braced by "labor and invention," the pilgrim of eternity lives in his "hour of vision" and we, his reader-spectators, live there with him. That kind of mental travel is part of the pilgrimage of eternity from which every age renews its own quest; it is addressed not to our vegetable existence but to our mental life.

27. *The Complete Works of Ralph Waldo Emerson* (Centenary ed.; Boston and New York: Houghton Mifflin, [1903]), I, 93. Cf. *VLJ*, p. 550, the passage beginning, "If the Spectator . . . ."

Babylon Revisited, or the Story of Luvah and Vala

JEAN H. HAGSTRUM

Blake may justly be considered the greatest love poet in our language. His pre-eminence does not lie in lyrical grace alone, although his verse, in its finest breathings, possesses crystalline beauty. Others, like Spenser, may surpass him in ringing celebrations of the beloved and of love, courtship, and marriage. Blake does something better. He probes the psychological, social, and political dimensions of love and embodies the combined excellencies of Richardson, D. H. Lawrence, and Freud. For range and resonance, for beauty, penetration, terror, pathos, for insights into revolutionary love and love as a restorer, it is difficult to think of his equal in verse.

The subtitle of this essay locates its temporal bounds: we are concerned with love and passion in the period of the great prophecies—*The Four Zoas, Milton,* and *Jerusalem,* when Satan has replaced Urizen as the arch-villain and the anti-man, when Orc has been sexualized and the political serpent has become phallic, and when the forgiveness of sins has replaced revolutionary indignation as a redemptive value. It is the period when Ona, Lyca, Thel, Leutha, Oothoon live on in the mind of the artist as emanations he fights to preserve for all eternity—as spirits that can emerge from the presses of art to help constitute the Wine of the Ages. But our immediate concern is not with these lovely and now sometimes shadowy recollections of past Innocence and Experience but with the Zoa of passionate love, Luvah, and his consort, Vala, who dominate a social-political-psychological landscape that is less like Urizen's rocky, stony, cavernous lunar death and more like Milton's lake of fire, with agonizing forms rising from its burning marl.

It would be hard to exaggerate the importance of the theme. Blake the older poet-prophet is more concerned than ever with those staminal virtues of humanity, the sexual appetites. He has shifted the emphasis from love as a singing joy in nature and from love as a force for revolutionary release to "the torments of Love & Jealousy," a preoccupation so central he made that phrase the subtitle of *The Four Zoas*. Innocent sexuality produced some of Blake's loveliest pages of composite art, and revolutionary sexuality some of his most memorable. But for richness of meaning and breadth of implication, both in its positive and negative aspects, it would be difficult to match even in Blake the love story of his late prophetic pages. The first adjectives that come to mind to describe this achievement are "powerful" and "inescapable." But "delicate" will also have to be used, since Blake is concerned with emotions that are evanescent and changing as well as searing, with creatures as gorgeous as they are dangerous, whose shifting forms are —if we may listen to a voice uncongenial in this setting—

Dipt in the richest tincture of the skies,
Where light disports in ever-mingling dyes,
While ev'ry beam new transient colours flings.[1]

Friendship is robust and can tolerate severe contentions. Love cannot—it flies into error, perversion, extremity, change.[2] Delicate in Innocence, it can become a glittering poison in Experience, tending toward death. And around the lovely, bestial, and protean forms of the late prophecies Blake weaves a complex network of meanings that coalesce, their main outlines, however, remaining firm and clear.

Our main concern is with fallen love, so vivid as picture, so salutary as prophecy, so close to our business and bosoms. It will help us see our fallen condition clearly if we begin with the ideal original and the ideal restored condition, though we intend no temporal sequence here, recognizing that the ideal and the real are states to which the prophetic vision—or its lack— can consign us here and now, at any moment of insight—or error. Vala, to begin with the derivative or secondary female principle, was, first, a city, a temple, or a garden. She was also the bride of Albion, the Eternal Man, and was, at the time of her birth, "the loveliest of the daughters of Eternity." The superlative perhaps ought to be toned down, since it comes from the mouth of the fallen goddess herself as she recalls her past. And when the fallen demons pay her the tribute of once having been a "fair crystal form divinely clear," we should of course pay them heed, remembering, how-

1. Pope, *Rape of the Lock*, II: 65–67.
2. "Altho' our Human Power can sustain the severe contentions / Of Friendship, our Sexual cannot: but flies into the Ulro" (*M* 41: 32–33). The statement just quoted is made by Ololon in despair, but it is a fair statement of Blake's own view in the years of tribulation.

ever, that they are under the spell of the seductress. Luvah, from whom Vala emanated as from a primary and more basic force, was her father, her lover, or her husband—always some kind of consort.[3] He was given the title of "prince of Love," a ruler over the east, the realm of the rising sun. But though he possesses a lofty title and a beautiful and extensive realm, his manner was more Christ-like than monarchical, for he was the "gentlest mildest Zoa." And his activities were rather those of servant than ruler: a cupbearer to the gods, he poured wine of delight and love, his pure feet stepping on the steps divine; a charioteer, he drove the horses of light and warmth; a weaver, he assumed a kind of feminine role, weaving fibres and threads for others to use.[4]

Considered ideally, these two—the Zoa of love and his consort—possess attractiveness and grace. But there is clear indication that their position is not the highest, the myth placing them more often than not in positions of service. All this, of course, befits a faculty or an appetite that is a part not the whole, that is powerful but not supreme, and that is gracious only when it is subordinate. Luvah and Vala in great eternity are not mighty monarchs but gentle angels ranged in order serviceable.

It is important to stress the qualities of gentle subservience ministering to harmony and proportion in the ideal state, because in the fallen state these beings assume the opposite characteristics. They become raging tyrants —burning, destroying, dominating. What could have been the nature of the fall that toppled them from a modest but noble station to swirl in vortexes of uncontrolled energy? Like all myths, Blake's provides alternative versions, each of which contributes an insight or an emphasis to round out the whole. There are at least four related but differing accounts of how Luvah and Vala got to be what we know them to be in life.

1. Luvah intoxicated Urizen, the god of light, with stolen wine—stolen, apparently, because the legitimate portion was of insufficient quantity to accomplish Luvah's mischief, which recalls Phaeton's, for he seized Urizen's horses and drove the chariot of the day.

2. While Albion and Urizen slept, Luvah and Vala awakened and flew up from the heart, their proper place, into the brain.

3. Luvah now aggressively assumed Urizen's territories to the south, leaving the east a gaping void.

---

3. See *J* 29: 36–37, 40; *FZ* V: *333*; *J* 80: 27; *FZ* V: *337*; *FZ* II: *311*.

4. See *FZ* I: *302*; *J* 24: 52; *FZ* V: *337*; *Thel* 3: 7–8; *J* 95: 16. Milton O. Percival suggests that Luvah's role as weaver points to feminine characteristics, since weaving in Blake is usually done by women. See *William Blake's Circle of Destiny* (New York: Columbia Univ. Press, 1938), p. 29. The implication of the passage in *Thel* cited, where Luvah appears first, is that he was associated with Apollo, the god of light.

4. Luvah and Vala divided into separate forms. Luvah was sealed in a furnace, as Vala fed the flames.[5]

These several versions say that the fall resulted in displacement and separation. The separation of Luvah and Vala need not mean anything so outlandish as that we were once literally androgynous and that in falling we became men and women. It means, more simply and relevantly, that passion is separated from tenderness, desire from affection, a disaster not unlike the one Freud described in "Degradation in Erotic Life."[6] The effect of separation is to leave tenderness a victim and passion a raw aggressor, both in the female and the male. The displacement does not mean literally that climates have been disordered at certain points of the compass, but metaphorically that heat has replaced light, that some places have become void and that others howl in thunder and cyclone. That is, some people most of the time and other people some of the time lament in loneliness and frustration, empty and deserted; and still other people most of the time and some people part of the time burn and freeze in passion. Blake is psychologist first and cosmologist second; the doctrine that all things fall to the center, leaving the east hollow, the south burning up in heat, and the west raging in storms is vastly more metaphorical than the modern tentative cosmology that disappearing stars have created black holes in the universe, small concentrations of matter of incredible density. As cosmology the modern formulation may turn out to be true. Blake's could not, though his psychology is valid. What Blake is saying in his four versions of the fall of Luvah is that within the human personality passion has supplanted reason, excess has supplanted control; the gentle passions have been replaced by violent ones, compassion by cruelty, love by prostitution.

All this is traditional enough, having been more or less present in human thought from the Book of Genesis to *Paradise Lost*; but Blake, radical humanist that he is, gives it a particular twist. The fall is a revolt not so much against God as against man. Luvah's ultimate blasphemy was that he murdered Albion, who is at once Blake himself, his culture, his nation, and, by extension, the eternal man in all of us. Luvah's own account reveals the full extent of his demonic and inhuman delusion, which was also close to Blake's own activities in the nineties. Both Blake and Luvah attack Urizen, Luvah believing that he would be able to blot out the human delusion of reason. Just how mistaken and impious he was, Luvah himself reveals when he says that he hoped "to deliver all the sons of God / From bondage of the Human Form" (*FZ* II: *311*). A tragic flaw and a hideous blindness! For

5. See *FZ* I: *301*; *FZ* V: *337*; *M* 19: 17–24; *FZ* VIIA: *351*; *FZ* II: *310*.

6. Freud, like Blake, believed that ideally the two kinds of love are united. See the reprinting of this essay of 1912 in Sigmund Freud, *On Creativity and the Unconscious* (New York: Harper Torchbook, 1958), p. 174.

Christ is the Human Form Divine. The attack on Urizen had turned round and become an attack on Jesus, that is, on man himself. Luvah, in what at the end of the eighteenth century seemed to be a justified aggression against the rational faculty, succeeded only in crucifying Christ afresh. It is difficult not to believe that in the fallen Luvah's confession Blake is making his own.

The raging fiery furnace that Luvah and Vala have now placed in the world is the central heating and energy system of Babylon. For all its religious and political significance, Babylon is a highly sexual zone, more intensely sexual than the milder Beulah. Both places are created by Blake in response to the inescapable presence in man of sexual desire. Both are places of erotic blandishments, of the physical melting of the will. Both are places of veils, coverings, death, and ecstasy, and Luvah and Vala, the creators of Babylon, appear in Beulah. But for all their similarities Beulah and Babylon are, of course, distinctly separate regions. When Albion in Beulah faints on the bosom of Vala, this ecstasy causes a wall to be built by heaven around Beulah, which is endangered by an excess of its own qualities. Beulah is a place of "soft Delight," of shadows, mirrors, delicate wings, crystal palaces, and "mazes of delusive beauty"; of dreams "in soft deluding slumber," a mild and pleasant refuge in "soft slumberous repose" from the evils of Urizen-land. Essentially, it is a place of mercy created by the Lamb of God, who through it does what Los and Enitharmon as artists also do: here bodies are created for that "insane, and most deformed" part of man that Blake calls spectral, bodies that can preserve the essential human being from eternal death, which is damnation.[7]

Babylon, on the other hand, drives inexorably on toward death or nonentity. It is a place, not where spectres are put in bodies or literary artistic forms, but where they remain pure spectres, unthwarted, preying on life. In Beulah the moon beams faintly; in Babylon, the sun—out of place, to be sure—is a fire that rages too close to the earth. Beulah preserves, Babylon consumes itself and others. Beulah is a place of soft coverings—of the womb, the vulva, the mother's arms enfolding the child. Babylon is a place where male and female energy bubbles and boils in vein and artery. Beulah is a place of sweet alluring dreams, Babylon of nightmares. In Beulah "every female delights to give her maiden [that is, her maidenhead] to her husband." But in Babylon, where all males become one male in a drastic sexual concentration, love is a "ravening eating Cancer." In Bunyan, Beulah is the last step on the way to heaven. In Blake, Beulah is the married state, the last station on the way to eternal bliss. But Babylon is prostitution, tottering on the edge of Blake's hell, Ulro. Beulah is Innocence, the place of

7. *FZ* VIIA: *351*; *FZ* I: *298–299*; *FZ* III: *320*; *J* 37: 21; *J* 33: 4.

Oothoon's palace, and of the grain of sand that Satan's watch fiends cannot find.[8]

And yet they do find it—in Lambeth. They call Beulah sin,[9] thus perverting it to Babylon. In the last analysis Beulah and Babylon, vastly different and yet mutually reminiscent, can best be thought of together: Babylon is a hideous perversion of Beulah. The coverings, counterpanes, sheets, and blankets of Beulah become Vala's veil in Babylon. The protection and tenderness of Beulah, with its "dimm religious light,"[10] become the mysterious and life-denying sexual religion of Babylon. The delicate sexual acts of Beulah, necessary for our salvation, are twisted into the Abomination of Desolation. Both places are profoundly autobiographical in ways we can only divine. Beulah was a distillation of the best moments of Blake's marriage with Catherine and his collaboration with that sweet and simple woman in creating the lovely forms—in word, line and color—of *Innocence, Thel, Europe,* and *Albion.* In the hell of Babylon, Blake concentrated his worst moments with Catherine, his lusts, his own temptations, and the powerful conflicts that his creation of "The Tyger," the early Orc, Bromion, Urizen, and Hell must have entailed upon his psyche.

There are two kinds of perversion, those that turn a pleasure from its normal course and those that drive it too far, past enjoyment to excess. We shall consider the second kind in discussing monomaniacal heterosexuality, perhaps the central characteristic of a Babylonian citizen. But there are also in Babylon the abnormal, deviant types of perversion, although these are rather hinted at than fully developed. Three such perversions can be distinguished: (1) the incestuous, (2) the narcissistic, and (3) the feminine-phallic.

1. Storge, *or love of parents for offspring.* The term *storge,* from the Greek στοργή, was known and used by Blake, his contemporaries, and his immediate predecessors, including Swedenborg, from whom the poet undoubtedly borrowed it.[11] The Swedish seer uses the term for a love that is physical and that is communicated by that same sense of touch that cements the physical bond between married people. But it is universal, providential, tender, peaceful, and innocent. In fact, it tends to recede as innocence itself does.[12] But the English seer, in the period of his major prophecies, sees

8. See *J* 69: 15; *J* 69: 2; *J* 35: 1–2.

9. See *J* 37: 19.

10. Milton, *Il Penseroso,* l. 160.

11. S. Foster Damon, *A Blake Dictionary: The Ideas and Symbols of William Blake* (Providence: Brown Univ. Press, 1965), under "Storge." The *Oxford English Dictionary* lists uses of this term in 1637, 1764, 1809, and later.

12. Emanuel Swedenborg, *The Delights of Wisdom pertaining to Conjugial Love* (New York: Swedenborg Foundation, 1949), sections 392–398.

storge as something other than beautiful and divine parental love. From "all powerful parental affection" spring "the silent broodings of deadly revenge," and Albion comes to loathe his sons in sexual jealousy as he sees them assimilate with Luvah and assume their man's estate. So Los, in an illustration to *The Book of Urizen*, looks with envious eyes on his son Orc. Blake has provided an unmistakable Oedipal triangle in visual form, as son and mother embrace while a bearded father (an unusual way to represent Los) looks on in deep love-jealousy as a red chain of envy binds his waist. In *The Four Zoas* the son provides ample reason for his father's jealousy, for he has conceived an Oedipal love for his mother. The howling sexual serpentine Orc comes to love with a craving "Storgous Appetite." One would have to say that among the "thrilling joys of sense," which the sexualized Orc enjoys in exploring the "hidden things of Vala," is an abnormal affection for his mother.[13]

Similarly, when Enion draws the spectre from Tharmas on her loom of vegetation, he emerges as a "wayward" infant and a "sullen" youth. Then, when he has fully achieved his masculine form, he mingles with his mother to produce a bright wonder that is "Half Woman & half beast," a "Beauty all blushing with desire." Blake of course shudders at all this; for within that "vast Polypus of living fibres" (*fibre* being a sexual term) which Vala and the other females spin amorously from their bowels and which is Ulro, they, like Sirens, "lure the Sleepers . . . down / The River Storge . . . into the Dead Sea." *Storge* or maternal love can lead to death.[14]

Strong maternal love, as Blake sees it, can dangerously prolong childhood. We need not go back to those aged children Har and Heva in *Tiriel* for this perversion. It exists in the Babylon of the major prophecies as well. Gwendolyn reduces the "mighty Hyle" to "a weeping infant," and the mother exults over her conquest: "Look. Hyle is become an infant Love: look! behold! see him lie!" (*J* 82: 37). Blake is capable of conceiving of sexual sin as Milton had before him. The Sin portrayed by the Puritan poet in a passage illustrated at least twice by Blake and obsessively by his generation is a "Snaky Sorceress" who is a daughter of Satan, with whom she has had the intercourse that produces Death, by whom she is later raped.[15]

2. *Narcissus.* Before being incestuously enjoyed, Milton's Sin is narcissistically conceived, self-begotten from the head of her father Satan. Blake,

---

13. See *J* 54: 9–10; *U* 21 (Trianon) ; *FZ* V: *334*.

14. See *FZ* I: *299–300*; *M* 34: 24–25, 27–30. The last passage may, of course, mean no more than what Damon (*Dictionary*, under "Storge") sees in it—birth through the female genital tract, or the acquisition of a body. My view is that *storge* is also associated with the parental affection that leads to brooding revenge—that is, with a psychological perversion, not merely with physical birth.

15. *Paradise Lost* II: 648–814.

too, conceives of sexual sin as narcissistic, a subcategory of that dreadful vice of Ulro, self-destroying self-love. That strange, perverted, grotesque beauty that Enion incestuously produced and that we have already commented on is also a "self-enjoying wonder." And one characteristic Albion acquires in his fallen state is a tendency to worship his own Shadow, which is only a "watry vision of Man." Paradoxically, this urge rises in him when he feels himself to be nothing. The pious man who sings in his chapel, "Oh, to be nothing nothing, Only to lie at Thy feet,"[16] is perceived by Blake's penetrating eye (so like Swift's on the subject of dissenting hypocrisy) as self-idolatrous. Whomever Blake is thinking about—and it is undoubtedly more than pious Christians pretending to be nothing—the projection of self can absorb Albion entirely, a self-idolatry at which even Vala trembles and covers her face in shame; for of course it is a total negation of the heterosexual love by which this Venus subsists. It is a tempting vision, not to be taken lightly. Although "watry," it is also a shadow of "living gold, pure perfect, holy; in white linen pure." However fair, it is no less evil. It springs from a "wearied intellect" as an "entrancing self-delusion."[17]

Narcissistic self-enjoyment, present in Babylon, had existed earlier in the sexually frustrated sons and daughters of Albion in the period of Experience and of Lambeth. The pining virgin herself awakens her womb in the days of Urizenic predominance to joys in the "secret shadows of her chamber." The lustful youth "forgets to generate" and creates "an amorous image / In the shadows of his curtains" (*VDA* 7: 3–7). Frustration, Blake perceived early, could lead to sexual dreams and imaginings and, doubtless, also to the *vice solitaire*. As in Urizen's Experience, so in Vala's Babylon.

3. *The phallic woman*. Freud believed that in the terrors of his uninstructed imagination a young boy might endow his mother with the male organ and masculinize the woman who sometimes threatens and punishes him as she denies him his wishes.[18] Blake too conceived of the phallic woman. In *America* (Plate 14) a submissive boy is being instructed by an early version of Rahab seated under a tree, her loins producing a phallic serpent whose forked tongue seems to spit menaces at the youth. The fully developed Babylon of the later prophecies includes a similarly perverse creation to express aggressive and unnatural female sexuality. In Luvah's own story of his past, he conceives of Vala's earliest condition in imagery that is phallic.

16. I here recall a song by Homer Rodeheaver, the singer of Billy Sunday's evangelistic campaigns. I have no notion that it was sung in a chapel in Blake's day, though I am sure its self-abnegating sentiment was frequently heard.

17. The Blake references in this passage are as follows: *FZ* I: *300*; *FZ* III: *320*; *J* 43: 35–43.

18. See *New Introductory Lectures* in Sigmund Freud, *Standard Edition of Complete Psychological Works* (London: Hogarth Press, 1933), XXII, 24, 126, 130.

He produces first an earthworm, who becomes a scaled serpent (hating him, incidentally) ; under his care she then becomes a winged dragon bright and poisonous—this phallic career preceding her birth as a weeping infant who grows up to be a producing mother.[19] Vala has had, to say the least, a phallic origin that apparently remains with her, to keep her femininity aggressive and warlike. The mature Vala is even capable of the masculine act, for she at one point is conceived of as a "Worm in Enitharmon's Womb / Laying her seeds upon the fibres" (*FZ* III: *320*).[20]

We must, of course, be careful not to insist always on literal sexual perversions when Blake, with his all-personifying faculty, is clothing other human monstrosities in vivid physical imagery. But Blake's personified figures, so unlike those of his eighteenth-century predecessors, are real and powerful in and of themselves; and there is no clear separation between tenor and vehicle as in allegory, which Blake loathed. Sexual perversion is a powerful metaphor in Blake for political and religious perversion because it is itself a real feature of Babylon. And the three irregularities we have noted—the storgous, the narcissistic, and the female phallic—are insistently present as realities. There may be others as well, and when Blake refers to "detestable births," "devilish arts abominable unlawful unutterable" (*FZ* VIII: *364*), he may refer to dark sexual perversions he does not choose to embody fully in his myth. Blake has a lot to say about Ulro. Of Alla, the errors of the heart, he has also much to say, even though he uses the term only twice.[21] This essay discusses the errors and perversions of Al-Ulro, the errors of the "Loins & Seminal Vessels." But of Or-Ulro, the errors of the "Stomach & Intestines," Blake has virtually nothing to say—except that the imaginations that arise from these lower gates are not only "wondrous" but also "terrible, deadly, unutterable" (*M* 34: 13, 15–18). Like Saint Augustine and Swift before him and like Yeats after him, Blake was conscious of the irony that man is born between the gate of seed and the gate of excrement. About this latter orifice Blake is reticent, but his own contemporary the Marquis de Sade and our own age of Freud can supply the details.

Relatively silent about the phallic woman, whose perversion is unnatural, Blake has much to say about the phallic predominance in heterosexual men, about the male who "phallicizes" all nature, including his own and his be-

19. See *FZ* II: *311*.

20. John E. Grant has almost convinced me that the two figures on the huge lily (*J* 28) are Albion and Vala. But if, as I suggest, Vala in one aspect has a darkly masculine side, the illustration may indeed refer to Jerusalem and Vala assimilating. See Grant's "Two Flowers in the Garden of Experience," in *William Blake: Essays for S. Foster Damon*, ed. Alvin H. Rosenfeld (Providence: Brown Univ. Press, 1969), pp. 354–362. Grant, to whom I am indebted for several parallels, calls my attention to details of *J* 75, where the woman (perhaps Rahab) has genital scales and perhaps a penis.

21. See *M* 34: 12, 14; and *J* 89: 58.

loved's brain. This driving of a natural passion to absorbing excess is characteristic of the age of the phallic Orc, who has replaced the political revolutionary Orc.[22] (More precisely stated, the phallic-political Orc has replaced the political-phallic Orc; for neither manifestation is without the sexual and political combined.) When that frosty tyrant Urizen explores the world of the new Orc, he sees a world where his horses must feed in fiery mangers, where holy oil burns in fury within caverns and rocks, where the bulls of Luvah breathe fire, where lions howl in burning dens. It is a hell, a lake of fire consuming itself in the flames of Orc. In a brilliantly condensed description, it is called "A Cavernd Universe of flaming fire." One understands the sexual Babylon only if one realizes that it is a place of both (1) raging fiery passion and (2) caverned restraint. Hence the individual sufferings and also the rages that tear nations and cultures apart. Los's mighty rivers must flow in "tubelike forms" as they sink to the place of seed to be divided into testicles. Everywhere there is the pressure of passion on the veins and arteries of the body, and the moony escapes of Beulah are not adequate to provide relief.[23]

Love has become burningly sexual, as Luvah becomes Orc and as all nature becomes serpentine. Beauty becomes scarlet, separated from familial love; and lust rages in the heart that was once the seat of delicate sensibility and fine feeling. The "new born king" does not rule in mercy mild but as the red Orc, "the King of rage and death" (*FZ* V: *333*).

The paradox about love that we shall return to at the end emerges here. Blake allows Orc to enjoy his fires, at least to prefer them to the snowy death of Urizen. In fact, Orc's reading of the fall is very much like that of the earlier revolutionary Blake. Why does the phallic worm wrap the tree of life in the garden and lead Eve and mankind to destruction? Because he is "A Worm compelld"—compelled by the restraints and deceits of Urizen. And now Orc "organizes" a serpent body for all nature, becoming himself a "dark devourer," precisely because rational and coldly moral limits have been put upon him.[24]

There is no evidence that Blake rejects Orc's analysis. But he does add a new dimension to it. The new Orc may be preferable to Urizen, but he is a tyrant nonetheless. He subjects Babylon to a new tyranny, that of obsessive phallic passion that burns alone, unattached to any love object, and that

---

22. Northrop Frye, who comments on the transformation of Orc, says that his erotic quality "increases in proportion to the frequency with which Blake calls him Luvah" (*Fearful Symmetry: A Study of William Blake* [Princeton: Princeton Univ. Press, 1947], p. 235).

23. See *FZ* VIIA: *346*; *FZ* VIIA: *352*.

24. See *FZ* VIIA: *347*; *FZ* VIIA: *349*.

then stalks abroad seeking whom it may devour. Destructive, it is also nasty; and scaly monsters, bred in the swamps of Orc-country, vomit up creatures that "annoy the nether parts of man." It is the age of the phallic predominance. All who love, including the quondam King of Love himself, Luvah, are now "reasoning from the loins in the unreal forms of Ulros night."[25]

If men reason from the loins, they do so because of the dazzling beauty of the fallen Vala, because of the dominance of what Blake feared as an anti-human blasphemy, the dominance of the Female Will, made possible by sexual power. Vala is the *agent provocateur* of sex in the head.

Vala meets the old Orc in *America* as the nameless "Shadowy daughter of Urthona." She encounters the new Orc as a "nameless shadowy Vortex," and the change in phrasing is eloquent. Vortex indeed! Swirling sexual energy meets the phallic Orc more than half way—in "the Caverns of the Grave [a place of sexual commerce] & Places of human seed." But, in actuality, she embraces his fire to dampen it. She apparently wants Orc to lose his rage and subside into meekness. Why does she stoop to the Urizenic tricks of beguiling humility? The reason is simple. She has become a tyrant, and like all tyrants she recognizes the value of humility-inducing opiates. But the meekness is intended for her victim, for she herself is far from being lowly of heart. In Beulah, the creation of Los and Christ, the woman is a sub-missive receptacle, a handmaiden of her Lord. In Babylon she is an aggressive "Sexual Machine," who, as we have seen, may be regarded as also a phallic mother, a glittering but threatening dragon-shape. She is a rival of the serpentine Orc himself. Small wonder he is jealous![26]

The aggressive Vala is a successful imperialist on a larger scale than we have hitherto seen. Conquering new territories, she takes on more than Orc, becoming even Los's harlot, poisoning and dominating the artistic imagination. She also becomes Urizen's harlot, adopting, as we have seen, his arts of "Pity & Meek Affection," but extending these far beyond the task of subduing the serpentine fires of Orc. She penetrates Beulah with "false / And generating Love." She extends to all parts of the body, a "hungry Stomach, & a devouring Tongue." The fires of her loins invade cities, nations, families, languages. Man is reduced by her to a phallic worm and, paradoxically, an effeminate phallus at that, a breeder of seeds. Whoever he is—pope or poet, king or philosopher—he is "Woman-born / And Woman-nourished & Woman-educated, & Woman-scorn'd!" The fallen Vala, or Rahab, conquers such a wide domain because through her daughter, the cruel Tirzah, she sexualizes everything, creating breasts and testes ("tying the knots of milky seed into two lovely Heavens"), a brain heated white,

25. See *FZ* VIII: *369*; *FZ* II: *311*.
26. See *A* 1: 1; *FZ* VIIB: *395*; *J* 39: 25.

and a "red hot heart." That is, in magnetizing everything by sexuality, she can dominate it through physical attractiveness, thus perverting our staminal virtues.[27]

Vala's assumption of Urizenic qualities, which we have already mentioned, deserves further comment. Why should the fatal beauty with the blue eyes, the sapphire shoes, the golden brow, the silver locks, the white garments, and the burning zone turn to institutions, the church and the state? Why should she, who is served by all nature—the elements, the birds, the "far beaming Peacock," the proud horse, and the strong lion—wish to imitate the cold-hearted tyrant, once god of light and reason, now fallen to intellectual and spiritual tyranny? Partly because fallen sexuality, for all its seeming power, brings no fulfilment by itself and partly because tyranny knows no limits. And so the dominant Female Will extends her sway from nature to philosophy, which she naturalizes into mechanism, and to religion, which she naturalizes into deism. She also annexes France, intellectually, making Voltaire and Rousseau her covering cherubs. She becomes an unappeasable fanatic calling for new worlds to conquer, and she embodies the Abomination of Desolation by challenging the province of Christ. She arrogates to herself the candle of the Lord: "The Imaginative Human Form is but a Breathing of Vala." With her red fires, she claims to have elevated sexual love into the region of brotherhood. She has indeed usurped the place of Jesus on the throne of human nature.[28]

But of course she is an Antichrist, the false Christ whom biblical prophecy sees as heralding the time of the end. A monomaniacal tyrant, she was driven to attempt the dethronement of the Human Form Divine because "I alone am Beauty." Vala—whose husband is the sun, whose veil is the moon, and whose daughter is Jerusalem—is nature wanting to be all and in all. What a contrast she provides to the lovely and tender Mother Nature of *Thel*, who exhales her milky tenderness over the lowly worm! Blake is dreadfully serious about the dominating Female Will. Vala's veil, woven of vegetable fibres, hardens and petrifies into Urizenic rock and iron. It becomes so impenetrable—this covering that separates Adam and Eve and all their children and that ultimately covers the earth—that only Christ on the cross will be able to rend it.[29]

The effect of Vala's becoming both Orc-like and Urizenic needs to be examined further. Her all-naturalizing power becomes responsible for two enormous perversions, sexualized religion and the sexualized state. These separate but related phenomena are the most prominent—and dreadful—

27. See *FZ* VIIB: *395*; *J* 17: 25–26; *J* 64: 8, 16–17; *M* 19: 55–60.
28. See *FZ* VIIB: *396*; *FZ* VIIB: *398–399*; *J* 66: 12; *J* 29: 49–30: 1.
29. See *J* 29: 48; *J* 30: 7–8; *Thel* 4: 8–9; *J* 55: 11, 16.

features of Babylon. As the shadowy female, Vala has absorbed both the science and art of Urizen and the fiery aggressiveness of Orc. She is a double-threat tyrant, ice and fire at the same time, seductive and cruel. "In the power of Orc," she insinuates herself into the state, altering the vortexes, changing the true centers of power, making both female attractiveness and female frigidity a motive power. As Urizen, she insinuates herself into religion; for she has, as we have seen, affected the arts of pity and humility. In different ways, then, venereal disease may be said to attack metaphorically the body politic and even the body of Christ. Christ's real body resisted "the festering Venoms bright" that threatened it when he forgave the Magdalen and took on her sins to forgive them. But his false body, the established church, no longer had such immunity because it had forgotten the art of forgiving sin.[30]

Metaphors have a way of taking over in Blake, and the insistent use of sexual imagery for religion and religious imagery for sexuality (not unlike Donne, by the way) suggests an interpenetration of essences that can only mean that when one is corrupted the other is too. Woman-dominated man has created woman-dominated religious institutions—Hebrew, Christian, druidic, or natural. Puritanical religion enshrines female fears of sexuality and makes them holy—a perversion so gross that it causes the Eternals to laugh "after their manner." What provokes mirth in the heavens is a self-denying religious ethic by which a man "dare hardly to embrace / His own wife, for the terrors of Chastity." Hebraic religion, transmuted to Roman and Anglican Christian establishments, is also woman-dominated, but perhaps in another way. The magical ark of the Covenant and its equivalents in Christian altars, along with its attendant ceremonies and rites, is seen by Blake as analogous to secret, furtive, guilty sexuality. Freud noted that the holy and the forbidden are in many languages designated by the same word,[31] and in Blake sexual terror and sacrifice for sin are imagistically tied together. Both the sex act and the religious rite are done in secret, dark, covert places, incensed and perfumed; and the conjugal bed, with its hangings, counterpanes, and curtains, is like the altar, with its rich cloths, its protecting covers, and its vestmented priests. The tabernacle, the place of the sacred elements, is one of Blake's images for the enclosing of the male organ by the female. Both fallen sexuality and fallen religion hide the bread and wine from the light of common experience. Fallen religion can

30. See *FZ* VIII: *361*; *EG*, p. *514*.

31. See "The Uncanny" (1919), in which Freud discusses, among other words, the German word *heimlich*, which ranges in meaning from the familiar to the concealed, from the "homey" to the holy; it finally becomes synonymous with its opposite *unheimlich* (*Creativity and the Unconscious*, pp. 125–131).

also be druidic, but that cruel religion is no less female-dominated than the puritanical and the Hebraic-Christian. Vala's daughters wield the stone knife of cruel sacrifice, becoming castrators and circumcisers, sacrificing innocent male lambs to their perverse delights.[32]

Such, then, is the "Synagogue of Satan." Such is Rahab, the "False Feminine Counterpart Lovely of Delusive Beauty." In the religio-sexual tabernacles of Babylon the true God, who is the true man, is buried.[33]

If sexualized religion is bad, the sexualized state is even worse. And in this aspect Luvah-Los may be worse than Vala-Urizen. Luvah tears forth from Albion's loins and flows in red blood all over Europe, and Blake intends us to understand that sexual energy has burst its dams and issued forth as aggressive warfare. "The Beast & the Whore rule without control."[34]

Let us consider the several stages that descend to this awful perversion of love into war, of Vala first into "Mystery the Harlot" and then into "Mystery the Virgin Harlot Mother of War, / Babylon the Great, the Abomination of Desolation!" The first stage, from Adam to Lamech, includes mighty hermaphrodites, menacingly narcissistic, full of evil promise. The second produces the "Female-Males, / A Male within a Female hid as in an Ark & Curtains"—that is, the sexualized religion we have just considered. The final stage, to which Blake's age had arrived, is the "Male-Females, the Dragon Forms / Religion hid in War." This is the period when an inversion has taken place from the second stage: the male within a female has become "A Female Hidden in a Male."[35] We have already confronted one manifestation of this condition in discussing the aggressive phallic female who, assuming the role of a man, impregnates another female. We now confront the anomaly of the female-insinuated man. He is aroused by the female whose sexual attractiveness invades his whole being, dominating every nerve and limb; but he is without relief. The anomaly is that he has not only absorbed the female's seductive charms; he has also adopted the female ethic based on frigidity and, censoring himself, he becomes his own restrainer. He has been made effeminate, an old fear that Blake revives with new meanings. Man has, to use a Freudian term, "internalized" the principle of feminine chastity and denial. The female in the male serves (1) to arouse and (2) to frustrate him. Unfulfilled love and unrealized desire produce one of the most prevalent discontents of civilization. And man, drunk with his own swallowed passion, reels off to aggressive wars.

32. The Blake references in this paragraph are as follows: *J* 32: 43–47; *J* 44: 11, 34–40; *J* 65: 56–78. For a visual rendition of castrators and circumcisers, see *J* 69.

33. See *FZ* VIII: *363–364*; *J* 30: 25–35.

34. See *J* 47: 4–5; "Annotations to *An Apology for the Bible*," p. *601*.

35. See *FZ* IX: *375*; *M* 22: 48–49; *M* 37: 35–43; *M* 40: 20.

> I am drunk with unsatiated love
> I must rush again to War: for the Virgin has frownd & refusd
> Sometimes I curse & sometimes bless thy fascinating beauty.
>
> (*J* 68: 62–64)

We have said that only Christ could rend the iron veil of Vala. Only Christ can overcome the devastations of the "Female hid within a Male."

> But Jesus breaking thro' the Central Zones of Death & Hell
> Opens Eternity in Time & Space; triumphant in Mercy.
>
> (*J* 75: 21–22)

In studying Blake's concept of sexuality we confront a changing and paradoxical complex of attitudes that is a blend of personal joy and pain, prophetic rage and optimism, love of love and disgust with love.[36] That complex does, finally, organize itself into a pattern of Christian respect for the body that needs to be redeemed because it has been woefully perverted but that even in its fallen state, when sexual appetites are untrammeled and free, can provide an earnest of salvation.

So harrowing was fallen sexuality, but at the same time so full of delightful promise, that Blake always kept Babylon and Beulah in perilous balance. He could worry "Lest the sexual Generation swallow up Regeneration" and declare "Humanity knows not of Sex"; but he could also exclaim: "O holy Generation [*Image*] of regeneration."[37]

What is the place of the sexual body in Eden? Are there traces of the perilous balance even here? There seem to be; and these appear, if we try to follow Blake's hints about the hierarchical order of the four Zoas, as those eternal powers in man, none of which can be eliminated but all of which must submit to order, an order that may imply rank. Blake's ambivalent and changing responses to so powerful an instinct as the sexual seem to affect the position of Luvah. After the marvelous Titianesque bacchanal of the Last Vintage of the Nations, a purgative ritual act absolutely necessary to the restoration of the highly compromised human faculties, Luvah is spread by the sons of Tharmas and Urthona as dung on the ground. And in the majestic coda of Night IX ("The Sun has left his blackness & found a fresher morning"), there is a place for Tharmas and Urthona but none for Urizen and Luvah. The latter two had been active in harvesting the grain and in pressing the grapes; but the bread is made and the wine of the ages is refined by Urthona, assisted by Tharmas. It is as though the one-

36. For a discussion of the persistence of Blake's pre-occupation with sexual love and its shifting emphasis, see John Sutherland, "Blake: A Crisis of Love and Jealousy," *PMLA*, 87 (1972), 424–431.

37. See *J* 44: 33; *J* 90: 37; *J* 7: 65.

time tyrants of the mind and the passions must, in the restoration of order, return to their instrumental and subservient positions—reason below imagination, physical love below the sensibility of the heart. It may be possible to go beyond a subordination by pairs—Urizen and Luvah below Urthona and Tharmas—and say that Luvah stands below Urizen as undoubtedly Tharmas stands below Urthona, Blake reserving the highest role for the artistic and human imagination. Since *intellectual* war brings about the reign of sweet *science*, and since these are mental acts close to the imaginative, Luvah must take a place below Urizen. Albion turns Luvah and Vala over to Urizen with the command that as servants they are to "obey and live," forgetting the wars of sexual violence and returning to peaceful love. They are remanded into their own place, "the place of the seed not in the brain or heart." In *The Four Zoas*, then, the ranking of these mighty faculties would appear to be: Urthona, Tharmas, Urizen, and Luvah.[38]

But that order hardly persists in Blake's other apocalyptic climaxes, and sexuality is given greater emphasis. The assimilation of the virgin Ololon into Milton is sexually conceived in a kind of climax that *The Book of Thel* lacked. The "Clouds of Ololon" wrap around the Saviour's limbs as "a Garment dipped in blood"—that is, as Luvah's garments, the garments of physical passion. And in the climax of *Jerusalem* the bow of salvation is masculine and feminine, the arrows are the arrows of love, and the chariot in which the new fourfold man rides is the "Sexual Threefold."[39] The East, the realm of Luvah, has its rivers of bliss, the "Nerves of the Expansive Nostrils," nostrils perhaps being a polite substitute for enlarged sexual organs.[40]

Blake said of redeemed humanity that it "is far above / Sexual organization; & the Visions of the Night of Beulah." In apocalyptic vision Beulah is transcended, and the sexual torments of the Luvah-Orc-Vala Babylon are burned away. Institutional marriage and the ritual giving in marriage do not exist in the fourfold Eden. But the body, threefold sexuality, clearly does. It is now on the periphery where it is prominent but not predominant; it is no longer at the center where it does not belong. But the Zoas ride in their chariots, and Blake's final view is that the body must unashamedly be accepted and accorded its proper place in the intellectual and artistic life. "Art & Science cannot exist but by Naked Beauty display'd." Sexuality remains and the body is redeemed, assuming an important though subordinate place.[41]

38. See *FZ* IX: *390*; *FZ* IX: *391–392*; *FZ* IX: *380*.

39. "The chariot is actually the vehicular form of the driver himself, or his own body" (Frye, *Fearful Symmetry*, p. 273).

40. See *M* 42: 11–12; *J* 97: 9–12, 98: 11, 16–17.

41. See *J* 79: 73–74; *J* 32: 49.

The final view, from the perspective of the imaginative eternity, upon the raging torments of love and jealousy is instructive. We have seen that one ordering places Luvah below Urizen in their eternal stations. But the positions are reversed in a retrospective glance on their fallen condition. For the production of pure mischief, essential and causative distress, the palm must go to the intellectual tyrant Urizen, whom Albion addresses as follows:

My anger against thee is greater than against this Luvah
For war is energy Enslavd but thy religion
The first author of this war & the distracting of honest minds
Into confused perturbation & strife & honour & pride
Is a deceit so detestable that I will cast thee out
If thou repentest not . . .

(FZ IX: 375)

It is difficult not to believe that Blake shared Albion's view that it is better to burn sexually than to suffer, "in misery supreme" and all alone, the deprivations of ungratified desire. If so, Blake's latest position reveals the essential integrity of his position on sexual love. The message of Lambeth had not been lost but modified to meet new individual and social conditions.

Philosophically, religiously, and artistically, the reason for Blake's preservation of the sexual body in Eden can be explained by the work of Los and Christ, who in the last analysis must sanction and support what is to be preserved. Los beats the "terrific Passions & affections" into wedges and draws them into nerves. In the looms of Enitharmon the affections are endowed with "the ovarium & the integument." Both the man and the woman of art labor through adversity to create the sexual body with its "milky fibres" of semen. Why? Not merely because generation is the image of regeneration, although it is that. More basically, because the sexual act and the sexual emotions belong to our essential humanity. Because art makes humanity its subject, the presses of Los could not make the wine of eternity without the grapes of Luvah. Art—and the salvation that it ministers to—depends as much on the presence as on the control and purification of the passions.[42]

Christ comes clothed in Luvah's red robes. In Great Eternity—when the faculties were in ordered stability—Luvah had been the most Christ-like of the Zoas, "the gentlest mildest." Even in his sufferings on earth Luvah goes through a crucifixion, mocked as a king of Canaan, wearing a crown of iron thorns. Christ assumed the body of passion in the Incarnation, and when

---

42. See *FZ* VIII: *362*; *J* 86: 39. This last passage, Plate 86 of *Jerusalem*, establishes beyond doubt the sexual meanings of "fibres."

he forgave Mary he also forgave that "melancholy Magdalen," the fallen
Vala. Blake's belief seems to have been that Christ's nature was like ours
even in possessing the passions, that his manhood included the natures of
Luvah and Vala. When he put off his generated body (that is, the body he
acquired from his mother by natural, not supernatural, generation) by
dying on the cross, it was not to fly up to a shadow-land of pure spirit but to
reassume his position as fourfold man. The Eternal Man, who is Christ,
rides a sexual chariot and is wrapped in a threefold sexual texture—the
head, the heart, and the reins; the forehead, the bosom, and the loins. In
Babylon, as we have seen, "a pompous High Priest" enters religion and sex
"by a Secret Place," and sexuality is confined to the genitalia as religion
is centered in the high altar. In eternity the genitalia remain and are respected, but love is extended to the whole body: "Embraces are Cominglings: from the Head even to the Feet."[43]

Some modern women may have much to object to in Blake's latest thought
about the relations of the sexes. But it is hard to believe that *l'homme moyen
sensuel* would reject the hearty bread and full-bodied wine the late Blake
is offering him. Or his wife either, for that matter: "let men do their duty
& the women will be such wonders" (*Marg.*, p. 585).[44]

43. See *FZ* VIII: *358*; *J* 24: 53; *J* 65: 56–57, 66: 23–26; *J* 65: 38; *M* 4: 4–5; 5: 6–9;
J 69: 43–44.

44. Clearly Blake's concept of the spiritual body is relevant to this article. For a
discussion, see my "Kathleen Raine's Blake," *Modern Philology*, 68 (1970), 82.

The Figure of the Garment in The Four Zoas, Milton, *and* Jerusalem

MORTON D. PALEY

The garment is an image which acquires a particular importance in Blake's later works. It occurs in association with a constellation of related images, some of which have been discussed by Sloss and Wallis, by Bentley, and by the present author.[1] Yet this important symbol has never been discussed in detail in its own right. Sloss and Wallis's definition of it ("the consequences in life of a religious or philosophical point of view, of which Blake did or did not approve"[2]) is far too limited, and it does not even find entry into S. Foster Damon's invaluable *Blake Dictionary*.[3] An understanding of the figure of the garment is nevertheless indispensable to an understanding of the later Blake.

"Garment" is not used by Blake in a symbolically significant way before *The Four Zoas*. The *Concordance*[4] records no usages at all in the singular prior to this work, while usages in the plural are either literal or decorative:

1. D. J. Sloss and J. P. R. Wallis, *The Prophetic Writings of William Blake* (Oxford: Clarendon Press, 1926), II, passim; G. E. Bentley, Jr., *William Blake: Vala or The Four Zoas: A Facsimile of the Manuscript, A Transcript of the Poem, and A Study of Its Growth and Significance* (Oxford: Clarendon Press, 1963), pp. 171–175; Morton D. Paley, *Energy and the Imagination: A Study of the Development of Blake's Thought* (Oxford: Clarendon Press, 1970), pp. 89–170.

2. Sloss and Wallis, *Prophetic Writings*, II, 206.

3. *A Blake Dictionary: The Ideas and Symbols of William Blake* (Providence: Brown Univ. Press, 1965).

4. David V. Erdman et al., *A Concordance to the Writings of William Blake* (Ithaca: Cornell Univ. Press, 1967), I, 780–781.

"let our winds / Kiss thy perfumed garments . . ."; "Thy breath doth nour-
ish the innocent lamb, he smells thy milky garments. . . ."[5] It is clear that
such examples (there are nine in all before *The Four Zoas*) are fairly
casual in meaning, a literary, sometimes pseudo-biblical flavoring, while
from *The Four Zoas* on the word not only occurs more frequently (twenty-
four times) but also frequently takes on a special Blakean meaning. This
development is related to the larger theme of weaving in the later works.
Our concern is particularly with the garment as an ambiguous symbol of
the body in the three long poems, but we must begin by considering the
weaving theme, as for Blake a garment was first of all a woven object. This
makes possible its ambiguity: it is associated with human identity yet is not
in itself human.[6]

I

Blake had a good practical knowledge of weaving, and its processes and
techniques came to his mind easily. His father had been a hosier, as was
his brother James, in whose shop the Exhibition of 1809 was held. Furthermore, the advertisement which Blake executed for Moore & Co. {1} in 1797
or 1798[7] shows, in detail, three different types of loom at work. Thus, when
Blake employs the imagery of weaving, it usually has a literal referent as
well as a symbolic meaning, whether it involves something as simple as the
distaff held by Enitharmon on Plate 100 of *Jerusalem* {38} or as complex
as the textile mill of *Jerusalem* 15: 14–20:

I turn my eyes to the Schools & Universities of Europe
And there behold the Loom of Locke whose Woof rages dire
Washd by the Water-wheels of Newton. black the cloth
In heavy wreathes folds over every Nation; cruel Works
Of many Wheels I view, wheel without wheel, with cogs tyrannic
Moving by compulsion each other: not as those in Eden: which
Wheel within Wheel in freedom revolve in harmony & Peace.

We can say the same of "weaving" and its associated words as has already
been said of "garment": earlier usages are occasional and casual, later ones

5. The examples are from "To Spring" and *The Book of Thel*, pp. *400, 4*.
6. Some aspects of the weaving theme, especially the veil, are brilliantly discussed
by Paul Miner in his "Visions in the Darksom Air," in *William Blake: Essays for S.
Foster Damon*, ed. Alvin H. Rosenfeld (Providence: Brown Univ. Press, 1969), pp.
256–292.
7. See Geoffrey Keynes, *Engravings by William Blake: The Separate Plates* (Dublin: E. Walker, 1956), p. 15; for the date, see David V. Erdman, "The Suppressed and
Altered Passages in Blake's *Jerusalem*," *Studies in Bibliography*, 17 (1964), 36, n. 34.

more frequent and different in meaning. Although we are not merely concerned with word-counting, it does give some dramatic evidence. Prior to
The Four Zoas the *Concordance* records four instances of "weave," three of
"woven," four of "wove," and none of "weaving"—a total of eleven occurrences. From *The Four Zoas* on, the total for the four words is 119! With all
allowances for the larger volume of Blake's works after Lambeth, it is clear
that the weaving motif suddenly assumed major importance in his later
writings. There is an equally clear difference in the *mode* of meaning when
we consider, for example:

Once a dream did weave a shade,
O'er my Angel-guarded bed,
        ("A Dream," *SI, p. 16*)

and then

                    Lo Joseph is thine! to make
You One: to weave you both in the same mantle of skin.
                        (*J* 68: 1–2)

The transition in meaning seems to occur in a long passage which Blake
added to Night VIIA of *The Four Zoas*, a passage which is of the greatest
importance to any study of the evolution of Blake's later symbolism.

I I

As is well known, after Blake had written what he thought would be the
end of Night VIIA, he made a series of additions which resulted in more
than three additional pages of text. This was an attempt to push the poem
into the phase of redemptive action leading to the Last Judgment of Night
IX: first Los is united with his Spectre (VIIA: *353–354*); then Los and
Enitharmon begin the collaborative activity which is urged by the Spectre:

Urthonas Spectre terrified beheld the Spectres of the Dead
Each Male formd without a counterpart without a concentering vision
The Spectre of Urthona wept before Los Saying I am the cause
That this dire state commences I began the dreadful state
Of Separation & on my dark head the curse & punishment
Must fall unless a way be found to Ransom & Redeem

But I have thee my [*Counterpart Vegetating*] miraculous
These Spectres have no [*Counter*(parts)] therefore they ravin
Without the food of life Let us Create them Coun[terparts]
For without a Created body the Spectre is Eternal Death.
                        (VIIA: *355*)

In Los's affirmative reply to this speech, he says to Enitharmon: "Turn inwardly thine Eyes & there behold the Lamb of God / Clothed in Luvahs
robes of blood descending to redeem" (p. 355). "Luvahs robes of blood,"
emblematic of the Incarnation, are no doubt derived from the scarlet robe
which Jesus was forced to wear while he was mocked and beaten (Matt.
27: 28; in Mark 15: 17, "they clothed him with purple"). This taking-on
of the garment becomes a model for what the Spectres must do with the help
of Los and Enitharmon. Los feels "Stern desire / . . . to fabricate embodied
semblances in which the dead / May live before us in our palaces & in our
gardens of labour . . ." (p. 356). The "Created body" previously referred to
by the Spectre is seen as analogous to a work of art, to be given form and
substance by the artist, and both are aspects of incarnation:

And first he drew a line upon the walls of shining heaven
And Enitharmon tincturd it with beams of blushing love
It remaind permanent a lovely form inspird divinely human
Dividing into just proportions Los unwearied labourd
The immortal lines upon the heavens till with sighs of love
Sweet Enitharmon mild Entrancd breathd forth upon the wind
The spectrous dead Weeping the Spectres viewd the immortal works
Of Los Assimilating to those forms Embodied & Lovely
In youth & beauty in the arms of Enitharmon mild reposing.
                                                              (p. 356)

(Although we need not be over-literal about this, it is amusing to find
William Hayley reporting of Catherine Blake that "the good woman not
only does the work of the House, but she even makes the greatest part of her
Husbands dress, & assists him in his art . . . ."[8]) In a closely related passage
in Night VIII this activity is elaborated further:

From out the War of Urizen & Tharmas recieving them
Into his hands. Then Enitharmon erected Looms in Lubans Gate
And calld the Looms Cathedron in these Looms She wove the Spectres
Bodies of Vegetation Singing lulling Cadences to drive away
Despair from the poor wandering spectres and Los loved them
With a parental love for the Divine hand was upon him
And upon Enitharmon & the Divine Countenance shone
In Golgonooza Looking down the Daughters of Beulah saw
With joy the bright Light & in it a Human form
And knew he was the Saviour Even Jesus & they worshipped.
                                                              (p. 358)

What is accomplished by the introduction of this weaving symbolism? To
answer this question, we must glance back at Blake's works of the 1790s

8. G. E. Bentley, Jr., *Blake Records* (Oxford: Clarendon Press, 1969), p. 106.

and at the earlier parts of *Vala*. In *The Marriage of Heaven and Hell*, Blake had affirmed through the voice of the Devil that "Man has no Body distinct from his Soul" and that "Energy is the only life and is from the Body . . ." (4: *34*). Here and in *Visions of the Daughters of Albion*, Blake celebrates the joys of physical existence, and yet at the same time there is a sense of being trapped in the body, as expressed by Oothoon:

They told me that the night & day were all that I could see;
They told me that I had five senses to inclose me up.
And they inclos'd my infinite brain into a narrow circle.
And sunk my heart into the Abyss, a red round globe hot burning
Till all from life I was obliterated and erased.
Instead of morn arises a bright shadow, like an eye
In the eastern cloud: instead of night a sickly charnel house.
(VDA 2: 30–36)

It is not institutional repression that is being attacked here—it is of course attacked elsewhere in the poem—but the very nature of the senses in the world as we commonly experience it. Similarly, there is a pathetic force to Thel's famous question which cannot merely be put down to her own sexual fastidiousness: "Why a little curtain of flesh on the bed of our desire?" (*Thel* 6: 20). Even in these relatively early works, as Blake attempted to go through the senses to another realm of being, he was uneasy about the nature of the senses themselves. The Fairy in *Europe* (1794) says that "the cavern'd Man" fails to pass into the eternal world through the window of touch because "he will not" (iii: 1, 5); but the presence of this speech in only two of the twelve copies of *Europe* (see *p. 725*) may indicate some ambivalence on Blake's part about this. In the Lambeth books of 1795 the attitude toward bodily experience becomes equivocal indeed. We might say—while remembering that Blake was in no sense a systematic philosopher—that Blake was a monist who found his mythology entrapping him in a dualistic position. In these poems there is a terrible sense of anguish about the mere fact of physical existence.

7. In anguish dividing & dividing
For pity divides the soul
In pangs eternity on eternity
Life in cataracts pourd down his cliffs
The void shrunk the lymph into Nerves
Wand'ring wide on the bosom of night
And left a round globe of blood
Trembling upon the Void.
(U 13: 52–59)

There is still the implication of a world elsewhere, like the Gnostic Pleroma, inhabited by Eternals; but this does not help us much in the world of Generation, which is why the characteristic tone of Blake's heroines (Thel, Oothoon, Ahania) is one of lamentation. The Lambeth books create a myth of revolutionary energy which will redeem or regenerate the fallen human body; but when this myth loses its basis in socio-political reality,[9] Blake is left with only the "fallen" aspect of bodily life:

Since that dread day when Har and Heva fled.
Because their brethren & sisters liv'd in War & Lust;
And as they fled they shrunk
Into two narrow doleful forms:
Creeping in reptile flesh upon
The bosom of the ground:
And all the vast of Nature shrunk
Before their shrunken eyes.

Thus the terrible race of Los & Enitharmon gave
Laws & Religions to the sons of Har binding them more
And more to Earth: closing and restraining:
Till a Philosophy of Five Senses was complete
Urizen wept & gave it into the hands of Newton & Locke.
                              (*Song of Los*, 4: 5–17)

Yet Blake himself had not stopped believing in the possibilities of joyful experience in the natural world. "I feel that a Man may be happy in This World," we find him writing to Dr. John Trusler in 1799: ". . . to the Eyes of the Man of Imagination, Nature is Imagination itself."[10] The contradiction may, to some extent, reflect a certain ambivalence in Blake's own attitude, a chafing at the limits of sensory experience while at the same time wishing to experience Oothoon's moment of desire as fully as possible. Yet an emphasis on the negative aspect of bodily existence is made almost inevitable by Blake's choice of myth. Creation-by-emanation provides an excellent vehicle for a cosmogonic poem; but as the human body thereby becomes the result of a series of "falls," body must then be seen as a prison for "soul"—despite Blake's insistence elsewhere on the unity of the two. Blake finds a way out of this contradiction by introducing the figure of the garment.

9. See Paley, *Energy and the Imagination*, p. 90.
10. *The Letters of William Blake*, ed. Geoffrey Keynes (Cambridge, Mass.: Harvard Univ. Press, 1968), p. 30.

I I I

If we return to the passage already quoted from *The Four Zoas* (VIII: *358*), we can see what difference is made by the weaving of garments of flesh by looms in Lubans Gate, looms which are called Cathedron. We have already seen that Blake had a practical knowledge of the working of looms, and that the process of weaving takes on a new meaning and importance in *The Four Zoas*. To reinforce the latter point: even the word "loom," of which the *Concordance* lists sixty-eight occurrences, is not to be found in Blake's writings before *The Four Zoas*! Much can be—and has been—said about the sources of the image, for it is a common symbol in Platonic and Neoplatonic writing, as is the garment which it produces; but our concern is not with Blake's sources but rather with what he does with them.[11] Blake's imagination seizes on the recurrence of a symbol in diverse myths as a confirmation of the view that all existing mythologies are at the same time derived from the Holy Ghost and yet debased versions of an original myth which the visionary poet must re-establish.[12] It is therefore reassuring to Blake to find the loom in such disparate places as *The Cave of the Nymphs*, the Bible, and Norse mythology transmitted via Gray. But however Blake may draw upon traditional sources for his symbols, those symbols take on new meaning in the context of his own works. In this particular instance, Cathedron must have a degree of personal reference, for not only Blake's wife but also his mother and his sister were named Catherine. Luban is, as Damon says, "the vagina, the Gate of Golgonooza which opens into this world."[13] It also appears in Night V, where it is built by Los after he builds Golgonooza: "Tharmas laid the Foundations & Los finishd it in howling woe" (*p. 333*). It is only appropriate for the Zoa of the senses to lay the foundations of this gate, though the Zoa of imagination finishes it and, as we have seen, later sits in it (VIIA: *355*). Though built in pain, it provides a way for the Spectres to find their way back to paradise through the world of Generation.

To demonstrate further the difference the figure of the garment makes in the tenor of Blake's mythology, we may compare the passage from *The Four Zoas* (VIII: *358*) with one from *The Book of Urizen*. In Chapter VIII of *The Book of Urizen*, Urizen encounters his "eternal creations" as "Sons & daughters of sorrow on mountains / Weeping! wailing!" (23: 10–11). Uri-

11. On the sources of Blake's loom-symbolism, see Paul Miner, "William Blake: Two Notes on Sources," *Bulletin of the New York Public Library*, 52 (1958), 203–207; Kathleen Raine, *Blake and Tradition*, Bollingen Series 35: 11 (Princeton: Princeton Univ. Press, 1968), I, 86–92.

12. See *MHH* 12–13: *38*.

13. *Dictionary*, p. 253.

zen curses these children of his, who correspond to the four elements, and
then in his wanderings he creates the web which "is a Female in embrio"
(25: 18). This web of twisted cords is called "The Net of Religion" (25:
23); in Chapter IX it brings about the creation of the human body as we
know it, in a parody of Genesis:

1. Then the Inhabitants of those Cities:
Felt their Nerves change into Marrow
And hardening Bones began
In swift diseases and torments,
In throbbings & shootings & grindings
Thro' all the coasts; till weaken'd
The Senses inward rush'd shrinking,
Beneath the dark net of infection.

2. Till the shrunken eyes clouded over
Discernd not the woven hipocrisy
But the streaky slime in their heavens
Brought together by narrowing perceptions
Appeard transparent air; for their eyes
Grew small like the eyes of a man
And in reptile forms shrinking together
Of seven feet stature they remaind

3. Six days they, shrunk up from existence
And on the seventh day they rested
And they bless'd the seventh day, in sick hope:
And forgot their eternal life.

                                        (25: 23–42)

This places the human body very far indeed from any redemptive agency,
and it is hard to see how creatures so debased are to become regenerate
merely by the removal of priests and kings. Therefore we are not surprised
when in the sequel, *The Book of Ahania*, Fuzon's revolt against Urizen fails.
The web or net is superficially similar to the woven garment; but it carries
with it only negative implications, implications of entrapment. In introducing the figure of the garment, Blake makes it possible for us to view the
body as a buffer zone between the drives and appetites which constitute
man as mere spectre and Beulah, the potential earthly paradise within:

Enitharmon wove in tears singing Songs of Lamentation
And pitying comfort as she sighd forth on the wind the Spectres
Also the Vegetated bodies which Enitharmon wove
Opend within their hearts & in their loins & in their brain
To Beulah & the Dead in Ulro descended from the War
Of Urizen & Tharmas & from the Shadowy females clouds

And some were woven single & some two fold & some three fold
In Head or Heart or Reins according to the fittest order
Of most merciful pity & compassion to the Spectrous dead.

(VIII: 358)

In a striking parallel in *Sartor Resartus*, Carlyle says of man:

Round his mysterious ME, there lies, under all those wool-rags, a Garment of
Flesh (or of Senses), contextured in the Loom of Heaven; whereby he is revealed to his like, and dwells with them in UNION and DIVISION; and sees and
fashions for himself a Universe, with azure Starry Spaces, and long Thousands
of Years. Deep-hidden is he under that strange Garment; amid Sounds and
Colours and Forms, as it were, swathed-in, and inextricably overshrouded: yet
it is sky-woven, and worthy of a God.[14]

Yet the garment is in itself an ambiguous symbol. It can be put on or taken
off; or it can become confused with one's real self. "Clothes have made Men
of us; they are threatening to make Clothes-screens of us."[15] Or, to go back
to Blake's own terminology, there is always the danger of becoming a dunce
like Satan, who "dost not know the Garment from the Man,"[16] of mistaking
the Individual and his State. Potentially redemptive, the garment of flesh
can yet be imprisoning and destructive, and in his three long poems Blake
gives considerable attention to each possibility.

I V

Other "garment passages" in *The Four Zoas* are closely related to those already discussed. In Night I, Enion is the weaver. In a passage which Blake
added to his original text,

Wondring she saw her woof begin to animate. & not
As Garments woven subservient to her hands but having a will
Of its own perverse & wayward Enion lovd & wept,

(p. 299)

what she has woven is the Spectre of Tharmas. Tharmas having "sunk down
& flowd among her filmy Woof" (*p. 298*), Enion gives form to the fallen
form of bodily sensation.

. . . every nerve

She counted.   every vein & lacteal threading them among
Her woof of terror.

(p. 299 [not added])

14. Edited by Charles Frederick Harrold (New York: Odyssey Press, 1937), p. 65.
15. Ibid., p. 41.
16. *For the Sexes: The Gates of Paradise* (c. 1818?), p. 266.

The spectrous product of "her shining loom" begins by accusing her of sin and jealously dominating her, and goes on to participate in the psychic wars which occur during the "death" of Albion. The garment Enion wove him, "a form of gold" (*p. 299*) expresses something of his nature. Enion's involuntary weaving of the Spectre of Tharmas (the drawing *Theotormon woven* {2} conveys a similar meaning) may be counterposed with Enitharmon's merciful weaving of garments for the Spectres in Nights VIIB and VIII. Such juxtapositions are of great thematic importance in *Jerusalem*. Another negative instance of weaving is found in Night II, where "The Daughters of Albion girded around their garments of Needlework / Stripping Jerusalems curtains from mild demons of the hills / Across Europe & Asia to China & Japan ..." (*p. 310*). These garments are meant to conceal and deceive, to assist in the demonic imposture of the Daughters. As David V. Erdman illuminatingly explains this passage, it is a way of saying that "the British textile industry strips wool from sheep, binds children to factory labor, and leads imperial armies as far as China in search of markets";[17] and we are once more reminded that for Blake the garment has a very literal existence as well as a symbolic meaning.

We have already touched on the descent of the Lamb of God in Luvah's robes of blood. The opposite of this redemptive assumption of garments is Urizen's attempt to take on the attributes of the God of the Old Testament, described as covering Himself "with light as with a garment," as stretching out "the heavens like a curtain," as having "bound the waters in a garment" (Ps. 104: 2; Prov. 30: 4). "Am I not God said Urizen. Who is Equal to me / Do I not stretch the heavens abroad or fold them up like a garment" (III: *322*); "The ends of heaven like a Garment will I fold them round me" (VIIB: *392*). Urizen in his Selfhood wants to wear the world like a garment. He cannot of course understand a taking-on of garments by which Selfhood is abolished:

When Urizen saw the Lamb of God clothed in Luvahs robes
Perplexd & terrifd he Stood tho well he knew that Orc
Was Luvah But he now beheld a new Luvah. Or One
Who assumd Luvahs form & stood before him opposite.
                                                                (VIII: *358*)

The fraternity which the French Revolution promised but failed to achieve (Orc in this aspect) has been replaced by a vision of brotherhood brought by Jesus. The Shadowy Female, too, mistakes the meaning of what has happened, saying "I see the murderer of my Luvah clothd in Robes of blood" (VIII: *360*). But Luvah, the Zoa of the passions, has not been murdered; he

---

17. *Blake: Prophet Against Empire*, rev. ed. (Princeton: Princeton Univ. Press, 1969), p. 332.

has taken on a new manifestation. Blake's most succinct explanation of this occurs in an addition to Night II:[18]

For the Divine Lamb Even Jesus who is the Divine Vision
Permitted all lest Man should fall into Eternal Death
For when Luvah sunk down himself put on the robes of blood
Lest the state calld Luvah should cease. & the Divine Vision
Walked in robes of blood till he who slept should awake.

(p. 315)

The benevolent creation or assumption of the garment of flesh is, then, to be opposed to the creation of a false garment, as it is also opposed to the *un-* weaving of the merciful garment. In Night VIII all these possibilities are encountered together.

We behold with wonder Enitharmons Looms & Los's Forges
And the Spindles of Tirzah & Rahab and the Mills of Satan & Beelzeboul
In Golgonooza Los's anvils stand & his Furnaces rage
Ten thousand demons labour at the forges Creating Continually
The times & spaces of Mortal Life the Sun the Moon the Stars
In periods of Pulsative furor beating into wedges & bars
Then drawing into wires the terrific Passions & Affections
Of Spectrous dead.   Thence to the Looms of Cathedron conveyd
The Daughters of Enitharmon weave the ovarium & the integument
In soft silk drawn from their own bowels in lascivious delight
With songs of sweetest cadence to the turning spindle & reel
Lulling the weeping spectres of the dead.   Clothing their limbs
With gifts & gold of Eden.   Astonishd stupified with delight
The terrors put on their sweet clothing on the banks of Arnon
Whence they plunge into the river of space for a period till
The dread Sleep of Ulro is past.   But Satan Og & Sihon
Build Mills of resistless wheels to unwind the soft threads & reveal
Naked of their clothing the poor spectres before the accusing heavens
While Rahab & Tirzah far different mantles prepare webs of torture
Mantles of despair girdles of bitter compunction shoes of indolence
Veils of ignorance covering from head to feet with a cold web.

(p. 362)

Here we have a full spectrum of meanings for the garment figure. As "sweet clothing" it makes possible erotic fulfillment in our river of space; but an alternative wardrobe exists, one which may entrap us in the torments of unsatisfied desire. If the first alternative occurs, the garment may simply be

18. Of the ten references to this aspect of the Garment theme in *FZ*, nine are either in added passages or in the very late Night VIII. The single exception is in Night IV, where the Daughters of Beulah address the Saviour, saying "in mercy thou / Appearest clothd in Luvahs garments that we may behold thee / And live" (*pp. 330–331*).

taken off at the Last Judgment, as the Lamb of God "puts off the clothing of blood" (*p. 362*) which he had assumed. Ironically, it is Rahab herself who must unwittingly assist in this in order to bring about her elimination from the poem:

But when Rahab had cut off the Mantle of Luvah from
The Lamb of God it rolld apart, revealing to all in heaven
And all on Earth the Temple & the Synagogue of Satan & Mystery
Even Rahab in all her turpitude Rahab divided herself.
                                                          (VIII: *365*)

This cutting away of the mantle is no doubt an allusion to the division of Christ's seamless garment in John 19: 23–24:

Then the soldiers, when they had crucified Jesus, took his garments, and made four parts, to every soldier a part; and also his coat: now the coat was without seam, woven from the top throughout.
    They said therefore among themselves, Let us not rend it, but cast lots for it, whose it shall be: that the scripture might be fulfilled which saith, They parted my raiment among them, and for my vesture they did cast lots. These things therefore the soldiers did.

(Cf. Matt. 27: 35, Mark 15: 24) What is "fulfilled" is Psalm 22: 18: "They part my garments among them, and cast lots upon my vesture." This episode is, of course, the subject of one of Blake's greatest paintings, *The Soldiers Casting Lots For Christ's Garments*.[19] For Blake, the seamless garment symbolizes man's perfect body, which must be divided as a prelude to resurrection. It is, furthermore, possible to view the garment from two perspectives at once, as "fallen" and as resurrected.

Los said to Enitharmon Pitying I saw
Pitying the Lamb of God Descended thro Jerusalems gates
To put off Mystery time after time & as a Man
Is born on Earth so was he born of Fair Jerusalem
In mysterys woven mantle & in the Robes of Luvah

He stood in fair Jerusalem to awake up into Eden
The fallen Man but first to Give his vegetated body
To be cut off & separated that the Spiritual body may be Reveald.
                                                          (VIII: *363*)

In this simultaneous double perspective, the body-garment is perceived as constituting at one and the same time the entrapping and the redemptive aspects which have hitherto been seen as opposed alternatives. Furthermore,

---

19. See David Bindman, *William Blake: Catalogue of the Collection in the Fitzwilliam Museum, Cambridge* (Cambridge: Heffer, 1970), pp. 22–24, and fig. 10.

a new ambiguity is introduced. If the vegetated body is a garment which is finally to be "cut off," what is the spiritual body but another kind of garment?

V

In *The Four Zoas* the weaving theme is for the most part added to the poem's original structure, but in *Milton* it and its associated images are deeply embedded in both the text and the designs of the book. From almost the very beginning of the poem, weaving is of the greatest importance: "Three Classes are Created by the Hammer of Los, & Woven / By Enitharmons Looms" (2: 26–3: 1). On Plate 4, added to copies C and D, women are pictured with spindles and distaffs, creating the "Sexual texture" referred to in the text (l. 4). Enitharmon's "Looms vibrate with soft affections, weaving the Web of Life / Out from the ashes of the Dead . . ." (6: 28–29). This Web of Life, in contrast to Urizen's Net of Religion in *The Book of Urizen*, does not carry vicious connotations. There are both positive and negative possibilities. Rintrah and Palamabron fear that the Daughters of Los "in deceit . . . weave a new Religion from New Jealousy of Theotormon!" (22: 37–38), and Los in turn warns them against becoming vegetated, "for Cathedrons Looms weave only Death" (24: 35). However, Los's view is from the perspective of eternity, according to which our very lives in this world of Generation constitute Eternal Death. In our own world, weaving can be perceived much differently, as for example in the beautiful passage describing "the gorgeous clothed Flies," every one of which "the dance / Knows in its intricate mazes of delight artful to weave . . . ." These are among the Sons of Los, "Visions of Eternity," "But we see as it were only the hem of their garments . . ." (26: 2, 3–4, 10, 11).[20] From this perspective the looms of Cathedron are once more places of benevolent weaving. In the sub-basement of Blake's universe, Entuthon Benython, "Souls incessant wail" until "The Sons of Los clothe them" (26: 26, 30).

And the herbs & flowers & furniture & beds & chambers
Continually woven in the Looms of Enitharmons Daughters
In bright Cathedrons golden Dome with care & love & tears[.]
(26: 34–36)

20. The hem of the garment is important in Old Testament ritual observances (Exod. 28: 33; Num. 15: 38), while touching the hem of Christ's garment effects miraculous cures (Matt. 9: 20 and 14: 36). Writing to Anna Flaxman in September, 1800, Mrs. Blake says that she and her husband "love & remember with affection even the hem of your garment . . ." (*Letters of Blake*, p. 39).

Each perspective conveys a possible reality, and we frequently find the same images viewed from different perspectives in both *Milton* and *Jerusalem*. Perhaps most interesting of all are those passages in which, as in the example from Night VIII of *The Four Zoas*, the two perspectives converge. Blake usually reserves this device for moments of extraordinary importance, such as the magnificent passage at the end of Book I of *Milton*:

But Enitharmon and her Daughters take the pleasant charge.
To give them to their lovely heavens till the Great Judgment Day
Such is their lovely charge.   But Rahab & Tirzah pervert
Their mild influences, therefore the Seven Eyes of God walk round
The Three Heavens of Ulro, where Tirzah & her Sisters
Weave the black Woof of Death upon Entuthon Benython
In the Vale of Surrey where Horeb terminates in Rephaim
The stamping feet of Zelophehads Daughters are coverd with Human gore
Upon the treddles of the Loom: they sing to the winged shuttle:
The River rises above his banks to wash the Woof:
He takes it in his arms: he passes it in strength thro his current
The veil of human miseries is woven over the Ocean
From the Atlantic to the Great South Sea, the Erythrean.

Such is the World of Los the labour of six thousand years.
Thus Nature is a Vision of the Science of the Elohim.

                                                        (29: 51–65)

Here the full ambiguity of the weaving activity is expressed. It is in one sense a terrible betrayal of human identity, reducing it to, in Yeats's words, "a tattered coat upon a stick." (Strikingly, Blake refers to himself in old age as "only bones & sinews all strings & bobbins like a Weavers Loom."[21]) Yet it is equally a regenerative activity, making it possible for the redemptive activity of the Seven Eyes of God to operate in the world of time and space. Perhaps it is no coincidence that in the Book of Zechariah, where Blake found the Seven Eyes,[22] there is also a vision of the high priest Joshua "clothed with filthy garments," followed by a vision in which he is clothed with clean garments, showing that he will keep the ways of the Lord (Zech. 3: 3).

Milton's own garment is one of the most important images in the symbolism of the poem. The very first action he performs is "[taking] off the robe of the promise and ungird[ing] himself from the oath of God" (14: 13). This divesting himself of the garment is also the subject of the full-page illustration on Plate 16. It is a step preliminary to his descent to the

21. To John Linnell, 1 August 1826, ibid., p. 159.
22. Zech. 4: 10. See Northrop Frye, *Fearful Symmetry: A Study of William Blake* (Princeton: Princeton Univ. Press, 1947), p. 128.

lower world which we inhabit, for Milton does not need to be clothed with a merciful garment of flesh as do the wailing spectres: he has *chosen* to descend in order to redeem his own past self, that part of him which wrote in fetters, as well as the nations. In his great speech on Plate 41, he represents this redemptive function as a bringing of new garments. He comes

To cast off the rotten rags of Memory by Inspiration
To cast off Bacon, Locke & Newton from Albions covering
To take off his filthy garments, & clothe him with Imagination.
(ll. 4–6)

Once more, there is an alternative, negative possibility: "the Sexual Garments, the Abomination of Desolation / Hiding the Human Lineaments as with an Ark & Curtains / Which Jesus rent"[23] (41: 25–27). We may recall that in *For the Sexes* a similar garment image appears:

When weary Man enters his Cave
He meets his Saviour in the Grave
Some find a Female Garment there
And some a Male, woven with care
Lest the Sexual Garments sweet
Should grow a devouring Winding sheet.
(ll. 21–26)

Even the "Sexual Garments," then, may be qualified in their meaning according to context and perspective. Here they are seen in two possible aspects. As Damon glosses this passage, "In the cave, or grave, which is this body, the sexes are formed, that desires may be gratified, otherwise the stagnation of death would overcome us, and we should be doomed forever to the flesh."[24] This contrast of two possible meanings of the garment figure is the subject of almost an entire plate of *Milton*, added by Blake to copies C and D. Here the Shadowy Female threatens to put on a false garment, ironically modelled in part upon the instructions for making Aaron's "holy garment" in Exodus 28.

I will lament over Milton in the lamentations of the afflicted
My Garments shall be woven of sighs & heart broken lamentations
The misery of unhappy Families shall be drawn out into its border
Wrought with the needle with dire sufferings poverty pain & woe
Along the rocky Island & thence throughout the whole Earth
There shall be the sick Father & his starving Family! there
The Prisoner in the stone Dungeon & the Slave at the Mill

23. The nature and meaning of such imagery is the subject of an important article by Paul Miner, "William Blake's Divine Analogy," *Criticism*, 3 (1961), 46–61.

24. S. Foster Damon, *William Blake: His Philosophy and Symbols* (Boston: Houghton Mifflin, 1924), p. 85.

I will have Writings written all over it in Human Words
That every Infant that is born upon the Earth shall read
And get by rote as a hard task of a life of sixty years
I will have Kings inwoven upon it & Councellors & Mighty Men
The Famine shall clasp it together with buckles & Clasps
And the Pestilence shall be its fringe & the War its girdle
To divide into Rahab & Tirzah that Milton may come to our tents
For I will put on the Human Form & take the Image of God
Even Pity & Humanity but my Clothing shall be Cruelty
And I will put on Holiness as a breastplate & as a helmet
And all my ornaments shall be of the gold of broken hearts
And the precious stones of anxiety & care & desperation & death
And repentance for sin & sorrow & punishment & fear
To defend me from thy terrors O Orc! my only beloved!
                                        (18: 5–25)

The "Human Form"[25] she speaks of is an ironical inversion of Blake's
typical meaning, for it is a defense against human gratification, a mere
simulacrum. Therefore Orc pleads with her to assume what would normally
be a lower order of garment in Blake's terminology, the female form. "The
Sexual is Threefold: the Human is Fourfold" (*M* 4: 5), but the sexual
garment sweet is to be preferred to a false human form which is really
"clothing of cruelty." Therefore Orc says

Wherefore dost thou Create & Weave this Satan for a Covering[?]
When thou attemptest to put on the Human Form, my wrath
Burns to the top of heaven against thee in Jealousy & Fear.
Then I rend thee asunder, then I howl over thy clay & ashes
When wilt thou put on the Female Form as in times of old
With a Garment of Pity & Compassion like the Garment of God
His garments are long sufferings for the Children of Men
Jerusalem is his Garment & not thy Covering Cherub O lovely
Shadow of my delight who wanderest seeking for the prey.
                                        (18: 30–38)

This address of Orc's to the Shadowy Female is reminiscent of Isaiah's
words to Jerusalem:

Awake, awake; put on thy strength, O Zion; put on thy beautiful garments, O
Jerusalem, the holy city: for henceforth there shall no more come into thee
the uncircumcised and the unclean.

                                        (52: 1)

25. For a full discussion of the human form in Blake's works, see Anne K. Mellor,
Blake's Human Form Divine, forthcoming from the University of California Press in
1973.

The Shadowy Female's false garment is opposite to the true garments which Isaiah alludes to, just as her jewels are opposite in meaning to Isaiah's:

I will greatly rejoice in the LORD, my soul shall be joyful in my God; for he hath clothed me with the garments of salvation, he hath covered me with the robe of righteousness, as a bridegroom decketh himself with ornaments, and as a bride adorneth herself with her jewels.

(61: 10)

Orc calls upon the Shadowy Female to be Jerusalem, but she elects to be Vala.

Plate 18 presents, once more, alternative garments; but just as Book I of *Milton* concludes with the garment seen simultaneously from two perspectives, so does Book II. This time it is Jesus who appears in his apocalyptic manifestations, clothed in a bloody garment:

> with one accord the Starry Eight became
> One Man Jesus the Saviour. wonderful! round his limbs
> The Clouds of Ololon folded as a Garment dipped in blood
> Written within & without in woven letters: & the Writing
> Is the Divine Revelation in the Litteral expression:
> A Garment of War, I heard it namd the Woof of Six Thousand Years.
> (42: 10–15)

This garment not only comprehends both the "Divine Revelation" and the "Litteral expression"—it also unites them. Yet the literal expression always threatens to supersede the revelation behind it, to become "a devouring winding sheet" in the terms of *For the Sexes*. Therefore the redemptive activity of the Seven Eyes with their Shadowy Eighth successor is necessary in order to structure human history. History itself is the Garment of War. Probably this "Garment dipped in blood" is an allusion to Jacob's prophecy in Genesis 49: "he washed his garments in wine, and his clothes in the blood of the grapes . . . ." (The "he" refers to Judah but could easily be mistaken as referring to Shiloh in the preceding line, and Shiloh is traditionally taken as a type of Christ.) Seen from such a double perspective, the garment is neither "good" nor "bad" but *necessary*. Although it may be perverted to destructive purposes, it may also mediate between the forces of history and an otherwise helpless humanity.

VI

Much of what we have said about weaving in *Milton* could also be said of *Jerusalem*. Once more, two types of weaving may be significantly juxtaposed: "Why should Punishment Weave the Veil with Iron Wheels of War / When Forgiveness might it weave with Wings of Cherubim" (22: 34–35). Once more there is merciful weaving "in bright Cathedrons Dome / Weaving the Web of life for Jerusalem" (83: 72–73); and once more there is destructive weaving, as in Plate 37:

The Shuttles of death sing in the sky to Islington & Pancrass
Round Marybone to Tyburns River, weaving black melancholy as a net,
And despair as meshes closely wove over the west of London . . .
(ll. 7–9)

Among the products of this weaving we again find, in all its ambiguity, the garment.

As in *Milton*, the sexual garment in its positive sense can be related to the Divine Vision.

In Great Eternity, every particular Form gives forth or Emanates
Its own peculiar Light, & the Form is the Divine Vision
And the Light is his Garment. This is Jerusalem in every Man
A Tent & Tabernacle of Mutual Forgiveness Male & Female Clothings.
(54: 1–4)

In contrast, we have the fallen garment which Albion assumes when he begins to worship Vala:

O how I tremble!   how my members pour down milky fear!
A dewy garment covers me all over, all manhood is gone!
At thy word & at thy look death enrobes me about.
(30: 3–5)

All through the poem, looms and spinning wheels work away, and much depends on what they produce. On Plate 59 {34} the Daughters of Los are pictured weaving amid flames, creating, among other things, the innocent animals whose exteriors are their garments: "the wooly Lamb & the downy Fowl" (l. 48). On Plate 56, Los urges the Daughters of Albion in pre-Whitmanesque rhetoric, entreating them to engage in the kind of merciful weaving that Enitharmon did in Night VIIA of *The Four Zoas*:

Entune: Daughters of Albion, your hymning Chorus mildly!
Cord of affection thrilling extatic on the iron Reel:
To the golden Loom of Love! to the moth-labourd Woof
A Garment and Cradle weaving for the infantine Terror:
For fear; at entering the gate into our World of cruel
Lamentation: it flee back & hide in Non-Entitys dark wild.
(ll. 11–16)

At this point in the poem, however, the Daughters of Albion are incorrigible. On Plate 66 they strip off their own "garments of needle work" and "sit naked upon the Stone of trial" (ll. 17, 19). As two of the daughters are "Gonorill" and "Ragan," Blake may well have been thinking of the importance of garments and the lack of them in *King Lear.*

O! reason not the need; our basest beggars
Are in the poorest thing superfluous:
Allow not nature more than nature needs,
Man's life is cheap as beast's. Thou art a lady;
If only to go warm were gorgeous,
Why, nature needs not what thou gorgeous wear'st,
Which scarcely keeps thee warm.
                    (II. iv. 266–272) [26]

At this point in *Jerusalem* things are reverting to the state of nature that Lear envisions. The next step, corresponding to Goneril and Regan's revenge on Gloucester ("*Reg.* Hang him instantly. / *Gon.* Pluck out his eyes." [III. viii. 4–5]) is the Daughters' sacrifice of the victim: "They take off his vesture whole with their Knives of flint: / But they cut asunder his inner garments" (66: 26–27). Similarly on the next plate, "They strip off Josephs Coat & dip it in the blood of battle" (67: 23), and Gwendolyn later boasts "I have stripd off Josephs beautiful integument for my Beloved, / The Cruel-one of Albion: to clothe him in gems of my Zone" (81: 11–12).

Joseph is another traditional type of Christ, and his coat of many colors is a symbol for Blake of the phenomenal universe. In *Milton*, there is a slightly different version of the biblical story: "Joseph an infant; / Stolen from his nurses cradle wrapd in needle-work / Of emblematic texture was sold to the Amalekite" (24: 16–19). The *Jerusalem* reference is of course closer to Genesis, in which "they took Joseph's coat, and killed a kid of the goats, and dipped the coat in the blood" (37: 31). Dipping Joseph's coat in the blood of battle may be ironically counterposed to the descent of the Lamb in robes of blood, the one destructive, the other redemptive. Furthermore, if the Daughters were to succeed in making Joseph and Skofield one, "to weave you both in the same mantle of skin" (68: 2), both the potential redeemer and the would-be destroyer of humanity would become subject to the imprisoning aspect of the garment. This would fulfill the confusion of States which the "Princes of the Dead" desire in *Jerusalem* 55: 15–16, "To make One Family of Contraries: that Joseph may be sold / Into Egypt: for Negation; a Veil the Saviour born & dying rends." The fact that those who strip Joseph are women may well be, as Damon suggests,[27] a conflation of two parts of his story, for Potiphar's wife "caught him by his garment,

26. On another aspect of the importance of garments to the Shakespearean imagination, see Cleanth Brooks's essay on *Macbeth*, "The Naked Babe and the Cloak of Manliness," in *The Well Wrought Urn* (New York: Harcourt, Brace, 1947), pp. 22–49.
    27. *Dictionary*, p. 224.

saying, Lie with me: and he left the garment in her hand, and fled, and got him out" (Gen. 39: 12). This is the subject of the striking water color *Joseph and Potiphar's Wife*, in which the garment is held up prominently by Joseph's accuser as she points with her other hand at her innocent victim.[28]

If the garment is a mediator between humanity and forces "without" and "within"—let us say cosmic forces and biological drives—we would expect this figure to be dispensed with at the Last Judgment. Yet in *Jerusalem* Blake's attitude is more complex than this. "Man in the Resurrection changes his Sexual Garments at will" (61: 51), seemingly in direct contradiction to the injunction of Deuteronomy 22: 5: "The woman shall not wear that which pertaineth unto a man, neither shall a man put on a woman's garment: for all that do are abomination unto the Lord thy God." Consequently, in Blake's Eternity "Embraces are Cominglings: from the Head even to the Feet" (69: 43), and there need be no "pompous High Priest entering by a Secret Place" (1. 44). The exchange of sexual garments is a perpetual source of pleasure to the risen body. Albion's "wormy Garments" (94: 17) are not abolished but transformed, so that he can be described on the next plate very much like a second Orc—"into the Heavens he walked clothed in flames" (95: 7). The picture on Plate 95 {35} confirms this ambiguity. Is or is not the rising Albion wearing a garment? At first he appears to be naked, but a sort of diaphanous train seems to be trailing from the rear part of his body. Although one can make this out even in the black and white copies, it is very much heightened in the unique colored copy E. As Erdman observes, "Blake has changed the flames to a sort of triple tail or threefold fleshly garment extending downward as part of the young man's back."[29] Also on the ultimate plate of *Jerusalem* {38} we see Enitharmon with a spindle in her upraised left hand and a distaff in her right, weaving, as Damon says, "the dark garment of the flesh."[30] Once more the visual meaning is further emphasized in copy E, where Erdman points out "a thick thread, passing from the distaff to the woman's right hand . . . was created, on this copy, by the addition of a black wash (making a corridor of the light brown print, for the thread) and reddish orange streaks."[31] Presumably the weaving of garments is not going to stop in Eternity.

28. See *The Blake Collection of W. Graham Robertson*, ed. Kerrison Preston (London: Faber and Faber, 1952), p. 123, and pl. 41; also reproduced by Thomas Wright in *The Life of William Blake* (Olney: Thomas Wright, 1929), pl. 56.

29. "Suppressed and Altered Passages," p. 35.

30. *William Blake*, p. 475. Cf. Mary's distaff in the *Paradise Regained* illustration, *Mary's lamentation for Christ*; also the right-hand figure in Blake's last engraving, George Cumberland's calling-card.

31. "Suppressed and Altered Passages," p. 39.

In November, 1808, we find an anonymous reviewer complaining of *The Death of the Good Old Man* in Blair's *Grave*, "What is yet more absurd, is to see the spirit of the good man borne aloft between two angels and clothed in the *same habilements* as the body that lies on the pallet below! Mr. Blake should have recollected, that when the Prophet Elijah was taken up to heaven in a chariot of fire, his mantle 'fell from him.' "[32] Mr. Blake did not need the *Antijacobin Review* to tell him about the prophet Elijah; his use of the "same habilements" is deliberate. In *The Soul hovering over the Body reluctantly parting with Life*, the male corpse wears a shroud that obscures the lines of his body while the female soul wears a filmy high-waisted gown that would have been quite modish at a Regency ball; and in *The meeting of a Family in Heaven* all the figures are clothed in garments whose drapery reveals rather than conceals the contours of the human body. In *The Day of Judgment* some of the rising blessed are similarly clothed while others are naked, showing that in these *Grave* pictures, as in *Jerusalem*, Blake does not conceive of the risen body as either necessarily naked or necessarily clothed. The male figure in *The Reunion of the Soul and the Body* even wears a trailing skirtlike garment similar to that pictured in *Jerusalem* 95 {35}, while the descending female's gown unfurling behind her echoes this motif. What is particularly impressive about the three pictures just referred to is the erotic nature of the embraces, whether the figures are clothed as the husband and wife meeting in heaven or naked as the couple at the lower left in *The Day of Judgment*. One feels that these figures are well on their way to comminglings from head to foot. Nor is the ambiguity of the Blakean body-garment an invention of our twentieth-century consciousness. Coleridge, in commenting on the *Songs*, complained about "the ambiguity of the Drapery" in the title-page illustration. "Is it a garment," he asked, "or the body incised and scored out?"[33] The answer is of course either, or both, for close-fitting, filmy clothing suggestive of being the body itself was already characteristic of Blake's pictorial vocabulary by 1789. Sometime during the composition of *The Four Zoas* such imagery developed further and took on a more deliberate, almost technical meaning in Blake's symbolism, with results, as we have seen, of even greater importance to *Milton* and *Jerusalem*.

32. Bentley, *Blake Records*, p. 205.
33. To Charles Augustus Tulk, 12 (?) February 1818, in Bentley, *Blake Records*, p. 252. H. M. Margoliouth notes that in Blake's pictures "clothes are often transparent or nearly so, only the edges of them making it quite clear that the figure is clothed." —*William Blake* (London: Oxford Univ. Press, 1951), p. 39.

Visions in Vala:
A Consideration
of Some Pictures in the Manuscript

JOHN E. GRANT

One might have expected that the publication of G. E. Bentley, Jr.,'s monumental Clarendon edition of *Vala or The Four Zoas* in 1963 would stimulate a tradition of commentary on the drawings. In fact, however, with the partial exception of one design (p. 26 {8}), nothing like this has developed. Among the factors contributing to this silence seem to be the difficulties in grasping the ideas of these particular drawings and the general feeling that Blake's words are more important than his pictures. Blake studies have, until recently, been hampered by a lack of the scholarly interaction that leads to a progressive growth of understanding. Certainly the predecessors of Bentley did little enough to set an example for cooperative systematic study of the *Vala* drawings: Damon in the twenties seems to have paid no attention to Keynes's descriptions and comments on the drawings, and Wright seems to have been indifferent to both Keynes and Damon; Margoliouth in the fifties was hardly more responsive or detailed.[1] Seen in the light of this

For making various corrections and suggestions to draft versions of this essay, I wish to thank Jean H. Hagstrum, Judith Rhodes, and Michael J. Tolley. My particular thanks are due to David V. Erdman for reading my draft text with the manuscript open before him and for making many helpful suggestions. Naturally, I accept full responsibility for any errors of fact that remain. My research was greatly assisted by a fellowship in 1968–69 from the American Council of Learned Societies.

1. The works referred to are as follows: Geoffrey Keynes, *A Bibliography of William Blake* (New York: Grolier Club, 1921), pp. 32–42; S. Foster Damon, *William Blake: His Philosophy and Symbols* (Boston: Houghton Mifflin, 1924), pp. 398–402; Thomas Wright, *The Life of William Blake* (Olney: Thomas Wright, 1929), II, 137–140;

tradition, Bentley's comparative lack of attention to the drawings and to his predecessors' comments on them is quite understandable. Moreover, he was faced with textual problems of formidable complexity, and these tended to pre-empt his attention. But it is not captious to complain that his remarkable work of scholarship exhibits a faulty sense of proportion insofar as it implies that an accurate perception of the drawings is to be considered of less importance than speculations about the evolution of the text. The generally brief descriptions of the pictures in Bentley's edition do not even take notice of all that can be ascertained from a study of the reproductions in his edition, let alone the manuscript; at times they seem to represent a step backwards from valuable identifications established by Damon and Margoliouth. Altogether, such emphases and practices tended to depress rather than stimulate the interest that the publication of these extraordinary drawings ought to have generated.

Bentley's data-filled chapter on the drawings raises a number of interesting questions and makes some valid interpretational points; but there are a number of errors in the data, and some major premises of his argument are too confidently and uncritically employed, at times after having been introduced in a tentative way. An example of this is the assumption that the emphasis in Blake's pictorial art generally changed from illustration, in which pictures correspond to a text, to illumination, in which no such correspondence is evident. Something like this development has been claimed by other critics as well, but in fact it is not clear that the percentage of such correspondence is much less in the case of the late *Jerusalem* than the early *Marriage of Heaven and Hell*. Even if in general Blake's art actually progressed in the direction alleged, this would not provide a valid basis for making inferences applicable to any particular page in the *Vala* manu-

---

H. M. Margoliouth, *William Blake's Vala: Blake's Numbered Text* (Oxford: Clarendon Press, 1956), pp. 97 ff; G. E. Bentley, Jr., *William Blake: Vala or The Four Zoas: A Facsimile of the Manuscript, A Transcript of the Poem, and A Study of Its Growth and Significance* (Oxford: Clarendon Press, 1963), passim. It is most convenient to include references to these works simply by page number in the body of the text, but because the reader will need to have the Bentley edition at hand to make the most of my article and because Bentley's own comments are usually to be found following the letterpress transcriptions, I shall eliminate page references in citing the Bentley edition. References to Blake's great series of 537 watercolor designs for Young's *Night Thoughts*, which have still not been reproduced, will be as follows: *Night Thoughts*, 11 (I, 6) means the eleventh picture in the entire series, otherwise the drawing on letterpress numbered page 6 of Night I. One further item in the literature on the *Vala* designs must here be noted: John Beer, "Appendix Three, 'Vala or The Four Zoas': Text and Illustrations," *Blake's Visionary Universe* (Manchester: Univ. of Manchester Press, and New York: Barnes and Noble, 1969), pp. 343–352, which I find practically worthless in detail; I invite the curious to compare what Beer has said with what I say in this essay.

script. In the first place, at any point in his career Blake was capable of aligning text and pictures on either nearby or considerably separated pages. Moreover, the fact that a picture in *Vala* has been altered tells nothing of when the alteration was done. Blake might in the space of a day or two have tried out several versions of a picture; thus the amount of ascertainable connection between any text—any *surviving* text, we must constantly recall, in this much-altered manuscript—and any version of the picture is much more likely to have an intellectual or aesthetic cause than to be the result of a Blakean stylistic or organizational predilection. Often it is possible to speak meaningfully about "early" and "late" alterations of the text, but no principle is in sight for comparable assertions about the pictures. Blake's initial conceptions of some pictures may possibly be dated subsequent to the publication of pictures by other artists from which they seem to derive, but this is another question.

In order to do completely reliable work on the *Vala* pictures one should have, in addition to the Bentley edition, a thorough verbal description of every picture, together with sketches of details rendered invisible in the Clarendon reproductions. He should also have infra-red photographs of every drawing, since these often reveal delineations otherwise invisible in the manuscript, at least under ordinary illumination. And ideally he should be able to consult the manuscript as frequently as necessary. I have had to work under less than optimum conditions. As a result of two lengthy periods of study of the manuscript I have some two hundred typewritten pages of verbal and sketch notes, but I did not have infra-red photographs of the pages reproduced for this essay until my text was almost completed. Such errors as may have crept in, however, should not in general be of the kind that will invalidate the interpretations I propose. I have tried to indicate wherever the data are problematic and the interpretations tentative or even speculative. At times I may incautiously drop the conditional and lapse into the assertive: instead of saying, "If this be so, then this meaning may follow," I may say "Since this is represented so, the meaning is so." But this last "is" may be hypothetical: "If everything is as it now appears, we can interpret the meaning of the picture as follows." Nevertheless, while the reader is to be cautioned against expecting either descriptions or interpretations to be conclusive, he should also not exaggerate the extent to which most of what Blake left us is problematic. Frequently one has to confront at most several possibilities, not an indefinite number. In discussing the pictorial aspect of a number of pages, I shall sometimes merely indicate the options that seem to have prompted Blake to treat his material first one way and then another. In so doing, I shall try to promote the ongoing study of this remarkable work. Thus I shall aim to set forth my observations in such a manner as to invite correction or refinement by other scholars following me; particularly I shall hope that the descriptive bases for all assertions will be made sufficiently clear.

Designs on the following pages of the manuscript will be considered in some detail: 2, 13, 19, 22, 25, 26, 43–76, 35, 37–42, 117–140. A number of other pages are also mentioned as they relate to the designs chiefly in question. No single theory dictates that exactly these be the pictures discussed. My basic reason for singling them out is that I believe I have something new to say about them, either descriptively or interpretationally. The sequence of pages 37–76 covers the pages of Nights III–VI; they constitute what should be a meaningful and manageable unit containing examples of most of the kinds of problems one encounters in dealing with the designs in this extraordinary manuscript. These pages fall into two distinct sections, pages 37–42, which are the last written in copperplate hand, and pages 43–76, which are the first on *Night Thoughts* proof pages and the first consecutive pages written in the ordinary manuscript hand. The existence of two Nights VII seems to make page 76 a convenient terminus. The designs on pages 38–42 also constitute the most excessively erotic sequence of pictures in Blake; in spite of extensive erasure, most of what he depicted is still ascertainable. In an aside to an earlier article I commented briefly on the place of erotic considerations in an adequate view of Blake.[2] Here I shall merely add the opinion that a would-be visionary who is not a sexologist can never be a seer. Perhaps it is not inconsistent with this principle, however, to ask that the reader earn his delectation of the earlier designs in Night III by laboring with a prior consideration of the somewhat dryer subsequent designs on pages 43–76. The last section of this essay is a study of the concluding designs, those for Night IX, to this manuscript which was never finished. Most of the drawings contain important details that have not previously been noticed in published commentary. In this section, as often elsewhere, when one sees what the drawings are about he is able to recognize that the selection of the *Night Thoughts* engravings was probably deliberate rather than accidental. The evidence here indicates that, though Blake may not have found time to complete his manuscript, he was working effectively to end his illuminated epic.

Some Key Pictures

Among the chief challenges for the scholar who wishes to say something useful about the *Vala* manuscript is to avoid making assumptions which

2. See "Two Flowers in the Garden of Experience," in *William Blake: Essays for S. Foster Damon*, ed. Alvin H. Rosenfeld (Providence: Brown Univ. Press, 1969), esp. p. 488, n. 35. In this article, on p. 360 and pp. 488–489, n. 36, there is also a discussion of *Vala*, p. 124.

prompt conclusions that may not correspond to Blake's purposes either initially, medially, or when he abandoned work on it. One of the commonest assumptions, for example, is that Blake was preparing a manuscript that would be eventually turned into an "illuminated book," that is, be made into a replicative engraved work to be published, like *Europe* or *Jerusalem*. But as Erdman has argued, there is not sufficient reason to make this assumption. The evidence is that Blake seldom bothered to make a refined intermediate copy of his texts before committing them to copper. Though the corrections made in the text written in copperplate hand, together with the less formal scripts and the proof pages employed later in the manuscript, indicate that Blake abandoned hope of employing the surviving pages for the purpose, it is evident that he must have intended at some point to produce a unique copy of an illuminated manuscript not designed for replication.[3] Other scholars have entertained such a thought when considering the problem of the licentious drawings, which are so much more uninhibited than most of Blake's published work, but before Erdman they had not clearly recognized that, perhaps at every stage, the most Blake may have intended was to produce a single unique copy of a work which would draw together the strands of myth and iconography utilized in his other work.

If indeed the work was to be a synthesis or consolidation of these elements, one would expect to find a number of recollections of Blake's earlier work as well as anticipations of his later work. That this is in fact the case has been often observed, particularly with respect to episodes described in the text, though, as Erdman has shown, it is very tempting to make unprovable assertions about which writing preceded which. Repetitions of pictorial motifs, or at least distinctly ascertainable variations on earlier motifs, are always noteworthy. For example, as Bentley points out (p. 182), the drawing on page 60 of two figures embracing near a third who is bound around the chest recalls *Urizen* 21, while the drawing on page 74 of a bearded man carrying a large round object closely resembles *Urizen* 23. It is also clear that the situation on page 62, a man and woman lamenting over a youth who is bound down, is much like the one depicted in *America* 1 and elsewhere.

Other close connections of this sort might be noted, in addition to those mentioned by Bentley. For example, the quite sketchy drawing on page 2, inscribed "Rest before Labour," which serves as a kind of frontispiece to the whole work, depicts a nude man rising with his left arm raised and bent back, his face directed upward, his legs drawn up considerably, carrying a long object with about six oval loops in it held backhand in his right hand,

---

3. See David V. Erdman, "The Binding (Et Cetera) of *Vala*," *The Library*, 49 (1964—delayed; London: 1968), pp. 112–129, esp. p. 125.

which hangs at his side.[4] This is certainly related to the small but significant
male figure at the upper left in *America* 3, the first page of the prophecy
proper, who rises with a different curve of the hips but who is otherwise very
similar, having, it is notable, his left arm in almost the same position. But
this figure dangles chains on both sides; undoubtedly they are tethers he
has broken in order to rise, whereas the man in *Vala* deliberately holds what
was possibly at first the draft of a walking-stick, subsequently modified into
six or more links of chain. And there are several light rays that spread out,
evidently from behind his back, probably from the burden in his left hand
(which is otherwise invisible); there is no sign of such a burden in the
America page, but perhaps we are to understand that the man in the frontispiece to *Vala* is carrying a sun. This possibility seems more certain when we
recognize that he is similar to the man depicted at the left, seen from behind,
in the last plate of *Jerusalem*, who carries the sun, as Erdman has suggested, like a hod—for building {38}. This figure, usually identified as the
finally civilized Spectre of Los, may be rising; but he seems also to be
walking. And if we study the drawing on *Vala*, page 2, we see that that man's
legs were originally extended with his (conventionally delineated) right

4. Bentley, *Blake: Vala*, p. 2, evidently considers it more probable that the man is
"lying on his back"—though he is aware of the alternative that the man may be soaring
upward. In his casual and intermittent notes on some twenty of the *Vala* drawings,
W. H. Stevenson, in *The Poems of William Blake*, with a text by David V. Erdman
(London: Longmans, 1971), p. 292, declares flatly that the drawing in question is of
"a reclining male figure." Conceivably, this figure could be reclining, but either his
head or his feet, or both, would have to hang over the edges of the undelineated couch.
As is the case with drawings by artists such as Egon Schiele and Picasso, Blake's drawing can sometimes be effectively seen from several orientations. In this case, however,
both the inscription and the binding indicate that a vertical orientation is the proper
one; no major designs in the *Vala* manuscript are to be viewed with ninety-degree
reorientation, as is the case with the full-page designs in *Jerusalem*, pls. 27, 51, and
100. Perhaps the tendency of both Blake editors to be absorbed with Blake's words
led them to think that this frontispiece *illustrated* the aphorism, whereas what one *sees*
is that the man is rising, no doubt to or in his "labour," after his "rest." Incidentally,
I also question Bentley's suggestion that the man's right foot "may be a cloven hoof."
The great toe, to be sure, is unnaturally separated from the rest of the foot, and the
other toes on the right foot are not delineated, as they are on the left foot, which is
drawn in Blake's usual manner. But though Blake sometimes drew sinister males with
a cloven hoof, his delineations of hoofs are quite different from the deeply cleft final
version. The anomalous foot (and the curious musculature of the lower leg) in this
drawing is not easy to explain, but it is perhaps to be understood as crippled, the mark
of a kinship between Los and Hephaestus. Alternatively, Blake may have wished to
connect this peculiar foot with the remarkable symbolism of the sandals in *Milton*.
    Accuracy requires some further notes on this drawing, which may have a bearing on
interpretation. The *America* 3 prototype figure itself had a prototype in the canceled
plate a (the canceled plate and *A* 3 from copy K are reproduced as illustrations 28 and
29 in *Blake's Visionary Forms Dramatic*, ed. David V. Erdman and John E. Grant

foot in the area of the "L" in "Labour" and his left to the right of the
word, rather than being drawn up. Without further redrawing, this man
would not have been able to hike, but his feet were delineated in what was
much more like a walking position; the evident draft of a walking-stick in
his right hand suggests that he was, at some point, conceived as an avatar
of Blake's pilgrim, a figure one would expect to find at the outset of a major
work. It should be considered as well that this nude figure of the pilgrim as
escapee and/or explorer tends to modulate into the nudes who, seen from
behind, leap off in *Vala*, pages 3 (above) and 139. I shall have more to say
about them at the conclusion of this essay.

An interpretational principle to be emphasized with reference to the drawing on *Vala*, page 2, one that also applies more or less to the analogies to
the drawings cited by Bentley on pages 60, 74, and 62, is that none of Blake's
drawings in *Vala* exactly repeats a design used elsewhere. For this reason
the scholar should not be unduly impressed by resemblances to other designs,
however striking. Neither, of course, should he be indifferent to them; they
are signs that he may be on the track of understanding the symbolic meaning of one or more of Blake's repeated images as it operates in a particular
context. I believe that *America* 3 and *Jerusalem* 100 are crucially important
to an understanding of *Vala*, page 2. But many other correlations, as well as
much restraint, may be necessary before a scholar can be confident that he
has worked out the meaning. Indeed, it is possible to doubt, considering that

---

[Princeton: Princeton Univ. Press, 1970]) ; the chief difference in the figures is that
in the former the man has his *right* arm raised and bent back and his left arm lowered
to his side, whereas in the final version it is the *left* arm that is raised and bent back
while his right arm hangs at his side. But Blake also added a loop that hangs in a
catenary from the left elbow down and up to the left armpit. In copy M, the Blake
Trust facsimile, the links of this chain are clearly distinguished, but the color within
the catenary is not the circumambient blue of the sky; rather, it is a pale grey, as
though to strengthen the suggestion that the man might be carrying something. There
is no doubt that this man's eyes are open.

In *Vala* it is not ascertainable whether the man's eyes are open or closed, an encouragement to those who wish to make much of "Rest" in the inscription, and his left arm
has been redrawn at least once in the present position, finally with distinct evidence of
a manacle on the wrist, but with no certain evidence either of a burden or of, on his
left side, a dangling chain. The six or more straight lines that radiate to his left,
which I take to be light-ray lines projected from a luminary burden, may simply have
been drafts of a variously outspread left arm. Other lines at one and five o'clock, however, seem only intelligible as light-ray lines. There are also three vague oval loops that
descend from his left armpit; these resemble the chain links that descend on his right
side, but the loops on the left blend into a much larger one at his hip, and this is connected to smaller ones near his haunch in such a way as to suggest clouds, certainly
not chains alone. The prototypes of this man in *America* are above the clouds, but
Vala is a bigger story, and this pilgrim of eternity has farther to go before he can
transform his chains for a stick and achieve liberation: *hic labor est.*

the drawing is not highly finished, whether Blake himself had arrived at a decisive meaning. Still, excessive skepticism should also be guarded against. Such cautions are highly necessary when one addresses himself to the question whether a particular picture can be said to "illustrate" a passage in a work. Most discussions of Blake's text and pictures have been content to seize on some major point of correspondence without even bothering to mention elements in either text or picture that do not correspond. Erdman's excellent article on the designs for *America* sets a new standard in the interpretation of Blake's designs because he does take notice of such discrepancies and is usually able to explain the rationale for them.[5]

What one finds in Blake's iconography, then, is a series of metamorphic variations on a large repertoire of key images, comparable to, but less standardized than, the flexions of words in an inflected language. Because he had not grasped this principle, Bentley was unable to recognize many of the connections the *Vala* designs have with other designs in Blake's work, and thus he tends to exaggerate their peculiarity. He spends considerable time denying that, with one exception, there is any connection between the *Vala* drawings and the *Night Thoughts* water colors, in spite of the fact that *Vala* was written on *Night Thoughts* paper and proof pages. But, as I pointed out in my review article of the Bentley edition,[6] the drawing on *Vala*, page 13 {5}, is rendered more intelligible when seen in the light of *Night Thoughts*, 179 (V, 24). Concerning the main figure in the *Vala* drawing, Bentley has only this to say: "a head with closed eyes which is resting on its right ear. A left arm extended beside the head ends in serpentine coils." What Blake drew is a man's close-cropped head bent forward, evidently resting on the left side of his chest, with closed eyes and puffed cheeks; the left arm, probably bare, bends around, and the hand seems to rest on the central loop of a huge triple-looped horn, the mouthpiece of which is just below the right eye, with the loosely drawn bell in the lower left corner. Evidently this picture has some connection with lines 13: 22–23 and 14: 3, especially: "Elemental Gods their thundrous Organs blew; Creating / Delicious Viands. Demons of Waves their watry Eccho's woke! / . . . With doubling Voices & [loud] Horns wound round sounding. . . ." The illustrative noncorrespondence between the exuberance described in the text and the lassitude shown in the picture is part of Blake's meaning, but before the viewer tries to account for this he must first recognize that what appear to be "serpentine coils" are actually part of a horn. In the related design for *Night Thoughts* there is a large horn much like this one, being blown by a bearded whirlwind god

5. See David V. Erdman, "*America*: New Expanses," in *Blake's Visionary Forms Dramatic*, ed. Erdman and Grant, pp. 92–114.

6. See "Blake: Original and New," *Modern Language Quarterly*, 25 (1964), 356–364, esp. p. 363.

who is diving at the sea. Even more striking is the resemblance of design 8 for Gray's "The Bard," which was also executed on the same batch of paper as the *Night Thoughts* and *Vala*. There a huge whirlwind god with six feathery wings, long curly-snaky hair, and a short curly beard is shown sleeping on his back on the sea, with his crossed arms slipped through the double loops of the same kind of horn with an asymmetrical bell as in the other two designs. Curiously, Irene Tayler in her fine commentary[7] overlooks the connections that Blake surely hoped some of his viewers would make between this design and the other two.

Other kinds of problems occur when the viewer tries to discern what is going on in pictures that are less finished and/or are erased and/or seem to have fewer distinct analogies, particularly because of their frankly erotic nature. Bentley's description of the pictures on *Vala*, page 19 {4}, is, for example, almost totally erroneous, and the correction in my review[8] considered only some of the main facts. Bentley says, "*Under* the writing (apparently) is a large vague pencil sketch, which seems to represent flowing hair. A large chin and open mouth are also decipherable. Evidently they were drawn when the page was larger, for they disappear off the right margin. At the foot of the present page, just below the writing, is sketched a small figure on its back, its arms extended; perhaps it is a babe in swaddling clothes. In the right corner a naked woman seems to be sitting with her hands in her lap. . . . Probably this page should follow page 22," presumably textually. Concerning *Vala*, page 22 {6}, Bentley adds: "*Under* the writing (apparently) and covering the whole page are many wavy pencil lines which may represent long hair. A chin and wide mouth are decipherable, but nothing else. The right margin is empty but the lines disappear off the left side of the page. If page 19 is placed beside the top left half of page 22, many of the vague lines seem to meet, though no coherent picture yet emerges. Probably a strip perhaps half an inch wide, is missing from between the pages."

To consider the picture under the writing on *Vala*, pages 19 {4} and 22 {6}, first, if one aligns the tops of the two pages and then rotates the pages 90 degrees so that half-page 19 is above, the original sheet is effectively reunified and a perfectly clear picture emerges. It is the full-face of a man

7. *Blake's Illustrations to the Poems of Gray* (Princeton: Princeton Univ. Press, 1971), p. 100; hereafter referred to as *Blake's Gray*. The blowing of serpent horns is not, of course, an unusual motif in Blake's work, occurring, for example, once in the fifth design for Gray's "Ode on the Spring," twice on p. 51 of Blake's *Notebook*, and twice on the last page of the *Job* designs. Whether anything should be made of the minor variations among these several horns need not be considered here. Perhaps Blake himself would have thought it more remarkable that some musicians are hirsute while others are skin-heads.

8. "Blake: Original and New," pp. 363–364.

with long hair, distinct left eye to the right of lines 8–14, nose with oddly enlarged nostrils just above the left shoulder of the woman, and erased right eye in the area of the rock to the viewer's left of the woman (according to the textual orientation) on page 19. On page 22 the mouth, with corners drooping and lips parted, is to the left of lines 13–22 (according to the textual orientation) and the beard falls quite naturally through the text. One at first supposes that this head has no necessary connection with the *Vala* text, but the considerable resemblance of this head to that of the image ostensibly of Urizen on the facing *Vala*, page 23, forbids our being categorical about it. Blake was undoubtedly working in various ways with many pieces of paper that have now been lost as he attempted to perfect *Vala*, and we can now know little about some of the expedients he employed. It is also worth noting that the head in *Vala*, pages 19 and 22, bears a close resemblance to the fine patriarchal portrait called by Keynes *Head of Job*.[9] Keynes insists that this portrait is a drawing of c. 1823 made in connection with the Job series, but the similarities between the two may imply a different occasion.

When we consider the drawing at the bottom of the textually oriented page 19 {4}, we discern a scene more amusing than that suggested by a recumbent babe and a sitting woman. Briefly, what is represented is a winged cupid astraddle a large triangular-shaped object; he has just discharged his bow, which is clearly visible in his left hand. Between him and the woman is a large, irregularly shaped hillock or rock. The woman, who is standing to the right of this hillock, with her weight on her left leg and with her right leg raised, is bent to her right, and with her right hand is holding her crotch; she has been hit there by a crudely drawn arrow with feathers, distinctly visible in spite of some erasure. Her left forearm has been more thoroughly erased. What no doubt especially prompted the erasure is that the woman when hit was apparently urinating into a large, tilted tapered-neck jug. The left side of this jug, some 2.4 cm. high, can be ascertained in the reproduction and it is somewhat clearer, despite erasure, in the original manuscript. Thus interrupted, the woman has an understandable look of consternation on her pretty face. How may these figures be identified? The boy must be Cupid himself, here depicted in a variation of the action depicted on *Vala*, page 4, where he kneels with drawn bow on the back of a conical-headed (in one version) Leviathan. Possibly the viewer is supposed to connect the wavy, rather serpentine curve of the right-side

9. Reproduced in *Drawings of William Blake: 92 Pencil Sketches*, ed. Geoffrey Keynes (New York: Dover, 1970) no. 74; hereafter referred to as *Drawings 1970*. See also *The Blake-Varley Sketchbook of 1819*, ed. Martin Butlin (London: Heinemann, 1969), p. 92, for a similar drawing, and Butlin's note, p. 27, concerning another similar drawing in the Vanderhoef Collection.

locks of hair of the underlying drawn head with the partially erased barbed
arrowhead between Cupid's legs and imagine an enormous phallic snake-
mount on page 19 as well. In any case, the fact that Cupid is astraddle an
arrowhead is a noteworthy aspect of Blake's pictorial justice. The usual
representation of Cupid is with infantine genitals, if any at all. But his real
identity is more intelligible as a prongsman. This figure and his mount foreshadow a number of others in the series; Cupid is conceptually related to
the figure on page 25 {7}, as we shall see, but the symbolic connections
occur later in the manuscript; on page 108 a wingless boy sits on the buttocks
of a howling woman while restringing his bow. On page 134 a wingless nude
figure with outstretched arms rides on the back of a walking bird that has
a human head on its long neck and a long looped serpentine tail. On page
136 {22} an extraordinary youthful male head with moustaches and four
hairy wings carries on its top a distinct, though sketchily drawn, human
figure who gesticulates downward with his left hand. This symbolism recalls Blake's awesome picture of *Ezekiel's Vision* of the four Zoas.[10]

The identity of the woman is no less certain because she has adopted the
classical Venus Pudica position, though with more visible cause than usual.
Cupid and Venus are shown working together in *The Judgment of Paris*, a
major design I have elsewhere discussed in some detail,[11] where Cupid de-

10. Reproduced in *William Blake: Water-Color Drawings*, ed. Peter A. Wick
(Boston: Museum of Fine Arts, 1957), unpaged. See my article "The Vision of Ezekiel,"
Blake Studies 4 (1972), 153–157. The symbolism of a human-headed walking bird with
a rider in *Vala*, p. 134, is sufficiently bizarre to invite a search for sources. I believe that
I have discovered one in Gillray's caricatures, which, as Erdman has shown, Blake had
elsewhere used for their symbolism. Between 6 November 1806 and 20 May 1807, dates
suggestive for the growth of the *Vala* manuscript, Gillray published five pictures fea-
turing a goose, four times with a small human head, twice with a human rider, four
times walking (never flying), though never with a serpentine tail. Particularly in his
Triumphal Procession of Little Paul the Taylor upon his new-Goose, pl. 325, in *The
Works of James Gillray* (1851; rpt. New York: B. Bloom, 1968), the goose and rider
are seen in profile, much as in the *Vala* design, except that Gillray's rider is clothed
and his arms are not outspread. However, in pl. 330, entitled *A Plumper for Paul!—or—
The Little Taylor done over!*—which is a kind of sequel to the other design—the rider
has been thrown from the goose, but his right arm particularly is outspread. The allegory of these designs is explained by Thomas Wright and R. H. Evans in *Historical
and Descriptive Account of the Caricatures of James Gillray* (1851; rpt. New York:
B. Bloom, 1968), pp. 281 ff. Whether Blake is likely to have cared enough for the con-
troversies of "Broad Bottom" politics to have been making a point contra Gillray, I
leave it for others to decide. It seems unlikely that this was his primary concern in
the *Vala* manuscript. The fact that the rider in *Vala*, p. 134, carries a goblet in his
right hand connects him with Blake's several depictions of the Whore of Babylon who
rides the human-headed Beast, which is sometimes serpent-tailed. Since this fearsome
pair return in all ages of history, not least in 1798, the very distinction between topi-
cality and vision must be applied with care.

11. See "You Can't Write About Blake's Pictures Like That," *Blake Studies*, 1

parts in triumph, brandishing his weapon, while Paris hands over the apple to Venus, who has face and hair similar to those of the woman in *Vala*, page 19, and whose body is similarly, though less extremely, bent, as she covers herself with her left hand. As I have pointed out, Venus shows both hands in this picture, but Athena hides the snaky armor in her left hand behind her. In the *Vala* pictures, the hidden-hand motif (suggested in page 19 only by erasure) is very important in page 32, where it accompanies another Venus Pudica figure, and it is noteworthy in pages 35, 58, and 64 (see also *J* 81).[12] In addition, Cupid and Venus are shown in collaboration in *Night Thoughts*, 162 (V, 7), where they have captured a poet who, both manacled and laurel-crowned, plays his pipe at the right to entertain naked Venus, who is looking at herself in a mirror, while her Cupid kneels on her legs and prepares to discharge his bow at some victim, one who has been spotted off the picture at the left. There is also a small vermiculate form on the ground by Cupid's foot and on the next page, no. 163 (V, 8), a figure bows before a huge erect serpent (cf. *V*, p. 96). The wound depicted in *Vala*, page 19, must have preceded the succession of erotic triumphs that have been enacted ever since the primal one on Mount Ida. If the additions to Night I are taken together as a unit, perhaps out of textual sequence, the woman on page 19 must be related to Enitharmon, whose stubbornly closed "gates" are discussed at length in lines 1–7 of page 20. But the picture is by no means an "illustration" of these lines. Indeed, they can be more closely related to an erotic design, *Falsa ad Coelum Mittunt Insomnia Manes* (c. 1790; reproduced in *Blake Newsletter*, 20 [1972], 238), which Blake engraved after Fuseli: there a cupid is about to shoot an arrow at a butterfly perched by the crotch of a nude woman.

Another drawing, that on page 25 {7}, is noteworthy partly because it contains a familiar Blakean motif which, however, was long unrecognized because of a simple change of scale. Here a kneeling figure, probably male, is shown from the rear as he wrestles with what Bentley calls "three alternate sets of poles (?) which meet in three round objects before him" (p. 26). The huge "poles," which are vigorously but unmistakably drawn in pencil and crayon, can only be giant compasses or dividers, complete with large round hinges.[13] These compasses are thrust up into the last stanza of the text, which describes the torments of Luvah in the Furnaces of Affliction as

---

(1969), esp. pp. 196–199. The drawing is reproduced in *The Blake Collection of W. Graham Robertson*, ed. Kerrison Preston (London: Faber and Faber, 1952), pl. 24.

12. See also the remarkably similar figure of "a daughter of man who leads the angel on without herself betraying interest" in the second design for the Book of Enoch in *Blake's Pencil Drawings: Second Series*, ed. Geoffrey Keynes (London: Nonesuch Press, 1956), pl. 46; hereafter referred to as *Drawings 1956*.

13. I first identified these objects in my review of the Bentley edition, "Blake: Original and New," pp. 362–363. I am pleased that W. H. Stevenson concurs in this identification.

he is subjected to Urizen's "iron power" (1. 43), but these instruments are the ostensibly innocent ones described on page 24, particularly "the golden compasses" (1. 12), now transformed into devices of oppression. There can be little doubt that the man trying to control these compasses is Urizen himself, who has risen from his reclining position in page 23. That his instrument has been triplicated here is no greater wonder than that Satan's watch fiend has a triple bow in *Jerusalem* 39, when he attempts to kill imagination. The fact that the compasses have become so big in *Vala*, page 25, bigger than any others in Blake, can be understood either as a sign that they are more proportionate to the creative task or that Urizen has shrunk until he is less competent to wield them.[14] The back-to-the-viewer position is sometimes sinister in Blake; when it is combined with these huge compasses, there is an intense reiteration of a horror. This impression is not mitigated by the lines of verse written over the compasses.

Vala, *page 26*

One consideration to be borne in mind while studying any particular picture is how it relates to others in the same section of the manuscript. At the beginning of Night II, for example, Blake links page 23, recumbent Urizen, with page 25 {7}, Urizen with monstrous compasses. Similarly, page 26 {8} stands as a sequel to page 24. On the earlier page a female, probably Vala, shows her back to the viewer; then on the later page she reveals her several fronts. At least this seems a reasonable hypothesis as to what one should understand by the sequence of four monstrous creatures on page 26. Still, the interpreter must be wary lest this plausible sequence lead him to assumptions concerning what the page is about, assumptions that cannot be confirmed. But since this page has attracted more comment than any other in the manuscript, most of it mistaken, I believe, one should not disregard what may be Blakean leads.

Kathleen Raine makes some mention of these drawings in her long book,[15] but the thought is dissolved within the diffuse discussion of Blake's use of the Cupid and Psyche myth, and the only point that comes through clearly is that Ceres was said in an Orphic Hymn to have become an obscure dragon. The reader is simply turned back to the pictures with the added consideration that they may somehow be the result of Blake's meditation on the Proserpine theme and on the face as opposed to the body of Nature. What this amounts to is another case of inconclusive commentary which adds little

14. For a good recent discussion of the compass symbol, see Robert N. Essick, "Blake's Newton," *Blake Studies*, 3 (1971), 149–162.

15. *Blake and Tradition*, Bollingen 35: 11 (Princeton: Princeton Univ. Press, 1968), I, 183–185.

to scholarship because of the premature attempt to explain the drawings before they have been properly studied.

The same fault is even more evident in an essay on the page by Piloo Nanavutty which tries to interpret the picture on the basis of alchemy and various alchemical designs.[16] Though Nanavutty's ideas seem to have been formulated many years ago (see Margoliouth, p. 107), her article is filled with inaccuracies in the descriptions of all Blake's figures, and none of the pictorial analogies she claims is as suggestively comparable as a reference to Dürer's delineation of harpies noted by Bentley (p. 27, l. 13 n). Neverthe- less, Erdman's attempt in a note to dismiss Nanavutty's whole ingenious interpretation because of inaccuracy of description does not seem, on the basis of reproductions, to be entirely persuasive in the crucial particular singled out: "The interpretation hinges ... on our being able to see, issuing from the dragon woman at the bottom of the page, 'a child whose head is held firmly in the mouth of the dove that has proceeded from the womb first' (p. 297). Such a vision must derive from poor photography; a fresh examination of the original manuscript disclosed no child, no dove; for this volume we ordered an infra-red photograph . . . , which leaves no lines in the drawing fainter than what the naked eye can see. To be very specific: all the lines drawn between the two shorter mermaid tails of the dragon are outlines of the scales on her long central tail."[17]

Rationally speaking, of course, such a dragon as Blake portrays would have no room for a birth passage between its legs because of the huge tail that extends from beneath its rump—unless one were to suppose it to be revealed by X-rays within the tail. Thus the viewer does not expect to see either a child or a bird in this area. But while there is no sign whatever of the child reported by Nanavutty, there is a combination of lines in the tail area of the dragon that in the reproductions looks somewhat like the head of a bird with open mouth pressed against the anus of the dragon. The "bird" seems to have a clearly dotted left eye and sketch lines that might possibly represent its left wing which run across the tail edge into the top curve of the dragon's left flipper. This "bird" is much too roughly drawn, however, to be identified as a "dove," unless one has faith that he has discovered a text explaining the symbolism. Indeed, as Michael Tolley reminds me, the osten- sible head (the clearest part) is not much different from those of the fishes depicted in *Vala*, page 64. And these fish do have large definitely dotted eyes, whereas the dot for the eye of the "bird" is so sharp as to arouse suspicion

16. "*Materia Prima* in a Page of Blake's *Vala*," in *William Blake: Essays for S. Foster Damon*, ed. Rosenfeld, pp. 293–302.

17. David V. Erdman, discussion note to Helen T. McNeil, "The Formal Art of *The Four Zoas*," in *Blake's Visionary Forms Dramatic*, ed. Erdman and Grant, p. 382 n and pl. 89.

that some accident caused the appearance of an eye. My notes certainly do not hint at such an improbable ancillary creature. And if no eye, no "bird" —or flying fish. But Erdman has just completed a further study of the page, which finally explains away this "eye" as accidental. Even in reproductions one can see that there are actually two spots in this area, but only the manuscript makes it clear that these are in ink, a medium not otherwise employed in any of the drawings on the page, though there are many other such spots here and there. Presumably these are due to accidental splattering when the text was being copied out in ink.

The rest of Nanavutty's essay makes no contribution whatever to an understanding of the picture. This means that so far the only scholarly progress that has been made in the study of this design is represented by Bentley's orderly if not detailed description (p. 27) and the suggestive comments of Margoliouth: "This drawing is one of the few which makes full use of the left margin as well as the bottom. There are four winged figures, highly sexual, which may, I think, represent stages in the development of Vala as seen by Luvah, though they do not closely correspond to his account. Pictorial development from the text is not uncommon. The fourth figure, 'a many-breasted serpent-necked woman-dragon' [according to Damon], is undoubtedly the fully developed Vala of Luvah's description" (p. 107).

One might wish to cavil that the members can be differently identified. The neck is perhaps more swanlike than serpentine and the effect of multibreastedness is curiously, even equivocally, achieved. About the first breast, the left one, there can be no question, but the second breast down is coordinated with the remarkably displaced right arm and, moreover, is divided from the viewer by a belly line in such a way as to indicate that it is a right breast rather than a second left one. And the third "breast" is shaped differently from the other two, being more gradually tapered and without a darkened nipple; the horrid thought occurs that this just might be her slack belly skin after a pregnancy or even her belly with a boil on it!

The various sketch lines, however, allow one to suppose that Blake altered this part of the anatomy to produce the overall effect of multibreastedness that most viewers quickly perceive. Thus there appears to be sufficient sanction to go on describing this aspect of the anatomy of the fourth avatar of Vala as though it were more certainly delineated than is in fact the case.

It would be unlike Blake to have labored to depict this imposing creature without having in mind an idea of the significance of her various members. A study of some of the woman-dragon's pictorial analogies and prototypes should help us to recognize what characteristics Blake wished to emphasize. The neck, wings, and serpentine looping tail are probably derived from the same iconographic tradition as the elaborately developed drawing of a dragon in a picture formerly thought to be by Leonardo, *Dragon Attacking a Lion*, which is now in the Uffizi.[18] Pseudo-Leonardo's dragon has a beast head but also has a long curved, though heavier, neck. The right wing (which is in the foreground, since the figure is reversed) is exceedingly like the left wing of Blake's dragon in that it has a similarly scalloped trailing edge, though the leading edge is smoother and without the series of curves on that of Blake's creature. It also has a long looping snakelike tail proceeding from the anal area, though partly because of the angle it is not seen to complete one loop. Pseudo-Leonardo's beast has two somewhat doglike hair-fringed hind legs, rather than feeble flippers like Blake's beast, and it has no fore-limbs at all, in contrast to the vermiculate segmented forearms with finny fans on Blake's beast. Neither is there any sign of an anal crest with three points such as appears on Blake's figure; since pseudo-Leonardo's dragon is a land beast whereas Blake's is obviously aquatic, such features would not have been appropriate even if one could see that area of pseudo-Leonardo's creature, as he cannot. It is also notable that pseudo-Leonardo's beast is decidedly male, having a prominent scrotum and penis-sheath, whereas Blake's beast is undoubtedly female.

I would not, of course, wish to imply that Blake had to have known this rather fugitive drawing, which is probably a copy of Leonardo's lost original, in order to have drawn his woman-dragon. No doubt verbal iconography, such as Spenser's Error in *The Faerie Queene* I, i, 14ff, may have contributed something to Blake's vision, as Michael Tolley has suggested to me. It is important, however, that in Blake's great tempera, *Spenser's Faerie Queene*, the dragon depicted as being trampled at the outset of the parade, which appears to be the dragon from Canto 12, does not look like the one in *Vala*, page 26, except that it has a somewhat similar anal crest. On the whole the dragon in *Vala* bears a closer resemblance to the pseudo-Leonardo drawing than to either Blake's own drawing for Spenser or to Leonardo's other dragons,[19] or to dragons by most other painters, though the iconography of dragons was quite conventional in the Renaissance. Among the antagonists of Saint George one may mention Ucello's, now in the National Gallery, London, which is of the same general type but which has much larger legs and smaller wings and tail.[20]

18. Reproduced by L. D. Ettlinger in *The Complete Paintings of Leonardo Da Vinci*, with Notes and Catalogue by Angela Ottino della Chiesa (London: Weidenfeld and Nicolson, 1969), p. 112.

19. Blake's design for *The Faerie Queene* is reproduced as pl. viii in S. Foster Damon's *A Blake Dictionary: The Ideas and Symbols of William Blake* (Providence: Brown Univ. Press, 1965) and is discussed at some length by Damon. For Leonardo's dragons, see "The Dragon Fight," in *Leonardo: Saggi E Richerche*, ed. Achille Marazza (n. p., 1952), pp. 223–227, and illus.

20. Reproduced by Marco Valsecchi in *National Gallery: London* [Text] (New York: Great Galleries Series, 1965), p. 25. Neither the Ucello nor the Leonardo dragons

Probably the only other multibreasted figure in Blake is that of Eris, the goddess of Discord, who makes such an imposing entrance at the upper left in *The Judgment of Paris*.[21] If Blake's woman-dragon is the descendant of Leonardo's beast and the sister of Discord, she is no less a sister to Blake's

---

have forelimbs, whereas Blake's beast has extraordinary ones. Carpaccio's great Venetian *St. George and the Dragon* features a dragon with four feet, but its wings are not very much like those of Blake's beast. Blake's master Raphael painted two noteworthy dragons with distinct forelimbs; not, indeed, the defeated beast in *St. Michael and the Demon*, but those in both the Paris and Washington versions of *St. George and the Dragon* (reproduced by Ettore Camesasca in *All the Paintings of Raphael* [London: Complete Library of World Art, n.d.], pt. 1, pls. 46, 48, and 62). The Paris version has no hind legs, but its outstretched three-toed right foot is distinctly webbed and thus is not unsuggestive of Blake's fan-feet. The webbing on the front feet of the Washington version is not distinct, though this dragon has all four feet, bat wings, and a looped tail. Raphael's dragons are all quite small, but Ucello's is larger than Saint George's horse; moreover, in Ucello's picture what would seem at first to be the dragon's lady prisoner seems actually to be leading it on a leash. Blake was undoubtedly familiar with the Germanic tradition of representing the serpent of the Garden of Eden as a woman-headed and breasted creature, but if he knew Ucello's or similar pictures he could easily have concluded that the lady was not in fact oppressed by the dragon but complicitous with, or even the instigator of, it. One thinks forward to *Jerusalem*, where the triple-headed giant Hand contains the woman:

Imputing Sin & Righteousness to Individuals; Rahab
Sat deep within him hid: his Feminine Power unreveal'd
Brooding Abstract Philosophy. to destroy Imagination . . .
Her name is Vala in Eternity: in Time her name is Rahab.
(70: 17–30)

When we have a whore within a giant, a female-male, we are clearly in the same area of symbolism as a woman's head on a dragon's body. The imagery is not interchangeable, and doubtless the implications are somewhat different as well, but we need have little doubt that these conceptions in picture and words tend to converge in meaning.

21. This picture was briefly discussed in my "You Can't Talk About Blake's Pictures Like That," esp. pp. 196–198. It is reproduced by Darrell Figgis in *The Paintings of William Blake* (London: Ernest Benn, 1925), pl. 85. Jean H. Hagstrum reminds me of the probable derivation of Blake's multibreasted figures from the imposing figure of the Diana of Ephesus, versions of which were designed by Rubens in *Nature Adorn'd by the Graces* and by Harris, *Nature and the Arts*, both of which are reproduced in Hagstrum's *The Sister Arts* (Chicago: Univ. of Chicago Press, 1958), pls. IV and V-B. Certainly the endorsement of this image of Nature by Rubens would have been quite enough to alienate Blake from it, even if he had not been inclined to reject it on other grounds. Hagstrum has also suggested the following speculation about the symbolism of Blake's dragon: what if the tail on the creature is to be understood as that of a male serpent that had imbedded himself head-first within her? To be conscious of this female-male possibility is to recognize a further range of symbolism in this composite monster, which is manifestly human and bestial, mammalian and reptilian, aerial and aquatic. My discussion of the lower figure in the margin will help to clarify the point that in this page Blake was much concerned with unnatural mixtures of the sexes.

Geryon, who is depicted in design 31 for the *Divine Comedy* as he carries Dante and Virgil on his back down to the lowest third of Hell.[22] Geryon has no wings, and his tail is tapered out of his human-feline torso without the suggestion of a rump, but it becomes undoubtedly scaled as it loops down-ward and then turns into eleven distinct lumpish segments before ending in a scorpion hook, as specified by Dante. This last section of tail is much like the segmented forearms of the woman-dragon, whereas Geryon is depicted with quasi-feline hairy forepaws. Geryon has a short neck and the (heavily lined, strained) face of a just man, as Dante specified; in this connection it is interesting to note that Blake first drew the woman-dragon with a short neck and with a human head before he decided on the elongated neck. With a short neck the woman-dragon would have looked much more like Dürer's Stymphalian Birds alluded to (somewhat misleadingly) by Bentley. Human-headed, short-necked, serpentine-tailed, winged tormentors, it should be noted, are also represented in design 32 of Blake's *Divine Comedy: The Seducers Chased by Devils.*

Certainly the image of a dragon was not so conventionalized in Blake's own time as not to allow the artist very considerable leeway. In Gillray's two pictures entitled *St. George and the Dragon*, the first, of 13 June 1782, shows the beast with the humanized body of a bull, though with large wings having various curves on their leading edges and bat-webbed trailing edges that are very similar to those of Blake's beast in *Vala*, page 26. Gillray's second, of 2 August 1805, has feathery-appearing wings very unlike Blake's, but the elongated serpentine body with long tail is rather more like Blake's beast.[23] But bat-webbed trailing edges were common iconographic features for portentous creatures in Blake's time: Fuseli's design for the *Tornado*, which Blake engraved, has wings of this sort.[24]

It should also be mentioned that the dragon-form of Vala, page 26, bears a very close relation in symbolism to the enigmatic pair of designs, above and below, in *Jerusalem* 11. Without attempting to ascertain the meaning, one observes that the dragon-form flies through the air quite as the Indian-looking woman speeds through her medium, evidently water, with out-stretched arms in *Jerusalem* 11. The curious pointed appendages she wears are quite comparable to the webbed part of Vala's wings. The pearls she

22. Reproduced by Albert S. Roe in *Blake's Illustrations to the Divine Comedy* (Princeton: Princeton Univ. Press, 1953); hereafter referred to as *Blake's Divine Comedy*. A prototype of Blake's Geryon is Fuseli's drawing *Virgil, Dante, and Geryon*, dated 1811, in P. A. Tomory's *A Collection of Drawings by Henry Fuseli, R.A.* (Auck-land: Auckland City Art Gallery, 1967), pl. 30. It bears little resemblance to the *Vala* drawing (p. 26), however.

23. Designs reproduced in *Works of Gillray*, pls. 4 and 300.

24. Reproduced by Ruthven Todd in *William Blake: The Artist* (New York: Dut-ton Pictureback, 1971), p. 42.

wears about her neck and wrists also connect with the recumbant Vala figure in page 128, as well as to the pearls that adorn Sabrina and one of her companions in the seventh design of the Huntington series for Milton's *Comus* {29}. The outspread arms of this woman also resemble the outspread bat wings of the third avatar of Vala, above (p. 26). Probably the neck of the *Vala* dragon should be called swanlike rather than serpentine, as I have already suggested, and her companion, Vala's third avatar, certainly has a birdlike neck as well as the head and beak of a bird; this closely relates them to the humanized swan that sits in the water and appears to be pursuing (or blowing) bubbles drifting before it. While swans exist in redemptive contexts in *America* and in Blake's Gray designs, the activity of the humanized swans in the pictures under consideration does not seem at all redemptive.

It would be possible and of some interest to set forth a complete correlation of the woman-dragon with all her other relatives in *Vala* from pages 4 and 7 on. Such an undertaking would help to make clear more of the pictorial structure of the work as a whole, though I doubt it would bring out much that is not implicit in the bright and poisonous image Vala declines into on page 26. And I do not think we would get much more light on the curious fans that occupy the place of hands on the forelimbs of the woman-dragon. It is at least conceivable that these fans were provoked by the detestable task of decorating handscreens for Lady Bathurst which Blake declined during his residence in Felpham. If so, this would suggest something about the dating of the drawing, but it could hardly be said to participate in the meaning of the picture.

The infra-red photography has brought out details of one other figure (the lower one at the left of the text) so much more clearly than in previous reproductions that some notice must be taken of it here. What one sees at first is a bat-winged personage, probably a woman with bulging hips, her arms clasped in front of her, and her head bent sharply to her left, probably with her mouth open. About all that seems puzzling is that there has been extensive erasure on her chest and beside her head and that there are curly lines at the sides of her hips which suggest clumps of hair. Only when one studies this drawing closely does one recognize that what was originally depicted was a bat-winged phallus and scrotum ridden by the woman, whose legs dangle behind and beneath the dual curve of the scrotum. The hair that is visible can be nothing other than the pubic hair of the winged phallus, a feature of anatomy that Blake almost never indicates, in spite of his espousal of the nude as the basis of his art.

The reader may at first be disinclined to accept this unconditional identification because the object described is considerably more indecent than any so far discussed in the manuscript. But the winged phallus reappears, unerased, on page 42 {14}, and the phallus and testes reappear, erased, without wings on page 39 {11}, both of which drawings I shall later discuss. The motif of a rider on the winged creature occurs quite often in Blake: for example, see page 136 {22}. There are three versions of a girl riding a bird on page 73 of Blake's *Notebook*, and there are many riders of birds and/or insects in the designs for Young and Gray. Probably the most famous design of this sort is the youth riding a swan above children riding a serpent in Plate 11 of *America*. This symbolism will be more fully discussed in the notes to Erdman's forthcoming edition of the *Notebook*.

Blake's symbolism in *Vala*, page 26, seems at first to be much more erotic than that he employs elsewhere; but many of the same motifs occur in *Jerusalem*, though the connections are not immediately striking. I shall mention only a few more, having already called attention to *Jerusalem*, Plate 11, in relation to the two lower figures in *Vala*, page 26. The fat butterfly-winged girl with an Afro hairdo and a belly largely misshapen into an enormous vagina reappears as Jerusalem herself, outstretched, with butterfly wings, at the bottom left of *Jerusalem*, Plate 2. But this figure has to be combined with the bat-winged vagina in the upper picture of *Jerusalem*, Plate 58, to approximate the angle and the symbolism. The hair of this figure, which closely resembles that of Vala, the topmost figure in *Jerusalem* 25, is comparably domed with hair that is undoubtedly pubic in intention. The lower figure in *Jerusalem* 58 is a skeleton in flames; he is apparently male, the frustrated counterpart of the horrific-pathetic female above him. They are modulated figures of the woman and man on the edge and under the sea in *America* 13, who are being eaten by beasts. The point of these analogies is to clarify the plight of the female figures in *Vala*, page 26; they are driven by desire but are unable to satisfy each other in spite of their ostensible readiness to do so. The results of so much unfulfilled promise are evinced below in images pathetic or horrific.

Concerning the Influence or Function
of the Night Thoughts *Engravings in*
the Vala *Manuscript, Pages 43–76, Nights III–VI*

It seems generally to have been assumed that the proof pages of *Night Thoughts* engravings were simply employed by Blake as paper for his manuscript and that, if the engravings per se were in any way significant, it was only formalistically, in their perhaps occasionally having prompted Blake to draw similar designs on facing pages. His work habits may have been as unorganized as that, but the evidence makes it appear at least equally possible that Blake saw significant relationships among the *Night Thoughts* engravings and many of the *Vala* drawings that face them and also some of the drawings on the versos of the engravings or elsewhere in the manuscript. The simplest form of this hypothesis is to suppose that Blake deliberately selected the engravings and then drew pictures variously stimulated by them. But the undoubted lack of correspondence between some engravings and any surviving drawings (to say nothing of the extra pieces of paper intercalated) indicates a more complex evolution. Perhaps some engravings were chosen to echo existing drawings while other engravings may have prompted drawings. Such factors as Blake's later additions to the text must have complicated the growth of the manuscript. At first one might suppose that the fact that some *Night Thoughts* proofs were used as many as three times, while others were used not at all,[25] is an insuperable objection to a more purposeful conception of the choice of pictures, but Blake may have hoped to be stimulated at some later time by engravings he was temporarily employing to make several different drawings and then to withdraw the duplicates. He might, of course, even have felt that repeating the same design would have a justifiable effect, one comparable to the refrains in the poem, an aspect of his verbal artistry every proper reader has appreciated. And it is certainly not inconceivable that he wished to employ some *Night Thoughts* designs again in his own epic. They were, after all, Blake's pictures, not Young's; perhaps he wished to liberate some of them.

What I propose to do in this section is to make a survey of all the designs from Night III to Night VI, beginning with the appearance of the first engraving in the manuscript in the middle of Night III. I shall concentrate especially on connections between engravings and drawings that seem noteworthy. I shall not usually try to relate either drawings or engravings to texts or to describe either kind of picture with much thoroughness. Perhaps some of the resemblances I shall point out would have seemed accidental to Blake, but I am quite confident that Blake himself thought about many of them and would have found it good to have retained such design connections if *The Four Zoas* had reached a highly finished form. So stated, this conjecture may have implications for some theories about the growth of the manuscript, but I do not see that it contains any serious contradictions of the Erdman theory I endorsed earlier. It would not have been more difficult for Blake to have treated an engraving as a draft for a final watercolor design than it would have been for him to have treated a pencil drawing in the same way when the time came (as it evidently did not) for him to prepare final copy of the illuminated manuscript. Blake was, for example, perfectly capable of making a fresh watercolor version of Nebuchadnezzar in *Night*

25. See Bentley's generally accurate "Table III: *Night Thoughts* Engravings Used in *Vala*," *Blake: Vala*, p. 209. Proofs survive for all four of the engraved designs not utilized. I plan to discuss these proofs in the forthcoming Clarendon Edition of *Night Thoughts*, co-edited with E. J. Rose and M. J. Tolley.

Thoughts, 299, (VII, 27), after having etched a Nebuchadnezzar for *The Marriage of Heaven and Hell*, Plate 24, and making at least three color prints of the same subject.

Where facing designs echo one another it is tempting to conclude that the drawing echoes the engraving, but it is by no means impossible that a particular engraving was selected because it echoed a drawing already present on the facing page of the manuscript. For convenience' sake and to systematize the exposition, I shall describe the features in the engraving first and then single out details in the drawings which respond or correspond to them. I wish to reiterate, however, that I do not necessarily assume that the engraving preceded or inspired the drawing in any particular case.

Page 43 {15} shows a bearded old man with a scroll on which Hebrew characters are inscribed, reclining on his left elbow and exuding many spear points. The inscription has recently been deciphered by Professor Leonard Kravitz of Hebrew Union College as (in mirror writing) "Lord You are Death, YHVH The fire was with the fire / You . . . dust."[26] This tends to intensify the connection between this figure and the last three lines of (palimpsest) text on page 42 {14}, particularly line 19, "Am I not God said Urizen. Who is Equal to me." Pictorially, the figure is also connected to a shrouded and possibly bearded adult figure, whose head is bent to his right beneath and into the word "black" in line 21 of page 42. What is probably the left hand, pointing upward, of this partially erased, previously undescribed figure is just to the right of the word "opake," though that side of his mantle may also extend to the vertical sketched line farther right; on his right side the heavily crayon-shaded area originally tapered down in a long triangle, suggesting rather a shadow than a coverlet. A great deal of erasure was later necessary to introduce the bent-over woman and to make other changes that I shall discuss in the next section of this essay. Here I shall merely add that the shrouded figure on page 42 is in a position that echoes the figure of Death on page 43; it also resembles some versions of the elemental aged spirit in *The Marriage of Heaven and Hell* 11 (top, center of design) and also the suicide tree at the right of Virgil in illustration 24 to Blake's *Divine Comedy*.

Page 45 {17} depicts Christ bending over and touching the left breast of a clean-shaven, nude man who is supported by his right elbow, which rests on a ground cloth—it had been, perhaps, his shroud—spread on a hillock, and raises his left arm, evidently in aspiration. Page 44 {16} shows a bearded man with his mouth open; he is braced on his left elbow and has his redrawn, possibly webbed, right hand raised. His left thigh is the more

26. Professor Kravitz's deciphering was communicated to me in a copy of a letter of 6 May 1971, addressed to Professor Judah Stampfer, and kindly transmitted to me by David V. Erdman.

prominent, and a low shaded peak rises above his right. In the left margin stands a woman with a curious pointed hat or crown and a Gothic triptych on her loins. Bentley and others have observed that the men with raised arms in the two designs are nearly mirror images of one another. The engraving (repeated on p. 97), which is rather distantly derived from Michelangelo's *Creation of Adam*, is perhaps a version of the Good Samaritan story (another engraved design [used for p. 129] illustrates it more closely), but it is more likely to be a version of the Raising of Lazarus, as Michael Tolley suggests. The man on page 44 is probably Tharmas, described in the text as shouting, though he is evidently depicted as *lying* on water—the "peak" being a wave—rather than *standing* on "the affrighted Ocean"; the closely related picture for *The Gates of Paradise* 10 makes an aquatic environment seem more likely in this picture. The woman, who is the unkind counterpart of Christ on page 45 {17}, is perhaps Enion, whom Tharmas is calling for; but she might also be the hovering Enitharmon, looking on fascinatingly and coldly. Her hat or crown is like the central core of that worn by the Wife of Bath in the engraving of the Canterbury Pilgrims.[27] The rest of the Wife's hat could be constructed by combining this pointed core with the turbaned sides of the Prester Serpent's hood depicted in *Vala*, page 98.

In any case, the association of the hat-crown worn by the woman in page 45 with the sinister spiked crowns often worn by royalty in Blake's pictures has, generally, a negative connotation, though it would be injudicious to say that everyone who wears a spiked crown is thereby condemned by Blake. On the other hand, the Gothic tabernacle on the woman's loins one might expect to be a beautiful center of "living form." Thus Butlin took it to be in his review of the Bentley edition,[28] perhaps incautiously, but Bentley had described the tabernacle as being mere scribblings on the woman's belly. The fact is that Gothic designs are sometimes employed in negative or equivocal settings, and they often tend to suggest further bondage or, at best, the mere possibility of redemption. In the Gray designs, for example, the pictures for "A Long Story," 3, and "The Progress of Poesy," 2, show Gothic architecture in basically favorable situations, but in "Ode for Music," 5, a Gothic church tower is framed and limited by Trees of Death, and in "The Bard," 9, the Gothic decorations on dreadful King Edward's throne are not redemptive enough to straighten him out. One could argue that this is because the niches within these decorations have been emptied of human forms. But then one would have to observe that there is a curious downward

27. Reproduced by Geoffrey Keynes in *Engravings by William Blake: The Separate Plates* (Dublin: E. Walker, 1956), pls. 27–30.

28. See Martin Butlin, "Blake's *Vala*, or *The Four Zoas* and a New Water Colour in the Tate Gallery," *The Burlington Magazine*, 64 (1964), 381–382.

pitched roof, as well as the central upward one, on the genital tabernacle on
the woman in *Vala*, page 44. Perhaps Blake's sketchy drawing is only
sufficient to make us realize that, in spite of appearances, all is not well here.
Perhaps this tabernacle, as Jean Hagstrum suggests, is decorated merely to
entice in some pompous high priest. These would then be the gates of har-
lotry, decked out to simulate the Western Gate.

Any apparent connection between the last drawing of a Night and the
initial engraving for the next Night seems more likely to be accidental than
connections within a Night, but Blake's principles of design are too little
understood to allow us to say that any such connections are unintended. The
connections between the designs on page 46 {18}, inscribed "End of the
Third Night," and page 47 {19}, always inscribed as the first of Night IV,
appear quite close. The engraving shows a man supporting a sick woman,
who is stretched out on a hillside above the sea, as both look up toward
Apollo and his horses, who drive by to the right in the great orb of the
sun. At the left, in a detail which illustrates no text in the *Night Thoughts*,
a Clytie spirit spreads her arms toward the passing figure of Apollo, though
she has not escaped being anchored in a large sunflower-type of plant.[29] On
page 46 a bearded man pushes through a substance, variously identified as
six-foot-tall grass or fire or a cloud, but which is surely water (at least on
the left—and the fact that the man's lower left leg is seen through a trans-
parency increases the probability of its being water) ; he is shouting and is
undoubtedly looking for the woman, who stands cowering in distress with
hands spread and raised under the curve of waves. The text makes it clear
that the man is Tharmas, who also closely resembles the man in page 44, and
the woman is surely Enion, though her resemblance to the doubtful woman
on page 44 is less clear than that of the man to his predecessor. Enion has
been described as naked, but she is undoubtedly wearing a dress, and she
bears a resemblance to the sick woman in the engraving on page 47, insofar
as can be discerned from the back. The posture of Tharmas generally resembles that of Christ as Cloud-unfolder, both as he is depicted in the *Night
Thoughts* engraving, *Vala*, page 114, and especially as he is drawn on *Vala*,
page 116, though there are important differences too. In any case, there is
a repetition of the sea motif in the engraving and the drawing. The upstretched arms of Clytie are also comparable to the raised and outstretched
arm gesture of Tharmas, though the meaning of this gesture is undoubtedly
different; originally it was Tharmas' right arm that was raised, while his
left was braced at his side. It is also noteworthy that Enion's posture and
appearance are much like that of the lower woman being scourged in the

29. See my essay, "The Fate of Blake's Sunflower," *Blake Studies*, 5 (1973), forthcoming, for a discussion of this design.

element of fire at the left in *Il Penseroso* 9,[30] although in *Vala* the woman is clearly within the element of water. So far as the engraving is concerned, it is hard to disregard the correspondence between the image of Apollo and line 5, page 47, "Red as the Sun in the hot morning of the bloody day."

Page 49 shows a man who has a snake wound around him, lying with outspread arms and with his back on a mound, while a kneeling woman tries to restrain a child from seizing a bird that flies away. This group can be seen as a modulation of that depicted in *Urizen* 21, which also has other analogies among the *Vala* drawings, with the enwinding serpent corresponding to the chain on the standing man in the *Urizen* design. In page 48 a seated man with outstretched legs looks upward; he is holding his right fist to his breast, evidently to stanch a wound that is dripping blood. His face and long flowing hair resemble that of the man in page 49, insofar as can be determined at the different angle. Evidently he is Los, as described on page 49, lines 7–10. His face is very similar, reversed, to that of the man gazing upward, on page 47. The fact that Apollo also has a similar profile is suggestive, though Apollo has tight curly hair and a less aquiline nose.

Page 51 shows the reveler, Belshazzar, spilling his wine in alarm as a spirit in a cloud points to the writing on the wall. Above the text box a shrouded corpse is laid out and is encircled by what is either one headless worm or two well-coordinated worms. On page 50 there is a woman whose right side exudes drops as she sweeps through waves with her left arm before her and her right arm trailing. She is nude except that she may be wearing a trailing headdress which, however, does not veil her face. She is probably Enitharmon, who in the text on this page is described by her separated partner Los. The connection, if any, with the facing engraving is oblique, but there is a more suggestive cluster of images when pages 50 and 51 are seen in sequel to page 48 and page 49. Belshazzar is seated in a position much like Los on page 48, though his leg is drawn up, and the worm-entwined shroud at the top of page 51 is a kind of sequel to the snake-enwrapped man on page 49. The bleeding chest of Los on page 48 is clearly related to the bleeding chest of Enitharmon on page 50, and the spilled wine of Belshazzar on page 51 is a kind of modulation of this image. Figures on pages 50 and 51 also bear a suggestive relationship to figures in Blake's great enigmatic Arlington Court picture. Enitharmon closely resembles in posture the sea goddess who (reversed) wields a vortex at the left in the Arlington Court picture. As I have pointed out in an article on that picture, this figure is the same as that of the vortex-woman in the *Whirlwind of Lovers*, illustration 10 for Blake's *Divine Comedy*. It is also noteworthy that

30. This design is reproduced and discussed in my article, "Blake's Designs for *L'Allegro* and *Il Penseroso*, Part I: A Survey of the Designs," *Blake Newsletter*, 4 (1971), 128–130.

the warning spirit in the engraving, page 51, has his arms in a position quite like that (reversed, and pointing, rather than gesturing) of the Conjurer in Red in the Arlington Court picture, a posture which, as indicated in my article, echoes that of John the Baptist in the frontispiece for *All Religions Are One* 2.[31]

Page 53 shows Death as an ancient bearded bellman with bow and arrow breaking in on and awakening a mature male sleeper who has beside him various implements: an hourglass, an inkstand, a lighted lamp, and an open book. On page 52 a crouching nude woman holds her left hand to her breast as she tries with her right arm to fend off a nude curly-haired man with an erection who kneels behind her. The man's redrawn left hand goes behind her back; his right was variously redrawn, having at one time been drafted straight up, but seeming finally to rest on his own right shoulder. Originally, he was probably drawn in right profile facing her; and then, in an intermediate version, his left knee was behind her buttocks, but the final posture represents his whole body at a more discreet relationship to her. The alarm of the woman in the drawing is generally comparable to that of the man in the engraving, and the compositions are comparable, but otherwise the pictures seem quite different. The man and woman in the drawing are probably Los and Enitharmon, as the text seems to indicate; she has the same headgear as the woman in page 50 and he generally resembles the man in page 48, though his close tight curls tend to resemble those of Orc as they are later depicted, rather than the more flowing hair exhibited by Los in page 48 or even Apollo in page 47. The antithetical relationship between man and woman particularly recalls the discord of Tharmas and Enion depicted in page 48. The difficulties of Los and Enitharmon on page 52 attend the reconstruction of Urizen, who is, no doubt, envisioned as the ancient Death figure in page 53.

The next pair of pictures has even less connection. In page 55 Christ walks as a benefactor with a star nimbus among a procession of people of various ages from infancy to old age. On page 54 there is a crude drawing, with various other probably unrelated sketches, of a globe that appears to be floating on a sea, a motif that also occurs in the *Night Thoughts*, notably 231 (VI, 10). Seated in right profile with its back to the right side of this globe, its head on its drawn-up knees, and its left arm raised above its head, is a crudely sketched figure, perhaps of a woman. It does not seem helpful to relate this closely to the various pensive women in the procession on page 55. Probably the planet depicted on page 54 is related to the spherical imagery mentioned in the text on this page. The seated woman could con-

31. See my "Redemptive Action in Blake's Arlington Court Picture: Observations on the Simmons-Warner Theory," *Studies in Romanticism*, 10 (1971), 21–26.

ceivably be Enitharmon, who was associated with the sea on page 50. Such alienation and waiting amidst desolation seem to have been the condition of humanity before the Advent; it is thus contrasted with the Christian community being formed by Christ in page 55. It must be added that the ostensible wave at the viewer's left of the globe tends to look like a snow-peaked mountain; the appendage on the right slope, which resembles a huge two-leafed clover, is not intelligible according to either hypothesis. Just possibly this appendage can be seen as the bald head, chest, backward-bent left arm, and perhaps the outline of the buttocks and bottom of the leg extending across the wave mountain in left profile.

The next paired pictures also lap over from one Night to the next and are not closely related. Page 57 shows Nimrod as a hideous naked king who holds up a crude spear in his right hand and leads a brace of curs with his left hand. He grins down horribly as a third greyhound-type of dog chews at the throat of a backward-bent nude male victim. In page 56 a preternatural figure is seated in right profile and draws toward itself, by the wrists, a curly-haired, smiling youth, who approaches on his knees. Behind this figure there is a partially erased figure, probably demonic, though it has been described as a child. Margoliouth (pp. 122–123) tried to relate this scene to the Christ-and-Children symbolism on the engraved recto, page 55, or with the Raising of Lazarus—in which he is echoed by Stevenson. Such an interpretation, however, necessitates a very mordant irony, since what is surely depicted is a seduction and, as such, the picture may be a kind of sequel to the scene on page 52. The violence of Nimrod and his hounds against the victim in the facing page 57 may also be seen as a counterpart to the incipient violation scene on page 56. The text on page 55 might be taken to contain a clue that the subject of the picture is the rape of Enitharmon by Urizen, but the figures might also both be males. The design itself is a compositional and conceptual variation of *Night Thoughts*, 69 (II, 36), which depicts two male friends who reach out toward one another to touch their wine goblets before drinking a toast. The dominant figure in the *Vala* drawing has an oddly domed head with no notching whatever between its forehead and the bridge of its nose, which results in a streamlined blending of these features. In this way it is closely related to the drawing of *The Head of the Ghost of a Flea* now in the Tate Gallery. This family resemblance to the bloodthirsty Flea makes the figure an appropriate counterpart of the engraved Nimrod on page 57. The two fearsome figures on pages 56 and 57 are also variants of the figures of Age and Mischance respectively in the fifth design to Gray's "Ode on the Spring."

That there is some relationship between the designs on pages 59 and 58 is easy to establish, but evaluating it is difficult, partly because there seems

also to be a relationship between the pictures and the texts, which is likewise hard to pin down. Basically, the engraving on page 59 is of Christ as
the Man of Sorrows, who displays the nails in his hands and feet, and also
his crown of thorns, as he makes his way through the tongues of flame in
Hell. He is humble and pathetic, a modulated declension from the image of
Christ the Minister depicted in the engraving on page 55. Beneath the text
on page 59 is a rough drawing of an exultant figure, called by Bentley the
"traffic-stopping" Christ, with upraised, outspread arms; it is accompanied
by a bank of clouds that go up the right margin. The analogies do indeed
suggest that this figure should be taken to be Christ, though the features
are not distinct enough to establish this identification. Part of the difficulty
in interpreting this figure is to determine, since it probably antedates the
text, whether it is still meaningfully a part of the picture and whether it
should be taken to represent "the new born king" (l. 21) actually being
born as a full-sized adult from the woman who lies stretched out, possibly
bound down, on a ground covering, with her face hidden in her right arm.
If she is merely sleeping, why is she being regarded so pensively by the
curly-haired nude boy who stands at her head looking down?

If this were a birth scene, the primary analogy would be the color print
of "Pity," who, as a "new-born *babe*" striding the blast, is seen from the
back and is much smaller but otherwise quite like the exultant figure on
page 58. In some respects, notably the upraised, not outspread, arms of the
babe and the twisted position of the mother's body, the picture more closely
resembles the preliminary pencil drawings for "Pity," while the exultant
figure is very like, though on a much grander scale, the Christ Child in the
tempera of *The Nativity*.[32]

This line of interpretation seems tenuous, however, once the viewer recognizes the action that was originally being observed by the youth. In a
preliminary stage of the drawing, the woman, who may as well be called
Enitharmon, was depicted on her back with upstretched arms (the imper-
fectly erased lines of which seem like bonds in the revised drawing) toward
a (doubtless) male figure who crouches over her to mount her. This, in
turn, may well be a sequel to the seduction scene on page 56, and themati-
cally it is closely related to the picture on pages 39 {11} and 40 {12}. What
Blake seems to have concluded is that the possible scene of copulation between Los or Orc and Enitharmon would be both too early and too late at

32. Reproduced by Anthony Blunt in *The Art of William Blake* (New York: Columbia Univ. Press, 1959), pls. 29a, 29b, and 35b. All these postures, of course, tend
to merge into the characteristic "Glad Day" posture of Blake's *Albion rose*, reproduced
also by Blunt (see 6c, 7a, and 7c), though truly regenerate man has his legs spread,
whereas the exultant figure on p. 5 has his close together.

this point in the manuscript. Perhaps without either the image of the new-born wonder or that of the primal scene, the loins of Enitharmon have sufficient interest for Orc (who is much the same figure as the curly-haired youth of page 56). That something more than a natural curiosity on the part of Orc is involved is suggested by his anomalous features, such as elongated right fingers (cf. the right hand of Urizen on page 23) and his left hand behind his back, which is the characteristic posture of a liar in Blake, as evidenced in *Jerusalem* 81. The contrastive relationship between the exultant man on page 58 and the rejected man on page 59 applies in another key to Orc as immature pensive witness on page 58 and Christ as mature victim on page 59, a condition that Orc himself will be brought to on page 62. Whereas Orc is absorbed by the center of desire, himself as yet unscathed, Christ crucified wanders among the flames of the furious desire of mankind in bondage, which even now are destroying this world. It is also noteworthy that Blake had laboriously re-engraved the head of Christ from the sharp right profile of the proof stage, used in *Vala*, page 111 (which was de-lineated in the same position in *Night Thoughts*, 121 [IV, 12]), to the three-quarters right profile, presumably to enhance the mildness and to erase the blood. He also utilized the final state of the engraving again on page 115, remarkably placing it opposite the engraving of Christ Triumphant, which was designed as the frontispiece to *Night Thoughts* and then used as the title page for Night IV. The proportion of accident to design in this sequence is a formidable question.

Pages 61 and 60 are also in a contrastive relationship. The spirit reaching down from the cloud to touch a planet is, though displayed in a *Night Thoughts* engraving, illustrative of the still untrammeled powers of Orc (p. 61, l. 23) ; it is the antithesis of the bound Los depicted on page 60, who can do no more than witness the endearments of Orc and Enitharmon, de-scribed in the text, which became somewhat more restrained as a result of redrawing. The imagery is much the same as that in *Urizen* 21, though the composition is quite different, but, as usual, Blake introduces various modify-ing details, such as making Orc as tall as Enitharmon and presenting Los kneeling. Actually, the pensive Orc of page 58 is about the same size relative to Enitharmon as the amorous Orc of *Urizen* 21; this is a further indication of connection with the design sequence in *Vala*. It is also striking that the left wrist of Los on page 60 has a very prominent hole mark which cannot have been accidental; following, as it does, the engraving on page 59 of the Man of Sorrows displaying the nails, the drawing makes it evident that Los must be suffering from a comparable stigma and passion. Whereas Orc had been the witness to a primal scene in the draft drawing in page 58, Los observes its incestuous counterpart in page 60. In view of the impending binding of Orc, it is appropriate to adapt one of the keys from *The Gates of Paradise*, "My Son! my Son! I treatest thee / But as thou hast instructed me" (*p. 266*).

Certainly pages 63 and 62 constitute an ironic pair in the depiction of the family romance, which is the explicit concern of all the drawings for Night V. In the engraving a father kneels within a canopied chamber and spans with his right hand a cheerful baby boy, held in the lap of his mother, who is abed. That something dreadful, not just harmless paternal mensuration, is occurring is indicated, however, by the three angels (the one at the left cut off; the one in the center a stupid-looking owl in an earlier proof stage) who sit on the roof of the building and mourn with averted faces. Later I shall mention a connection between this design and the more explicitly appalling scene on page 42. In the drawing on page 62 is the familiar group of lamenting Los and Enitharmon and the bound-down Orc that is a staple in Blake's symbolism, as Bentley observed, from *America* 3, to an engraving dated 1812.[33] Among the noteworthy details are the facts that the face of the crouching Enitharmon closely resembles in position and delineation that of the mother in the engraving on page 63 (the suggestion of wings on Enitharmon in the drawing I take to be an accident of the shading) and that the locks of Los's hair extend in five or more flamelike points. There are important connections in the flaming hair symbolism between this figure of Los and the two drawings entitled by Keynes *Los Supporting the Sun* and *Los Kneeling*.[34] In the former a figure, seen from the front and with legs apart, is similar to that of the central man in *Vala*, page 66, seen from the back, with legs together, who supports the sun on his head (in a Herculean posture). In the second drawing a vigorous male brandishes a bow (not a sickle, as Keynes would have it[35]) in his right hand and an arrow in his left, above the quiver on his left shoulder. Such a dreadful Los confirms the validity of the "Augury" that reminds us that "The Poison of the Honey Bee / Is the Artist's Jealousy" (*p. 482*).

The figure of Los also quite clearly resembles that in the puzzling full-page drawing of a man on page 76. The two lines emanating from the right heel of Los evidently pass through his right foot and seem to continue to the feet of Enitharmon and thence, by means of the line that appears also to delineate the contour of a hillock, first to the outstretched right hand of Orc

33. The continuity of Blake's imagery is summarized by Martin Butlin in *William Blake: A Complete Catalogue of the Works in the Tate Gallery*, rev. ed. (London, 1971), p. 30; hereafter called *Tate Catalogue*.

34. Reproduced in *Drawings 1956*, pls. 24 and 25.

35. His description was accepted uncritically by Anne T. Kostelanetz in a review that appeared in *Blake Newsletter*, 2 (1968), 5, and corrected in a riposte by Frederic Cummings in *Blake Newsletter*, 2 (1968), 47. Unhappily, Keynes did not make this correction in his *Drawings 1970*, pl. 50.

and then to the right side and perhaps beyond. Though these lines might be explained as merely delineating the contours of the landscape, I believe they should be recognized as "influence lines" of the kind I have briefly discussed as occurring in *The Judgment of Paris*.[36] As in that picture, the viewer who has attained angelic perspective will understand that both tyrants and victim are bound together in a frightful eternal moment.

The relation between pages 65 and 64 is evidently that of admonition and plight. In the engraving the God of Thunder arouses the alarmed poet, who kneels by the sea and looks up in consternation with ineffectually crossed arms. The drawing on page 64 underwent a large number of alterations which would take long to describe, but probably what is finally depicted is yet another version of the cuckolding of Los. This event takes place in a narrative sequence between the events depicted on pages 63 and 62 and represents an intensification of the event depicted on page 60. Or, in psychic terms, it seems still to be going on despite the ostensibly decisive binding of Orc depicted on page 62. At the left Los sits on his heels and is bent forward, in left profile, with his outstretched arms holding a net which is connected at an angle to a rope. The net is presumably the one being made on page 29 and the rope the one being handled on page 14. Between the net and the rope on page 64 is a roughly drawn fish head, with large-dotted eye and open mouth, and another fish head protrudes from the reticulation of the net. The horizontal line that cuts off the first fish beneath the eye, ends the rope abruptly, and crosses the base of the left toes of Los indicates the surface of water. Behind Los's back the lusty Enitharmon with upturned head is being kissed from behind by Orc as she reaches back and grasps his large phallus in her left hand. His sketchily indicated left hand extends beneath her left armpit and a crab advances toward her crotch. This scene may be regarded as a version of the cuckolding of Hephaestus by Aphrodite and Ares. According to Homer, the illicit lovers were netted by Los's prototype, but here Blake's blacksmith-to-be seems snared in his own (Urizenic) gins, or at least is too preoccupied with his work to heed the warnings of the fishes. One recognizes the resolute distraction of Los more vividly when he observes that Los was at one stage sketched full-face, with his face on the left side of his head, peeking back over his left shoulder, attempting to see what was going on behind his back. The alterations in this drawing were extensive: originally the torso of the Los figure was bent sharply back so that the chest line was about 1.2 cm. below the letters of the text and the head was in the present area of the upper arm and back of Enitharmon. What

36. "You Can't Write About Blake's Pictures Like That," pp. 198–199. Not all scholars recognize Blake's use of this symbolism, but I continue to regard it as certainly present in *The Judgment of Paris* and probably present in *Vala*, p. 62, and elsewhere.

other action may then have been delineated is conjectural, though if one
recognizes the connection between this version of the drawing and the design for *Jerusalem* 25, in which the bound Albion has his head in the lap
of the fascinating Rahab, one can almost reconstruct a side view of a
similar situation for the draft drawing. Because in posture the backward-
bent figure in the draft resembles a male in the *Jerusalem* design, because
he is ultimately delineated as a male, Los, and because there is no indication
of female breasts in the draft version, I conclude that this figure was originally a male, possibly the bound Orc, as he appears on page 78. It is also
conceivable that Blake had originally considered drawing Enitharmon in
this backward-bent position. Both later (p. 122) and earlier (p. 41) a woman is drawn in a similarly backward-bent position, however; and this may
be evidence in favor of this hypothesis, which was suggested to me by David
Erdman. The connection between *Jerusalem* 25 and page 41, which I shall
discuss below, gives the similarity a special suggestiveness.[37] It is noteworthy
that the dual motif of an upturned head with another head above it in the
facing pages 64 and 65 ironically contrasts Enitharmon in the final version
of the drawing with the awakened poet, and Orc with the Thunder God.

The design on page 67 is engraving 33, which was derived from water
color 119 (IV, 10) in the *Night Thoughts* series. Although the symbolic
message is simple and unmistakable, the beautiful dancer-like gestures of
Eve and Adam are repeated Blakean motifs and have an especial interest
because of this. Moreover, if the gestures employed on page 66 are seen as
modulations of those on page 67, they appear to be less enigmatic. Recently
there has come to light a monochrome wash drawing, enscribed *Donald the
Hammerer*,[38] in which a man and woman gesticulate, in ways much like
Eve and Adam, to exhort a blacksmith who is standing back to his forge,

37. Another consideration is the fondness of Blake's friend Fuseli for Romantic
Mannerist stretched-out postures, both for victims of violence and for lovers engaged
in passionate kissing. A sketch by Fuseli dated 1790–1800, *Nackter Mann nach ruck-
wärts in die Arme zweier knieden Männer sinkend*, pl. 89, in Paul Ganz, ed., *Die
Zeichnungen Hans Heinrich Füsslis* (Bern-Olten: Im Urs Graf-Verlag, 1947), pretty
clearly set a precedent for *Jerusalem*, pl. 25; the presence of a dominant woman in the
background above the male victim is particularly suggestive of a connection in the
compositions. On the other hand, Fuseli did a whole series of erotic sketches and
drawings that recall the *Vala* designs: see Ganz, pls. 94, 96–99. The earliest datable
design (1812–1813), pl. 97, *Jungen Mann, eine am Spinet sitzende Frau küssend*, indicates that Fuseli found Blake's erotic design in *Vala*, p. 64, damned good to steal from,
even though he made a less licentious drawing after seeing it. Once again the artistic
interaction can be observed within what Hagstrum, with a nice ambiguity, refers to as
"The School of Blake."

38. It is described by Robert Essick, "The Blakes at UCLA," *Blake Newsletter*, 4
(1971), 75–77, with the reproduction on p. 76. See also the discussion by John Beer,
"Blake's 'Donald the Hammerer,' " *Blake Newsletter*, 5 (1971–72), 165–167.

{1} *Moore and Company Advertisement* (engraving). *By courtesy of the Trustees of the British Museum.*

{2} *Theotormon Woven* (pencil drawing). *Victoria and Albert Museum.*

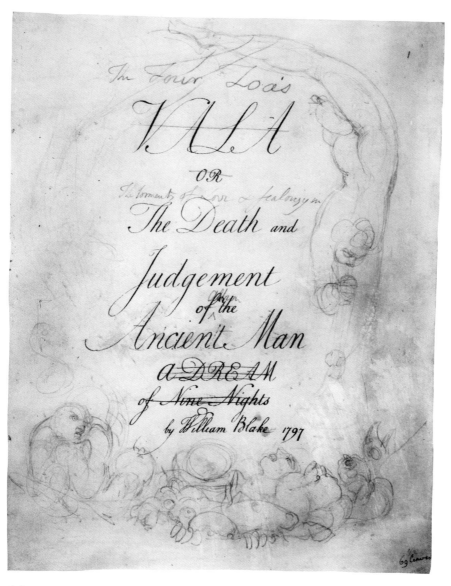

{3}   *Vala*, p. 1 (infra-red photography). *By courtesy of the Trustees of the British Museum.*

{4} *Vala*, p. 19 (infra-red photography). *By courtesy of the Trustees of the British Museum.*

{5} *Vala*, p. 13 (infra-red photography), detail. *By courtesy of the Trustees of the British Museum.*

Luvah replied Dictate to thy Equals. am not I
The Prince of all the hosts of Men nor Equal know in Heaven
If I arise into the Zenith leaving thee. to watch
The Emanation & her Sons the Satan & the Anak
Sihon & Og. wilt thou not rebel to my laws remain
In darkness building thy strong throne & in my ancient night
Daring my power wilt arm my Sons against me in the dark Atlantic
My deep. My night which thou arising hast assumd my Crown
I will remain as well as thou & here with hands of blood
Smite this dark sleeper in his tent then try my strength with thee

While thus he spoke his fires reddend o'er the holy tent
Urizen cast deep darkness round him Silent brooding death
Eternal death to Luvah. raging Luvah pourd
The Lances of Urizen from chariots. round the holy tent
Discord began & yells & cries shook the wide firmament
Beside his anvil stood Urthona dark. a mass of iron
Glowd furious on the anvil prepard for spades & coulters All
Thy sons fled from his side to join the conflict pale he heard
The Eternal voice he stood the sweat chilld on his mighty limbs
He dropd his hammer. dividing from his aking bosom fled
A portion of his life shrieking upon the wind she fled
And Tharmas took her in pitying Then Enion in jealous fear
Murderd her & hid her in her bosom embalming her for fear
She could arise again to life Embalmd in Enions bosom
Enitharmon remains a corse Such thing was never known   In Eden that one died a death never to be revivd
Urthona stood in terror but not long his spectre fled
To Enion & his body fell. Tharmas beheld him fall
Endlong a raging serpent rolling round the holy tent
The Sons of war astonishd at the Glittring monster drove
Him far into the world of Tharmas into a cavernd rock

But Urizen with darkness overspreading all the armies
Sent round his heralds secretly commanding to depart
Into the north Sudden with thunders sound his multitudes
Retreat from the fierce conflict all the Sons of Urizen at once
Mustring together in thick clouds leaving the rage of Luvah
To pour its fury on himself & on the Eternal Man

Sudden down fell they all together into an unknown Space
Deep horrible without End Separated from Beulah far beneath
The Mans exteriors are become indefinite opend to pain
In a fierce hungry void & none can visit his regions

{6} *Vala*, p. 22 (infra-red photography). *By courtesy of the Trustees of the British Museum.*

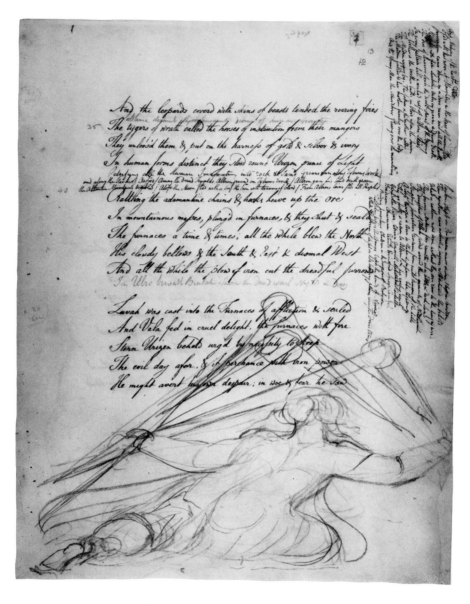

{7} *Vala*, p. 25 (infra-red photography). *By courtesy of the Trustees of the British Museum.*

Vala incircle round the furnaces where Luvah was clos'd
In joy she heard his howlings, & forgot he was her Luvah
With whom she walkd in bliss, in times of innocence & youth

Hear ye the voice of Luvah from the furnaces of Urizen

If I indeed am Valas King & ye O sons of Men
The workmanship of Luvahs hands: in times of Everlasting
When I call'd forth the Earth-worm from the cold & dark obscure
I nurturd her I fed her with my rains & dews, she grew
A scaled Serpent, yet I fed her tho' she hated me
Day after day she fed upon the mountains in Luvahs sight   50
I brought her thro' the Wilderness, a dry & thirsty land
And I commanded springs to rise for her in the black desart
Till she became a Dragon winged bright & poisonous
I opend all the floodgates of the heavens to quench her thirst

                                    And

{8}   *Vala*, p. 26 (infra-red photography). *By courtesy of the Trustees of the British Museum.*

{9} *Vala*, p. 37 (infra-red photography). *By courtesy of the Trustees of the British Museum.*

Infolded in thick clouds, from whence his mighty voice burst forth

O bright ~~Ahana~~ a Boy is born of the dark Ocean
Whom Urizen doth serve, with Light replenishing his darkness
I am set here a King of trouble commanded here to serve
And do my ministry to those who eat of my wide table
All this is mine yet I must serve & that Prophetic boy
Must grow up to command his Prince & all my kingly power
~~But~~ Vala shall become a Worm in Enitharmons Limb
Laying her seed upon the fibres soon to issue forth
And Luvah in the loins of Los a dark & furious death
Alas for me! what will become of me at that dread time?

Ahania bowd her head & wept seven days before the King
And on the eighth day when his clouds unfolded from his throne
She raisd her bright head sweet perfumd & thus with heavenly voice

O Prince the Eternal One hath set thee leader of his hosts

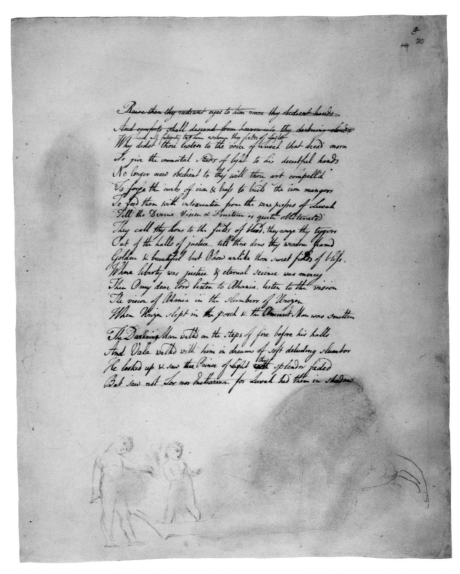

{11} *Vala*, p. 39 (infra-red photography). *By courtesy of the Trustees of the British Museum.*

Of a soft cloud outstretched across, & Luvah dwelt in the cloud

Then Man ascended mourning into the splendors of his palace
Above him rose a Shadow from his wearied intellect
Of living gold pure, perfect, holy; in white linen pure he hover'd
A sweet entrancing self delusion, a watry vision of Man   50
Soft exulting in existence all the Man absorbing

Man fell upon his face prostrate before the watry shadow
Saying O Lord whence is this change thou knowest I am nothing
And Vala trembled & cover'd her face, & her locks were spread on the pavement
I heard astonishd at the Vision & my heart trembled within me
I heard the voice of the Slumberous Man & thus he spoke
Idolatrous to his own Shadow words of Eternity uttering
O I am nothing when I enter into judgment with thee
If thou withdraw thy breath I die & vanish into Hades
If thou dost lay thine hand upon me behold I am silent
If thou withhold thine hand I perish like a fallen leaf
O I am nothing & to nothing must return again
If thou withdraw thy breath. behold I am oblivion

He ceasd: the shadowy voice was silent, but the cloud hover'd over their heads

{12} *Vala*, p. 40 (infra-red photography). *By courtesy of the Trustees of the British Museum.*

In golden wreathes, the sorrow of Man & the balmy drops fell down
And Lo that Son of Man, that shadowy Spirit of the Fallen One
Luvah. descended from the cloud; In terror Man arose
Indignant rose the Awful Man & turnd his back on Vala

Why roll thy clouds in sickning mists. I can no longer hide
The dismal vision of mine Eyes, O love & life & light;
Prophetic dreads urge me to speak. futurity is before me
Like a dark lamp. Eternal death haunts all my expectation
Rent from Eternal Brotherhood we die & are no more

Here I heard the Voice of the fallen One starting from his sleep

Whence is this voice crying Enion that soundeth in my ears
O cruel pity; O dark deceit; can love seek for dominion

And Luvah strove to gain dominion over the mighty Albion
They strove together above the Body where Vala was inclosd
And the dark Body of Man left prostrate upon the crystal pavement
Covered with boils from head to foot. the terrible smitings of Luvah

Then frownd the Fallen Man & put forth Luvah from his presence
(I heard him: frown not Urizen: but listen to my Vision)

{13} *Vala*, p. 41 (infra-red photography). *By courtesy of the Trustees of the British Museum.*

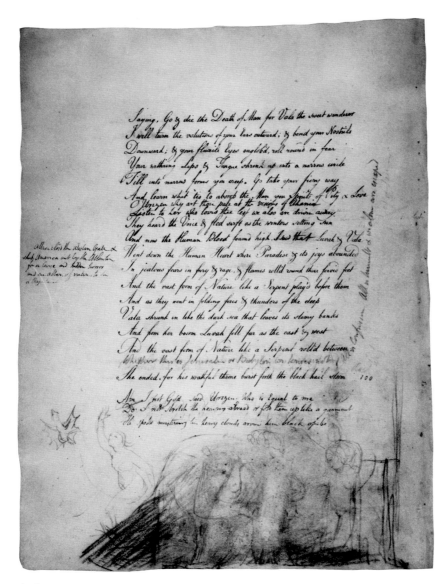

{14} *Vala*, p. 42 (infra-red photography). *By courtesy of the Trustees of the British Museum.*

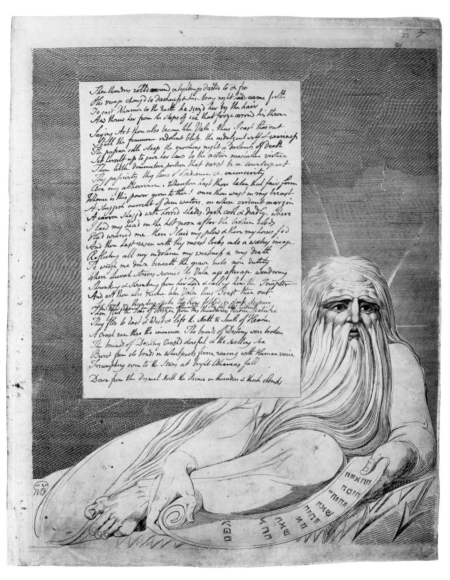

{15} *Vala*, p. 43 (engraving). *By courtesy of the Trustees of the British Museum.*

{16} *Vala*, p. 44 (infra-red photography). *By courtesy of the Trustees of the British Museum.*

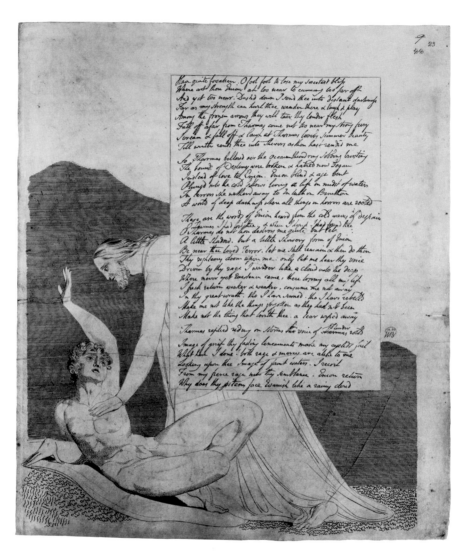

{17} *Vala*, p. 45 (engraving). *By courtesy of the Trustees of the British Museum.*

{18} *Vala*, p. 46 (infra-red photography). *By courtesy of the Trustees of the British Museum.*

{19} *Vala*, p. 47 (engraving). *By courtesy of the Trustees of the British Museum.*

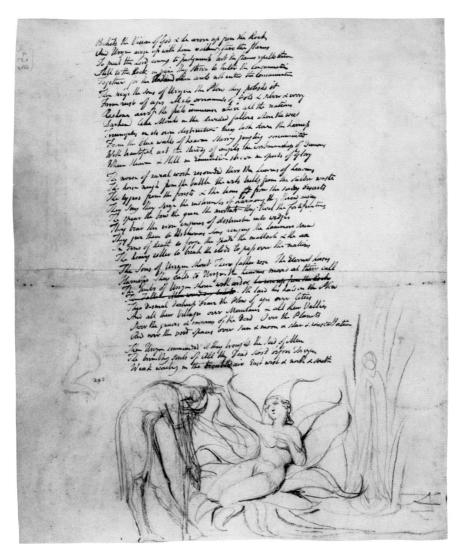

{20} *Vala*, p. 124 (infra-red photography). *By courtesy of the Trustees of the British Museum.*

{21} *Vala*, p. 126 (infra-red photography). *By courtesy of the Trustees of the British Museum.*

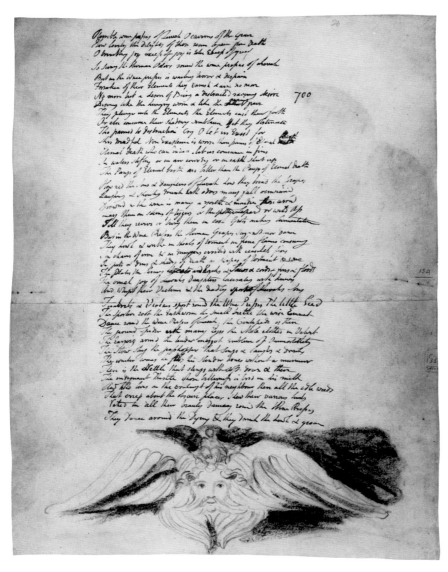

{22} *Vala*, p. 136 (infra-red photography). *By courtesy of the Trustees of the British Museum.*

{23} For *Comus* (water
color, no. 1) : [Comus
and His Rout Surprise
the Lady]. *By
permission of the
Huntington Library,
San Marino,
California.*

{24} For *Comus* (water
color, no. 2) : [Comus,
Disguised as a
Villager, Addresses
the Lady]. *By
permission of the
Huntington Library,
San Marino,
California.*

{25} For *Comus* (water
color, no. 3) : [The
Brothers Seen by
Comus Plucking
Grapes]. *By
permission of the
Huntington Library,
San Marino,
California.*

{26} For *Comus* (water
color, no. 4) : [The
Brothers with the
Attendant Spirit in
the Wood]. *By
permission of the
Huntington Library,
San Marino,
California.*

{27}   For *Comus* (water
        color, no. 5) : [Comus
        with the Lady
        Spellbound at the
        Banquet]. *By
        permission of the
        Huntington Library,
        San Marino,
        California.*

{28}   For *Comus* (water
        color, no. 6) : [Comus
        Driven Out by the
        Brothers]. *By
        permission of the
        Huntington Library,
        San Marino,
        California.*

{29} For *Comus* (water
color, no. 7):
[Sabrina Disenchants
the Lady]. *By
permission of the
Huntington Library,
San Marino,
California.*

{30} For *Comus* (water
color, no. 8): [The
Lady Returns to
Her Parents]. *By
permission of the
Huntington Library,
San Marino,
California.*

Before Ololon Milton stood & perceivd the Eternal Form
Of that mild Vision; wondrous were their acts by me unknown
Except remotely; and I heard Ololon say to Milton.

I see thee strive upon the Brooks of Arnon. there a dread
And awful Man I see. oercoverd with the mantle of years.
I behold Los & Urizen. I behold Orc & Tharmas;
The Four Zoa's of Albion & thy Spirit with them striving
In Self annihilation giving thy life to thy enemies
Are those who contemn Religion & seek to annihilate it
Become in their Feminine portions; the causes & promoters
Of these Religions, how is this thing? this Newtonian Phantasm
This Voltaire & Rousseau; this Hume & Gibbon & Bolingbroke
This Natural Religion! this impossible absurdity
Is Ololon the cause of this? O where shall I hide my face
These tears fall for the little-ones; the Children of Jerusalem
Lest they be annihilated in thy annihilation.

No sooner she had spoke but Rahab Babylon appeard
Eastward upon the Paved work across Europe & Asia
Glorious, as the midday Sun in Satans bosom glowing:
A Female hidden in a Male. Religion hidden in War
Namd Moral Virtue; cruel two-fold Monster shining bright
A Dragon red & hidden Harlot which John in Patmos saw
And all beneath the Nations innumerable of Ulro
Appeard, the Seven Kingdoms of Canaan & Five Baalim
Of Philistea, into Twelve divided, calld after the Names
Of Israel: as they are in Eden. Mountain River & Plain
City & sandy Desert intermingled beyond mortal ken

But turning toward Ololon in terrible majesty Milton
Replied. Obey thou the Words of the Inspired Man.
All that can be annihilated must be annihilated
That the Children of Jerusalem may be saved from slavery
There is a Negation, & there is a Contrary
The Negation must be destroyd to redeem the Contraries
The Negation is the Spectre; the Reasoning Power in Man
This is a false Body; an Incrustation over my Immortal
Spirit; a Selfhood, which must be put off & annihilated alway
To cleanse the Face of my Spirit by Self-examination.

{31}   *Milton*, pl. 46, copy D. *Library of Congress, Rosenwald Collection.*

{32}   *Milton*, pl. 50, copy D. *Library of Congress, Rosenwald Collection.*

{33}　*Jerusalem*, pl. 1, copy E. *From the Collection of Mr. and Mrs. Paul Mellon.*

{34} *Jerusalem*, pl. 59, copy E, detail. *From the Collection of Mr. and Mrs. Paul Mellon.*

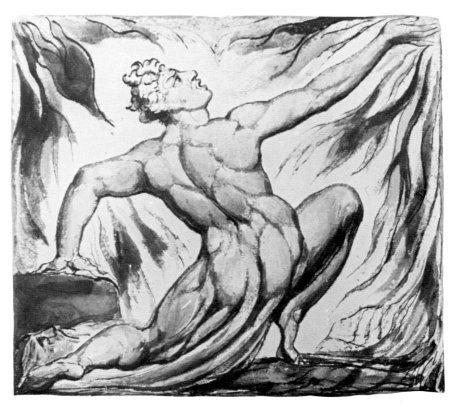

{35} *Jerusalem*, pl. 95, copy E, detail. *From the Collection of Mr. and Mrs. Paul Mellon.*

{36} *Jerusalem, pl. 76, copy* E. *From the Collection of Mr. and Mrs. Paul Mellon.*

All Human Forms identified even Tree Metal Earth & Stone, all
Human Forms identified, living going forth & returning wearied
Into the Planetary lives of Years Months Days & Hours reposing
And then Awaking into his Bosom in the Life of Immortality.
And I heard the Name of their Emanations they are named Jerusalem

The End of The Song
of Jerusalem

{37}   *Jerusalem*, pl. 99, copy E. *From the Collection of Mr. and Mrs. Paul Mellon.*

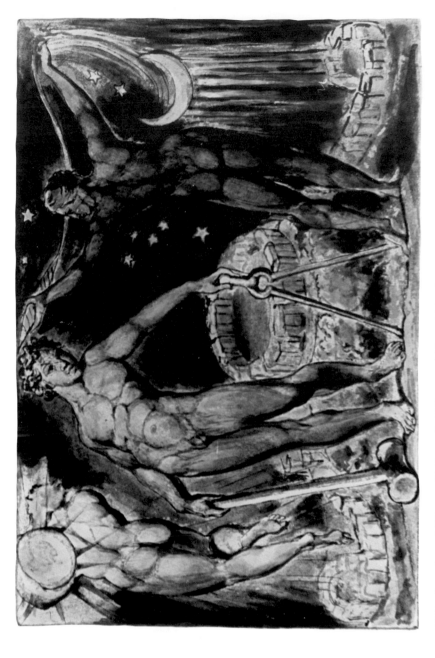

{38}   *Jerusalem*, pl. 100, copy E. *From the Collection of Mr. and Mrs. Paul Mellon.*

holding in his left hand the handle of a hammer and grasping with his right
the handle of a sword. The admonishing man, the first figure at the left,
stands back to the viewer, as Eve does in *Vala*, page 67; he wears an apron
over his tunic, and he gestures upward with his open left hand but points
off to the left as he looks, in three-quarters right profile, at Donald. The
woman at his right stands facing the viewer, as Adam does in *Vala*, page
67, and gestures upward with her right hand and downward with her left,
like Adam. She is clothed, however, in a long empire-style dress and wears
a headdress. Except that her raised and lowered arms are reversed and that
she carries nothing in either hand, she is extremely similar to the woman
in the tempera entitled *Evening*[39] and is more generally related to the
central woman in violet in the Arlington Court picture, as has been noted
by Robert Simmons and Janet Warner.[40] The figure of Donald is not fugitive, as is the wayfarer in the *Vala* engraving, but neither is he resolutely
laboring as is the Conjurer in Red, the central man in the Arlington Court
picture, nor yet victorious like Los the blacksmith at the end of *Jerusalem*.
But if he turned around he might control the sunny globe.

The connection of this dereliction with page 66, the first full-page design
in *Vala* since the frontispiece, page 2, is predictably oblique. Full-page
designs ought to be synoptic rather than ancillary, and this vantage point
would be an excellent one from which to look forward to the end. Margoliouth recognizes some of the problems raised by this design, but does not
appreciate the imaginative issues: "If the drawing is late enough, it may
represent the risen Eternal Man and his four spiritual sense of 'Life's' or
Zoas. It cannot represent the Los of Night V" (p. 126). But a full-page
representation of Los *as victim* is precisely what is not wanted at this point,
after so many images of failure; if Los is ever going to set things straight—
or if the Eternal Man is ever going to reanimate—it is quite time to give a
pictorial indication of what the new age has in store. In this hinge design
between the first and second parts of *Vala*, we are shown the central man
from behind, just as in *Jerusalem* 76 {36} we are shown from behind the
still potentially regenerate Albion, standing with outstretched arms before
Christ crucified. His position as master of the sun in *Vala*, page 66, also
prefigures that of the Spectre of Urthona, who bears off the sun in *Jerusalem*
100 {38}; he, as I have argued above, is derived from the man in *Vala*,
page 2. The text on page 65 bespeaks Urizen's resolve to explore the graves,
as he is shown doing in *Urizen* 23 and later in *Vala*, page 74. But in time
only Los can control the sun when, as in *Jerusalem* 1 or 97, he assumes the

39. Reproduced by Geoffrey Keynes in *The Tempera Paintings of William Blake: A
Critical Catalogue* (London: Arts Council of Great Britain, 1951), pl. 2.

40. "Blake's Arlington Court Picture: The Moment of Truth," *Studies in Romanticism*, 10 (1971), 9.

burden of our friend Diogenes the Grecian. One also recalls the prophetic presence who appears in *Songs* 28, the frontispiece to *Experience*, with an angelic child on his head. When the god displays a human form rather than appearing as a light, a halo, it is a sign that things are gathering to an end.[41] Or, to translate Blake's picture on *Vala*, page 66, into Greek, if the central man has temporarily raised the temporal sun he is Hercules-Los; if he has finally mastered the eternal Sun he is Atlas-Albion. Admittedly the Greek stories told of their heroes holding up the *sky*, rather than the *sun*; but Greek fabulators were notoriously evasive of apocalypse and continued to cherish dark mysteries. We are here concerned with what the Greeks were driving at, even if they did not quite recognize it. And notice the curious curved lines related to this sun, which has been brought under control: may not these lines delineate the rest of the sky reordered? Consider the similar lines surrounding the defeated, if defiant, Satan on page 111 of Blake's *Notebook*.

The subordinate figures in this picture are two men with outstretched arms who fly beneath the arms of Los and two women who sit crouching below them; thus they cannot represent all four Zoas, as previous critics have suggested. There are several kinds of clues to their identities: the two men are in a back-to-front relationship, like Eve and Adam in the facing engraving; this seems to be a sign of positive balance. The analogies in *Urizen* indicate that the man facing the viewer at his right is Urizen himself, here beardless, as portrayed with upraised hands and knees in *Urizen* 12. The figure at the viewer's left bears a resemblance to the Earth-explorer in *Urizen* 10 who, in turn, is the same figure represented from the front in *The Gates of Paradise* 3 as the spirit of Earth and is thus identifiable as Los (toiling in his temporal dimension). Almost the same figure is represented as Satan in the first design for *Paradise Regained*;[42] in idea, this similarity

41. As has sometimes been observed, this redemptive image is modulated and magnified as *The Whirlwind: Ezekiel's Vision of the Cherubim and the Eyed Wheels*. See my article on this picture, mentioned in n. 10 above. A front view of the central man of *Vala*, p. 66, is given in the drawing that Keynes calls *Los Supporting the Sun*, reproduced in *Drawings 1956*, pl. 24, which is also related to the other drawing I refer to in n. 34 above. Though very intense and with legs spread, this figure, the obverse of the central man in *Vala*, is the positive alternative to such heroic villains as Nelson, as I explain in further detail in a review of Morton D. Paley's *Energy and the Imagination: The Development of Blake's Thought* in *English Language Notes*, 9 (1972), 210–216. The fact that the sun in this drawing exudes lightning correlates with the bolt of the benign Thunder God of *Vala*, p. 65; and, as will be noted, the central man of *Vala*, p. 66, is also flanked on the right side with bolts.

42. Reproduced in David Bindman, *William Blake: Catalogue of the Collection in the Fitzwilliam Museum, Cambridge* (Cambridge: Heffer, 1970), pl. 23. It is also suggestive that in this picture of the *Baptism of Christ* the almost nude central figure of Christ is flanked to the left by John the Baptist, whose back is toward the viewer,

of delineation between Los and Satan may foreshadow that time in *Jerusalem* when Los becomes able to face the infernal in himself. On page 66 Los seems first to have been represented either with a cracked head or as a naked brain, but the final version in black crayon shows him in three-quarters right profile, with upturned face; presumably the cracks or striations are still there, but they have been reintegrated by an outline. Los's right arm was redrawn at a greater angle from the vertical, but he evidently remains enwrapped in the cloud visible at his right. The figure seated beneath him, also redrawn several times to emphasize greater alertness and even readiness to arise, can be none other than Enitharmon herself. The figure of unbearded Urizen at the right may well be veiled (or, if under water, he may be identified as Tharmas). This figure may be wielding a spear in his left hand while his right hand conducts down a sketchy bolt of lightning; it seems to touch him on the right side of the chest and then continue down either to smite the bound hair of his downtrodden Emanation, Ahania, who is hunched up in despair, or else to spend itself behind her. This bolt recalls that of the admonishing Thunder God on the recto. One infers that, in reaching for the sun, both Los and Urizen have lost track of their obligations to their Emanations. Perhaps the distinct pencil marks on the right shoulder blade of the central man is the sign of a primal scar that is healing but is still uncured. If he were Adam's successor Albion, this would be no wonder. Some viewers may be unwilling to see these marks as a scar at all, but if one recalls the symbolism of the chest wounds (in the front, to be sure) of Los on page 48 and Enitharmon on page 50 he should not be unprepared for such speculations.

The pair of pages 69 and 68 does not stand in a clearly illustrative relation to the text; and yet there has been a persistent tradition in the work of Damon, Wright, and Margoliouth (see p. 132) to identify the woman in the drawing as one of the three daughters of Urizen encountered by her father in this episode, which is partially derived from the encounter of Satan with his daughter Sin in *Paradise Lost*. Once again Blake's pictorial initiative becomes more apparent, if not perfectly clear, when one considers the choice of the engraving as deliberate, rather than accidental. In the text of *Night Thoughts* that accompanies the original design for page 69, the large woman is identified as Reason, displaying the balanced scales of Justice to her scribal daughter, Faith, who sits beneath her, looking up attentively with her pen poised on a large sheet of paper in her lap. It is evident in the context of Young's poem as interpreted by Blake that this dominance of

and to the right by a woman who faces the viewer. In the next two pictures of the *Paradise Regained* series, the main figures, Christ and Satan, and Andrew and Simon Peter, stand in a back-to-front relationship to the viewer, as in the *Vala* designs in question.

Reason is sinister; small clues, from the spiked crown on Reason's head to her concealed left foot, substantiate this interpretation. The beautiful head-on drawing of the woman with dangling head and flowing hair on page 68 can thus be seen either as a sequel to page 69, with Reason now downcast, or as a complement to it which presents the third of Urizen's daughters. It is suggestive to recognize that the woman on page 68 is closely related to the figure of the mourning Eve in the late tempera version of *The Body of Abel Found by Adam and Eve*, though Eve is less symmetrically presented in the group design. This figure is also related to Job's mourning wife in *Job 6, Satan Smiting Job with Sore Boils* (the tempera is a companion picture to the *Body of Abel*, in which Cain has the same face as Satan[43]), who, in turn, is derived from the mourning woman depicted in the last plate of *America,* 16, whose hair turns into a veritable waterfall—as does the hair in *Vala,* page 68. When faces are thus hidden, it is particularly difficult to supply names for identification, but the woman on page 68 can hardly be Faith per se, for Faith is represented on page 69 with a very lank head of hair; it would take some of Reason's luxuriant growth to make such a waterfall as on page 68.

Both the engraving on page 71 and the drawing on page 70 have distinct textual connections, but the relationship between the designs does not become clear until one recognizes the bridge design for *Night Thoughts*, 494 (IX, 76). In that picture the entire right edge and bottom of the design are given over to jaws with triangular teeth like those of the monster in *Vala,* page 70. But in the *Night Thoughts* design this monster, "dread Eternity," has a long curving tongue on which a crouching female figure is holding her head and crying out in horror at her imminent fate. Her terror is an intensification of the consternation of the alarmed poet in *Vala,* page 71, who has just been awakened by the onset of the Urizenic figure of Death the bellman; indeed the large bell with its clapper, together with the arrow-head that is visible, constitutes a veritable mouth that would be sufficient cause for alarm if perceived. Textual connections on page 71 (second portion) to the engraving include the "bed" and "rising" of Urizen (ll. 30, 32) and his "pen" and "books" (ll. 35, 39). The drawing of the wonderful dragon with short tail, human hands and feet, and a navel, is correctly related by Bentley to the alligator in Hayley's *Ballads* because of its gaping jaws. It is also a kind of consolidated foreshadowing of the epiphany of Leviathan and Behemoth in *Job* 15.[44] Margoliouth (p. 132) connects the beast with the "dishumanized men" mentioned in the text, line 31; and of course the visions of "monsters" (l. 20), "serpents . . . stretched out enor-

43. These pictures are reproduced in *Tate Catalogue*, nos. 54 and 55.
44. Reproduced by Geoffrey Keynes in *William Blake's Engravings* (London: Faber and Faber, 1950), pls. 38 and 59; hereafter called *Engravings 1950*.

mous length" (1. 33), "ribbd / And scaled monsters" (ll. 34–35), also in
the text on page 70, are all relevant, as is the "fierce scorpion glowing with
gold" on page 71 (first portion), line 1. All these creatures and objects—
the consolidated dragon, the various percepts in the text on page 71, and
the awakened sleeper, his literary accoutrements, and his supernatural
awakener in the engraving on page 71—can be understood as identities of
Urizen and products of his several metaphysics. As with the angel in *The
Marriage of Heaven and Hell*, it depends upon the eye of the beholder.

The texts on the lower half of page 72 and the top half of page 73 are
taken up with a lament of Urizen over the "poor ruind world" (p. 72, l. 35)
which has fallen into desolation, just as he himself has:

Where joy sang in the trees & pleasure sported on the rivers
And laughter sat beneath the Oaks & innocence sported round
Upon the green plains . . .

(p. 72, l. 39—p. 73, ll. 1–2)

He is trapped in "this world of Cumbrous wheels / Circle oer Circle" (p.
72, ll. 22–23), where a web follows him "from Vortex to Vortex" (p. 73,
l. 33) down to "the dark horrors of the Abysses lion or tyger or scorpion"
(p. 73, l. 39). With this final identity we are back with one of the terms for
the dragon on page 70, but it applies practically as well for the great python
dragon of the engraving on page 73, which the woman in this design is
attempting to escape, with appeals directed above. But there is only a vacuum there and her only support is a waning moon. In the *Night Thoughts*
watercolor sequel, no. 79 (III, b), it is made clear that the beast succeeds
in swallowing both his tail and his lady, and she is shown howling deep
within while the snake smiles contentedly. The drawing on page 72 of *Vala*
may likewise be a kind of sequel to the engraving. In the final state of the
drawing, three women (as many as seven were drafted) languish in various
postures of despair underneath one branch of a large-trunked, somewhat
serpentine, dead tree that projects another broken bifurcated limb up the
right margin. The largest of these women has long flowing hair and she is
seated within what is probably a roughly drawn scythe. These are undoubtedly the three daughters of Urizen seen before on pages 68 and 69. The
suggestion that the tree is a kneeling, headless man is strengthened by the
undersketching within the trunk of a kneeling figure, in a robe, who has
a head. This tree is quite similar to the dead one at the left in the middle
design for the second page of "The Little Girl Lost" (*SE* 35), the hint that
a tree is inhabited by a sinister human presence is indicated in some versions
of "Holy Thursday" (*SE* 33), and the quoted line of verse about the "Oaks"
recalls the "Ecchoing Green" (*SI* 6). The serpentine tree of *Vala*, page 72,
is Urizen himself, who is alternatively symbolized by the great python on

page 73. One also recalls such animated trees as those in *Milton* 16 and 42.

Whereas the connections between engraving and drawing in the pairs immediately preceding are not at once obvious, in the case of pages 75 and 74 the connections are perhaps less close than they at first seem to be. Because of the obvious imagistic relationship between the drawing on page 74 and the design in *Urizen* 23, in which Urizen carries a sun like a bowling ball, and perhaps also because Apollo hides his head on page 75 within the very orb of the sun, it is usually assumed that Urizen is depicted in page 74 as carrying the sun. Moreover, we are reminded in the text (p. 74, l. 35; p. 75, l. 3) that he carries a "globe of fire." But if one looks carefully, he sees that Urizen is carrying a *vortex* (which emits no beams), not a globe; it is a *way* of looking at things, a *prejudice*, rather than a source of illumination of reality, which is what our prophetic friend Diogenes the Grecian (*MHH* 13: *38*) tried to teach all men to understand.[45] Urizen's left arm was redrawn several times, though never in the straight-arm position of *Urizen* 23: first it was a short withered arm ending in a claw, then a regular-sized arm with only the stump of a hand, and finally with the hand raised and pressed against the edge of the paper—evidently. When the pages of the manuscript were mounted, the person responsible was so mechanical as to lay down the verso sides on the edge of framing paper, rather than to glue down the edges of the engraved rectos, which have no comparable interest in this part of the manuscript; however, this ill-considered system of display only rarely obscures the manuscript.

In the text of *Night Thoughts* it is clear that the engraving on page 75 shows Apollo covering his eyes so as not to see the Crucifixion of Christ. Since in page 74 Urizen is said to be approaching the crucified Orc, the utilization of this engraving can hardly be coincidental. There is a sense in which Apollo with his team of four horses can be said to *be* Urizen, as in the case of *Job* 14.[46] Thus the facing designs reveal Urizen first bringing his prejudices with him on his self-selected, fact-finding mission and then hiding his eyes from the facts that appear too horrendous to be faced.

Night VI ends, as did Night V, with a full-page design. As Margoliouth notes (p. 133), Keynes, Damon, and Wright all identify the figure here as a nude woman, descending, but Margoliouth insists "it is a man with a well-

45. I realize that the object here declared to be a vortex will not seem sufficiently different from what I simply declare to be a sun on p. 66 to satisfy all readers that Blake intended to make a distinction. Apart from the fact that the sun on p. 66 has beams of sorts—below and on either side of the curves I have taken to indicate the sky—and that what Urizen carries on p. 74 is shaped like a roughly drawn helix or vortex ring (a "Slinky"!), there is no great difference in delineation, but perhaps none is to be expected. It is worth considering that the word "vortex" enters Blake's prophetic vocabulary with *Vala*, and that the vortex is not otherwise depicted in the designs.

46. Reproduced in *Engravings 1950*, pl. 58.

developed chest," while Bentley cautiously indicates that it is a man "in the attitude of 'Glad Day,' his arms outstretched, dancing toward us." Stevenson also sees the figure as a male. Margoliouth further suggests that the genitals were erased, "probably as a preliminary to the substitution of scales" (p. 133). The erasures in the genital area have been so thorough that one cannot say for certain, but it appears that initially the figure was a male with a large erect phallus and scrotum. The genitals were then erased, but there remain visible two lines which need to be accounted for. The first consists of three connected curves and a loop in the navel area; they suggest neither scales nor pubic hair, the conjectures that first come to mind. The second curve is in the crotch and, in itself, would naturally indicate a vagina. Possibly at this stage the breasted effect was increased, but Blake never added the large nipples that would have been necessary to make this figure unequivocally female. Where a figure indubitably female is depicted, as in *Vala*, pages 44 {16} and 50, such details are not necessary. It is consistent with the puzzlement associated with the various drafts of Night VII that this figure could be connected either with the engraving of the serpent-entwined crucified *man* of Night VII [a], page 77, or with the engraving of the diving *woman* with downstretched arms who tries to awaken the thorn-vine-entwined poet in Night VII [b], page 91. The fact that the male form of the figure on page 76 is related to the first page of this Night, supposedly the *later* version, whereas the altered version that looks more like a woman is more closely related to the first page of the Night, supposedly the *earlier* version, seems at first rather confusing. But the reader must bear in mind that the meaning of the terms "earlier" and "later" depends on the aspect of the manuscript one is studying. It is quite possible that Blake became reluctant to indicate the sex of the figure unequivocally because he might have had to change the figure, which had already been first male, then scaled, then female, yet again before he reached a final solution to the problem of the intractable Night VII.

Bentley does well to draw our attention to the Glad Day analogy, but whether we are thinking of *Albion rose* or of the tiny man in the second tendril frame at the left in the *Introduction* to *Innocence* (*SI* 4), the characteristic posture of Glad Day is to rest on his *left* foot, with the arms raised above the shoulders, if at all, at a less steep angle. A comparable figure resting on his right foot with out-thrust right hip and genital scales is Satan, in the design, mentioned above, for *Job* 6, *Satan Smiting Job with Sore Boils*, though his arms are also outspread horizontally.[47] Another detail of the drawing not mentioned previously is the fact that the rather dim face of the figure is distinctly framed with a roughly circular line that could hardly

47. Ibid., pl. 48.

have been the draft for a head, because the scale would obviously have been too small. Quite possibly this is to be understood as the facial opening in a helmet. A similar figure of a helmeted warrior, stepping on his left foot, however, but with comparably upstretched arms, is to be found in the fourth design for Gray's "Triumphs of Owen."[48] The style of Owen's helmet does differ a little, in that it has an extra cheekbone curve, but it is otherwise quite similar; moreover, Owen wears a very hairy "feathered" crest that extends down to the back of his neck and thus creates an effect quite like the faint wisps of hair surrounding the head of the figure in *Vala*, page 76. These locks of hair also bear a considerable resemblance to the aforementioned flames of hair displayed by Los on page 62. I may add that in Bentley's reproduction there are to the left of this figure's nose two distinct irregular lines that were not remarked in my notes. I am informed by Erdman that these are in the original, but I am unable to guess what they may have been intended to represent; tears are very improbable. Erdman speculates that these might be deletion marks: the nose and mouth certainly needed more delineation.

Concerning the breasted effect of the figure, which Bentley suggests was increased in revision, comparable effects have proven puzzling in other Blake pictures, notably *The Little Boy Found* of *Innocence* (*SI* 14).[49] In the drawing there is certainly more suggestion of breasts than, for example, in the comparable figures of Albion, Satan, or Owen, already mentioned. There is more too than is to be seen on the chest of Cain in the drawing of *Cain and the Body of Abel*,[50] a comparable full-chest drawing of about this period in Blake's career. The figure of Cain there rushes off with his legs in practically

48. Reproduced in *Blake's Gray*, design 90.

49. Thomas E. Connolly and George R. Levine, "Pictorial and Poetic Design in Two Songs of Innocence," *PMLA*, 83 (1967), 257–264; David V. Erdman, "Note," *Blake Newsletter*, 1, i (1967), [9]; John E. Grant, "Recognizing Fathers," *Blake Newsletter*, 1, ii, (1967), 7–9; Thomas E. Connolly and George R. Levine, "Recognizing Mother," *Blake Newsletter*, 1, iii (1967), 17–18; John E. Grant, "Mother of Invention, Father in Drag or Observations on the Methodology That Brought About These Deplorable Conditions and What Then Is To Be Done," *Blake Newsletter*, 2 (1968), 29–32, and 50–54. Fuseli's ambiguous representations of sexuality are discussed by Tomary, *Drawings by Fuseli*, p. 9.

Evidence is accumulating that Blake too was sometimes at pains to indicate sex changes in delineating figures. One bizarre case occurs in the *Night Thoughts* material: In the title page for Night II, no, 36 (II, a) and in the commonest state of the engraving, p. [17]—one of four designs not employed in *Vala*—the figure who stands in the crotch of Time is unquestionably male. Yet in an alternative state utilized in some published copies this figure was given carefully engraved bare female breasts. Such matters will be considered in detail in the forthcoming Clarendon Edition of Blake's illustrations for the *Night Thoughts* (see n. 25 above).

50. Reproduced in *Drawings 1970*, pl. 47.

the same position as those of the tiny figure of the alarmist who rushes to the left to awaken the spectator in the sixth design for *L'Allegro*, where, as I have argued,[51] what seems to be delightful entertainment is actually dereliction of duty on the part of the youthful poet. The alarmist is thus the redemptive counterpart of Cain, that primal troublemaker, just as Albion is the redemptive counterpart of Satan, the sender of disease. The upraised arms of the figure in *Vala*, page 76, which are without weapons such as Owen had, must be a positive sign that remained constant, if indistinct, through the various metamorphoses of the figure. But this figure, through his gesture and the intent look in his eyes, rather than through words, has to communicate what is needful to know to complete the visions of *Vala*.

In order not to complicate unduly the deliberations about this important though enigmatic figure, I have not yet considered another set of hypotheses that, if they are found satisfactory, might substantially solve some of the mysteries of *Vala*, page 76. Let us suppose, as Tolley suggests, that the man was depicted by Blake as having a sceptre-headed erect phallus and let us further suppose, as Erdman suggests, that the genital erasure was done by the subsequent possessor of the manuscript who made comparable erasures elsewhere. If that were the case, what we see in the navel area is not the remnant of genital scales (which are not employed elsewhere in the manuscript) but the tip of the scepter head, the rest of the phallus having been erased. The suggestion of a vagina line that appears in the present state of the drawing might only be an accidental remnant of the scrotum delineation. If the figure had distinctly male genitals, the amount of breasted effect would not make it seem either inordinately female or peculiarly androgynous. Moreover, I am bound to say that, despite the resemblance of this figure to helmeted Owen, the helmeted effect could have been another accident of drafting a full-face image; the device of drawing inner guide lines to the area of facial features is a familiar one in portraiture, though Blake

---

51. See "From Fable to Human Vision: A Note on the First Illustration," in *Blake's Visionary Forms Dramatic*, ed. Erdman and Grant, p. xiii. See also my "Blake's Designs for *L'Allegro* and *Il Penseroso*," pp. 127–128. Another representation of the alarmist figure occurs at the center of the powerful water color entitled *Fire*, reproduced as pl. XXVIII in G. E. Bentley, Jr., *The Blake Collection of Mrs. Landon K. Thorne* (New York: The Pierpont Morgan Library, 1971). But this figure is seen from the right rear rather than from the front, thus differing from the figure in *Vala*, p. 76. A more striking analogy, an alarmed rather than alarmist figure, is that of Oothoon as she is represented running from the pursuit of a flaming sky-god on the title page of *Visions of the Daughters of Albion*. She is in a position almost exactly like that of the problematic figure in *Vala*, p. 76, except that she is looking backward. It is noteworthy that this figure of Oothoon is hardly breasted at all, even less so than the figure in question. The subsequent images of Oothoon in *Visions* are not, however, markedly flat-chested.

does not employ it as mechanically elsewhere in this manuscript. The wavy lines that I take to be the plumes of a helmeted figure are also sufficiently intelligible as Blakean floating hair. The reader is invited to judge between these two divergent accounts of the facts. I hope that one or the other will be adequate to cover the case.

The First Designs for Night III, Pages 37–42

The five pictures after the first of Night III occur on the last sheets in the manuscript before the proof pages of *Night Thoughts* were utilized. Before erasure, they were undoubtedly the most extravagantly erotic sequence of designs Blake is known to have made. It is possible that the expurgatorial erasures were done by some of the Linnells when they possessed the manuscript, but it is also possible that Blake himself did them "as a first step to changes which would have made these particular drawings publishable," as Margoliouth conjectures (p. xv). This form of the theory of Blake's own responsibility seems untenable, however, except as a very preliminary step: the erasures of pages 38–40 are so extensive as to leave no real basis for making more publicly presentable designs even if the erasures had been very thorough—which, in the case of page 40 {12}, they certainly were not. Moreover, page 41 {13} is rather faintly and equivocally drawn, but it is hardly erased; it would have been quite impossible in Blake's time to have "published" a clearly delineated version of this erotic fantasy. At this point we must recall Erdman's theory that Blake's having employed a good copperplate and modified copperplate orthography for transcribing the text seems to bespeak an intention for "publication" only as a unique illuminated manuscript, rather than as a work to be replicated by printing. Thus one is driven back to supposing that Blake himself made some erasures, doubtless before he gave the manuscript to Linnell, or that the Linnells made them, or that both contributed to the censorship, but only in the expectation that some viewer might find this unique manuscript distressing if it were unexpurgated. In any case, the fact that although most of the erasure smudging seems to be the product of a white eraser, some of it seems to be the product of a red one, may be a reason to prefer the hypothesis of joint responsibility. Scraping seems also to have been employed in some places in the manuscript. An added consideration is that India rubber erasers, I have been told by an art historian, were not available in Blake's time and artists commonly employed bread to make erasures. If true, this would have a bearing on which erasure Blake might have been responsible for. But my present notes on methods of erasure are not thorough enough for me to make a reliable report here. Rather than attempt conjectures, I wish merely to bring these matters up in the hope that they will be duly considered in subsequent scholarship. Insofar as possible, I shall also avoid discussion of the textual problems presented by this Night.

What must be recognized immediately, however, is that though there have been relatively few alterations in the text on any of these pages except page 42 {14} (and even that page was not very extensively altered in comparison with others of the manuscript), the pictures do not stand in a close "illustrative" relationship to the text in any of the pages after the first. It is as though Blake chose to present pictorial highlights from one or two episodes which are alluded to dimly if at all in the accompanying text. Yet the evidence does not permit the conjecture that these pictures may not have been intended to accompany these pages of text, since the drawings carefully avoid the text and (with one exception) never touch more than a few words, including catchwords. Blake seems sometimes to have used any blank paper at hand for impromptu sketching, but these designs do not seem the products of such impulses. Indeed, the single instance where the drawing has not carefully avoided the text is on page 37 {9}, which is the one picture undoubtedly illustrative of a text on the same page, even though in this case the lines impinge upon an appreciable number of words.

As is often the case, however, Blake's "illustrative" work adds or alters material beyond anything that could have been inferred from the words themselves, thus presenting the interpreter with a challenge as soon as he has finished his preliminary work of objective description. In page 37 {9}, executed in black crayon and pencil, there is depicted a seated figure, doubtless male, with long hair or a headdress, who is staring to his right, with his right hand raised to his chin and his right elbow resting on the knee of his right leg, which is drawn up under his long robe so that his right foot rests on the neck of the draped figure, unquestionably female, who kneels before him. In his right hand, raised to his chest, are two roughly drawn parallel lines; these probably indicate a book. In her right hand the female figure holds his left foot, the toe of which is at her eye level; it had first been drawn (perhaps as a hoof) down at the bend of her arm in an area subsequently shaded over. As I pointed out in my previously mentioned review article,[52] even a mere description must also mention the fact that, while the man's left foot is human, the toes of his foot are drawn as a crude triple (or quadruple) birdlike claw, and are indicated with the darkest lines in the picture—except for those delineating the eye of the woman. It is conceivable that the lines in question might be taken to be merely crude indications of

52. "Blake: Original and New," p. 363.

the woman's hair, but most viewers have no trouble recognizing the claw-
foot, which was introduced by Blake as an afterthought in crayon. The depiction of such a member certainly makes a sardonic relationship of picture
to text which begins with a description of regal Urizen's "splended feet"
(l. 2). The anxiety manifested in Urizen's facial expression does correspond
to the concern expressed in Ahania's speech (ll. 5 ff), but the viewer must see
what a monster the starry king himself really is. Evidently Blake changed
Urizen's right foot into a claw, to symbolize the bondage that Ahania
suffers without recognizing the cause. Moreover, the distinct horizontal
lines that cross her lower right leg indicate that she is kneeling in water.
Since water is probably also indicated in page 42 {14} and certainly evidenced in pages 44 {16} and 46 {18}, it seems highly probable that Blake
had begun the first design for Night III by employing this discrediting
symbolism.

Blake, of course, could have no sympathy with such obsequiousness as
that of Ahania before either God's priest or king and perhaps even intended
that she be given a black or opaqued eye for her reward (which is much
like the eye of the deluded Los on page 64—and no other in the manuscript)
in addition to having to bear the burden of the claw. It takes a certain kind
of blindness to accede to the demands either of sexism or of more generalized tyranny. For Protestant Blake, genuflection at the feet of another
smacked of papism;[53] thus the angels who obediently lower their sceptres to
the authority of the fat pope in *Europe* 11 earn serpents' tails from the satirical artist. An even closer analogy occurs in *Night Thoughts*, 396 (VIII, 50),
where a simpering priest bows down to kiss the foot of a fat pope, which is
represented as a cloven hoof. Another related design is the third for Blake's
Divine Comedy, the upper section, where a bisexual-appearing priest kneels
before the God of this world who, more appallingly Miltonic than Dantesque,
wields conical vortices and also reveals a cloven hoof to his intimate. This
imposing, difficult picture, which has not so far received adequate comment,
contains a large amount of explicit symbolism bearing on what came before
and what comes after in the Dante designs. In a much simpler way, *Vala*,
page 37, has comparable status as a pivotal design.

---

53. Any recollection of the humility of the Magdalen before Jesus only increases the
irony of Ahania's demeaning conduct: we are not told that Urizen first stooped for her.
The motif of a bowing figure was first tried out in p. 18 before the diving figure was
delineated, but p. 31 is a clear prototype, in which an undoubtedly female figure is
huddled up in genuflection before an evanescent youth. Ahania is naturally to be
understood on p. 37 as going into a crouch after her dive, which is depicted on p. 36.
The appearances of Urizen on pp. 23, 25, and 27 are all more or less compatible with
his appearance on p. 37; this is particularly true because of the turban-hair shown on
p. 23.

It is not, however, as Margoliouth has claimed (p. 114), that page 37, dealing with the appeal of Ahania, is complemented and concluded by page 46, which he supposed, erroneously, has to do with the casting-out of Ahania by Urizen. As I have argued above, page 46 seems to make most sense as a depiction of Tharmas in search of Enion. Nevertheless, both page 37 and page 46 have much to do with the relationship between the sexes, even if the actions shown in these designs are not of the sort ordinarily thought of as erotic. When, however, page 46 is seen as the sequel to page 44, which is undoubtedly erotic, the erotic charge latent in page 46 becomes manifest. Something similar is involved in the relation of the sequence of pages 38–42 to page 37.

Four of the five erotic drawings in *Vala*, pages 38–42, contain distinct, hardly erased figures who observe the action depicted. There is a continuity of this theme from the penultimate design of Night II, *Vala*, page 35, in which, at the right, a young girl looks in alarm and dismay at a man, seen from behind, who is crouched, apparently to defecate. There has been considerable erasure, as well as the addition of foliage, in this area of the drawing, but less in the central area, where two prominent kneeling women watch two others who are gathering vegetated phalluses. The analogy to *The Gates of Paradise* 1 might encourage an identification of these stems as mandrakes, but they show no hominid characteristics. Other details in this complex picture include a third witness seated behind the central kneeling one and, at the left, a standing woman who wears pajamas and carries on her head a characteristic basket filled with the kind of foliage added at the right. Whether this is to camouflage a load of phalluses is uncertain; at least three still grow among the screening foliage at the right, but the central vegetated phallus was subsequently extended to indicate the trunk of a sapling that rises up and out of the picture. The relationship of expurgatorial erasure and redrawing to dispassionate Blakean alteration is highly problematical in many of these designs, and the exegete cannot afford to forget this fact in looking for either the representation or the message. It must be noted that in this, the only page of the manuscript without any textual alteration, there is little that can be thought of as illustrative connection between text and picture. Within Night III, of course, there is a pronounced imagistic continuity between the previously mentioned staring figure of Urizen (as well as the benighted vision of Ahania) in *Vala*, page 37, and the scopophilia and scopophobia of the subsequent designs.

Though infra-red photography rather mitigates the effect, the left pictorial area of *Vala*, page 38 {10}, is one of the most thoroughly erased in the manuscript. Usually the censorship was less effective; as Damon commented of the expurgations as a whole: "the smeared blanks in the designs leave too much to the imagination, as may be seen by tilting the page so that a shadow fills the grooves made by Blake's pencil."[54] But as in other complex erased pictures, the problem is less to discern residual line grooves than to ascertain what stage of pictorial intention one is considering. That Blake seems to have tried out various ideas for the approximately six figures in this picture before final erasure is suggested by the alterations in the two largely unerased figures at the right. This complicates the interpretation of what one is able to make out, but the location of the figures is not in doubt.

The first figure is clearly indicated by the large head, seen in right profile to the left of lines 4–8. The head itself, which, though faint, is hardly erased, is very similar to that of Urizen as presented on page 37 {9}; and since Urizen also speaks most of the text there need be no hesitation in identifying this figure as the "Prince of Light." But he is not "infolded in thick clouds"; as far as can be made out, his body is a large, thick tube that bends inward down the left margin, perhaps over the word "O" in the last line, and then blends into the assembled smaller figures before disappearing. There is much erasure in what would be the right shoulder area, where three or more residual lines converge above the knobbed top of another object indicated by two straight lines; this area extends down from line 6 to almost the bottom line of the text. If this were simply some schematic shoulder and book, there would be no expurgatorial reason to erase the area so thoroughly. We are thus led to conjecture that the "body" is actually a pointed phallic tip to which a human head was somehow attached. Three curved lines to the left of Urizen's head may be representations of clouds, though they are very small. There are two other appendages: one is two parallel, lightly drawn, curved lines in the eight o'clock area; the other is an appendage, 7 cm. long, that extends down to the lower left corner. At times this looks like the draft of a thin leg and large foot, but at other times it seems like an erased tail.

There are three erased figures beneath the text: I shall refer to them, left to right, as the second, third, and fourth figures, respectively. The head of the second, which is curly-haired and which looks out with two distinct eyes and a perhaps merry mouth, is below and to the left of the word "O" in the last line. The rest of the body is unclear; it appears that, at one stage, the right arm of this figure was thrown outward in the eight o'clock area and the right leg went down to seven o'clock; if so, the genitals in this version were severely erased. In this delineation the right arm would be bent across the chest and the left leg drawn in a bent-up position. If this was the form of the first version, the body of this figure was altered to a right profile in which the navel and crotch, to the right of what at first seems the left leg but turns out to be the drawn-up right leg in profile, were distinctly enough drawn to survive erasure. The visibly heavy erasure would thus fall in the

54. *Blake: Philosophy and Symbols*, p. 399.

buttocks area—for no clear reason. The context certainly implies that this figure is Orc.

Just to the right, under the word "Prince," the head and left shoulder of the third figure are indicated, rather dimly and with little erasure, perhaps gazing at the second figure. The third figure bears a considerable resemblance, even in position, to the head at the lower left and also to the head of Enitharmon at the upper right in *Jerusalem* 87.

The fourth figure is much the most difficult to make out. It seems to have been variously drawn under the word "Eternal." The clearest detail is the left leg and foot of a standing figure about 1.5 cm. below the horizontal line. At times the figure seems to wear a conical hat, the tip of which is indicated by a dot under the letter "n" in "Eternal." The body may have been either lean and rather shapeless, or else very fat with its belly extending to the bent right knee of the modified form of the second figure. In the latter case the fourth figure was probably represented as kneeling, rather than standing, with the left knee touching the right knee of the second figure.

If the fourth figure does not kneel, the fifth must have been drafted at one point with its left leg bent back under it, though in what remains of the picture it is the extended form of the underside of this leg and sketched foot that makes the main horizontal line, which extends to within 4 cm. of the left edge of the page. The fifth figure twists back to embrace the sixth figure. It is probably male (despite the suggestion of a right breast) with a fat belly, heavily erased and, probably, a vertically erect phallus which ejaculates in a parting stream above the erased area. The twice-redrawn fat head has a curly forelock and a flabby, rather repellent, face. Damon calls it a Silenus figure.

The sixth figure is undoubtedly a woman, who half-kneels on her right knee in a small depression, while keeping her right foot on the ground. She was first drafted with head and leg farther to the right, head downcast into her raised arm (unless we should take this sketched but unerased figure as an alter-ego) ; but then she was relocated in her present position. There she looks back, with evident alarm, though probably not at Silenus, whose fingers are in her curly hair and whose right arm is under her right arm, which was resketched, but not fully redrawn, as dangling down in front of her. The belly of this woman is unusually slack for a Blakean figure who is not clearly fat; this may be due, in part, to the twist of her body. Her wide-eyed, open-mouthed expression differs sharply from the unpleasing languor of her companion.

The primary analogues in *Vala* for the fourth and fifth figures are to be found on page 52, where a crouching woman attempts to repel a kneeling man, and on page 56, where a seated figure draws toward him a smiling youth on his knees. To these aforementioned drawings may be added that on page 118, where three (or four) figures—the leftmost one of whom may be a longhaired male (though there is an indication of a breast)—appear to be wrestling pleasurably or participating in a "group grope." The twisted posture of the man in page 38, together with his unpleasant fat face, which resembles that of the fat pope in *Europe* 11, gives him a distinctly repulsive appearance. One also recalls other figures, such as fat Simon, who is shown crawling at the left in *The Pit of Disease: The Falsifiers*, in Blake's *Divine Comedy* 58 and 58E, while being watched by Virgil and Dante. If I were to hazard a guess as to the identities of the two visible figures in *Vala*, page 38 {10}, I would say they are a vision of Urizen grown decadent in trying to emulate Orc and of Ahania grown youthful, but more disturbed by what she sees than what she does not feel. In *Vala*, page 37 {9}, Urizen had been alarmed by what he saw, and Ahania had been absorbed in a degrading act of love and obeisance. Here, despite the fact that the text has Urizen describing the supposed activities of a bright boy identifiable as the licentious Orc, it is Ahania who looks alarmed at the erotic vision, while her enfeebled partner derives what pleasure he may. We cannot now say with certainty what it is that Orc, the second figure, was doing that seemed so alarming; but the fact that he was doing it either next to (or even within) the phallic body of censorious Urizen must have made it seem particularly inordinate.

The primal scene, witnessed by two children in *Vala*, page 39 {11}, is much less fully obliterated, but such are the tensions and hazards of describing erotic scenes that there are appreciable discrepancies between the accounts that Damon and Margoliouth give of the largely unerased children. The former would have it that two "boys" are pointing "with glee" (p. 400), while the latter declares that the two children are "horrified" (p. 114) at what they could see. Bentley is probably more accurate in describing the children as a boy and a girl with erased genitals; he describes the girl as shocked, but does not mention the obvious pleasure the indubitable boy at the left takes in the scene he is witnessing. As the last line of text indicates, these children are to be identified as Los and Enitharmon, unobserved as they watch the dreamlike erotic adventures of the "Darkning Man" and Vala. Vala is the larger figure who, as the unerased lines indicate, is seated in left profile with her left leg stretched out almost to Los's left knee, while her right leg is drawn up with her knee close to the left hand of Enitharmon. She is leaning against something and her torso is twisted toward the viewer, with her breasts clearly visible and her sketchily drawn right arm raised beneath them to her left arm, while her sketched left arm is hanging down behind the mound that braces her. The torso position is quite like that of the recumbent woman in *The Marriage of Heaven and Hell* 2, below, while the legs are positioned like those of the woman in *The Marriage of Heaven and Hell* 3, above. Only the head is difficult to make out. It is clear that, in this version, she is not obviously enjoying the lovemaking, but neither is she making much of an attempt to resist the Darkning Man.

He is more fully erased, but is distinctly visible, probably smaller than she, standing crouched between her legs and, at least in one version, probably embracing her around the neck as he pulls her head up to meet his, though her back must have been in a different position to effect this kiss, unless he had decapitated her. The most distinct form of his erased head, which impinged upon the last two words of text, shows him in right profile with a grotesque (possibly caricatured negroid) face and with curly hair. There are drafts of at least three curly heads in this area, which seem to be the result of drawing the two figures first with their heads together kissing and then with them separated. The viewer is inclined to suspect a scene of fellatio here, but there are no certain indications of such action. There seems to be evidence that the man was depicted as having a long, hoselike phallus.

There is no doubt that before erasure the boy Los was depicted with an erection; also previously unmentioned is the presence in the left margin of an enormous phallic object, at least 19.5 cm. tall, which is quite clearly discernible even in the Bentley reproduction. It is possible that this object, which is symbolically a modulation of the sea serpent in the left margin of *Vala*, page 4, was drawn with facial features on the head; and it is certain that at the bottom, diagonal lines meet to form a kind of V-neck collar above swellings that would represent the testes in the scrotum, if it is simply phallic. But these swellings might also represent the breast if the figure were given a human head, presumably of a female with an elongated neck, rather like Tenniel's Alice in the second chapter of *Wonderland*. There are three distinct bumps (the lower one of which is tipped) on the outside of the phallus opposite the first three lines in the last paragraph; they could be taken to be either breasts or huge boils. It must also be noted that the phallus is inner-lined on both sides about 1 cm. from the edge and extending the length of the shaft; possibly this might be the depiction of a sort of seminal reservoir.

It is noteworthy how many continuities of posture and arrangement there are between the facing drawings on pages 38 and 39: Ahania views with alarm as Enitharmon does, and their faces are similar in spite of the difference in their ages. Some of the gestures of Ahania are paralleled in the arm positions of Vala. The Darkning Man presses his affections on a noncompliant Vala, as Urizen had done on Ahania, but Vala's seated and twisted position is much like that of Silenus-Urizen. The postures of the erased figures in page 38 are too problematic for certain analogies, but the shaft-body of phallic Urizen is very comparable to the schematic phallus displayed in the left margin on page 39.

Los and Enitharmon had appeared before in *Vala*, pages 8 and 9, first as infants and then as children. That they should not appear again, at least as children, until this design, is a striking and suggestive consideration in the presentation of this visual story.

The basic positions of the three figures in right profile on page 40 {12} are not in serious question despite the extensive erasure in the middle of the drawing. A woman, with her head at the right and her forearms and hands bent back above her head, lies prone. Between her legs another figure, presumably male, crouches, with his head above her back, and thrusts forward his arms, which are being held by the woman. It appears that neither figure was more than sketched; the back of her head is curiously delineated so as to suggest a nose and face. In several other pictures Blake, likewise, indicates faces in the backs of heads. Damon says that the man is trying to turn over; but Bentley correctly remarks that the position seems to indicate coitus from the rear—there are no remaining lines that make it certain whether vaginal or anal coitus is intended, however. On the rump of the crouching figure is seated, in right profile, a small bird-winged Cupid with an indistinct old face and sketchily indicated outstretched arms in which he holds reins (or less probably a wand) some 7.5 cm. in length, which extend to the man's face. That he was drawn after the man is probable, since the man's rump line shows through Cupid's thigh and knee. On his right foot he wears a distinctly drawn spur with a starred rowel, unquestionably designed to goad his mount on to greater efforts.

This bowless Cupid is doubtless related to the Cupids of *Vala*, pages 4–6, 19, and 108, and his position as rider anticipates that of the wingless riders in pages 134 and 136, previously mentioned. He also has a striking analogue among the *Night Thoughts* designs, 162 (V, 5). Bentley calls attention to the analogy to the winged scribes mounted on the Assyrian beasts in *Jerusalem* 41.

It seems probable that *Vala*, page 40, is a sequel to page 39, in which the sexual union is not face-to-face, perhaps because of the lapsarian sense of shame on the part of both sexes. When desire degenerates into compulsion, a drive, the delights of love cannot be enjoyed as between equals. The next design can be best understood as a further stage of erotic degradation.

Vala, page 41 {13}, certainly represents an erotic fantasy; but, considering that there was only a little erasure, which seems not to have been part of the pattern of expurgation, to describe exactly what is happening is not as easy as it might seem. With a few modifications, Bentley's simple candor describes quite well what the viewer tends to see: "a pencil sketch of a voluptuous nude woman lying on her back, her right leg extended, her left leg bent [back], her back arched, breasts thrust forward, mouth open, who stretches her arms far back to . . . lines which seem to represent the enormous

penis and scrotum of a nude [male torso] kneeling behind her." One could
say more about the obvious delight the woman derives from her activity, and
the curious headless torso needs discussion, but the most noteworthy detail
unmentioned by Bentley or other describers is that the woman is unmistakably experiencing anal penetration from a large and long phallic object that
seems unattached to either the male or anything else in the picture. The fact
that the right side has no line of closure makes the object an uncertain
representation of a dildo. What the viewer sees is physiologically impossible,
but impossible accomplishments are common in pornography, and students
of Blake know that his characters must be contortionists even in more commonplace encounters. Whether the woman is to be understood as merely
manipulating a penis and scrotum, as Bentley says, or whether the torso is
indeed headless and limbless, or only drawn in such a position as to render
these members invisible, the overall scene becomes more intelligible when
the interpreter relates the picture to the text and recognizes the two figures
as Vala and the Ancient Man—Albion.

The male "body" being played with by Vala evidently lies on its back,
with the head probably sunken into the chest and the thighs widespread; the
left thigh ends in a rather pointed knee, and the calf is invisible. The large
penis, which is held in the left hand of Vala, is pushed against the left thigh,
and was drawn without any tip; the shaft is crossed by the point of Vala's
hair. There are many curly lines, partially rubbed out, on the right thigh at
both sides of Vala's right hand; one initially supposes them to be pubic hair,
but because of their asymmetrical arrangement they are probably representations of Albion's boils, which are, of course, Job's traditional venereal
boils. Unless the viewer recognizes that Albion's penis is represented without a tip and that the object attached to Vala's buttocks is indeed phallic, and
until he further understands that he is being shown an erotic *fantasy*, he may
"doubt from what he sees" and find the action unintelligible in some particulars. In sequence and in context, however, the only puzzling lines are the
two nearly parallel ones crossed by a curve near Vala's right shin. I suspect
they are a quick attempt on the part of the artist to sketch the basis of some
detail that was proving difficult to render, but I do not know with certainty
which detail.

The continuity of symbolism from pages 40 and 41 confirms the indications of anal eroticism delineated in the latter, which might otherwise seem
too improbable. As in relationships between wrestlers and dancers, Albion
first has Vala down; but then she gets loose and reciprocates in her fashion.
A more external and less conventionally shocking view of the relationship
on page 41 {13} is indicated in *Jerusalem* 25. We have already observed
how the draft version of page 64 is related to this plate in *Jerusalem*, but in
this case both *Vala* drawings seem more closely related to the later drawing

than they are to one another. In *Jerusalem* 25, if the gelded or harnessed figure of Albion in this plate were rotated fifty degrees, the cruel charmer Rahab, who is seated on a suggestively phallic stone, could easily get into a position to re-enact amatory adventure of her mother depicted in *Vala*, page 41. In doing so, she would utilize such other details from *Jerusalem* 25 as the bent left leg of Tirzah, she would substitute phallic manipulation for the navel-cord manipulation preferred by her sister, and she would employ a two-handed strategy like Vala's in this plate; here she spreads rooty toils to trap the man, but elsewhere in Blake (including a *Night Thoughts* engraving [6 E], p. 10, notable by its absence from the manuscript) her avatars, called Sin, spread plagues in this manner. And that is the right-handed strategy in *Vala*, page 41.

There is a continuity of the motif of erotic manipulation between pages 41 and 42, and the sense of grotesqueness of the action in the latter design is probably increased by the implicit contrast with the designs on page 41 and earlier which depict relationships between more or less consenting adults— though often witnessed by interested children. In page 42 {14}, a scene partially described in the previous section of this essay, a large woman span-measures the penis of a boy who looks up smiling at her, with his right hand resting on her back and his left arm crooked confidently at his side, with a twofold object, some 1.5 cm. in diameter, hanging from it; this toy has four fairly distinct dots on it and might be a butterfly. If so, it would represent a variation of the *Night Thoughts* motif of boy pursuing bird used in pages 49 and 77. The span-measurement motif is also a variation of a *Night Thoughts* motif, that performed by the father in page 63.

The events on page 42 occur in a foreground area sharply set off from the background by the very heavily shaded horizontal line to the viewer's right, which has been considerably erased, and the diagonal line at the viewer's left, the lower triangular area of which is unerased. These curtains seem originally to have been the encompassing robes of a central, rather sphinx-like, figure, whose nose is clearly discernible under the "b" in the word "black" in the last line, even though it has been blended into the top of the head of the bent-over woman. When this area was annexed to the woman, the spirit was more dimly indicated at two different angles, with eyes nearly under the letters "a" and "k" in "black." The small-but-breasted girl who stands composedly, though with legs crossed, and looks on was probably added at the same time. I suspect she was relocated from a position which originally had her standing with her head where the woman's shoulder is now. To make room for her there, the raised left arm, or staff, or even tree trunk, of the superintending spirit was erased. But the fact that the girl stands with her left arm bent rather seductively behind her head may indicate that she is oddly holding hands with the man she loves. As a modulation of a motif on page 40 this seems the more probable. It is noteworthy that the shadow at the left is distinctly delimited and (so far as the deplorable British Museum mounting allows us to see) this delimitation occurs, unevenly, all across the bottom. This, together with the fact that the lower legs of none of the three standing figures are indicated, makes it clear that they are all standing in water (or mud).

These figures are curtained off from the area at the left in the background where another nude woman (an alter-ego?) is apparently in pursuit of a very clearly delineated and unerased bat-winged phallus.[55] I have already pointed out how this creature is prefigured in the phallic symbolism on pages 26 and 39, and it can also be recognized as a variation on the symbolism of the boy with a butterfly, who is being erotically manipulated in the foreground of this picture. Another noteworthy detail is that, though the woman is less distinctly delineated than the bat-winged phallus, she is drawn with a slack belly and a ponytail, and her raised right hand has an indication of a glove, or at least a cuff, on it. In this detail there is a suggestive relationship to the weirdly gloved left hand of the distorted woman at the lower left in *Jerusalem* 31. The forward curve of the fingers on the raised hand of the pursuing woman forbids us to think her hand is held in a backhand position, as the bend of her arm might lead us to suppose. Curiously, she must be pursuing the bat, in spite of the fact that there are two clear and distinct, curved string lines that turn upward on either side of her; they would seem to be tether lines on the creature, although neither is quite clearly connected to it. The nearer string, indeed, appears to come from the woman's almost invisible left hand, though the secure for the other is not indicated. The motif of trying to catch a bat-winged creature occurs also in *Jerusalem* 13, where the pursuer is a man and the creature more like a flying

55. Jean H. Hagstrum, *William Blake: Poet and Painter* (Chicago: Univ. of Chicago Press, 1964), p. 89, traces the origin of Blake's motif, utilized in *Thel* 6 and *America* 11, of children riding a serpent to the ancient Priapian cult statuary of a child riding a phallus. The example he gives, pl. XLIX–A from Herculaneum, shows that the phallus also has wings, though not imposing ones. In Richard Payne Knight's *A Discourse on the Worship of Priapus and its Connection with the Mystic Theology of the Ancients* (London, 1786), Blake could have seen engravings of other winged phalluses without riders that more closely resemble the one in *Vala*, p. 42. Especially on pl. [VII], entitled *Phallic Figures Found in England*, Blake would have been impressed by Fig. 3, which has large wings near the rear, and Fig. 4, which has triangular bird wings in the same area. Both have extra phalluses appended and are depicted as walking on hind legs, rather than flying, and neither has bat wings; but Blake would certainly have found in them corroboration of or license for his fantasy. Payne Knight himself tried to suppress this book, and as a result it was very rare, thus adding to its piquancy. It was published with an introduction by Ashley Montagu, in company with Thomas Wright's *The Worship of the Generative Powers* (1866), as *Sexual Symbolism* (New York: Julian Press, 1957).

insect. It appears that bat-wingedness is never a favorable sign in Blake's pictorial symbolism, partly because of the overwhelmingly sinister image of the bat-winged spectre in *Jerusalem* 6. Thus one suspects that, even if she should catch her quarry, the pursuing woman in *Vala*, page 42, will not experience satisfaction from it. Blake did not love life the less for it, but he seems to have observed more clearly than most libertarians in the eighteenth century how the pursuit of natural happiness tends to lead insensibly toward a quest for the unnatural. It was also apparent to him that neither prudence nor authority is able to offer useful guidance in the necessary task of discriminating the desirable from the compulsive. Since they cannot bear to envision enough, traditional arbiters cannot be believed when they try to say what is too much. If we look carefully at *Vala*, page 42 {14}, we can see that the lines, far from leading the bat-winged phallus, must be reins that are dropped down by it to lead the woman on and on. The bat-winged phallus is a further metamorphosis of Cupid's image, as the God of Love appeared to the viewer in page 40 {12} spurring on to greater efforts and directing with the reins the most extreme exertion the Darkning Man was capable of. In page 42 there is a variously perverse scene which is ripe for the intervention of the engraved Urizen-Death on page 43 {15}, whose message of the spears is always "Thou Canst Not," whatever the message of the scroll may say.

Blake's Art of Concluding: The Designs for Night IX

Here I propose to make a rapid survey of some visual strategies employed by Blake to bring his story of *Vala* to a conclusion in Night IX. The last drawing for the previous Night, page 116, is an optimistic and effective drawing of Christ walking (originally striding) and pushing the clouds aside. And the first engraving for Night IX, page 117, shows the rescue of an individual spirit by angels after death, which may be taken to prefigure "The Last Judgment" announced in the subtitle. But then, in quick succession, we are shown, in page 118, the erotic entanglement that is certain to get nowhere; a spirit pointing down from a cloud to the earth—doubtless a trouble spot—in page 119; a pining woman in page 120; a dying man, though attended by a friend and by good spirits, in page 121; an exhausted woman in page 122; a tethered poet in page 123; and then, page 124 {20}, a scene in which a crippled man leans on a crutch and receives a fascinating or compassionate touch on the forehead from a nude young woman who is seated on a kind of lily. This scene is backed by some vegetation that may be flaming, and contains within it a draped, probably female, figure. Other details, such as that the man's head was probably first bent so as to look at the woman's prominent vulva before he rectified his posture and received his blessing, or that he was crippled by the loss of his left foot, or that there is water to the lower right—all these details are compatible with the interpretation of the picture as a meeting of Albion and Vala.

Something of this message must be getting through to the man in page 125, as the moments of time bring truth to one seated in a poet's chair. But in page 126 {21} a terrifying flying ghost bursts through the text, looking at the reader with huge eyes that (*pace* Bentley) only Blake could have made and brandishing spears that meet near the head of a man in the left margin, who is helpless before this onslaught. The sketch lines that cross in the lower part of the text indicate that the monster goes, as well as flies, through the world (in this like the figure of departing Time in the facing page 127); but the lines also prefigure the resisting knight who is sketched in much the same way when he beats off the returning spook in page 132. The other two figures in page 126 are those of a downtrodden giant, sunk in the landscape at the right, and a small shepherd with crook who strides on unafraid in much the same posture as Time on the facing page 127. But this shepherd will save the world lost to Time. The huge sketched legs in page 126, which touch both the energetic shepherd and the sunken giant, are the alternative modes of transport used by the Spectre of Time in his progress through the world, as the facing engraving makes clear. At the left they have attached to them a third leg that smashes into the thighs of the man in the margin; he is being overwhelmed by this onset. That this third leg is a phallic weapon should hardly seem surprising at this stage in the study of Blake's symbolism. But skeptics may wish to check the extraordinary twentieth design for *Pilgrim's Progress*, entitled *Christian Beaten Down by Apollyon.*[56] There, in what is almost a developed and simplified version of *Vala*, page 126, Apollyon has huge wings, though he advances on his legs, brandishing spears in both hands against Christian, who kneels between the wide-eyed demon's legs and looks up in horror, unable to raise his sword, though protecting himself to some extent with his shield. But what particularly holds Christian down is Apollyon's enormous, fiery phallus, which is even longer than his thighs. No doubt Bunyan, as well as Blake, recognized Ezekiel's Covering Cherub and John's Antichrist in the figure of Apollyon and his less sectarian successor, the reactionary ghost of Orc in *Vala*, page 126.

In page 128, we see the figure of Vala as exhausted dancer, unable to manipulate her tambourine wheel, but still dressed to fascinate like the Whore of Babylon. At the left, probably in her dream, a woman and man

56. *The Pilgrim's Progress.* Illustrated in 29 watercolor paintings by William Blake now printed for the first time. With a new introduction by Geoffrey Keynes (New York: Limited Editions Club, 1941).

engage in what seems to be simultaneous games of Indian wrestling and marbles. Perhaps this would not be the worst way to kill time. Above Vala a woman looks up meaningfully from her pipe to communicate a message to the reader, while the man with her plays a large lyre. Their sport redeems our time. Then on page 129 Jesus appears as the Good Samaritan, addressing his solicitude to the victim who as yet cannot face what is good for him. Once again on page 131, the expiring man appears, as he did earlier in this Night in the same engraving (page 121). In the facing drawing on page 130 he is Albion revealed: peeled, aged, and half-sunk in water, but still daring to look up, refusing to despair—like other intrepid sufferers in Blake, notably the unintimidated witness who remains unbowed at the left side of the color print of *The House of Death*;[57] he will not be blind to the abominations of the sky god who, with his plaguey hand, is a smiter with disease.

The sketch lines for drafts of knees, subsequently shaded over, and for the head of the man in page 130 make it clear that he was at first conceived of as writhing or as averting his eyes, like the Strong and Ugly Men in *The House of Death*. But in his final position of composure, though he is in bonds of bones, his position is an easily recognizable modulation of the famous "skeleton reanimated" image of *Night Thoughts*, 37 (II, 3)—and of Blair's *Grave*—which Blake had employed as an engraving in *Vala*, page 105, at the middle of Night VIII. In page 130 we see Albion at the limit of deprivation, unable to see an image either of his tormentor (himself) with an arrow or of his reanimator (himself) with a horn. The horn he wants for Judgment was drawn sounding for all the inhabitants of the pit in *Vala*, page 1 {3}. His depilated condition is a more advanced case of that of the man drawn in *Vala*, page 27, though his *position* is a modulation of that of the woman, Vala, in the same design, as well as of that of Tharmas (though without a gesture) in *Vala*, page 44 {16}, prefiguring the posture of the woman in *Vala*, page 138, even closer to the end. In position he also forshadows the recumbent or supine men in *Jerusalem* 14 and 19.

The atmosphere of eschatology quickens from here to the end. In *Vala*, page 132, there is a sketchy restatement of the problem, which has ultimately two aspects, war and love. Above is the shouting monster, much like the Covering Cherub as he appeared on page 126, though he was invisible to Albion on page 130. He is still flinging down his spears and arrows; but he has no distinct wings to fly with, perhaps—Blake's curious mode of delineation demands some such explanation—because he gets all the support he needs from his antagonist, who has taken over the legs of the demon as they appeared on page 126. Albion, now aroused, assumes the posture of a man-at-arms (like a warrior in Blake's *Gray, Sisters* 10) to defeat him. But

57. Reproduced in *Tate Catalogue*, no. 22.

in so doing he assumes a posture much like the aforementioned Apollyon in the Bunyan designs. Though drawn from the back (but with the suggestion of a face on the back of his head), he shows an enormous, crudely drawn scrotum and penis comparable to Apollyon's wondrous member; and he too has a man bowed down and almost groveling between his legs. After this, a description of his armaments may seem excessive; but what one finally sees is that the brand he is swinging back for a master stroke has two legs—like a huge pair of compasses. The rounded object with three straight lines on it, which crosses the base of the compasses-sword near his hand, is unclear to me; one could argue that it is a sketch of a measuring-scale for the compasses, but not with much conviction. And the shield at his side shows on its inside three ropelike circular loops; is it possible that these too are signs of a vortex, somehow related to that of the snake-man in the fragment of the manuscript called page 144?

The contrary vision of his alter-ego—between his legs and obsequiously bowing—is evidence of the power of love that succeeds where violence cannot, though the militant Beast must be in league with this Whore. She appears as a nude woman, with dripping hair, who stands in water just below her knees and looks down on her admirer. Her hands are at her side, but we recognize that the two are re-enacting the Judgment of Paris: he, as Paris with nothing more to give; she, as Aphrodite with no need to fear anything's being taken. I suppose they are Albion and Vala again, but they can be whatever other pair we care to name.

In *Paradise Lost* the woman is Sin and the horrific spirit with arrows is Death. Perhaps it is unrealistic to ask that Albion triumph over the former unaided—without reciprocation what would such a triumph be but the continuation of the bondage of sexism? But Albion's stand against Death is seen to have turned things around in *Vala*, page 133, the engraving for *Night Thoughts*, 20 (I, 15), a design used previously as page 81. Giving up the struggle against Albion as Saint George, Death the spoiler has twisted the two kings of this world together[58] and treads them underfoot as he turns his attention above and furiously attacks the sun that shines on the just and especially the unjust in temporal existence. His assault arrow is a modulation in imagery of the sickle and flail of Urizen (V 132: 2, 133: 34).

Earlier in my text and in footnote 10 I discussed the bizarre symbolism of *Vala*, page 134, with its human-headed, serpentine-tailed bird and the nude rider who holds a goblet in the hand of his outspread left arm and tries to direct his mount with a long wand in his outstretched right arm. The motif of a rider with a goblet on a strange beast is bound to suggest the Whore of Babylon, "Mystery," who carries her "cup"; and since the text mentions

58. Cf. Erdman, "America: New Expanses," p. 108.

Mystery in *Vala*, page 134: 5 ff, it is natural to suppose that it is she who is represented on this page. Partly because the human head on this absurd, rather than formidable, Beast looks quite female to me, however, and partly because the rider looks masculine to me, I tend to think that there is meant to be an ironic reversal in the picture of the genders indicated in the text. When one recognizes the derivation of this imagery from Gillray's political cartoon, which I have discussed, it is easy to see the picture as the temporary triumph of political man, who is the necessary devotee of the Goddess Mystery, a triumph which is an illusion and will not last long. The picture also stands in a complex relationship to the episode in the text on page 135, with its imagery of "wine of ages" and "Waggons" (ll. 22, 29) ; but the various strands would take long to discriminate.

The composition of *Vala*, page 135, is rather comparable in that the bent-over figure of Time has his head, feet, and scythe in positions quite like that of the goose in *Vala*, page 134, and his unfurled left wing delineates an area much like the curious shadow area above the back of the goose. On page 133 Death had felled the kings and was assaulting the sun; here Time has taken a toll of nobility and warriors and his scythe sweeps on to revelers, who are in the "wine presses of Luvah" (136: 1) ; even the sober folk at the left have only a little longer exemption.

I continue to think that *Vala*, page 136 {22}, depicts a scene far above the excessive joy described in the text, that what we are shown is the true triumph of man much as it appeared in Ezekiel's vision of the cherubim. When one studies the great human face in the mount, he begins to discover a resemblance under the whiskers, not only to the face of *Satan in his Original Glory* but even to that of the *Man that Taught Blake Painting*.[59] Then when one looks to either side of the face, amidst the hair, there appear cartoon faces of a droop-eyed bird on the right (viewer's left) and of a blinded, smiling ape on the left (viewer's right).[60] Finally, looking above the fore-

59. Reproduced in *Tate Catalogue*, nos. 31, 51, 52.

60. I believe Blake wanted to tease his viewers by introducing these whimsical avatars of two Zoas in a picture otherwise observant of the decorum of the portentous sublime. These presences are so unlikely that previous commentators have not even mentioned them, though they are unerased and perfectly visible. Blake's exact purpose in thus caricaturing two of his giant forms at this point in the work is not clear to me. A more ample context for interpretation is provided by a survey of representations of the Zoas as they appear in three of their best-known pictures: *The Four and Twenty Elders Casting Their Crowns Before the Divine Throne, Beatrice Addressing Dante From the Car* (reproduced in *Tate Catalogue*, nos. 40 and 74 respectively) and the *Second Title Page for Genesis* (reproduced in Damon's *Dictionary*, pl. II). In the first the Zoas appear, above the figure of God, as eagle, then man, to the viewer's left, and bull, then lion, to his right. But then the Zoas are also repeated in cascades of variously caricatured forms as framing borders on either side of the picture: on the viewer's left there are at least eight representations of the eagle, together with **eyes**

lock at what is indubitably a seated man, one notices that perhaps he holds
something in his left hand, which is stretched down and out. Is it a pen he
holds, or is he simply trying to point out to us something on the sheet of paper
or opened book that at last we recognize to be delineated particularly by
the diagonal line extending down from his left hip? Is the light area above
his right shoulder the indication of a nimbus, or does the flattened, symmetrical, grey curved area above his head constitute a halo? Is the name of
this man Los? William Blake? Is his text now *The Four Zoas*? One reason
it is necessary to look and learn is that the same motif of showing the word
occurs on the very last page of the manuscript, *Vala*, page 140.

The engraved design *Vala*, page 137, looks as though it is unrelated to
either the text on this page or the design on the previous page; but once we
know the subject, which in *Night Thoughts* is Jacob wrestling with the
angel, we are able to recognize how, narratively, it is the precondition to
the triumph envisioned on page 136 {22}. Strikingly, Blake has taken pains
to complete the drawing of both figures within the text area and then has
carefully avoided the added lines with his text, as though to indicate that
this picture, at any rate, contains a motif that is a meaningful part of the
manuscript, not an excrescence. Formerly I thought that the figure in the

---

for at least two more, but only one man, distinctly delineated. On the viewer's right
there are three bulls and two lions, together with eyes enough for five more creatures.
Of all these images of the Zoas, the eagle at eleven o'clock, and the lion at two-thirty
(above the hominid one) bear considerable resemblance to the side breasts in *Vala*,
page 136, particularly the eagle. The purpose for the distortion and proliferation of the
beasts in this water color is not, however, clear to me.

In *Beatrice Addressing Dante* the Zoas are differently arranged: beside Beatrice, to
the viewer's left, the lion is placed behind and the eagle in front; to the viewer's right,
the bull is above and the man, who is distinctly Christ-like, in front. Here the eagle
(though decorated with laurels!) is not unlike the bird in *Vala*, p. 136; and the comic
lion might not be unlike the ape, but he is seen from the front rather than in profile,
so the connection cannot be firmly established. In the *Second Title Page for Genesis*
the Zoas are lined up while bathing their feet in the Jordan just outside Eden. From
left to right they are man, eagle, lion, ox, which is different from the order of the other
two but is closer to the former. Interestingly, the three beasts are not here greatly
caricatured, but the man is appallingly rendered, showing a jack-o'-lantern mouthful
of teeth and serpentine tongue in right profile, after having been originally drawn as
a downcast full-face; the nose of this version has not been fully integrated into the
jaw of the revised profile portrait.

While these representations of the Zoas perhaps raise more problems than they
solve, the use of caricature in all three pictures and the quite close resemblances in
several cases to the problematic faces on the winged head should remove all doubt that
Blake fully intended them to be recognized as Zoas in *Vala*, p. 136. We must now admit
that Blake inclined to whimsy in many of his representations of the Zoas. There is no
evidence, however, that he was being unserious in thus presenting the powers of
Albion.

foreground must be the angel because, though bent, he has the stronger wrestling hold (and only a superhuman creature could perform such a contortion), but this idea is perhaps rendered untenable by the fact that it is the nearer figure who is draped, a piece of corporeal modesty more likely to be affected by a human than by a champion angel. The Apollonian curls of the upright figure are also more divine than the disheveled wavy locks of Jacob the man. If he is shown as having the stronger hold and making impossible efforts, that is what he must have had to do to hold out all night.

Now "the Sun has left his blackness & has found a fresher morning" (p. 138, l. 20). In the end the general redemption is assured, and in the text it is the male figures, and particularly Urthona, who take charge. The evidence is, however, that an equal part of Blake's concern is reflected in his decision to make the three last pictures those of women. On page 138 there is a fine drawing of a nude woman who lies on her left side, no doubt in water, looking up pensively while waiting for the end. It seems to have been generally overlooked that she is the prototype of the woman who lies on her left side in water, against a background of flames, at the bottom of *Jerusalem* 93. Both figures should surely be identified as Enitharmon, about to be reunited with Los.

The last picture has the commentators curiously divided as to its sex. Damon and Margoliouth saw plainly that the figure, shown from behind, leaping like a dancer off the little curve of earth and flying up, is a woman. But both Bentley and Stevenson assert that the figure is male, probably because in page 139, lines 4 and 7, Urthona is spoken of as arising. Since the sex of the prototypical figure in *Night Thoughts*, 139 (IV, 30), is also ambiguous,[61] the only decisive clue as to the sex of the figure in *Vala*, page 139, is its delineations: the large rounded buttocks and the long hair which is blown upward. If one compares the back view of Albion as "Glad Day" in *Jerusalem* 76 {36}, one will remain in little doubt that the figure in *Vala*, page 139, is supposed to be female. Though seen from a somewhat different angle and without a male in sight to greet her, she is the prototype of the fulfilled woman who rises to embrace the father in *Jerusalem* 99 {37}. If her name in the engraved work is Jerusalem, her name in the manu-

---

61. Cf. also *Night Thoughts*, 208 (V, 53), 217 (VI, b), 227 (VI, 6), 229 (VI, 8), 231 (VI, 10), 250 (VI, 29), 268 (VII, d), 280 (VII, 8), 321 (VII, 49), 428 (IX, 10), 453 (IX, 35) and 454 (IX, 36)—the upraised arm of the first has its counterpart in the lowered chains of the second (472 [IX, 54]). About half of these figures are clearly female, but several are ambiguous. The most closely related figures in *Blake's Gray* are in *Poesy* 8 and 12, both of which are female, though the guide in the last design is in a similar position but seen from the front. He, of course, is male and so is the spirit in the first of the Gray designs, *Spring* 1, who is related in symbolism, though not much in bodily position.

script would naturally be Vala. We must not overlook the fact, however, that another female figure who is almost her mirror image on a smaller scale has appeared on page 3 (above), though the earlier woman does not leap with her hand raised so decisively, and she looks to her left rather than upward. Perhaps the woman on page 3 (above) is looking in the direction of page 2 in order to assess the progress in liberation thus far achieved by the image of Los, who is there delineated. In that case the woman on page 139 would be identified as Enitharmon, who is launching from the earth to meet Urthona among the stars.

There is one further implication in the symbolism of page 139 that is all too easy to be persuaded of if one accepts uncritically the evidence of the page as it appears in the Bentley reproduction. As is evident, however, if one looks at page 140, the verso, there was a defect in the paper some 10.7 cm. long, which extends down from the top of the sheet in a slightly irregular crease. Such paper would naturally be most appropriate for engraving proofs, and Blake initially employed it simply for the purpose of printing an impression of the first of his *Night Thoughts* engraved designs. But when Blake came to utilize the unengraved recto for his last drawing in *Vala*, probably after he had scribbled out his text in ink, that crease in the paper attracted him as a draftsman. He drew the leaping woman's right arm through the tail on the terminal "m" in the last word "Dream" and made the tip of her crudely delineated index finger almost touch the end of the paper crease, which actually touches the fingers and stops in the first knuckle area. I am informed by David Erdman that the crease was not at all marked, even with pencil, by Blake, and that in actuality the crease does not appear to be a line, although the impression that it is a line increases in photography as a result of an accumulation of dust in it, doubtless since Blake's day.

These being the facts and physical probabilities, is the interpreter justified in treating the crease as though it had no significance, like the coincidental "bird's eye" on page 26 which Erdman has now convincingly explained away? I do not think the cases are identical. The chief difference is that the crease on page 139 undoubtedly influenced the drawing and placement of the right hand of the figure. The body of this woman has been given a mannerist twist quite extreme even for Blake—somewhat less extreme, admittedly, than the twists exhibited by the mildew blowers in *Europe 9*— and the thrusting of her arm through the tail of a letter bespeaks a further attraction of the draftsman, at any rate, to this crease. I would, moreover, maintain, on the basis of Blake's usage in several of the water colors for *Night Thoughts*, that he was given to employing crease lines, whenever possible, as horizon lines and the like in ways that do have significance in the delineating of his pictures. While it is important that Blake did not strengthen the crease on page 139, one could argue that he did not do so because he felt that the crease was distinct enough for his purposes, which, at this point in the development of the manuscript, could have been no more than to arrive at a text and delineations worthy of more careful renderings. I do not, of course, assert that this was the case, but only that the grounds for supposing that the crease had significance are sufficient to make it reasonable to attempt to set forth what significance it could be supposed to have had.

The gesture of Enitharmon's upraised right hand (a very similar gesture is made by a wayfaring male traveler in *Night Thoughts*, 168 [V, 13]) certainly indicates that she is pointing upward in the strenuous pursuit of her destiny. This is no less true whether one takes the crease into account or whether he disregards it. But if the crease is brought into the reckoning, it becomes an indication of the way to be followed in striving to return to the eternal home. The most famous occurrence of this motif in Blake is in *Jerusalem* 77, the introduction to the last chapter, where there is a small picture of a child following a clue of string through the forest of error (the motif is derived from *Night Thoughts*, 362 [VIII, 16]) ; and it is accompanied by the famous Blakean motto:

I give you the end of a golden string,
    Only wind it into a ball:
It will lead you in at Heaven's gate,
    Built in Jerusalem's wall.
              (*J* 77: 229)

But what one sees is also confirmed by the *Night Thoughts* engraving of a resurrection of a woman that is the subject on the verso, *Vala*, page 140, the actual last page of the manuscript. Blake would have thought it uncreatively repetitious to have shown the soaring of a man at the end of *Vala*, since that aspiration in action had been sufficiently delineated in the frontispiece to the whole work, which as I have said, shows Los rising to his redemptive task. I think Blake meant us to notice that both these resurrections are individual, rather than communal, no doubt because a last judgment passed over these individuals. When the Last Judgment comes, as shown on the *Vala* title page, it will be up to mankind to discover that we are all, men and beasts, the four Zoas. Till then, as we are shown on the last page of *Vala*, Death will have his day between Life and Immortality. But I think we must see even here that the Soul of Sweet Delight will not be finished by what Death can do or what our fate would disregard.[62]

62. For an interpretation of this design, see my essay, "Envisioning the First *Night Thoughts*," in *Blake's Visionary Forms Dramatic*, ed. Erdman and Grant, pp. 331–335.

On Reading The Four Zoas:
Inscape and Analogy

MARY LYNN JOHNSON

BRIAN WILKIE

Two of Blake's most famous comments on his visual art suggest the way we think *The Four Zoas* should be read if the individual is to experience for himself that rejection of error and embracing of truth which Blake calls a Last Judgment. In discussing his painting of the subject he urges the "Spectator" to "Enter into these Images in his Imagination approaching them on the Fiery Chariot of his Contemplative Thought," to "make a Friend & Companion of one of these Images of wonder" (*VLJ, p. 550*). To Dr. Trusler he wrote in 1799, "That which can be made Explicit to the Idiot is not worth my care. The wisest of the Ancients considerd what is not too Explicit as the fittest for Instruction because it rouzes the faculties to act" (*p. 676*). Our reading of *The Four Zoas* in this essay depends, in ways that we hope are obvious, on learned commentaries. But we want most to encourage the sort of visceral and personal response to this deeply introspective poem that we believe Blake demands of his readers.

Although Blake cancelled his original subtitle, "A DREAM of Nine Nights," the phrase is descriptive of the cosmic, but more especially the personal, nightmare universe of the poem and seems to be more than a synonym for "extended vision" or a bow to Young's *Night Thoughts*. We need not insist on the dream-form as crucial in itself, but we must recognize that the movement of the poem, like that of dreams or free association or the other vehicles of introspection which happen to have been developed most fully by psychoanalysis, yields its meaning in proportion to our willingness to examine what happens within us. The displacements and incongruities of dreams defy all our ordinary expectations of coherence, working apparently by

purely arbitrary narrative laws; yet in them we recognize meaning, profound or casual, having to do with our deepest needs and psychic concerns
or merely dredged up from the activities of the preceding day. Much the
same combination of arbitrariness and verifiable truth emerges from *The
Four Zoas*, as dreams are a union of universal symbols (all buildings represent the human body, says Freud) with our private psychic articulations
(the building we went to school in). The verifiable portion that is in the
public domain, the "mythic" part that inheres in man's literary or otherwise
shared symbolism, has been explored by Northrop Frye and used by all of
us who have learned from him. A more personal verification is what we wish
to emphasize in this reading, though we hope also to show that individual
experience recapitulates collective human experience, as the Romantics seem
to have assumed. As a corollary, we hope to show that the poem has a
demonstrable pattern of continuity, though this artistic pattern depends
significantly on patterns in the psyche that we can arrive at only through
introspection.

Two different kinds of evidence in support of a subjective reading of the
poem seem relevant here. One is a recent essay by Helen T. McNeil on the
form of *The Four Zoas*, which makes several incisive points: that, unlike
most of Blake's works, the poem exists without a context, even such a personally Blakean one as that given in the expository parts of, say, *Milton*; that
the mythology of the poem is offered to the reader bluntly, as a *fait accompli*
without explanation or justification; that the poem's meanings can be
derived only from its hectic and disruptive scenes themselves; that the form
of *The Four Zoas* threatens the mimetic mode as such and offers either a
return to pre-Homeric primitivism or a sophisticated advance in literary
form; that the poem has some affinity with dream narrative.[1] The last of

1. Helen T. McNeil, "The Formal Art of *The Four Zoas*," in *Blake's Visionary
Forms Dramatic*, ed. David V. Erdman and John E. Grant (Princeton: Princeton Univ.
Press, 1970). We are indebted to many other Blake critics whose ideas have inter-
penetrated so organically that they have become the common property of Blakeans.
The most influential commentators for us have been the following: G. E. Bentley, Jr.,
ed., *William Blake: Vala or The Four Zoas: A Facsimile of the Manuscript, A Trans-
cript of the Poem, and A Study of Its Growth and Significance* (Oxford: Clarendon
Press, 1963); Harold Bloom, *Blake's Apocalypse: A Study in Poetic Argument* (New
York: Doubleday, 1963); S. Foster Damon, *William Blake: His Philosophy and
Symbols* (Boston: Houghton Mifflin, 1924); Northrop Frye, *Fearful Symmetry: A
Study of William Blake* (Princeton: Princeton Univ. Press, 1947); H. M. Margoliouth,
ed., *William Blake's Vala: Blake's Numbered Text* (Oxford: Clarendon Press, 1956);
and J. Middleton Murry, *William Blake* (London and Toronto: Jonathan Cape, 1933).
Some of our ideas coincide with those of Thomas A. Vogler, *Preludes to Vision: The
Epic Venture in Blake, Wordsworth, Keats, and Hart Crane* (Berkeley and Los Angeles:
Univ. of California Press, 1971). We recognize that something like our approach has
been tried before by Margaret Rudd, *Organiz'd Innocence: The Story of Blake's*

these points is made briefly and in passing; but it is a telltale, for all the characteristics just summarized—especially the arbitrariness—are typical of dream structure. All suggest the personal demands, far greater than most literary works require, that this poem makes on the reader. A work like Blake's *Songs*, subtle though it is, is approachable by established critical routes in a way that is not true of *The Four Zoas*; the former is to the latter almost exactly as *Dubliners* is to *Finnegans Wake*, another dream poem which relentlessly forces us to look into our own psychic mechanism.

The other piece of evidence is experiential. Many of us who have taught *The Four Zoas* to seasoned readers who are Blake novices can testify that they frequently are shaken or frightened or exhilarated by the poem while claiming not to understand very much of it. If they inch along, Damon and Margoliouth and Frye and Bloom at the elbow, trying to keep track of the characters and to remember the episodes in succession, they are baffled and frustrated. Yet typically, when these readers are asked to take an uninhibited stab at what a certain scene means, their account is in at least rough accord with what veteran Blakeans find in the poem. Often they appeal to parallels in their own experience. The discovery that their primary response to the poem has validity then dissolves their paralysis and encourages them to study the criticism in order to sharpen and refine their basic intuitions. But introspection is the first step in comprehension.

Our reading goes through the first six Nights only, although anticipatory remarks about the last three Nights occur occasionally. The main reason for this abbreviation is that to read the whole poem in the kind of detail necessary to illustrate our approach would take more space than is appropriate for this volume. Furthermore, in the last three Nights the poem's denouement broadens (especially in Night VIII) to include historical and religious references that bring to individual psychology a new dimension more obviously public and polemical. We deal with the fall in the first three Nights, the state of fallenness in the central three, and leave the resurrection to unity in the last three Nights to all whom Blake summons as converts.

A few other explanations are in order. (1) Although introspection of personal experience seems to us almost the only way to read the poem that does not make it recondite phantasmagoria, we recognize the danger of merely eccentric interpretations. That this essay has two authors will lessen that danger, we trust. (2) Although some of our interpretations are allegorical, most are meant to be *analogies* which readers are urged to supple-

---

Prophetic Books (London: Routledge & Kegan Paul, 1956), but our reading is plainly different from hers. On dream narrative as a literary form we acknowledge a debt to Samuel Di Christina, a graduate student at the University of Illinois who is working on that subject in connection with De Quincey.

ment with others of their own. We hope they will understand the examples in whichever way they think works best or helps most. (3) On one level the Zoas and their Emanations are objective dramatic characters with distinctive personalities, and the relationships between these males and females almost certainly reflect what Blake saw as a real difference between the ways in which men and women think and behave. For example, apart from their symbolic burden, the Emanations show a delicate psychological attunement to one another, an intuitive sisterly sympathy in failure or success, that will strike many readers as realistically feminine. But both Zoas and Emanations are ultimately psychic elements in both men and women. The point that Blake's characters are both forces in the psyche and psychologically plausible men and women, often taken for granted, bears repeating here because it is a premise for what follows. (4) We have tried not to summarize the action for its own sake; but a certain amount of recapitulation is necessary in order to anchor the commentary. Not everyone, even among Blakeans, has the plot of *The Four Zoas* firmly memorized.

Night I. Although the poem opens in a world of epic superhumanity, as "The Song of the Aged Mother which shook the heavens with wrath / Hearing the march of long resounding strong heroic Verse" (I: 297), we are reminded immediately that this cosmic superstructure is to be internalized in our understanding of our human selves. As though Blake were taking special pains not to be misunderstood, he says that the heroic verse is being prepared for "the day of Intellectual Battle" (I: 297). A deleted passage says that if "Whosoever reads" comprehends "with his Intellect the terrible Sentence," the universe will quake in fear of the mental warfare to come. The entire opening passage implies Blake's concern with reader psychology and perhaps an earlier intention to attract a wider audience than a private manuscript could command. The poem is to sing of the "Four Mighty Ones" in "every" man; and the refocusing of the original subtitle, "The Death and Judgement" of the Eternal Man, as "The torments of Love & Jealousy" in his death and judgment, implies again a turn to the familiar, the troubled heart and psyche. The nature of the Zoas is known to the "Heavenly Father only" (I: 297); but the remoteness so suggested is immediately dispelled, for "Father" also directs us ahead to the first Zoa whose plight is described, the "Parent power" Tharmas, the most childlike and instinctual of the personified mental powers. One implication here is that unless we become as children (who could elucidate his visions easily, as Blake wrote in the 1799 letter to Dr. Trusler) we shall not understand this poem. We must trust our intuitions.

Tharmas has been described as innocence, instinct, the binding force of the human personality, and the body. All these are valid identifications, except that in this context the "body" must not be understood as that of adult sexuality, which is closer to Blake's Luvah. Tharmas is the body as a child knows it, unselfconsciously and without question, the body of Wordsworth's child that *feels* its life in every limb. Tharmas is the "Parent" power in the sense that the child is father of the man. He is the innocent's trust, his sense of wholeness, as in the *Songs of Innocence*; and more than any other Zoa he has an affinity with that pastoral mood and state that Blake calls Beulah. Just as children are uncannily alert to indefinable atmospheres long before either mind or emotion can identify them, so Tharmas and his Emanation Enion are throughout the poem an early-warning system that scents the fall and, conversely, the possibility of reintegration before any of the other Zoas, or human faculties, does. Thus the fall of Tharmas is described first.

What Tharmas has sensed is the generic human fall, considered either as that mysterious historical and evolutionary leap which awakened humanity simultaneously to its unique gifts and its unique capacity for evil or as the more individual lapse which caused each of us to be divided from others and against ourselves. Its most salient symptom and cost are sexual, the torments of love and jealousy, and therefore we can all recognize it through what we underwent at adolescence and to some extent at that even earlier climacteric called "the age of reason." We encounter Tharmas and Enion in the middle of a terrifying quarrel, reminiscent of that between Milton's Adam and Eve, in which they have both realized their nakedness, though for Blake that means emotional nakedness. Both feel loneliness combined with poignant longing, and in their speeches his key word is "pity," hers "terror." They feel paranoid selfconsciousness, and their dialogue is riddled with contradictions; Tharmas says he has hidden Jerusalem, then that Enion has abducted her, then that he has taken Enitharmon in and cannot cast her out. It is clear that the human instinctual powers have been thrown into panicky confusion, and their feeling of sinfulness and victimization at once reflects the new kind of psychological guilt that afflicts them. Their dialogue can hardly be called that at all; he assumes her resentment before she expresses it, and their speeches are self-enclosed or at least oblique, parallel dramatic monologues in which neither listens to or responds to the other's comments, questions, accusations. The sexual attraction-repulsion familiar in adolescence has also been awakened; Tharmas sees Enion alternately as a root growing in hell to draw him to destruction and as a celestially beautiful, expanding flower.

Enion draws out from Tharmas his "Spectre," the male version of the sexual and personal possessiveness that in Blake balances the shadowy "Female Will." This Spectre emerges finally as a golden idol, narcissist and megalomaniac; filled with desire and contempt, he calls the cowering Enion —in a deleted passage—a "Diminutive husk & shell / Broke from my bonds" (*p. 741*). The adolescent has learned, partly through female encouragement, the locker-room parody of virility as well as the whole Adam's-rib psychology as understood by feminists. Blake puts his condemnation of spectral love into the mouths of the Daughters of Beulah, feminine protectiveness at its best: "The Spectre is in every man insane & most / Deformd" (I: *299*). Protecting man from the most primitive of nightmares, the dream of falling, the Daughters follow sleepers, "Creating Spaces lest they fall into Eternal Death" (I: *299*), including a space for that ultimate home of the spectral that Blake names Ulro. This is the first of several hints by Blake at an elusive-to-define providence, an economy of preservation for man, that operates almost independent of his will. The same motif occurs later in Night I in the description of the Council of God in Eternity (I: *306*). Perhaps Blake means to suggest no more than the hope or expectation that somehow human regeneration will occur. His attitude toward fallen humanity is that of a parent who trusts, even during the ordeal of growth, that his confused and dislocated child will turn out all right.

After their mutually infecting quarrel Tharmas and Enion copulate and give birth to Los and Enitharmon. They, in the end, will be the agents of redemption in the poem; but for a long time they are repellent figures. Since these embodiments of man's power to see and shape are the offspring of Tharmas and Enion, Blake seems to be saying that the first panicky impulse, after man has recognized instinctively his division, is to evoke, just as instinctively, the power to *do* something— *anything*—about it; for this creative power, however misguided, is still a dynamic, a potential for change that makes redemption possible. Like Shelley, Blake sees the regenerating force in man not as mind or even heart in itself but as an imaginative, creative force arising from instinctive sources.

There follows for the human imagination an interval of heady though ill-founded bliss; the youthful couple re-enact their parents' decline, living at first happy and naked in Beulah but soon falling into contentious shame and jealousy: "Alternate Love & Hate his breast; hers Scorn & Jealousy / In embryo passions" (I: *301*). In the world of Tharmas, now fallen into Generation, they delight in the suffering of their parents and eventually come into Urizen's sphere of influence. With the nasty elusiveness that will later half-madden Los, Enitharmon recommends ingratitude and scorn toward their parents in order to insure their continued attention. On the dramatic level, the tensions of the generation gap have seldom been better delineated; but the point goes deeper: in their rejection of instinct, the primitive parent, and in their allegiance to fallen reason, they show what is all too likely to happen to imagination in man's confused condition. Blake had in mind, no doubt, the excessive rationalism of eighteenth-century art; but a more personal analogy is available in the cocky cerebralism of certain

older children and adolescents. The youthful Shelley, with his Enlightenment necessitarianism, is a case in point. Enitharmon is especially prone
to sexual fantasies that feature her, sometimes in the guise of Vala, with
both Albion and Urizen, whom she calls on for help when Los threatens her.
Los himself, benightedly, tells her that the world of their joy is in the
human *brain* "Where Urizen & all his Hosts hang their immortal lamps" (I:
302); but he has not lost all of the visionary faculty as Enitharmon has:
when Urizen declares himself sole and eternal God and offers Los power
over reason's arch-enemy Luvah, "The Prince of Love the murderer," Los
refuses to bow to Urizen's law. He sees that, like Satan in *Milton*, Urizen is
"one of those who when most complacent / Mean mischief most" (I: *302*).
Urizen's reply is worth quoting, since it is the ultimate anti-Blakean blasphemy and defines through negation the path to human reintegration that
Blake will eventually map:

Art thou a visionary of Jesus the soft delusion of Eternity
Lo I am God the terrible destroyer & not the Saviour
Why should the Divine Vision compell the sons of Eden
to forego each his own delight to war against his Spectre
The Spectre is the Man the rest is only delusion & fancy.
                                                (I: *303*)

There is ironic accuracy and lucidity here, but fallen reason reads black
where Blake reads white.

Still, the power of imaginative making is seriously ill, too ill to recognize
even blatant error: Los humbles himself before Enitharmon, and their
union on this basis is celebrated at a great feast presided over by Urizen.
The banquet scene is one of the great set pieces in Blake, a kind of Black
Mass which solemnizes the total denial of the human and imaginative, a
blasphemy that will be directly reversed in the poem's last Nights. Urizen's
hosts sing to the sulky newlyweds a terrible song of Experience in which
the humane labors of harvest and vintage are despised and replaced by
bloodshed. The utilitarian triumphs over the human. The enemy is declared
to be Orc, the fallen incarnation of passion, who is to be chained by imaginative power. Blake's lament at this triumph of genteel and academic art
over the vigor of passion and its replacement by the sham aesthetic vigor of
warfare is powerful; and like much great epic poetry it exemplifies the
imaginative fascination of the horrific. We must remember that this whole
demonic hymn is directed at the human imagination, now reduced to torpid
conformity.

The touching antiphon is sung by Enion, the now weakened and distant
shadow of human instinct. She mourns tenderly over the animal victims of
the very blood-sacrifice that Urizen's hosts have just celebrated so gleefully.

Feebly, the instinctual warning system in man, despite the depraved form of imagination it has produced without so intending, tells us that there is something dreadfully wrong in a world where creatures survive only by preying on others. Her lament is a refutation of all complacent rationalizations about chains of being and ecological life-cycles which would, for example, render meaningless the subtle terrors of Frost's poem "Design" or Tennyson's outcry against nature's waste and bloodiness.

The last movement of Night I returns to Blake's hopeful sense of a salutary providence. The Eternal Man has sunk down in sleep upon the Rock of Ages; but a Council of God, personified in Jesus, meets in Eternity and hears the frightened report of the fall from Beulah's messengers, who typically shrink from conflict among the Zoas. Heretofore we have had the fall presented as it appears to the human being actually undergoing the new horror of fragmentation; but now it is told from the more universal viewpoint, as it were, of Eternity and the Divine Vision, for the innocence of Beulah is to the state of Eternity as Tharmas, whose distress we observed at first, is to Albion, or to any one individual. The messengers see the fall in terms not of its symptoms but of its causes, not in terms of stunned instinct or confused imagination but as a conspiracy and power struggle between Luvah and Urizen, desire and restraint, the two ultimate powermongers in man. Like Tharmas, the messengers represent the bewilderment of the innocent psyche at the new turmoil that afflicts it; and like our typical adolescent they sense the fall as a conflict between passion and restraint—a dilemma all too familiar in scores of fictional accounts of the ravages of puritanism. The messengers, like Saint Peter, want the Saviour to act directly, violently, by cutting this new and troublesome Gordian knot. But the Saviour is not this kind of *deus ex machina*. Instead, Seven Eyes of God are elected to watch over fallen man—Jesus, the seventh, watching with particular solicitude while the Daughters of Beulah guard the fallen man's Emanation, Jerusalem, who is now debarred from Beulah by the jealous Enitharmon. The salvation of man must be achieved by a spiritual and internal effort, as later Nights will show.

Night II. That this Night was at one time meant to open the poem is revealing. The Zoas are sometimes seen as four different but co-ordinate powers in man; in fact they function as two pairs: Urizen and Luvah-Orc, Tharmas and Urthona-Los. Urizen and Luvah are ultimate energies in man, the *fuel* of his psyche; Tharmas and Los, on the other hand, are *instruments* or ways of organizing human energies, or directions they can take. If the first pair is like electricity, the second is like circuitry. Blake sees the psychic war as, essentially, one between Urizen and Luvah, and his earlier plan to open the poem with their conflict as depicted in Nights II and III (and anticipated

near the end of Night I) was logically correct. His later decision to begin
with Tharmas and then Los changed the strategy to a psychological one
which starts from our *recognition of* and *response to* our fallen division.
Now he is ready to depict the *causes* of the fall.

Albion, having heard Enion's voice, decides to abdicate. Though he recognizes reproachfully Urizen's part in the rebellion described in Night I
by Beulah's messengers, he feels that the immediate and main threat is
Luvah, and so he does what we are all prone to do in our panicky times of
crisis: he summons the psychic policeman Urizen, the force of mental law
and order. He says to himself, not "Let's find ourself," but "Let's think this
out and get a grip on ourself." (It is no coincidence that our society keeps
the child safely in school during his first two climacterics.) Urizen's response is characteristic too; he is only too happy to assume power (as in the
first line of *The Book of Urizen*) ; yet almost immediately he sees how impossible his position is: "No more Exulting . . . Pale he beheld futurity"
(II: *309*). Though man has been perverse enough to enthrone the very
power of rationalism and "practicality" that had helped subvert him, his
reason itself has enough acuity to know that alone it is inadequate. But at
the same time reason is horrified enough by the other human faculties (as
the superego is horrified by the id) to attempt this quixotic solo enterprise;
and thus Urizen proceeds with his task, in the mood of gloomy fatalism that
will be typical of him in his fallen state.

His mission is to build the "Mundane Shell," a labor that requires many
new mechanical tools. The human imagination is petrified into rock and
sand. Psychologically this Mundane Shell is the world seen as recalcitrant
matter that threatens us and that we can do little human with or about. Man
has "objectified" his world; Reuben and Levi, sons of Albion, "behold /
What is within now seen without" (II: *310*). This is the "sensible" view of
matter, the attitude that in older children replaces the desire to hug or kick
what pleases or injures them. In the unfallen state, Blake believes, we would
have this intimate, human-like response to *all* objects, which would be
"thou's" instead of "it's." In "The Eolian Harp" Coleridge feels that he is
being daring when he speculates that all of animated nature may tremble
into thought when a creatively intellectual breeze sweeps over it, but Blake
pushes the idea toward the inanimate as well. Reason's task, Urizen's task,
is to make man ashamed of such feelings, as Coleridge's Sara does.

Blake now shows what happens to the libidinal energies under this rule
of "reasonableness." Luvah, the Zoa of passion, is cast into a furnace, his
Emanation Vala feeding the furnace with fire, under the supervision of a
Urizen who dreads Luvah. Vala's inability to recognize the inmate of the
furnace as her once-innocent lover reflects a new awareness by man, now
ruled by fallen reason, of sexual desire as a destructive force. The imprison-

ment of Luvah is the fig leaf, the chaperone, censorship, Victorian morality. A little later in the poem we see Luvah finally melt with woe and Vala's fires grow cold as she falls beneath the furnaces, a heap of ashes. Now the furnaces can be tapped of their molten metal, which runs out in channels cut by a plow held by Urizen but drawn by Luvah's bulls. Here is a succinct verbal emblem both of the internal process of sublimation and of the external diversion of passionate energies into socially acceptable intellectual competition. The manipulation is reason's, but all the energies are those of passion.

Before he melts, Luvah speaks a fervid poem in which truth is mixed with ghastly error; for this is *fallen* passion speaking, "Reasoning from the loins" (II: *311*). The account he gives of his nurturing of Vala from an earthworm through a serpent through a bright and poisonous winged dragon refers in part to the development of his penis and also to the emergence of the female sex organs as a horror and threat (cf. Blake's drawing on MS page 26 {8}). Luvah's embryological synopsis implies man's growing awareness of sex as a powerful evil. As all the Emanations are products or externalizations of the Zoas, Vala is the specific externalization of fallen love: a sexually alien Other. Luvah mourns her loss and describes the incipient triumph of psychic discord; he himself, once love, is now hatred; Urizen, once faith and certainty, is now doubt. So far, so good; but Luvah then goes on to define what he conceives to have been his mission: "to deliver all the sons of God / From bondage of the Human form" (II: *311*), which is blasphemy paralleling Urizen's in Night I. The fallen libido would also make a good tyrant. It makes all the mistakes it must make when it undertakes to operate alone, when reasoning comes from the loins. Urizen-Luvah parallels like this one are recurrent in the poem and constitute one of its central structural principles.

Certain of the children of man see "these visions" (presumably the activities of Urizen and Luvah) and are appalled; but others go obliviously about their business—measuring the sun's course, buying and selling, forming schools and instruments. They hide from the knowledge of the psychic breakdown by applying the anodyne rationalism that Coleridge describes in the sixth stanza of the "Dejection" ode. They keep themselves going, in a limited way, by means of a dissociation of sensibility. Blake is also satirizing, with laconic grimness, the assumption that the inner life as revealed in art, literature, emotional and spiritual experience, and dreams is less real than, say, the fluctuations of bonds or the latest findings in celestial spectroscopy.

Meanwhile, with scales and compasses, under the direction of the "Architect divine," the builders continue to work on the geometrical Mundane Shell, which turns out to be also the palace of Urizen. Later in the poem the universe of eighteenth-century deism will emerge—that is, the world of absolute imaginative death that we would all inhabit if, for example, we considered "an unusually sizable concentration of crystalline carbon" to be an adequate description of the Hope diamond. What we have here in Night II is an earlier model of the universe (earlier both historically and developmentally) which is highly intellectualized but also beautiful, the universe of Ptolemy or Dante rather than that of Newton or Gradgrind. It is a fallen world, but not devoid of a certain kind of poetry, of mathematical "elegance," as reflected in the sumptuous appointments of Ahania's chambers in the palace. (The setting and mood of Ahania's rooms are both like Keats's "Chamber of Maiden-Thought" and like what Verdi creates for Amneris in *Aida*.) And the stars, though now moving in the measured courses of rationalism, are still seen poetically: they renew their wasted strength in winter and reappear fresh in the summer skies. Some capacity to humanize his vision of the sky still remains for man.

When Urizen returns from his work on the cosmic construction project he discovers with dismay that a rift now exists between him and his dutiful spouse Ahania. The familiar pattern repeats itself: jealousy, possessiveness, and (as we shall see in Night III) the sense of sin that Urizen can feel even more acutely than his brother Zoas can. The definitive account of this separation will appear in Night III; but even here, in the Night devoted to the fall of passion, Blake reminds us that reason's megalomania is not only aggressive but self-destructive, opposed to what is loveliest in reason itself. In an apparently deliberate parallel, Blake gives us almost immediately a lament by Vala for her lost Luvah. (This is one of many suggestions in the poem of the intimate interdependence of the Emanations; one is reminded of Eliot's claim that all the women, as well as all the men, in *The Waste Land* are one.) Vala is suffering, along with other female slaves of the construction project; the objects of love are now seen as mere utilitarian objects—another point that parallels charges by feminists. But we also learn that, despite her professed love, Vala is never aware of Luvah when he does appear to her and despises him in spite of her professions—which is the male counter-argument. In any case, the sexes are sorely embattled, love is indeed sick.

When Los and Enitharmon reappear, they are bent on a cruel plot to divide Urizen and Ahania by bringing to Ahania an awareness of the outcast Enion. (As it will happen, the implementation of this plan will be mainly the work of Los.) The imaginative power has pitted itself against instinct; reason has dominated passion; now it is reason's turn to be victim of imagination. The methods used by imagination seem demonic, but Blake probably meant to show it here as doing something that is salutary in the long run. If creativity is ever to perform its saving work, it must abjure the cold rationalism it has heretofore obeyed. But that is not an easy task, as we now discover. Most of the remainder of Night II is an especially detailed and horrible account of the destruction of imagination through guilty and possessive love, love being the central motif of this Night. The third side of the triangle is Urizen, whom Enitharmon plays off against Los with enormous skill at amatory strategy, "the game." In much fuller psychological detail than in Night I, Blake describes their fall from power and sensory flexibility to the torments of jealous division. Enitharmon's tactic is to cripple Los by instilling in him a sense of sin so deep that even when she is not around to watch him he will never be able to delight in other women, or the beauty of the world; he now can be trusted contemptuously to monitor himself, somewhat like the degraded Winston Smith at the end of Orwell's *1984*. She sings her fierce canticle of the "Female Will," the anthem of all attempts to castrate men. In her assumed mood of sexy, languorous faintness, she entices Los to approach her, only to fade and flee when he takes the bait. Los has fallen victim to the combination of sensuality and celestial otherworldliness that drive and deride the young boy in Joyce's "Araby." This whole strategy is abetted by Enitharmon's allegiance to Urizen, her "God," who is something between her protector and her lover, a sort of intellectual Cupid.

Los's revenge is to attack Urizen where he is most vulnerable, in his attachment to Ahania, whom Los wishes to draw into the vacuum of exile where Enion now exists. Enion's great lament follows, in which she reproaches herself for having ruined or rejected everything that had been valuable to her. She and Tharmas had once been the instincts of Innocence; but now she has learned the high price of Experience. She has come to see that ease of mind is possible only for those who live in comfort, only so long as the universal misery surrounding them does not touch them personally. The terror of her song is enhanced when we remember that she and Tharmas are basically children. Her initiation into the horrors of life, like the fallen Titans' bewildering discovery of pain in the primeval world of Keats's *Hyperion*, ought to affect us as the hard lot of myriad Dickensian waifs does. The special pointedness of Enion's lament is in its juxtaposition with the cruelty of Enitharmon and Los, for Enion is their mother. In giving birth to the defensive force of imagination, instinct seems to have ruined both love and imagination itself, with reason soon to follow. For Enion's inability to remain callous in the face of suffering reaches to Ahania's voluptuary palace and bed, where it awakens her to insomniac sympathy. Ironically, Enion is unaware that Los's plot against Ahania will drive Enion herself further into nonentity (II: *318*); what happens to one Emanation affects them all. Ahania's response to Enion's lament is like what happens to a young student when his bliss is soured by awareness of social ills, when out of a desire to make learning accountable he decides that to enjoy the life of the mind for its own sake is irresponsible. In Night III, Ahania, the mind's delight in its activity, will bow before a colder notion of reason which holds that the pleasurable element in thought is merely a coddling of that dilettante Imagination. To enjoy learning will no longer be an innocent activity.

The latter half of Night II is so impressive, dramatically and lyrically, that it seems to be a direct depiction of human behavior. But Blake is still creating a psychodrama, a map of the mind. The repression of desire already portrayed will produce an intolerable strain on the imaginative powers that disrupts their uneasy subjection to rationality. The product of creativity, Enitharmon, is still officially in the service of Urizen; but that a revolt has taken place on a deep level is shown by Los's stirring up of Enion, the voice of instinctual innocence, just as earlier Los himself had been called into action by the parent power of instinct. The plot against Urizen is cruel but it has to happen, and the alliance of imagination with instinct will survive, though sometimes uneasily, until it is ready to take a more positive turn in Night VIIA.

Night III. The leading motif of this Night is the suicide of reason, whose tenure as regent of the psyche has been short-lived. In order to feel properly the self-destructiveness of reason here, its utter irrationality, we must be aware of the beauty, the sensuality even, that Blake can attribute to the un-fallen mind of certainty and faith. That condition is described nostalgically in the last chapter and plate of *The Book of Ahania* in some of the most sensual lines Blake ever wrote. There Urizen, as plowman, lover, and teacher, has a "lap full of seed," the "seed of eternal science" (5: 29, 34). Ahania herself, reason's epiphany, is one of the loveliest and most loving women in Blake—wise but also elegant and even voluptuous. She is the embodiment of everything graceful and urbane and human about the intel-lectual life; in Night III she is introduced with "her bright head sweet perfumd & ... heavenly voice" (III: *320*). She is a combination of Desde-mona and a Near Eastern princess, and in Night III Urizen is a jealous Othello, a base Indian who throws away a pearl.

The Night begins with Ahania's attempt to reassure Urizen about his control of the new starry universe (perhaps conceding him more power than he really has, but that is the kind of dutiful wife she is) and her plea that he not darken present joy with fears of futurity. The link with her misgiv-ings at the end of Night II is not explicit, since Blake is trying to show not a fully conscious recognition by reason but a dim intuition, born of sym-pathy with suffering, that man doth not live by mathematic thought alone. This intuition has to come to Urizen obliquely, through his consort, the side door of his psyche. His answer is an outright repudiation of her pleas and warnings. He does fear futurity, the day when he must eventually serve "that Prophetic boy" (III: *320*)—an epithet for Los in Night I (*p. 301*) and in this passage not exclusively, as commentators have generally assumed, a reference to Orc. Despite his dread, Urizen *decrees* that Vala and Luvah "shall" descend into the womb and loins of Enitharmon and Los; he wants to punish Los by cursing him with the rearing of these unruly children, yet he fears the reappearance of Luvah in an unknown form. His willed decree, which in its fear and fatalism recalls Herod's reaction to the Nativity, is part of the whole motif of suicide in Night III. What he predicts and conjures is the union of imaginative power, which until now has been pretty much under his control, with the libidinal or emotional powers. He feels uneasily that he has been set on a spurious throne for the real purpose of serving, not ruling, the human imagination. Like the legendary Boston censor, he suffers from the prurient conviction that lascivious poetry or any art that avoids restraint will rip the fabric of the mental and social order. More generally, Urizen's fear is the familiar one that the exuberance which is beauty will turn into lust, that if a man lets his feelings go he may not be able to keep his religious beliefs or his political principles.

In still another account of the fall, Ahania puts the essential blame on Luvah's deceitful assumption of Urizen's steeds of light. Despite the attractiveness of her wifely bias toward Urizen, we know from the more reliable narration of the messengers of Beulah in Night I that Ahania's version of the fall is misleading. (Elsewhere in this volume [see pp. 183–185] John E. Grant points out that Blake's drawing, on MS page 37 {9}, of Ahania's self-abasement before Urizen has sinister implications.) In Ahania's vision, Albion, walking with Vala, sees a shadow arise "from his wearied intellect" (III: *320*)—which, of course and ironically, is Urizen, though Ahania seems unaware of that fact. This pure and perfect golden monster is the embodiment of holiness in the negative sense that Blake detests so heartily and that Orc excoriates so wrathfully in Plate 8 of *America*. Caught *in flagrante delicto*, Vala cowers predictably before this Sunday School idol; and Albion himself worships it idolatrously as the very ground of his existence. Ahania trembles in astonishment, and indeed mind itself should be able to see through this sham deity on purely intellectual grounds. But we are now in a world of mental sickness where puritanical conscience exerts absolute tyranny, as in the excruciating struggles of a man to maintain a rigidly orthodox faith even when the best part of his mind rejects it. It is the world where, as Shelley puts it, "the loftiest fear / All that they would disdain to think were true" (*Prometheus Unbound*, I: 619–620). The surprising thing, at least superficially, is that Luvah, sexuality, emerges as a cloud from the shadowy idol—which accords dramatically with Ahania's refusal to implicate her husband but also indicates something deeper. She recognizes—perhaps in spite of herself, for she still seems to see Luvah as the aggressor against Albion—that excessive purity is linked with the libidinous, as with Saint Anthony's temptations and perhaps the sick imaginings of Hawthorne's young Goodman Brown. Albion himself shares Ahania's distrust of Luvah (at least in her vision), turns his back on Vala, and drives Luvah away, cursing the latter's senses and shrinking them up; the two flee down to the human heart. Ahania now fears the same fate for Urizen and herself if he will not listen.

Ahania's loving and sensible advice produces the same response that Desdemona's intelligent and well-meant advocacy of Cassio does: Urizen feels insanely jealous rage. He insists on his power as sole God, and while continuing to feel Ahania's beauty casts her from his throne by the hair, misrecalling their past, implying that she is a harlot, and saying:

Shall the feminine indolent bliss. the indulgent self of weariness . . .
Set herself up to give her laws to the active masculine virtue
Thou little diminutive portion that darst be a counterpart
Thy passivity thy laws of obedience & insincerity
Are my abhorrence.

                                                                (III: *322*)

This is male chauvinism with, quite literally, a vengeance. The imagery and situation recall the ugly scene between Tharmas and Enion in Night I, where pathological pseudo-masculinity is also exposed for what it is. Both the golden Shadow of Holiness in this Night and the golden form of the Spectre of Tharmas in Night I are narcissistic idols, glorified self-images. Their anti-feminist psychology is so nearly identical that in cancelled lines Blake once gave Tharmas almost the same phrase for Enion that Urizen uses against Ahania: "Diminutive husk & shell" (*p. 741*).

The casting-out of Ahania is another of Blake's most awesome and ironic passages. Urizen has done just what Enion accused herself of doing at the end of Night II; he has destroyed everything that makes him happy. Reason's better half (literally true here) has given him a true insight into the death-like nature of "holiness," and his reply is to deny hysterically the truth. This is what every intellectual does when he substitutes for delight in his work a desiccated notion of scholarship as pain; he is likely then to distrust beauty and joy in the life of the mind and even to disapprove of zest and attractiveness in his colleagues. There is also a close analogy between the exile of Ahania and a certain common kind of nervous breakdown. Though warned by both Enion and Ahania, both by instinct and by what is still best in his reason, that mental constructs cannot subsist in isolation from the rest of the psyche, the victim insists on being governed by his perverted notion of pure rationality until he loses not only what is best in his mind but even the compulsively rigid rationality that he had tried to maintain; he starts screaming and smashing things.

Disasters follow one another apace. Ahania falls like lightning, Urizen like its echoing thunderbolt ("Reason topples from its throne," as the cliché runs), their sons flee, Destiny breaks its bounds. The fragile clockwork of the mathematic universe and psyche has been shattered, indirectly through instinct and, beyond that, through the assault from imagination that Los had launched in Night II. Urizen's fall is to a world of despair and hope, the insomniac Ahania's to the edge of nonentity where Enion had been before. A horrible groan arises; and Tharmas appears, sobbing and struggling to achieve the voice and features of man. Though he still feels hatred toward Enion, he also misses her more than ever. She, blind and age-bent, utters her third lament, pleading to be allowed to survive near him even in the most minimal way. Both have become shadows, mists, inaudible voices of the indefinite and chaotic. The very instinct for survival, what doctors used to call "the will to live," is very nearly gone. The fall cannot proceed any farther without the total disappearance of man, or of his psychic reality, which for Blake is the same thing. It remains to be seen how the imprisoned or broken or faded human faculties will cope with their, and our, grim world.

Night IV. Nights IV through VI comprise the poem's middle movement, and, although this section hints at better days to come, it is essentially a portrait of dreariness. The human psyche is in chaos. Reason has been fragmented and stupefied. Passion has hidden itself in merely natural forms such as corporeal violence, lust, sex for its own sake. Instinct has become shapeless and has lost most of its power of psychological bonding. The imaginative power is afflicted almost as sorely; Los and Enitharmon are still active but are badly handicapped by division, from others and between themselves. The last three Nights will present a redemptive process, however painful; and the first three have had at least the adrenal excitement of present tragedy, the fall itself. Now, in the middle part, man must face his severest test: living with a state of fallenness that seems to be a permanent condition. One may bring to the ordeal of an amputation temporary, emergency resources of strength; but living from day to day without the limb is the supreme test.

The first movement of *The Four Zoas* begins with the response to the fall by instinct and imagination and then proceeds to passion in Night II and reason in Night III. The middle three Nights have a similar construction; in Night IV instinct and reason limit the fall, after which the poem focuses on passion in Night V and reason in Night VI. In the final movement of recovery man's powers are redeemed in the same order. Imaginative impulses, set in motion by instinct, create new forms in Night VIIA; in the Lamb of God's assumption of Luvah's robes of blood and the Crucifixion of Night VIII, love transforms violent energy; and in Night IX, among many other apocalyptic events, reason at last abandons all effort to repress the other powers and is liberated from an obsessive concern with futurity.

Night IV is difficult and confusing, partly because it must depict psychic confusion, partly because of the ambiguity inherent in the very concept of a "lowest point." It is both depressing and strangely comforting to know that things cannot possibly get any worse; thus all episodes in this Night are heavily ambiguous. Psychiatrists say that no patient can be helped until he is desperate, until the bottom has fallen out and he has hit a new and final low, until he feels in his soul that there is nowhere to go but up. Sad as it is to lie flat on the basement floor, it is reassuring to know there *is* a floor. Moving on a continuum between the fullest possible being and utter non-being, man is in danger of ceasing to exist, that is, of falling into a state best imagined as permanent psychosis. But the fall is arrested at the Ulro-point; the limits of time, space, matter, the human body are set. The species and most individuals do survive, though just barely—through Tharmas, the vestigial voice of instinct that tells us that all this unhappiness and waste are absurd, through Los, the power that makes possible even in our fallen state moments of ecstatic vision, and through that mysterious providence, or hope, that Blake calls Jesus, the Council of God.

As in Night I, we begin with Tharmas, who inaugurates the defensive process. He wants to die, but fortunately for man that is impossible; even at his worst there is something that makes the human being want to recuperate. Like the dying Mercutio with Romeo and Tybalt, Tharmas puts the curse of "an honest man" (IV: *325*) on Urizen and Luvah, for honesty is Tharmas's hallmark; instinct cannot really lie, any more than the knee-jerk reflex can be faked. A new tenderness for Los and Enitharmon arises at the same time as a longing for Enion. In the hope that creative activity will somehow restore Enion, Tharmas commands Los to rebuild the universe (though a universe of death and decay) and Enitharmon to weave forms (though soft delusive ones) for man. Instinct is terribly confused, but it is operative.

Los's immediate response is to tell Tharmas to keep his distance and to assert his own allegiance to the fallen Urizen. Los is denying his origin in instinct, preferring a "higher" alliance with reason. We have seen his efforts to subvert Urizen's dominance; but now in his fastidiousness he is appalled by the chaotic instinctual principle that Tharmas represents, somewhat as militantly cerebral poets of the 1920s and 1930s were embarrassed by the overt expression of feeling. In his repeated sneers at his parent power as "father of worms & clay" (IV: *325*), Los rejects what Yeats calls the "foul rag-and-bone shop of the heart." Enitharmon is even more dismayed by Tharmas, for the architectural world of Urizen was to her a "sweet world" symbolizing the Urizenic relationship which she had tried to establish with Los. Still further self-divided, Los claims that although he was once Urthona, Urthona is now nothing more than his shadow. What Blake is showing here, probably, is the megalomania that the creative principle is capable of when it takes itself too seriously and refuses to remain in touch with the instinctive needs that man feels he should satisfy through art. Los's attitude toward art is the arrogant or complacent one that Keats's Moneta attacks so strongly in *The Fall of Hyperion*. The creative power in man now sets itself up not as a prophet but as an oracle and dictator. Doubting Tharmas (a pun on Thomas, no doubt), like the proverbial Missouri skeptic or the man in the street who distrusts the pretensions of art and knows what he likes, denies Los's claims and declares himself to be the sovereign ruler.

Like Los and Jesus later in Night IV, Tharmas now does something ambiguous but crucial. He carries Enitharmon away from Los—separating art from its productive activity for the time being—and thereby causes the Spectre of Urthona to emerge from Los. The spectral Tharmas of Night I and the spectrally holy Urizen-Luvah of Night III had been golden statues; Urthona's Spectre is a statue-like figure too, but a leaden one. Like all Blake's Spectres, this one is a repulsive, chilling figure; the base metal suggests the defeatist dreariness of creative power in its uninspired, day-to-day moments of dullness. Yet his appearance is salutary; he becomes a meek apprentice who is not above the lowly tasks that Los needs help with. What instinct has done is to take High Art down a peg by reminding it of its roots in craftsmanship. Sir Joshua Reynolds is reminded that it is better to paint than to pontificate; computer composers are reminded that they might learn to play the piano; novelists are reminded that they must write and not just utter opinions at symposia; and all of us are reminded that it is better to make things and thus improve vision than merely to deplore the cultural wasteland.

Significantly, the Spectre now recognizes Tharmas as an old friend from the days in Eternity, though both are now decayed in beauty; and Tharmas, once "the mildest son of heaven," is now "a Rage / A terror to all living things" (IV: *326*). The Spectre gives still another version of the fall, this time from the viewpoint of Urthona and Tharmas, the most reliable narrators among the Zoas. Their basic guiltlessness in that event, implied earlier by Beulah's messengers, is corroborated here. And in Tharmas's warm response to his "old companion, / With whom I livd in happiness before that deadly night / When Urizen gave the horses of Light into the hands of

Luvah" (IV: *327*), neither Urizen nor Luvah is blamed, or blamed solely, but the point is confirmed that some kind of confusion of the primal powers of love and reason had caused the fall. The cycle of recognitions between instinct and imagination is completed a few lines later (*p. 327*) when Tharmas sees Los as the fallen Urthona. The immediate consequence of the fall, as the Spectre remembers it, has been the separation from Urthona of his Emanation. At the same time, his loins broke forth into veiny pipes and englobed; as with Luvah in Night II, the externalization of the sexual organs merges psychologically with the appearance of the female as a separate, alien being. But just as the mutual recognitions among these Zoas foreshadow their eventual reunion as one man, so tentative gestures toward their Emanations offer dim hope in this dark Night that the feminine portion of the psyche will some day be restored. In a further attempt to bring about the reappearance of Enion, Tharmas enjoins the Spectre to carry Enitharmon back to Los and to assist him in binding Urizen. Tharmas hopes one of the new forms brought into being by the Los group will embody Enion.

Los now begins an ambiguous but creative act, and the return to him of his productivity emblemizes a renewed ability to act and make. This collaboration between Los and his Spectre and the partial reunion with Enitharmon anticipate the critical turning point in Night VIIA, where the action will be unequivocally positive and humane. Los's task, with the help of these divided portions of his being, is to build a new order on the ruins of Urizen's world, to incarnate reason in the human body as we know it, and to create time as well. Like most events of Night IV, this act is both tragic and saving. The parallel with adolescence is clear and immensely powerful. The child's former unselfconscious confidence in the rightness of his body and his creative powers is gone now; his all-flexible senses had already rigidified into rationalism, and now that too has failed. The new body, the new sense of the limitations of the physical and the entrapment by time and circumstance that succeeds childhood, is a terrible thing; "Shades of the prison house begin to close / Upon the growing boy." Life is now a dreary prospect stretching ahead into an unexciting future, like human life after the postdiluvian covenant between God and Noah, when God promises to let life run its course without spectacular interventions but makes man settle for a very limited kind of happiness. On the other hand, what might have been a *total* catastrophe, the madness of retreat from the senses into the psychosis of pure rationality, is averted; for the newly sensed body that catches colds, needs eyeglasses, and cannot fly is also the body that hears melody, inhales fragrance, and embraces others. Our limited bodies confirm our fallenness but also provide avenues for the achievement of an eternity even better than what was lost; Blake is adapting the Christian and epic *felix culpa* theme. It is important that, after the skull, skeleton, and heart have been forged on Los's anvil, the "pangs of hope" begin when the first of the sensory organs takes shape. Los cannot see the good in what he is doing; after all, he has been acting unwillingly, driven by an instinct he detests, "Raging against Tharmas his God & uttering / Ambiguous words blasphemous filld with envy firm resolvd / On hate Eternal in his vast disdain" (IV: *329*). Imagination can see no more than that the human person is in for a bad time.

But before the terrible dance that shakes Los at the end of Night IV, Blake has introduced his note of reassurance, the Council of God. The application to his poem of the Raising of Lazarus in John 11—the passage that so moved the timid magdalen Sonia in *Crime and Punishment*—is a brilliant tour de force, but it also suggests powerfully the tenderness of Blake's sympathy with fallen man. For the third time in this Night, this time on a cosmic level, he reminds man that he need not wholly die. The Daughters of Beulah appeal to Jesus, the Divine Vision, in the form of a double female (Mary and Martha of Bethany), the "Feminine Emanation." They speak as simple, sad, trusting but troubled women, saying that, if the Saviour had been there, their brother (Albion-Lazarus) had not died.[2] The Saviour replies that, if they have faith, their brother shall live again. He does not say, "Albion, come forth," for salvation is to come from man himself; but he finds or sets limits to the fall. As Blake wrote in his annotations to Watson, "Jesus could not do miracles where unbelief hinderd . . . . The manner of a miracle being performd is in modern times considerd as an arbitrary command of the agent upon the patient but this is an impossibility not a miracle neither did Jesus ever do such a miracle" (*p. 606*). The first two limits, of opacity and contraction, are *found* by Jesus; they are in Albion's bosom; inherently the lower limits of human nature, they exist independent of Satan and Adam, after whom they are named. The third limit, to the Starry Wheels, is *put*, not found. This means first that the dreary cycles of time and nature, the "many wheels resistless" (IV: *328–329*) which Los had been rolling from furnace to furnace, will come to an end. Psychologically it means that human beings need not resign themselves to permanent fallenness but can hope for an apocalypse of vision. On both levels the apathy implied in Noah's covenant has been implicitly reversed.

The passage about Jesus' intervention separates two identical passages which appear in different contexts: "terrified at the shapes / Enslavd humanity put on he became what he beheld" (IV: *329, 331*). The relationship between *beholding* and *becoming* is altered after Jesus intervenes. Before this dividing point in the poem, all the Zoas and Emanations have caused what they beheld to come into being. Their perceptions of each other have

2. The mood of this passage is strikingly like that of the second section, the choral duet for female voices, of Bach's Cantata No. 78, *Jesu Der Du Meine Seele.*

taken on objectified, externalized reality: as each Zoa has rejected his Emanation, for instance, the most intimate portion of himself has become a threatening alien. The characters in the poem have responded to others not as persons in themselves or as psychic forces which have a right to exist, but as images, creations of the beholder, projections. After Jesus' intervention this activity becomes reflexive. These images and creations take possession of their creators. Los becomes what he beholds *and* "what he was doing" (IV: *331*); as he limits Urizen, he is himself enslaved. The image on his anvil is so frightening that it remakes Los himself; his idea of Urizen becomes his idea of himself as well. There is an extreme example of this phenomenon in Byron's relationship to his Harold, though Byron *wants* to become his creation:

'Tis to create, and in creating live
A being more intense that we endow
With form our fancy, gaining as we give
The life we image, even as I do now.
What am I? Nothing: but not so art thou,
Soul of my thought! with whom I traverse earth,
Invisible but gazing, as I glow
Mix'd with thy spirit, blended with thy birth,
And feeling still with thee in my crush'd feelings' dearth.
                    (*Childe Harold's Pilgrimage*, III, vi)

Just as when Shelley's Prometheus beholds the "execrable shapes" of the Furies, mankind's foul ideas, "Methinks I grow like what I contemplate, / And laugh and stare in loathsome sympathy" (*Prometheus Unbound*, I: 450–451), so Los, when he sees humanity distorted under the shapes he imposes, turns this new distortion on himself. The first time we were told that Los became what he beheld (before Jesus' intervention), there was nothing good about this development; Los had cursed Tharmas, had been filled with blasphemy, envy, hate, and disdain, had heard the howls and groans of Urizen and Enitharmon gratefully. But after he has completed his task and has become both what he beheld *and* what he was doing (after Jesus' intervention), he suffers along with his victims. He is thrown into spasms of involuntary sympathy with them; like Coleridge's Christabel with Geraldine, he passively imitates Urizen and Enitharmon (who is the personification, among other things, of his pity). Every time Urizen howls, Los's lips move silently, against his will, and his loins wave; as Urizen's bones hurtle, Los's bones twinge and his sinews bend. Every time Enitharmon shrieks, Los's knees knock. This pain in Los is a hopeful sign; it indicates that these men and women, and these fragments of the psyche, are really part of one another, whether they know it or not. Los is feeling like the legendary Siamese twin, cut apart from his brother, who still twitches when his brother is hurt. The sympathy thus born, like the limits defined in this Night, is presented in negative terms; but it is an augury of salvation.

Night V. This Night, paralleling the torment of Luvah in Night II, begins with the birth of Orc, fallen passion, from Los and Enitharmon. Now separated far from his cold furnaces and the bound Urizen, Los shrinks with Enitharmon into fixed space as a dreadful winter and darkness settle in and the earth shakes convulsively in sympathy with Enitharmon's labor throes. The scene recalls *Europe,* Plate 3, and "To Winter" (*pp. 60, 401–402*). Since in Blake mind and object correspond, Orc is both an external phenomenon and the mental state that projects it. Something similar appears in Night VI: both nature as seen by Newtonian rationalism and the stuntedness of reason itself. In Orc we see both fallen passion and nature experienced as a "life force" unredeemed by human vision—nature as evolutionists regard it, for example, when they feel awe and admiration for its ruthless but inexorably "right" violence. It is the fallen view of the cycle of nature, as *The Book of Thel* is the unfallen view of it. Later this violent nature will be identified more precisely with Vala, the outward embodiment of passionate vitality. We must remember too that Orc's birth follows immediately the shaping of a body for Urizen and for man; the first fruits of our awareness of the utter physicality of the body are, as in adolescence, the imperatives of sexuality and of raw physical energy. Although both the incarnate Urizen of Night IV and this newborn Orc of Night V show traces of their Edenic potential, neither is fully human. Fallen sexuality, for example, is a reminder of the energy of Eternity; but it is also the motive force of corporeal war.

These new images of mind and nature are solemnized in the fierce hymn prophesying the birth of Vala, sung by enormous demons who awake when Orc is born. There follows the account, as in *The Book of Urizen,* of the rearing of Orc, the formation of Los's chain of jealousy, and his binding down of his fourteen-year-old son. This binding, also requiring help from the Spectre of Urthona, is clearly parallel to the binding of Urizen in Night IV; both intellect and passion, the original powers in rebellion, have to be imaginatively restrained before they can be released in the reintegration of Albion. In binding Urizen, Los had acted under the command of Tharmas, instinct. In binding Orc, Los is under no compulsion but his own jealousy. It is hard to understand why Blake gives Los the motivation of jealousy, not only in the binding of his son but in his dealings with Enitharmon, Urizen, and the others. Since the evil of jealousy is as fundamental an idea as any in Blake, Los's display of this weakness certainly underlines the sickness of imagination. Yet in a psychic state where fallenness seems a permanent fact, even jealousy may be seen as stemming from the imagination; at least it is better than cold indifference.

The ambiguity in sexuality and in adolescence is now dramatized in a powerful passage which shows the bound Orc as both suffering horribly and enjoying gigantic delights, as though he were at once the clod and the pebble. He howls in flames; but at the same time spirits are ransacking the universe, hurrying on errands to bring him wine, food, and the most literally far-fetched joys of the senses. His loins are inwoven with silken fires; and he is close to nature, both her grand phenomena and her intimate secrets. As a portrait of adolescent energy—both as anyone can remember it and more particularly, perhaps, as it has emerged in recent self-portraits of the youth culture and adult images of it—this passage can hardly be surpassed, though it is matched in intensity by the dialogues between Orc and Urizen in Night VIIA (*pp. 346–348*) and Plates 7–8 of *America* (*pp. 52–53*). Though Blake still feels much of the admiration for such Orc-energy that he had expressed in earlier works, he is now more ambivalent toward it; for he has "Spirits of strength" (V: *335*) rejoicing in their palaces over the slain. Slogans like "Make love, not war" offer no real alternatives if both love and war are waged in the same spirit of exuberant egoism. And in placing Orc in such intimate contact with nature Blake is implicitly questioning the quasi-worship of it that has traditionally been ascribed to the Romantics. Nature is seductive but finally subhuman.

Just as, after binding Urizen, Los had been horrified by his handiwork, so now he and Enitharmon repent of what they have done to Orc. They return from Golgonooza, parental love impelling them to unchain their son. But it is too late; in grim and insistent detail Blake tells us that the chain of jealousy has taken organic root in the rock and in Orc's limbs, even to the center of the earth, "a living Chain / Sustained by the Demons life" (V: *336*). After a parent has repressed his child, the repressions and the child's rebellion are a part of him; it is useless now for the parents to be sorry. On another level we are to understand that the inseparability of love and jealousy is apparently an inexorable law in the fallen world which this middle part of the poem describes, a dismal law of existence unalterable by even the most heroic effort. Yet this seeming hopelessness is like the demonstration of a magician who proves something impossible before proceeding to perform it, for later in the poem jealousy *will* be annihilated. In Jesus' parable the wheat and the tares cannot be separated in the normal course of things but must await a final, apocalyptic harvest which for Blake is an overthrow of man's mere "nature."

Even now, though, something immensely significant has happened. For the first time we see Los and Enitharmon acting in a spirit of unselfish sacrifice; the involuntary fellow-feeling experienced earlier by Los has begun to yield something more positive, though still painful. The motif is reduplicated immediately in the parents' return to Golgonooza, when Enitharmon's heart, which she had sealed earlier against Los (I: *308*), bursts open and closes again in pain. Enitharmon senses Vala within her and beholds the abyss where Ahania weeps; we observe again the delicate attunement of the Emanations to one another. Enitharmon also feels the sufferings of Orc; a deep distress has humanized the parents' souls. The kind of sympathy, born of suffering, that George Eliot venerates and that moves Shelley's Prometheus to retract his curse has become an element in the human imagination. In later Nights the beneficial fruits of that change appear: Los is enabled to see within (VIIA: *355*) and to enter into Enitharmon's bosom "now the Obdurate heart was broken" (VIII: *358*). But for the present Los and Enitharmon, like the sexes in "To Tirzah," rise to work and weep.

Now both reason and passion, drawn into natural forms in this Night and the preceding one, go into operation in the familiar way of the world. Orc's life-force awakens its symbiotic counterpart in Urizen; desire awakens restraint, the prolific the devourer, in the dynamic of opposition Blake had delineated in *The Marriage of Heaven and Hell*. There the dialectic had been a healthy one which only a religious fool would try to mitigate; here it is more ambiguous. Urizen's lament (in the quatrains Blake often uses for the poem's arias) is surprisingly sympathetic in tone, perhaps because Urizen is now humanly embodied. He mourns the loss of the blissful past, as it was described in *The Book of Ahania*, when the delights of the mind were sensual in their intensity, and like any conservative idealizing the good old days, he contrasts that time with the present. In lines that recall "The Garden of Love," we read that "The gardens of wisdom are become a field of horrid graves" (V: *336*). We hear another version of the fall, in which Urizen concedes that both he and Luvah were at fault because of a disastrous exchange of Urizen's steeds for Luvah's wine. Urizen is now capable of nostalgic sympathy for Luvah and Vala, probably because Luvah has now become Orc, a far more threatening figure than the unfallen Luvah. Reason had tried to pre-empt desire even when it had been a force of beauty and purity, but Urizen had not known when he was well off, and now he has a revolutionary on his hands. The psychology is like that of the preacher who reviles his daughter for wearing nail polish until she strikes back by becoming the town harlot.

The Night ends with Urizen's decision to explore his dens (which are also those of Urthona [V: *336*]) to locate the pulsation of Orc that is shaking his cavern-world from the other end of reality; things have become polarized. Reason moves toward passion, if for no other reason than to assess its strength, and speculates that "perhaps this is the night / Of Prophecy & Luvah hath burst his way from Enitharmon / When Thought is closd in Caves. Then love shall shew its root in deepest Hell" (V: *337*). Urizen had foreseen and decreed that event in Night III (*p. 320*) as revenge for his own submission to Los, and it is hard to tell now whether his surmise indicates trepidation or subconscious hope on his part. In any case, reason and passion are now opposed in their archetypal way; both are operative in a subterranean world like that of Plato's cave, which is where most human beings live most of the time.

Night VI. Having seen how love actually operates under the conditions of our confused existence, we turn in Night VI to the world fallen reason creates. Like a general reviewing his troops and securing his garrison against a rumored offensive, Urizen responds to Orc's pulsations—that is, to the brute vision of nature and the threat of immorality—with a rationalist survey of the world. This is what Blake means by Urizen's exploring his dens; his economical treatment of the same subject in Chapter VIII of *The Book of Urizen* helps greatly in reading Night VI.

At the outset Urizen comes to a river and is denied drink by three women who turn out to be his daughters and shrink into dry channels when they recognize him; his turning water into rock is a reversal of Moses' miracle in the wilderness. The passage, apparently allegorical, is problematic; but a note that will recur throughout Night VI emerges clearly: mind cannot communicate with this new world. Reason, when it was faith and certainty, was at one with the physical universe; now this world seems a threatening enemy to be conquered by domineering mental fiat. But reason is capable of appreciating what it has lost, and so Urizen mourns the days when these his sweet offspring—the physical world as understood by unfallen reason, or perhaps even the mathematic but still elegant order in Night II—were in harmony with him and he had showered them with gifts. The tone is typical of the fallen Urizen, tearful nostalgia combined with anger; for he goes on to curse his offspring, to bring into existence through his own gloomy pessimism the very evils he deplores or pretends to deplore. As always in Blake, we become what we behold and vice versa. He half predicts, half wills, that his children may curse Tharmas, Los, and Orc. He is like a parent who after a quarrel with his child says, "Go ahead, leave home, hate me, go ruin yourself." Throughout Night VI nature will shrink in terror from this loving, despotic, tearful father; for he half-forces it to do so by his gloomy mistrust of himself and of it, his refusal to let people and things obey their own laws, or rather (since law and uniformity are Urizen's own invention) their own natures, or rather (since nature is Luvah's invention) their own eternal selves. We recognize instinctively and perhaps even rationally what *The Book of Thel* teaches: the world around us will not betray the heart that loves her but will always betray the mind that treats her as an enemy to be controlled, spectrally systematized. Yet our fallen reason insists that we do those things. Newton could have seen his apple as a uniquely beautiful being of reds and yellows that, mother-like, nourished an infant worm; but he chose to reduce it to the controllables of mass and distance for the same reason that he chose to unweave the rainbow. Urizen attempts this kind of domination all through the sixth Night.

Such rationalist tyranny arouses a deep-seated opposition in human instinct, and so at this point a furious Tharmas reappears. Urizen's worldview is utterly irreconcilable with man's need for wholeness and health. Since he would rather die than truly absorb the deist view of reality, Tharmas now reverts to his earlier expressed death-wish, offering Urizen a madly illogical bargain by which they would commit mutual murder, the penalty for non-compliance also being mutual murder. Inevitably, Urizen totally ignores this childlike illogic and continues his arduous exploration, Tharmas fighting in retreat like a Parthian archer. To the rational mechanist the feeble objections of humanist instinct are unworthy of notice or rebuttal, a situation reflected in scientists and utilitarians at their most unimaginative. We think of the Benthams, the Gradgrinds, the mechanist science not only of the Enlightenment but perhaps even more exactly of the late Victorian era—when biblical controversy, for example, was a contest between inflexible scientism and naive piety. Yet instinct survives; like Dickens' Sissy Jupe it fights a rearguard action against a demented reason.

Urizen's journey in this Night is closely modeled on Satan's journey through Chaos in Book II of *Paradise Lost*, as well as the highway construction by Sin and Death later in that poem; and such echoing is appropriate to Blake's vision of mind confronting a universe unshaped by mental effort—a mere dust storm, disorganized, hostile to human needs, and meaningless. The healthy way to organize chaos is a humanizing through imagination, and perhaps that is why Urizen's dens are identical with Urthona's and Los's, but fallen reason's method is to create mechanical patterns, models, laws. In Chapter XIII of the *Biographia Literaria* Coleridge writes that "all objects (*as* objects) are essentially fixed and dead," and fallen reason is contented with or resigned to such death so long as it can measure and reduce. This is what Urizen does. His journey is over a terrifying terrain where he is afflicted by monsters, incessant conflict with refractory matter and biological data. Los broods over this darkness which Urizen tries to illumine with a globe of fire, his intellect and perhaps also the fallen sun—Wordsworth's "light of common day" or the unimaginative sunlight of *The Ancient Mariner*.[3] The ruined spirits, afraid of their own sighs, who

3. See Robert Penn Warren, "A Poem of Pure Imagination: An Experiment in Reading" (1945–46), in *Selected Essays* (New York: Random House, 1958).

mope and suffer in this world were once Luvah's children as well as Urizen's, humanized by healthy love and mind; but now all natural beings are "dishumanizd men" (VI: *340*) locked up in their own senses and selves. Again Blake is describing both mind and object: considered as human persons, the spirits are dishumanized men because they have exchanged their full imaginative life for a truncating rationalism; as objects, the spirits— lions and tigers, for instance—are dishumanized *by* men who see them as merely external beings, not as related to human imaginative needs in the way beloved household pets are. Urizen cannot communicate with these objects; he is like the man who speaks "The Tyger" and unlike the child who speaks "The Lamb":

> in vain the Eloquent tongue. A Rock a Cloud a Mountain
> Were now not Vocal as in Climes of happy Eternity
> Where the lamb replies to the infant voice & the lion to the man of years
> Giving them sweet instructions Where the Cloud the River & the Field
> Talk with the husbandman & shepherd. But these attackd him sore ...
> (VI: *341*)

Urizen, seeing that his children are already suffering beyond his cruelest wish, tries to retract his curse. His repentance, however, does no more good than that of Orc's parents in Night V, for the fetters of his victims are now growing from their souls. Nor can he calm the elements, being himself "subject." Nowhere does Blake make clearer what he means by mind-forged manacles. The mechanist world-view seems to have become an ineluctable datum of human consciousness. Yet, just as the strength of jealousy had been dramatized in Night V so that we could appreciate better the magnitude of its later annihilation, so with this rationalism, which also will be destroyed in the imaginative triumph of the last Nights.

Arriving at Luvah's East, now vacant and storm-beaten, Urizen finds himself sinking, whirling in bottomless space. But he is sustained by "The ever pitying one" (VI: *341*), who creates a bosom of slimy clay on which Urizen can rest and begin a cycle of continual life, death, and rebirth. This organicizing is apparently a salutary qualification of his otherwise unmitigated vision of death, since the organic belongs to Luvah, Urizen's contrary. The only constant throughout these cycles is Urizen's books (they are both discursive works and account books, for Urizen has to "regulate" them from time to time), which survive without harm their author's successive deaths. This is a sardonic comment by Blake, one feels sure, on the ability of rationalism to survive any one of its versions; at the same time, by providing a counterpart of the "Orc cycle," Blake underlines the ultimate affinity-by-opposition between fallen passion and fallen reason. The middle section especially of *The Four Zoas* is full of such ironic parallels.

Urizen has also begun to create "Vortexes," which on one level correspond to what we mean when we say we are "going through" something. In a broader sense, a vortex is a way of looking at things, an orientation, a pathway through chaos. As reason throws itself into meaninglessness, it both organizes and limits raw experience and data. But at least there is a sense of direction and equilibrium that results from establishing the vortex, the system. This is hard and heroic work; nothing falls into place of itself. When Urizen gets to the end of what he has established, where a vortex has ceased to operate, every direction is upward. The only stable equilibrium is where he is, but that is not good enough; he wants a godlike vantage point above reality, or a foundation point beneath it. Either one of these positions would be a void; Urizen cannot cope with plenitude or piedness, he only works reductively. If he labors upward and looks back, the point he has just left is also upward; if he lets himself go, he falls through immensity. The labors of fallen intellect are a rowing upstream in order to stay level. All of this corresponds to our common complaint that just when we get things organized we see much more than a particular system, or vortex, will accommodate; we wish we could find one solid position from which to sight *all* possibilities. Like Archimedes, reason wants a point in space to give it leverage to move the world.

Urizen therefore decides, quasi-literally, to take a stand; "Here will I fix my foot" (VI: *343*), his bodily foot and that of his Newtonian compass. He wants law and order; and for him that means order *through* law, the last refuge of rationalist man appalled at the world's complexity. Like Milton's Mammon, he envisages subterranean riches; and like the deist he hopes to create an obedient universe where futurity and contingency will be bound. Unimaginative man posits such a Creator, is all too willing to concede Urizen's claim that he is sole God. Urizen invents instruments, not just to measure the immense but to "fix" it; for in this ghastly parody of the "sweet Science" mentioned in the last line of the poem the only reality is what can be dealt with in terms of one's own "discipline." To a behavioral scientist rats *must* be essentially similar to people, since rats are available for experimentation, and hunger and sex are of first importance *because* food pellets and copulations can be counted. Everything shrinks under this standardization. Urizen will not allow uncertainties, the feeling of always falling, of always being in the place where a vortex has ceased to operate; everything that does not fit is just ignored. Every human soul, we are told, is terrified by this development, but Urizen cannot be bothered about that; like behaviorists at their most arrogant, he thinks he knows what man needs or ought to feel he needs. Power is Urizen's aim; mere instinctive humanists are put on the defensive and made to feel like dilettantes.

Urizen is aged now, and as he wanders a web like a spider's follows him, the product of his agedness, "A living Mantle adjoind to his life & growing from his Soul" (VI: *343*), like so many phenomena in Blake. If we can take *The Book of Urizen* as a gloss, this is the net of religion, but it also has psychological correlatives. We are told that everyone refuses to open within into eternity as he is capable of doing. One of the captions in *The Gates of Paradise* reads, "Perceptive Organs closed their Objects close" (*p. 262*), and that is what happens here in Night VI; the beautiful and circumambient winglike tent of the universe, which the immortal man can raise or lower at his will, vibrates, quivers, closes. The tent is both the biological eyelid and the eye's objective correlative, the friendly and complaisant sky that, as we read in *Milton* (29: 4–18), accompanies a man whenever he moves from one place to another. We note that the dislocations of mind and sense perception with which most of Night VI has been concerned are intimately allied with religious dislocations. This Night outlines the fallen thought-process which leads Blake to connect Newton and the deists with the moral accuser who is the God of this world and the cleansing of sensory organs with the supreme human charity of forgiveness. Night VI is one of Blake's most lucid testimonies to the cohesiveness, for better and worse, of religion, psychology, and perception.

A little earlier, Urizen had questioned creatures such as scorpions; now he does not ask but merely contains and limits. He wanders on, finally reaching Urthona's world, seemingly his point of departure; it is not for nothing that Blake makes Urizen the king of circles. Like Milton's Satan, he beholds from a peaked rock the world of Los where Orc exults and suffers. Here Tharmas, like the proverbial cornered rat obeying instinct, turns to meet the inexorable pursuer he has been fleeing from and fighting; and he is joined by the Spectre of Urthona, no longer in his humble guise as a blacksmith's apprentice but accoutered in what is almost a parody of warlike might. It turns out that, after all, the aggressions of puffed-up intellect can in the direst moments of stress be met most effectively by lowly instinct in alliance with the human faculty of working with the hands and body. The battle seems to be joined.

Not so, however; Urizen retires to think things over. He has not yet confronted Orc. The warring parties, as at the end of a fourth act in Shakespeare, hesitate and ponder on the brink of a climactic decision. There is a *fermata* on the edge of resolution. This uncertainty will continue through the melodramatics of Night VIIA, until near the end of that Night the decision is made to abandon the whole habit of competitive thinking and feeling that has heretofore dominated human life and this poem; the apocalypse is launched and all the depressingly familiar rules of human behavior will be discarded like outgrown, constricting old garments. Night VI ends on a note of uncertainty that in the context of the dreary middle of *The Four Zoas* ought to be a relief from the apparent certainty of despair and darkness. That pinprick of uncertainty will let the light of redemption into the poem; and the experience of that same uncertainty in each individual opens in him, according to the Blakean gospel, the possibility of a healing struggle for new life.

Say First! What Mov'd Blake?
Blake's Comus Designs and Milton

IRENE TAYLER

"Milton lov'd me in childhood & shew'd me his face," wrote Blake in 1800; and perhaps by that date he had already come to consider Milton his own great prophetic forebear. But aside from the famous passage in *The Marriage of Heaven and Hell*, he appears scarcely to have mentioned Milton before his trip to Felpham. Then, an explosion—for then began those critical transmutations of Milton's art, through prophecy and exhaustive illustration, that form such a large and important part of Blake's canon.

Certainly Blake had at his disposal at Felpham more Milton materials than he ever before had access to. Hayley had recently published (1794–97) a large, handsome edition of Milton, with a "Life" written by himself and with illustrations by Westall; in 1800, he was preparing for publication Cowper's translations of the Latin poems and comments on the major English poetry. The artist Romney had been visiting Hayley in 1792 when the Hayley Milton was in preparation—he made then a pastel portrait of Cowper later used by Blake—and wrote his son of the stimulating atmosphere: "Hayley is writing the life of Milton, so you may imagine that we were deep in that poet, everything belonging to him was collected together, and some parts of his work read every day."[1] These materials "collected together" were presumably still in Hayley's possession when Blake arrived eight years later, and indeed one of Blake's important jobs on his arrival was the painting of a series of "Heads of the Poets" to decorate Hayley's fine library. Among these heads there were portraits of Cowper (after Romney) and of Milton, in whose faces Blake wrote that he had "the happiness of seeing

1. *William Blake's "Heads of the Poets,"* ed. G. L. Conran and William Wells (Manchester: William Morris Press, n.d.), p. 28. (At that time Hayley lived in Eartham.)

the Divine countenance . . . more distinctly than in any prince or hero."[2]

In this setting Blake began his own work on Milton; his first project was a group of eight designs illustrating *Comus*. By October, 1801, he had a buyer in the Reverend Joseph Thomas, Rector of Epsom. Blake wrote Flaxman: "Mr Thomas, your friend to whom you was so kind as to make honourable mention of me, has been at Felpham & did me the favor to call on me. I have promis'd him to send my designs for Comus when I have done them, directed to you" (p. 53). The Reverend Thomas proved a devoted collector of Blake's work: he commissioned several illustrations to Shakespeare, and even went to the trouble of copying unique works owned by others. In 1805 Nancy Flaxman wrote her husband, mentioning that Mr. Thomas "wishes as a great favor the loan of *Blake's Gray* . . . he wishes to make a few copies from it—to keep with his Young's Nights Thoughts & some other works he has of Blakes[.] he wishes to collect all B—— has done, & I have a little commission to give Blake for him [.]"[3] But the choice of subject for these first designs does not appear to have been Mr. Thomas', as Blake seems already to have been at work on them when he and Thomas first met.

I think Blake's reasons for choosing *Comus* lay in what he felt to be the importance of the work to an understanding of Milton. I said that Blake had scarcely mentioned Milton before his trip to Felpham; but critics have nonetheless found some strong Miltonic connections in his earlier work, perhaps chiefly in *Thel*. "This poem," says S. Foster Damon, "is a reconsideration of the idea on which *Comus* is based."[4] Certainly the situations of the two young virgins are similar; both stand at the point of maturity, both evade sexual experience: Milton's virgin reaches—still virginal—the safety of her parents' home, and Thel flees shrieking to the vales of Har. Blake's *Thel* could, I think, be read as a comment on the inadequacy of Milton's solution, but the poem surely has other purposes as well.

The illustrations to *Comus*, on the other hand, are directly concerned with certain strengths and sterilities in Milton's vision. I suggest that Blake chose *Comus* because at this time of renewed, attentive excitement, he saw the masque freshly as a kind of synopsis of Miltonic vision and error: further, that his work with the designs, in turn, led him to recognize the need for a far more powerful, broader, and more deeply personal confrontation with the older poet—in short, that these designs moved him to undertake his great prophecy *Milton*; and finally that the residue of their influence is

2. *The Letters of William Blake*, ed. Geoffrey Keynes (Cambridge, Mass.: Harvard Univ. Press, 1968), p. 98. All citations from Blake's letters are from this edition and are given in parentheses in the text.

3. G. E. Bentley, Jr., *Blake Records* (Oxford: Clarendon Press, 1969), p. 166.

4. "Blake and Milton," *The Divine Vision: Studies in the Poetry and Art of William Blake*, ed. Vivian de Sola Pinto (London: Victor Gollancz, 1957), p. 92.

clearly visible in the prophecy itself, and especially so in the visionary forms of its conclusion.

In what sense a synopsis of vision and error? A virgin lost in the forests of the night is tempted by a shape-changing enchanter, yet manages to retain her Human Form Divine and reach at last, in the opening morning light, the safety of her parents' home. Obviously such a history may be adopted by different parties: Milton's emphasis on sexual restraint could hardly be shared by the Blake we know, and yet a shape-changing son of Circe embodies dangers that Blake would be as eager to expose as Milton had been before him. What meaning, then, *might* Blake have found in Milton's masque? The answer must surely lie in the nature of Comus' enchantment and of the lady's release, so it is not surprising to find, in the designs that illustrate these points, peculiarly Blakean twists: the chair on which Comus holds the lady enchanted is decorated by Blake with women serpent-bound, images of fallen sexuality and moral law; and in the next design, as her brothers drive Comus away, the entire scene of enchantment disperses in a cloud that rises steamily from about the lady herself, suggesting that the entire drama may really have been played in the theater of her own mind, where the darkness has been, in Oothoon's words, "impressed with reflections of desire" (*VDA* 7: 11). In brief, I think Blake saw the lady's encounter with Comus as the product of that frightened girl's fantasy: her bondage, the bondage of sexual fears; her release, the release from them.

Joseph Wittreich has observed that "these illustrations are characterized by their literal quality,"[5] and it is true that to follow them is to trace visually the action of the masque—drama and dance in eight frames. Still, as I have already implied, to follow them closely is to trace certain other kinds of action as well. Let us consider masque and pictures together.[6] There are, as readers of the poem know, only six main characters, excepting the parents and friends who join in celebrating the masque's conclusion: the lady and her two brothers, who are making a night journey through the forest to be present at the festivities at Ludlow Castle; Comus, who meets and tempts the lady; the Attendant Spirit, sent by Jove to aid her; and Sabrina, nymph of the River Severn, who breaks the lady's enchantment at last.

Milton's masque opens as the Attendant Spirit descends and explains the situation to us all; but hearing Comus' approach he retires to disguise himself as a country shepherd. Then Comus enters with his rout of monsters,

5. "William Blake: Illustrator-Interpreter of *Paradise Regained*," in *Calm of Mind: Tercentenary Essays on Paradise Regained and Samson Agonistes in Honor of John S. Diekhoff,* ed. J. A. Wittreich, Jr. (Cleveland: Press of Case Western Reserve Univ., 1971), p. 98.

6. This section, interpreting Blake's *Comus* designs, appeared separately as an article in *Blake Studies,* 4 (1972), 45–80.

singing the praises of night and love, but breaks off his dance as he hears the "chaste footing" of an approaching virgin; at last she enters, while Comus, disguised and hidden in the hope of learning her business, overhears her sing to Echo, asking news of her two lost brothers and calling them a "gentle Pair / That likest thy Narcissus are."[7] The first of Blake's eight designs {23} telescopes these three stages of the action, violating chronology with curious effect; at the top left the Attendant Spirit is still present in his sky robes, watching as Comus and his crew plunge diagonally across the center, carrying charming rod, glass, and torches; but at right, below, the lady is there too, depicted not as we see her when she enters Milton's stage, but apparently as she had sat earlier waiting for her brothers—yet she appears already to see Comus, and to see him indeed in his full, rowdy, undisguised form, surrounded by his crew of beasts.

The second design {24} follows Milton a little more closely: Comus, now disguised, approaches the lady full of questions and compliments, as in the text; but Blake again adds the Attendant Spirit—quite an eye-catching figure here, bearing in his right hand the golden flower of the protective root haemony, as yet unmentioned by Milton. (In the colored original the flower stands out brightly.)

Comus tells the lady he had seen her brothers earlier that evening, "what time the labour'd Oxe / In his loose traces from the furrow came" (ll. 290–291), that they had been gathering grapes and seemed in their beauty to be a fairy vision "I was aw-strook, / And as I past, I worship" (ll. 300–301). Blake shows the flashback as Comus has recounted it—the time-setting ox, the grape-gathering boys, Comus at worship {25}. But he has added in the distance the lady beneath her tree, at the spot marked by the Attendant Spirit, who hangs in the air above her. Also he has placed an odd emphasis on a kind of fluttery femininity in the boys: the view might be sanctioned by Comus' description of their fairy-like beauty, which is itself presumably based on the lady's hint in her song that her brothers are "likest thy Narcissus"; but the emphasis is still remarkable.

The lady now goes off with the disguised Comus to search for her lost brothers, and Milton's scene changes to find the boys themselves discussing their sister's dangers; the older brother has been describing, in fervid detail, the powers of their sister's "chastity" and "true Virginity" (ll. 419, 436) when the Attendant Spirit enters, dressed as the shepherd Thyrsis, and tells them her true plight, offering them a root more medicinal even than the moly that Hermes gave Odysseus to protect him against Circe's charms. (Circe, of course, was Comus' mother.) The shepherd boy who gave him

7. *Comus*, ll. 235–236. Quotations from Milton's masque follow the text of *The Works of John Milton*, ed. Frank Allen Patterson (New York: Columbia Univ. Press, 1931–38), I, i, 85–123. All subsequent citations will appear within parentheses in the text.

the root, says Thyrsis, told him that in another country—not here—it bore a bright golden flower. Blake consistently shows not the root described by Milton, but the golden flower itself {26}.

The oddity of the design is in the way the three figures are hemmed in, enclosed first by the trees that meet above them, then by that draped female overhead, guiding her chariot of fiery dragons. This strange figure is not in Milton's masque; Blake may mean her to suggest the moon-goddess Cynthia who "checks her Dragon yoke, / Gently: o're th'accustom'd Oke" in *Il Penseroso* (ll. 59–60)—though she does not much resemble his rendering of those lines when he comes, years later, to illustrate them in their own context. But the chief allusion is probably to Medea, niece of Circe and votary of the triple Hecate, the three-formed goddess who is at once Luna (in the sky), Diana or Cynthia (on earth), and Proserpine (in the underworld). By making Comus Circe's son, Milton has made him Medea's cousin; so Blake merely literalizes and makes explicit the connection, visualizing her in her famous dragon-car as Comus' extension, or female form. Certainly she is a dark and urgent female power, and she rides hard over the men in this picture.

The scene shifts, in word and picture {27}, to a stately palace in which Comus has seated the lady in an enchanted chair—one can just make out the serpent-bound women that decorate it—and offers his dangerous glass. She refuses angrily:

Thou canst not touch the freedom of my minde
With all thy charms, although this corporal rinde
Thou hast immanacl'd, while Heav'n sees good.
(ll. 662–664)

This opens the climactic debate in which Milton expounds the ideas that animate the masque. Comus accuses the lady of "inverting" the covenants of her trust with Nature in refusing gentle enjoyments, to which the lady of course replies that the issue is not one of inversion, but of proper use: "None / But such as are good men can give good things" (ll. 701–702), things that will please a "well-govern'd and wise appetite" (l. 704). To Comus' arguments against abstinence, then, the lady argues for temperance; but moving to the height of her fervor she shifts her ground and alludes darkly to "the sage / And serious doctrine of Virginity" (ll. 785–786); he is not fit to hear of such things, she says, but if she *should* try to speak of them,

the brute Earth would lend her nerves, and shake,
Till all thy magick structures rear'd so high,
Were shatter'd into heaps o're thy false head.
(ll. 796–798)

Comus is impressed—"She fables not" (l. 799)—but is still dissembling weakly when the brothers rush in with their swords drawn {28}. Comus flees, and we see the crew evaporating in the night, clinging to their last show of shadowy life along his wand, while the cloud dispersing from be-hind the lady's chair reveals once more the forest setting with which we began.

But Comus has escaped with his rod, leaving the lady still fastened in her chair with no apparent way to reverse the spell—until the Attendant Spirit invokes the nymph Sabrina, who rises with her nymphs {29}, singing her presence and readiness "To help insnared chastity" (l. 908). She undoes the spell by asking that the lady look on her as she sprinkles water on the lady's breast, finger, and lip, and finally touches the "glutenous" seat with "chaste palms moist and cold" (ll. 916, 917). She then leaves, with the thanks of the Attendant Spirit, as the lady rises from her seat to go and join the com-pany at her father's residence and "double all their mirth and chere" (l. 954).

Blake's picture shows Sabrina breaking the lady's enchantment, but with none of the gestures described by Milton: the attention of the group seems rather to be centered on the brothers, who bow as if in prayer to Sabrina. The Attendant Spirit, at left, seems already to be suggesting the departure, his pointing finger illustrating the last lines of his speech:

Com let us haste, the Stars grow high,
But night sits monarch yet in the mid sky.
                    (ll. 955–956)

In the background is the suggestion of sunrise, but with stars still visible beyond the V-shaped tree trunk that frames the sky, the same tree we saw in the last picture beyond the clearing clouds; the rooty trunk supporting the lady is her enchanted seat, now returned to its natural form.

Milton concludes his masque at Ludlow Castle on the stage of the theater itself, where the "Noble Lord and Lady bright" receive their children amid dancing and festivity as the Attendant Spirit departs, leaving players, par-ents, and guests to join in an all-including pageantry of dancing and music. But Blake shows no scene of public rejoicing, no mingling of spectators and participants, no castle or lord and lady bright {30}. Rather the parents seem humble, somewhat careworn, even wistful, as they draw their daughter to them at the door of what appears to be a very simple cottage. The brothers watch in wonder as the Attendant Spirit, once more winged and wearing his sky robes, flies "Up in the broad fields of the sky" (l. 978) westward, to the gardens of Hesperus, where, we are told, Adonis heals his wounds in Venus' company and Cupid makes Psyche his eternal bride at last—a land of healing and fulfilled love: Blake's Beulah. The masque concludes with the words of the Attendant Spirit:

Mortals, that would follow me,
Love vertue, she alone is free,
She can teach ye how to clime
Higher than the Spheary chime;
Or if Vertue feeble were
Heav'n it self would stoop to her.
          (ll. 1017–1022)

He flies, then, in Maynard Mack's words, "beyond the music of the spheres —the limits of the universe—to the throne of God."[8] Blake shows him in a posture familiar to those who know Blake's pictures: body bent back, arms spread wide paralleling his angel wings, toes pointed as in a ballet leap. It is the posture of the lark at morning in the *L'Allegro* designs, the Christ Child at birth in the *Nativity Ode*, and of Christ in Resurrection, not in one picture only, but in many.[9]

Questions enough have been raised by details of visual handling, despite the impression of literalness that the designs do seem to give: there are the lady's initial view of Comus undisguised, the uncalled-for appearances of the Attendant Spirit, Medea in her dragon-car riding over the woods, the golden flower depicted in explicit opposition to the text, the curious decorations on the lady's enchanted chair and the clouds that arise from around her, Sabrina's address directed to the brothers rather than the lady, the Attendant Spirit's impressive departure, and the muted privacy of the homecoming that in Milton's text is the very public celebration for which the masque was commissioned in the first place. And many of these details suggest images familiar from Blake's other art.

Milton has written an allegory of the human pilgrimage from adolescence into maturity, or perhaps more largely through mortal life. The danger besetting the young lady pilgrim is that she may fall under the spell of false desires that will cloud her mind and reduce her to a state less than human: those who succumb find "their human count'nance, / Th' express resem-

8. *Milton,* ed. Maynard Mack, 2nd ed. (Englewood Cliffs, N.J.: Prentice-Hall, 1961), p. 66 n.
9. The rising lark is reproduced by Geoffrey Keynes in *John Milton, Poems in English with Illustrations by William Blake, Miscellaneous Poems* (London: Nonesuch Press, 1926), facing p. 28; the newborn Christ appears in the same volume, facing p. 4. A good example of the figure of Christ in Resurrection is that in the Fogg Museum, formerly in the Butts Collection. It is reproduced in the Blake Trust facsimile, *William Blake's Illustrations to the Bible,* comp. Geoffrey Keynes (London: Trianon Press, 1957), p. 148.

blance of the gods, . . . changed / Into som brutish form" (ll. 68–70). For defense against such perversion she welcomes faith, hope, and—not charity, or Christian love—but chastity. (And the greatest of these is chastity!) Her answer to Comus stresses "the holy dictate of spare Temperance" (l. 766); but when she comes actually to confront him at the pitch of argument, it is not the arguments for chastity or temperance that seem most to shatter his assurance. Rather it is her mention of the "sage / And serious doctrine of Virginity" (ll. 785–786) that leads him to concede: "She fables not, I feel that I do fear / Her words set off by som superior power" (ll. 799–800). Is virginity, then—total sexual abstinence—Milton's ultimate advice to a proper pilgrim? It would appear that chastity alone should suffice for most moral purposes, assuring, for one thing, the virginity of unmarried ladies like the young daughter of the Earl of Bridgewater while permitting in time the chaste intercourse of marriage. What is, then, the virtue that allows mortals to climb beyond the music of the spheres? Total sexual denial?

In fact, Milton changed his mind on the question. The version of *Comus* actually performed at Ludlow Castle did not have the lines about the doctrine of virginity, but allowed Comus to interrupt the lady much earlier with his impatient "Com, no more, / This is meer moral babble" (ll. 805–806). So in the earliest versions of the masque, while the lady argues for temperance in response to Comus' broader arguments for enjoyment, she offers no answer at all to the specifically sexual charge, and thus her response—as far as it goes—is that of moral maturity, strict, but not extreme; and her emergence at dawn from that ominous wood would be her emergence into discerning young womanhood. She would have shown herself ready to join her parents and their guests in the life of social and ceremonial responsibility and love.

But between 1634 and 1637 Milton thought again, and the result was that he lengthened the lady's speech and gave her the opportunity to respond—in the most heated lines in the masque—to Comus' specific urgings to sexual enjoyment. One would expect these added lines to continue the direction of her earlier argument for temperance, to extend them to temperance in matters of sex: namely, chastity. (In *Christian Doctrine* Milton defines the matter explicitly: "*Chastity* consists in temperance as regards the unlawful lusts of the flesh."[10]) But not so here at all. Instead she offers the famous and emphatic doctrine of virginity. Her position and her fervor certainly do appear to cripple Comus, but they very nearly cripple the entire masque as well. Certainly they complicate and confuse the whole question of its moral message.

Now Blake, coming to this poem, must have seen in it many of the marks

10. *Works of Milton*, ed. Patterson, XVII, 217.

of true vision: the spectrous beasts that prowl and riot in the night soul and pervert the Human Form Divine; the forests of night, solitude, and affliction; the price of experience—it is not bought for a song. The story in outline must have seemed clear to him: the young virgin lost in the forest, her bondage in darkness and fear, her final release into the light of a new morning. It is surely on one level a rite of puberty in Milton's view and Blake's as well. But what different function such a rite has for these two poets! Add to that the crippling divisions in Milton's own mind, and Blake's sensitivity to such divisions in Milton anyway, and we have the makings of a spiritual war.

For Blake the great bondage in our life of the body is unfulfilled desire, which is in turn ultimately a matter of fear expressed through jealousy or self-righteousness or repressive cruelty:

Selfish father of men
Cruel jealous selfish fear
Can delight
Chain'd in night
The virgins of youth and morning bear.
(*SE, pp. 18–19*)

The great task of puberty, then, of achieving sexual maturity, is to learn to unchain delight, to accept without fear or shame these new stirrings of desire, to recognize in them the energy of life. In *The Book of Thel* that young virgin, seated at her own grave plot "where the fibrous roots / Of every heart on earth infixes deep its restless twists" (6: 3–4), heard a voice of sorrow ask why the maturing body must know such anguish:

Why cannot the Ear be closed to its own destruction?
Or the glist'ning Eye to the poison of a smile?

Thel's response to the voice was, as we all know, immediate flight:

The Virgin started from her seat, & with a shriek,
Fled back unhinderd till she came into the vales of Har.
(6: 21–22)

Blake's first design for *Comus* {23} shows this virgin lady, too, seated among fibrous roots in a kind of cavern of the grave, and what she hears and sees cavorting above her does seem like "her own destruction" in "the poison of a smile"—possibly alluring, certainly threatening. One can see her body steeled (indeed "clad in compleat steel" [l. 420]) against those who might "dare to soyl her Virgin purity" (l. 426). Her shoulders are turned, she clasps her hands as if in prayer, and her eyes express a kind of tremulous anxiety. In the distance the Attendant Spirit surveys the entire scene with dismay: the release of this young lady is going to take some doing! Blake collapses sequence here to show us, in effect, the spiritual state in which the lady's night journey begins; a spirit of life is there to protect her, but she is divided from it by her virgin fears, embodied in Comus and his unruly crew.

In the second design {24}, the lady addresses the disguised Comus and makes her appeal for help; she is still in a kind of cavern, though formed here by the trees whose branches bend and twist above her head (branches and roots are often similar signs in Blake). At the right descends the At-tendant Spirit with his golden flower. By now we should begin to suspect why Blake has disregarded the "root" of Milton's text and chosen instead the golden flower itself as the Spirit's counter-charm against Comus' en-chantments. It is, surely, one of those "sweet flowers" that grew in the garden of love before it became a place of graves with "Thou shalt not, writ over the door" (*SE, p. 26*); the "bright Marygold" or "Golden nymph" (*VDA* 1: 5, 8) plucked by Oothoon and put to glow between her breasts; the "sweet flower" that was offered to Blake but that he passed over for his "Pretty Rose-tree" (*SE, p. 25*); in other words, sex experienced as delight. That it should be proffered here by the Attendant Spirit himself suggests that Blake read Milton as he said he read the Bible: "thou readst black where I read white" (*EG, p. 516*). In Blake's eyes, an Attendant Spirit sent by the gods to help a virgin on her troubled way to maturity could bring no better charm against evils than a flower from the garden of love. It must have seemed to Blake that Milton's true prophetic insight had prompted him to place the Spirit's home in the gardens of Hesperus, that is, the west (or in his own term, Beulah), which is Blake's region of sexual instinct and the body, and to locate there also such mythological emblems of love as Venus and Adonis, and especially Cupid and Psyche, from whom will be born, in Milton's lines, the twins of Youth and Joy. Of course Comus, too, invokes Hesperus in his opening line, and also offers sexual experience; but his manner is frighten-ing to the lady, and his charms bind down the body and pervert the human to the bestial. In a moment I will examine more fully the reason why this is so, and why the golden flower is the specific antidote.

Let us pass designs 3 and 4 again rather quickly; design 3 {25} shows Comus "worshipping" the brothers as they gather grapes, looking in Comus' words like "a faëry vision / Of som gay creatures of the element" (ll. 297–298). Yet I still think it is the lady's own description of them as "most like Narcissus" that Blake points to in showing them feminized, dreamy, in-dolently self-admiring; even their swords are laid aside and suggestively intertwined in narcissistic mirror-love. In design 4 {26} the brothers have their swords in hand again as the Spirit commends to them the golden flower. Hard above them, closing them into that dark woods, rides the serpent lady.

Designs 5 and 6 should now be considered in some detail, for they explain much of what has gone before and what will follow. The first of these {27} shows the lady enchanted by Comus, who stands before her, his wand held over her head in a kind of phallic dominion. The lady is transfixed in his power, that is, in her fear of him, and covers her bosom in a gesture of chaste self-protection. The decorations on her chair might be considered emblems of the state of her spirit; she is herself serpent-bound by her fallen view of moral law and of the relation between the sexes, by her own Female Will, to use Blake's term. The decorations themselves have many counterparts familiar from Blake's other art: the figure of Sin at the gates of Hell in *Paradise Lost*, for example, or the bound lovers in the "heavens of Venus" section of Blake's ninth illustration for *Il Penseroso*—lovers who illustrate the condition that Blake elsewhere refers to as "spiritual Hate, from which springs Sexual Love as iron chains" (*J* 54: 12); similar female figures are wound and tangled among serpents in *Jerusalem*, Plate 75, in a design that S. Foster Damon interprets as Rahab and Tirzah in "the Warfare of moral virtue."[11] All coalesce in the image of the binding serpent as mortality, hence generation, the fallen life of the divided sexes.

Blake's point of departure is something like this: when a thing is divided, reunion seems like death to the separated parts—as indeed it *is* death to their separateness. When women are divided from men, they fear sexual union as a type of that total union that would annihilate their separate identity and so, as they think, somehow put them in the power of men. So they seek to pervert intercourse to purposes other than true union, to teach the laws of chastity and morality—that love is sin and abstinence virtue—and to harness sexual energy into the service of feminine power. Men encourage this when they idealize women, and especially virgin women, in their society and in their church, as in the tremendous importance placed on the virginity of the mother of God. All ordinary conception, being not immaculate and therefore thought to partake of "original sin," must itself be sinful and the desire for it sinful. Thus women, by refusing themselves in love, become by a terrible irony *more* valued, more "pure." "Who shall I send," says Enitharmon in *Europe*, "That Woman, lovely Woman, may have dominion? / . . . Go! tell the Human race that Womans love is Sin" (6: 2–3, 5). The relationship of generative nature to this will for power, based on fear and exercised through sexual dominion, is characterized by Blake in many of his female figures—most complexly in Vala, the "Mother of the Body of death" (*J* 62: 13). At her worst, "Satanic Holiness triumphd in Vala / In a Reli-

11. *William Blake: His Philosophy and Symbols* (Boston: Houghton Mifflin, 1924), p. 473. The illustration of Sin from *Paradise Lost* is reproduced by Keynes in *Poems in English*, facing p. 48; that from *Il Penseroso* in the same edition, facing p. 35. Plate 75 of *Jerusalem* can be seen in the Blake Trust facsimile of the poem (London: Trianon Press, 1950).

gion of Chastity," when "Head & Heart & Loins, closed up in Moral Pride" (*J* 60: 47–49).

Now this is the position of the lady rooted to her serpent-wound chair, confronting Comus. In him she sees the imagined form of sexual man as enemy, trying to "trap" her, as Milton has her say, "With lickerish baits, fit to ensnare a brute" (ll. 698, 699). Her mixed attraction and angry contempt express (to quote Blake again) that "spiritual Hate, from which springs Sexual Love as iron chains."

Comus' wand is his phallic power, as I have already suggested; but his cup is pertinent too. It is a version of Vala's "Poison Cup / Of Jealousy" (*J* 63: 39–40) that so often catches the shrieks and groans of suffering men, elsewhere called the "Cup of Delusion"; Los laments to his love,

Why wilt thou rend thyself apart & build an Earthly Kingdom
To reign in pride & to opress & to mix the Cup of Delusion
O thou that dwellest with Babylon!

(*J* 85: 30–32)

In other pictures the Whore of Babylon herself carries such a cup, as does Chaucer's Wife of Bath.[12] "Mystery, Babylon," dwells in Satan's bosom:

. . . here is her secret place,
From hence she comes forth on the Churches in delight
Here is her Cup filld with its poisons, in its horrid vales
And here her scarlet Veil woven in pestilence & war.

(*M* 38: 23–26)

The cup is, then, another expression of the serpent bondage pictured on the lady's chair—that deluded desire for power through chastity that too much dominates the persons and institutions of the natural world. The lady is far more in the power of Comus—of her own fears—than she thinks. She had, we recall, taunted Comus,

Fool, do not boast,
Thou canst not touch the freedom of my minde
With all thy charms, although this corporal rinde
Thou hast immanacl'd, while Heav'n sees good.

(ll. 661–664)

But in Blake's view there is no question of Comus' touching the freedom of her mind—he is himself the very expression of her mind's terrible bondage.

12. The Whore of Babylon may be seen in *William Blake's Illustrations to the Bible*, pl. 168; and on the title page of Young's *Night Thoughts*, Night VIII, reproduced as Plate X in *William Blake: Essays for S. Foster Damon*, ed. Alvin H. Rosenfeld (Providence: Brown Univ. Press, 1969). The Wife of Bath appears in Blake's illustration of Chaucer's Canterbury Pilgrims, of which an engraved version is reproduced in Bentley's *Blake Records*, pl. XXXIIb.

She is immanacled precisely insofar as he *is* the creation of her mind. She is, in Blake's view, as surely and absolutely right to refuse that cup as she is in Milton's; the difference is that for Blake it is her own fears that urge it upon her, arguing with Satanic appeal that it will make her happy. But though she is a frightened woman, she is not so completely immanacled as to have lost all powers of discrimination. "None," she says, "but such as are good men can give good things" (ll. 701–702); and Blakean and Miltonic virgin alike recognize that Comus is not a good man.

But who are good men?—in Milton's lady's view? and in Blake's? Basically, her brothers are, in both: but for Blake they have much to learn. Our first view of them, we recall, had been through Comus' eyes; and I have been arguing that Comus is, in turn, a projection of one aspect of the lady's mind. He had seen and "worshipt" the brothers as they were gathering grapes, and there they seemed very dainty creatures indeed. Good men, then, are in this view sexually unthreatening men: they have laid their swords aside (literature did not wait for Blake to suggest that swords are emblems of masculine potency) and regard not their work, but each other, with wistful impotence. Comus admires and approves, of course, precisely because the lady does; narcissism is by no means antithetical to Comus' own state of being; in fact, for Blake, Comus and Narcissus are really expressions of the same assumptions about the split between self and other.

Robert Simmons, writing about Blake's *Book of Urizen*, has shown the pertinence of the Narcissus myth to Blake's myth: "the story of Narcissus' perception of his own image in the water [is] a parable for the origin of the philosophical problem of the split between subject and object. It is the perception of this distinction between "self" and "other" that creates the divided physical world—a world everywhere in Blake associated with water."[13] The division of man from woman is, of course, an aspect of the divided physical world; and the association with water Milton generously supplies for Blake here with the nymph Sabrina, another example of what Blake must have regarded as uncanny prophetic self-insight. As Blake saw it, not only Milton's story, but his very language, was laced with images of division: a virgin lady mistrustful of desire and lost from her brothers invokes the aid of Echo (her own reflecting voice) to find boys "like Narcissus." Narcissus-like men are "safe" in that their love is inward-turned, and so by definition innocent of sexual union, or any union whatever. It is pertinent to recall that Narcissus' plight resulted from his unwillingness, or inability, to return the love of Echo. Thus the lady's choice of Echo and Narcissus as the appropriate lovers to invoke in her time of trouble is almost comically appropriate to Blake's view of the lady as a virgin afraid of union,

13. *"Urizen:* The Symmetry of Fear," *Blake's Visionary Forms Dramatic,* ed. David V. Erdman and John E. Grant (Princeton: Princeton Univ. Press, 1970), p. 151.

protecting her separateness. Her brothers are also, of course, quite in the power of female religion, piously voicing its doctrines and invoking its heroines: the older brother recounts how "Som say no evil thing that walks by night / . . . Hath hurtfull power o're true Virginity" (ll. 431, 436), and notes approvingly that Diana, "silver-shafted Queen for ever chaste" could "set at nought / The frivolous bolt of Cupid" (ll. 441, 443–444) [14]: likewise Minerva, "unconquer'd Virgin," "freez'd her foes to congeal'd stone" with "rigid looks of Chast austerity" (ll. 447, 448, 449). He argues, in fact, that saintly chastity can so purify the body as to make it become immortal. In short: sexual denial raises woman to the powers of godhead—truly Satan's own temptation,[15] and not so different, in its ultimate effect, from Comus'. Both temptations are founded on a belief in the separateness of man from woman, and both build on and encourage the strife that results from that separateness.

When the Attendant Spirit arrives and finds the brothers engaged in this discourse, he offers them a chance to free their sister through the use of haemony, which in Blake's picture (again) is no root, but the golden flower of love—that is, of sexual love experienced as delight rather than as power struggle. One may recall that in this picture the boys have taken up their swords at last, though perhaps not yet with much conviction.

In other words, the Spirit is arming the brothers for an attack on the Female Will, that veiled tyrant of women that makes them tyrants over men; I take Medea and her dragons riding above the three figures in the same design to be an embodiment of that enemy, seeking to oppress and enclose the three, and prevent them from a task so dangerous to her well-being. (The more distant allusions to Circe and Hecate would of course be quite appropriate in this context.)

The sixth design {28} at last shows the attack itself: the brothers have arrived, swords now held high, and their rush of "dauntless hardihood" (l. 649) has swept away palace, table, even Comus' lordly gown; one has seized his glass, too, but the enchanter escapes with his wand in its cluster of shadowy creatures and a last, flickering lamp. The clouds that contain the entire company disperse from their source around the lady, revealing once more the natural world of woods and stars.

Thus Blake seems to have seen the entire encounter with Comus as the

14. If Blake does have Cynthia's dragon yoke from *Il Penseroso* in mind in design 4 {26}, it would probably be an allusion also to Milton's reference to her here. Cynthia (Diana) was especially worshiped by women and perhaps was once considered a spirit of woods, according to *The Oxford Companion to Classical Literature* (Oxford: Clarendon Press, 1937), p. 143.

15. This view seems to be implicitly shared by the lady in her warning that her talk of virginity would have the power to move inanimate things.

lady's fantasy, based on her fears of sexual man as a dangerous enchanter whose powers, if she should succumb to them, would destroy her human identity. Her brothers share her views at the outset; and all three children must learn, in Blake's reading of the Comus story, to accept the golden flower and put its power to use, driving notions of Comus away from the lady, and allowing the brothers to resume their swords.

But Milton had added another step to the lady's disenchantment, and called on the nymph Sabrina {29}. We have observed Blake's departure from his text in having Sabrina in effect disenchant the brothers rather than the lady: they are now the center of attention—ours, the lady's, and Sabrina's. Female deities are necessarily ambivalent—at best—in Blake, and especially virgin ones; Milton had stressed Sabrina's virginity.[16] Blake shows the nymphs holding shell-cups; the nymph at the far right holds a shell in a cup ominously similar to Comus'. The shell in Blake is usually an emblem of the mortal body—the circumference of the spirit, which is one reason why he calls west "the Circumference" (*J* 12: 55)—and sea shells are especially clearly so, since water itself is an emblem of the material world, as noted in connection with Blake's use of the Narcissus myth. Nymphs are spirits of generation—the reason Oothoon saw her golden flower "now a flower; / Now a nymph" (*VDA* 1: 6–7)—and specifically spirits of water. Blake says 64,000 of them "guard the Western Gate"! (*J* 13: 28). So they are always in danger of falling into the patterns of sexual strife. Yet they are also shadows of those waters that Blake says "wash off the Not Human" and that he calls "the Waters of Life" (*M* 41: 1).

It is therefore appropriate that the brothers, with the Attendant Spirit's help, should release the lady's mind by freeing it of the fears that are Comus, and of his enchantments that are the resulting urgings of the Female Will; but it is also appropriate that the *nymphs* must release her body, for they *are* the body. They do so through the brothers, I think, because female freedom cannot be achieved without male freedom as well, a point Blake has already forcibly made in *Visions of the Daughters of Albion* and broadly implied here in his emphasis on the swords. The brothers' devotional posture shows their freedom to be at best partial; for the nymphs, being

16. Milton himself is in something of a tangle here, as the appeal to Sabrina is made in the name of various water powers, among them "sirens sweet" (l. 877). But Comus had associated his mother Circe with the sirens. Certainly both Circe and the sirens are types of women whose love lures men to their destruction, as would also seem to be the nymphs "with wily glance" mentioned a few lines later (l. 883). Sabrina's family connections might well raise eyebrows. It may be a very distant allusion to these connections that prompts Blake's lines that open *Jerusalem*, Plate 75:

Rahab, Babylon the Great, hath destroyed Jerusalem.
Bath stood upon the Severn with Merlin & Bladud & Arthur,
The Cup of Rahab in his hand, her Poisons Twenty-seven-fold.

elements of this physical world, "know not of Regeneration, but only of Generation" (*M* 31: 19) ; their waters (as I said) are only shadows of the waters of life. It is the Attendant Spirit who knows of Regeneration, as he has already shown and as he implies here again by pointing up and away. His pointing finger in this design balances Comus' starward gesture in the first one; Comus was welcoming night and its dark confusions, while the Spirit here urges the company away from them:

Com Lady while Heaven lends us grace,
Let us fly this cursed place,
Lest the Sorcerer us entice
With som other new device.
                    (ll. 937–940)

In the last design {30} we see the lady arrived out of the forest and into the morning, "Image of truth new born" (*SE, p. 31*). She has been freed into sexual life, not yet eternal life—she approaches her parents' house, not, as does the Attendant Spirit himself, Beulah or the "throne of God." Yet the time will come, Blake has said, when all creation will appear "infinite and holy"; and this time will be brought about by "an improvement of sensual enjoyment" (*MHH* 14: 38). This improvement she is now ready for; but if we may judge by the appearance of the lady's parents, there will still be much suffering to pass on the way to eternity.

At Felpham and before, Blake had been working, reworking, striving to understand himself in *Vala*. What he found in *Comus* was a kind of Dream in One Night, a story of temptation and release deeply appealing to his own visionary grasp of one of man's major patterns of experience. But according to Blake, it is the idea of sexual love as bestial and corrupting from which we must be freed. The argument against "violation"—the notion of "soiling" virgin "purity"—is itself the wily and dangerous deceiver. It is, as I have said, a defensive argument, based in fear for the integrity of one's "self." But one's "self," in its very selfishness, is already a divided and diminished thing; and it drives men to self-righteous brutality or self-loving narcissism —not very different states—and women to a nightmare of destruction and cold self-refusal that finds its limit in total stasis among grotesques.

Milton's argument had shown a virtuous and cautious virgin reach maturity by resisting her wily male attacker. Blake found there the story of a frightened virgin who reached maturity by breaking free of her benighted state of self-isolating fear of her own desires. She has had a lost traveler's dream under the hill—Blake so pictures her in the first design," "dreaming" Comus' unruly approach—but weary night does pass and the sun rises on her homecoming at last.[17] The cottage and older couple are simple and

17. The design accompanying the poem I paraphrase here—Blake's "Epilogue" to

generalized because, for Blake, the lady has not arrived at Ludlow Castle to join through shared ceremony the world of social relationship, but rather has arrived from a spiritual journey to reach the inner world of womanhood. She has escaped being Thel and readies herself to become Oothoon, to pluck that glowing flower of sweet delight.

Vala has been subtitled "The Death and Judgement of the Ancient man," but when Blake changed the title to *The Four Zoas*—possibly about the time of illustrating *Comus*—he expanded his subtitle to read "The Torments of Love & Jealousy in The Death and Judgement of Albion the Ancient Man" (*FZ, p. 296*). This is a significant shift; and the *Comus* designs define that jealousy as the Selfhood's struggle for survival.

Thel had fled back from the voices of sexual experience; the lady in Blake's *Comus* designs surmounted them, having understood their source and meaning; but Milton himself had yet to learn that male integrity means not exclusions but inclusion. Northrop Frye has observed that "the image of the emanation, the aggregate of all that a poet loves visualized as a bride"[18] is missing from Milton; though he could portray the sinister Female Will with devastating accuracy, as in his portrait of Dalila, there are no women whose love inspires, redeems, and fulfills the poet-prophet, no Beatrice for this Dante. Thus Blake depicts Milton as "Unhappy tho in heav'n" (*M* 2: 18) because he is divided from his female selves—biographically his three wives and three daughters—by his misunderstanding and resentment of them, and theirs of him.

Blake's portait of Milton for Hayley's library shows the poet surrounded by a coiling serpent offering an apple of temptation; the allusion is to *Paradise Lost*, of course, but more largely to the whole complex of human error resting in our mistaken notions about the nature of the generative life. The serpent is also one of those that coil about the lady's chair in *Comus*; the apple (from the tree of knowledge), another version of the cup of mystery and the divisive moralities of good and evil that mystery promotes. Blake probably did not know that the stern arguments promoting virginity were Milton's afterthought, emphasizing the already strong spirit of denial almost at the price of the work's artistic unity. But he sensed clearly enough

---

the series suggestively entitled *For the Sexes: The Gates of Paradise* (pp. 256–266) — displays at the top of the plate a serpent with about thirteen numbered coils (the age of puberty?) and below Satan oppressing the traveler. That the Satanic dream arises in part from repressed sexual desire Blake indicates by having Satan arise from the phallus of the sleeper (see the placement of Satan's right foot). The design may be seen in Kathleen Raine's *Blake and Tradition*, Bollingen Series 35: 11 (Princeton: Princeton Univ. Press, 1968), I, 288.

18. *Fearful Symmetry: A Study of William Blake* (Princeton: Princeton Univ. Press, 1947), p. 352.

the fear and anger that led Milton to make the changes. They are Milton's Selfhood, which he must return, in *Milton*, to destroy.

The Bard's Song that opens the first book of *Milton* alludes to the issues of self-love and jealousy. But Blake expands them to include his larger prophetic concerns; for sexual division is a type of all division—a root of political and religious tyranny, of slavery to the sword and moral law. The counter to such slavery, the path to liberty, is through self-annihilation, as Milton also knew. But in Blake's view a great part of Milton's trouble was that he saw self-annihilation as something too much like submission to the will of an external God (a notion capable of breeding self-righteous doctrinal rigidity), whereas for Blake it meant washing off the "Not Human" (*M* 41:1), free and total acceptance of all that is alive in one's self and nothing that is not alive—meaning, at one level, the repudiation of Selfhood and reunion with one's emanations. Such a state is sexless in the sense that it is undivided, yet active with the "severe contentions / Of Friendship" (*M* 41:32–33); a state so wearing, though joyous, that one must recede from it occasionally into the moony and idyllic separateness of Beulah, which is marriage expressed as luxurious romantic dalliance and soft mother-love rather than fiery consummation. It is the state to which the virgin in Blake's eighth *Comus* design {30} can aspire, against which she can measure the happiness of the sexual love for which she is now ready; but, though eternity will never be reached by one who has not the capacity for such lovingness, Beulah is not itself eternity. A "threefold" state that assumes the division of the sexes, it is always in danger of collapsing into that sinister world of division ruled by the triple Hecate and all she represents in the way of Female Will and fallen vision. In its collapsed state, this is the world of Milton's Comus, his fallen Eve squabbling bitterly with her husband, and his Dalila; it is the world to which Milton descends in search of his emanation, Ololon.

And Milton said, I go to Eternal Death! The Nations still
Follow after the detestable Gods of Priam;   in pomp
Of warlike selfhood, contradicting and blaspheming.
                                        (*M* 14:14–16)

Like the virgin in *Comus*, he will make a night trip in search of a spiritual morning:

I will arise and look forth for the morning of the grave:
I will go down to the sepulcher to see if morning breaks:
I will go down to self annihilation and eternal death . . .
What do I here before the Judgment? without my Emanation?
                                        (*M* 14:20–28)

So he descends, through Beulah to the vegetative world, where he enters Blake through his left (material) foot: at this a "black cloud," widely interpreted as Milton's puritanical religion, splits off from them, and

Then Milton knew that the Three Heavens of Beulah were beheld
By him on earth in his bright pilgrimage of sixty years

In those three females whom his Wives, & those three whom his Daughters
Had represented and containd, that they might be resumd
By giving up of Selfhood.

(M 15: 51–52, 17: 1–3)

This is a crucial matter: freed from his "black cloud," and by means of Blake's illustrations and present prophecy, Milton will be seen to have had in fact a fuller vision of Beulah than he knew. Milton had the capacity, though he exercised it only obscurely: indeed it was buried in *Comus*, in the figure of the Attendant Spirit and his golden flower. Blake's role as brother prophet is now to help Milton engage in spiritual warfare against the Satanic Urizen that dwelt inside him and distorted his art, and so to lay bare the true prophetic meaning of his vision. To underscore the importance of this moment in which "Milton knew"—the moment is really a kind of visionary synopsis of the entire prophecy—Blake offers a full pictorial display of its meaning (in some copies interrupting the crucial lines at their center, after "sixty years") : on the lower half of the plate a vigorous young Milton pulls down the aged Urizen and his stone tablets of law into the waters of the river Arnon, "a river of possessive love, the jealousy of the Selfhood," as Harold Bloom observes.[19] But above we see what will be the result of this powerful act: in the light of the morning sun—that image of truth new born—stands a handsome, haloed young bard with his lyre, while about him play his joyous emanations pictured as Daughters of Beulah. These are the Heavens of Beulah that Blake says Milton beheld unaware and that will be restored in the vision that concludes this prophecy.[20]

Milton's long struggle with Urizen on the Arnon is variously detailed in the plates that follow; Los, the prophetic power, enters Blake's soul (*M* 22: 12–14), and we are shown how earth suffers under the dominion of Urizen and the Female Will, how the living yearn, in their state of war and

19. See Harold Bloom's "Commentary," in *The Poetry and Prose of William Blake*, ed. David V. Erdman (Garden City, N.Y.: Doubleday, 1970), p. 352.

20. I am aware of the negative or ironic interpretation that Damon (e.g., *A Blake Dictionary: The Ideas and Symbols of William Blake* [Providence: Brown Univ. Press, 1965], p. 44) and others have placed on Blake's use of the term "Heavens of Beulah," but here the context seems to define them clearly in their positive, regenerative sense.

oppression, for the new awakening that prophecy can provide. Meanwhile Ololon, who in her role as Milton's fulfillment is here envisioned as the River of Life in Eden (compare the role of Sabrina, the Severn, in *Comus*), decides also to descend, to join Milton in his act of self-annihilation; as her decision is made in the spirit of Jesus the Saviour, Blake imagines Him coming with her "in the Clouds of Ololon" (*M* 21: 60).

Her actual descent as a female figure begins in the second book; and predictably the descent is made through the state of Beulah, which here receives the fullest and loveliest description Blake ever gave it. Beulah laments for Ololon as she passes through; and in this beautiful lamentation, which concludes with an echo from the Song of Solomon ("Men are sick with Love" [*M* 31: 62]), Blake introduces two figures who will gain in importance as the prophecy draws toward its close: the lark, who is the bird of morning; and the wild thyme, who leads the morning's "sweet Dance" (*M* 31: 53).

As Ololon prepares to leave Beulah and continue her downward journey, Blake adds a final "Song of Beulah," spoken by the "Divine Voice" himself to a wife identified as "Virgin Babylon Mother of Whoredoms" (*M* 33: 20). She is of course the inverse of Jerusalem, the Whore of Babylon of Revelation, the Female Will in our entire civilization. The song is correspondingly an inverse of the Song of Soloman, for it sings not of the love that redeems —man and woman or Jesus and his people—but of the love that destroys by jealousy. When woman rids herself of that, "then alone begins the happy Female joy / As it is done in Beulah" (*M* 33: 19–20), a release that will be signaled by the wife's bringing Jerusalem to "give her into the arms of God your Lord & Husband" (*M* 33: 23). Beneath these lines Blake provides his famous diagram of "Milton's track," the path that Milton took in his own descent. That this diagram of an event that happened some twenty plates earlier should appear only now suggests that it is offered as the balance, the other half (as it is literally the other half-plate) of the song that is sung above it; for it shows that Milton's descent must pass between Urizen and Luvah (the power of love) and through the dark fires of Satan, the Selfhood. The destructive cruelties of Babylon's female jealousy and Milton's male Selfhood are aspects of the same negating spirit, just as Medea could be an aspect of Comus.

As he had prepared for descent, Milton had cried:

I in my Selfhood am that Satan: I am that Evil One!
He is my Spectre! in my obedience to loose him from my Hells
To claim the Hells, my Furnaces, I go to Eternal Death.

(*M* 14: 30–32)

Milton's furnaces are his creative art, "hells" in the vigorous sense depicted
in *The Marriage of Heaven and Hell* if the prophet works unhindered and
in joy, but "hells" in the terrible Satanic sense if, as was the case with the
historical Milton, the poet's Selfhood is at war with his own prophetic vision.
Milton's path of descent is thus a re-examination of the roles of love and
reason in his life and art (as he passes between Urizen and Luvah), a confrontation with Satan (through his fires), and a return to his Adamic state
(the limit of contraction and the destination of his "track") to unite with
his redemptive emanations. These are at once the women in his life and the
products of his art, with whom his reunion will achieve eternal life for himself ("What do I here before the Judgment? without my Emanation?") and
for them—both as they are his female family and as they are his prophetic
art, the products of his furnaces.

"There is a Moment in each Day that Satan cannot find," writes Blake,
"Nor can his Watch Fiends find it" (*M* 35: 42–43); it is the moment of
inspiration, and at such a moment the poet Blake had his vision of the
descent of Ololon to his garden in the form of a virgin twelve years old. The
time is identified as morning—though "nor time nor space was / To the
perception of the Virgin Ololon . . . / for the Satanic Space is a delusion"
(*M* 36: 17–18, 20)—and the occasion is heralded by those morning figures
introduced before, the lark and wild thyme. But here they are transformed
by Vision; the wild thyme defines (with a pun) the time:

Just in this Moment   when the morning odours rise abroad
And first from the Wild Thyme . . .
The Wild Thyme is Los's Messenger to Eden,
                         (*M* 35: 48–54)

and the lark, the place:

Just at the place to where the Lark mounts . . .
. . . & the Lark is Los's Messenger.
                    (*M* 35: 61–67)

It is a morning moment, when in the eyes of the poet Nature is transformed
into Vision.

Allow me, then, my own moment of—irresponsibility. Imagine Blake
early one morning in 1801, or perhaps 1802. He has finished, or is just fin-
ishing, his illustrations to *Comus* and is troubled by the Miltonic errors he
finds there—perhaps more troubled than before because he is closer to
Milton than before, deeply involved in his works and the making of his
portrait. He has seen that Milton's error lies in his stern spirit of denial, the
fear and anger that are the expressions of his raging Selfhood, the Satan in

him that struggled against his prophetic vision and almost ruined *Comus*. And he has seen that while the effects blast human endeavors as far-flung as philosophy, politics, religion, and art, the trouble itself can be defined in terms of a failure in sexual love: the poet-prophet's failure to envision his emanation, an experienced vision of himself in Beulah—which is the state of "marriage." As Comus was the product of the virgin lady's frightened fantasy in Blake's reading, so *Comus*—with its unspoken assumption that human sexual love leads inevitably to Ulro, the dominion of Hecate, Circe, and the Female Will—was the product of Milton's frightened fantasy.

So on this morning that I am suggesting we imagine, Blake walks in his garden thinking about his great prophetic forebear; it is a period when the natural landscape around Felpham is still a joy to him, and the sounds and smells of morning perhaps especially so. Suddenly, his vision comes: lark and thyme (available to his imagination from nature and literature alike) are transformed into messengers of Los, and they prepare him for his momentous insight: the arrival of Ololon, who is the pale prepubescent lady of Milton's *Comus* metamorphosed by Blake's vision into precisely what Blake realized Milton had been unable fully to create for himself, the "image of the emanation, the aggregate of all that a poet loves visualized as a bride."

Strikingly, the lark and thyme, while the messengers of Los indeed, are also recognizable versions of the Attendant Spirit and his haemony. We have already seen that the departing Spirit in *Comus* {30} assumes the posture and bears the angel wings that Blake will later use for the lark in the second design for *L'Allegro*, and we are advised in *Milton* that though he looks like a bird to Ulro eyes, "the Lark is a mighty Angel" (*M* 36: 12).[21] Similarly the wild thyme seems to the inhabitants of Ulro "Terrible, deadly & poisonous," "a mighty Demon" (it is, after all, the root of the flower of love), and therefore appears in Ulro vision (in Milton's *Comus* for one!) as "a small Root creeping in grass" (*M* 35: 56). Milton had described haemony as "a small unsightly root," adding that "in another Countrey" it bore a bright golden flower. To this country Blake hoped to bring the elder prophet.

To return to the dramatic situation:

Walking in my Cottage Garden, sudden I beheld
The Virgin Ololon & address'd her as a Daughter of Beulah.
(*M* 36: 26–27)

He invites her into his cottage; but she is firm to her purpose and says she has come to seek Milton whom she has driven from Eternity. But Milton himself cannot yet hear her; rather, her words bring Milton's Shadow "in

21. The connection of the lark to the twenty-seven churches might possibly allude, in this reading, to the Attendant Spirit's self-expressed role as the agent of the gods.

Selfhood deadly" (*M* 37: 10), bearing "the Gods of Ulro" in him, "down into my Cottage / Garden: clothed in black, severe & silent" (*M* 38: 7–8). It is time for the final battle between Milton's true humanity and the Satan inside him. Blake himself knows of this spiritual condition, and sees before him the desolation of Satan's bosom, in which dwells Babylon with her poison cup and the enchained Jerusalem in a setting of horrid architecture that recalls the imprisoned lady and the tempting cup in the palace of *Comus.* But as the brothers had confronted the enchanter there, now the true Milton confronts the Satan of his Shadow and orders him, in the name of Jesus, to "be no more" (*M* 39: 2). The words herald a mighty change:

Suddenly around Milton on my Path, the Starry Seven
Burnd terrible! my Path became a solid fire, as bright
As the clear Sun & Milton silent came down my Path.
(*M* 39: 3–5)

This is the fully cleansed Milton at last, divested of his black-clothed Puritan shadow; and in a momentous vision Blake sees Albion begin to arouse himself as the last traces of the "Not Human" are cleansed from England's great prophet.

Book I had concluded with a description of the world of Los, the natural world seen in poetic vision; in a sense this is also where Blake's *Comus* illustrations concluded, with the young virgin ready to assume sexual life. Freed from virginal stasis by the nymphs, who "know not of Regeneration, but only of Generation," she could then partake of that "improvement of sensual enjoyment" which is necessary in this world to bring about the time when all creation will appear "infinite and holy." You cannot see Golgonooza, says Blake in *Milton*, "till you become Mortal & Vegetable in Sexuality, / Then you behold its mighty Spires & Domes of ivory & gold" (35: 24–25); in descending, in Book II, from her state as the waters of life in Eden to her present state as a virgin on Blake's garden walk, Ololon coalesces with the mortal virgin lady of *Comus* to take up where that virgin left off, to ready her cumulative self to meet the man who loves her and the poet who created her. She sees in her own vision his far-reaching struggles with the powers of Selfhood—Urizen and Satan—and she recognizes the part her own fears and jealousies have played in those trials. "Is Ololon the cause of this?" she asks. As if to answer in what sense she is implicated, Rahab Babylon appears:

A Female hidden in a Male, Religion hidden in War,
Namd Moral Virtue; cruel two-fold Monster shining bright
A Dragon red & hidden Harlot which John in Patmos saw.
(*M* 40: 20–22)

Milton's self-righteous support of religious war and his vision in *Comus* of the "virtue" of prim virginity are both examples of the whoredoms and error that consolidate at Apocalypse. It is Female Will—in men and women —and as such it is the Selfhood, the negation, that must be annihilated. Below the lines describing Rahab Babylon's appearance, across the bottom of the plate, Blake shows a dense wood in which a naked figure holds terrible combat with a serpent and monster-headed beast like those that menace the lady in *Comus*—but here it is Milton himself battling down the spectres of the night forest of his own vision {31}.

All the nations of Ulro appear as Milton gathers together the catalogue of negations that must be destroyed "That the Children of Jerusalem may be saved from slavery" (*M* 40: 31). He has come

To cleanse the Face of my Spirit by Self-examination.

To bathe in the Waters of Life; to wash off the Not Human.
                                    (*M* 40: 37—41: 1)

He will cast off rational demonstration, memory (as opposed to inspiration), and all who advocate or practice false art, the destroyers of Jerusalem and murderers of Jesus. All these, he says,

   are the Sexual Garments, the Abomination of Desolation
Hiding the Human Lineaments as with an Ark & Curtains
Which Jesus rent: & now shall wholly purge away with Fire
Till Generation is swallowd up in Regeneration.
                                    (*M* 41: 25—28)

This is Ololon's final step as well, though a frightening one: terrified, she admits that in her separate, sexual form, she cannot survive total regeneration:

Altho' our Human Power can sustain the severe contentions
Of Friendship, our Sexual cannot: but flies into the Ulro.
                                    (*M* 41: 32—33)

In Beulah she can survive as her separate self, but that is the very danger of Beulah, the reason why Beulah-love can so easily slip and fall into Ulro jealousy and hate. But at this climax she chooses the "Eternal Death" of total union, and with a shriek (like Thel's) her virgin self flees into the depths of Milton's Shadow, as the bloody wars of earth become—for the regenerated—the intellectual wars of Eternity. Jesus, who had come in the clouds of Ololon, now wraps them around him as clouds of blood and enters the bosom of Albion, sleeping England, as the trumpets announce the Apocalypse to come.

Blake can endure the vision no longer—that moment in his morning garden is over—and he falls outstretched to wake and wait for his own day of judgment "in the Vegetable Body," as Catherine, his "sweet Shadow of Delight," stands trembling by his side. The lark and odorous thyme are themselves again:

Immediately the Lark mounted with a loud trill from Felphams Vale,
And the Wild Thyme from Wimbletons green & impurpled Hills.

(*M* 42: 29–30)

Los and Enitharmon turn to their prophetic duties on earth; Oothoon weeps over her "Human Harvest" (in "Pity for the suffering of restrained womanhood," Damon suggests[22]); and all the earth prepares, in the words of the final plate, "To go forth to the Great Harvest & Vintage of the Nations. Finis."

On this last plate {32}, standing with arms outstretched as if to support the "Finis" above her, stands a lovely girl between two wing-lapped creatures that look like stalks of wheat similar to those on the lady's chair as she was being released from Comus' bondage. Damon interprets the design as representing "the Soul in ultimate ecstasy, between Seraphim of Love,"[23] and that is surely true. It is also a prefiguring of the human harvest announced at the conclusion of *Milton*: the millennium. But it is clearly also Ololon come home to her eternal parents, as the lady had come home to their sexual shadows in the world of generation. Blake himself has made the connection explicit, for on the back of a sketch for this final design of *Milton* he wrote: "Father & Mother, I return from flames of fire tried & pure & white" (*p. 730*). Not "pure" in the language of Milton's errors, but truly pure, tried by the flames of self-annihilation and free at last of the "female dream" that had blasted the wheat of *Europe*.

Of course I am not suggesting that we reduce *Milton* to *Comus*' terms; all of the ideas and most of the method could grow easily enough out of Blake's own earlier prophecies. But in the second book, as the figure of Ololon expands in importance and approaches her ultimate union with Milton, the imaginative connections with *Comus* assert themselves more and more insistently. What seems clear—yet once more—is that Blake saw how in that revealing masque Milton was unable to detect his own enemies. The context of Blake's awareness is accordingly held in residue in the prophecy that seeks to provide Milton's errors with their necessary correction. That Blake was himself intimately familiar with the same source of misery and mangled art, that "enemy of conjugal love" as he writes in a letter to William

22. *Blake: Philosophy and Symbols*, p. 429.
23. Quoted by Keynes in the Blake Trust facsimile of *Milton* (London: Trianon Press, 1967), unpaginated notes at the end.

Hayley (Keynes, p. 106), is clear from his deep interest in the subject, his clarity about its implications, and his own elaborate role as a character in the prophecy itself. But that is perhaps a question for biography.

Ololon is a fulfilled version of the lady of *Comus* as she is a maiden seeking fuller humanity, which Milton refused her in the conscious argument of his poem. But he undermined his own intention by his powerfully visionary Attendant Spirit, who shoots from Heaven "Swift as the Sparkle of a glancing Star" (l. 80), as did Milton himself in Blake's vision. And Milton grasped far better than he knew the powers of the magic root haemony, that true and loyal messenger of Los. So Ololon is also in an important sense the product of Milton's own prophetic imagination, whose form Blake has not so much created as clarified. She is Milton's bride, but ultimately also the Bride of the Lamb and all mankind whose name entitles Blake's final prophecy—*Jerusalem*. The prim virgin of Milton's *Comus* has come a long way; but as she achieves the fulfilled "Liberty" displayed on the final plate, so does her prophet-creator who loved Blake in childhood and "shew'd [him] his face"; Blake can at last in good conscience write "Finis" to his answering labor of spiritual warfare and brotherly love.

"The Hem of Their Garments":
The Bard's Song in Milton

JAMES RIEGER

"Few are the readers," Gilchrist warns us, "who will ever penetrate beyond the first page or two" of *Milton*.[1] Impatience got the better of Blake's first biographer at the place where readers are still turned back, that is, at the bottom of Plate 2. "A Bards prophetic Song" breaks forth among the Eternals, the Sons of Albion, whom it confuses and annoys, and who murmur against it when it ends on Plate 13. "From this point on," Harold Bloom observes, "*Milton* becomes a majestic and relatively simple poem, overwhelmingly rewarding the reader who has been patient with the necessary complexities of the Bard's Song."[2]

When Blake addressed his "Sublime Allegory . . . to the Intellectual powers," he was not speaking to anything like the critical intelligence as we ordinarily define it; much of his meaning would remain "altogether hidden from the corporeal Understanding."[3] Still, the unhidden or discoverable portion ordinarily predominates. The personages and events of Blake's myth can usually be translated into the "corporeal" terms of history, aesthetics, and faculty psychology. But the pure sublimity of the Bard's Song forces us to abandon every level of traditional exegesis except anagogy. As the most strictly prophetic episode in all the so-called prophecies, it is aimed finally and singly at the "Intellectual powers." The Bard demands that Moses' prayer, slightly misquoted by Blake at the end of the "Preface," be

1. Alexander Gilchrist, *Life of William Blake*, "*Pictor Ignotus*" (London: 1863), I, 196.
2. *Blake's Apocalypse: A Study in Poetic Argument* (Garden City, N.Y.: Doubleday, 1963), pp. 355–356.
3. Letter to Thomas Butts, 6 July 1803, *The Letters of William Blake*, ed. Geoffrey Keynes (Cambridge, Mass.: Harvard Univ. Press, 1968), p. 69.

fulfilled in each hearer's imagination: "would God that all the Lord's people were prophets, and that the Lord would put his spirit upon them" (Num. 11: 29).

I

Characterization in the Bard's Song is so elusive and the narrative thread so hard to follow that critics who would ordinarily shun the biographical fallacy have followed S. Foster Damon's reading of its central episode, Palamabron's contest with Satan, as a dark conceit for Blake's own difficulties with his patron William Hayley.[4] Although he accepts the identification, Northrop Frye warns that it is only partly useful; total interpretation along these lines would reduce the Song to "a grotesquely over-written account of a squabble between a sulky megalomaniac and a conceited dilettante."[5] One may go further. Such an interpretation would convict Blake the author of "the Self righteousness / In all its Hypocritic turpitude" (38: 43–44) that Blake the character, merged with Milton, puts off in "Self annihilation" later in the poem. And if Blake was in fact vindictive, would the Bard's Song not be, again in Frye's words, "the most futile revenge ever taken"?[6] His Sublime Allegory was "to be a Memento in time to come, & to speak to future generations."[7] Did he fancy that the future would also breed researchers equipped to find the poetaster Hayley beneath loud, thundering Satan, "Coming in a Cloud with Trumpets & with Fiery Flame" (39: 23)? If he did, he was correct; but he was also an obscurantist, "mad Blake" indeed.

The last objection can also be lodged against historical interpretation. David V. Erdman, admitting that "the clues are slight," sees Satan as Cromwell and Napoleon, Palamabron as Parliament, Rintrah as Pitt, and Leutha as Marie Antoinette.[8] Because the etched copper for the title page promised "a Poem in 12 Books" (corrected to "2 Books" in the first two of the four known copies), Erdman assumes that ten books are missing and that they "seem to have constituted a visionary account of the English Revolution." Blake did of course compose visions of the American and French

4. S. Foster Damon, *William Blake: His Philosophy and Symbols* (Boston: Houghton Mifflin, 1924), p. 175.

5. *Fearful Symmetry: A Study of William Blake* (Princeton: Princeton Univ. Press, 1947), p. 327.

6. Ibid.

7. *Letters*, ed. Keynes, p. 69.

8. *Blake: Prophet against Empire*, 2nd ed. (Garden City, N.Y.: Doubleday Anchor, 1969), pp. 424–426.

Revolutions, and Erdman has documented them thoroughly. But in the present case his identifications are totally arbitrary, and his logic with regard to ten missing books will not stand in the face of the poem's manifest wholeness. More basically, any historical allegory in the Bard's Song, if it is there, is so recondite that only a scholar will be able to find it. It is unlikely that Blake desired to limit his audience so severely. *Milton* does demand expertise in scriptural history, but the Bible is the heritage and study of every Christian, whatever his formal schooling.

To argue against biographical and historical interpretation of the Bard's Song is not to disallow *application* of the myth to life and society, Blake's or our own. The difference in approach is crucial. Once we know that during the "three years" it took Blake to "write all these Visions" in his "beautiful / Cottage" in "Felphams Vale" (36: 23–24) he was chafing against his patron's solicitude, we may, if we wish, hear echoes of his exasperation in Leutha's complaint against Satan:

To do unkind things in kindness! with power armd, to say
The most irritating things in the midst of tears and love
(12: 32–33)

or in Palamabron's prayer:

O God, protect me from my friends, that they have not power over me
Thou hast giv'n me power to protect myself from my bitterest enemies.
(9: 5–6)

And certainly Blake had someone like Hayley in mind when he made Milton resolve

To cast aside from Poetry, all that is not Inspiration
That it no longer shall dare to mock with the aspersion of Madness
Cast on the Inspired, by the tame high finisher of paltry Blots,
Indefinite, or paltry Rhymes; or paltry Harmonies.
(41: 7–10)

To say that Palamabron, toiling in the Satanic mills, suggests Blake illustrating Hayley's ballads is to note an actual resemblance; but it is not to make a valid critical statement. One can as meaningfully apply the myth to the experience of past or "future generations." When Palamabron labors out of his vocation, he looks like Milton sacrificing bodily and spiritual vision as Cromwell's Latin Secretary, or like any steward of the Word who hides his talents. It is, for instance, methodologically proper to speculate that Elynittria's chastity and jealousy explain why "my Shadow of Delight . . . is sick with fatigue" (36: 31–32); whether or not Elynittria is an eternal type of the vegetated Shadow, the Shadow is herself a character in the poem, not the historic Catherine Blake. But it is fallacious (as well as the loosest chatter about the dead) to assert, even as cautiously as Damon did, that Mrs. Blake's "arrows of jealousy kill inspiration,"[9] or that Leutha is "the personification of Hayley's unconscious homosexuality."[10]

The Bard begins by commanding the Sons of Albion to "Mark well my words! they are of your eternal salvation" (2:25), and he repeats the injunction six times in the Song. After it ends, he defends himself against the Assembly's condemnation of "this terrible Song" by exclaiming,

I am Inspired! I know it is Truth! for I Sing

According to the inspiration of the Poetic Genius
Who is the eternal all-protecting Divine Humanity
To whom be Glory & Power & Dominion Evermore Amen.
                        (13:51—14:3)

If we accept the Bard's self-estimate, as Milton does immediately, then his words are Evangel, which every human soul must understand in order to survive. In the remainder of the poem, humanity is represented by the composite, regenerating figure of Milton, Los, and the persona of Blake. Clearly, much more is involved than an artist's unpleasant working conditions, Parliament's pusillanimity before Cromwell, or, for that matter, Blake's practical aesthetics and his theory of psychological types.

In a recent article, Eve Teitelbaum has noted similarities between Rintrah, Palamabron, and Satan and the Strongest Man, Beautifullest Man, and Ugliest Man in Blake's water color of *The Ancient Britons*: Rintrah and Palamabron stand for the energetic and rational components of art, the sublime and the beautiful.[11] Teitelbaum also argues that Rintrah and Satan derive their occupations and personalities from the Plowman and Miller depicted in *Sir Jeffery Chaucer and the nine and twenty Pilgrims on their journey to Canterbury* and analyzed in the *Descriptive Catalogue*. Suggestive as Teitelbaum is, a full reading of the Bard's Song must expand to include Blake's pure aesthetics, salvation through the "Imagination / Which is the Divine Body of the Lord Jesus" in every man (3:3-4). The warfare within the imagination—that is, among the Sons of Los—is an affective rather than a facultative psychomachia.[12] The heroes are pity, love, and

9. *Blake: Philosophy and Symbols*, p. 409.

10. S. Foster Damon, *A Blake Dictionary: The Ideas and Symbols of William Blake* (Providence: Brown Univ. Press, 1965), under "Leutha."

11. "Form as Meaning in Blake's *Milton*," *Blake Studies*, 2 (1969), 37-64.

12. In his unpublished paper, "The Bard's Song: A Study in Critical Approaches," L. Edwin Folsom, Jr., suggests that the Classes of the Reprobate, the Redeemed, and the Elect may be partially understood in terms of the medieval divisions of the soul into *sapientia*, *scientia*, and *sensus*.

wrath at injustice. The enemy is the Satanic perversion of these attributes of Christ into "the Selfish Virtues of the Natural Heart" (*J* 52: *199*). The opposed conditions often look alike, yet differ completely; they resemble each other, in T. S. Eliot's words, "as death resembles life." Let us first consider this civil war of brothers in the light of corporeal understanding, and then examine the identity and the idiom of the Bard.

The first question that comes up in any discussion of Blake's permanent *dramatis personae* is whether they remain the same characters from poem to poem. Satan presents few problems; for except when he comes forward as "the Devil," Blake's ironic spokesman in *The Marriage of Heaven and Hell*, he is the spectral Selfhood, the rational Negation, the accuser of sin. Rintrah and Palamabron are more elusive. The former first roars in "The Argument" of the *Marriage* as the prophetic "just man," who "rages in the wilds" like Elijah or John the Baptist. He reappears in *Europe*, four years later, as a furious king of fire, whom his mother Enitharmon sends with his brother, "Palamabron horned priest," to "tell the Human race that Womans love is Sin!" (8: 3; 6: 5). The two are now missionaries of the very mistake that kept "Lavater & his cotemporaries" from seeing that the only vices are hindrance and omission of act.[13] As for Palamabron, his horning equates him iconographically with Moses, who, according to Frye, is sometimes "the spirit, as opposed to the letter, of the law" and sometimes "an evil being, the spokesman of the morally virtuous Satan who wrote the ten commandments."[14] It also suggests cuckoldry, inversely accomplished on Plate 13 of *Milton*, where Leutha, who represents female secrecy among other things, is smuggled by night into Palamabron's tent by his Emanation, Elynittria. The brothers continue their Urizenic career on Plate 3 of *The Song of Los*, where they foist "Abstract Philosophy" on "Brama . . . Trismegistus . . . Pythagoras Socrates & Plato."

Rintrah and Palamabron turn up next in Night VIII of *The Four Zoas* along with Satan, now also their brother, as children or fragments of Los, with the curse of Adam and all postlapsarian history upon them. Los identifies them and himself as

> that shadowy Prophet who six thousand years ago
> Fell from my station in the Eternal bosom. I divided
> To multitude & my multitudes are children of care & Labour.
> (VIII: *365*)

Bloom writes that "what *Milton* draws upon is a reading knowledge of the abandoned *Four Zoas*. Armed with our memories of that ambitious poem,

---

13. Annotations to Lavater's *Aphorisms on Man*, p. 590.
14. *Fearful Symmetry*, p. 334.

we can understand the Bard's Song."[15] But our actual memories are not what Blake, who did leave the poem in manuscript, could have expected them to be. Moreover, Erdman argues in the textual notes to his and Bloom's edition that, "The writing of VIII . . . must have occurred after Blake had begun if not completed *Milton* and *Jerusalem*" (*p. 738*). Nevertheless, the manuscript account of the contest for the harrow and the ensuing trial is close enough to the Bard's Song in certain details so that comparison will prove useful later in this discussion.

On Plate 22 of *Milton* Rintrah and Palamabron guard the gate of Golgonooza against the composite "Shadow terrible" of Milton, Blake, and Los. And in *Jerusalem* the brothers are found hard at work in the forge of Los: "the thundring Bellows / Heaves in the hand of Palamabron . . . thundering / The Hammer loud rages in Rintrahs strong grasp . . ." (16: 8–11). They are last mentioned by Enitharmon, who laments their desertion of her and recalls "that terrible Day of Rintrahs Plow & of Satans driving the Team" (*J* 93: 10). Among the Giants of Albion, she continues, Merlin was like Rintrah and Judah like Palamabron. The apparent inconsistency of the brothers from poem to poem may be resolved if one chooses to see them as degenerate when they serve their mother or Urizen and regenerate when they work for their father. But let us return to *Milton*.

The traditional and mistaken identification of Palamabron with pity and Rintrah with wrath in the Bard's Song[16] derives from a later passage in which Los mourns the apostasy of twelve other sons, the tribes of Israel:

Still my four mighty ones are left to me in Golgonooza
Still Rintrah fierce, and Palamabron mild & piteous
Theotormon filld with care, Bromion loving Science.
                    (*M* 24: 10–12)

The four mighty divisions of Los *now* bear the same relationship to him that the Zoas bear to Albion. His adverb "still" draws attention to the fictive sequence of eternal events. The falling away that Los recounts here (eleven plates after the Song) was a consequence of the miscreative fantasies of Palamabron that ended the Bard's narrative:

In dreams she [Leutha] bore Rahab the mother of Tirzah & her sisters
In Lambeths vales; in Cambridge & in Oxford, places of Thought
Intricate labyrinths of Times and Spaces unknown . . .
                    (13: 41–43)

According to Los, the twelve lost sons were generated because "They left me, wandering with Tirzah" (24: 4). If they have become male camp-

---

15. *Blake's Apocalypse*, p. 340.
16. The tradition begins with Damon's *Blake: Philosophy and Symbols*, p. 175.

followers of a whore's daughter, may not the four loyal sons have changed for the better in the thousands of years that separate the erotic nightmare that spawned Rahab and Tirzah from the present time of the poem? This is indeed the case. Los and his children have cleansed their diseased affections.

In the Bard's Song "Theotormon & Bromion contended on the side of Satan / Pitying his youth and beauty" (8: 30–31). As for the sentiment that misled them, pity was the specious vice of Los and Satan, not of Palamabron, who was "alas blamable" for a different sort of moral cowardice: when Los reassigned the harrow of the Almighty to Satan, Palamabron "fear'd to be angry lest Satan should accuse him of / Ingratitude" (7: 10–12). It was Satan who drove "the Harrow in Pitys paths" (12: 28), just as it was his "incomparable mildness," "brothers tears," and "pretence of pity and love" that effected the usurpation (7: 4, 15, 26). Pity was the science of Satan. Because he lacked the science of wrath, he rent the two qualities "asunder, and wrath was left to wrath, & pity to pity" (9: 46–47). All of this makes it ironic that Palamabron should have caught the blame:

So Los said, Henceforth Palamabron, let each his own station
Keep: nor in pity false, nor in officious brotherhood, where
None needs, be active.
(7: 41–43)

Los scolded Palamabron because he could not yet see that he himself had erred by giving in to the "most endearing love" of Satan (7: 5). When Los at last recognized his mistake, he did so in terms that provide the key to the quarrel:

Mine is the fault! I should have remember'd that pity divides the soul
And man, unmans . . .
(8: 19–20)

Satan negates imagination, emasculates the human existence itself, by fracturing the soul into Zoas, sons, fratricidal and fallen emotions. True pity and humanity, the image of God, usually masquerade as shadowy, female cruelty (18: 19–20). Conversely, as we know from *Songs of Innocence and of Experience*, cruelty apes mercy's human heart, and Satanic jealousy counterfeits pity's human face. That is why the partially regenerated Palamabron and Rintrah, inept in theodicy but sensing the basic issue, later rebuke Los at the gate of Golgonooza:

O mild Parent!
Cruel in thy mildness, pitying and permitting evil
Tho strong and mighty to destroy, O Los our beloved Father!
(23: 18–20)

Wrath is to be understood in the same dramatic terms, as an epidemic throughout Eden. The contrary to pity enters *Milton* when Los assigns to Satan the work of Eternal Death: "Get to thy Labours at the Mills & leave me to my wrath" (4: 14). Los "became what he beheld" (3: 29) even earlier in the poem when in panic he malformed the body of Urizen, the body of his own sickness and dismal woe, whom he will later recognize as the Satan he now enslaves. This is to say that all he and we behold in the course of the Bard's Song is a negative projection of Urthona as he continues to fall. It should not surprise us, then, that his son Satan, the reductive and murderous miller, should look exactly like Rintrah, his suffused wrath:

But Rintrah who is of the reprobate: of those form'd to destruction
In indignation. for Satans soft dissimulation of friendship!
Flam'd above all the plowed furrows, *angry red* and furious,
Till Michael sat down in the furrow weary dissolv'd in tears.
Satan who drave the team beside him, stood *angry and red*.
                                        (8: 34–38; my italics)

The visual similarity between Satan and Rintrah becomes a virtual identity in the trial in Palamabron's tent. This crucial episode must be quoted at length:

Mark well my words, they are of your eternal salvation

Then rose the Two Witnesses, Rintrah & Palamabron:
And Palamabron appeal'd to all Eden, and recievd
Judgment: and Lo! it fell on Rintrah and his rage:
Which now flam'd high & furious in Satan against Palamabron
Till it became a proverb in Eden. Satan is among the Reprobate.

Los in his wrath curs'd heaven & earth, he rent up Nations . . .
He displacd continents, the oceans fled before his face
He alter'd the poles of the world, east, west & north & south . . .

For Satan flaming with Rintrahs fury hidden beneath his own mildness
Accus'd Palamabron before the Assembly of ingratitude! of malice:
He created Seven deadly Sins drawing out his infernal scroll,
Of Moral laws and cruel punishments upon the clouds of Jehovah
To pervert the Divine voice in its entrance to the earth . . .

Thus Satan rag'd amidst the Assembly! and his bosom grew
Opake against the Divine Vision . . .

Astonishment held the Assembly in an awful silence: and tears
Fell down as dews of night, & a loud solemn universal groan
Was utter'd from the east & from the west & from the south
And from the north; and Satan stood opake immeasurable
Covering the east with solid blackness, round his hidden heart,

With thunders utterd from his hidden wheels: accusing loud
The Divine Mercy, for protecting Palamabron in his tent . . .

And Satan not having the Science of Wrath, but only of Pity:
Rent them asunder, and wrath was left to wrath, & pity to pity . . .

Then Los & Enitharmon knew that Satan is Urizen
Drawn down by Orc & the Shadowy Female into Generation.

$$(9: 7–52; 10: 1–2)$$

It is customary to read this difficult passage as follows: Rintrah appears as
a witness for Palamabron against Satan, but is himself unjustly condemned
for his righteous indignation; the triumphant Satan crows over his acquittal
by appropriating and perverting Rintrah's wrath, thereby joining for a moment the Class of the Reprobate; Los, angry at the miscarriage of justice,
curses the created world; Satan carries his own rage so high that he invol-
untarily reveals himself to the now repentant Assembly as the true culprit
and the Urizenic limit of opacity. This is more or less the received interpretation.[17] It seems the obvious one; but it is undermined two plates later by
an Eternal's explanation of what has, in fact, happened:

And it was enquir'd: Why in a Great Solemn Assembly
The Innocent should be condemn'd for the Guilty? Then an Eternal rose

Saying. If the Guilty should be condemn'd, he must be an Eternal Death
And one must die for another throughout all Eternity.
Satan is fall'n from his station & never can be redeem'd
But must be new Created continually moment by moment
And therefore the Class of Satan shall be calld the Elect, & those
Of Rintrah. the Reprobate, & those of Palamabron the Redeem'd
For he is redeem'd from Satans Law, the wrath falling on Rintrah,
And therefore Palamabron dared not to call a solemn Assembly
Till Satan had assum'd Rintrahs wrath in the day of mourning
In a feminine delusion of false pride self-deciev'd.

$$(11: 15–26)$$

This speech elucidates the trial. It appears that "Rintrah," the rage that
flamed high and furious in Satan after judgment was given, had been annexed by him in the day of mourning that *preceded* the trial, when both had
burned "angry red" over the plowed fields. As a clever lawyer, Palamabron
had seized this opportunity to compel Satan "to / Defend a Lie, that he may
be snared & caught & taken" (8: 47–48). Rintrah appeared as a trial witness
not in his own person, but as a self-defeating irateness "in" Satan the ad-

17. See, for instance, Bloom's commentary on 8: 46—9: 52 in *The Poetry and Prose of William Blake*, ed. David V. Erdman (Garden City, N.Y.: Doubleday, 1970), pp. 826–827.

versary. Satan raged even higher after the verdict because, although the "Rintrah" in him had borne the brunt of the judgment, he himself had been cast out for safe-keeping in the Class of Election.[18] This is to say that whereas honest wrath must suffer in atonement for the Satan who can so corrupt it, the corrupter himself is likewise hurled down. When Leutha offers herself as ransom for Satan's sin, she does so because she has "beheld Satans condemnation" (11: 28). Wrath, a quality as chameleonic and dangerous as pity, spreads from the judged to infect the judges as well: "Los in his wrath curs'd heaven & earth," and the Eternal reveals that the "judgment" falling on Rintrah was itself "wrath."

An understanding of Blake's scheme of Election, Redemption, and Reprobation justifies the verdict, the ways of Eden to itself, and reveals the true identity of the antagonists. When Blake inverts these Calvinistic classes, as he did "good" and "evil" in *The Marriage of Heaven and Hell*, he does not deny their reality, nor, strictly speaking, is it *he* who turns them topsy-turvy. Rather, it is the "Modern Church" that "Crucifies Christ with the Head Downwards."[19] Like the states defined later in the poem, the three classes "Created by the Hammer of Los" (2: 26) must be distinguished from their temporary membership, as Los explains by way of introducing the story of the trial in *The Four Zoas*:

There is a State namd Satan learn distinct to know O Rahab
The Difference between States & Individuals of those States
The State namd Satan never can be redeemd in all Eternity[.]
                                              (VIII: *366*)

When the Eternal says that what he calls Satan, the Class of the Elect, "is fall'n from his station & never can be redeem'd," he does not mean that individuals in that State will fail to see salvation. The Bard knows that on the Day of Judgment

18. Cf. *The Four Zoas* VIII: *366*:

Wherefore Palamabron being accusd by Satan to Los
Calld down a Great Solemn assembly Rintrah in fury & fire
Defended Palamabron & rage filld the Universal Tent.

When Los adds here that "Satan not having the Science of Wrath but only of Pity / Was soon condemnd & wrath was left to wrath & Pity to Pity," he apparently means that Satan, as a novice in the school of wrath, simply bungled. He had not yet mastered the hypocritical "science" of this stolen quality, as he had that of pity. Like his counterpart in *Milton*, Satan was then sentenced to protective exile in "Enitharmons Moony space." It will be noticed that in *this* version, Rintrah does appear as a defense witness for Palamabron.

19. *VLJ*, p. *554*.

The Elect shall meet the Redeem'd. on Albions rocks they shall meet
Astonish'd at the Transgressor, in him beholding the Saviour.
And the Elect shall say to the Redeemd. We behold it is of Divine
Mercy alone! of Free Gift and Election that we live.
Our Virtues & Cruel Goodnesses, have deserv'd Eternal Death.

(13: 30–34)

Likewise, the enraged individual whom Los and Enitharmon recognize as
Urizen will be restored to his place in fourfold human perfection. As Lucifer
(the First Eye of God) explains,

States Change: but Individual Identities never change nor cease:
You cannot go to Eternal Death in that which can never Die.

(32: 23–24)

Lucifer's "that" is individuality, and we shall presently find Urizen's individuality on its way to regeneration. But the Satanic State itself, the Spectre
or Negation, must be utterly destroyed "to redeem the Contraries" (40: 33).

Wrath divides the soul as tragically as pity does. It splits Los's soul into
two aspects, Rintrah and Urizen-Satan, who look exactly alike to the corporeal eye. The first may be compared to honest indignation, which, according to Blake's Isaiah, "is the voice of God" (*MHH* 12: 38). The other steals
a brother's science in order to accuse a second brother of sin in the self-
righteous anger which, Blake says elsewhere, defines hell.[20] The identity
of Urizen-Satan and Rintrah in their irate father, incidentally, explains why
"the Plow of ages" driven by Urizen in the Last Judgment that ends *The
Four Zoas* (IX: *379*) becomes Rintrah's in the Bard's Song and why the
mourning Los, preparing to be wrathful, calls it "my Plow" (8: 20).

Rintrah's expiation of Urizen's Satanic guilt dramatizes the profound
paradox that defines Blake's Christianity. The elect of this world and the
pharisees of natural religion despise, reject, and execute the Messiah as a
reprobate, a transgressor and "an Abettor of Criminals,"[21] whom it nevertheless pleased the Lord to bruise, in Isaiah's words (53: 10). The Eternal
in the Bard's Song appears to be saying that the true Christian virtues are
fallen and tainted, that one aspect of them has petrified into what are later
called the "Idol Virtues of the Natural Heart" (38: 46) and the accusation
of sin. On the one hand, there is the just wrath of such a prophet as Jere-
miah, of Jesus driving the money changers from the temple, of the Lamb
returning in judgment on the Last Day, and of the lion, whose wrath is the
wisdom of God (*MHH* 8: *36*). On the other, there is that of the fallen Urizen, "the satanic desire to murder opposition," in Damon's apt phrase,[22] God

20. Ibid.
21. Ibid.
22. *Dictionary*, under "Wrath."

Almighty who "comes with a Thump on the Head."[23] This form of wrath becomes the deadly *ira*, just as false pity and love are subspecies of *acedia*.

The Sons of Albion reject the Bard's Song on the grounds that "Pity and Love are too venerable for the imputation / Of Guilt" (13:48–49). But they have just heard of the havoc raised by hypocritical pity, and readers of the *Songs of Experience* know that the self-congratulatory glow we feel when we contribute a mite to alleviate social misery "would be no more, / If we did not make somebody Poor."[24] There are clod-love and pebble-love, agape and eros speciously united as a single English abstraction, as well as Satan's "soft / Delusory love to Palamabron" (12: 6–7). Lucifer and the Seven Angels warn that "Affection or Love becomes a State, when divided from Imagination," which is not a State but "the Human Existence itself" (32: 33–34). "Without Forgiveness of Sin," Los states in *Jerusalem*, "Love is Itself Eternal Death" (64: 24). Los will not be able to tell his Sons that "we live not by wrath. by mercy alone we live!" until he too has "embracd the falling Death, he is become One with me" (*M* 23:33–34). Pity and love move Los and Milton to voyage through Eternal Death, merged with each other and with the generated Blake. The same generosity leads the Christ of *Paradise Lost* to ask his Father to "Account mee man" (III: 238). The Almighty replies that by such means

> Heav'nly love shall outdo Hellish hate,
> Giving to death, and dying to redeem,
> So dearly to redeem what Hellish hate
> So easily destroy'd . . .
>   (III: 298–301)

Despite its surface complexity, *Milton* demands simply and relentlessly that the incarnation, passion, and resurrection of Christ be repeated in every man. True wrath, pity, and love purge themselves of their Satanic counterfeits by taking on the imputation of guilt that boggles the legalistic understanding of the Sons of Albion. Therein consists the great mercy of the Assembly's condemnation of Rintrah for his brother Satan. Only the scapegoat can save iniquitous men, the fragments of degenerate Imagination, from dying "one . . . for another throughout all Eternity." Los, the parent power of Imagination, explains in *The Four Zoas* that Satan's fall from his high station into the Class of the Elect is actually his preservation, through "Jerusalem pitying," until "Jesus Came & Died willing beneath Tirzah & Rahab" (VIII: *366*). The fallen Vala mercifully takes guilty individuals into her protective custody until they can be ransomed from their States:

23. *VLJ*, p. 555.
24. "The Human Abstract," *p. 27.*

Thus in a living Death the nameless shadow all things bound
All mortal things made permanent that they may be put off
Time after time by the Divine Lamb who died for all
And all in him died. & he put off all mortality.

(VIII: *368*)

The Bard's Song, then, is a prophet's account of the fall of prophecy itself, Los "the Spirit of Prophecy the ever apparent Elias" (24: 71). He confesses to Rahab in *The Four Zoas* that through "pride & wrath," the first two of the ecclesiastical deadly sins, he has pierced the Lamb of God and disintegrated into multitudes, the children of care and labor; he invites his daughter Rahab, the Babylonian parody of Christian liberty, to "Hear me repeat my Generations that thou mayst also repent" (VIII: *365*). His male progeny include Rintrah, Palamabron, Theotormon, Satan, Adam, the tribes and kings of Israel and Judah, Saint Paul, two Christian emperors, and the reformers Luther and Milton. Because these fragments of Los are also the heirs of Cain, the fratricidal moral virtues, the Bard's Song is generically a tragedy of the sort defined by Hegel and A. C. Bradley: "The essentially tragic fact is the self-division and intestinal warfare of the ethical substance, not so much the war of good with evil as the war of good with good."[25] Wrath and pity, judgment and mercy, the ethical qualities of the Old and New Testaments, battle in the imagination envisioned and served by Blake as similar antitheses do in the *Oresteia* and *Hamlet* read by Bradley. The relevance of the Bard's Song to the remainder of *Milton* is that these attracting and alienating qualities devastate each other in the soul of any revolutionary, but unregenerated, poet whose self-pity assigns blame or praise to the constituent qualities of human existence instead of justifying them to each other in a sublime theodicy. The wrath of such an artist against corporeal or spiritual enemies—Scholfield, Hayley, the second Caroline court—projects outwardly, ineffectively, the self-contempt that scorches Eden. As Bradley puts it, "*any* spiritual conflict involving spiritual waste is tragic."[26]

The tragedy becomes druidic sacrifice in *Jerusalem*, where the contraries are "decided," etymologically cut in half, into

a World of Mercy, and
A World of Justice: the World of Mercy for Salvation
To cast Luvah into the Wrath, and Albion into the Pity
In the Two Contraries of Humanity & in the Four Regions.

(65: 1–4)

25. A. C. Bradley, "Hegel's Theory of Tragedy," in *Oxford Lectures on Poetry*, 2nd ed. (London: Macmillan, 1909), p. 71.
26. Ibid., p. 87.

Los knows at this point that the dialectic of contraries must yield to an Edenic union, and he expresses his rejection of mental strife in a parody of the Book of Common Prayer: "Pity must join together those whom wrath has torn in sunder" (*J* 7: 62). Pursuing the allusion to the marriage service, one might conclude that God is the joiner together and man the divorce lawyer. But the Prayer Book's agents of wedding and separation become in Blake parallel lines of human expression—the Holy Word and, below it, the False Tongue, the sensuously contracted Adam enslaved by Satanic opacity.

Narrative time is a mere device in *Milton* and *Jerusalem*, a sequential representation of two eternal moments that by definition lack extension. Nevertheless, Frye correctly regards one as Resurrection and the other as the Last Judgment, "corresponding to the first and second coming of Jesus."[27] Each is its own split-second, but one follows the other. The two should be seen as stages in the conversion of Los the prophet, roughly as the conviction of sin and the dawn of grace, epitomized by the infinitives that introduce and conclude *Milton*. Blake's epigraph on the title page refers to the overt purpose of *Paradise Lost*, "To Justify the Ways of God to Men." The poem fulfills this intention by annihilating the Selfhood that first disaffects a man from the Emanations he fears to love, and then coaxes him into an expense of spirit, the division of his ethical substance against itself. *Milton* ends with another infinitive, alone and unpunctuated on Plate 43: "To go forth to the Great Harvest & Vintage of the Nations." *Jerusalem* depicts this gathering together of the fruits of vegetated, temporal existence as the garnering of all human forms into the bosom of Albion, "in the Life of Immortality" (99: 1–4). The promise of *Milton* is fulfilled by the joy of Los in *Jerusalem*, by the cry that goes up "from the great City of Golgonooza in the Shadowy Generation" (*J* 98: 55). For Golgonooza, the palace of art, is built with the bricks of "pity and compassion." It is an advanced human stage in which the wrecked fields of *Milton*, plowed with the salt of tears and anger and harrowed into madness by Satan, become literally civilized:

The stones are pity, and the bricks, well wrought affections:
Enameld with love & kindness, & the tiles engraven gold
Labour of merciful hands: the beams & rafters are forgiveness.
                                   (*J* 12: 29–32)

T. S. Eliot once disagreed with the Grecian Urn's opinion that beauty is truth: "this line strikes me as a serious blemish on a beautiful poem; and the reason must be either that I fail to understand it, or that it is a statement which is untrue. . . . The statement seems to me meaningless: or perhaps,

27. *Fearful Symmetry*, p. 324.

the fact that it is grammatically meaningless conceals another meaning from me."[28] The success of more recent critics of Keats's ode shows that Eliot did not try hard enough; his deprecation of his own abilities masked his unwillingness to take the poet seriously. Anyone reading the Bard's Song for the first time faces the same question, whether to blame himself or the author for his confusion. The Bard's Song is perhaps the most puzzling episode anywhere in the poetry published by Blake himself. Is that because one's normal expectations of narrative do not apply in this case, or because Blake was on the Homeric nod when he wrote it? Frye has on different occasions suggested both alternatives: first, that the Bard's Song "does not relate a sequence of events, but tells the story of the dispute of Palamabron and Satan and then brings out its larger significance by a series of lifting backdrops";[29] second, that a sequence does appear if the editor eliminates Plate 5 and reorders the others to read 2, 7, 4, 6, 3, 8 ff.[30] Either the narrative structure is a ruse, then, or Blake garbled it.

My own reading implies a radical restatement of Frye's earlier view. Explanations are offered—the backdrops are lifted—in a narrative sequence that runs counterclockwise, as it were, to that of the fable itself. First we are told that Satan is really Urizen, then that he has been cast out although he seemed to have been vindicated, then that the jury was as wrathful as the litigators, then that Palamabron knew all along, as we did not, that his brothers had assumed each other's appearance in the day of mourning. And it is only after the Bard ends his Song that the Sons of Albion blurt out the point of the story by piously denying it: pity and love were the issue from the outset, and their protean personifications are the culprits. We have been worse than inadequately informed; we have been deliberately misled.

II

The nature of the Bard and the nature of the Sons of Los mandate the obscurity of the Song. Prophetic irony is the opposite of obscurantism, although it is essential to the divine strategy that the two look the same in the cataracted eyes of the gentiles. The inner sense of the "words . . . of eternal salvation" must be virtually invisible. Angus Fletcher states the distinction exactly:

28. "Dante" (1929), in *Selected Essays*, 2nd ed. (New York: Harcourt, Brace, 1950), p. 231.

29. *Fearful Symmetry*, p. 332.

30. Northrop Frye, "Notes for a Commentary on *Milton*," in *The Divine Vision: Studies in the Poetry and Art of William Blake*, ed. Vivian de Sola Pinto (London: Victor Gollancz, 1957), p. 130.

... when "difficult ornament" is most "difficult," it is usually because the poetry is prophetic, like the prophetic books of the Bible or Blake's prophetic poem *The Four Zoas*. The poet can always justify his obscurity, no matter how deep, because he claims to be presenting an inspired message. This is not mere allegorical cleverness. It is the attitude of the prophet who in turn is reading the mind of some higher Being. Whether we can believe in this view is a matter of private metaphysics.[31]

The reptilian "Bard of Albion" in *America* (15:16) perhaps represents the Poet Laureate; and in a letter to Hayley, Blake describes the youthful Edward Garrard Marsh as "my much admired & respected Edward the Bard of Oxford."[32] Otherwise, Blake identifies the bards of medieval Wales with the Hebrew prophets, and the imposition of the Norman yoke on Britain with Jerusalem's exile and enslavement in Babylon. Bardic and prophetic sublimity is to the culture of the usurper as the Bible and Blake's prophecies are to the classics revered in the oppressor's universities. The first sentence of the "Preface" to *Milton* echoes the Saviour's rejection of Greek and Latin in *Paradise Regained*, draws the line of battle, and announces that the disinherited bard is once again about to raise his voice: "The Stolen and Perverted Writings of Homer & Ovid: of Plato & Cicero, which all Men ought to contemn: are set up by artifice against the Sublime of the Bible."

The "Introduction" to *Songs of Experience* shows through grammatical ambiguity that bards and prophets do more than denounce conquerors, chasten backsliders, and reveal the immediate pleasure of God. Their words are the divine utterance itself, by which the world and man were made:

Hear the voice of the Bard!
Who Present, Past, & Future sees
Whose ears have heard,
The Holy Word,
That walk'd among the ancient trees.

Calling the lapsed Soul
And weeping in the evening dew ...

The present participle in line 6 identifies the bardic "voice" with the "Word" by modifying them both. Together they constitute the Logos, the demiurgic Son of God who created Adam in His own image and now pursues His fallen and shamefaced replica through the overgrowth of the Garden. Blake consistently glosses the shaping aspect of Christ as the imagination, which he personifies in his myth of the Zoas as Los, whose name contracts *logos*.

31. *Allegory: The Theory of a Symbolic Mode* (Ithaca: Cornell Univ. Press, 1964), pp. 277–278.
32. Letter of 27 January 1804, *Letters*, ed. Keynes, p. 87.

Blake's union with Los in *Milton* intensifies in *Jerusalem*, where the author's prayer echoes and further identifies him with the bard of *Experience*:

I see the Past, Present & Future, existing all at once
Before me; O Divine Spirit sustain me on thy wings!
That I may awake Albion from his long & cold repose.
                              (*J* 15: 8–10)

The Word is invariably misunderstood and resented by its primary audience. Earth answers the bard of *Experience* reproachfully because she thinks she hears the "Selfish father of men" rather than the prophet of the Son of Man. The Bard's Song in *Milton* so incenses the Sons of Albion that the singer takes terrified refuge in Milton's bosom (14: 9). Finally, "Oxford, immortal Bard!" speaks "the words of God" to Albion in *Jerusalem*. Like his predecessor, he tells of "the Plow of Jehovah, and the Harrow of Shaddai," which will arouse the dead to Judgment. But once again, "Albion turn'd away refusing comfort" (*J* 41: 7–16).

To what extent can Earth, Albion, and his Sons be blamed for their deafness to the Word, which in Blake as in Scripture clothes itself in rhetorical darkness? Robert Lowth outlined the paradox in the Latin lectures he delivered, beginning in 1741, as Praelector of Poetry at Oxford: "The immediate design of all prophecy is to inform or amend those generations that precede the events predicted; and it is usually calculated either to excite their fears and apprehensions, or to afford them consolation." Nevertheless, "prophecy, in its very nature, implies some degree of obscurity, and is always, as the apostle elegantly expresses it, 'like a light glimmering in a dark place, until the day dawn, and the day-star arise.' "[33] Lowth became Bishop of London in 1777, in which capacity he appears as the moribund "Londons Guardian" in *America* (15: 9). His lectures, translated into English in 1787, rediscovered the principle of parallelism in Hebrew versification, thereby rescuing that body of poetry from those academic slaves of the sword who had undertaken to defend it by torturing isolated lines to fit the classical hexameter model.[34] Tempting though it is to speculate that Blake read Lowth, it is unnecessary to regard the two as anything but equally sensitive exegetes. Blake detested Mystery; yet he echoed the Word mysteriously expressed, and he painstakingly distinguished the songs of his bards from their druidic context. Because he, like Lowth, studied in its minute particulars the artistry of the Bible, he saw the same soul making or breaking paradox.

33. Robert Lowth, *Lectures on the Sacred Poetry of the Hebrews*, tr. G. Gregory (London: 1847), p. 224.

34. For the historic significance of Lowth's biblical criticism, see Murray Roston, *Prophet and Poet: The Bible and the Growth of Romanticism* (London: Faber and Faber, 1965), pp. 21, 58, et passim.

The stylistic paradox of darkness and clarity mirrors the ethical inconsistency between judgment and mercy, wrath and pity. It is familiar, perhaps notorious, to all readers of Scripture. The Lord commands Moses to
do wonders before Pharaoh: "but I will harden his heart, that he shall not
let the people go" (Exod. 4: 21). He commissions Isaiah: "Go, and tell
this people, Hear ye indeed, but understand not; and see ye indeed, but
perceive not. Make the heart of this people fat, and make their ears heavy,
and shut their eyes; lest they see with their eyes, and hear with their ears,
and understand with their heart, and convert, and be healed" (Isa. 6: 9–10).
Jesus explicitly glosses this passage in defense of his own parabolic style:
"For whosoever hath, to him shall be given, and he shall have more abun-
dance: but whosoever hath not, from him shall be taken away even that he
hath. Therefore speak I to them in parables: because they seeing see not;
and hearing they hear not, neither do they understand" (Matt. 13: 12–13).
It all seems rather unfair, especially to such presumable innocents as the
first-born of Egypt. Calvin's dogma of predestined election or reprobation
rests, of course, on such instances of divine caprice. But Blake's Christianity
emphasizes conversion and abundant grace, the "break of day" promised
by the bard of *Experience* and confirmed by his "immortal" counterpart in
Jerusalem. Neither Earth nor Albion is condemned to "turn away" forever
from the Word, the rising day-star looked for also by the apostle (2 Pet.
1: 19).

When Jesus speaks of salvation, he often adopts a negative or exclusive
manner: "Verily I say unto you, Except ye be converted, and become as
little children, ye shall not enter into the kingdom of heaven" (Matt. 18: 3).
Blake writes rather more hopefully to and of his fellow men, most of whom,
he trusts, will "delight" in the prophetic parabolism of his designs. And
delight, for Blake, is Christian joy:

> But I am happy to find a Great Majority of Fellow Mortals who can Elucidate
> My Visions, & Particularly they have been Elucidated by Children, who have
> taken a greater delight in contemplating my Pictures than I even hoped. Neither
> Youth nor Childhood is Folly or Incapacity. Some Children are Fools & so are
> some Old Men. But There is a vast Majority on the side of Imagination or
> Spiritual Sensation.[35]

Blake's earlier statement in this letter that "What is Grand is necessarily
obscure to Weak men" does not imply contempt for his audience. "That
which can be made Explicit to the Idiot is not worth [his] care" because he
seeks to transform the imbecility of the natural man into the wisdom of the
little child who, according to Isaiah (11: 6) and the bardic speaker of "The

35. Letter to Dr. Trusler, 23 August 1799, *Letters*, ed. Keynes, p. 30. All subsequent
quotations from Blake in this paragraph are from the same letter.

Little Girl Lost," will lead all brutes into the peaceable kingdom. Like the wise men before him—and he names Aesop, Homer, and Plato as well as Moses and Solomon—Blake and his bards speak in parables because their aim is heuristic. They point the way by challenging men to find it for themselves: "The wisest of the Ancients consider'd what is not too Explicit as the fittest for Instruction, because it rouzes the faculties to act." The sublime of the Bible and of Blake's allegory is named obscurity by men who think they are listening to a cruel, selfish, jealous, divine obscurantist. Once again, Blake shares Moses' hope that the deaf and the deluded may all become prophets.

Rhetorically, *Milton* exists on four levels of discourse, corresponding to the four worlds of Blake's myth. The highest voice is, of course, the sublime of pure vision, the Edenic mode of the Bard's Song. The lowest is the False Tongue, the sense of touch, equivalent to "Ulro, Seat of Satan" (27: 45–46). Between them lie the voice of the Daughters of Inspiration in Beulah and, beneath that, the language of "Albions land: / Which is this earth of vegetation on which now I write" (14: 40–41). The utterances of any higher realm are only partially intelligible to the inhabitants of the worlds below it. That is the central stylistic problem of the poem.

For instance, to the "Mortal eyes" of Generation and "those of the Ulro Heavens," the mighty angel who is Los's messenger appears in the form of a lark (36: 11–12). Likewise, the lamentation of Beulah over Ololon sounds in vegetated ears like a song of spring, the repeated trills of the lark leading the choir of day (31: 28–31). The difficulty of the Bard's Song is therefore as much the author's weakness as our own. The dispute between Satan and Palamabron is a thrice-told tale when we hear it, the bardic music recorded by the Daughters of Beulah, who must in turn pour their "mild power" into Blake's hand, "descending down the Nerves of my right arm" (2: 5–6). The sublime of the Holy Word is difficult of access because the Lord wills it to be contaminated by such vehicles as the "uncircumcised lips" of Moses, "slow of speech, and of a slow tongue" (Exod. 6: 30; 4: 10). Blake's prayer in *Milton* confesses to traditional prophetic clumsiness:

O how can I with my gross tongue that cleaveth to the dust,
Tell of the Four-fold Man, in starry numbers fitly orderd
Or how can I with my cold hand of clay! But thou O Lord
Do with me as thou wilt! for I am nothing, and vanity.
(20: 15–18)

Like Isaiah, "a man of unclean lips" dwelling "in the midst of a people of unclean lips" (6: 5), Blake fears that he will profane his mission. That is why he invokes the Daughters of Beulah at the outset. They are types of the seraph who cauterized the corruption from Isaiah's mouth with a live coal.

"If there is a single central image in *Milton*," Bloom remarks, "it is the garment, from the weavings of Enitharmon's looms that cover the three classes of men through Milton's taking off the robe of the promise on to the appearance of Jesus in the apocalyptic 'Garment dipped in blood' that emerges from the dispelled clouds of Ololon on the forty-second plate."[36] One may add to this list the cruelty in which the Shadowy Female clothes the image of God, Jerusalem's long sufferings as the garment of God, and the vegetable world that Blake binds on as a bright sandal to walk forward through eternity (18: 19–20, 36–37; 21: 13–14). The verbal ornament of each descending level of discourse may be similarly viewed as travesty of the truer idiom of the level just above it. Because Milton, like Blake, is not only a Christian but a Christian poet, he sees the self-annihilation that leads to salvation as a purgation of his rhetoric, which he expresses by the metaphor of divestment. In his climactic speech on Plates 40 and 41, the spectral and Satanic incrustations over his immortal spirit, the filth he washes from his face and the "rotten rags" he casts from his body, profane the Word in both its fideistic and artistic manifestations, which are the same. The rationalism that veils faith in the Saviour is equated in two consecutive and grammatically parallel verses to the tawdry, mnemonic art that denies inspiration (41: 3–4). The poetry of remembrance looks outward to nature's images, "the Sexual Garments . . . Hiding the Human Lineaments as with an Ark & Curtains" (41: 25–26). It is ripe for burning in the fire of regeneration because it is a soiled costume, a patchwork of inductive reasoning that burlesques imagination, the true clothing of Albion.

When Milton invades Blake's foot on Plate 21, he entrusts himself to the fiction of the poem *Milton*, to the garments of its author's language as well as to those of his body. Reciprocally, the invocation that precedes the Bard's Song parodies the openings of *Paradise Lost* and its detested classical models. The march forward through eternity is a kind of three-legged race in which each hobbled partner—stammering, that is, and half deaf—assists the other to an apparent goal, revealed at the end of the poem as a condition of openness, preparation, and strength for further labor in the human harvest viewed by Rintrah and Palamabron (42: 36–39). The poem has advanced upward, as well as forward, towards the Edenic perspective of the Bard's Song. Neither Blake nor Milton understood the Song when it was dictated to the former and when it moved the latter, like the music it is, to self-annihilation, to an imitation of Christ that seemed to him at first eternal death, the Satanic negative of incarnation.

The progress is also inward, a stripping of the veils of allegory from the body of truth. Lowth remarks that "the prophetic, indeed, differs in one

36. *Blake's Apocalypse*, p. 396.

respect from every other species of the sacred poetry: when first divulged, it is impenetrably obscure; and time, which darkens every other composition, elucidates it." History is the means by which "the Holy Spirit has itself condescended to remove the veil" from "sacred institutions."[37] Blake's view coincides with Lowth's. Los, the very spirit of prophecy, "is by mortals nam'd Time," and "Time is the mercy of Eternity; without Times swiftness . . . all were eternal torment" (24: 68, 72–73). The narrative time or history of the poem releases the reader from the pain of confusion. He begins to penetrate the prophetic ethos through the mortal drama of Milton and Blake, which works out the Bard's issues of pity, love, wrath, contrariety, and negation. One's forward, upward, and centripetal journey is blocked, however; the reader does not quite arrive at the far goal of time, full knowledge. That is because the characters themselves do not get there either. *Milton* is merely the prelude to vision.[38]

The idiom of the Bard's Song is to the Holy Word as nature is to eternity. Both are garments, and both may be called the Sons of Los. Los identifies the Bard's mythic antagonists with the generated world when he reintroduces the Prince of the Starry Hosts, Urizen-Satan:

Thou seest the Constellations in the deep & wondrous Night
They rise in order and continue their immortal courses
Upon the mountains & in the vales with harp & heavenly song
With flute & clarion: with cups & measures filld with foaming wine.
Glittring the streams reflect the Vision of beatitude,
And the calm Ocean joys beneath & smooths his awful waves!

These are the Sons of Los, & these the Labourers of the Vintage[.]
(25: 66—26: 1)

The redemption or humanization of Urizen-Satan began on Plate 20, where Milton struggled to re-sculpt him from Adamic clay. Los next introduces the "gorgeous clothed Flies," also his children, who elsewhere in the poem represent consciousness with all its gates open. Finally, he shows us his *prophetic* Sons:

37. Lowth, *Lectures*, p. 128.
38. Thomas A. Vogler's *Preludes to Vision: The Epic Venture in Blake, Wordsworth, Keats, and Hart Crane* (Berkeley and Los Angeles: Univ. of California Press, 1971) was received too late for consideration in the body of this essay. Distinguishing between the "content" and the "function" of the Bard's Song (pp. 43–47), Vogler perpetuates the notion—unsupportable, in my view—that the Song contains "a vision of Blake's own struggle with the Urizenic Satan within himself which is objectified in Hayley" (p. 47). But we substantially agree on the question of what the Song *does*: "The situation is one in which a poet, in a poem, tries to create the relationship that ideally should exist between a poem and a reader" (p. 46).

> thou seest the Trees on mountains
> The wind blows heavy, loud they thunder thro' the darksom sky
> Uttering prophecies & speaking instructive words to the sons
> Of men: These are the Sons of Los! These the Visions of Eternity
> But we see only as it were the hem of their garments
> When with our vegetable eyes we view these wond'rous Visions.
>
> (26: 7–12)

The last two lines define the proper approach to the idiom and the personages of the Bard's Song. The Bard's language and the fallen ethos whose
self-division it describes are both vestments of the Word; the English to
which Blake is confined in reporting the Song reveals only the edge of those
garments. The natural world of stars, insects, and trees is also a prophecy,
written as it were in the universal tongue but with the characters of an
unknown alphabet.

Scripture itself, appearing in the sky at the end of the poem, is a similar
garment of war and time, the woof of the six thousand years of human
history:

> One Man Jesus the Saviour. wonderful! round his limbs
> The Clouds of Ololon folded as a Garment dipped in blood
> Written within & without in woven letters: & the Writing
> Is the Divine Revelation in the Litteral expression.
>
> (42: 11–15)

Saint John the Divine beheld the same figure, "clothed with a vesture dipped
in blood," on which there was "a name written, KING OF KINGS, AND LORD
OF LORDS" (Rev. 19: 13, 16). The Apocalyptic Christ is also "called Faithful and True . . . and his name is called The Word of God" (19: 11, 13).
None of these appellations "calls" him correctly, because each is like the
swaddling- and grave-clothes in which he entered and left corporeal existence. None reveals the other "name written, that no man knew, but he
himself" (19: 12).

The woven letter is the irreducible, atomic symbol, the cipher that en-
codes what Eliot called the "word within a word, unable to speak a word, /
Swaddled with darkness." Eternity remains invisible and silent, aloof from
the texture of history and language, in which it nonetheless manifests itself
slowly and partially. The prophet's literal expression, his allegory of plows,
mills, and harrows, is therefore our most hopeful possession while we live
in merciful time. We must try as cryptologists to penetrate this sublime rag
of language and nature, as Blake insists that we see through, not with, the
window of the vegetated eye.[39] When the Bard demands that we mark words
well, he demands all.

39. *VLJ,* p. 555.

Blake's Radical Comedy:
Dramatic Structure as Meaning in Milton

W. J. T. MITCHELL

This essay grew out of an attempt to answer a fairly simple question about Blake's *Milton*: why these things in this order? This question seems to me a necessary counterpoint to the usual approach to Blake's prophecies, which locates meaning in an encyclopedic, schematic system of cross-references.[1] While that kind of reading is indispensable, it is also important to see Blake's images as existing in an evolving, unfolding drama, and not as referring to a stable system of fixed meanings.

From this approach I have learned a few preliminary lessons: (1) we must give up the idea that any character in the poem speaks for Blake—even Blake himself—just as we recognize that Dante as a character in *The Divine Comedy* must be distinguished from Dante the author; (2) we must avoid the abuse of systematic allegory involved in assigning rigid moral identities to Blake's characters; Los can make mistakes; Satan and Urizen are capable of prophetic perception and action; a character's consciousness must be evaluated in terms of what he is saying and doing at a particular moment in the poem; (3) we must make ourselves more aware that the symbolic implications of action and interaction serve as controls upon the

Limitations of space have prevented me from recording all my departures from and debts to previous readings of *Milton*. I assume the reader's familiarity with the work of Northrop Frye, David V. Erdman, Harold Bloom, and S. Foster Damon, the four pillars of my understanding of the poem. I would like to thank the American Philosophical Society and the Ohio State University Summer Research Fellowship in the Humanities for their help. My largest debt is to my Ohio State University graduate students in the Blake seminar of Spring, 1971, whose detailed scrutiny of *Milton* made a grasp of its overall form possible.

1. Frye and Damon are the most important proponents of this method; their followers (which include myself) are legion.

symbolic implications of images and personifications; irony and humor are as much a part of the texture of Blake's prophecies as the eclectic radiance of the language; (4) we must be more attentive to the metaphorics of dramatic framing; *Milton* is not a lyric sung in solitude, but a dramatic poem which is conscious of its relation to an audience.

It will be no surprise to readers of *Milton* that as a dramatic poem it seems to be a comedy. I call it a *radical* comedy in order to call attention to a number of things. First, it seems to me that the poem does not reveal in Blake a growing conservatism or a flight into romantic idealism,[2] but rather that it expands and deepens the religious and political radicalism of Blake's earlier work. Second, I use the word *radical* in the sense of "root" or fundamental. *Milton* describes the basic turning point in Blake's career as a poet, the point at which an artistic decision became inseparable from a life decision. The comic "resolution" of *Milton* would have been impossible if Blake had not decided to give up Hayley's patronage and return to London. (*Jerusalem* is also a comedy, but seems to me less radical because less closely connected to a root situation in Blake's life.) Finally, I use "radical comedy" as a theatrical metaphor, a way of seeing *Milton* as a kind of living theater, open-ended, inconclusive, and reaching out to involve its audience in the action.

This metaphor can be applied to the literal action of the poem, which attains a comic resolution only to have it vanish and be replaced with an announcement that the *real* struggle is about to begin. There is a similar open-endedness at the conclusion of *Jerusalem*, where we are given a picture of eternity, not as resolution, rest, or static transcendence, but as a continuing process of "living going forth & returning wearied" (99:2). *Jerusalem* does seem, however, to have raised the dialectics of existence to a new plane, beyond the compulsive repetitions of history. *Milton* is a radical comedy because it returns to the root situation, London of the 1800s, where the work of the prophet is just beginning.

The theatrical metaphor also puts the relation of the poem to its audience in a clearer perspective. *Milton* is an exploration of the limits of poetry as a force for inciting people to imaginative action, and a prophecy of the breaking-down of those limits, a democratization of the poetic genius. Book I explores the limitations of individual prophets in a hostile society: the Bard, Milton (who assumes the roles of Moses and Jesus among others), Los, and Blake himself. Book II prophesies a time when all the Lord's people become prophets, cast off their passivity (personified as the feminine form

2. Recent readings of *Milton* which advance this view are Harold Fisch's "Blake's Miltonic Moment," in *William Blake: Essays for S. Foster Damon*, ed. Alvin H. Rosenfeld (Providence: Brown Univ. Press, 1969), pp. 36–56, and Peter Alan Taylor's "Providence and the Moment in Blake's *Milton*," *Blake Studies*, 4 (1971), 43–60.

of Ololon), and renovate the world. This prophecy is presented as the dilation of a privileged moment of insight, a tantalizing glimpse of a comic resolution which is promptly dissolved to return the reader to his own world—presumably with, as Stevens puts it, "a new knowledge of reality." Also, it is to be hoped, with something to do with that knowledge.

I

Blake's prophecies before *Milton* asked the reader to contemplate the events of history from an eternal perspective. Revolution is depicted as something that must break out as surely as the annual birth of spring or the onset of puberty. The creation and fall of man are presented as a panorama of sacred history, which the reader may contemplate along with the bard, seeing past, present, and future contained in one giant image. *Vala* or *The Four Zoas* expands this image, articulating its members with more characters and relationships, increasing the number of perspectives from which it could be seen, and bringing its total form into focus—the form of the Giant Man as container of the cosmos. Blake worked slowly toward the epic-prophetic strain, not printing any books for over ten years. With *Milton*, he breaks that long silence and fulfills the promise which had been latent in his earlier prophecies. *Milton* calls the reader, not to contemplation, but to action. It dramatizes the eternal perspective only to subvert its detachment from history and to force the reader to abandon the position of aesthetic disinterest.

The heightened didacticism of *Milton* is most directly apparent in the rabble-rousing "Preface," with its call for artists to rebel against fashionable and oppressive "classics," which is a thinly disguised summons to political and psychological revolution as well. England is to be rebuilt, all the Lord's people are to become prophets. No one will be allowed to remain on the sidelines and contemplate the building of the new order if Blake has anything to say about it:

I will not cease from Mental Fight,
Nor shall my Sword sleep in my hand:
Till *we* have built Jerusalem,
In Englands green & pleasant Land.
                    (1: 95; my italics)

Blake's deletion of this preface in late versions of *Milton* is balanced by his expansion of the Bard's Song, the primary call to action within the poem, with its resounding refrain: "Mark well my words! they are of your eternal salvation." The central, thematic action of the poem might be defined, in fact, as call and response. The first thing Blake asks his muses is "what mov'd Milton" to abandon his contemplative position, "pondering the intricate mazes of Providence / Unhappy tho in heav'n." The secondary actions all reflect this central theme of being moved to act: Ololon follows Milton's example and leaves the false heavens of Albion to descend into Ulro; Los recalls "an old prophecy" and descends into Lambeth's Vale; when Ololon arrives in Blake's garden, he immediately assumes that she brings a summons to action, asking "What am I now to do."

This was far from being an aesthetic question for Blake, as investigations into the circumstances surrounding the composition of *Milton* have clearly shown.[3] The affliction that his messengers of providence might send him into was not symbolic but real. Why should he leave a life of relative ease, material security, in a pastoral refuge from the tensions of London, for the almost certain poverty that would face him if he dropped Hayley's patronage? Why, especially if no one would read, much less understand the poems he was sacrificing so much for, and if he was himself sometimes fearful that his gift of vision was an "abstract folly" luring him away from duty and reality?[4] We can only say that apparently he heard a very strong call and that from whatever perspective we choose to approach *Milton*—as an expression of Blake's attempt to come to terms with his life, as a rhetorical gesture to an audience, as a poetic structure with a particular action—we find the call to action and the response an essential part of that perspective.

Milton, in other words, is Blake's attempt to bridge the gap between the ironic, critical view of the world that had permeated his earlier prophetic books, and a comic, redemptive view of a new order. *The Marriage of Heaven and Hell* asserts the imminence of apocalyptic renovation but enacts it poetically only in epigrammatic flashes. Night IX of *The Four Zoas* dramatizes a major vision of apocalypse, but without a fully realized organic connection to the other eight Nights of fallen history. *Milton* supplies the connection between history and apocalypse; that is why it so frequently evokes the imagery of millennium, the thousand-year golden age which, in the Christian tradition, is the preparation for the final unveiling of the heavenly city Jerusalem. It is also why *Milton* addresses the reader so directly. Blake's vision of a providential resolution to history does not depend upon the aid of a transcendent provider who will make the apocalypse happen. "We" will build Jerusalem in England's green and pleasant land.

Blake dramatizes this heightening of the reader's role with his use of the "Eternals," that vague group of characters that first appear in his poetry in *The Book of Urizen*. The Eternals function in the early prophecies as muses

3. I assume the reader's familiarity with Blake's biography, and particularly with the letters of the Felpham period.
4. See Blake's letter to Butts, 11 September 1801, *pp. 685–686.*

(they dictate the words and visions of *Urizen*), as a chorus detached from the action and commenting on it, or as a quasi-transcendent "Divine Council" sitting above the action of the poem. Their only action is a hasty retreat from involvement in the action: in *Urizen* they deputize Los to close off the fallen world in its own separate shell so they will not have to look at it. Blake makes it clear, however, that they are not to be seen as an infallible, transcendent perspective, in spite of their seemingly indefinite capacity for retreat, withdrawal, and detachment.[5] In *Milton* the Eternals are not allowed to remain on the sidelines but are drawn into the action, ultimately to play the decisive role in the poem. They begin with an expansion of their earlier roles, as the judges in the "Great Solemn Assembly" which is convened in the Bard's Song. Another group of Eternals is presented as the audience of the Bard's Song. They react in dismay to the Bard's message and to Milton's descent into the fallen world. They are later seen driving out that portion of Milton which stayed behind in their heavens. In repentance for this act, multitudes of them unite to follow Milton's descent, at which point they acquire the name of Ololon and become a major character in the poem.

Milton's Eternals at their banquet tables have the same function as the guests at the Ancient Mariner's wedding feast: they are there not just to heighten the drama but to represent the audience in the poem and to define its relation to the poem. The fact that the Assembly of Eternals occasionally coalesces into "One Man, even Jesus" (21: 58), is not flattery of the reader, but Blake's definition of his audience's potential. More frequently this audience is seen in disarray and doubt, making faulty judgments, or actively persecuting the poet. Blake goes a step beyond Coleridge's dramatization of audience, however. The Ancient Mariner leaves behind him a "fit audience" of one chosen listener who undergoes a conversion as a result of hearing a poem. The other wedding guests remain in an ambiguous position: were they ignored by the Mariner because they, unlike the chosen guest, are worthy to attend the wedding feast? Or were they ignored because the Mariner's penetrating eye saw that they are unworthy and, therefore, would be unreceptive to his tale? Blake, like Coleridge, gives a dramatic role to the one listener who can receive the poetic message, in the person of Milton; but then he goes on to dramatize the reaction of the unreceptive portion of the audience, and to analyze its prospects for salvation. In *Milton* the immediately fit audience is few indeed, but the ultimate audience is everyone. No one is to be cast into outer darkness at Blake's wedding feast. In fact, the guests are not to remain a detached audience or a passive bride;[6] but ultimately they will unite around the image of the bridegroom himself.

5. See my discussion of the role of the Eternals in "Poetic and Pictorial Imagination in Blake's *Book of Urizen*," *Eighteenth-Century Studies*, 3 (1968), 88–89.

6. As her final act, Ololon casts off the bridal form of the Twelve Years Virgin.

II

Blake dramatizes his theme of call to action and response in three distinct phases: the Bard's Song (2: 25—13: 44), Milton's descent (13: 45—29: 65), and Ololon's descent (30: 1—finis). The Bard's Song is the call to which Milton responds. Milton's descent, in turn, becomes the call to which Ololon responds, and Ololon's descent becomes the call for a multitude of responses, some presented within *Milton* (the unveiling of the Covering Cherub, the stirring of Albion, the descent of Jesus), some projected outside of *Milton*, either in its sequel *Jerusalem*, or (to return to the spirit of the "Preface") in the reader himself.

Looking at the poem as a closed structure, however, we see at least two overlapping rhythms governing the dramatic movement, the first of which is the series of three waves or cycles I have just described. If we look more closely at the internal narrative patterns of these three waves, we discover that each plays a variation on the basic comic pattern of disintegration and restoration of order. The Bard's Song tells the story of the break-up of a family and the establishment of a new, albeit very imperfect order, in which Satan has a very strong position. The next phase begins with the disintegration of the assembled Eternals in the heavens of Albion as Milton decides to return to the fallen world. Milton's descent is also viewed from below as the advent of a destructive force, a sign that "Satan shall be unloosed upon Albion." When the union of Milton, Blake, and Los is complete, however, a new—still very imperfect—order is celebrated in the vision of nature as a creation of the imagination that concludes Book I. The final phase begins with the disruption of the peaceful world of Beulah at the apocalyptic descent of Ololon and culminates in the glimpse of a visionary new order, which is apparently perfect but which passes like a lightning flash to return Blake "To Resurrection & Judgment in the Vegetable Body" (42: 27).

It is important to note that these phases are simultaneously cyclical and progressive (i.e., dialectical). The disintegrating movement in the Bard's Song is a "fall" or primal crime, combining the themes of usurpation, murder, and the creation of both the world and the social order ("Three Classes are Created . . . *when* Albion was slain"). The disintegrating movement in the next section is an ambivalent combination of overtones of the fall and the redemption. Milton's decision to go to Eternal Death reminds us of Christ's offer in *Paradise Lost*; and yet his descent is perceived as the fall of a star, the sign of the death of the hero, and, in particular, of the fall of Satan in *Paradise Lost*. The disintegrating movement in Ololon's descent seems completely positive: the Daughters of Beulah, although they lament the approaching violence, perceive Ololon's appearance in purely apocalyptic terms, as the revelation of divine order.

The three comic cycles of *Milton* are thus contained in an overall cycle. The pattern of disintegration and restoration of order that structures the parts is also the structure of the whole. The Bard's Song is the Book of Genesis and *Paradise Lost*, initiating the disintegrating movement with its account of creation and fall. Milton's descent, like *Samson Agonistes* and *Paradise Regained*, depicts the struggle of the Christian hero in the fallen world. Ololon's descent is the apocalyptic renovation, the Second Coming of *Milton*. A good index to the progress of this cycle is the way in which the forces of evil are manifested in each phase. Satan's true nature is presented as a complete surprise both to himself and to his adversaries in the Bard's Song, and, with the help of an ambiguous judgment from the Eternals, he "triumphant divided the Nations" (10: 21). Satan's nature is more apparent in the next phase, although still veiled by being presented in the characters of Urizen and the Shadowy Female; and Milton's struggle with his adversary might best be described as ending in a draw. When Ololon descends, however, Satan is manifested as an encyclopedic summation of all the previous villains and is given all the trappings of omnipotence, only to be rendered, ironically enough, completely impotent.

It is far too pat, however, to see *Milton* as a sequential narrative poem with internal cycles of rising and falling action. Running against both the cyclic and progressive movements of the poem is a current in Blake's language that I can only describe as "apocalyptic pressure," a sense that the system of words before the reader is continuously straining to explode into a new order. No doubt this is partly a response to Blake's radiant obscurity, which makes reading him a continuous process of discovery, and partly a function of his frequent use of the rhetoric of violence and noise, with silence reserved for climactic moments like Milton's confrontation with Urizen. But it is chiefly a result, I think, of his frequent and calculated use of apocalyptic imagery. The Bard's Song, which functions as the Genesis of the narrative in *Milton*, seems almost ready at several points to become its Revelation. Leutha's description of Satan's work with the harrow (12: 25–26) makes him sound like the dragon of Revelation rather than the usurping brother; the quarrel of Satan and Palamabron begins to sound more like Armageddon (8: 26–40) than Cain and Abel; the Assembly's judgment begins to look like a Last Judgment when it calls up "Two Witnesses" as did John of Patmos. These echoes remain ironic and unactualized in the Bard's Song; but they create a sense that "the time," in some sense, is always potentially at hand in Blake's world and is not dependent on a scheme of progressive development or cause and effect.

The diagrammatic view of *Milton* as a progressive series of cycles is subverted, then, by the local textures of the poem, which, in the manner of the Sons of Los, expand and contract the moment at will, and walk up and down before the ever-present mural of Six Thousand Years. The diagram-matic view may help the reader orient himself in the dramatic movement, and it may help put to rest the notion that Blake's major prophecies are form-less grab-bags full of exciting ideas and bad poetry. It is becoming more and more evident that almost "every word and every letter *is* in its fit place," and that Blake's discovery in *Milton* of the full range and power of his prophetic voice was also the discovery of a form adequate to that voice.

It is also important to remember that, for Blake, form was not a closed, autonomous phenomenon, but a living process. *Milton* is not just a demon-stration of Blake's imagination at work. It is also propaganda for the read-er's imagination—an allegory that "rouzes the faculties to act" as a means of rousing the young men of the new age to be just and true to their own imaginations, not to rest in contemplation of Blake's artistry, much less the artistry of Greek and Roman models. Blake is so much concerned to empha-size this power of poetry to overcome aesthetic disinterest that he opens his poem, not with a leap into the middle of the action, but with a dramatiza-tion of poetry as incitement to action, "A Bards prophetic Song."

I I I

There is certainly some irony in the fact that the Bard's Song, the most explicitly designated call to action in *Milton*, is the least explicit in its meaning. Blake seems to have tinkered with the obscurities of this section considerably, moving plates around, deleting and adding, and generally heightening the complexities that make this the most difficult section of the poem. The reader almost inevitably, I suspect, forgets the dramatic frame-work of the Song and enters into it as an action directly narrated by Blake, rather than as a poem-within-a-poem. When the Song ends, the audience is definitely not moved to act; it behaves more like the audience of a scholarly lecture, raising objections based on prior value judgments ("Pity and Love are too venerable for the imputation / Of Guilt" [13: 48–49]), or ques-tioning the credentials of the speaker ("Where hadst thou this terrible Song" [13: 51]). The audience finds its preconceptions about justice and truth subverted by the Bard's Song: it questions the disposition of guilt, innocence, and judgment in the story; and it wants to know "if the acts have been perform'd"—where, when, and in what sense is there any truth to the Bard's story.

The Bard's narrative divides naturally into three phases: (1) a brief account of the origin and creation of the world in which the action will take place; (2) the quarrel of Satan and Palamabron that destroys this world-order, a destruction that culminates in the divisive judgment of the Solemn

Assembly; (3) the reactions to the judgment, with the resultant creation of a new order by Enitharmon and the Assembly. If the action of the Bard's Song is a sequential alternation between the activities of creation and destruction, the Bard's opening definition of his action compresses this kind of alternation into a single moment: "Three Classes are Created by the Hammer of Los, & Woven / By Enitharmons Looms when Albion was slain upon his Mountains / And in his Tent" (2: 26—3: 2).[7] At least four possible relationships between creation (the making of three classes) and destruction (the slaying of Albion) can be seen in this summary of the action: (1) three classes were created to restore the order which was lost when Albion was slain; (2) the creation of three classes was an oppressive, divisive act which caused Albion's death, his "fall into Division" (cf. *FZ* I: *297*); (3) the creation of three classes and the death of Albion are two ways of describing the same event; (4) the creation and death are two events which occurred simultaneously, but the first seems to be still going on, while the latter happened in the past. The Bard's statement of theme is calculated to send the listeners' minds spinning back and forth among these possibiliites, a condition which is only accelerated when we ask for such details as who did these things where. Creation is presented as the work of both male and female representatives of the imagination, "the Hammer of Los, and the Looms of Enitharmon." But what about Albion's death, which seems to have occurred in two places at once? It may help to note that these two places also carry sexual connotations: was Albion slain "upon his Mountains," an unreprieved Isaac sacrificed by and to a father, "And in his Tent," like Sisera (Judges 5), the victim of a female assassin? If two events can happen at different times and appear simultaneous, why not one event occurring simultaneously in two different places?

At this point we may begin to notice that the Bard's syntax and grammar are designed to subvert our notions of "objective" time, space, and identity and to replace them with a linguistic world in which these modalities are subject to the shaping power of the imagination.[8] The Bard even subverts the logical law of contradiction by placing all the possible relationships between the apparent opposites of creation and destruction into a single matrix. He tells us that they are equivalent, or that one causes the other, or that they are merely coincidental, or all of these things simultaneously. When we try to apply his statement of theme to the subsequent action of his song, we find no mention there of the death of Albion. He fades into the background as a macrocosmic container for the main action, which is

7. I follow Erdman's text, based on the last copy of *Milton* (Copy D) that Blake printed.

8. See my "Poetic and Pictorial Imagination in Blake's *Book of Urizen*" for a discussion of Blake's use of temporal and spatial ambiguity.

the creation of the three classes of men, first, as the main activity of Los's family before the quarrel disrupts their labors and, second, as part of the judgment of the Assembly: "And therefore the Class of Satan shall be calld the Elect, & those / Of Rintrah the Reprobate, & those of Palamabron the Redeem'd," is the pronouncement of the Assembly, which seems not to have noticed that the classes were created before the quarrel (see 4:4; 5:11–14, 38; 7:1–3). The three classes, in other words, are presented both as the order that Satan destroys when he usurps Palamabron's role and as the new order that is established by the Assembly after the quarrel. Fortunately the Bard's opening lines have prepared us to read without expecting causal, sequential order and to view creation and destruction as closely intertwined, perhaps even equivalent phenomena, rather than simple antitheses. At best, those lines affirm the power of creative activity to counteract death. At worst, they suggest that the first of the fine arts may indeed be murder.

The opening phase of the Bard's Song continues to play variations on the ambiguous matrix of relationships between creation and destruction. Los begins by creating a form for Urizen, who has fallen into a disorganized, indefinite stupor. But Los's creation is in itself something of a destructive act; for it is only the formation of a disintegrated human form, fragments of a body rolling in a void on the border between chaos and creation. It must, however, be seen as the creation of some minimal kind of order in response to the complete disorganization of Urizen. This creation quickly becomes a destructive force in itself: when Los beholds his work, he begins to fall apart himself, falling into division and sexuality. He quickly creates a new order among the members of his burgeoning family, subduing his Spectre and building a workshop. This new order, however, contains a rebellious youngest son named Satan, whose usurpation will shatter Los's world. Los keeps the quarrel under control for the moment; but if the reader thinks this uneasy peace is to be seen as prelapsarian harmony, he is quickly disabused by the Bard's digression on the activities of mankind (the Sons and Daughters of Albion) under Los's reign. They are busy lamenting the restrictions of the fallen body (5:19–37) and helping to create the three classes, but their only attempt to overcome their condition is the preparation of animals for sacrifice (4:25). The equilibrium of Los's world is perhaps more humane than the new one which will be established after the judgment of the Assembly, when "Satans Druid Sons / Offer the Human Victims throughout all the Earth" (11:7–8).

The rapid interplay between creation and destruction, which governs the introduction, is slowed down in the next phase of the Bard's Song by Los's attempts to preserve the order of his realm, in spite of the chaos which results from Satan and Palamabron's exchange of duties. Los first applies pity, which sympathizes with both sides of the quarrel and refrains from judgment. He simply calls for a return to proper roles: "Henceforth . . . let each his own station keep" (7: 41–42). Los immediately perceives that this method only covers up the conflict without resolving it: "Mine is the fault! I should have remembered that pity divides the soul / And man, unmans" (8: 19–30).[9] So Los turns to the technique of cleansing, purgative wrath: "follow with me my Plow. this mournful day / Must be a blank in Nature: follow with me, and tomorrow again / Resume your labours, & this day shall be a mournful day" (8: 20–22). Los does not know that the day of mourning will get out of control, and that there will be no resumption of labors the next day. The reign of Los is about to give way to that of his son, Satan.

Nevertheless, Los's decision to apply the science of wrath to the quarrel and allow the antagonists to reveal themselves fully is the first turning point in the Bard's Song. For the first time, the destructive phase of the cycle begins to have regenerative overtones. The plow breaks up the old order to permit the planting of new life, and the Armageddon which develops among the field hands leads into something that looks like a Last Judgment. These overtones remain ironic and unrealizable, however, in the context of the Assembly's questionable judgment. With the introduction of this body of judging Eternals, the Bard begins his most direct satirical attack on his audience, the Eternals listening to his song in the heavens of Albion.

The Assembly faces the classic problem of justice in a fallen world: how do we judge when no one is innocent? There are two principal ways of handling the dilemma. The first is the theory of ordinary moral justice, which ignores the complicity of society in the guilt of its criminals and pretends that they are solely responsible for their deeds. The second is the theory of atonement, which selects an innocent scapegoat as ransom for men's sins. We tend to think of the first alternative as civilized and rational, if somewhat imperfect, and of the second as primitive and superstitious, but more satisfying to absolute conceptions of justice. Christian societies tend to preach the second and practice the first.

The judgment of the Assembly is an unsuccessful attempt to patch together the apparent virtues of both ideas of justice: their judgment falls "on Rintrah and his rage: / Which now flam'd high & furious in Satan" (9: 10–11), leaving us to wonder exactly who has been condemned—the innocent Rintrah or the wrathful Satan. The first alternative is highlighted when the question is asked, "Why in a Great Solemn Assembly / The Innocent should be condemn'd for the Guilty?" (11: 15–16). But the rationalization of the verdict by one of the Eternals merely amplifies the ambiguity: it appears

9. Los may also be referring to his initial mistake of giving the harrow to Satan out of pity.

one moment as if Rintrah had been used as an atonement ("If the Guilty should be condemn'd he must be an Eternal Death / And one must die for another throughout all Eternity" [11: 17–18]), and the next moment as if Rintrah were only a kind of snare into which Satan had been lured so he might reveal himself before the Assembly ("Palamabron dared not to call a solemn Assembly / Till Satan had assum'd Rintrah's wrath" [11: 24–25]). Leutha perceives the judgment only as a condemnation of Satan; and the reaction of the audience to the Bard's Song completely ignores the explicit condemnation of "Rintrah and his wrath," seeing only the ironic imputation of guilt to "Pity & Love," the masks that hid Satan's envy from everyone, including himself.

The Assembly's verdict probably breeds more chaos than Satan's exchange of duties with Palamabron. Los is so angry that he destroys the order of his own creation. Satan rushes in with a new order of "Moral laws and cruel punishments," revealing himself as the Jehovah of accusation and judgment. The shocking revelation of the chaotic "World of deeper Ulro" within the breast of the advocate of law and order begins to make Los's reign look like a golden age by comparison. In this context, the Eternals' pronouncement that Palamabron "is redeem'd from Satan's Law" by Rintrah's sacrifice must seem quite ironic. Imagine the effect if, in Saint John's vision of the Last Judgment, the Messiah had turned on Elijah and cast him out with Satan in order to redeem Moses. It begins to be apparent that the real object of the Bard's attack is not Satan, who has only to be recognized to be rejected, but Palamabron and his class of "Redeemed" souls, who continually escape judgment by allowing the Elect to find Reprobate scapegoats for them. The audience of the Bard's Song is right to sense the ironic imputation of guilt, not merely to the self-deceptive "Pity & Love" of Satan, but more particularly to the custodian of pity, Palamabron, who is doubly guilty in that he consciously suppressed his true feelings and sold out to Satan.[10]

The fact that Palamabron probably represents Blake in this section of the poem does not lessen the probability that he is being treated ironically. Blake seems to have been more interested in understanding what it means to be a prophet in an age that does not believe in prophets than in making himself look good at the expense of Hayley. Insofar as he "serv'd / The Mills of Satan as the easier task" and hid his wrath during his stay in Felpham he had jeopardized his whole prophetic mission. Hayley's loss of

10. In "A Poison Tree" in *The Songs of Experience*, Blake presented the suppression of wrath as the creation of the tree of knowledge, the occasion of the primal crime. The speaker and his foe, like Palamabron and Satan in *Milton*, are presented as equally guilty.

temper only redeemed Blake from the charge of ingratitude; it did not solve the problem of how to be a prophet. Like Milton (14: 30), Blake must have seen that Satan was not primarily Hayley or the Establishment but his own Selfhood, that part of him which doubted his calling enough to keep him in Felpham for three years. Placing this Satanic Selfhood among the Reprobate was only half an answer, because it meant continuing to operate in terms of the atonement—the scapegoat theory of redemption. The other half of the problem was to restore Satan, "That he may go to his own Place Prince of the Starry Wheels" (3: 43). The annihilation of the Selfhood or Spectre is only the prelude to the creation of a new Selfhood which will serve the imagination.

So Satan needs a redeemer, a fact which is dramatized in the concluding episode of the Bard's Song: "But when Leutha (a Daughter of Beulah) beheld Satans condemnation / She down descended into the midst of the Great Solemn Assembly / Offering herself a Ransom for Satan, taking on her his Sin" (11: 28–30). Leutha's offer is the second turning point in the Bard's Song, applying the science of pity as an antidote to the science of wrath with which Los brought the conflict to a crisis. For the first time we encounter a character capable of willing self-sacrifice, an exemplar for Milton's "unexampled deed." Once again the echoes of Apocalypse resound; but this time, instead of an inconclusive battle and an ambiguous judgment, we glimpse a resolution to the struggle in the institution of the Seven Eyes of God (a promise that history will end) as a response to Enitharmon's creation of "a New Space to protect Satan from punishment" (13: 13). The Bard's final prophecy of a time when "The Elect shall meet the Redeem'd" (13: 30) and acknowledge their errors is presented as a consequence of the healing, forgiving female imagination, not the warlike activities of Los and his Sons, a point which is restated when Milton's descent to contend with the errors of the fallen world remains inconclusive until his female counterpart Ololon follows in his path to renew that world to life.

Milton's act is both incited and brought to fruition by female characters, Daughters of Beulah like those who stand guard around the moment in which the poet's work is done (28: 48). It is an appropriate irony that Leutha, who takes upon herself all the faults Milton ever ascribed to women, becomes the one to show him what he must do. If the Whore of Babylon can be imagined making her peace with the poet, even becoming his muse, however unreliable (13: 36–44), then it may be possible to liberate Satan himself. Milton accepts the challenge and goes forth, not to repeat the error of placing Satan among the Reprobate, but "to loose him from my Hells" (14: 31) and to reclaim these hells to their proper function, as the furnaces of the imagination.

I V

The audience understands the major ironies of the Bard's Song but rejects them. Like the Assembly within the Song, it would prefer to leave wrath to wrath and pity to pity (9: 47), to allow the judgment to fall on Rintrah, not on Palamabron or his mild Satanic benefactor. Milton does not respond until the Bard takes refuge in his bosom (14: 9), perhaps a suggestion that the effectiveness of the song for Milton is not so much in hearing the words as in uniting with the point of view of the speaker. In the course of Milton's descent this idea is cumulatively reiterated until Blake, Los, Milton, and the Bard have become one person.

It is interesting to compare this picture of the nature of poetic effectiveness with Coleridge's hypnotic theory—the notion of the poet as someone who casts a spell over his listener with his look and his words. Blake's Bard has no such power, but like the Mariner he seems to know the man who must hear him, and he flees for refuge to that man. Milton responds immediately, possessed not be a superior power but by love: "Milton rose up from the heavens of Albion *ardorous*!" (14: 10; my italics). The transfer of poetic message, its effectiveness as a call to action, is presented as a matter of karmic affinity between speaker and hearer. The wider, general audience of Eternals does not share this affinity and is moved to act, not by poetry, but by Milton's exemplary action.

The only good listener to the Bard's Song, then, is the one who not only understands the ironies, but applies them to himself ("I in my Selfhood am that Satan" [14: 30]), and transforms the Bard's ambiguities into immediate, personal action. Milton sees that the Eternal's pronouncement, "One must die for another throughout all Eternity" (11: 18), means only that "someone else must die for me" to the Redeemed of this world.[11] He sees that Leutha's offer of herself has redemptive potential insofar as it is an act of love, but is misguided in that it still operates as a "Ransom" to tyrannical justice. Milton tries to enact the prophetic part of these perverse doctrines of Atonement and to shed their legalistic, authoritarian features by descending to Eternal Death, not primarily as a sacrifice for others, but as a paradoxically selfless act of self-interest: "I will go down to self-annihilation and eternal death / Lest the Last Judgment come & find me unannihilate / And I be siez'd & giv'n into the hands of my own Selfhood" (14: 22–24).

Despite Milton's attempt to translate the complexities of the Bard's Song

11. Blake amplifies the theme of the perverted atonement in *Jerusalem*. See in particular *J* 39: 25–56, where Los asks, "Must the Wise die for an Atonement? does Mercy endure Atonement? / No! It is Moral Severity & destroys Mercy in its Victim." *Self*-sacrifice is a different matter.

into unambiguous action, his act is not understood by any of the characters in the poem, including Blake himself.[12] His descent, as we have noted, is perceived from this world as the fall of a star, the sign of the defeat of a hero; and in *Paradise Lost*, Milton's own simile for the fall of Satan. From the perspective of the eternity he has left behind, Milton also appears as a threatening figure. The Eternals in the heavens of Albion apparently see no threat in the normal course of spiritual striving, which goes "inward to Golgonooza" on its journey to eternity and which works to open gates from the fallen world into a better one. But Milton's act is a heretical reversal of the direction of the spiritual journey: he passes "outward to Satan's seat" in an implicit rejection of the heavens where he had been silent, but unhappy, until he heard the Bard's song. The reaction of the Eternals to the spurning of their heavenly abode is understandable: they say, in effect, "You can't quit! you're fired!" and drive Milton and his seven attendants out of their heavens. In a parody of Satan's expulsion in *Paradise Lost*, the Eternals "rend the heavens round the Watchers in a fiery circle," forcing Milton and his cohorts to "flee with cries down to the Deeps: / Where Los opens his three wide gates, surrounded by raging fires!" (20: 46–48).

Milton's act is ambiguous even from his own point of view; or, to put it more precisely, Milton does not have a single point of view. As he begins his return to the fallen world, his "Self" splits into three portions that correspond to the three classes of men described in the Bard's Song. The Reprobate portion is Milton's "real and immortal Self," which remains above the fallen world until the Eternals drive it out. This "real" Milton is presumably aware of the acts of his lesser selves, but this awareness is not reciprocal: "to himself [the portion that descended] he seemed a wanderer lost in dreary night" (15: 16). Milton's Redeemed and Elect selves—those divisions of both society and psyche which are indicted by the Bard—are presented in a composite form as Milton's "Shadow, / A mournful form double" in that it is bisexual but, more important, in that it refers to Milton as both the traveler and as the world he travels through. Milton beholds his Shadow as an external being, the twenty-seven–fold Polypus which envelops the whole fallen world, and as separate figures within that Polypus—his three wives and three daughters, the Shadowy Female, and Urizen. These portions of Milton, which can best be described as projected or created selves, correspond to the Elect in psyche and society; and they struggle against, tempt, or simply surround as environment Milton's Redeemed portion, that part of his Shadow which travels through and strives with the world he has entered. Blake becomes part of Milton's struggle with himself when Milton enters his left foot, the Redeemed portion of the Shadow entering Blake, the Elect

12. Blake probably does not know that it is Milton who has entered him until Ololon's descent reaches his garden (37: 15).

portion remaining externalized as "a black cloud . . . spread over Europe" (15: 50).

Milton's return thus seems only to perpetuate the indecisive dialectic between creation and destruction which the Bard's Song criticizes. His descent as a redeemer is taken as a sign that "Satan shall be unloosd upon Albion" (17: 32), perhaps in the form of a new round of European wars. His Shadow seems to cancel itself out by being identified with both sides of the conflict in the fallen world. His "Real Human" portion, which is probably responsible for his decision to descend, like Christ, from heaven to this world, has left behind it only an empty couch in a tabernacle (20: 47–48), which suggests that his sacrifice, like Christ's, has been co-opted by the forces of Mystery. The Eighth Eye of God (Milton), like the Seventh (Jesus), has had his ministry corrupted. The Bard's concluding account of the Seven Eyes of God (the seven attempts of God to manifest himself in history) had made precisely this point in describing the fate of Jesus' descent to Eternal Death: "For then the Body of Death was perfected in hypocritic holiness, / Around the Lamb, a Female Tabernacle woven in Cathedrons Looms" (13: 25–26). The mystique of Milton and Christ entombs their prophetic messages in hollow, allegorical shells. They become "classics" to oppress the imaginations of the young men of the new age. Such "creations" ultimately become destructive forces in themselves: "Miltons Religion is the cause: there is no end to destruction! / Seeing the Churches at their Period in terror & despair: / Rahab created Voltaire: Tirzah created Rousseau" (22: 39–41). That is, a new body of self-righteous judges, worshiping the gods of Reason and Nature, has succeeded the Puritan Elect. *Paradise Lost* is no longer a force for Christian liberty, but serves as a mirror for magistrates and imperialists, "Shewing the Transgressor in Hell, the proud Warriors in Heaven: Heaven as a Punisher & Hell as One under Punishment" (22: 51–52).

It begins to look, in other words, as if the creative imagination has become completely corrupted in the service of the Elect. The creations of artists, the systems they develop to liberate their minds from the systems of others, become, in their turn, enslaving systems for future generations, an artist's "Orc-cycle." It must have occurred to Blake that his own system was not necessarily exempt from this vicious circle. Both wrath (Rintrah) and pity (Palamabron), the two principal emotional allies of the artist, are in constant danger of departing to the camp of the Elect, prophetic wrath degenerating into tyranny and warfare, pity lapsing into hypocritical sentimentality. Blake dramatizes this low point in the life of the imagination in Los's response to Milton's expulsion from heaven:

Los saw them and a cold pale horror coverd o'er his limbs
Pondering he knew that Rintrah & Palamabron might depart:

Even as Reuben & as Gad; gave up himself to tears.
He sat down on his anvil-stock; and leand upon the trough
Looking into the black water, mingling it with tears.

(20: 51–55)

This is the nadir of the poem. Milton's descent has not only proved inconclusive: it has apparently become the occasion for further fragmentation
of the imagination.

But it is also the turning point: "At last when desperation almost tore his
heart in twain," Los recollects "an old prophecy" which predicts that
Milton's journey will "set free Orc from his Chain of Jealousy" (20: 56–
61). There is an unmistakable element of the ridiculous in the convenient
timing of Los's memory here. Blake seems to be trying to strain the reader's
suspension of disbelief to the breaking point, pulling an old prophecy out
of the hat when no logical turning point can be developed from the action
itself. It seems to me that the credibility of this moment in the poem can be
preserved only by the reader's recollecting another prophecy which has just
recently been sung to the harp at an immortal feast, the song that moved
Milton. The Bard's Song is so novel and obscure that no one understands it;
perhaps Los's prophecy is so old that no one remembers it. In any case, the
point is surely that Los's descent to unite with Blake is spurred by a poem,
just as Milton's was. Insofar as the Bard's song is an ironic exhortation,
urging the redeemed souls in the heavens of Albion to see the hollowness of
their salvation and to return to the fallen world, the song is a "prophecy" of
Milton's descent into Felpham's Vale—not prophecy as prediction, but as
self-fulfilling call to action. We still ought to see, however, a certain amount
of humor in Blake's making poems the major causes of action in his drama,
in view of the fact that he knew the world was completely ignorant of his
work and likely to remain so. The same kind of bravado allowed him to treat
his isolation as a joke in *The Marriage of Heaven and Hell*, when he threatens to unleash his "Bible of Hell, which the world shall have whether they
will or no (*MHH* 24: 43). Is it not somehow appropriate that the point at
which tragedy becomes comedy be marked by a joke?[13]

The real turning point of the poem is, of course, taking place offstage, in

13. I use the word "joke" rather than "irony" to describe this episode, because the
humor liberates and releases tension rather than maintaining it in some ironic, ambiguous equilibrium. The situation, I agree, is devastatingly ironic: It has just occurred
to Los that Milton's descent may destroy the last vestiges of prophetic possibility;
Rintrah and Palamabron (the prophet and poet) may abandon Los's mission. But Los
does not dwell upon this irony. He finds release from the black waters of melancholy
through a hilariously improbable flash of memory. The moment is a microcosm of the
whole poem, which, far from being ironic, is a comedy about the personal triumph of
a prophet in an unprophetic age. Blake's joke here, as in *The Marriage of Heaven and
Hell*, is a minute comedy, raising ironies and difficulties only to dispel them.

the audience of Eternals which rejected both the Bard's Song and Milton's interpretation of it, and which is now having second thoughts (22: 15—23: 4). Within the fallen world, however, this reversal is heard only indistinctly and fearfully, "as the poor bird within the shell / Hears its impatient parent bird" (21: 28–29), so let us delay consideration of this event until its meaning becomes more distinct.

Los's renewal of confidence, and his subsequent union with Blake and Milton, does not mean that the struggle to keep together what is left of the imaginative family has been won. Los has had a faint glimpse of a providential resolution to the issues of history, but he still cannot convince even his own Sons and allies that Milton's descent is a hopeful sign. Rintrah and Palamabron argue that Milton's work has become indistinguishable from the oppressive systems which perpetuate the fallen world and that the proper course is to "throw him into the Furnaces" (22: 32) and start over fresh. From his Sons' perspective, Los is perhaps getting a little too detached and "mythic" in his role of cosmic historian, "Pitying and permitting evil" (22: 30) rather than casting it out. Los finds himself arguing for the potentially reactionary virtues of patience and trust in providence, counseling Rintrah and Palamabron against premature actions. His warnings to avoid martyrdom and holy war make sense, but they also seem rather unconvincing to Rintrah and Palamabron, who are seeking to avoid the unchaining of Orc and Satan (22: 33–34), and for whom martyrdom and war have been deplorable facts (22: 44, 59) rather than desired tactics. Los even seems to be defending the new religions of Reason and Nature developed by Rahab and Tirzah (22: 41) when he argues that "These lovely Females form sweet night and silence and secret / Obscurities to hide from Satans Watch-Fiends, Human loves and graces" (23: 39–41). In answer to his Sons' questions, "How long shall we lay dead in the Street of the great City / How long beneath the Covering Cherub give our Emanations" (23: 11–12), Los can only reply with a more positive form of the question: "O when shall we tread our Wine-Press in heaven; and Reap / Our wheat with shoutings of joy, and leave the Earth in peace" (23: 45–46). Los can only argue that he comprehends history more fully, not that he knows the way out of it: "We were placed here . . . / With powers fitted to circumscribe this dark Satanic death / And that the Seven Eyes of God may have space for Redemption. / But how this is as yet we know not, and we cannot know; / Till Albion is arisen" (23: 51–54).

The debate at this level proves inconclusive. Rintrah and Palamabron remain "Indignant, unconvinced by Los's arguments & thunders rolling / They saw that wrath now swayd and now pity absorbd him / As it was, so it remaind & no hope of an end" (24: 45–47). They do see, however, the cost of refusing to cooperate with their father, when his wrath begins to make him look "Like the black storm, coming out of Chaos" (23: 21), an image of the apocalypse as destruction of all order. Perhaps one has to believe in providence, even when all the evidence is against it, and go to press, not merely in the face of a doubting world which will not read or understand what one has to say, but even in the face of one's own doubts about the message.

So Los, Rintrah, and Palamabron descend to the wine-press (the printing-press of Los, in this context, I think) and meet with more opposition and disbelief from the "Labourers of the Vintage," and Los produces more half-convincing rhetoric. He promises an imminent awakening to Eternal Life, but argues that it will come only by continuing to create the structures of the fallen world, the three classes and the Mundane Egg. He promises liberation from those "Who set Pleasure against Duty" (25: 51) in the same breath that he asks his workers to "abstain from pleasure & rest" while they do their duty at the wine-press. "Lightnings of discontent" are the only response to this attempt to justify the ways of imagination to man.

So Los abandons the argumentative mode of address, stops exhorting his followers either to action or inaction, and calls them instead to contemplation:[14] "Thou seest the constellations in the deep & wondrous night" (25: 66). The remainder of this phase of the poem is an extended meditation on the entire "Vegetable World" as a creation of the imagination. Probably this is the most frequently quoted section of *Milton*, perhaps because it is an apotheosis of the masculine version of reality. The entire cosmos is described as the fabrication of the human imagination. Time and space are pliable material to be shaped by the human will. In many ways it seems an extremely optimistic vision: if the world is what we make it, then we can give it the form of our heart's desire and create Jerusalem in England's green and pleasant land. But the monologue does not ignore the sad truth that we have in fact created a world which seems to frustrate, not gratify, human desire. The concluding summary, "Thus Nature is a Vision of the Science of the Elohim," is double-edged and brings us back to the basic dilemma of all Blake's poetry: if we create our nature, why do we botch the job, and how do we set things right? Los has no answer. He and his family prevent things from becoming total chaos; occasionally they salve the misery of the fallen world with delightful ornaments. But in themselves, they simply perpetuate the system rather than freeing men from it. In spite of the beautiful exuberance of most of the meditation, the sombre conclusion

14. The speaker of this section is not explicitly identified. Dramatic continuity would seem to make it primarily Los's voice; but since he has united with Milton and Blake, we should listen for all three.

in which the creative forces are seen perverted (29: 53) casts a shadow over the whole, leaving us with the same dilemma we found in the Bard's Song.

The apotheosis of Los's family at the end of Milton's descent, then, is only the groundwork for further action. It is an epiphany of the "Whole Vegetable World," designed to provide for the reader the alteration in perspective which Blake received when Milton and Los entered him. We should recall, at this point, that both Los and Milton reconstruct the "nether regions" of Blake's imagination, his left foot. When Milton enters Blake, "all this Vegetable World appeared on my left Foot / As a bright sandal formd immortal of precious stones & gold" (21: 12–13). After Los recollects his old prophecy he binds on Blake's sandals to prepare him for the journey through eternity. Blake's meditation on creation gives the reader a similarly miniaturized, portable encyclopedic vision of the world, compressed into the pulsation of an artery. This vision, like Blake's sandal, is still ambiguous: a bright artifact of precious stones and gold, or (from Rintrah and Palamabron's point of view) "a fibrous left Foot, black" (22: 35); an image of the heavenly city, or the vegetative Polypus. The reader must strap on this vision and proceed.

V

The faint echoes of a providential resolution to history, which Los heard only "indistinct in fear" during Milton's descent, become a triumphant chorus as Ololon descends. We can return now to that turning point with a somewhat clearer sense of its significance. Milton's descent has revealed the limitations of the masculine, active imagination, showing its contentions finally coming to rest in bemused contemplation of its own creation. Ololon's descent will provide the incarnation of the female imagination, the inspiration which can regenerate the Mundane Shell created by the Sons of Los and which can break out of the divided, cyclical consciousness that splits the imagination into masculine and feminine stereotypes.

Los found his glimmer of hope only after reflecting on the "black water" of melancholy and despair. His faith in providence is presented as an absurd and paradoxical affirmation of the need to continue creating when creation seems to have become a cycle of oppression and destructive reaction. Ololon's conversion involves the same paradoxical sense that "if the fool would persist in his folly, he would become wise." Ololon rejects the Bard, then Milton. But at least they[15] have been forced to act and have been prevented

15. I use the third person plural to refer to Ololon except for the brief episode of

from remaining passively in their false, detached heavens. Since they would not defend truth, they have been forced to defend a lie, which turns out to be more educational than defending nothing. Ololon's persistence in folly leads to the potential wisdom of remorse, and finally to the actual wisdom of repentance. The moment when Ololon begins to lament their error, providence begins ("at this time all the Family / Of Eden heard the lamentation, and Providence began" [21: 23–24]). Ololon (whose name is probably derived from "ululation," the wailing of mourners) personifies a kind of regenerative guilt and sorrow, in contrast to Leutha, who expresses a similar remorse but with a self-accusing sense of sin that stymies her regenerative possibilities. Ololon's guilt does not seek an accuser whose justice must be satisfied, but a course of action which will redeem the error itself. Their first impulse is to imitate the descent of Milton: "Let us descend also, and let us give / Ourselves to death in Ulro among the Transgressors" (21: 45–46). The Divine Family (which has coalesced as one man in response to Ololon's lament) cautions them, however, that they have a different task. Milton goes to Eternal Death, annihilating himself like Christ. Ololon's duty is to "Watch over this World, and with your brooding wings, / Renew it to Eternal Life" (21: 55–56), like the Holy Spirit.

Ololon's renewal of the world is divided into three phases: first, they descend into Beulah to transform it from a peaceful refuge into a staging area from which revolution can be launched; second, they descend into the heavens of Ulro to serve as messengers of providence and to provide escape hatches from the Mundane Shell; third, they descend into Generation (Felpham's Vale) to provide an encyclopedic revelation of their own errors and Milton's and to give Blake the inspiration "To go forth to the Great Harvest & Vintage of the Nations," which Los promised but was unable to deliver. These three phases are arranged spatially as concentric spheres containing various sublevels. Ololon's journey toward the center combines the images of space travel with the journey beneath the earth, through the labyrinth, and into the living creature.

In the first region of Beulah, Ololon immediately appears as an image of apocalypse. The residents of Beulah and the nations of the earth see "The Lord coming / In the Clouds of Ololon," and lament the approaching affliction. Their lamentation, like Ololon's, is the kind of regenerative sorrow which manifests itself as a providential vision of nature transformed into an ecstatic, harmonious dance. The region of Beulah, we must recall, is seen from the point of view of our world, Generation, as a dreamlike refuge from

---

the poem when she becomes a female. This may produce some awkwardness for the reader of this text, but it is essential to an accurate rendering of Ololon's role as "multitudes."

the normal state of nature as struggle for survival. As Ololon descends into Beulah, this picture of nature is turned inside out, and the strife of Generation is seen as contained in a larger order of regeneration and love. The moment of inspiration at dawn is no longer drowned by the clarions of common day (21: 25), but becomes the keynote for the entire day. The voices of the lark and the nightingale, the dance and scent of the wild thyme, are not surrounded by hostility or indifference as in Generation, but spread their "effluence Divine" throughout creation: "All Nature listens silent" and then "all the birds begin their Song" and "every Tree, / And Flower & Herb soon fill the air with an innumerable dance" (31: 36, 39, 60–61).

Blake ends this celebration of nature as an order of love with a note of discordance, a reminder of the message of the Bard's Song: "Men are sick with love" (31: 61). In Blake's hands, this worn convention of romantic love becomes the point of departure for an analysis of the pathology of sexual love. In early copies of *Milton* he continued immediately with an account of the perversion of love by female jealousy (pl. 33), a Song of Beulah in which the more sombre, critical perspectives of "The Divine Voice" and Ololon replace the joyous voice of Beulah herself. In later copies he balanced this account with Milton's "vision & dream beatific with the Seven Angels of the Presence" (32: 2), which reminds us that the male Spectre's predatory pursuit of the female Emanation is equally responsible for making love a sickness (32: 5).[16] Milton reviews his descent in sexual terms and sees that the portion of himself which descended to explore the heavens of Ulro like "a wanderer lost in dreary night" (15: 16) was his Spectre, hunting the footsteps of his Emanation like a wolf after its prey. The Seven Angels of the Presence instruct Milton that it is precisely this spectrous, elect portion of himself which must be annihilated. The task of the egotistical male will is to muster sufficient courage to will its own death. Milton, like Satan, abstracts himself from "female loves"—not, however as the accuser of sin (cf. 12: 47–48) but in order to "Redeem the Female Shade" (33: 11) by annihilating the masculine consciousness that makes women into commodities such as virgins and harlots.[17] Even in this critique of love, then, the songs of Beulah continue to sound "comfortable notes / To comfort Ololon's lamentation" (34: 1–2) by suggesting the cure for the sickness of love. The annihilation of male will and the relenting of female jealousy are in the process of occurring in the descents of Milton and Ololon. Their assumption of the stereotyped roles of masculine and femi-

16. Plate 32 (Milton's dream) was added in copies C and D. It comes after Plate 33 (the Divine Voice in the Songs of Beulah) in C, before it in D.

17. Blake consistently equates the virgin with the harlot in the figure of Rahab Babylon.

nine consciousness is dramatized so that sexual love can be consumed in the order of human love.

Ololon's descent must continue, then, by carrying the vision of regenerated love into that region which most needs it, the Ulro "where the Contraries of Beulah" (including the sexes) "War beneath Negations Banner" (34: 23). Ololon follows in Milton's track, widening it into a road and, like Milton, encountering visions of the fallen world which are really visions of their fallen self. Milton saw the Polypus as his own Shadow (14: 36); Ololon sees it as a web woven by the sixfold female, the sexual portion they have come to transform. Until they enter into this form and become "Mortal & Vegetable in Sexuality" (35: 24), their perspective on the world will still be detached from and ignorant of the world's continuing struggle to attain consciousness of itself. As long as Ololon remained outside the fallen world, in other words, "they / Could not behold Golgonooza" (which is, literally, the "new skull" or consciousness that evolves inside the structure of the old [35: 18]); Ololon has descended only to the level of the "Watchers of Ulro," the refuge of the Starry Eight (Milton plus the Seven Angels) which Ololon drove out of Beulah. There is no dramatic confrontation at this point because the real conflict of the poem is between Milton's spectrous form and Ololon's female portion, their modes of being inside the Polypus. Ololon's descent into the heavens of Ulro, the starry void around the world, is, like the descent into Beulah, only a prelude to the return to Generation, the world of the Sons of Los, Blake, and the reader. If Beulah gives Ololon a vision of regenerated nature, Ulro gives them an overall perspective of degenerated nature. The problem is to bring these two visions together and to allow the first to transform the second.

Ololon begins this work immediately, as an invading multitude rushing through all the breaches in the Mundane Shall, cleansing all the windows through which eternity is glimpsed in the fallen world. The lark and the wild thyme, the animal and vegetable agents of inspiration, are united with the fountain and the rock, the mineral version of the "opened center."[18] These minute particulars of inspiration in the phenomenal world do not spread irresistible, spontaneous influence as they did in Beulah; rather, their activities are now surrounded by hostile forces, they must occasionally put on a threatening appearance themselves (35: 55), and their influence must be multiplied by "the Industrious" (35: 43). Ololon is approaching Golgonooza, where inspiration and love become the basis for work, at which

18. For a good discussion of this concept, see Edward J. Rose's "The Symbolism of the Opened Center and Poetic Theory in Blake's *Jerusalem*," *Studies in English Literature*, 5 (1965), 587–606.

point, "Ololon and all its mighty Hosts" appear as "One Female . . . a Virgin of twelve years" descending into Blake's garden in Felpham.

Ololon's arrival produces in and around Blake an instant epiphany of Milton's Shadow as a summation of the religions of Western man. The "heathen" deities of Egypt, Greece, and Asia Minor are summed up as the Gods of Ulro, the Twelve Sons of Albion, and Satan. The patriarchs and prophets of the Judao-Christian tradition from Adam to Luther are united in the images of the Covering Cherub and the churches or heavens of Beulah. What Blake consistently attacks in these religions is their attachment to mystery and violence, the perversions of female and male will respectively. The revolutionary zeal of the prophets becomes the pretext for tyranny and holy war in the hands of organized religion; the genuine mysteries of divine love and inspiration become the secret allegorical property of a priesthood. Perhaps Blake seems over optimistic in thinking that these things need only be manifested clearly to be rendered ineffectual, but then that is only half his point. The other half is that the prophets themselves are responsible in part for what happens to their ministry, and they must prevent it from being co-opted. The struggle is not primarily to recognize and correct the external evils of the world, but of the self as an image of that world. Blake sees "the Covering Cherub & within him Satan / And Rahab, in an outside which is fallacious"; he knows that "within / Beyond the outline of Identity, in the Selfhood deadly" (37: 8–10) is the place to find the real Satan. The climax of Milton and Ololon's descent can best be epitomized in the words of Walt Kelly: "We have met the enemy and he is us."

The meeting of Milton and Ololon, then, is simultaneously a revelation of the archetypal errors of masculine and feminine consciousness and a redemption of these errors. Ololon redeems the "pity & love" which we had seen usurped by false benevolence in the Bard's Song. Milton redeems the usurper himself, as well as the wrath which was cast out along with him, refusing to annihilate Satan and become a greater in his place. The law of Satan's heaven is power and violence; "but Laws of Eternity / Are not such: know thou: I come to Self Annihilation / Such are the Laws of Eternity that each shall mutually / Annihilate himself for others good, as I for thee" (38: 33–36). Volumes could be written on what Blake means here by "Self Annihilation." The concept has overtones in the mystical idea of ego-death and Nirvana, the Christian idea of the death and rebirth of a new man in Christ, the existentialist concept of the self as an entity which is continuously created and destroyed, Saint John's "Dark Night of the Soul," Gandhi's doctrine of creative, militant nonviolence, to name just a few. I suspect that long arguments could be waged over which of these is closest to Blake's meaning. But the first thing we could agree on is that the concept surely involves a radical redefinition of the central epic virtue of courage. Milton does not come to teach passivity or quietistic humility; that is the lesson of Satan: "Thy purpose & the purpose of thy Priests & of thy Churches / Is to impress on men the fear of death; to teach / Trembling & fear, terror, constriction; abject selfishness" (38: 37–39).

The second thing we ought to notice is that the courage required for self-annihilation is not in itself sufficient to redeem either the self or the world. Milton's act would remain within the fruitless cycle of creation and destruction which continues to trap the male imagination, even after his descent, if it were not for Ololon's response, her renewal of life to balance his descent to death. Ololon's final transformation into an ark and a dove, the bearer and messenger of life amidst the annihilating flood, occurs when she casts off her false femininity. Her seeking-out of Milton reverses the traditionally passive role of the virtuous heroine in epic and romance, but she does not escape this role by becoming a female warrior, a woman in the armor of a man, "A Female hidden in a Male, Religion hidden in War" (40: 20). On the contrary, she sees that the stereotypes ruling the behavior of both sexes are the basis for the vicious cycle which entraps the best efforts of Milton and the Sons of Los, and that these roles must be annihilated and recreated as human relationships before the cycle can be broken and transformed into the fruitful, liberating dialectic of contraries.

VI

Milton's act of self-annihilation, which has been promised from the beginning as the central event of the poem, is never described. In the apocalyptic climax of the poem, we see Ololon's transformation, but Milton's deed seems to occur offstage, if at all. It seems to me that this apparent omission is Blake's way of dramatizing the most fundamental difference between the acts of Milton and Ololon. Milton's self-annihilation is not a particular act which he performs at the end of his descent; it is a continuous process which begins when he first sheds the robe of the promise to return to the fallen world and which continues beyond the end of the poem. The apocalyptic visions which Blake sees in Felpham's Vale do not mean the end of Milton's struggle with Urizen or his labors in the "Chasms of the Mundane Shell" (39: 57). Milton comes "to teach men . . . to *go on* . . . annihilating Self" as a way of living in and dealing with Satan's world. Blake's description of himself in William Upcott's album, "Born 28 Novr 1757 in London & has died several times since," suggests that he saw Milton's lesson as operative in his own life.

Milton's descent, in other words, shows the limits and possibilities of that pole of the imagination which struggles within the fallen, historical world and within an imperfect self. Milton is both Saint George and the Dragon, Jesus and Satan, the lost traveler and the wilderness he travels through. Ololon's descent, on the other hand, shows the limits and possibilities of that pole of the imagination which glimpses the direction and goal of history and sees this world from an eternal perspective. Milton moves through a world which is himself. Ololon begins as a group of passive observers dwelling on the banks of a river named Ololon. Do we move through our world, or does it move through us? Blake seems to be suggesting that imaginative activity is the dialectic between these two points of view. When one tries to negate the other we have, at best, the dilemma of the active imagination creating its own prison ("Nature as a Vision of the Science of the Elohim") and the passive imagination fleeing into quietistic contemplative refuges.

The meaning of *Milton*, then, is in the reverberations between the descents of Milton and Ololon. We can look at them as representing the active and passive poles of consciousness, the maker-destroyer of systems versus the principle of life and inspiration in both the maker and his system. The two books of *Milton* can be seen as a drama of the relationship between theodicy (the historical, argumentative attempt to vindicate providence) and theophany (the direct vision of God which makes arguments about him worth having). Most important, Milton and Ololon's descent dramatizes the restoration of imaginative rapport between a poet and his audience, the isolated Reprobate artist "who never ceases to believe," and the redeemed multitudes of his public "who live in doubts and fears" (25: 7–8). Ololon's descent in Milton's track as a multitude is a vision of all the Lord's people becoming prophets and working out their redemption, rather than allowing the Elect to find Reprobate scapegoats for them. A Marxist could read the poem as an allegory of the masses awakened from the opiate of their false heavens, descending into the real world to reclaim it for humanity.

As we move further from the poem, Milton and Ololon's relationship resolves into the dialectic of death and life: Milton comes to teach men to die and to struggle in an inconclusive war; Ololon comes to teach them how to live and to hope. The argument of the first book is that a man must be a maker, giving life even to the forces of evil, death, and destruction. The argument of the second book is that "Whatever can be Created can be Annihilated" (32: 36). The systems, states, artifacts, and Selfhoods that men create are not ends in themselves, but instruments in the liberation of consciousness. Thus, Los is presented "striving *with* [i.e., by means of, *and* against] systems, to deliver Individuals from those systems" (*J* 11: 5). A work of art is not eternal; it is a created entity, a State, and "the Imagination is not a State: it is the Human Existence itself" (*M* 32: 32).

Blake created a system in his poems lest he be enslaved by another man's;

but his real problem, it should be clear, was to design a system that would self-destruct. Milton, the character, is transformed in the course of his poem into just such a paradoxical entity, a State called "Eternal Annihilation." *Milton*, the poem, is built to embody the same paradox. The elaborate and obscure machinery of the poem, the multiplicity of characters and scenes, the encyclopedic fabric of Six Thousand Years, are all rendered equivalent to the single, visionary flash of insight, the pulsation of an artery. The reader, like Blake, has been lifted by this vision only to be dropped back into this world to listen with Los to "the Cry of the Poor Man" (42:34). At this point the formal structure converges with the didactic point of the poem as a call to action and as propaganda for the reader's imagination. We are propelled out of Blake's universe into our own. The whole thing (history? or the poem?) was (is?) a dream and a joke, a Divine Comedy whose ending has been glimpsed—but not yet realized.[19]

19. This essay was completed before I came across Stanley E. Fish's concept of the "self-consuming artifact," which was elaborated first in *New Literary History*, 2 (1970), 137–138, and more recently and very fully in *Self-Consuming Artifacts: The Experience of Seventeenth-Century Literature* (Berkeley and Los Angeles: Univ. of California Press, 1972). Although we come to the idea from different directions, I think we are talking about essentially the same thing.

William Blake and
His Reader in Jerusalem

ROGER R. EASSON

Repeatedly, in his correspondence, in his marginalia, and in his poetry, William Blake expresses an abiding concern with his audience; and that concern becomes more evident as Blake's disenchantment with his audience —especially with his patrons—becomes more pronounced. Blake's patrons expected from him an art of clarity but received an art of obscurity; Blake expected from his patrons spiritual friendship but received instead only corporeal friendship. This was unsettling to a poet who believed that " 'He who is Not With Me is Against Me.' " "There is no Medium or Middle state. . . . if a Man is the Enemy of my Spiritual Life while he pretends to be the Friend of my Corporeal," Blake wrote to Thomas Butts, "he is a Real Enemy—but the Man may be the friend of my Spiritual Life while he seems the Enemy of My Corporeal, but Not Vice Versa."[1] *Jerusalem*, Blake's last illuminated book, is the product of the poet's disillusionment with the audience he had hoped would receive him according to his merit. With its rhetorical density and allegoric opacity—both functions of Blake's search for an honest reader—*Jerusalem* is a poem about itself, about the relationship between the author and his reader. A grand allegory concealed by a rhetorical veil of error, *Jerusalem* may be read as a poem about the experience of reading *Jerusalem*; it is a poem that enjoins the reader to participate with its writer in the creative process.

For this reason, it is important to examine Blake's understanding of the reader-writer relationship—a relationship that he continually defines in terms of the one that exists between teacher and pupil. But this teacher-

1. *The Letters of William Blake*, ed. Geoffrey Keynes (Cambridge, Mass.: Harvard Univ. Press, 1968), p. 67. Hereafter referred to as *Letters*.

pupil relationship was, for Blake, marked by failure, by the pupil's lack of appreciation for the teacher, and finally by a mutual rejection. Within *Jerusalem* Blake underscores his pursuit of spiritual friendship by including in the midst of a complicated narrative section these clear and comprehensible lines:

I have tried to make friends by corporeal gifts but have only
Made enemies: I never made friends but by spiritual gifts;
By severe contentions of friendship & the burning fire of thought.

                                                    (91: 15–17)

Jerusalem, then, is a severe contention of friendship, and reading it requires entering the burning fire of thought. *The Marriage of Heaven and Hell* expresses the hope that Blake's last illuminated book fulfills:

If the doors of perception were cleansed every thing would
appear to man as it is, infinite.
For man has closed himself up, till he sees all things thro'
narrow chinks of his cavern.

                                                    (14: *39*)

Jerusalem's reader is the citizen of a fallen world; his perceptual abilities are obstructed by the values and concerns of that fallen world. Each fallen reader approaches *Jerusalem*, initially at least, in the spirit of the Spectre— unloving, unbelieving, unforgiving, and reasoning. Blake does not conceal *Jerusalem* from the reader, but rather the reader, by not attentively obeying the preface, "To the Public," makes, like Swinburne, a "sea of words"[2] out of a meticulously ordered and intricately wrought poem. In *Jerusalem* the reader's ability to understand the nature of the allegory is a function of his ability to love. Odd as that may sound in this age of academic objectivity, or might have sounded in the age of reason where disinterestedness was highly esteemed, this is exactly what Blake desires. In fact, in the first paragraph of the preface, love and friendship are identified as the highest rewards a reader can give to Blake for his creative labor.

The preface is important because it is there that Blake speaks plainly about the relationship he hopes to develop with his reader. And this is a demanding relationship, devoid of the usual considerations given to friendship in the fallen world. When, in the second paragraph of the preface, Blake begins to consider the reader, he hopes the reader will not take offense at the "Enthusiasm of the following Poem." For Blake's contemporaries, more perhaps than for ourselves, enthusiasm was what Blake suggests his might seem, "presumptuousness or arrogance" (3: *144*). Johnson defines

2. Algernon Charles Swinburne, *William Blake: A Critical Essay* (London, 1868), p. 187.

the word, using a quotation from Blake's archenemy, John Locke, which sounds surprisingly like Albion's first lines (4: 24) :

1) a vain belief or private revelation; a vain confidence of divine favor or communication. "*Enthusiasm* is founded neither on reason nor Divine revelation, but rises from the conceits of a warmed or overweening brain," Locke. 2) Heat of imagination; violence of passion; confidence or opinion. 3) Elevation of fancy; exaltation of ideas.[3]

Blake's *Jerusalem* is a poem of enthusiasm; and in an age of reason and an age of reason's religion, Deism, such pretense was a very real offense against taste. *Jerusalem*, by displaying in every line the heat of imagination, the violence of passion, and the actual confidence of divine communication, was a calculated affront to contemporary belief and taste. The poem is tactless and rudely unobservant of the dictates of eighteenth-century literary norms and traditions. But then, Blake fairly shouts that "JERUSALEM IS NAMED LIBERTY AMONG THE SONS OF ALBION" (26: *169*). *Jerusalem* is stylistic liberty, liberty from the bondage of literary tradition, from commercial considerations, even from the requirements of minimal communication. Seldom in Western literature has the onus of communication fallen so heavily upon the reader.[4] Blake might be seen more accurately as a brilliantly cunning manipulator of his reader, rather than as a scholar of esoteric wisdom or an other-worldly artist. He is the trickster poet who has recognized that in the fallen world "deep dissimulation is the only defence an honest man has left" (49: 23).

Thus, there are two classes of reader: the reader who is not offended by Blake's enthusiasm or his other literary offenses, and the reader who is offended and is incapable of the "continual forgiveness of Sin." There is no medium state. Either the reader is forgiving or he is unforgiving: either loving and believing, or accusing and unbelieving. For the one, Blake reserves an inheritance of "Wisdom, Art, and Science" (*J* 3: *144*), for the other, "bitterest Enmity" (1: 8). This duality in approach, it should be noted, is anticipated in one of Lavater's *Aphorisms on Man*, which Blake

3. E. L. McAdam, Jr., and George Milne, eds., *Johnson's Dictionary: A Modern Selection* (New York: Random House, 1965), p. 166.

4. The modern reader should find in *Jerusalem* a challenge similar to that in Joyce's *Ulysses* or *Finnegans Wake* or Yeats's *A Vision* or Proust's *À la recherche du temps perdu*. Stanley E. Fish suggests in *Surprised by Sin* (Berkeley and Los Angeles: Univ. of California Press, 1971) that Milton may have been as manipulative as Blake. The reader of Blake should not take the communication process for granted; he should recognize that his perceptions are being controlled by the author and that his responses are at least as important as the author's style. Blake has so ordered his poem that, according to the initial responses the reader makes, it will have either opacity or translucence. But no matter how the reader begins, *Jerusalem* is never perfectly lucid; it is still the furnace of burning fires of thought.

underscored approvingly: "Who, with calm wisdom alone, imperceptibly directs the obstinacy of others, will be the most eligible friend or the most dreadful enemy" (p. 583). In order to create a poem that would be the locus both of visionary instruction for spiritual friends and of intellectual warfare for spiritual enemies, Blake constructed *Jerusalem* around two warring and diverse structures. The first of these is the sublime allegory, a visionary drama detailing Albion's fall and abrupt salvation. The second is the great obscuring veil of narrative, the system of error that, if investigated by a reasoning reader, becomes a tormenting and eternal labor of frustration.

When the reader enters *Jerusalem* in the spirit of reason and unbelief, he is confronted by a narrative structure which so completely usurps his attention that he fails to perceive the perfect fourfold drama it conceals. This narrative is composed of four elements—authorial intrusion, dramatic narration, visionary narration, and visionary definition—which represent different aspects of *Jerusalem*'s narrator. The four narrative aspects progress in complexity and obscurity until the reader is hurled into frustration and confusion. This is not to suggest, however, that the narrative is without value and meaning. Rather it is to suggest that the narrative conceals a thing of greater beauty and value and that to read *Jerusalem* it is necessary to identify the narrative and isolate it from the drama.

The simplest aspect of the narrative veil is the intrusion of Blake, the author, into the fabric of the poem.[5] This is the same voice we hear in the four prefaces, "the voice of the Bard! / Who Present, Past, & Future sees" (*SE, p. 18*). This is *Jerusalem*'s anchor in the vegetable world: the visionary eye which, though bound in this world of formlessness, is the vortex of vision out of which the poem emanates and into which the reader is drawn. The narrator stands apart from the visionary stage upon which the allegoric drama takes place; however, he is the vehicle for our perception of that action. The speeches of authorial intrusion are usually marked by the appearance of "I see," or "I hear," and by a rhetoric more penetrable than its context.

Dramatic narration is perhaps the most common of the narrative aspects and usually precedes or follows the individual speeches of the allegoric drama. Directly relating one speech of the drama to the next, or immediately explaining the movements of the visionary characters—Albion, Enitharmon, Jerusalem, Los, Vala—the lines are stage directions and reflect the visionary narrator's function as stage manager.

5. The following lines involve authorial intrusions: (1) 4: 1–5; (2) 5: 16–26; (3) 5: 35–39; (4) 9: 7–31; (5) 10: 20–21; (6) 15: 6–34; (7) 26; (8) 34: 28–29; (9) 34: 40–44; (10) 36: 58–60; (11) 41: 25–28; (12) 47: 13–18; (13) 61: 33; (14) 74: 14–57; (15) 98: 40–45; (16) 99: 5.

Visionary narration is often a direct extension of the dramatic narration. Here the narrator becomes the visionary interpreter and commentator, extending the stage directions into a discourse upon the action or into a description of the effects of the speech upon the inhabitants and landscape of the "Valley of Vision" (22: 9) within *Jerusalem*. For example, when in Plate 4 the Saviour cajoles Albion to accept his love and friendship but is rejected as the "Phantom of the over heated brain!" (4: 24), lines 33–35 are simple dramatic narration describing Albion's immediate behavior after the speech. Lines 1–15, immediately following on Plate 5, however, belong to a visionary narration describing the alteration in the landscape resulting from Albion's expressions of revenge, jealousy, and rejection.

By far the most complicated and seductive aspect of this narrative web is visionary definition, the lines that seem to be clues to an explanation of Blake's visionary system. Definition is scattered throughout the poem in different guises, often in fragmented form.[6] This strategy creates the illusion that the pieces of definition must be collected and fitted together. Blake uses a host of rhetorical ploys to achieve this illusion, such as parenthesis (5: 58–59), appositive (5: 37–38), aphorism (91: 2), analogy (32[36]: 23–24), simple equivalency (5: 34), and amplification (10: 7–16). Visionary definitions are anything but rational definitions as we know them. Rather they are indefinite descriptions of a system Blake created to save himself from enslavement. "I must Create a System, or be enslav'd by another Mans" (10: 20). And, conversely, if another man's system would have enslaved Blake, what does his system do to other men? It clearly is intended to enslave them. But by enslaving, Blake hoped to force his readers into "Striving with Systems to deliver Individuals from those Systems" (11: 5).

Visionary definitions are frequently as ambiguous and enigmatic as what they seem to define. The illusion that the visionary definitions are capable of illuminating the chaos that besets the reasoning reader constitutes one of the major errors of the reasoned approach to *Jerusalem* and is reinforced by the seductive quatrain placed at the beginning of Chapter IV:

I give you the end of a golden string,
    Only wind it into a ball:

6. In approaching *Jerusalem*, we should not equate the confusion of the scattered visionary definition with disorder and carelessness, for then we would be judging Blake's technique without taking all options into account. Besides the regular and expected kinds of order, there are other kinds of organization which it would be unfair to ignore. Random placement, for instance, is not necessarily chaos, but rather the absence of order, as darkness is the absence of light. How should Blake better illustrate his anger towards a society that has made a religion of reason than to offer these definitions in an order and manner devoid of logic and reason?

It will lead you in at Heavens gate,
  Built in Jerusalems wall.

                              (*p. 229*)

S. Foster Damon expresses the usually accepted meaning of this little poem:
"Blake scattered his clues broadcast throughout his writings. They form a
prodigious jigsaw puzzle. Pieces are missing; pieces which ought to belong
don't quite fit. Nevertheless, assembling what we can, we find that not only
does a section fit together, but that it also makes amazing good sense which
might have been obvious from the first."[7] Of course, were this true Damon's
prodigious labor would have solved the puzzle and explained the enigma.
But it did not.

The ambiguity of this quatrain is generally underestimated, and its use
in justifying the fragmented "puzzle" approach to Blake's system is questionable. Though the metaphors of piecing together a puzzle and of winding
up a ball are similar, they are far from identical. Perhaps the most crucial
difference may be realized by recalling the origin of the string metaphor in
the Theseus myth, where Ariadne shows Theseus how to escape from the
labyrinth after he has killed the Minotaur—he is to wind up the ball of
string he unwound as he entered. Traditionally, the guide gives the ball of
string to the adventurer as he enters the confusion of the labyrinth. Here,
however, Blake hands the reader the end of the string, which is unwound,
indicating that the reader is in the depths of the labyrinth already. In this
case, though, to follow the mythic parallel to its conclusion, before the reader
can begin to wind up the ball of string, he must conquer his spiritual Minotaur, the selfhood. At that point, winding up the string may, in fact, lead the
reader "in at Heavens gate, / Built in Jerusalems wall"; for he will then
be traveling in the "Spirit of Jesus" which is "continual forgiveness of Sin."
If, however, the reader does not subdue the selfhood, then the essential task
enjoined by the metaphor—the destruction of the Minotaur—is unfulfilled
and the reader succumbs to the selfhood, leaving *Jerusalem* a literary puzzle
without solution.

As we have noted before, *Jerusalem* mirrors the state of the reader; and
if the reader is still dominated by the spectral reason when he attempts to
thread his way through the verbal maze, then he will be led deeper and
deeper into the enigma, into the darkness of Blake's allegoric night. It has
been said that "the essential mission of the maze was to defend the 'Centre'
—that it was, in fact, an initiation into sanctity, immortality and absolute
reality. . . . At the same time, the labyrinth may be interpreted as an apprenticeship for the neophyte who would learn to distinguish the proper

7. *A Blake Dictionary: The Ideas and Symbols of William Blake* (Providence:
Brown Univ. Press, 1965), p. x.

path leading to the Land of the Dead."[8] Blake's poem demands just such an apprenticeship of the reader; for the reader must learn to forgive, to love, and to enter into the spirit of Jesus by throwing off selfhood. The apprenticeship ends when the reader gains spiritual maturity and perceives the infinite in all things. It is no accident that parallel with, and to the left of, this quatrain on Plate 77 are the lines, " 'Saul Saul' / 'Why persecutest thou me' " (*p. 229*). The reference to Saul of Tarsus (Acts 26: 14) is meant to provide a parallel to the reasoning and condemning reader. Saul is like the reader who, not being able to understand *Jerusalem* completely, condemns it as a flawed and defaced work of art, the product of unusual haste, or inattention, or illness. Just as Saul was overcome by the spirit of Jesus on the road to Damascus, so too the reader must be overcome, and must cast off the reasoning selfhood. In Acts 26: 18 Jesus tells Saul that he has appeared to him so that Saul may minister to the Gentiles, "To open their eyes, and to turn them from darkness to light, and from the power of Satan unto God, that they may receive forgiveness of sins, and inheritance among them which are sanctified by faith that is in me." The vision Saul experiences and the apocalypse of vision the reader experiences as he reads *Jerusalem* are analogous. In *Jerusalem* Blake strives to open the reader's eyes, to turn them from the darkness of doubt into the light of forgiveness and love. *Jerusalem* strives to turn the reader from the power of the Satanic reason to God, a balanced psychic integrity, that he may forgive Blake's rhetorical sin and receive the inheritance of "Wisdom, Science, and Art" contained in *Jerusalem.*

These four narrative constructs—visionary definition, visionary narration, dramatic narration, and authorial intrusion— conceal Blake's allegory, but they are important to the poem's sublime nature. Morton D. Paley has surveyed the background of the "sublime" in terms of Longinus and others without perceiving the word's alchemical associations.[9] Blake defines sublime allegory, in the famous Butts letter of 6 July 1803, as "Allegory address'd to the Intellectual powers, while it is altogether hidden from the Corporeal Understanding . . ." (*Letters*, p. 69). Discussing the same idea of poetry, Blake puts it yet more chemically: "What is it sets Homer, Virgil & Milton in so high a rank of Art? Why is the Bible more Entertaining & Instructive than any other book? Is it not because they are addressed to the Imagination, which is Spiritual Sensation, & but mediately to the Understanding or Reason? . . . Consider what Lord Bacon says: 'Sense sends over

8. I quote from Mircea Eliade, *Tratado de historia de las religiones,* as paraphrased by J. E. Cirlot, *A Dictionary of Symbols,* trans. Jack Sage (New York: Philosophical Library, 1962), p. 167.

9. *Energy and the Imagination: A Study of the Development of Blake's Thought* (Oxford: Clarendon Press, 1970), pp. 1–29.

to Imagination before Reason have judged, & Reason sends over to Imagination before the Decree can be acted' " (*Letters*, p. 30). In chemistry the verb "sublime" means that a substance may pass from solid to gas without passing into the intermediate liquid state. So, too, Blake is using the word. Sublime allegory is poetry that speaks to the intellectual powers without penetrating the intermediate stage of the corporeal understanding. It is poetry that is, quite literally, beyond reason. Consequently, it is best suited for dethroning reason within the reader who does not understand that the dominance of reason in his own mind prevents his entering the life of eternity. He is, thus, in his Spectre's power and is deluded as Albion is deluded. It is for this reader that Blake inscribes, in reverse writing, upon the scroll of Plate 37:

Each Man is in
  his Spectre's power
Untill the arrival
  of that hour.
When his Humanity awake
And cast his Spectre
  into the Lake.
        (p. 182)

Sublime allegory is designed to arouse the intellectual faculties by its grandly manipulative obscurity so that the individual's humanity may awake and cast off the dominance of reason. The power and terror of the sublime reside in its ability to communicate nonrational intellectual content to the intellectual faculties, thereby overcoming and bypassing that psychic agency which, in the age of reason especially, so fashioned an individual's perception of reality. Sublime poetry terrifies the reasoning mind, because it denies the centrality and dominance of the reasoning faculty. And, in this way, it threatens to disorient the reader, to overthrow reason, and to let loose the disintegrating forces of chaos.

One of the major problems in interpreting the allegoric nature of *Jerusalem* is simply seeing the allegory. The external structure Blake gives the poem, of four chapters each introduced by a preface, has little to do with its real nature. The major structural illumination comes when the reader realizes that *Jerusalem* is composed of an allegoric drama embedded in an obscuring matrix of narration.[10] The second critical task, after identifying

10. For other approaches to the structure of *Jerusalem*, see Harold Bloom, "Blake's *Jerusalem*: The Bard of Sensibility and the Form of Prophecy," *Eighteenth Century Studies*, 4 (1970), 6–20; Northrop Frye, *Fearful Symmetry: A Study of William Blake* (Princeton: Princeton Univ. Press, 1947), pp. 356–403; Karl Kiralis, "The Theme and Structure of William Blake's *Jerusalem*," in *The Divine Vision: Studies in the Poetry and Art of William Blake*, ed. Vivian de Sola Pinto (London: Victor Gollancz, 1957),

the nature of the narrative veil, is neither to define the exotic vocabulary nor to catalogue Blake's images, but rather to strip the narrative veil away from the body of the drama. Before the reader can comprehend the totality of *Jerusalem* he must, like an aggressive lover, strip away the obscuring cloak of narration and behold the exposed perfection of the visionary drama. Then, and only then, can the symbolic consummation of understanding and illumination occur. The design on Plate 99 {37} of *Jerusalem* suggests that the apocalypse of vision is like the ecstasy of consummation. The visual pun is underscored by the consuming fires that play around the united lovers.

Perhaps, the best way to begin this second critical task is to go through the poem carefully, transcribing those lines which are clearly spoken by members of Blake's allegoric cast.[11] Once this task is accomplished, the

---

pp. 141–162; Henry Lesnick, "Narrative Structure and the Antithetical Vision of *Jerusalem*," in *Blake's Visionary Forms Dramatic*, ed. David V. Erdman and John E. Grant (Princeton: Princeton Univ. Press, 1970), pp. 391–412; Edward J. Rose, "The Structure of Blake's *Jerusalem*," *Bucknell Review*, 11 (1963), 35–54; and Joanne Witke, "*Jerusalem*: A Synoptic Poem," *Comparative Literature*, 32 (1970), 265–278.

11. As clarification, I submit this formula of the transcript of the visionary drama: CHAPTER I, SCENE 1: Saviour, 4: 6–21; Albion, 4: 23–32. SCENE 2: Spectre, 7: 9–50; Los, 7: 51–8: 20; Los, 8: 30–40; Los, 10: 29–36; Spectre, 10: 37–59; Lament of Erin and the Daughters of Beulah, 11: 17–12: 4; Los, 12: 5–15. SCENE 3: Los Soliloquy, 17: 16–47; Los, 17: 59–63; The Cry of Hand and Hyle, 18: 11–35. SCENE 4: Jerusalem, 20: 5–10; Vala, 20: 12–20; Jerusalem, 20: 22–41; Albion, 21: 1–49; Vala, 22: 1–15; Albion, 22: 17–18; Jerusalem, 22: 19–24; Albion, 22: 26–32; Jerusalem, 22: 34–35; Albion, 23: 1–7; Jerusalem, 23: 9–12; Albion, 23: 16–19; Albion 23: 29—24: 60; Voice from Beulah, 25: 3–13.

CHAPTER II, SCENE 1: Albion, 28: 6–12; Spectre, 29[33]: 5–16; Albion, 29[33]: 29–34; Vala, 29[33]: 36–30[34]: 1; Albion, 30[34]: 2–16; Los, 30[34]: 23–40; The Voice from the Furnaces, 31[35]: 9–18. SCENE 2: The Eternal Ones, 32[36]: 44–49; Those in Great Eternity who contemplate on Death, 32[36]: 50–56; Los, 33[37]: 2–9; The Divine Family, 34[38]: 14–26; London, 34[38]: 30–39. SCENE 3: Los, 35[39]: 15; Albion, 35 [39]: 16–23; Los, 35[39]: 25–26; The Friends of Albion, 36[40]: 11–20; Four Zoas, 38[43]: 8–11; Los, 38[43]: 12–79; Bath, 40[45]: 3–32; Oxford, 41[46]: 10–15; Albion, 42: 9–16; Los, 42: 19–45; Albion, 42: 47–54; Spectres of the Dead, 42: 63–65; Spectres of the Dead, 42: 71–74; The Voice Divine, 43[29]: 6–26. [Though no narrative section of any length intervenes between these scenes, it is clear they are separate, for a division is indicated by the departure of the Divine Family.] SCENE 4: Enitharmon and the Spectre, 43[29]: 29–41; *Albion* [as reported by Enitharmon and the Spectre], 43[29]: 42; Enitharmon and the Spectre, 43[29]: 44–46; *Albion*, 43[29]: 47–52; Enitharmon and the Spectre, 43[29]: 53–58; *Albion*, 43[29]: 59–60; Enitharmon and the Spectre, 43[29]: 60–65; *Albion*, 43[29]: 66–71; Enitharmon and the Spectre, 43[29]: 72–82; Los, 44[30]: 21–40; Los, 45[31]: 29–38: Jerusalem, 45[31]: 45–49; Vala, 45[31]: 50–66; Erin, 48: 54—50: 17; Daughters of Beulah, 50: 24–30.

CHAPTER III, SCENE 1: Spectre, 54: 16–24; Those who disregard Mortal Things, 55: 4–5; Others said, 55: 5–16; Yet Others Said, 55: 17–18; The Divine Family, 55: 36–46; Many Conversed Saying, 55: 49–53; The Voices of Living Creatures, 55: 56–66; The Great Voice of Eternity, 55: 69. SCENE 2: [I have departed here from my usual

visionary drama will appear a perfect fourfold entity telling the double story of Albion and Los. Its sixteen scenes are divided into two cycles of eight scenes each, a Los cycle and an Albion cycle. The Albion cycle presents the fall of Albion and the resulting ruined state of *Jerusalem*, while the Los cycle details the struggle Los endures to protect the Divine Vision in time of trouble. Moreover, these two cycles are carefully interlaced in a nearly mathematical symmetry.

The Albion cycle consists of the following scenes: Chapter I, scenes 1 and 4; Chapter II, scenes 1, 3, and 4; Chapter III, scene 3; Chapter IV, scenes 1 and 4. These tell consecutively of Albion's denial of the Divine Vision, his desire for Jerusalem, his rejection of his Friends, his final collapse into death, the forgiveness of his Emanation, and his final and somewhat abrupt redemption. The Los cycle consists of a parallel sequence of scenes: Chapter I, scenes 2 and 3; Chapter II, scene 2; Chapter III, scenes 1, 2, and 4; Chapter IV, scenes 2 and 3. These portray Los's attempt to hold the forces of his vegetating and enslaving system in check, lest they imprison him as they have Albion. They depict consecutively Los's confrontation with his Spectre, his endurance of the accusations of Hand and Hyle, the first eternal conclave where Los warns Albion of his rising Spectre, the eternal conclave that finally sends Los to investigate the fallen condition of Man, his confrontation with Vala and the Sons of Albion, his confrontation with the prophecy of Gwendolen and Cambel, and finally the confrontation with

---

manner of determining what is a speech and what is not. Usually I take Blake at his word, seeing as speeches those he says are speeches. Here the speeches are well marked, though the speaker is not. I realize that these lines are repeated elsewhere when such an interpretation is not possible. The added choric effect of question and answer seems, to me, in keeping with what follows. Cf. 30[34]: 25–26.] Los, 56: 3; Daughters of Albion, 56: 3; Los, 56: 3; Daughters of Albion, 56: 4; Los, 56: 5–7; Daughters of Albion, 56: 8–10; Los, 56: 11; Daughters of Albion, 56: 12–17; Los, 56: 18–25; Daughters of Albion, 56: 26–28; Los, 56: 29–37; Daughters of Albion, 56: 39–40; Los, 56: 42–43; Great Voice of the Atlantic, 57: 8–11. SCENE 3: Song of the Lamb, 60: 10–37; Jerusalem, 60: 52–64; Divine Voice, 60: 66—61: 2; Vision of Mary and Joseph: *Mary*, 61: 4–5; *Joseph*, 61: 5–6; *Mary*, 61: 6–13; *Joseph*, 61: 14–27; Voice Among the Reapers, 61: 34–35 [Vala?]; Another Voice, 61: 36–46 [Jerusalem]; The Voice Jerusalem Hears, 61: 50—62: 1 [Saviour]; Jerusalem, 62: 2–17; Jesus, 62: 18–29. SCENE 4: Los, 63: 26–31; Vala, 64: 12–17; Los, 64: 18–24; Spectre Sons of Albion, 65: 29–55; Daughters of Albion, 67: 44–68: 9; Spectre Sons of Albion, 68: 11–70.

CHAPTER IV, SCENE 1: Jerusalem, 78: 31–80: 5; Vala, 80: 16–31. SCENE 2: Gwendolen, 80: 83—82: 9; Gwendolen, 82: 22–44; Los, 82: 81—83: 65; Daughters of Beulah, 83: 85–84: 28; Los, 85: 22–86: 32. SCENE 3: Los, 87: 3–11; Enitharmon, 87: 12–24; Los, 88: 2–15; Enitharmon, 88: 16–21; Spectre, 88: 38–43; Los, 90: 28–38; Los, 90:52–57; Los, 91: 1–30; Los, 92: 1–6; Enitharmon 92: 8–12; Los, 92: 13–27; Enitharmon, 93: 2–16; Los, 93: 18–26. SCENE 4: Brittannia, 94: 22–27; Albion, 96: 8–13; Jesus, 96: 14–16; Albion, 96; 20–22; Jesus, 96: 23–28; Albion, 96: 33–34; Albion, 97: 1–4; The Cry of the Living Creatures, 98: 46–53.

Enitharmon. In Chapters I and IV Albion controls the first and final scenes, whereas Los controls the internal ones. In Chapters II and III, however, the control of the scenes is exactly reversed. Those scenes which Albion controls in Chapter II are in the control of Los in Chapter III. Graphically, if we let A stand for the scenes Albion controls and L stand for those controlled by Los, then the pattern looks like this: ALLA / ALAA / LALL / ALLA. This is an outline of the divine allegory freed from its obscuring matrix of narration, and it is to this allegory that we should address our interpretative energies.

Like most allegories, *Jerusalem* has a cast of allegoric forms, which interact to tell a story whose meaning is metaphorically implied. It is not an allegory about the fall of man generally, but about the fall of one man in particular—the reader. The drama within *Jerusalem* details the confrontation between the intellectual forces of the reader as represented by Albion and the Sons and Daughters of Albion, and the intellectual forces of the author as represented by the Friends of Albion, the Divine Family, the Saviour, Los, the Spectre, Enitharmon, and a host of lesser characters. The artifact, the poem *Jerusalem*, in which this allegoric confrontation occurs, is represented by the characters of Jerusalem (the drama) and Vala (the narrative).[12]

Blake does not intend that these metaphorical relationships be obscured completely, and therefore he translates the hopes, desires, and commands of the preface into the allegoric confrontations of Chapter I, scenes 1 and 2. Further, the poem is designed so that the reader is forced to return repeatedly to the preface. *Jerusalem* is not a linear poem. It does not allow the reader to read easily from beginning to end. In fact, the rhetorical density of Blake's narrative web varies sharply from the relative simplicity of the authorial intrusions and prefaces to the opacity of such passages as the one detailing the building of Golgonooza (12: 21—13: 55). The effect of this variation is to place rhetorical barricades in the reader's path, forcing him to return to the first eleven plates in order to see what information he has missed that might assist him in finding his path again. To go beyond Gol-

12. There are three main groupings of speaking characters within the visionary drama: (1) Those who represent the intellectual forces of the reader: Albion, the Sons of Albion, Hand, Hyle, the Daughters of Albion, Gwendolen. (2) Those who represent the intellectual forces of the author: the Saviour, Los, Spectre, Erin, the Eternal Ones, those in Great Eternity who contemplate Death, the Divine Family, London, the Friends of Albion, the four Zoas, Bath, Oxford, Spectres of the Dead, the Voice Divine, Enitharmon, those who disregard mortal things, Voices of Living Creatures, the Great Voice of Eternity, the voice among the Reapers, the Lamb, the voice Jerusalem hears, the Great Voice of the Atlantic, Brittania, Jesus. (3) Those who represent the forces of the artifice within which the poem dwells: Jerusalem, Vala, Mary, Joseph.

gonooza without seeing the parity between the preface and scenes 1 and 2 is to be woven into the narrative deceit by Enitharmon's loom or to be caught up in the system Blake designed to destroy all systems. The barrier of 12: 21—13: 55 successfully emphasizes these crucial scenes and their relationship to the allegory.

The Saviour of Chapter I, scene 1, is the personification of the Spirit of Jesus defined in the preface on Plate 3 as "continual forgiveness of Sin." The synonyms "Jesus" and "Saviour," which provide the link from preface to poem, are underscored by the use of the phrase, "Saviours kingdom," in the same paragraph. The Saviour's kingdom is that state of mind exemplified by continual forgiveness of sin. In the second paragraph on Plate 3 Blake hopes the reader will be with him "wholly One in Jesus our Lord." Therefore, when the Saviour of Chapter I, scene 1, says, "I am in you and you in me, mutual in love divine" (4: 7), he is assuming that Albion has already become one with him, that the hope of the preface has been translated into allegoric fact in the poem. We also should respond to the Saviour's phrase, "we are One; forgiving all Evil" (4: 20), because it is almost an exact paraphrase of the notion of the author/reader becoming one in Jesus, whose primary trait is forgiveness. We can in this way relate Albion to the reader, because it is the reader, Blake hopes, who will assume the state of union in Jesus.

But Albion is not the obedient reader. He denies this union, using a phrase very similar to that in the preface, "We are not One: we are Many . . ." (4: 23). Though we may not understand at this stage how *Jerusalem* can be the reader's emanation, we should already have grasped that, if the reader and author figure in the allegory, an allegoric character bearing the poem's name should represent the poem itself, and that the poem is somehow hidden as a consequence of Albion/Reader's rejection of the Saviour.

While the first scene of Chapter I makes the main equivalencies between the allegory and its metaphorical relationships in the preface, it does not furnish us all the keys to the kingdom. Its main function is to give the attentive and obedient reader enough of the basic relationships to allow him to begin inductively constructing the pattern of the allegory. Whereas the reasoning approach to *Jerusalem*, which includes demonstration and deduction, hurls the reader into the enslavement of the system, the approach Blake seems to demand necessitates inductive leaps based upon the ability to accept as fact the outrageous claims of the preface. Reason must work in harness with faith and love to draw the fiery chariot of inspiration.

The second scene of Chapter I is not as carefully connected to the preface, but it should not require great observational skills to recognize, once the initial relationships have been established, that Los, working at his furnaces, is a good facsimile of the "God of Fire" lauded in the preface. But even without that observation few readers should pass the furious warnings without thinking they were somehow meant for them:

... As thou art now; such was he O Spectre
I know thy deceit & thy revenges, and unless thou desist
I will certainly create an eternal Hell for thee. Listen!
Be attentive! be obedient! Lo the Furnaces are ready to recieve thee.
I will break thee into shivers! ...
                                        ... if thou
Desist not from thine own will, & obey not my stern command!
                                        (8: 6–12)

These furious commands and threats, though highly amplified and allegoric, are comparable to the commands of the third paragraph in the preface. With little additional insight, Los will be seen to be another author figure and the Spectre to be like the reader. If the reader heeds these warnings, he will certainly begin to search the poetry more carefully and take the assertions of the preface more seriously. Perhaps the most difficult assertion to accept, and one of the most crucial, is contained in the last paragraph of the preface, where Blake writes: "Every word and every letter is studied and put into its fit place: the terrific numbers are reserved for the terrific parts—the mild & gentle, for the mild & gentle parts, and the prosaic, for inferior parts: all are necessary to each other" (3: *144*). But this is a test of faith, an assertion which is anathema to the reasoning reader. The reader still in his Spectre's power will attribute this assertion to Blake's over-heated rhetoric and thus will begin his progress into indefinite demonstrations. But the reader who accepts this statement, as least hypothetically, and who gives Blake a chance to prove its validity will not go unrewarded.

If the reader successfully passes the test of initiation in the preface, then he will come to see that within the allegoric drama there are two distinct cycles of events, related yet independent of each other. In the Albion cycle the allegoric fall occurs. The intellectual forces of the reader, as represented by Albion, fall from perfect communication, collapse into a state of frustrated non-communication, and suddenly regain entry into grace. Meanwhile, in the Los cycle, the forces of the author, as represented by Los and his brethren, react to the fall of Reader/Albion by fathering a system of allegoric dissimulation and obscurity designed to free individuals from systems, and they broodingly work to control the system lest the obscurity be permanent and the poem share the same fate as the spectrous reader. As a consequence, Los treads a fine line between making his allegory too opaque or making it too transparent.

Albion as reader sins and falls from perfect communication when he denies that he is one with the author. That denial casts him into the power of the Spectre and out of the Spirit of Jesus. It affirms that he is entering the reading of *Jerusalem* by the normal intellectual skills of fallen man: reason, analysis, and evaluation. When Albion/Reader sins in this manner he hides his emanation, Jerusalem (both poem and character), by being no longer able to perceive her perfection and integrity. In the fourth scene of Chapter I, when he re-enters the dramatic context, his first words are accusations:

O Vala! O Jerusalem! do you delight in my groans
You O lovely forms, you have prepared my death-cup:
The disease of Shame covers me from head to feet: I have no hope . . .
                                        (21: 1–3)

But even before Albion himself enters the drama, his sons, Hand and Hyle, have been accusing *Jerusalem* of whoredom and corruption:

Cast! Cast ye Jerusalem forth! The Shadow of delusions!
The Harlot daughter! Mother of pity and dishonourable forgiveness
Our Father Albions sin and shame! But father now no more!
Nor sons! nor hateful peace & love, nor soft complacencies
With transgressors meeting in brotherhood around the table . . .
                                        (18: 11–15)

Albion/Reader, unable to relate to *Jerusalem* in any reasoning and analytical manner, turns in frustration and anger to accusation and condemnation. Albion, sinning, has fallen into shame and doubt; shame that the poem resists the reader's skill and doubt that there is any value to the poem. Albion/Reader finds himself frustrated, unable to penetrate the narrative veil he is struggling to comprehend. "I have erred! I am ashamed! and will never return more . . ." (23: 16). His last conscious volley of accusation ends with the curse of Albion (23: 38–40). This curse marks the lower limit of Albion's fall, for in it he curses not the poem he cannot understand, not the author who created it, but the suppressed Humanity both seek to liberate.[13]

13. Since Manhood is the state of humanness, Humanity is its synonym. The suffixes "-ity" and "-hood" have approximately the same meaning. Albion feels that his selfhood is being destroyed, that his ability to control his perceptions successfully is being eroded, and that he finally may have to admit his frailty and seek assistance, as he does in the last scene of Chapter IV. When he does admit that he is no longer self-sufficient, that he needs help to rule his state of being, the Humanity is aroused, and Albion is saved from Eternal Death. But while still in this state of collapse, the selfhood, raging at its defeat, wishes that defeat would also result in the defeat of the Humanity— "death," in the allegory, translates well in this reading of intellectual warfare into "defeat." Albion does not realize that in wars of the intellect, thoughts are themselves "swift arrows" and deadly. Then Jesus, as the Divine Humanity, is also slain. As Jesus says in Matthew 25: 40: "Inasmuch as ye have done it unto one of the least of these my brethren, ye have done it unto me." To wish that death and annihilation were the

> . . . Therefore O Manhood, if thou art aught
> But a meer Phantasy, hear dying Albions Curse!
> May God who dwells in this dark Ulro & voidness, vengeance take,
> And draw thee down into this Abyss of sorrow and torture,
> Like me thy Victim. O that Death & Annihilation were the same!
>
> (23: 36–40)

From this point onward in the poem Albion/Reader is in delusion. He pays homage to the reasoning Spectre in Chapter II, scene 1, and accepts Vala/Narrative as the only beauty worth perceiving (cf. 29[33]: 48—30 [34]: 16). Los/Author makes one final effort to rouse Albion. In scene 3 of Chapter II he calls forth the "Friends of the Giant Albion" in a situation which is the reverse of *Everyman*, the morality play. Here, like Everyman, Albion/Reader asks, "Will none accompany me in my death?" (35[39]: 19). But Albion rejects the assistance of all those who offer advice and help, such as London, who offers to give himself for Albion (34[38]: 30–39), and flees into eternal death unheeding. Others step forth, yet Albion does not want their assistance. Albion/Reader is unlike Everyman, who sought companionship from aspects of this vegetable world, became disillusioned with them, and finally accepted as his companion, Good Deeds, the aspect of his spiritual life, to accompany him to death. Instead Albion/Reader rejects the approach of spiritual friends and accepts the council of spiritual enemies (cf. 42: 1), an act that leads to his utter frustration:

> . . . O thou deceitful friend
> Worshipping mercy & beholding thy friend in such affliction:
> Los! thou now discoverest thy turpitude to the heavens.
> I demand righteousness & justice. O thou ingratitude!
> Give me my Emanations back[,] food for my dying soul!
> My daughters are harlots! my sons are accursed before me.
> Enitharmon is my daughter: accursed with a fathers curse!
> O! I have utterly been wasted! I have given my daughters to devils . . .
>
> (42: 9–16)

Los/Author responds to the accusations of Albion/Reader's frustration at being unable, through the arts of demonstration and unbelief, to comprehend the poem by saying, "I have innocence to defend and ignorance to instruct: / I have no time for seeming; and little arts of compliment . . ." (42: 26–27). Los/Author in his own cycle, then, carries on the twin tasks of defending the poem from the attacks of spectrous readers and of instructing the fallen reader in the arts of perception. To do this Los first

---

same is to wish that, because the body must die, the soul should also die, or to interpret the allegory, because the reasoning critic cannot understand *Jerusalem*, it must be incomprehensible.

casts out his Spectre—divides from him—and subjugates him. Since the Spectre represents reason and vengeance, these attributes of the author are controverted and made to work with the inspired method of the poet's humanity.

The author's problem in *Jerusalem*, that of Blake and Los and the Saviour, is very complicated. How shall he teach an unloving, reasoning audience to love, obey, and have faith without seeming either too gentle, pitying, and benign, or too revengeful, angry, and impatient? Yoking his reasoning faculty with inspiration, Los/Author creates a great system which is represented by his emanation, Enitharmon. This system, like all systems, is designed to enslave fallen Albion/Reader and to protect the wisdom and art of *Jerusalem* from his accusations and condemnations. Thus Los/Author's Reason or Spectre always works with Enitharmon's system to clothe Albion/Reader in the garment of error. The allies of Enitharmon are identifiable by their trade—they all are weavers and all, except the Spectre, are female.[14] They all contribute to the generation of Albion, to the

14. Blake has utilized an ancient strategy in the construction of his allegory of intellectual warfare. The obscuring forces are represented by females because:

... Was it not said of old
Set your Son before a man & he shall take you & your sons
For slaves: but set your Daughter before a man & she
Shall make him & his sons & daughters your slaves for ever!
(45[31]: 51–54)

But there are several allegoric females of seemingly inconsistent intent. Vala, the emanation of Luvah (love, here turned to hate), the allegoric representative of the narrative web, is only as aggressive as the reader makes her. To attack the narration, analyzing vocabulary, allusion, and myth and condemning it for its stylistic deviation, is to invest Vala with great strength. To recognize the narrative, though, as a deceit and a veil to be initially dismissed and ripped away from the drama, is to neutralize her, is to cease attacking her and to accept her as she is. Then Jerusalem is freed, the reader perceives the drama's perfection and brings on the apocalypse of vision which cleanses his doors of vision.

Enitharmon, the emanation of Los (the inspired poetic imagination) is also part of this motif. She says to Los: "You are Albions Victim, he has set his Daughter in your path." Los is Albion's victim if the reader never reaches the perception of *Jerusalem*'s double form of narrative web and visionary drama. But if the reader grasps this requirement and enters into love, forgiveness, and friendship, then—

The Poets Song draws to its period & Enitharmon is no more.
For if he be that Albion I can never weave him in my Looms
But when he touches the first fibrous thread, like filmy dew
My Looms will be no more & I annihilate vanish for ever[.]
(92: 8–11)

Read "reader" for Albion and "the delusion" for Enitharmon, and the allegory translates well.

confining of the spiritual being of Albion/Reader within the web/veil/
cloak of flesh, the trademark of mortal and fallen man. Thus enclosed in
death, his only salvation is to hurl himself into the furnaces of Los/Author
to have his portals of perception cleansed by the corroding fires of thought
and to have consumed the garment of error he has donned. To accept the
system, whose indefinite explanation is contained within the narrative of
Jerusalem, and to work within its confines is to remain in the world of
death. That is exactly what the spectre within each man desires, for it en-
thrones reason and demonstration and unbelief that are in control of perception. Thus Albion/Reader is deluded if his perceptions (the Daughters
of Albion) are directed by reason. His responses (the Sons of Albion) then
become deranged and lead him further into error and death.

The majority of Los/Author's energy is consumed in the struggle to
control the system that has emanated from him lest the slavery it directs be
permanent. As we see in scene 3 of Chapter IV, Enitharmon refuses Los/
Author's dominion and threatens to hurl Los into vegetable death along
with her victim, Albion. If communication and salvation were never to be
the lot of Albion/Reader, then Los/Author must fail in his attempt to save
Albion from his death to spiritual reality. And then Los/Author must subside into being "mad Blake" who wrote that unintelligible poem, *Jerusalem.*
Jerusalem, in this way, would itself become a forgotten artifact of beauty
and oddity, fit only for collectors of literary curiosities.

Los/Author's reply to this threat asserts his control over Enitharmon:

... Man cannot unite with Man but by their Emanations
Which stand both Male & Female at the Gates of each Humanity
How then can I ever again be united as Man with Man
While thou my Emanation refusest my Fibres of dominion?
                    (88: 10–13)

We return once again to the desire voiced by Blake in the preface and by
the Saviour in scene 1, the desire for union in the Spirit of Jesus; and it is
within this context that the most complex requirement of the poem exists.
If Los/Author must control his emanation to facilitate communication, it
follows that Albion/Reader must control his emanation Jerusalem/*Jerusalem* as well. In Chapter I, scene 4, Jerusalem talks about a time gone by
when Albion and Jerusalem were in harmony:

O Vala what is Sin? that thou shudderest and weepest
At sight of thy once lov'd Jerusalem! ...
          ... O! if I have Sinned
Forgive & pity me! O! unfold thy Veil in mercy & love ...
When Albion rent thy beautiful net of gold and silver twine;
Thou hadst woven it with art, thou hadst caught me in the bands
Of love; thou refusedst to let me go: Albion beheld thy beauty

Beautiful thro' our Love's comeliness, beautiful thro' pity.
The Veil shone with thy brightness in the eyes of Albion,
Because it inclosd pity & love; because we lov'd one-another!
Albion lov'd thee! he rent thy Veil! he embrac'd thee! he lov'd thee!
Astonish'd at his beauty & perfection, thou forgavest his furious love:
I redounded from Albions bosom in my virgin loveliness.
The Lamb of God reciev'd me in his arms he smil'd upon us:
He made me his Bride & Wife: he gave thee to Albion.
Then was a time of love: O why is it passed away!

(20: 22–41)

Once Albion loved, and Jerusalem was loved, and Vala was embraced. Once Albion/Reader saw Vala's (narrative's) beauty and understood its great complexity and compassionate design of mercy and love. Identifying the system, the reader/lover separated it from Jerusalem (the drama) and loved it, studied it, and delighted in its wisdom. At such a time *Jerusalem* becomes controlled by, not controller of, Albion: as poem, *Jerusalem* becomes the conscious creation of Albion/Reader, because he has drastically altered his perception of its form. In this epiphanic moment, the union of Los/Author and Albion/Reader "in Jesus our Lord, who is the God of Fire and Lord of Love" is effected. The allegoric figure of Albion at this point, and only at this point, becomes a double allegoric form. He is both Albion/Reader who creates a fallen Jerusalem/*Jerusalem* by his reasoning perceptions of demonstration and the arts of unbelief, and Albion/Author whose fury threatens to destroy *Jerusalem* through the arts of reason, by building an enslaving system of occult references and obscure historical allusion. Albion/Author is English Blake, the generated Eternal, whose historical context and personal experience threaten to overcome the Spirit of Jesus, the Divine Humanity, which resides in every mortal breast.

Los/Author seeks to overcome both the fact of the generated reader's death to the perception of eternity and the possibility that the sublime obscurity the bard cultivates in *Jerusalem* may not succeed in overcoming that visionary lethargy. The bard must at once ensure that *Jerusalem* survives as a viable literary work, which will encourage the reader to labor at the furnaces of Los, and ensure that those readers who do not enter in forgiveness and faith will endure throughout a frustrating, though alluring, labyrinth. This labyrinthine poem is rooted both in Blake's disappointment with his contemporary audience and in his hope that one day an audience would receive him as he desired, transforming itself by a new awareness of its own infinite nature. This aesthetic creates within *Jerusalem* a cunning and magnificently ordered rhetorical screen to separate the sheep from the goats, the saved from the damned, the forgiving, faithful readers from the accusing, rational ones. Consequently, Blake's rhetorical apocalypse is more perfectly structured than rational men have acknowledged.

Blake's aesthetic is epitomized in a pair of aphorisms, one by Lavater and one by Blake himself. Blake underlined Lavater's Aphorism 157 and punctuated it with double exclamation marks: "Say not you know another entirely, till you have divided an inheritance with him" (*p. 576*). Blake's own aphoristic comment upon the art of knowing reads: "He who has sufferd you to impose on him knows you" (*MHH* 9:42). These two aphorisms mark two sides of the relationship Blake has entered into within *Jerusalem*. Lavater's is written from the point of view of one who has something to give, as Blake does in his gift of prophecy, while Blake's is written from the point of view of one who receives something, as the honest reader of *Jerusalem* undoubtedly will. Blake has a great inheritance of visionary wisdom, art, and science that he invites the honest reader to share with him. And Blake is determined to know the kind of reader with whom he shares it. Consequently, he has ensured that only those who allow him to impose upon them will share his enlightenment, his expanded vision.

The faith Blake vested in a hypothetical audience of the future is cause for amazement. He entered into the Herculean labor of producing his magnificent graphic-literary artifact during those years when his reputation had sunk into obscurity, and when he was depending upon patrons for his livelihood. More amazing still is the internal strength of conviction with which he pursued such an aesthetic of imposition in the face of nearly universal neglect and commercial failure. Blake was not merely writing poetry of great beauty; he, in fact, sacrificed those vegetable traits we call beauty for another order of beauty altogether—an eternal, sublime beauty, capable of restoring the fallen reader to a new and expanded vision. His gift to his fellow men is not majestic words or bold histrionics; it is a cataclysm of vision, a most extraordinary education.

The Structures of Jerusalem

STUART CURRAN

*The greater part of the city is built upon a high hill, which rises from an
extensive plain . . . . It is divided into seven rings or huge circles . . . , and the
way from one to the other of these is by four streets and through four gates, that
look towards the four points of the compasse.*

— Tommaso Campanella

To assert from the start that *Jerusalem* is the most lucid of Blake's major
prophecies would appear an act of critical impudence were it not for the
manifest obscurities of the unfinished *Four Zoas* and of the Bard's Song
that in *Milton* stands like a Covering Cherub before the entrance to the
sublime paradise of the Felpham garden. But even if one considers *Jerusalem* apart from its predecessors, its consistent artistic control must be
acknowledged. Difficult it may be, but no sophisticated reader confesses
himself lost in its midst, unable to comprehend the plate he is reading. In
addition to the range and subtlety of the epic style, in *Jerusalem* Blake attains a clarity and a sense of driving purpose beyond his previous efforts.
Yet to acknowledge Blake's clarity is not to suggest that *Jerusalem* is an
easy poem. As all its readers comprehend, it is as great an intellectual
challenge as its predecessors; and it is that because, though the reader is
generally sure of the immediate ground he treads, the path before and after
may be swept with mists. That, one might submit, is at once a structural
enigma and a triumph of art.

The architecture of *Jerusalem* has elicited a number of learned and
ingenious analyses, but has yet to be satisfactorily explained. For that task
must necessarily dissipate the mists of obscurity through which we view
this epic, and most attempts have merely cast a light upon them. Karl
Kiralis has suggested a development paralleling the three ages of man,

329

from childhood to adulthood to old age, from Judaism to Deism to Christianity.[1] Objecting to the order of this progression, Edward J. Rose sees each chapter dominated by one of the four Zoas and the entire work organized according to fourfold patterns such as the parts of the day and the seasons.[2] These interpretations probably stem from Northrop Frye's view of the poem as biblical history, tracing the fall, its effects, redemption, and apocalypse.[3] Henry Lesnick has recently concentrated with perception on the symbolic values in Blake's designs, but he does not descend into the text to support his thesis that the poem offers dual perspectives, the historical and the eternal.[4]

The tendency in accounting for the structure of *Jerusalem* is to play for big stakes and not fret about the pennies. To look closely at any of the structures suggested is to find them imposed on a generally resistant poem. Frye's scheme, for instance, implies that the sacrificial orgy at Stonehenge represents the redemptive crucifixion of Christ, even though events darken considerably thereafter and even though the slaying of Luvah has been recounted a half-dozen times previously. The movement from childhood to adulthood to old age is not parallel to the unhistorical sequence of Judaism, Deism, and Christianity, as Kiralis suggests; and, if anything, as Rose rightly points out, the movement of *Jerusalem* would be the reverse, from senility to rebirth. But then Rose's Zoas are recalcitrant to his will: Tharmas, who should dominate Chapter I, is mentioned there only in the catalogue of Golgonooza; Luvah, who should be the principal Zoa of Chapter II, becomes the sensationally martyred major figure of Chapter III. Beyond these overly rigid demarcations, Rose's diurnal and seasonal rotation raises fundamental questions about Blake's art. Should we unquestioningly assume that Blake, who constantly proclaimed the imagination's freedom from nature, would so easily resort to cyclical patterns to inform a work demanding our independence from them? Can we even assume after the recasting of time values in *Milton* that Blake would organize his structure around a temporal progression, even one more religious than historical, as Frye would have it? Not only does Blake's abandonment of the chrono-

1. "The Theme and Structure of William Blake's *Jerusalem*," in *The Divine Vision: Studies in the Poetry and Art of William Blake*, ed. Vivian de Sola Pinto (London: Victor Gollancz, 1957), pp. 141–162.

2. "The Structure of Blake's *Jerusalem*," *Bucknell Review*, 11 (1963), 35–54.

3. *Fearful Symmetry: A Study of William Blake* (Princeton: Princeton Univ. Press, 1947), pp. 357–358.

4. "Narrative Structure and the Antithetical Vision of *Jerusalem*," in *Blake's Visionary Forms Dramatic*, ed. David V. Erdman and John E. Grant (Princeton: Princeton Univ. Press, 1970), pp. 391–421.

logical scheme of *The Four Zoas* for the blinding revelation of *Milton* suggest a philosophical and aesthetic denial of the commonsense view of
history, but the minute particulars of *Jerusalem* strongly imply a determined affront to that same view. As must be obvious, the most perceptive
comments on *Jerusalem* have proceeded from sensitive critical intuition
which is almost always grandly general; sometimes it is grandly wrong.
Yet, no consideration of the structure of *Jerusalem* that ignores its specific
details for the sake of clarity can long support its validity. Such a stance is
as specious as Thel's belief that she can attain vision without submitting to
the welter of experience. Worst of all, the partial truths of generality restrict critical efforts to realize the whole and leave us as far as ever from
comprehending the artistic form of Blake's greatest achievement. Harold
Bloom, in his commentary to the Erdman edition, succinctly states the
critic's task: "the problem may be only that the poem has not had enough
accurate and close readers as yet; in time it may seem no more and no less
difficult in structure than *The Faerie Queene* or *The Prelude,* works curiously and wonderfully put together but each on a basis not so discursive as
it may first appear."[5]

Let us begin, as Blake would have it, *in medias res.* When Luvah is
sacrificed at the center of Chapter III, it should surprise no attentive reader:
he has been slain twice before in the progress of the poem. In the first
chapter Albion calls upon Vala to perform upon him the same savage act
she directs in Chapter III:

But come O Vala with knife & cup: drain my blood
To the last drop!   then hide me in thy Scarlet Tabernacle
For I see Luvah whom I slew.

(22: 29–31)

Shortly thereafter Albion, confronting the enormity of the sacrificial
morality he has taught his children, curses his "Manhood," which is Luvah,
then in shocked remorse confesses to druidic rites.

What have I said? What have I done? O all-powerful Human Words!
You recoil back upon me in the blood of the Lamb slain in his Children.
Two bleeding Contraries equally true, are his Witnesses against me
We reared mighty Stones: we danced naked around them . . .

(24: 1–4)

5. *The Poetry and Prose of William Blake,* ed. David V. Erdman (Garden City,
N.Y.: Doubleday, 1970), p. 843. Bloom here suggests that the Book of Ezekiel is the
structural model for *Jerusalem,* a thesis expanded in "Blake's *Jerusalem*: The Bard of
Sensibility and the Form of Prophecy," in his book *The Ringers in the Tower: Studies
in Romantic Tradition* (Chicago: Univ. of Chicago Press, 1971), pp. 65–79. Bloom's
intent, however, is not to establish a strict structural analogy with Ezekiel, but to

The dead Luvah is, of course, a figure for Christ, and at the conclusion of Albion's monologue, which except for the ritual lament of Beulah ends the chapter, Albion discerns the similarity:

Dost thou appear before me who liest dead in Luvahs Sepulcher
Dost thou forgive me!   thou who wast Dead & art Alive?
                                    (24: 57–58)

It would appear more than lightly paradoxical that Albion calls upon Vala to slay him for the murder of Luvah in exactly the terms in which Luvah is to be slain two chapters later, and then implies that Luvah had been slain in that manner himself. However enigmatic it is, it is clear through Blake's reiterations at the end of Chapter I that Luvah is dead.

In the second chapter we discover the Daughters of Albion "divid[ing] Luvah into three Bodies" (30: 46) as Los constricts Reuben's senses. Vala later confesses her fear that Luvah will be slain, and almost immediately we perceive the Sons of Albion in conflict with him.

Hark! the mingling cries of Luvah with the Sons of Albion
Hark! & Record the terrible wonder!   that the Punisher
Mingles with his Victims Spectre, enslaved and tormented
To him whom he has murderd, bound in vengeance & enmity.
                                    (47: 13–16)

Is it merely a coincidence that in both these instances—at the end of Chapter I and the end of Chapter II—Albion utters the same words and performs the same act?

Look not so merciful upon me O thou Slain Lamb of God
I die! I die in thy arms tho Hope is banishd from me.
                                    (24: 59–60)

Shudder not, but Write, & the hand of God will assist you!
Therefore I write Albions last words.   Hope is banish'd from me.

These were his last words, and the merciful Saviour in his arms
Reciev'd him . . .
                                    (47: 17—48: 2)

These parallel double deaths suggest that we must consider the recurring sacrifice of Luvah within the larger context of Albion's repeated deaths. After his initial rejection of the Divine Vision at the beginning of *Jerusalem* Albion does not directly figure until Plate 19. Los first describes him as "Sleeping" (5: 30) but then, as he surveys his responsibilities, claims that

identify the prophetic mode responsible for a number of devices and dramatic relationships in Blake's epic.

"Albion is dead! his Emanation is divided from him!" (12: 6). And in Plate 15, where Blake's voice returns to set Los's labors within the visionary perspective, he claims to "see Albion sitting upon his Rock in the first Winter" (15: 30) and asserts that "Albion sat in Eternal Death" (15: 33): "Albion groans in the deep slumbers of Death upon his Rock" (16: 27). Moreover, in the designs for Plates 9, 14, and 19, Albion is pictured as dead. He re-enters the poem in conflict with his Sons, with Jerusalem, and with Vala, and his hopelessness drives him to the death that concludes Chapter I. He returns, of course, to the consternation of the uninitiated reader, in the fifth line of Chapter II, but quickly attempts suicide. As the efforts of his Friends to save him fail, he is at last left in direct confrontation with Los, who opens his furnaces to him: Albion "turn'd sick! his soul died within him" (42: 4). By the end of the chapter he is again dead. Yet once more at the beginning of the third chapter Albion appears, now driving the Plow of Nations and fleeing from the Divine Vision as always. The episode is dealt with briefly, but in an order reversing normal expectations: first, as Los explains how Albion fell beneath the plow (56: 35–36), then as narrative exposition (57: 12–16), with Albion fleeing, being plowed under, and seeking the Rock of Ages where he reposes until Plate 95. It is, one presumes, the same rock on which Blake envisioned Albion sitting in Plate 15, as the plow was that over which Albion recounted Vala's extending her power in Plate 30.

Conversant readers may find this extended rehearsal of Albion's deaths a belaboring of the obvious, and yet it is remarkable how many of the obvious problems of *Jerusalem* have been avoided in favor of attaching a logical consistency to the recondite. Repeated death, needless to say, violates human capacities and epic logic. Yet, puzzling as the pattern here traced may be, it does have the virtue of simplicity. In each of the first three chapters Luvah is sacrificed; in each Albion dies. In Chapter IV both Luvah and Albion are restored to life. Only by stretching the meaning of the word beyond its customary associations can such a pattern be called narrative.

Furthermore, if this pattern is, as it would seem to be, intentionally prominent, it is not unique. Much of the meaning of *Jerusalem* is lodged in the parallels and contrasts Blake develops both in text and design. The epic repetition evident in the concluding plates of Chapters I and II is a constant device in the poem, culminating in the moment of regeneration at the end:

As the Sun & Moon lead forward the Visions of Heaven & Earth
England who is Brittannia enterd Albions bosom rejoicing.
                                        (95: 21–22; cf. 96: 1–2)

Previous commentators, notably Edward J. Rose and Henry Lesnick, have delineated some of the clear contrasts between the final plates of Chapters II and IV. Erin's long and moving lament for the fallen world, "Where Fish & Bird & Beast & Man & Tree & Metal & Stone / Live by Devouring" (50: 6–7), is transfigured into a universal hymn of joy in which "All Human Forms [are] Identified even Tree Metal Earth & Stone" (99: 1). The parallel between the concluding plates of Chapters I and II must be, for many new readers, the first indication of a structuring force in the epic, and the ritualized laments of these plates differ only in the greater length and depth of the second. The conclusion of Chapter III also has its clear precursor, in the organization of Golgonooza and of the counties in the British Isles that Blake places at the center of Chapter I. With this parallel, however, one must immediately acknowledge that, though a strong bipartite structure is suggested, the chapters cannot be assumed to be absolute units: structural patterns may cut across the main divisions of the epic.

If no utterly consistent pattern is to be discovered in a structure of balanced chapters (and to expect one is to underestimate Blake's multiform purposes in *Jerusalem*), it would profit us to ignore the chapter divisions for the moment and inquire into other possible units of structure. As Frye advanced and George Mills Harper elaborated, in Blake's late works four is a concept whose antithesis is three.[6] These numbers roughly represent the eternal and the fallen. At the end of each of *Jerusalem*'s four chapters Christ the Eternal is invoked. But if we divide the poem into three parts, we find ourselves confronting climactic symbols of the fallen state. In Plate 35 Albion repulses the Divine Vision and rushes to his expected suicide within the Gates of Los at Tyburn, the English Golgotha. In Plates 66–67 at a second place of sacrifice, Stonehenge, Luvah is crucified.[7] As we have gathered from Chapter I, Albion's despondency arises from his having slain Luvah. The repetition of the act by his Sons and Daughters not only emphasizes a degenerate existence as the continuing creation of

6. See Frye, *Fearful Symmetry*, pp. 368–369, and Harper, "The Divine Tetrad in Blake's *Jerusalem*," in *William Blake: Essays for S. Foster Damon*, ed. Alvin H. Rosenfeld (Providence: Brown Univ. Press, 1969), pp. 235–255.

7. Blake's rearrangement of the plates for Chapter II, which occurs in two copies and has been followed by Keynes, is a vexing question that deserves a complete analysis never accorded it. If that is manifestly beyond the scope of this essay, the fact of the rearrangement must affect any conclusions about the structure of Chapter II. Significantly, the revision does not greatly alter the basic divisions of the original that I cite. Blake transformed material from late in the dramatic sequence to its beginning and then, apparently dissatisfied with his attempt at sharper juxtapositions of events, returned to the original sequence. This testifies to the dramatic, rather than a logical or narrative, ordering of events in the poem. In respect to the climax of the first third, the rearrangement emphasizes the binding of Reuben's senses (Plate 34 [30]) rather than Albion's attempted suicide. Clearly, the restriction of man's sensual nature is a

man's perverted will, but underscores man's struggle with Luvah as his principal dilemma. And yet, if this three-part division, which operates as counterpoint to the chapter units, does add to our understanding of the structural rhythm of *Jerusalem*, the interplay is insufficient in itself to represent the outstanding peculiarities of the epic's development. As the spectacular drama of Luvah's sacrifice leads a reader to see the tripartite division, the curious fragmentation of Chapter I would suggest an expansion of that division.

Jerusalem is by design a relatively simple poem until the beginning of Plate 18, when we depart from the grand perspective that has witnessed the building of Golgonooza and the organization of the universe to confront an infernal council scene, a parody of Book II of *Paradise Lost*, in which the Sons of Albion squabble for power and banish Jerusalem. The disparity between the two parts of Chapter I is actually stronger than that between Chapters I and II: clearly Blake has forced a structural period. Should we divide the tripartite structure, however, the initially inconsistent resolves within a balance of six equal parts. An introductory section, Plates 1–17, outlines the basic themes, tensions, and perspectives of the poem; the second section, beginning with the council of the Sons of Albion and ending with Albion's attempted suicide (Plates 18–35), centers on Albion's assertion of moral law and his horror at its effects; in the third part, concluding with Erin's elegiac lament, we watch a concerted attempt to save Albion collapse in successive failures; in the fourth division the principles of a woefully fallen humanity culminate in the sacrifice of Luvah in Plates 66–67; the fifth section slowly builds toward the internecine warfare of the Sons and Daughters of Albion, issuing in the transformation of Hand and Hyle (Plate 82) and the Daughters' appeal to Los for salvation (Plate 84); and the final section, Plates 84–100, delineates how Los transfigures universal destruction and fear into apocalypse. Such a balanced division allows us to retain the major triad wrought by climactic acts of death, as well as the strong break at the end of Chapter II. At the same time, it furnishes a rationale for the rupture in Chapter I and structurally supports the obscure but crucial importance of Plates 84–85.

Still, such a division does not represent the immediate experience of reading *Jerusalem*. To balance the work in four, in three, or in six divisions is to view *Jerusalem* from distinct points of reference combining clarity and symbolic progression. But to read the poem is to be involved in a crescendo of turmoil, of contradiction, of seemingly spontaneous changes

---

major motif throughout the epic: the binding of Reuben is a more austere version of the bloody crucifixion of Luvah in Plates 66–67. Thus, if the original sequence stresses two distinct but complexly related events symbolic of man's fallen nature, the revision accentuates variations of the essential destructive act.

of course. As I have argued elsewhere, the model for this four-book epic is Milton's *Paradise Regained*, whose epic mode is one of dialogue.[8] The reader of *Jerusalem* occupies the center of a constantly shifting dialectic: between Blake and his vision, Los and his Spectre or Emanation, Vala and Jerusalem, Albion and Jerusalem, the Sons and the Daughters of Albion, and so on. This is the underlying source of the poem's confusion, and any structural analysis must be capable of expressing this basic characteristic. Numerology, one must recognize, is easily susceptible to over-manipulation; and yet it is necessary to pursue such divisions as we have noted further if we are to fit the immediate reality within its larger patterns.

The dialectical basis of *Jerusalem* is symbolically the same as that of *Paradise Regained*: the antithesis of Christ and Satan, as Blake openly suggests in the lyric that begins Chapter IV. The divisions supporting the large design of the poem, when transferred into each chapter, outline this dialectic. Roughly speaking, each chapter is susceptible of a division into four and into three parts: if we attend to the tripartite, we confront various manifestations of the Satanic; if we emphasize the quadripartite we encounter exemplars of the eternal vision which is Christ. In Chapter I Plates 7–8 introduce the battle between Los and his Spectre which will recur later; in 17–18 we are introduced to the Sons of Albion. In contrast, both Blake and Los assert the vision motivating their labors in Plate 5; the creation of Beulah is represented in Plate 11 and the forging of Golgonooza begins on Plate 12; the Friends of Albion and Jerusalem enter the poem on Plate 19; and both Christ and Beulah come forth to evidence their love for Albion in Plates 24–25. The three stresses on the fallen world in Chapter II occur in "To the Jews," Plate 27, where the Spectre is identified as Satanic, in Albion's flight from the Divine Vision, Plate 35, and in Albion's instructing his Spectre to destroy Los in the great confrontation of Plate 42. To divide this chapter into four parts is to encounter the Divine Vision in Plate 31, the Friends of Albion and four Zoas in Plates 37–39, the revelation of the Divine Vision in Plate 43, and the prayers of Erin and Beulah on Plates 49–50. Again, the prose and lyric of "To the Deists" (Plate 52) centers on the causes for our fallen state; Plate 60 represents both the beginning of the druidic emphasis of Chapter III and, in the long lament of Jerusalem, reveals her insanity and her doubt of the Divine Vision; Plates 66–67 have been previously cited as enacting the bloody sacrifice of Luvah, as representing the Sons and Daughters of Albion reduced to a state of savagery. Once again, the contrast is manifest. In Plate 55 we witness the extended

8. "The Mental Pinnacle: *Paradise Regained* and the Romantic Four-Book Epic," in *Calm of Mind: Tercentenary Essays on Paradise Regained and Samson Agonistes in Honor of John S. Diekhoff*, ed. J. A. Wittreich, Jr. (Cleveland: Press of Case Western Reserve Univ., 1971), esp. pp. 145–155.

debate of the Eternals and their election of the Seven Eyes of God; in Plates 61–62 the Divine Vision descends to comfort Jerusalem and erase her doubts; Plate 69 ends the druidic sequence with a revelation of the contrasting life of eternity; and at the end of the chapter Rahab is at last revealed and Jesus breaks the fallen cycle of history. The tripartite structure of Chapter IV lays stress on the false and devouring religion of Caiaphas in "To the Christians" (Plate 77), the terrible fury of the demonic Hand in Plate 84, and either the battle between Los and his Spectre in Plate 91 or Enitharmon's attempt to preserve her integrity against Los, the final confrontation, in Plate 93. The fourfold accents fall on the self-defeat of the Daughters of Albion and Los's consequent sense of his eternal powers in Plates 80–82, the rapturous hymn to Jerusalem and description of the triumphant Los on Plate 86, the ending of time on Plate 94, and the attainment of the eschaton on Plate 99 {37}. That these divisions are not mathematically exact does not diminish their value for distinguishing the rhythms of *Jerusalem*. The analysis demonstrates that the horrors of man's fallen state, so fully documented as to seem the principal substance of *Jerusalem*, are consistently balanced by the revelation of eternity struggling with all its powers to redeem the degenerate humanity. However much the course of the dialectic alters, the underlying pattern remains: the contention of Christ and Satan for the soul of man.

A further structural division derives from this, and after the preceding distinctions its validity should be obvious. Plate 50, like Plate 99, is an absolute division, the end of a dramatic act that begins not so much with Plate 27, the inception of Chapter II, as with Plate 18. Similarly the movements of Chapter III cross the boundary of Chapter IV and are not turned back until the Daughters of Albion seek Los's protection in Plate 84. As Plates 18–50 and 51–83 constitute sequences, so do Plates 1–17 and 84–100. Indeed, one might suggest that between Plates 18 and 83 we are elaborating the basic conflicts enumerated in Plates 1–17 in order to understand how we can translate the imaginative organization of human reality, Golgonooza, into the eternal organization whose lines begin to form in Plate 84. The unified historical structure of Six Thousand Years, which Los is said to have formed in Plate 85, is this symbolic vision of human history achieved in the central two-thirds of *Jerusalem*. These central plates, 18–83, constitute a prolonged parenthesis in the eternal order, as does human life, naturalized and imprisoned within a fallen conception of reality. But paradoxically, to structure the world of Albion, the effort of Plates 18–83, is to illuminate the flaw in the foundation of Golgonooza, so that the world of Los (Plates 1–17, 84–100) may be regenerated with Albion.

A final structural pattern, cutting across the other patterns but at the same time through points of contact rendering them more emphatic, lends cohesiveness and context to the complementary structures of *Jerusalem*. The cohesiveness is eschatological; the context the Book of Revelation. In a major prophetic poem one would, of course, expect allusions to Revelation, but Blake recalls as well its movement through seven visions, stressing their general character in multiples of fourteen. *Jerusalem* begins, like the Book of Revelation, with Christ's appearance to his scribe. As John's initial task is to examine the churches of the earth, Blake begins by outlining the nature of the fallen and visionary worlds, climaxed by his survey of Golgonooza, the city of art. This unit concludes with Plate 14, where Blake originally intended to end the first chapter. John's second vision concentrates on the judgment of God; Blake's concentration on human judgment is epitomized in Plate 28 with a description of the Tree of Moral Virtue, which man has substituted for the Tree of Life and which is responsible for the suicidal and sacrificial urges that dominate the ensuing plates. In John's third vision, of the seven angels with their trumpets, God allows the separation of the wicked and faithful: now "the court which is without the temple . . . is given unto the Gentiles: and the holy city shall they tread underfoot forty and two months" (11:2). Not only does the confrontation between Albion and Los in Plate 42 recall this numerically, but in Los's firm defiance of Albion and his Sons it similarly testifies to the power with which God has armed the faithful. The weak in faith, however, cannot keep their vigil: in Plate 42 the Friends of Albion, despairing, give in to the false security of Rahab. (It is worth noting that neither Plate 28 nor Plate 42 was affected by the alternative ordering Blake attempted in Chapter II, an indication of their importance to a larger structural pattern.) In John's fourth vision the church is beset by a dragon and beasts, and the Lamb of God appears: Blake suggests a similar juxtaposition of apocalyptic contrasts in the election of the Seven Eyes of God in Plate 55 and Los's attack on the Female Will (the Great Whore is carried by the Beast with seven heads and ten horns) in Plate 56. John's fifth vision, of the plagues attendant upon God's wrath, is balanced by Blake's depiction of the wine-presses of warfare and sacrifice on earth: in Plate 70 the Sons and Daughters of Albion aggregate in Hand and Rahab, types of the Antichrist and Whore of Babylon, allowing Blake to undertake the catalogue of the fallen world that ends Chapter III. God's judgment on Babylon and the appearance of Christ for battle comprise John's sixth vision, transformed by Blake into the self-destructive power play of the Daughters of Albion that provokes the voracious Hand to turn upon them. Once again united in Rahab, the Daughters beseech Los for salvation, effecting the turning point in the epic. Here in Plate 84 Los is, like Christ, at last victorious. John's final vision, of the great battle and of Jerusalem descending, corresponds to Los's hymn to Jerusalem and to his leading the regenerate Albion to victory and union with his Emanation. The Antichrist's defeat occurs in Plate 98. Thus, though *Jerusalem* can hardly be conceived of as a simple revision of the Revelation of John, it establishes strong structural analogies with its predecessor.[9]

To summarize, then, Jerusalem discloses the following seven structures: a primary structure of four divisions, obviously linked by calls to various classes of readers; a two-part structure delineating the marked contrast between Ulro and Eden; a three-part structure whose pivots are climactic representations of the fallen state; a threefold and a fourfold division within each chapter stressing the dialectical mode of the poem; a sixfold division emphasizing the continuity of major events; a second three-part structure, derived from the sixfold, which surrounds the central two-thirds of the work, the world of Albion, with the perspective of Los's visionary labor; and a sevenfold structure stressing the poem's genre as epic prophecy and recalling its heritage within the tradition of Christian apocalypse. That such interrelated structures can be compatible should be obvious from Blake's exemplum, the multistructured *Paradise Lost*, which also distorts normal chronology through the imposition of an eternal perspective.[10] Yet if Blake did look to *Paradise Lost* for artistic instruction, *Jerusalem* is far more complex and consequently more radical in its structural innovations. From a two-dimensional viewpoint it could be best depicted in reference to Renaissance charts of the cosmos or zodiac in which the great circle envelops a series of intersecting arcs of complementary circles. To attempt a

9. So involved a matter as the relationship of the Book of Revelation to Blake's achievement in *Jerusalem* can only be lightly sketched here: it deserves detailed study like that accorded *Paradise Lost* by Michael Fixler ("The Apocalypse within *Paradise Lost*," in *New Essays on Paradise Lost*, ed. Thomas Kranidas [Berkeley and Los Angeles: Univ. of California Press, 1969], pp. 131–178). It is evident that Blake positions certain events and descriptions to correspond with analogues in Revelation: so the escape and report of Enitharmon and Los's Spectre on Albion's interior state recall the two witnesses of Revelation 11. The identification of Rahab at the end of Chapter III is exactly analogous with Christ's revelation of the Great Whore, even to the same words, and Los's hymn to Jerusalem is John's vision rhapsodized and humanized. But just as obvious as these parallels are altered contexts, revisions, even parodies. The twenty-four elders around the throne of God can be contrasted with the twenty-four Friends of Albion whose good intentions make their failure even more disastrous or (structurally apposite) with the parodic assembly of the Sons of Albion in Plate 18.

10. It is, of course, true that multiple structures invest *Paradise Regained* as well, though in the second epic Milton seems consciously to make them subtle and implicit rather than immediate and unmistakable to the reader as in *Paradise Lost*. See John T. Shawcross, "The Balanced Structure of *Paradise Lost*," *Studies in Philology*, 62 (1965), 696–718.

three-dimensional perspective would require the imaginative grasp of Shelley, picturing the exuberant harmony of the regenerated Spirit of the Earth in *Prometheus Unbound*, Act IV. To borrow his happy phrase, the structure of *Jerusalem* is comprised of "intertranspicuous spheres."

To identify the patterns of *Jerusalem*, even to suggest the form in which they coexist, is not to elucidate the purpose for which Blake organizes so involved a structure. And it is that purpose which has so plagued the poem's commentators. The foregoing analysis would seem at least to imply that Blake is attempting to serve a variety of purposes within the context of a synoptic form. Yet, if the several principles of structure here identified enlarge the concerns and shape the outlines of *Jerusalem*, they are nonetheless framed by the four chapters into which Blake molded his poem. To understand how these function we must return not alone to the classes of readers to whom they are addressed, nor to the four Zoas nor the four elements nor the four seasons, though Blake may possibly have wished such connections to be drawn; we must return to the events, if they may be called that, which inform the chapters. As was noted earlier, both Albion and Luvah die during each of the first three chapters. In each of those chapters both Vala and Jerusalem lament their state. In each there is a catalogue of the organization of the British Isles; in each an extended analogy—social, political, geographical—with the organization of Palestine. The parallels, which could be multiplied almost at will, are obvious sinews of the structure, and the reader is just as obviously intended to grasp their similarities. But to what end? Is there an essential difference between the laments or the deaths of Chapters I and III? The question, in other words, is whether these parallels are set as marking-stones on a narrative progression whereby the reader may more surely discern the logical development of events. If they were, they would presumably alleviate exactly those problems that most trouble our comprehension. More likely, the parallels stress differences in degree. The death of Luvah is scarcely alluded to in Chapter I, but becomes a central focus of Chapter III. Conversely, Albion's death forms the primary substance of Chapter II, but recurs in a mere five lines in Chapter III.

Were one to subtract from the text all those descriptions and events repeated elsewhere in a parallel or contrasting form, little of significance would remain in the poem. Except for the apocalyptic concluding plates there are few distinct events in *Jerusalem*, which is why the reader feels himself caught in a labyrinth, fated to return again and again to the same landmarks without discovering an egress. And that, of course, must be Blake's point. There is no narrative progression whatsoever in the first three chapters of *Jerusalem* because, from Blake's point of view, there is no narrative progression in the life of man. The "silly Greek and Latin

slaves of the Sword" (*M* 1: *94*) who destroyed Troy and Carthage transferred their compulsions to the medieval madmen who spent centuries
trying to reclaim Jerusalem by force. Since Jerusalem is an imaginative
attitude, no amount of heroic action will bring the actor—or the spectator
—within her walls.

For Blake, to discard narrative as the *primum mobile* in the epic is only
to follow the course marked by Milton in *Paradise Regained*. And like
Milton, Blake substitutes for narrative a heroic enlargement of comprehension. Los greatly resembles Milton's Christ, but more significant than
similarities are the differences. Christ has the fortunate capacity to expand
his consciousness logically, beginning with an assessment of basic needs
and continuing through a gradually enlarging sense of priorities until he
realizes his divinity. Los struggles in the dark, and even the most puzzled
reader must sense the near tragic dimensions of Blake's hero who knows
what must be done but cannot find the means to achieve it. Los's striving is
for comprehension, and progression in Blake's epic derives from the slowly
maturing consolidation of error by which Los defines the logic of man's
fallen state. What Los consolidates, significantly enough, is archetypes, and
the underlying structure of *Jerusalem* is a single archetypal pattern successively repeated until Los can fathom the symbolic meaning of its "Universal Attributes" (90: 32) and use it to transfigure the fallen into the
regenerated. The mind expands within like a spiral that at last encompasses
the universe.

A recent commentator on *Jerusalem*, Joan Witke, has registered the profound, if wholly unsupported, intuition that the four chapters of *Jerusalem*
should be read in terms of the four gospels; and she helpfully adduces a
tradition of the respective audiences for the gospels corresponding to
Blake's classes of readers.[11] To go further and try to determine how each of
Blake's chapters recapitulates one of the gospels, however, is to muse Blake
with the Daughters of Memory rather than the Daughters of Inspiration. A
rewriting of the gospels as structural basis for an epic poem is obviously
in accord with Blake's conception of the Christian vision as the true heroic
subject. But Blake's method departs as sharply from the apostolic narrative
as from that of orthodox writers of epic. To Blake the crucial drama of
Christ's life covers the briefest of spans: the judgment, agony, crucifixion,

11. *"Jerusalem*: A Synoptic Poem," *Comparative Literature*, 32 (1970), 265–278. A
further attempt at defining the movement of *Jerusalem*—Anne K. Mellor, "The Human
Form Divine and the Structure of Blake's *Jerusalem*," *Studies in English Literature*
11 (1971), 595–620—sees the four chapters as respectively comprehending the Human
Form Divine Albion rejects, and the abuses of the body, of the mind, and of the
imagination. Although the inadequacies of previous commentary are admirably exposed, this study, pressing a thesis that is totally unconvincing, is generally weak in
evidence and impressionistic in approach.

and resurrection.[12] These compose the archetypal morality play Blake rehearses throughout *Jerusalem*.

Following the brief invocation, Christ's call to man's soul and man's refusal to heed it are the immediate events introducing *Jerusalem*. The subsequent poem proceeds to expand upon the dynamics of this confrontation. Albion's spurning of Christ is a moral judgment resulting in crucifixion, symbolizing man's commitment to his own spiritual death. The repeated sacrifice of Luvah is analogous; and, as we concentrate our vision upon it in the third chapter, we perceive that spiritual death is itself synonymous with viewing Christ as a fertility god, to be sacrificed to the powers of the natural cycle. But the judgment and death of Luvah is not singular, but microcosmic. The death of Albion is its result, the logical next step in the necessitarian world created by man's degenerate mind. Albion stands self-condemned and flees to death as a last refuge. The chain-reaction implicates the Sons and Daughters of Albion who, having succumbed to the religion of nature which is death, turn upon one another a suicidal fury born of frustration. Although these are separate acts linked in a causal relationship, they also represent permutations of a single act which is the crucifixion of Christ. And that itself is the archetypal symbol of man's inescapable fate as a natural being. As Blake continually refocuses his poem, the repeated laments of Albion and of his children demand our compassion. Faced with the necessity of death, they cannot live their lives free of its menace. "The passage through / Eternal Death" (*J* 4: 1–2) is long and inescapable, distorting, perverting, and debasing man. It undermines any security he attains and, continually reducing him to the material with its specious appearance of stability, effectively destroys his liberty. In man's struggle with death, whoever breaks the barriers of materialism, egocentricity, or morality that man has set against death appears most to betray him. That agent, whether in his naturalized form of sexuality or in his spiritual form of imaginative desire, is Luvah.

Although the development of *Jerusalem* is achieved through variations on an archetypal dramatic relationship—the dialectic between the Divine Vision and fallen man—and although the same fundamental events are repeated again and again, the emphasis does change. If we return to the climactic points dividing the threefold structure, Albion's suicide and Luvah's sacrifice, we can easily discern the shift in perspective. The central two-thirds of *Jerusalem* is governed by the distinction invoked by Los when he rallies the Zoas to his aid in order to protect the divine virtues

12. One must, of course, recognize that Christ's ministry is analogous to the labors of Los and of Blake, and that the birth is of great symbolic importance to the epic; but the major emphasis of the epic's dramatic encounters is on the final days of Christ. There are also a number of omissions, notably the baptism.

against man's wish "That they may be condemnd by Law & the Lamb of God be slain" (38: 30) ! Plates 18 through 50 concentrate on the judgment of Christ within each man; Plates 51 through 84, on his crucifixion. Albion's imposition of a code of moral law to save him from mutability and impulse produces the moral vacuum, Ulro, he finds himself imprisoned within. Much of the second chapter concerns Los's attempt to free him from this rigid morality. And the failure of the Friends of Albion, the cathedral and university cities which must be intended to represent humanistic achievements, forces us to understand their limitations when confronted with an elementary disease of the soul. Those institutions reflecting man's most humane impulses are impotent to save a society that has rejected their motives. They remain outside, islands whose commerce has been severed with the mainland. The urgency with which Los, and after him Erin and Beulah, appeal to the Divine Saviour reflects their sense of the inadequacy of all salvation but that stirring in the depths of man's own perverted soul. Yet that salvation is itself dependent on man's having first plunged to the bottom of the Ulro he has embraced. He must experience his own crucifixion repeatedly until he comprehends that his defenses against death have walled him apart from life, that the logical outcome of his craving for "a solid without fluctuation" (*U* 4: 10) is death. Thus we discover ourselves forced from the relatively static despondency of Plates 18–50 into the raging warfare of Plates 51–84. The culmination of this section is the Daughters' feminist rejection of male supremacy and their subsequent attempt to reduce the male to the dependency of an infant. For the sake of survival, they would project into a social norm the symbol of the Virgin Mother with her child, which in Los's celebration of Mary's adultery to Jerusalem (Plates 60–62) is seen to be a perverse misconception of Vala's. Indeed, the demand for virginity that issues in the crisis of Plates 82–84 is introduced at the very start of this central two-thirds of the epic when Albion and his Sons attack Jerusalem as a harlot and lodge their faith in Vala as the paragon of virtuous chastity. Plates 82–84 achieve the turning point in Los's long struggle with Ulro because at last that struggle has bred a perfect antithesis of the archetype. Gwendolen and Cambel assume the role of the Virgin Mary, casting Hand and Hyle as dependent Christ; but what they create is exactly the opposite of their desires, a universal force of reduction. Hyle becomes the winding worm of death, devouring a life that refuses generation; and Hand becomes a monster, identified in 84: 20–25 as the Antichrist.

At this point Los has at last codified the Manichean antithesis implicit in Albion's original rejection of the Divine Vision. To see the forces of death in all their dimensions is necessary before Los can discover the source from which they emanate. The antithesis has been strongly marked and defined with increasing explicitness in the prefatory plates to each chapter. From the necessity of accepting the "continual forgiveness of Sin," which is Blake's definition of Christ in "To the Public," the poet proceeds to survey his own London world and identify himself as the murderer of Christ in the lyric of "To the Jews," to return to the medieval crisis of church and corrupt state in the "Monk of Charlemaine" lyric of "To the Deists," and to retreat further in time to confront the archetype which has motivated his epic in the vision of Caiaphas and Christ in "To the Christians." Caiaphas' "Wheel of Religion" (77: 13), proceeding "From west to east against the current of / Creation" (77: 4–5), depends on a fundamental driving force in all men, that which arises at the end of Plate 5 "Westward, a black Horror" (5: 68), introducing Los's Spectre to *Jerusalem*.[13] The Antichrist in every man is his Selfhood that would destroy the world to preserve its integrity. The momentous realization Los comes to in Plate 91, recapitulating Blake's in "To the Jews," is his own responsibility for the evil he has labored against so valiantly. And in his annihilation of the Spectre, Los at last releases the visionary potential of man from the barriers erected to enclose it.

This heroic achievement releases the archetype from its fallen bondage, and in the final plates we at last perceive its underlying truth. The most powerful of the ironies that suffuse *Jerusalem* is that the repeated acts by which it is structured do not end with the apocalypse. The judgment and crucifixion recur once more and indeed forever, but transfigured, as Christ gives himself for Albion's salvation and Albion rushes to defend his intercessor from the forces of the Antichrist. The crucifixion of Luvah by which his heart was ripped away is elevated to the arrows of love that "Open the hidden Heart in Wars of mutual Benevolence Wars of Love" (97: 14). The acts by which Albion and his children committed themselves to Ulro were the essential acts of their release, which underscores the truth of Los's celebratory exclamation:

O holy Generation [*Image*] of regeneration!
O point of mutual forgiveness between Enemies!
Birthplace of the Lamb of God incomprehensible!
                              (7: 65–67)

As an epic *Jerusalem* assembles a cast of mythological human attributes all of whom are aspects of one another and whose continuing readjustments

13. A similar analogy can be drawn between Enitharmon, who "divided in pain, / Eastward toward the Starry Wheels" (5: 67–68), and Jerusalem's flight to the east. Such analogies reinforce one's conviction that the early plates of Chapter I contain in microcosm the subsequent development of the epic, comprising a center from which the visionary mind reaches out to comprehend the particulars of human life and history.

take place independent of an external space-time continuum. Its form departs radically from the customary epic depiction of a culture's organizing mythology: rather it analyzes what to Blake is *the* mythology of Western man—"the Divine- / Humanity, who is the only General and Universal Form" to plumb the basic truths of its symbolism. The symbolism is itself pure in its integrity, as capable of perversion as of total revelation. Los's purpose as epic protagonist is to force the symbolic to reveal its truth, and if it cannot be attained directly, then man must achieve it negatively. Only in Plate 85, when the Daughters of Albion accept Gwendolen's Falsehood as offering the solitary escape from the rapacious Hand, do we comprehend the truth of Los's assertion, that he labors on "That he who will not defend Truth, may be compelld to defend / A Lie" (9: 29–30), thus "Giving a body to Falshood that it may be cast off for ever" (12: 13).[14] The structure accompanying that heroic labor represents it exactly, for the Eternals have no sense of the fallen progression of time: Golgonooza is in existence (5: 29) before it is created; Albion is dead before he dies. The visionary mind, creator of epic perspectives and epic deeds, shares the capacity of the Eternals viewing man's lapsed universe:

> listning to the weeping clods till we
> Contract or Expand Space at will: or if we raise ourselves
> Upon the chariots of the morning. Contracting or Expanding Time!
> (55: 43–45)

The intertranspicuous structures of *Jerusalem* continually repeat the rhythms of a fundamental dramatic event, demanding that we hold in perfect equilibrium within our minds the archetypal act, the potentials of its variation, and an expanding consciousness of its symbolic meaning. Where the mind contracts, it perceives a microcosmic dialectic; where it expands, it discovers the cosmos of all human history. If it strains that expansion to the breaking point, it transfigures the myth and creates an infinity of realized human potential. The apocalyptic plates of *Jerusalem*'s conclusion, so extraordinary in conveying the visionary's release from the fallen struggle, are the reward of the mental efforts the preceding plates have demanded of both poet and reader. But paradoxically, that struggle is not waged to move history inexorably to a perfect communitarian anarchy: its purpose is to free man from that very sense of history, from the logical succession of events that constitutes narrative. Blake's epic purpose is not reformation,

---

14. This principle, or a variation of it, is reiterated at crucial moments in *Jerusalem*. In Plate 66, during the sacrifice of Luvah, the indirect release of humanity is enunciated: "He who will not comingle in Love, must be adjoind by Hate" (66: 56); and just before the Daughters of Albion turn to Los for protection a similar statement is made: "he who will not bend to Love must be subdud by Fear" (81: 16).

but conversion. The structure he created to encompass it is not so much a sublime allegory as it is the more and more detailed analysis of *the* sublime allegory of Christ's life and death. Blake's maturest poem is in structure a painting, to be viewed in its parts and as a whole in the same imaginative act. To read it, as a Christian would demand, with our whole heart and soul, is to create from the static form a *tableau vivante*. Only once in *Jerusalem* does Blake epitomize his meaning simply and totally upon a single plate. On the full-page illumination of Plate 76 {36}, Albion, stretching his arms wide in unconscious sympathy, contemplates the crucified Christ. The structure of *Jerusalem* continually returns its participants— Albion, Los, Blake, the reader—to this essential symbol until our contemplation attains the visionary penetration that transforms the pathos of suffering humanity into the sublime of willed self-annihilation. In this sudden, imaginative act, which rolls stones aside and breaks seals from sacred gates, we liberate Christ, Jerusalem, and their exiled race from bondage.

Yet if we, as readers, achieve our heroism in a revelatory flash, we are acutely conscious of the sustained imaginative act, emphasized by Blake's repeated instrusions pleading for comprehension, that the artist has undertaken in order to liberate his art from the bondage of false traditions. *Jerusalem* is Blake's greatest poem because, though not his last, it is ultimate, an eschaton to which the complexities of his vision surge and in which at last they can be resolved. The analogy with man's yearning for the heavenly city Jerusalem is not only pronounced but complete. Jerusalem is perfect form. What man must do to regain his divine heritage, Blake must accomplish to realize his masterpiece. If history, warfare, determinist theology, materialism, and social hierarchies proceed from a single source, from it too comes a literature of narrative progression; and the artist must create a form capable of encompassing, of comprehending, all of these without surrendering to them. Blake's foundation is Christ, the elemental symbol, and upon that simplest of bases he erects an edifice of multiple structures, enlarging, contracting, interacting, continually shifting in their combinations of focus—truly "Visionary forms dramatic" (98: 28). For us to attempt to define the whole from the parts is to engage in a dynamic of mental expansion unique even in the history of that most comprehensive form, the epic. What Blake sought and achieved in *Jerusalem* was a literary form of true Gothic dimensions. In divorcing himself from the classical (and neoclassical) epic, represented by Homer and Virgil, Blake left his own discerning commentary on his greatest poem:

Grecian is Mathematic Form Gothic is Living Form Mathematic Form is Eternal in the Reasoning Memory. Living Form is Eternal Existence.

("On Virgil," *p. 267*)

Delivering Jerusalem

K A R L   K R O E B E R

Albion hears not Jerusalem's Song of Mildness & Clarity!
Albion contracts throughout a thousand Classrooms, dividing
Into Druidic Commentators; his fibres of Learning
Englobe to a labyrinth, concealing the naked Vision:
A Spectre of Prophecy to destroy Prophecy!

I am tempted to parody Blake's most beautiful, and once neglected, prophecy, because today the poem needs to be delivered not from oblivion but from its interpreters. Although erudite and ingenious exegeses sink eventually to inoffensive footnotes, until sedimentation is complete we lose the illumination of *Jerusalem*'s graphic clarity. And because *Jerusalem* is not a prophecy of our age, it could provide a valuable perspective upon present intellectual culture and its origins. But we miss this perspective if we reduce the poem to proto-twentieth-century literary mythicism. To Northrop Frye, for example, there is no significant difference between *Jerusalem* and *Finnegans Wake*: "In Blake the quest contains the cycle and in Joyce the cycle contains the quest, but there is the same challenge to the reader, and the same rewards for him."[1] Although Frye does admit that there are differences between Joyce and Blake, his desire to identify them is revealed by the fuzziness of the adjectives by which he strains to conflate their work: "Blake's work is middle-class, nineteenth-century, moral, romantic, sentimental, and fervently rhetorical, and these were the cultural qualities that Joyce ... most deeply loved and appreciated."[2]

1. Northrop Frye, "Quest and Cycle in *Finnegans Wake*," *Fables of Identity* (New York: Harcourt, Brace, 1963), p. 264.
2. Ibid., p. 256. To prevent misunderstanding, I state here unequivocally that I am

If Blake and Joyce are to be joined by so blurry a term as "middle-class," it is fair to insist that the former is "blue collar" and the latter "white collar." *A Portrait of the Artist*, let alone Richard Ellmann's comprehensive biography, testifies that the taste and the life-style of Dublin's most celebrated exile had nothing in common with those of Protestant English Blake, who served a full apprenticeship, worked with his hands every day of his life, and never left the ambiance of London. Radical differences between the personalities and life histories of Joyce and Blake suggest how surprising it would be were *Jerusalem* and *Finnegans Wake* much alike. There are, of course, similarities. Both are "night visions" and mytho-poetic; and both appear so complex as to be fully comprehensible only to specialists. But the "difficulty" of each work is entirely distinct, as may be illustrated by a contrast of brief but representative passages.

There's many's the icepolled globetopper is haunted by the hottest spot under his equator like Ramrod, the meaty hunter, always jaeger for a thrust.[3]

Against this, one may set Blake's contrast between Regenerated and Generated love.

Embraces are Cominglings: from the Head even to the Feet;
And not a pompous High Priest entering by a Secret Place.
                                (*J* 69: 43–44)

The passages differ as do shield and spear. Joyce presents us an en-wrought circular surface. Puns, portmanteau words, language-crossings ("jaeger"), all are whorls of a decorative design. The sentence leaves us at the same emotional-perceptual level at which we began. Our pleasure lies in moving through an arabesque which endlessly turns back into itself rather than carrying us on to new domains of language and observation. It is no denigration of Joyce's linguistic skill to observe that the verbal richness of *Finnegans Wake* is based almost exclusively on what are, broadly, puns. The fun of the book (and why it ought to be read aloud) lies in Joyce's skill at utilizing foreign words, invented and newly combined words, and misspellings and mispronunciations to create a continuous intellectual interplay among all verbal elements as verbal elements. The total interplaying, however, implies circularity; a pun is a

---

an admirer of Professor Frye. Like all students of Blake, I am indebted not only to the wisdom of his criticism but also to the enthusiasm he has infused into Blake scholarship for more than a quarter of a century. It happens, however, that I believe Professor Frye to be mistaken on the point at issue in this essay, a point of some importance.

3. James Joyce, *Finnegans Wake*, 3rd ed. (London: Faber and Faber, 1968), p. 435, ll. 12–14.

self-enclosed system. *Finnegans Wake* can end appropriately only with the words which begin it.

It is a fair guess that, for Blake, Joyce's style would epitomize what he castigated as "the same dull round," self-imprisonment within an externalized mechanism. Punning is a verbal turning of "wheels without wheels"; "globetopper," for example, is controlled by the "external" reference of "globetrotter." *Jerusalem*'s language thrusts through the verbal surfaces in which Joyce delights; for it is a spare, efficient weapon of attack, fashioned out of a belief that the sharpest linguistic effect results from a continuous, dynamic connection with the nonlinguistic. The prophecy contains little verbal or rhetorical ingenuity. The two lines I have quoted are typical in being declarative exposition. The "joke" of the second line (especially interesting because systematized etymology was scarcely developed in Blake's time) depends upon the history of each word *in itself*, verbal wheels *within* wheels. Thus "pompous" contains within itself the root meaning of "inflated," and "Secret" its original connection to "separate," "put apart." Blake doubtless learned to utilize word histories (particularly of latinate terms) from Milton. But his exploitation of etymology owes as much to his conviction that wisdom comes from penetrating to the inner workings of phenomena and to his impulse to link the verbal to the nonverbal, words to gestures, acts of imagination to bodily processes. The "point" of line 44, Plate 69, depends on a pictorial rather than an auditory identification of a stately display of public ritual with the "secret" of a phallus entering a vagina. The quotation epitomizes the style of *Jerusalem*: minimal Joycean phonic "play," but persistent identification of intellectual with visceral, psychic with physical, linguistic with pictorial.

The thrust of Blake's verse is anti-paradigmatic.[4] Insofar as his identification of sexual intercourse and institutionalized religion delineates a "pattern," the pattern is delineated to be broken. What we now know, the "truth" of the identification, is to be superseded by what we have not yet known, embraces that are comminglings from the head even to the feet. The purpose of *Jerusalem* is to help us reject the kind of "archetypal" truth exposed in line 44, to see something beyond the recurrent patterning of fallen existence.

Blake's poetry is uniquely graphic. No one today would deny that the pictures and ornamentations of *Jerusalem* are integral to its meaning. But the poetry as poetry also is "graphic." This pictorial quality makes the

4. I have borrowed the terms "paradigmatic" and "syntagmatic" from linguistics. I recommend G. N. Leech's essay, "Linguistics and the Figures of Rhetoric," in *Essays on Style and Language*, ed. Roger Fowler (London: Routledge and Kegan Paul, 1966), pp. 135–156, as illustrating the applicability of this categorization to literary analyses.

verse resistant to the favorite methods of contemporary criticism, which
tend to be narrowly specialized. Frye's *Anatomy of Criticism*, for instance,
is of small use to an art historian. All of Frye's basic terms (*mythos*, for
example) are derived from and are applicable to the sequentiality of literary
art and are not intended to elucidate graphic modes. But *Jerusalem*'s poetry
adheres to visual as well as auditory constraints; its "freedom" is freedom
from restrictive regulation by a single aesthetic mode. *Jerusalem*'s poetry,
literally engraved words, is itself a kind of composite art which is to a
degree distorted by conventional literary analysis. For illustration I cite
Plate 99 in its entirety.

All Human Forms identified even Tree Metal Earth & Stone. all
Human Forms identified, living going forth & returning wearied
Into the Planetary lives of Years Months Days & Hours reposing
And then Awaking into his Bosom in the life of Immortality.

And I heard the Name of their Emanations they are named Jerusalem.

These lines are difficult to scan, first, because they are long. Psychologists
have discovered that most people can perceive six like elements in a perceptual field as six items but have difficulty apprehending seven, and only
a few can apprehend as many as eight in a single perceptual act. Blake's
lines all contain at least seven feet; they are difficult for most of us to apprehend as metrical unities. And, as Blake warns in his prefatory note on
his versification, he has freed himself not merely from the bondage of
rhyme but also from the bondage of Miltonic blank verse. Blake's verse is
"free," for his theme is freedom, just as the difficult metrical unity of each
line is appropriate to his central purpose, to enable us to break through the
limitations of conventionalized perception, to expand our powers of apprehension so that we will not end where we began.

What free verse is free from is a predictable pattern of line rhythm and
length. Scansion of one line of free verse does not provide a reliable guide
for scanning the subsequent line. Free verse fits "graphic" poetry, because
patterns of graphic composition are free in analogous fashion. Repeated or
corresponding linear elements in a picture are not fitted to a "prede-
termined" sequentiality of form, simply because drawing is not a temporal
art, as is poetry or music.

In Plate 99, moreover, no word "stands for" or "represents" anything
other than itself, just as in the poem as a whole Albion does not represent,
say, mankind. Albion does not play the role of Everyman; Albion *is* man's
uniting humanness. On every level Blake's style is anti-archetypal, anti-
paradigmatic. He does not urge us to "imitate" Christ, but, rather, to recognize—to see—that Christ is within each of us, individually. He urges us
not to accept any given pattern of existence but to realize the free creative-

ness of energy by which we should organize our existence. Actual existence, true reality, is contrary to the illusory patterning of being which is, in fact, evidence of our fallen condition. *Jerusalem*, therefore, is not cyclical but repetitive.[5] Throughout the poem Blake repeats words, phrases, lines, groups of lines, not to mention syntactic patterns and rhetorical structures. Analogously, Los is always and everywhere in the poem Los. He has no other names, no other titles, and his occupation scarcely admits of variations. The style of *Jerusalem* (both graphically and poetically) is not that of allusive complexity, not of baroque richness, but of classical austerity, reiterating simple, primal features.[6]

In Plate 99, for instance, one observes astonishing repetitiveness, even to the placing of ampersands. The last word of line 1 and the first three of line 2 repeat the opening four words of the plate (so that the first line opens and closes with "all," this, I think, for dramatic juxtaposition with the final word on the plate, "Jerusalem"—one who is all). The last half of line 1 and the last half of line 3 are parallel lists; the sequence of "living," "returning," "reposing," "Awaking," is made forceful by grammatical parallelism; and not only are there participial forms in each of the first four lines, but each contains a single more-than-trisyllabic word, "identified," of course, appearing in both lines 1 and 2. As these few observations make clear, repetition enables Blake to establish strong contrasts without recourse either to overtly unusual syntactic arrangements or to spectacular metaphors. Thus the final line of Plate 99 is powerful in part because in it, for the first time in the plate, we encounter a personal subject and conjugated verbs. The final line, furthermore, contains a potent because unobtrusive syntactic reversal, what a modern linguist might be tempted to call a transformational dramatization. The portion of the line following the caesura is passive voice, present tense, with a plural subject, whereas the opening phrase is active, past, with a singular subject; and its object, the noun "Name," is transformed into the verb "named" in the second part of the line. This reversal within grammatical operations gives vitality to

---

5. The length of the prophecy in part is a consequence of Blake's "redundant" style. Many of *Jerusalem*'s lines could be omitted without distorting the fundamental "story line" (as is true of the *Iliad*), although the poem's aesthetic quality would be destroyed. Excising many passages (I am tempted to say *any*) from *Finnegans Wake* would ruin the structural unity of the book, in large measure because its allusiveness is highly articulated.

6. Blake's style is indubitably to be associated with what some art historians call "linearism," a later eighteenth-century anti-Rococo style, of which Blake's friend Flaxman was an important practitioner. Robert Rosenblum's *Transformations in Late Eighteenth Century Art* (Princeton: Princeton Univ. Press, 1967) treats this subject and is essential to any balanced understanding of Blake's poetry as well as his engraving.

a sentence which appears—superficially—to be flatly prosaic. The reversal, moreover, embodies the primary macrofunction of Plate 99: here, at last, the condition of true, Regenerated reality is attained, a condition in which time, activity and passivity, individuality and collectiveness, as we have known them in Generation, are transcended.

There is no such point, no Blakean Regeneration, in *Finnegans Wake*, which concludes by beginning again; and this feature of macroscopic structure is reflected in the microstructure of subordinate passages.[7] The rich variety of Joyce's language creates circular correspondences, cycles being appropriate for the rendering of archetypal, that is, recurrent, patterns. *Jerusalem*, however, moves inward to a point of transformation. Moving in to transformation is reflected in the microstructure of the poem's verses, for example, by their syntagmatic organization; that is, what counts is each word in itself, and the dominant relation of any given word is to other words in the sentence or line in which it appears. This organization explains Blake's preference for simple, undeformed syntax. And the Joycean paradigmatic pun—e.g., Ramrod-Nimrod, "Nimrod" not actually appearing in the text but being mentally substituted for "Ramrod" by the reader— must play an insignificant role in *Jerusalem*, which moves steadily forward, like fine calligraphy. Like good calligraphy, Blake's poetry is clear and consistent, an aid rather than an impediment to *progressive* understanding. Just as a gifted calligrapher always forms his letters in the same fashion (so a "g" always looks like a "g" and does not need to be "interpreted" as a variant of a "g" pattern), so Blake's poetry is consistent, that is, repetitious. Surprisingly few passages allude to other passages. In *Jerusalem* allusion is replaced by simple repetition, which explains, for example, why Albion "dies" so often.[8]

Modern critics assume that poetry is in essence metaphoric. Yet there are relatively few metaphors in *Jerusalem*. I suggest that this paucity of metaphor is integral to Blake's pictorial, calligraphic, syntagmatic verse.

---

7. A succint and perceptive description of the style of *Finnegans Wake* is provided by Robert M. Adams, *James Joyce: Common Sense and Beyond* (New York: Random House, 1968), pp. 172–216. Adams specifies exactly the premise upon which *Finnegans Wake*'s style is founded: "It is a condition of the world as Joyce sees it that nothing happens or, if something does, its happening is part of a cycle which has neither meaning nor direction, only an immemorial shape. *Plus ça change, plus c'est la même chose*" (p. 185).

8. Reiteration permits fluidity of structure; to a degree plates can be rearranged because re-ordering does not upset patterns of allusion. Analogously, it is simple repetition, most apparent to us in formulae, which permits the fluidity of oral epics. Repetition (especially of numerical features) as well as vividly pictorial language are, of course, among the outstanding features of the immediate and dominant "source" for *Jerusalem*—the Book of Revelation.

Metaphor customarily consists in some violation of a common, expectable pattern of semantic meanings. Blake prefers figures which emphasize, over-determine, a psychologist might say, expectable patterns of language-use and so make us aware of the false limitations imposed by conventionality upon the potency of verbal forms. The prevailing rhetorical mode of *Jerusalem* is that of declarative exposition, bringing forth the "literal" meaning of words and sentences, foregrounding their intrinsic significance rather than suggesting new references, connotations, or combinations they can be made to yield. Blake does not subject language to Joycean torture. As Plate 99 illustrates, he even avoids (as much as possible) modifiers; adjectives and adverbs tend to obscure the integrity, as it were, of the words they modify. His preferred part of speech is the noun. *Jerusalem*'s poetry is remarkably denotative, as is suggested by the prominence in Plate 99 of "mere" parallel lists of substantives: "Tree Metal Earth & Stone . . . Years Months Days & Hours."

All these stylistic features are congruent with the central aim of *Jerusalem*, to reveal the beautiful *is* hidden by an ugly *seems to be*. The prophecy strives to reveal an ever-present truth existent within fabrications of false appearances. Blake, as I have said, does not urge us to imitate Christ, but to recognize that our individuality *is* the liberation of Christ within each of us. He proposes no pattern to be followed, but, instead, the attainment of a liberating mode of perception, one creative of its own "rules." So he is not interested in Joycean ingenuity, invention, originality—recyclings of received forms of meaning and reference. He concentrates on graphic ex-position. He wants us to see what is *in*, not what may be done *with*, each word. Thus in Plate 99 the potency of "Planetary" depends on its root, its origin "hidden" within it, the meaning of "wandering." And the *placing*, the syntagmatic location, of "Planetary" is meant to help waken us to the intrinsic meaning of the word. By *placing* I mean physical positioning in the line and on the page. Blake's poetry results from two constraints, that of the rules of English and that of graphic rhythms between words and letters as visual forms. This feature of his art needs to be examined ex-tensively and in detail. Here, for brevity, I merely point to an obvious illustration in his most famous lyric. In the line "Tyger, Tyger, burning bright" there is a distinct graphic rhythm established by the letters that "rise" ("T," "b," "h," "t") and those that "fall" ("y" and "g"). In *Jerusalem* word length and total shape are, I think, more important in placing than letter-structure. But the spatial relations between words are significant. The progressive movement of *Jerusalem* as a whole is meant to bring us to a point of transformation at which we awake to the existent reality which we have been concealing by self-created illusions. At that point we see all the words in all their significance, *both* as verbal symbols *and* as visual artifacts. Blake is indifferent to Joycean phonic-semantic play because he concentrates on unification of visual-verbal rhythms.

Jerusalem affirms the goodness of fundamental life-processes of our cosmos, both physical and mental, those we can represent verbally and those we can represent visually. The poem reveals that life is—simply—the thrust of spiritual energy, and, however warped by our ineffectual and misguided exercise of that energy, in it alone lies salvation. We feel "instinctively" (as we now say) that vital impulses are good; in fact, says Blake, they are. Although he wishes us to be Regenerated, the state of Regeneration he envisions is no mere antithesis of Generation but the complete realization of the power which is incompletely exercised (and therefore distorted) in the state of Generation.

It is this conviction, that the world as it truly is is good, rather than any desire to elucidate psychological or mythical patterns, which leads Blake to construct *Jerusalem* as a "mythopoetic night vision." Its "plot" is the commonplace act of falling into sleep and awakening. Sleep is our chief means of natural regeneration. Falling asleep is a process of detaching oneself from one's ordinary "identity," what Blake calls "selfhood," what today we call one's sense of one's role. In this respect, at least, sleep is a temporary "death" containing within it the potentiality of renewed life. I propose that this simple-minded, rather naturalistic understanding of *Jerusalem*'s form, an understanding encouraged by the style of the prophecy, may lead us to useful evaluations of the poem's strengths and weaknesses and its special position in the cultural history of Western Europe. Thorough exposition of this thesis must await a full-length study of *Jerusalem*; here I sketch some outlines of my understanding of the poem, omitting many important matters and making no effort to defend particular readings.

From the opening of the prophecy, Albion's death is presented as part of a process of potential regeneration, because his salvation lies within himself:

I am not a God afar off, I am a brother and friend;
Within your bosoms I reside, and you reside in me . . .
                              (4: 18–19)

Inward expansion is perhaps the key to *Jerusalem*, and I shall have more to say about it. But first I want to stress that for Blake it is a process. When he speaks of a "state," we tend to think of a static condition. But to him stasis is nonentity. Existence is movement, that is, kinetic energy. He conceives of sleep (like any other "state") as continuous movement, away from waking consciousness to the depth of sleep, what I call the point of anti-consciousness, then a contrary movement to awakening and refreshed consciousness. To me, then, the crucial word in the first lines of Plate 4 is "passage":

Of the Sleep of Ulro! and of the passage through
Eternal Death! and of the awaking to Eternal Life.
                          (4: 1–2)

Jerusalem records a journey, a passage from disintegration to reintegration. But it is a journey inward.[9] Chapter I initiates the passage by detailing
various processes of self-division. After the separation of Albion and Jesus
in Plate 4, other divisions occur, these constituting the "characters" who
dominate the prophecy until Albion's reawakening. Culminating the separations of Chapter I is Albion's anguished cry, "If God was Merciful this
could not be" (24: 53). How can the world we know, so filled with sense-
less suffering and meaningless evil, testify to the existence of a merciful
God? To that question *Jerusalem* is the answer. We, not God, are the
creators of suffering and evil. Albion, falling away from the God within,
initiates a chain-reaction of multiplying divisions which are the state of
Ulro.

The first and most important "figure" to be separated after the original
division of Albion and Jesus is Los, the artificer, the impulse of divine
energy toward Regeneration which prevents Albion from slipping into annihilation, nonentity. But Los exists as a separate entity only because of
Albion's fall; and all that Los does, in one sense, is the reverse of true
nobility and divinity. Los is "good," one might say, only in his motivation:
"for Albions sake / I now am what I am" (8: 17–18). But Los is, here and
throughout the poem until his resurrection, "a horror and an astonishment / Shuddring the heavens to look upon me" (8: 18–19). Los asserts
that his "business is to create" (10: 21), but what he creates is the consolidation of error (9: 29–30, 12: 10–15). Los is creative spirit struggling
in a fallen cosmos, and therefore admirable; but his creativity—"Striving
with Systems to deliver Individuals from those Systems" (11: 5)—is almost a parody of Christ's creativity, which makes reality out of "nothing,"
truth out of delusion.

(But whatever is visible to the Generated Man,
Is a Creation of mercy & love, from the Satanic Void).
                          (13: 44–45)

The "bright Sculptures of / Los' Halls" (16: 61 ff) are the finest achievements possible in a fallen world but only faint adumbrations of the visionary forms dramatic that are the easy creations of each man when he is joined
to the Christ within him.

Los is a smith, a forger of things. However impressive his creations, they
contribute to the multiplex system of artifacts from which we must break

9. The famous first plate, Los stepping through a doorway, is unmistakably a human
figure in the act of *entering*.

free to find salvation. Los's creations are externalities, projections, parts of the system of "wheel without wheel, with cogs tyrannic / Moving by compulsion each other" (15: 18–19). His works are consolidations of what Blake calls "withoutside" (19: 17), in one word implying both separated externality and lack of definite form. The "art" of Los is illusory, for it is made up of and represents that

. . . Outside . . .
Beyond the Outline of Identity both ways, which meet in One:
An orbed Void of doubt, despair, hunger, & thirst & sorrow.
                                                                      (18: 2–4)

In short, Joyce's successor, Beckett. Los fabricates, with the full "willfullness" of a dreamer (see 17: 39–41), "a distorted & reversed Reflexion in the Darkness / And in the Non Entity" (17: 42–43). The artist divided from Christ creates mere reflections of what is outside, that is, a copy of a copy; for what is "reflected" originates inside the artificer. The true creative center—and circumference—of reality (whence visionary forms dramatic arise) is inside each and every individual, who is the center—and circumference—of the universe.

The Vegetative Universe, opens like a flower from the Earths center:
In which is Eternity. It expands in Stars to the Mundane Shell
And there it meets Eternity again, both within and without,
And the abstract Voids between the Stars are the Satanic Wheels.
                                                                      (13: 34–37)

Jerusalem is a passage inward, a penetration into the depths of psychic energy. This penetration alone enables us to know the difference between what actually exists and what "seems," what we think exists but does not except as evidence of the disorganization of our psychic and perceptual processes. Once self-divided, man's creative spirit itself becomes a potential source of other divisions and a shaper of an imprisoning world of external "things." The owner of valuable paintings has a strong lock on his door. If we are to understand *Jerusalem*, we have to recognize that Los, too, must be resurrected, since it is his "inadequacy" which enables us, finally, to grasp the nature of the visionary forms dramatic which are the ultimate potential within every human being, if we redeem the fallen world, the only world in which "Los" can exist.[10]

10. In an important review-essay which appeared after this essay was written, *Modern Philology*, 69 (1972), pp. 261–266, Jerome J. McGann elucidates the role of Los throughout Blake's later work, not just in *Jerusalem*. McGann observes that "one of his [Los's] most difficult functions is to give way before the Redeemer"; Los himself must "undergo the death through which his own *dire* but merciful inventions

The existence of Los is evidence of Albion's dividedness, and from that dividedness springs all evil. Evil is lack of integrity. Lacking integrity, a man sees shamefulness in the behavior of others, because, as Blake makes plain in the later plates of Chapter I, he feels shame, that is, he is ashamed of himself:

The disease of Shame covers me from head to feet: I have no hope
Every boil upon my body is a separate & deadly Sin.
Doubt first assaild me, then Shame took possession of me
Shame divides Families, Shame hath divided Albion in sunder!
                                        (21: 3–6)

Filled with shame, a man lacks the power of self-forgiveness, from which forgiveness of others arises. And whereas forgiveness unites, doubt and shame divide. What we see in the later plates of Chapter I is Albion's increased self-anatomizing producing the separations that are Vala and his Sons. Disintegrating, Albion sees these phantasms as reality (23: 1–2), nature becomes sin, and the unity of an infinite universe of minute particulars becomes a single globe of matter. Minute particulars cannot be recovered by analysis of this unitary globe, because it is a phantasm, an inaccurate perception of reality. Analysis, the primary method of rationality, only divides the analyst, leading him finally to a despairing vision of an infinitely divisible, hence meaningless, universe. Reason, separated from man's integrative functions, becomes a spectre, a creator of spectrous existence.

The Infant Joy is beautiful, but its anatomy
Horrible ghast & deadly! nought shalt thou find in it
But dark despair & everlasting brooding melancholy!
                                        (22: 22–24)

Chapter II shows disorganization becoming death, a continuing descent from waking awareness to a point of absolute anti-consciousness, Albion's "final" death in Plate 48. By entering into a state, one attains the possibility of passing through it (what Thel refuses to do). Because we fall asleep we can awaken refreshed. The core of the conception of mental states as regions to be traversed and of the moment of deepest sleep as a total inversion of consciousness is contained in Blake's idea of "limit."

---

drive all *things*" (my italics); and "Los is Jesus' instrument just as Los's Spectre is the instrument of the Eternal Prophet." McGann recognizes that Los (whose name, I believe, links him to, yet distinguishes him from, *loss*) is crucial to Blake's ideal "of a form of art which would not imprison later generations . . . knowing that his visions were not ours any more than his own perceptions were ritually repeatable." It is encouraging that from critics such as McGann *Jerusalem* needs no deliverance.

There is a limit of Opakeness, and a limit of Contraction;
In every Individual Man, and the limit of Opakeness,
Is named Satan: and the limit of Contraction is named Adam.
(42: 29–31)

Blake's limits are not impassable boundaries (as Voltaire in Chapter IV thinks them) but critical points, equivalent to thirty-two degrees Farenheit for water. Contracted to Adam, mankind attains the possibility of the redeeming Christ. Reaching the limit of "Opakeness" which is Satan, man attains the possibility of total luminescence, Lucifer, complete emanative power, the power of giving forth light instead of casting shadows, making spectres. By plunging into the depth of sleep, man attains the possibility of re-awakened life, rebirth. At our farthest remove from ordinary consciousness our conventional and imprisoning (because spectral) identity dissolves, we are least our usual waking selves, so at that point or limit we attain the possibility of becoming totally self-organized. Only then are we freed from the inhibiting pressure of those "systems" external to us which contract and darken individuality into Selfhood.

Blake believes we expand by moving inward and contract by moving outward.[11] Asleep, our perceptions are focused—literally—on our inner being, the physiological processes which constitute our vital body, to which we are blinded when awake by the multitude of sensations streaming in upon us from the external world. True vision, seeing into, is the power of beholding multitude as one, that is, of apprehending the unity of processes which organize discrete phenomena ("organize"—give purpose to, without diminishing the integrity of, each phenomenon). True existence, true life, consists in activities, processes, not things, circulation of blood, not blood. To sleep is not to attain true vision but sleep leads toward true vision, perception of the unity of diversity, the perception that reality *is* organizing power.

We live as One Man; for contracting our infinite senses
We behold multitude; or expanding: we behold as one,
As One Man all the Universal Family; and that One Man
We call Jesus the Christ: and he in us, and we in him.
(34: 17–20)

The nature of the unity of diversity is suggested by Albion, fallen, becoming "The Reactor" (29: 9). The Reactor must be "a Punisher" (29: 16), because his activities are compulsive, initiated by forces outside him-

11. Most of us recognize the possible truth in this paradox, for, when we speak of something spiritual as distinct from the physical, we refer to something whose "inside" is not determined by its exterior dimensions. Usually, in fact, we mean by "spiritual" what is bigger "inside" than "outside."

self. To forgive, on the contrary, is to act in a genuinely spontaneous fashion. In ordinary speech the nominal equivalent of the verb "forgive" almost never occurs; "a forgiver" sounds odd, as "a punisher" does not. The latter designates not a person but a role. One cannot genuinely forgive another by playing the role of "forgiver." Christ, then, is man totally spontaneous, individualized, uncircumscribed by any role; and Albion's fall is descent from individuality of existence to spectrous existence through a multiplicity of roles. To fall is to enslave oneself to seemings, to have one's individual identity devoured by a multiplex, illusory Selfhood (33: 16–24). Ulro is archetypalism, an archetype being the form of a role.[12] The self-organizing power that is vitality diminishes as it accepts any non-self-created pattern of existence.

Blake describes loss of individuality as a hardening of the minute particulars (31: 20) that make up living reality. Taking upon itself a pattern of being, the vital, spontaneous, self-energizing potency of actual life freezes. The essential generosity of living interactions congeals; the minute particulars, which are in essence impulses of mutual forgiveness, become things instead of processes. Fallen, we think of things, such as flesh, as "more real" than processes, such as metabolism. Blake's central term for the hardened

12. One could argue cogently that—in Blake's view—because we are fallen we tend to think archetypally. In any case, elucidations of archetypal patternings help us to understand how Blake *used* his aesthetic and theological inheritance. One may miss the point and force of Blake's imagination if one fails to recognize how he transforms traditions, iconographic as well as intellectual-religious, within which he worked. Yet I feel that Blake studies have suffered from what C. S. Lewis called the "type of criticism which always takes us away from the actual poem and the individual poet to seek the sources of their power in something earlier . . ." ("The Anthropological Approach," in *English and Medieval Studies Presented to J. R. R. Tolkien*, ed. Norman Davis and C. L. Wrenn [London: G. Allen and Unwin, 1962], p. 223). Because they are so graphic, Blake's prophecies are especially distorted by modes of criticism which seek, as it were, to pass beyond a text's concrete specificity. Blake's method of publication, which makes each "copy" of a given work unique, reverses conventional publication procedures that produce thousands of identical copies—of *Finnegans Wake*, for example. Even *Jerusalem*'s mode of publication, then, requires that we respect it as a particular existential artifact. Many younger critics' insistence that Blake's art be analyzed as "composite art" is attractive because it enforces such respect. In a context less restrictive than this brief essay I hope to explore the possibility that the "problem of myth" in Blake's work is to a degree terminological only. I should like to extend and refine upon Professor Frank Kermode's valuable suggestion that we "distinguish between myths and fictions. Fictions can degenerate into myths whenever they are not consciously held to be fictions. . . . Myth operates within the diagrams of ritual, which presupposes total and adequate explanations of things as they are and were; it is a sequence of radically unchangeable gestures. Fictions are for finding things out, and they change as the needs of sense-making change" (*The Sense of an Ending: Studies in the Theory of Fiction* [New York: Oxford Univ. Press, 1967], p. 39).

world is "fibre." Fallen world and fallen man are composed of fibres, sub-
stantial, intricate, entangling filaments which are, so to speak, contracted
mockeries of the mobile organizedness of truly living processes. He almost
surely picked up the term "fibre" from the biology of his times. From the
early seventeenth century, fibres had been regarded as composing a major
portion of animal and vegetable tissue. And in 1756 Linnaeus had identified
as a species of freshwater polypus (this name is introduced by Blake in
Chapter I) the hydra, a fibrous animal which, when cut apart, becomes
two animals. In the hydra-polypus is crystallized Blake's understanding
of the fallen natural world, a condition of endless multiplication through
division.[13]

For Blake, fibres are not real; they are spectres. By their *seeming* sys-
tematizations they epitomize the disorganization of our perceptions, which
leads us to regard the external as more real than the internal, solid, "opake"
things as more actual than insubstantial processes of vitality. And he does
not restrict fibres to organic growths. He sees our civilization as constructed
of fibres of a more pernicious kind than those making up organic tissue:

> But Albions sleep is not
> Like Africa's: and his machines are woven with his life.
> (40: 24–25)

For us today, living in a society entirely dependent on a network of electrical
wires, his vision of modern life as a tangled web of mechanized fibres seems
unbelievably prophetic. Less attractive to many is his linking of fibres with
the feminine and identifying the feminine as deceit.

For Blake, what we see as "feminine" is only the spectrous result of
Albion's divided integrity. Apprehension of sexual categories is evidence
of disorganized perception. To perceive a human being as "female" is to
fail to perceive "her" as a full human being. Sexual differentiation de-
grades both perceiver and perceived. The appearance of "woman," a class
of human being distinct from "mankind," is primary testimony that our
world is deceitful, a "pretence" of reality:

> A pretence of Art, to destroy Art: a pretence of Liberty
> To destroy Liberty. a pretence of Religion to destroy Religion.
> (38: 35–36)

To accept pretense for reality is to entangle oneself in the nets (fibres) of
Vala, who is nature, a multiplicity of veils, fabricated concealments of
actuality. This is why Blake associates our fallen sexuality with our reason.

---

13. I suspect that Blake knew, beside Linnaeus, Erasmus Darwin's discussion of the
"Polypodium Barometz" or "Tartarian Lamb," strikingly illustrated in *The Botanic
Garden*, Part II ("The Loves of the Plants"), 4th ed. (London, 1799), II, 37.

After all, most people still say that sexual differentiation is the most reasonable thing in the world. But so to differentiate is to obscure a sense for the humanness which encompasses male and female, to subjugate inhibited interaction between human beings to the labyrinthine complexities of feminine (partially human) delusion, to veil, darken, the simple truth of the unity of diversity:

... their Daughters govern all
In hidden deceit! they are vegetable only fit for burning:
Art & Science cannot exist but by Naked Beauty displayd.
(32: 47–49)

A "reasonable" man's relation to the natural world is the same as a male to a female in sexual matters, an entangling of oneself in an illusory labyrinth of veils. What Blake calls a "deist" is today usually a scientist or technocrat, one who believes only the evidence of "nature" and "reason" and rejects "revelation." A deist's relation to the natural cosmos is that of a stupid man to a clever woman who has seduced him: self-imprisoned in a mesh of delusive desires of whose character, even existence, he is unaware, he is at the mercy of her whims, even as he prides himself on his virility.

Chapter III focuses on this "limit" of fallenness, "The Female hid within a Male" (75: 18). Sexuality is presented as the epitome of natural being; here Albion's original integrity dissolves into an incomprehensible multiplicity of sexual relations; man becomes labyrinth, reality becomes appearance. This is not, however, the deepest anti-consciousness. In Chapter III a return to consciousness, reawakening, begins. The nature of the process can perhaps best be understood through a comparison with psychoanalysis. To the analyst, the value of his patients' dreams is that they are fantasies. Because they are not "true," they are a means, a pathway, to "truth." A woman, let us say, dreams of snakes. The snakes are dreamed, not real; they are the patient's "creations." By helping her to concentrate—not on real snakes—but on how and why she creates, fantasizes, snakes, the analyst can bring his patient to recognize an actuality, her real if self-concealed feeling, shall we say, about her husband's phallus. One reaches reality only through a labyrinth of illusion, even as the passage to eternal life is through the door of natural death.

As death, the focus of Chapter II, results from the divisions of Chapter I, so the sexuality of Chapter III is a consequence of death. Sexuality is the ultimate codification of division; sexuality is death's system for making more dead bodies. Our sexuality is a delusive veil, because it is mere responsiveness to illusion, not an expression of the force of inner reality. Our sexuality is an inversion of the processes of true energy. Sexual activity is temporarily enervating; the exercise of genuine energy increases its potency. For Blake true energy does not function entropically because it is an organizing impetus—the second law of thermodynamics is precisely the defining condition of natural life, fallen existence.

True energy is a giving or flowing forth from inside, from real being, the impetus, one might say, to organize life more effectively; and this is why Blake uses the term "emanation" for Jerusalem.

In Great Eternity, every particular Form gives forth or Emanates
Its own peculiar Light, & the Form is the Divine Vision
And the Light is his Garment. This is Jerusalem in every Man . . .
                                            (54: 1–3)

Only what possesses "Definite & Determinate Identity" can emanate: for "The Infinite alone resides" in "minutely organized Particulars" (55: 64, 62). Only what is infinite can release energy without diminishment of potency.

The condition of Regeneration, Great Eternity, is vibrantly, heroically sexual: Comminglings from the head even to the feet. Our sexuality is a perversion of the free flowing-forth of *bodily* energy, the ceaseless emanating which is the characteristic of redeemed life. Regenerated, we shall know a bodily potency of interchange, a real sexuality, of which in our fallen state we can scarcely conceive. Again one sees why Blake associates sexuality with reason. What is reasonable is not, by definition, impossible. What appears impossible is, necessarily, unreasonable. But it is precisely the limits of the possible that Jesus expands:

Jesus replied. I am the Resurrection & the Life.
I Die & pass the limits of possibility, as it appears
To individual perception.
                        (62: 18–20)

Jesus in this quotation comforts Jerusalem, who in the third chapter is condemned repeatedly as a harlot. The whole chapter, in fact, is keyed to exposing the evil of distinguishing between wife and harlot, a distinction Blake identifies as fundamental to civilization as civilization. All civilizations are druidic, bureaucratically "Unhumanized" (63: 18), because they are systems of regulations concerning unreal distinctions which derive ultimately from sexual division. In Plate 61 Blake retells the Joseph and Mary story in such a way as to leave no orifice for the Holy Ghost.

And Mary said, If thou put me away from thee
Dost thou not murder me? Joseph spoke in anger & fury. Should I
Marry a Harlot & an Adulteress? Mary answer'd, Art thou more pure
Than thy Maker who forgiveth Sins & calls again Her that is Lost . . .

Ah my Mary: said Joseph; weeping over & embracing her closely in
His arms: Doth he forgive Jerusalem & not exact Purity from her who is
Polluted.

(61: 4–16)

The reworking of the story is no joke but essential to Blake's belief. If
Christ is within each of us, and "There is none that liveth & sinneth not"
(61: 24), the true relation between Joseph and Mary must be as he presents
it. Refusal to recognize this truth is the basis of the destructive pride,
cruelty, and divisiveness of all civilizations:

What is a Wife & what is a Harlot? What is a Church? & What
Is a Theatre? are they Two & not One? can they Exist Separate?
Are not Religion & Politics the Same Thing? Brotherhood is Religion
O Demonstrations of Reason Dividing Families in Cruelty & Pride!

(57: 8–11)

Representation of sexuality as the fountainhead of civilization's deceitful divisiveness prepares us for the revelatory awakening of Chapter IV,
in which imagination, the awakened intellect, passes beyond the limits of
seeming to what truly is. Liberative and expansive reality, eternal life,
exists, and because it is eternal always does exist inside our labyrinthine selfhoods. Retreating within ourselves, penetrating through anti-consciousness,
we find:

The Female hid within a Male; thus Rahab is reveald
Mystery Babylon the Great: the Abomination of Desolation
Religion hid in War: a Dragon red, & hidden Harlot
But Jesus breaking thro' the Central Zones of Death & Hell
Opens Eternity in Time & Space; triumphant in Mercy.

(75: 18–22)

So the final chapter embodies a complex movement of expansion through
completion of a process of interiorization, discovery within, for

What is Above is Within, for every-thing in Eternity is translucent:
The Circumference is Within: Without, is formed the Selfish Center
And the Circumference still expands going forward to Eternity.

(71: 6–8)

The simplest analogy for expansion through interiorization is provided by
a water drop under a microscope. To the naked eye a drop looks small; seen
through a microscope it turns out to be a richly complex "cosmos." The
analogy is useful, too, because seeing the drop magnified (in Blake's terminology, seeing through, not with, the eye) expands one's consciousness, and
the revelation of Chapter IV is, simply, increased awareness of actuality.

The chapter's thematic center is the city, the unified reintegration of many human beings that true consciousness within each individual makes possible. Just as the water drop is a universe, so the individual is a city, and a city is the individuals within it, as the universe is a coherence of minute particulars. The "ghost towns" of the American West are buildings without inhabitants. In Blake's view, London is a "ghost city," because it contains no truly living inhabitants, only spectres. Conversely, each individual is a "Seed of a city," that is, a potentiality of the creation of self-organized, fully humanized, emanatively mutualized collective existence—the goal of all life processes, of all energy:

The land is markd for desolation & unless we plant
The seeds of Cities & of Villages in the Human bosom
Albion must be a rock of blood . . .
                              (83: 54–56)

Full realization of man's organizing energy in a collectivity of mutual forgiveness (which is recognition of the integrity of oneself and each other person as a minute particular) is an act of consciousness, dependent upon an awakening from delusion. Hence the first portion of Chapter IV is a series of laments, which recur to earlier events in the poem. But lamentation is an expression of awareness, and hence a beginning of the creativity realized in the final plates. A lamentation finally awakens Albion, who rises in wrath, re-energized, annihilative of the Druid spectres of his sleep. But Albion's wrath means more: he calls to Jerusalem to "Open the hidden Heart in Wars of mutual Benevolence, Wars of Love" (97: 14). Eternal Life is life at its most vital, least passive and least inhibited, most emanative. Albion awakening releases the stored energy within him which is Jesus; and Jesus is assertive, outgoing love:

Jesus said. Wouldest thou love one who never died
For thee or ever die for one who had not died for thee
And if God dieth not for Man & giveth not himself
Eternally for Man Man could not exist! for Man is Love:
As God is Love: every kindness to another is a little Death
In the Divine Image nor can Man exist but by Brotherhood.
                              (96: 23–28)

Wars in eternity are activities of love. Mutual forgiveness is a creative act, assertive selflessness: "kindness to another is a little Death." Only Jerusalem identified, the many recognized as one and the one recognized as many, only *that* makes creative socialness, individuality and brotherhood together—in fine, human city-life—possible.

In Chapter IV Los "falls" and is resurrected. All Los can do during Albion's sleep is to consolidate error, work *toward* regeneration. Regeneration attained, Los as Los disappears, merging back into the Jesus-Albion unity. This reintegration is testimony to the inherent divinity of the cosmos: "Nor can any consumate bliss without being Generated" (86:42). As on the vegetative level sleep is necessary to refreshed life, so Generation is no accident but a necessity of Eternal Life. The material universe as it is, not as it seems to deists, not regarded as the deceitful abstraction "Nature," is the dwelling place of the divine energy of mercy which is Jesus. Salvation comes not from another world, not from another life, but from within this world, from within the life of each of us.

The total movement of *Jerusalem* from division through death and sexuality to civil reintegration is the process of "identifying" Albion's emanation, Jerusalem. What the process affirms is that we *can* re-establish our true identity, attain full livingness. "Identity" means, primarily, being oneself and not another. Yet the word can be utilized to mean "exactly like another." Identical twins have individual identities. This is Blake's point, why for him Jerusalem is simultaneously woman and city, an individuality and a collectivity. All men are identical, not in the sense of being carbon copies of a divine original, but in being equally unique embodiments of the energy which is Jesus Christ. "Identity," furthermore, refers to the capacity to remain the same under varying conditions, and "identify" can carry the meaning of attesting to something's being what it purports to be. *Jerusalem* attests to the continuing reality of eternal life. Living is what it purports to be, better than nonentity, because true life is a passage into ever more intensely realized livingness.

Read in the manner I have so rapidly sketched, *Jerusalem* appears less a labyrinthine hunting-ground for erudite archetypalists than a relatively straightforward exposition of a religious vision pertinent to many current secular issues. Its practical relevance, to be sure, is restricted. Blake, for example, fails to understand the intricate articulation of a complex society. For him, "society" is a collection of individuals. He does not recognize "society" to be an organization of sub-societies. Hence some readers feel that, however impressive Blake's explanation of what is good and bad in personal relations, his thought is useless to contemporary conditions of social living. He defines what is needed to make urban life tolerable and rewarding, in two words, mutual forgiveness. But modern New Yorkers may find his definition of little practical use. Their problems spring from the fact that the personal relations of eight million people are significantly determined by their varied participation in the multiple sub-societies which constitute the articulated organism of the city. Blake never grapples with problems posed by levels of organization.

Jerusalem, nevertheless, provides an illuminating perspective upon contemporary life because it marks a critical point, a Blakean limit, in European cultural history. Blake introduces into religiously oriented literature a new understanding of the Fall of Man. For the *felix culpa* of *Paradise Lost* he substitutes a psychological inevitability deriving from the distinctively human impulse to *reify*, to apprehend human phenomena as if nonhuman or suprahuman. He attacks our tendency to treat products of human action as if something other than artifacts. He sees special danger in mental artifacts. He opposed belief in established mythologies, and he surely would be as hostile to those of modern technology and psychology as he was to that of pagan Greece. To believe in, that is, passively to accept, a mythological system is to surrender one's creative potency, the source of the energy of belief, and thus to "unhumanize" the world.

Yet Blake sees such unhumanizing as inevitable. Life to be life must be creative. What is created takes on an autonomous existence, which then functions as an obstacle to further exercise of the creativity which brought it into being. Myth-making is an expression of creative power, but myth-making produces mythologies, in whose names new myth-makers are discouraged, persecuted, killed. Man is everywhere in chains *because* he is born free.

From this conception emanate Blake's most prophetic declarations. Only long after his death did the sociologist Durkheim observe that the essence of all formal religions is a division of the world into two segments, one sacred, the other profane. The purpose of *Jerusalem* is to attack this foundation of institutionalized religion, which Blake represents as Druidism. For him, setting stones on end to mark sacred spots epitomizes the idiocy of arbitrary segregations of places, persons, or times. Everything that lives is holy; every atom of the universe is equally sacred. The "conflict" within *Jerusalem* is between those who try to divide the universe—who distinguish between wife and harlot—and Jesus Christ, the intrinsic divinity of every minute particular.[14]

Because he does not admit the existence of the profane, Blake's vision of Regenerated Life may impress us as more intellectual than religious.

And they conversed together in Visionary forms dramatic which bright
Redounded from their Tongues in thunderous majesty, in Visions
In new Expanses, creating exemplars of Memory and of Intellect
Creating Space, Creating Time according to the wonders Divine
Of Human Imagination, throughout all the Three Regions immense
Of Childhood, Manhood & Old Age . . .

(98: 28–33)

14. Blake, of course, perceived that "sacred" and "profane" ooze out from religion to infect all aspects of secular life (just as priesthood provides the primal model for secular bureaucracies). He had no difficulty, for instance, seeing through the "sacredness" of property rights.

One is tempted to call such a passage super-Kantian, for it envisions man's having the potency to create the categories, the psychic organization, by which he will perceive and conceive. And this passage alone is evidence enough that Blake is not opposed to science, philosophy, or intellectuality. What *Jerusalem* denounces is blind faith—in religion, reason, art, politics, anything. And, as the very style of the prophecy tells us, the modern world is threatened not by overt blind faith (as were earlier civilizations) but by the concealment of it. This is why Blake identifies as his chief enemies neither religious nor political leaders, but intellectuals: Bacon, Locke, Newton, Voltaire. It is the modern intellectual who most effectively conceals, especially from himself, the irrational foundation of his activities, his blind faith in intellectuality.

It is not the reasonable man's reason Blake condemns, but his unexamined confidence in reason. The condemnation is a clue to the special cultural moment which *Jerusalem* dramatizes. The prophecy expresses a major transformation in the history of religion, a transformation initiated by the Protestant Reformation. But *Jerusalem* (more explicitly than its literary predecessors at least) identifies religiosity with the active *creation* of belief. The prophecy castigates passive acceptance of anything. Blake's religion is in a real sense without faith (even as it is without temples, holy places, other than all human bodies). Each believer creates his own belief; such creation is the core of imaginative activity. Because Blake devised a style capable of graphically characterizing this literary-religious innovation, *Jerusalem*, aside from its aesthetic merit, is an essential document for understanding the genesis of modern culture.

Index

Abrams, M. H., 54–55

Adam, 66, 112, 172–73, 175, 222, 238, 271, 272, 274, 279, 304, 358; fall of, 35; limit of contraction, 77; state of, 253; curse of, 263. SEE ALSO Eve

Adams, Robert M., 352

Adonis, 242

Adultery, 69–70, 343

Advertisement for Moore & Co., 120

Aeschylus, 271

Aesop, 277

Aesthetics, 259

Ahania, 124, 175, 183–85, 188, 189, 213, 214–15, 216, 217, 218, 226

Ahania, Book of, 53, 126, 215, 226

Albion, 15, 16, 18, 19, 20, 44, 73, 93, 94, 98, 103, 104–5, 107, 108, 114, 116, 117, 172, 174, 175, 180, 181, 191, 195, 196, 197, 199, 209, 222, 224, 256, 284, 286, 295, 296, 297, 336, 338, 339, 346, 360; lament of, 15; sleep of, 63, 71–72, 210; death of, 71, 73, 128, 289, 318, 331–32, 332–33, 334, 335, 340, 342, 345, 354; regeneration of, 96, 344, 364; as Eternal Man, 102, 283; fainting of, 105; garments of, 136, 138; and Luvah, 211, 217, 342; and holiness, 216; rejects Divine Vision, 275, 313, 318, 320, 332, 333, 334, 336, 342, 343; fall of, 312, 321, 359; as reader, 316, 319–26; spectre of, 318, 336; reunion with Jerusalem, 318, 339; curses humanity, 322; on Rock of Ages, 333; as symbol, 350; separated from Jesus, 355; division in, 357; wrath of, 364. SEE ALSO *Jerusalem*

—daughters of, 108, 128, 136, 290, 319, 332, 334, 336, 337, 342, 343, 345; as perception, 325; appeal for salvation, 335, 338; war with sons of Albion, 335; aggregate as Rahab, 338; as falsehood, 345

—friends of, 323, 333, 336; as representatives of Blake, 319; despair of, 338; and elders of Revelation, 339; as humanistic institutions, 343

—sons of, 87, 108, 290, 304, 318, 319, 332, 333, 334, 336, 338, 339, 342, 357; as responses, 325; war with daughters of Albion, 335; aggregate in Hand, 338; and elders of Revelation, 339

Albion rose, 168, 179

Allegory, 11–12, 86, 91, 93, 99, 109, 205–6, 280, 309, 310, 314; sublime, xiii, 23–24, 259, 260, 277, 312, 315, 319, 346; veils of, 278; systematic, 281. SEE ALSO titles of individual works

All Religions Are One, 166

Altizer, Thomas J. J., xv

America, xv, 148, 159, 216, 225, 274, 275; as prophecy, 27; meeting of Vala and Orc, 111; copies of, 147

—Blake's designs for: pl. a: 146; pl. 1: 145; pl. 3: 146, 147, 170; pl. 11: 160, 193

American Revolution, 260–61

Ancient Britons, The, 262

Androgynous symbols. SEE Symbolism

Antichrist, 34, 44, 88, 112, 195, 338, 339, 343, 344

Antijacobin Review, 139

TEXT DESIGNED
BY IRVING PERKINS
JACKET DESIGNED BY KAREN FOGET
MANUFACTURED BY HERITAGE PRINTERS, INC., CHARLOTTE, NORTH CAROLINA
TEXT IS SET IN BODONI BOOK, DISPLAY LINES IN BODONI

Library of Congress Cataloging in Publication Data
Curran, Stuart.
Blake's sublime allegory.
Includes bibliographical references.
1. Blake, William, 1757–1827. I. Wittreich,
Joseph Anthony, joint author. II. Title.
PR4147.C8   821'.7   72–1377
ISBN 0–299–06180–9